AF725109

AI-Augmented Optimization and Control for Engineers

by

ant

Table of Contents

Front Matter

The landscape of engineering is undergoing a profound transformation, driven by the rapid advancements in artificial intelligence and machine learning. These powerful computational tools are no longer confined to theoretical research; they are now integral to solving complex, real-world problems, offering unprecedented capabilities in perception, decision-making, and optimization. In the realm of control systems, the integration of AI promises to unlock new levels of performance, adaptability, and robustness that were once considered unattainable. This book is born from the conviction that a deep understanding of this synergy is essential for modern engineers.

Our journey begins with a concise review of fundamental control concepts, setting a common ground for readers from diverse engineering backgrounds. We then delve into the mathematical underpinnings of optimization, a critical tool for designing efficient and effective control strategies. The core of this book, however, lies in bridging the gap between data and control: how to learn system dynamics from observations, how to leverage reinforcement learning to achieve optimal control policies through interaction, and how to embed safety and constraint satisfaction into these learning processes. We explore advanced topics such as AI-augmented Model Predictive Control and adaptive control, illustrating how learned components can enhance established control methodologies.

Throughout this book, we aim to strike a balance between theoretical rigor and practical applicability. We provide intuitive explanations, illustrative examples, and insights into industrial case studies, enabling readers not only to grasp the concepts but also to envision their implementation. This book is intended for advanced undergraduate and graduate students, as well as practicing engineers, who seek to expand their expertise by integrating cutting-edge AI techniques into their control engineering workflows. We assume a solid foundation in mathematics and basic control theory, and our writing style is formal yet accessible, prioritizing clarity and precision. The ultimate goal is to equip you with the knowledge and tools necessary to design intelligent, safe, and high-performing control systems for the challenges of today and tomorrow.

The field of control systems has long been a cornerstone of modern engineering, enabling us to regulate, optimize, and automate complex processes across virtually every industry. From the thermostats in our homes to the autopilots in aircraft, control theory provides the mathematical framework for achieving desired system behaviors. Traditionally, control design has relied heavily on mathematical modeling of physical systems and the application of well-established analytical techniques. However, the increasing complexity of modern systems, coupled with the availability of vast amounts of data, necessitates a paradigm shift. Artificial Intelligence (AI) and Machine Learning (ML) have emerged as powerful complements and, in some cases, alternatives to traditional approaches, offering new avenues for designing intelligent and adaptive control systems.

This book explores the exciting intersection of AI and control theory. We aim to demystify how machine learning techniques can be harnessed to enhance control system design, implementation, and performance. Our target audience includes advanced undergraduate and graduate students in control systems, mechanical engineering, electrical engineering, and computer science, as well as practicing engineers seeking to integrate AI into their control engineering practice. A foundational understanding of calculus, linear algebra, and basic control principles is assumed.

We will begin by revisiting fundamental concepts in optimal control and convex optimization, providing the mathematical bedrock upon which more advanced topics are built. Subsequently, we will delve into the crucial area of learning system models from data, a vital step for creating data-driven controllers and for augmenting analytical models. The power of reinforcement learning for designing controllers that learn optimal policies through interaction will be a significant focus, exploring both foundational algorithms and their deep learning extensions. Furthermore, we will address the paramount importance of safety and constraint handling in AI-augmented control systems, presenting techniques to ensure reliable and secure operation. Throughout the book, we will illustrate these concepts with relevant examples, ranging from robotics and autonomous vehicles to industrial processes, demonstrating the practical utility and transformative potential of AI in shaping the future of intelligent control systems.

Chapter 1: Foundations in Optimal Control

The bedrock of modern engineering, from the simplest household appliance to the most complex aerospace vehicle, lies in the sophisticated orchestration of control systems. At its core, a control system is a mechanism designed to manage, command, and direct other devices or systems to achieve a desired outcome. These systems are not merely about automation; they are about precision, stability, and efficiency, ensuring that complex processes operate as intended, often under varying conditions and in the presence of disturbances. The ubiquity of control systems is such that we interact with them constantly, often without explicit recognition. Consider the humble thermostat in your home. It acts as a control system, sensing the ambient temperature and adjusting a heating or cooling element to maintain a user-defined setpoint. Similarly, the cruise control system in an automobile monitors the vehicle's speed and modulates the engine's power to maintain a constant speed, even when encountering inclines or declines. These everyday examples, though seemingly simple, embody the fundamental principles that govern more intricate engineering applications.

A typical control system comprises several key components, each playing a vital role in the feedback loop that enables regulation. At the most basic level, we have the
plant or the **process** to be controlled. This could be anything from a chemical reactor in a manufacturing plant, the flight dynamics of an aircraft, to the speed of an electric motor. To understand the state of the plant, **sensors** are employed. These devices measure physical quantities such as temperature, pressure, position, velocity, or acceleration, converting them into signals that the controller can interpret. The **controller** is the "brain" of the system. It receives the sensor measurements, compares them to the desired setpoint or trajectory, and computes an appropriate command signal. This computation is based on a predefined control strategy or algorithm. Finally, the **actuator** is the

component that translates the controller's command signal into a physical action on the plant. For instance, a valve opening or closing, a motor adjusting its speed, or a rudder changing its angle are all actions performed by actuators.

Control systems can broadly be categorized into two main paradigms: open-loop and closed-loop. In an
open-loop control system, the control action is independent of the system's output. The controller dictates a command based on a model or a predetermined sequence, without monitoring the actual result. A classic example is a simple toaster: you set the timer, and the heating elements operate for that duration, regardless of how brown the toast actually becomes. While simple and often cost-effective, open-loop systems are susceptible to inaccuracies if the system's behavior deviates from the expected model or if external disturbances occur. There is no mechanism for correction.

In contrast,
closed-loop control systems, also known as feedback control systems, continuously monitor the output of the plant and use this information to adjust the control action. This feedback mechanism is what allows closed-loop systems to achieve higher precision and robustness. The thermostat and cruise control are prime examples of closed-loop systems. The thermostat senses the room temperature (output), compares it to the setpoint (desired state), and adjusts the heating or cooling (control action) accordingly. The cruise control system senses the vehicle's speed, compares it to the set speed, and adjusts the throttle (control action) to maintain the desired speed. This feedback loop, involving sensing, comparison, and action, is fundamental to achieving stability and desired performance in dynamic systems.

The architecture of a closed-loop system can be visualized as a cycle:

1. **Reference Input:** This is the desired value or trajectory for the system's output (e.g., the desired room temperature, the target speed).
2. **Controller:** Compares the reference input with the measured output and generates an error signal. Based on this error, it computes a control signal.
3. **Actuator:** Receives the control signal and applies it to the plant.
4. **Plant (System):** The physical process being controlled. Its behavior is influenced by the actuator's action and any external disturbances.
5. **Sensor:** Measures the output of the plant.
6. **Feedback Signal:** The measured output from the sensor, which is fed back to the controller for comparison with the reference input.

The continuous comparison between the desired state and the actual state, and the subsequent adjustment of the control action, allows the system to counteract disturbances and maintain performance. This feedback principle is not only central to engineering but also appears in biological systems (e.g., maintaining body temperature) and economic systems.

The performance of a closed-loop control system is often evaluated based on several criteria:

Stability: The most crucial aspect. A stable system will not exhibit unbounded oscillations or diverge uncontrollably. In a closed-loop system, stability is achieved through careful design, often involving analysis of the system's poles and the feedback gain.
Accuracy: How closely the system's output tracks the desired reference input. This is often measured by the steady-state error, which is the difference between the desired and actual output after the system has settled.
Transient Response: How the system behaves when subjected to a change in the reference input or a disturbance. Key metrics include rise

time (how quickly it reaches the desired level), settling time (how long it takes to settle within a tolerance band), and overshoot (how much it exceeds the desired level before settling).
Disturbance Rejection: The ability of the system to minimize the impact of external disturbances on its output. A well-designed feedback controller can effectively reject many types of disturbances.
Robustness: The ability of the system to maintain satisfactory performance despite uncertainties in the plant model or variations in operating conditions. This is a particularly important consideration for systems operating in unpredictable environments.

Historically, control system design relied heavily on mathematical modeling of the plant dynamics and analytical techniques to derive controller parameters. This approach, often referred to as classical control, utilizes tools like transfer functions, state-space representations, and frequency domain analysis (e.g., Bode plots, Nyquist criteria). While effective for many linear time-invariant (LTI) systems, these methods can become cumbersome or insufficient when dealing with highly complex, nonlinear, or time-varying systems, which are increasingly prevalent in modern engineering.

This is precisely where the integration of Artificial Intelligence (AI) and Machine Learning (ML) becomes transformative. Traditional control design often requires a precise mathematical model of the system being controlled. However, obtaining such models can be challenging, if not impossible, for many real-world systems. Factors such as unmodeled dynamics, nonlinearities, parameter drift, and external disturbances introduce uncertainties that limit the effectiveness of controllers designed based on simplified analytical models. Machine learning offers powerful tools to address these limitations. By learning directly from data, ML algorithms can:

Build Accurate System Models: System identification techniques, powered by ML, can create highly accurate, data-driven models of complex systems, even those with significant nonlinearities or unmodeled dynamics. These learned models can then be used within established control frameworks like Model Predictive Control (MPC) or for simulation and analysis.
Develop Direct Data-Driven Controllers: In some cases, ML algorithms, particularly reinforcement learning, can learn control policies directly from interactions with the system, bypassing the need for an explicit system model altogether. This is especially useful for complex tasks where defining a precise model is intractable.
Enhance Existing Controllers: AI can augment traditional controllers by providing intelligent tuning, adapting parameters online in response to changing conditions, predicting future disturbances, or optimizing performance objectives in ways that are difficult to achieve with fixed analytical methods.
Improve Robustness and Safety: ML techniques can be employed to explicitly design controllers that are robust to uncertainties or to incorporate safety constraints, ensuring that learned systems operate reliably and within safe boundaries.

The journey through this book will begin by establishing a common understanding of control system fundamentals. We will revisit the core concepts that define what a control system is, its constituent parts, and the fundamental paradigms of open-loop and closed-loop operation. This foundational understanding is crucial because the subsequent chapters will explore how AI and ML techniques can be integrated with, or even drive, these control systems. By leveraging data, learning, and optimization, we aim to design control systems that are not only more effective and efficient but also more adaptable and intelligent, capable of tackling the increasingly complex engineering challenges of the 21st century. Whether controlling a fleet of autonomous vehicles, optimizing energy grids, or enabling sophisticated robotic manipulation, the principles of control systems, augmented by the power of AI, form the cornerstone of future technological advancements.

The quest for superior performance in any engineered system inevitably leads us to the concept of optimality. We don't just want a system to work; we want it to work as well as it possibly can, according to some well-defined criteria. In the realm of control, this translates to designing strategies that minimize costs, maximize profits, reduce energy consumption, or achieve desired objectives with the utmost efficiency and speed. This pursuit of the "best possible" outcome is the essence of optimal control, and at its heart lies a profound and elegant idea: the Principle of Optimality.

This principle, a cornerstone of dynamic programming and a fundamental tenet of optimal control theory, was famously articulated by Richard Bellman. It offers a powerful recursive framework for solving complex decision-making problems, especially those that unfold over time. In essence, the Principle of Optimality states that if a particular sequence of decisions or controls is optimal for a given problem, then any subsequence of those decisions or controls must also be optimal with respect to the state encountered at the beginning of that subsequence. Put more simply, an optimal path to a goal must consist of optimal subpaths leading to intermediate stages.

To grasp this intuitively, let's consider a common, everyday problem: finding the shortest path between two locations on a map. Imagine you need to travel from City A to City D, and you know there are intermediate cities, B and C, forming various possible routes: A to B to D, or A to C to D, or even A to B to C to D. Suppose the shortest path from A to D is discovered to be A → B → D. The Principle of Optimality asserts that the

segment of this path from A to B must be the shortest possible path from A to B. If there were a shorter path from A to B, say A → X → B, then we could substitute this shorter segment into our original path, resulting in A → X → B → D. This new path would clearly be shorter than A → B → D, contradicting our initial assumption that A → B → D was the shortest path from A to D. Therefore, the path from A to B
must be optimal, and similarly, the path from B to D *must* be optimal with respect to the starting point B. This recursive structure is key: the optimal overall path is composed of optimal sub-paths.

This principle is incredibly powerful because it allows us to break down a large, complex problem into smaller, more manageable subproblems. Instead of trying to determine the entire optimal sequence of controls from the initial state to the final state all at once, we can focus on finding the optimal control for the next step, knowing that future decisions will also be made optimally. This recursive decomposition is the foundation of dynamic programming algorithms, which are widely used to solve optimal control problems.

Mathematically, the Principle of Optimality can be formalized. Let $J^*(x0, t*0)$ represent the optimal value of a performance index (which we aim to minimize or maximize) starting from state $x*0$ at time $t*0$. If $u^(t)$ is the optimal control policy for the time interval $[t*0, tf*]$, then for any intermediate time $t*1$ within this interval, the control policy $u^(t)$ for $t \in [t*1, tf]$ must be the optimal control policy for the problem starting from state $x(t*1)$ at time $t*1$. In other words, the future optimal control is independent of how the initial state $x(t*1)$ was reached.

Consider a system described by a state vector $x(t)$ and governed by a differential equation $\dot{x}(t) = f(x(t), u(t))$, where $u(t)$ is the

control input. We seek to find a control policy $u(t)$ over a time horizon $[t
0, tf]$ that minimizes (or maximizes) a cost functional, often expressed as:

$J = \Phi(x(t
f)) + \int{t0}^{tf} L(x(t), u(t)) dt$

Here, $\Phi(x(t
f))$ is a terminal cost associated with the final state $x(tf)$, and $L(x(t), u(t))$ is the instantaneous cost rate.

The Principle of Optimality, when applied to this continuous-time optimal control problem, leads to the Hamilton-Jacobi-Bellman (HJB) equation. Let $V(x, t)$ be the optimal cost-to-go function, representing the minimum cost from state x at time t to the final time t_f. The HJB equation is a partial differential equation that characterizes this function:

$\frac{\partial V}{\partial t} + \min_{u} \left\{ L(x, u) + \nabla V(x, t) \cdot f(x, u) \right\} = 0$

with the boundary condition $V(x(t
f), tf) = \Phi(x(t_f))$.

The term $\nabla V(x, t) \cdot f(x, u)$ represents the rate of change of the optimal cost with respect to time, considering the system dynamics and the chosen control u. The minimization is performed over all admissible control inputs u. This equation essentially states that the rate of decrease of the optimal cost of-to-go must balance the instantaneous cost incurred plus the change in cost due to the system's evolution under the optimal control. The optimal control policy $u^(x, t)$ is then found by determining the u that achieves this minimum at each state and time.

The recursive nature implied by the Principle of Optimality is fundamental to how we approach solving these problems. If we were to consider a discrete-time system, the Bellman equation takes a more direct discrete form:

$V
k(xk) = \min{uk} \{L(xk, uk) + V{k+1}(x{k+1})\}$

where $V
k(xk)$ is the optimal cost-to-go from state xk at stage k, uk is the control at stage k, and $x{k+1} = f(xk, u_k)$ is the next state. Again, this shows how the optimal cost at the current stage depends on the optimal cost at the next stage, propagating backward in time (or stages).

The implications of the Principle of Optimality are far-reaching for control system design. It allows us to structure algorithms that can find optimal control policies for complex systems. For instance, in robotics, when a robot arm needs to move an object from point A to point B, the Principle of Optimality would suggest that the path taken by the arm to reach an intermediate point must itself be optimal for reaching that intermediate point from the start. This recursive decomposition is what enables dynamic programming and related techniques to tackle problems that would otherwise be computationally intractable.

Consider another example: optimizing the fuel efficiency of a vehicle. The overall goal is to travel a certain distance with minimum fuel consumption. According to the Principle of Optimality, any segment of the optimal journey must also be fuel-efficient for that particular segment. If the vehicle is traveling at a certain speed and approaching an incline, the optimal strategy for the next few moments (e.g., adjusting throttle, gear) must be optimal for that immediate situation, assuming the remainder of the journey will also be completed optimally. This doesn't mean making locally optimal decisions without regard for the future; rather, it means that the sequence of decisions, when viewed as a whole, is optimal, and every part of that sequence, viewed in isolation from its starting point, is also optimal.

This principle forms the theoretical underpinning for many advanced control strategies. It guides the development of algorithms that can adapt and optimize system behavior in real-time. Without this principle, the problem of finding optimal control sequences for dynamic systems would be exponentially more complex, often involving an exhaustive search through all possible control histories. The Principle of Optimality provides a structured way to prune this search space by ensuring that we only consider optimal sub-solutions.

Furthermore, the Principle of Optimality highlights the interconnectedness of decisions in sequential problems. An optimal choice at one stage not only affects the immediate outcome but also influences the set of possible states and the associated costs in all future stages. This foresight is implicitly captured by the recursive structure of dynamic programming and the Bellman equation, allowing the system to "look ahead" by evaluating the optimal future costs from each potential next state.

The mathematical formulation of the Principle of Optimality, particularly the Hamilton-Jacobi-Bellman equation, is a critical tool in continuous-time optimal control. It provides a way to characterize the optimal cost function and, by extension, the optimal control policy. While solving the HJB equation analytically can be challenging for all but the simplest systems, it provides a theoretical foundation and motivates numerical methods for approximating the optimal control law. These methods often involve discretizing the state space and time, transforming the continuous problem into a discrete one where dynamic programming can be applied more directly.

In summary, the Principle of Optimality is a profound insight that simplifies the design of optimal control strategies. By asserting that an optimal overall solution is composed of optimal sub-solutions, it enables a recursive approach to problem-solving. Whether we are navigating the complexities of autonomous driving, optimizing chemical processes, or managing financial portfolios, this principle provides the intellectual bedrock for designing systems that achieve their objectives in the most efficient and effective manner possible. It is a testament to the power of decomposition and recursion in taming complexity and finding the best path forward.

The pursuit of optimal control strategies for dynamic systems inherently involves minimizing or maximizing a performance index, which often takes the form of an integral over time. This is precisely where the mathematical discipline of the Calculus of Variations becomes an indispensable tool. It provides the formal framework and analytical machinery to determine functions (or trajectories, in our context) that extremize (minimize or maximize) a given functional. A functional, unlike a standard function that maps numbers to numbers, maps entire functions to numbers. In optimal control, the performance index is a functional because it depends on the entire time history of the system's state and control inputs, not just their values at a single point in time.

At its core, the Calculus of Variations deals with finding an unknown function, say $y(x)$, that makes a functional $J[y]$ stationary (i.e., a minimum, maximum, or saddle point). The functional $J[y]$ is typically expressed as an integral of some function F, which may depend on $y(x)$ and its derivatives:

$J[y] = \int_{a}^{b} F(x, y(x), y'(x)) dx$

where $y'(x) = \frac{dy}{dx}$. To find the function $y(x)$ that extremizes this integral, we employ the concept of a "variation." Much like in differential calculus where we perturb a variable x by an infinitesimal amount δx to analyze the change in a function $f(x)$, in the Calculus of Variations, we consider a small perturbation, or variation, $\delta y(x)$, to the function $y(x)$. This variation $\delta y(x)$ is itself a function of x, and it is assumed to be zero at the endpoints of the interval, i.e., $\delta y(a) = \delta y(b) = 0$, if the boundary conditions are fixed.

The varied function is then $y(x) + \epsilon \eta(x)$, where ϵ is a small parameter and $\eta(x)$ is an arbitrary function such that $\eta(a) = \eta(b) = 0$. The change in the functional $J[y]$ due to this variation is given by:

$\delta J = J[y + \epsilon \eta] - J[y] = \int_{a}^{b} F(x, y + \epsilon \eta, y' + \epsilon \eta') dx - \int_{a}^{b} F(x, y, y') dx$

The first variation of the functional, δJ, is defined as the coefficient of ϵ in the Taylor expansion of $J[y + \epsilon \eta]$ around $\epsilon = 0$. If the function F is sufficiently smooth, this can be computed as:

$\delta J = \frac{d}{d\epsilon} \left. J[y + \epsilon \eta] \right|_{\epsilon=0}$

$\delta J = \int_{a}^{b} \left(\frac{\partial F}{\partial y} \eta(x) + \frac{\partial F}{\partial y'} \eta'(x) \right) dx$

For the functional $J[y]$ to be stationary, its first variation δJ must be zero for all admissible variations $\eta(x)$. This condition is analogous to setting the derivative of a function to zero to find its extrema.

To proceed, we can use integration by parts on the second term in the integral:

$\int_{a}^{b} \frac{\partial F}{\partial y'} \eta'(x) dx = \left[\frac{\partial F}{\partial y'} \eta(x) \right]_{a}^{b} - \int_{a}^{b} \frac{d}{dx}\left(\frac{\partial F}{\partial y'}\right) \eta(x) dx$

Since $\eta(a) = \eta(b) = 0$, the boundary term vanishes. Thus, the first variation becomes:

$\delta J = \int_{a}^{b} \left(\frac{\partial F}{\partial y} - \frac{d}{dx}\left(\frac{\partial F}{\partial y'}\right) \right) \eta(x) dx$

For δJ to be zero for any arbitrary function $\eta(x)$, the term multiplying $\eta(x)$ inside the integral must be identically zero. This leads to the fundamental equation of the Calculus of Variations, known as the Euler-Lagrange equation:

$\frac{\partial F}{\partial y} - \frac{d}{dx}\left(\frac{\partial F}{\partial y'}\right) = 0$

This is a second-order ordinary differential equation for the unknown function $y(x)$. Solving the Euler-Lagrange equation subject to appropriate boundary conditions (which could be fixed values of $y(a)$ and $y(b)$, or other constraints) yields the function $y(x)$ that extremizes the functional $J[y]$.

In the context of optimal control, the independent variable is typically time, t, and we are looking for an optimal control function $u(t)$ and a corresponding state trajectory $x(t)$ over a time interval $[t_0, t_f]$. The performance index is a functional $J[x, u]$ that we want to minimize or maximize. A common form of this functional, as introduced earlier, is:

$J = \Phi(x(t_f)) + \int_{t_0}^{t_f} L(x(t), u(t), t) dt$

Here, $x(t)$ is the state vector, $u(t)$ is the control vector, L is the

Lagrangian or instantaneous cost rate, and Φ is the terminal cost. The system dynamics are described by a set of differential equations:

$\dot{x}(t) = f(x(t), u(t), t)$

The Calculus of Variations, when applied to control problems, often requires a slight extension. Instead of finding a single function $y(x)$, we are now seeking optimal functions $x(t)$ and $u(t)$ that satisfy the system dynamics and extremize the performance index. This leads to the development of the Euler-Lagrange equations in a form suitable for systems with control inputs and state variables. To handle the constraint imposed by the system dynamics, the method of Lagrange multipliers is employed. We augment the integrand $L(x, u, t)$ with terms involving the system dynamics multiplied by costate variables (Lagrange multipliers), denoted by $\lambda(t)$. The augmented Lagrangian becomes:

$\bar{L}(x, u, \lambda, t) = L(x, u, t) + \lambda^T(t) (f(x, u, t) - \dot{x})$

Here, λ is a vector of costates, with the same dimension as the state vector x. The functional to be extremized is now considered as:

$J = \Phi(x(t_f)) + \int_{t_0}^{t_f} \left[L(x(t), u(t), t) + \lambda^T(t) (f(x(t), u(t), t) - \dot{x}(t)) \right] dt$

We treat $x(t)$ and $\lambda(t)$ as independent functions to be varied,

in addition to the control $u(t)$. The variations $\delta x(t)$ and $\delta \lambda(t)$ are considered. For the terminal state $x(t
f)$, we might have free boundary conditions, or fixed values. If $x(tf)$ is free, the variation $\delta x(t_f)$ is non-zero. The variation of J with respect to $x(t)$ and $\lambda(t)$ will yield the Euler-Lagrange equations.

The variation with respect to $\lambda(t)$ is straightforward. Let $\bar{L} = L + \lambda^T (f - \dot{x})$.

$\delta J{\lambda} = \int{t0}^{tf} \delta (\lambda^T (f - \dot{x})) dt = \int{t0}^{t_f} (\delta \lambda^T (f - \dot{x}) + \lambda^T \delta (f - \dot{x})) dt$
If we consider the variation only with respect to λ, then $\delta x = 0$ and $\delta u = 0$. So $\delta f = 0$, and $\delta \dot{x} = 0$. Thus, $\delta J{\lambda} = \int{t0}^{tf} \delta \lambda^T (f - \dot{x}) dt$.
For this to be zero for any $\delta \lambda$, we must have $f(x, u, t) - \dot{x} = 0$, which is precisely the system dynamics constraint. This confirms that the Lagrange multiplier approach correctly incorporates the system dynamics.

Now, we consider the variation with respect to $x(t)$ and $\lambda(t)$.

The variation of the integral part with respect to $x(t)$ is:
$\int{t0}^{t_f} \left(\frac{\partial L}{\partial x} + \lambda^T \frac{\partial f}{\partial x} \right) \delta x(t) dt$

The term involving $\lambda^T \dot{x}$ needs careful handling. Let's rewrite the integral term as $\int
{t0}^{tf} L(x, u, t) dt + \int{t0}^{tf} \lambda^T f(x, u, t) dt - \int{t0}^{t_f} \lambda^T \dot{x}(t) dt$.
The last integral can be integrated by parts:

$-\int{t0}^{tf} \lambda^T \dot{x}(t) dt = -\left[\lambda^T(t) x(t) \right]{t0}^{tf} + \int{t0}^{t_f} \dot{\lambda}^T(t) x(t) dt$

Combining these parts, the total variation of J (assuming $x(t 0)$ is fixed, so $\delta x(t0) = 0$) is:
$\delta J = \left(\frac{\partial \Phi}{\partial x(tf)} - \lambda^T(tf) \right) \delta x(tf) + \int{t0}^{tf} \left[\left(\frac{\partial L}{\partial x} + \lambda^T \frac{\partial f}{\partial x} + \dot{\lambda}^T \right) \delta x(t) + \frac{\partial L}{\partial u} + \lambda^T \frac{\partial f}{\partial u} \delta u(t) \right] dt$

For δJ to be zero for arbitrary variations $\delta x(t)$, $\delta u(t)$, and $\delta \lambda(t)$ (though $\delta \lambda$ is implicitly handled by the dynamics), we equate the coefficients of these variations to zero.

The coefficient of $\delta x(t)$ in the integral must be zero for all $t \in [t0, tf]$. This yields the costate (or adjoint) equations:

$-\dot{\lambda}^T(t) = \frac{\partial L}{\partial x} + \lambda^T \frac{\partial f}{\partial x}$

Or, in vector form, $\dot{\lambda}(t) = -\left(\frac{\partial L}{\partial x} + \frac{\partial f}{\partial x}\right)^T \lambda - \left(\frac{\partial L}{\partial x}\right)^T$.

Note the sign convention. If we define the Hamiltonian $H(x, u, \lambda, t) = L(x, u, t) + \lambda^T f(x, u, t)$, then the costate equations are $\dot{\lambda} = -\frac{\partial H}{\partial x}$.

The boundary condition for the costate at $t f$ is derived from the term multiplying $\delta x(tf)$:

$\lambda^T(t
f) = \frac{\partial \Phi}{\partial x(tf)}$

If $x(t
f)$ is fixed, then $\delta x(tf) = 0$, and this boundary condition is not imposed. If the terminal cost Φ is zero, then $\lambda(t_f)=0$.

The coefficient of $\delta u(t)$ in the integral must be zero for all $t \in
[t
0, tf]$:

$\frac{\partial L}{\partial u} + \lambda^T \frac{\partial f}{\partial u} = 0$

This equation, when solved for $u(t)$ as a function of $x(t)$, $\lambda(t)$, and t, gives the optimal control law in terms of the state and costate. This is often expressed in terms of the Hamiltonian:

$\frac{\partial H}{\partial u} = 0$

This set of equations—the system dynamics, the costate equations, the optimal control condition, and the boundary conditions—forms the foundation for deriving optimal control policies. These are known as the Pontryagin Minimum Principle (PMP) if we are minimizing the cost. For a maximization problem, it is sometimes called the Pontryagin Maximum Principle, though the derivation is analogous.

Let's consider a classic problem to illustrate the application of these principles: the brachistochrone problem. The word "brachistochrone" comes from Greek words meaning "shortest time." The problem is to find the path between two points that a particle, starting from rest and sliding under gravity, will traverse in the shortest possible time.

Suppose we want to find the path from $(0, 0)$ to (xf, yf) where $y_f < 0$ (assuming the y-axis points upwards and gravity acts in the negative y direction). The particle starts with zero velocity.
The speed of the particle at any point (x, y) can be determined from energy conservation. Initial kinetic energy is zero. At height y (where y is measured from the starting point as zero), potential energy lost is $-mg y$. So, $\frac{1}{2}mv^2 = -mg y$, which gives $v = \sqrt{-2gy}$ (if we consider y as positive downwards from the start). If we consider y as positive upwards and the start at $y=0$, then the height is $-y$, so $v = \sqrt{2g y}$ for $y>0$ downward. Let's assume y is positive downwards. So, $v = \sqrt{2gy}$.

The time taken to traverse an infinitesimal segment ds along the path is $dt = \frac{ds}{v}$. The total time is $T = \int dt = \int \frac{ds}{v}$.

We can express ds in terms of the path's shape. If the path is given by $y(x)$, then $ds = \sqrt{1 + (y'(x))^2} dx$.
So, the functional to minimize is:

$T[y] = \int
{0}^{xf} \frac{\sqrt{1 + (y'(x))^2}}{\sqrt{2gy(x)}} dx$

This is a functional of the form $J[y] = \int_{a}^{b} F(y, y') dx$, where $F(y, y') = \frac{\sqrt{1 + (y')^2}}{\sqrt{2gy}}$.

The Euler-Lagrange equation for this functional is $\frac{d}{dx}\left(\frac{\partial F}{\partial y'}\right) - \frac{\partial F}{\partial y} = 0$.

Here, F does not explicitly depend on x. In such cases, there is a conserved quantity, analogous to energy in mechanics. The Beltrami identity states that if F does not depend on x, then $F - y' \frac{\partial F}{\partial y'} = C$ (a constant).

Let's compute the required partial derivatives:

$\frac{\partial F}{\partial y'} = \frac{1}{\sqrt{2gy}} \cdot \frac{1}{2\sqrt{1 + (y')^2}} \cdot 2y' = \frac{y'}{\sqrt{2gy}\sqrt{1 + (y')^2}}$

Now apply the Beltrami identity:

$F - y' \frac{\partial F}{\partial y'} = C$
$\frac{\sqrt{1 + (y')^2}}{\sqrt{2gy}} - y' \left(\frac{y'}{\sqrt{2gy}\sqrt{1 + (y')^2}} \right) = C$
$\frac{1 + (y')^2 - (y')^2}{\sqrt{2gy}\sqrt{1 + (y')^2}} = C$
$\frac{1}{\sqrt{2gy}\sqrt{1 + (y')^2}} = C$

Squaring both sides and rearranging:

$1 = C^2 (2gy) (1 + (y')^2)$
$\frac{1}{C^2 2g} = y (1 + (y')^2)$

Let $k = \frac{1}{C^2 2g}$. This is a constant.

$k = y \left(1 + \left(\frac{dy}{dx}\right)^2 \right)$
$\left(\frac{dy}{dx}\right)^2 = \frac{k}{y} - 1 = \frac{k-y}{y}$
$\frac{dy}{dx} = \sqrt{\frac{k-y}{y}}$

This is a separable differential equation. However, it is more convenient to parameterize the solution. The equation $\frac{dy}{dx} = \sqrt{\frac{k-y}{y}}$ describes the slope of the curve. If we consider a cycloid, which is generated by tracing a point on the rim of a circle as it rolls along a straight line, its parametric equations are well-suited.

A cycloid traced by a circle of radius R rolling on the x-axis, with the point starting at the origin, is given by:
$x(\theta) = R(\theta - \sin \theta)$
$y(\theta) = R(1 - \cos \theta)$

Let's find the slope $\frac{dy}{dx}$ from these parametric equations:

$\frac{dy}{d\theta} = R \sin \theta$
$\frac{dx}{d\theta} = R(1 - \cos \theta)$
$\frac{dy}{dx} = \frac{dy/d\theta}{dx/d\theta} = \frac{R \sin \theta}{R(1 - \cos \theta)} = \frac{2 \sin(\theta/2) \cos(\theta/2)}{2 \sin^2(\theta/2)} = \frac{\cos(\theta/2)}{\sin(\theta/2)} = \cot(\theta/2)$

Now let's look at our differential equation $\frac{dy}{dx} = \sqrt{\frac{k-y}{y}}$.

Substitute $y(\theta) = R(1 - \cos \theta)$:
$\sqrt{\frac{k - R(1 - \cos \theta)}{R(1 - \cos \theta)}} = \sqrt{\frac{k - R + R \cos \theta}{R(1 - \cos \theta)}}$
For this to match $\cot(\theta/2)$, we need a specific relationship between k, R, and θ.
We know that $1 - \cos \theta = 2 \sin^2(\theta/2)$.
Also, $\cot(\theta/2) = \sqrt{\frac{1+\cos\theta}{1-\cos\theta}}$.
So, $\frac{dy}{dx} = \sqrt{\frac{1+\cos\theta}{1-\cos\theta}}$ is not directly what we derived from the cycloid.

Let's re-examine the derived differential equation:
$\left(\frac{dy}{dx}\right)^2 = \frac{k-y}{y}$.

From the cycloid equations: $x = R(\theta - \sin \theta)$, $y = R(1 - \cos \theta)$.
$\frac{dy}{dx} = \cot(\theta/2)$.
So, $\cot^2(\theta/2) = \frac{k - R(1 - \cos \theta)}{R(1 - \cos \theta)}$.
Using $\cos \theta = 1 - 2 \sin^2(\theta/2)$ and $1 - \cos \theta = 2 \sin^2(\theta/2)$:
$\cot^2(\theta/2) = \frac{k - 2R \sin^2(\theta/2)}{2R \sin^2(\theta/2)}$
$\frac{\cos^2(\theta/2)}{\sin^2(\theta/2)} = \frac{k}{2R \sin^2(\theta/2)} - 1$
$\frac{\cos^2(\theta/2)}{\sin^2(\theta/2)} + 1 = \frac{k}{2R \sin^2(\theta/2)}$
$\frac{\cos^2(\theta/2) + \sin^2(\theta/2)}{\sin^2(\theta/2)} = \frac{1}{\sin^2(\theta/2)} = \frac{k}{2R \sin^2(\theta/2)}$
This implies $1 = \frac{k}{2R}$, so $k = 2R$.

Substituting $k=2R$ back into $y = R(1-\cos\theta)$:

$k = 2R$, so $R = k/2$.
$y = \frac{k}{2}(1 - \cos \theta)$. This equation confirms the form of y.
Also, $x = R(\theta - \sin \theta) = \frac{k}{2}(\theta - \sin \theta)$.
These are the parametric equations of a cycloid. The parameter θ is related to the angle of rotation of the rolling circle. It can be seen that y ranges from 0 to $2R$ as θ ranges from 0 to π. For $\theta > \pi$, the cycloid starts to curve back.
The solution $y(x)$ that minimizes the time is a segment of an inverted cycloid. The specific cycloid is determined by the final destination $(xf,

yf)$. The starting point $(0, 0)$ corresponds to $\theta=0$. The end point (xf, yf) determines the value of θ_f and the radius R.

This brachistochrone problem beautifully demonstrates how the Calculus of Variations can be used to find an optimal trajectory that minimizes a time integral, a common objective in control problems. The derivation leads to a differential equation whose solution is a curve that might not be immediately obvious. The identification of the solution with a cycloid is a classic result, showcasing the power of this mathematical framework.

The Calculus of Variations is not limited to finding paths in 2D. In optimal control, we are often dealing with multi-dimensional state spaces and control inputs, and the performance index can be a more complex functional. The Euler-Lagrange equations extend naturally to these cases, becoming a system of differential equations for the state and costate variables. The Hamiltonian formulation derived via the augmented Lagrangian provides a structured way to handle these complex scenarios.

The Hamiltonian $H(x, u, \lambda, t) = L(x, u, t) + \lambda^T f(x, u, t)$ plays a central role. The optimality conditions can be written concisely as:

$\dot{x} = \frac{\partial H}{\partial \lambda}$ (which is $f(x, u, t)$)
$\dot{\lambda} = -\frac{\partial H}{\partial x}$
$\frac{\partial H}{\partial u} = 0$ (for minimizing L)
Boundary conditions for $x(t0), x(tf), \lambda(t0), \lambda(tf)$.

The term $\frac{\partial H}{\partial \lambda}$ yields $\dot{x} = f(x, u, t)$, as λ is not part of f in the standard formulation and H

is linear in λ. If H is linear in λ, i.e., $H = L + \lambda^T f$, then $\frac{\partial H}{\partial \lambda} = f$.

The condition $\frac{\partial H}{\partial u} = 0$ is the key to finding the optimal control $u^(t)$. This equation implicitly defines $u^$ as a function of x, λ, and t, provided that H is differentiable with respect to u and that $\frac{\partial^2 H}{\partial u^2}$ is non-singular for the optimal solution. If the control u is constrained to a set $\mathcal{U}$, then the condition becomes that $\frac{\partial H}{\partial u}$ must be such that $u^$ achieves the minimum of H over $\mathcal{U}$. If u is unconstrained, we simply set the gradient to zero.

The boundary conditions are also crucial. For the state $x(t)$, they are usually given as $x(t
0) = x0$ (initial condition) and $x(tf)$ may be fixed or free. For the costate $\lambda(t)$, the boundary condition is derived from the terminal cost $\Phi(x(tf))$. If $x(tf)$ is free, then $\lambda(tf) = \frac{\partial \Phi}{\partial x(tf)}$. If $x(tf)$ is fixed, then $\lambda(tf)$ is determined by the costate dynamics. If $\Phi=0$ and $x(tf)$ is free, then $\lambda(t_f)=0$.

Solving these coupled differential equations (system dynamics and costate equations) with the optimal control law and boundary conditions typically requires numerical methods, especially for nonlinear systems. This is because the costate equations depend on x and λ, and the optimal control $u^$ also depends on x and λ. This forms a Two-Point Boundary Value Problem (TPBVP), which is generally more difficult to solve than an initial value problem.

The Calculus of Variations, therefore, provides the theoretical foundation for deriving the necessary conditions for optimality. It transforms the problem of finding an optimal function into solving a system of differential equations. While it doesn't always yield an explicit solution, it offers a powerful analytical tool and the basis for numerical algorithms used in modern optimal control. The elegance of the Euler-Lagrange equation and the structured approach provided by the Hamiltonian formulation are cornerstones of optimal control theory.

The framework established by the Calculus of Variations, while powerful, primarily yields necessary conditions for optimality. For optimal control problems, a more direct and broadly applicable tool is Pontryagin's Minimum Principle (PMP). Developed by Lev Pontryagin and his colleagues in the Soviet Union, PMP provides a set of necessary conditions that an optimal control must satisfy. It is a significant advancement because it can handle a wider range of problems, including those with non-linear dynamics and constraints on the control inputs and states. At its heart, PMP is an extension of the ideas from the Calculus of Variations, but it frames the problem using the concept of the Hamiltonian, which elegantly incorporates both the system dynamics and the performance index.

The core idea behind PMP is to define a Hamiltonian function, often denoted by H, which is constructed from the system's Lagrangian (the instantaneous cost or reward rate) and the system dynamics. For a system described by the state equation $\dot{x}(t) = f(x(t), u(t), t)$ and a performance index to be minimized in the form $J = \Phi(x(t f)) + \int{t0}^{tf} L(x(t), u(t), t) dt$, the Hamiltonian is defined as:
$H(x, u, \lambda, t) = L(x, u, t) + \lambda^T(t) f(x, u, t)$
Here, $\lambda(t)$ represents the vector of costate or adjoint variables, which are essentially Lagrange multipliers associated with the system dynamics. These costate variables are crucial as they capture the sensitivity of the optimal cost to changes in the state variables.

Pontryagin's Minimum Principle states that if $u^

(t)$ is an optimal control for the time interval $[t0, tf]$, and $x^(t)$ is the corresponding optimal state trajectory, then there must exist a costate vector function $\lambda(t)$ such that for all $t \in [t0, tf]$:

1.
State Equation: $\dot{x}^(t) = \frac{\partial H}{\partial \lambda}(x^(t), u^(t), \lambda(t), t) = f(x^(t), u^(t), t)$. This is simply the original system dynamics.

2.
Costate Equation: $\dot{\lambda}(t) = -\frac{\partial H}{\partial x}(x^(t), u^(t), \lambda(t), t)$. This equation describes the dynamics of the costate variables. It shows how the adjoint variables evolve backward in time (or forward, depending on the convention and problem formulation).

3.
Minimization Condition: $H(x^(t), u^(t), \lambda(t), t) \le H(x^(t), u, \lambda(t), t)$ for all admissible control values u at time t. This condition implies that the optimal control $u^(t)$ must minimize the Hamiltonian at each instant of time, given the current state $x^(t)$ and costate $\lambda(t)$. If the control u is unconstrained, this condition simplifies to $\frac{\partial H}{\partial u}(x^(t), u^(t), \lambda(t), t) = 0$.

4.
Boundary Conditions: The initial state is typically fixed, $x^(t0) = x0$. The terminal state $x^(tf)$ may be free or constrained. The costate boundary conditions are coupled with the terminal cost function Φ. If the terminal state is free, then $\lambda(tf) = \frac{\partial \Phi}{\partial x}(x^(tf))$. If the terminal state is fixed, this condition is not imposed. If the terminal cost Φ is zero and the terminal state is free, then $\lambda(tf) = 0$.

The power of PMP lies in its ability to transform an optimal control problem into a two-point boundary value problem (TPBVP). We have the system dynamics evolving forward in time from $t
0$ and the costate dynamics, which are often solved backward in time from tf. The minimization condition at each time step provides the optimal control law $u^(t)$ as a function of $x^(t)$ and $\lambda(t)$. When combined, these form a set of differential equations with conditions specified at both the initial and final times, which can then be solved, often numerically.

Let's consider an example to illustrate the application of Pontryagin's Minimum Principle. Suppose we want to minimize the time taken to reach a target state for a simple one-dimensional system.

Consider a system with state $x(t)$ and control $u(t)$, described by $\dot{x}(t) = u(t)$. We want to drive the system from $x(t0) = x0$ to $x(tf) = xf$ in the minimum possible time tf. Let $t0=0$ and $x0=0$, and we want to reach $xf > 0$. The performance index to minimize is simply $J = tf$. This can be written in the standard form by introducing a dummy state variable, say $s(t)$, such that $\dot{s}(t) = 1$ with $s(t0)=0$, and the objective becomes minimizing $s(tf)$. The terminal state $s(tf)$ is not constrained, but we want to minimize it. The terminal cost Φ is zero.

The system dynamics are:

$\dot{x}(t) = u(t)$
$\dot{s}(t) = 1$

The performance index is $J = s(t
f)$. Here, $L(x, u, s, t) = 0$ (instantaneous cost is zero) and $\Phi(x(tf), s(tf)) = s(tf)$.

The control is subject to constraints, typically $|u(t)| \le U{\max}$, *where* $U{\max}$ is a positive constant. This constraint is crucial and demonstrates the strength of PMP over methods that assume unconstrained controls.

The Hamiltonian is given by:

$H(x, u, s, \lambdax, \lambdas, t) = L + \lambdax \dot{x} + \lambdas \dot{s}$
$H(x, u, s, \lambdax, \lambdas, t) = 0 + \lambdax u(t) + \lambdas (1)$
$H(x, u, s, \lambdax, \lambdas, t) = \lambdax u(t) + \lambdas$

The costate equations are:

$\dot{\lambda}_x = -\frac{\partial H}{\partial x} = -0 = 0$
$\dot{\lambda}_s = -\frac{\partial H}{\partial s} = -0 = 0$

The boundary conditions for the costates are derived from the terminal cost $\Phi(x(t
f), s(tf)) = s(t_f)$:
At $t=tf$, $\lambdax(tf) = \frac{\partial \Phi}{\partial x(tf)} = 0$.
At $t=tf$, $\lambdas(tf) = \frac{\partial \Phi}{\partial s(tf)} = 1$.

From $\dot{\lambda}
x = 0$, we get $\lambdax(t) = C1$. Using the boundary condition $\lambdax(tf) = 0$, we find $C1 = 0$. So, $\lambdax(t) = 0$ for all $t \in [t0, t_f]$.
From $\dot{\lambda}s = 0$, we get $\lambdas(t) = C2$. Using the boundary condition $\lambdas(tf) = 1$, we find $C2 = 1$. So, $\lambdas(t) = 1$ for all $t \in [t0, t_f]$.

Now we apply the minimization condition for the Hamiltonian:

$H = \lambdax u(t) + \lambdas = 0 \cdot u(t) + 1 = 1$.
The Hamiltonian is $H=1$, and it does not depend on u. However, we must satisfy the constraint $|u(t)| \le U_{\max}$. The minimization condition states that the optimal control $u^(t)$ must minimize H over the admissible set of controls. Since $H=1$ is constant with respect to u, any u satisfying the constraints would yield the same Hamiltonian value. This seems to suggest that the minimum is achieved for any admissible u.

However, PMP states that $u^(t)$ must minimize H. If H were dependent on u, say $H = g(u)$, we would choose u to minimize $g(u)$. In this specific time-optimal problem, the minimization condition should be interpreted as finding u such that H is minimized. If H is $ \lambda
x u + \lambdas $, and $\lambdax = 0$, the term involving u vanishes. The Hamiltonian is simply $\lambdas = 1$.

Let's reconsider the minimization condition in the context of constrained control. The condition is $H(x^
, u^, \lambda) \le H(x^, u, \lambda)$ for all admissible u.
In our case, $H = 0 \cdot u + 1 = 1$. So, $1 \le 1$ for all admissible u.
This suggests that the optimal control might be related to the sign of $\lambdax$ if $\lambdax$ were non-zero. The fact that $\lambdax = 0$ is peculiar for time-optimal control. This is a known characteristic of time-optimal problems for systems where the control directly affects the state derivative. The transversality condition (boundary condition for costate) for time-optimal problems often results in $\lambdax(t_f)=0$.

The control $u^(t)$ should be chosen to minimize H. If H were $ \lambda
x u + \lambdas $, and we had $\lambda_x \neq 0$:
If $\lambdax > 0$, we would choose $u = -U{\max}$ to minimize H.
If $\lambdax < 0$, we would choose $u = +U{\max}$ to minimize H.

Since $\lambda_x = 0$, this direct approach doesn't yield a unique control.

This situation suggests that the control might be bang-bang, switching between $+U
{\max}$ and $-U{\max}$. For the system $\dot{x} = u$ with $x(0)=0$ and $x(tf)=xf$, to reach a positive xf in minimum time, we intuitively should use $u(t) = +U{\max}$ for the entire duration. If this is the case, then $x(t) = U{\max} t$ and $tf = xf / U{\max}$.

Let's verify if this control satisfies PMP. If $u^(t) = U
{\max}$ for all $t \in [0, tf]$, then:
$\dot{x}^(t) = U{\max}$. With $x^(0)=0$, we get $x^(t) = U{\max} t$. If $tf = xf / U{\max}$, then $x^(tf) = U{\max} (xf / U{\max}) = xf$. So the state reaches the target.
The costate equations and boundary conditions $\lambdax(t)=0, \lambdas(t)=1$ are satisfied.
The minimization condition: $H = \lambdax u + \lambdas = 0 \cdot u + 1 = 1$.
The condition is $H(x^, u^, \lambda) \le H(x^, u, \lambda)$ for all admissible u.
$1 \le 0 \cdot u + 1$, which is $1 \le 1$. This inequality is always true for any u.

The ambiguity arises because the Hamiltonian is linear in u and the coefficient λ_x turns out to be zero for the entire interval. In such cases, the minimum of the Hamiltonian might be achieved over an interval of control values. However, for time-optimal control problems of this form, the solution is known to be bang-bang. The minimum time is achieved by always applying the maximum possible control effort in the direction that increases the state towards the target.

This example highlights that PMP provides necessary conditions. While it helps identify candidate optimal controls, further analysis might be needed to confirm optimality. For many systems, especially with non-linear dynamics or more complex cost functions, PMP yields a unique optimal control law.

A key strength of PMP is its ability to handle control constraints explicitly. When the control u is constrained to a set $\mathcal{U}$, the minimization condition becomes:

$u^(t) = \arg \min_{u \in \mathcal{U}} H(x^(t), u, \lambda(t), t)$. This means that at each time t, we find the control u from the admissible set $\mathcal{U}$ that results in the smallest value of the Hamiltonian.

Consider another example: a system with $\dot{x}(t) = -x(t) + u(t)$, with $x(0)=1$, and we want to drive $x(t)$ to 0 in minimum time t_f. Assume $|u(t)| \le 1$.

The performance index is $J = t_f$. So $L=0$, $\Phi=0$, and we introduce $\dot{s}=1$, $s(0)=0$.
The Hamiltonian is $H = \lambdax \dot{x} + \lambdas \dot{s} = \lambdax (-x + u) + \lambdas (1)$.
Costate equations:
$\dot{\lambda}x = -\frac{\partial H}{\partial x} = -\lambdax (-1) = \lambda_x$
$\dot{\lambda}s = -\frac{\partial H}{\partial s} = 0$. With $\lambdas(tf)=1$, we get $\lambdas(t)=1$.

Boundary conditions:

$\lambdax(tf) = \frac{\partial \Phi}{\partial x(t_f)} = 0$.
$\lambdas(tf) = \frac{\partial \Phi}{\partial s(t_f)} = 1$.

From $\dot{\lambda}
x = \lambdax$, the solution is $\lambdax(t) = C e^t$. Using $\lambdax(tf) = 0$, we get $C e^{tf} = 0$, which implies $C=0$. Thus, $\lambda_x(t) = 0$ for all t.
The Hamiltonian becomes $H = 0 \cdot (-x + u) + 1 = 1$.
Again, the Hamiltonian is independent of u.

The problem $\dot{x} = -x+u$ with $x(0)=1$ to $x(t
f)=0$ in minimum time is a standard example where the control should be $u^(t) = -\text{sgn}(x(t))$. However, this requires knowing the sign of $x(t)$ beforehand. PMP is supposed to give us this information. The issue here is the $\lambdax=0$ situation.

In cases where $\lambda_x=0$ for a duration, it might indicate a singular arc, where the control is not bang-bang and cannot be determined solely from $\partial H/\partial u = 0$. This means that H might be constant with respect to u over the interval. For such singular arcs, one might need to look at higher-order conditions or alternative optimality conditions.

However, for the specific problem $\dot{x}=-x+u$, $x(0)=1$ to $x(t_f)=0$ with $|u|\le 1$, the optimal control is indeed $u^(t) = -\text{sgn}(x(t))$. Let's analyze this control.

If $x(t)$ is positive, we want to decrease it, so we choose $u=-1$. If $x(t)$ is negative, we want to increase it towards zero, so we choose $u=+1$. The differential equation is $\dot{x} = -x+u$. If $u=-1$, $\dot{x} = -x-1$. The solution for $x(0)=1$ is $x(t) = -1 + 2e^{-t}$. This is positive for small t. As t increases, $x(t)$ decreases and approaches -1.

If $x(t)$ becomes negative, we switch u to $+1$. $\dot{x} = -x+1$. The solution for $x(t1) < 0$ is $x(t) = 1 + (x(t1)-1)e^{-(t-t_1)}$. This trajectory will approach $+1$.

The optimal trajectory must reach $x=0$. The control $u^(t) = -\text{sgn}(x(t))$ implies that if $x(t)>0$, $u=-1$; if $x(t)<0$, $u=1$.

Let's test $u(t) = -1$ for all t. Then $\dot{x} = -x-1$, $x(0)=1$. $x(t) = -1 + 2e^{-t}$. This trajectory asymptotically approaches -1. It never reaches 0.
Let's test $u(t) = 1$ for all t. Then $\dot{x} = -x+1$, $x(0)=1$. $x(t) = 1$. This trajectory stays at $x=1$.

The issue might be in the interpretation of the boundary condition $\lambda
x(tf)=0$ for time-optimal problems when the terminal state is free. For free terminal state, time-optimal control does not impose a condition on $\lambdax(tf)$ directly from $\partial \Phi / \partial x(tf)$. Instead, the condition is on the Hamiltonian at tf. For a time-optimal problem, $H(tf) = \lambdas(t_f) = 1$.

Let's assume a bang-bang control $u(t) = \text{sgn}(\lambda_x(t))$.

From $\dot{\lambda}x = \lambdax$, we have $\lambda_x(t) = C e^t$.
The Hamiltonian is $H = \lambdax u + \lambdas$.
If $\lambdax(t)$ is never zero, $u^(t) = \text{sgn}(\lambdax(t))$.
If $\lambdax(t) = C e^t$, for $C \ne 0$, then $u^(t)$ is either e^t or $-e^t$. This suggests $u^(t)$ changes sign, but e^t is always positive.
This implies $\lambdax(t)$ should have a constant sign if $C \ne 0$.

The problem $\dot{x}=-x+u$ with $x(0)=1$ to $x(t_f)=0$ is known to have a solution where $u(t)$ switches. For example, $u=-1$ initially to drive x down, and then potentially switches to $u=+1$ to fine-tune near zero.

If we try to reach $x=0$ from $x=1$ using $u=-1$: $\dot{x}=-x-1$, $x(0)=1$, $x(t)=-1+2e^{-t}$. This approaches -1. It seems impossible to reach 0 with a constant u.

The issue arises because the specific system dynamics $\dot{x}=-x+u$ coupled with the costate equation $\dot{\lambda}
x = \lambdax$ leads to $\lambdax*(t)=0$ if we apply the terminal condition $\lambdax*(t_f)=0$.
For time-optimal control, a common strategy when the Hamiltonian is linear in u and λ_x becomes zero is to consider higher-order derivatives of the Hamiltonian with respect to u and time, or to analyze the structure of the control.

Consider the generalized Legendre-Clebsch condition, which is a higher-order necessary condition for optimality. If $\frac{\partial H}{\partial u} = 0$ gives a singular arc (i.e., it does not uniquely determine u), we examine $\frac{d}{dt}\left(\frac{\partial H}{\partial u}\right) = 0$ and subsequent derivatives.

$\frac{\partial H}{\partial u} = \lambda_x$.
$\frac{d}{dt}\left(\frac{\partial H}{\partial u}\right) = \dot{\lambda}_x$.
If $\lambdax *= 0$ and $\dot{\lambda}*x = 0$, this suggests a singular arc.
However, if $\dot{\lambda}x *= \lambdax*$, then if $\lambdax*=0$ at $t*f$, it implies $\lambdax*=0$ for all t backwards from $t*f$ if the time interval is sufficiently large.

Let's re-evaluate the problem formulation and boundary conditions for time-optimal control. The condition $H(t_f)=1$ must hold.

$H = \lambdax u + \lambdas$.
$\lambdas(t)=1$ always. So $H = \lambdax u + 1$.
If $u^(t) = -\text{sgn}(\lambdax(t))$, then $H = \lambdax (-
\text{sgn}(\lambdax)) + 1 = -|\lambdax| + 1$.
For H to be minimized, we want to minimize $-|\lambdax|+1$. This is achieved when $|\lambdax|$ is maximized.

Let's consider the case where $x(t
f)$ is free. The boundary condition is that the Hamiltonian evaluated at tf must be -1 for a minimization problem of $-\int L dt$ or $+1$ for a maximization problem of $\int L dt$. If the objective is time minimization, and $J=tf$, then $\Phi=0$. The Hamiltonian condition is $\lambdas(tf)=1$ (from $\partial \Phi / \partial s$). The value of H at tf is not directly constrained to ± 1 as in some formulations.

The key is that PMP gives necessary conditions. For problems with constraints, the conditions are:

1. $\dot{x} = f(x, u, t)$
2. $\dot{\lambda} = -\partial H / \partial x$
3. $u^(t) = \arg \min_{u \in \mathcal{U}} H(x, u, \lambda, t)$
4. Boundary conditions.

In $\dot{x}=-x+u$, $|u|\le 1$, $x(0)=1$, $x(t
f)=0$, minimum tf.
$H = \lambdax(-x+u) + \lambdas$. $\lambdas=1$. $H = \lambdax(-x+u) + 1$.
$\dot{\lambda}x = \lambdax$. $\lambdax(tf)$ depends on whether $x(t_f)$ is fixed or free.
If $x(tf)$ is fixed to 0, then $\lambdax(tf)$ is not determined by Φ. However, typically for $\dot{x}=f(x,u)$, the costate $\lambdax(tf)$ is determined by $\partial \Phi / \partial x(tf)$. Here $\Phi=0$, so $\lambdax(tf)=0$.

This leads to $\lambda_x(t)=0$ for all t. Then $H=1$, and $u^$ is any value in $[-1,1]$ that minimizes H. Since H is independent of u, any $u \in [-1,1]$ is a candidate. This means there might be a singular control or a family of optimal controls.

This suggests that maybe the problem is not a simple bang-bang control.
For $\dot{x}=-x+u$, $x(0)=1$, $x(t_f)=0$.

Let's try to find a $u(t)$ that drives x from 1 to 0.
If we use $u=-1$ for $0 \le t \le t1$, $x(t) = -1+2e^{-t}$. $x(t1)=-1+2e^{-t1}$. For $x(t1)$ to be ≤ 0, we need $2e^{-t1} \le 1$, so $e^{-t1} \le 1/2$, $t_1 \ge \ln 2$.
At $t1 = \ln 2$, $x(t1) = -1 + 2(1/2) = 0$. So, with $u(t)=-1$ for $t \in [0, \ln 2]$, we reach $x=0$ at $t_f = \ln 2$.
This is a valid solution. The minimum time is $t_f=\ln 2$.
The control is $u(t)=-1$ for $t \in [0, \ln 2]$.
Let's check if this satisfies PMP.
$\lambda_x(t)=0$ for all t. $H=1$. Minimization: $H=1$ for $u=-1$, $1 \le 1$. This is satisfied.
The state equation: $\dot{x}=-x+u$. If $u=-1$, $\dot{x}=-x-1$. $x(0)=1$. $x(t)=-1+2e^{-t}$. At $t=\ln 2$, $x(\ln 2)=-1+2e^{-\ln 2} = -1+2(1/2)=0$.
So, $u^(t)=-1$ for $t \in [0, \ln 2]$ is the optimal control.

This example shows that sometimes the optimal control might be constant, even for time-optimal problems, and $\lambda_x=0$ is consistent with this. The key is that the Hamiltonian must be minimized over the admissible control set. If the Hamiltonian is constant with respect to u, any admissible u that results in the minimal Hamiltonian value is a candidate.

Beyond these foundational aspects, PMP also provides a framework for problems with state constraints. If the state $x(t)$ is constrained to remain within a certain region, additional conditions, known as generalized Legendre-Clebsch conditions or similar adjoint variable boundary conditions, are required. These conditions essentially ensure that the optimal trajectory does not violate the state constraints and that the costate variables are adjusted accordingly when the trajectory hits a boundary.

The derivation of these conditions for state constraints is more involved. It typically involves introducing additional Lagrange multipliers associated with the state constraints and deriving their dynamics. The essential idea is to extend the Hamiltonian framework to incorporate these additional constraints, leading to a more complex system of differential equations and boundary conditions. However, the fundamental principle remains: minimizing the Hamiltonian with respect to the control input, now over a feasible region that respects both control and state constraints.

In summary, Pontryagin's Minimum Principle is a cornerstone of optimal control theory, offering a powerful and systematic approach to determining optimal control strategies. By defining a Hamiltonian function and deriving necessary conditions based on its properties, PMP transforms complex optimization problems into solvable systems of differential equations. The principle's ability to handle control constraints and its theoretical elegance make it an indispensable tool for analysis and design in a wide array of engineering and scientific applications. While it provides necessary conditions, for many practical problems, these conditions are also sufficient for optimality, especially for linear systems or under certain convexity assumptions. The principle's generalization to handle state constraints further solidifies its position as a fundamental theoretical construct in modern control theory.

The Linear Quadratic Regulator (LQR) stands as a seminal technique within the field of optimal control, offering a systematic and elegant solution for a specific, yet pervasive, class of problems: controlling linear systems to minimize a quadratic cost function. Its enduring popularity stems from several key attributes: the simplicity and tractability of the underlying mathematics, the guaranteed stability and performance of the resulting controller, and its role as a foundational benchmark against which more complex, often heuristic or data-driven, control strategies are measured. LQR provides a concrete framework for understanding the trade-offs between control effort and system performance, making it an indispensable tool for both theoretical analysis and practical engineering design.

The core of the LQR problem formulation lies in its two primary components: the system dynamics and the cost function. We consider a continuous-time linear time-invariant (LTI) system, described by the state-space representation:

$\dot{x}(t) = Ax(t) + Bu(t)$

Here, $x(t) \in \mathbb{R}^n$ is the state vector of the system at time t, representing its internal configuration. $u(t) \in \mathbb{R}^m$ is the control input vector, which we can manipulate to influence the system's behavior. A is the $n \times n$ state matrix, characterizing the system's internal dynamics (how the state evolves without external input), and B is the $n \times m$ input matrix, dictating how the control inputs affect the state. We assume that the system is controllable, meaning that it is possible to steer the system from any initial state to any final state using the available control inputs.

The objective in LQR is to find a control input $u(t)$ over a specified time horizon, say from $t=0$ to $t=t_f$, that minimizes a quadratic performance index. This cost function penalizes deviations of the state from a desired target (often the origin, $x=0$) and the magnitude of the control effort. The general form of the quadratic cost function for a finite-horizon LQR problem is:

$$J = x(t_f)^T S_f x(t_f) + \int_{0}^{t_f} (x(t)^T Q x(t) + u(t)^T R u(t)) dt$$

In this expression:

- $x(t_f)^T S_f x(t_f)$ represents a terminal cost, penalizing the final state error at time t_f. S_f is a symmetric positive semi-definite matrix ($S_f \ge 0$). If the terminal state is not of critical importance, S_f can be set to zero.
- $\int_{0}^{t_f} x(t)^T Q x(t) dt$ is the integrated state cost, penalizing deviations of the state from the origin over the entire time horizon. Q is a symmetric positive semi-definite matrix ($Q \ge 0$), where diagonal elements represent penalties on individual states.
- $\int_{0}^{t_f} u(t)^T R u(t) dt$ is the integrated control cost, penalizing the effort expended by the control inputs. R is a symmetric positive definite matrix ($R > 0$), where diagonal elements penalize individual control inputs. The requirement for R to be positive definite ensures that excessive control effort is always penalized, thereby preventing unbounded control actions and leading to a well-posed problem.

The matrices Q and R are tuning parameters. By adjusting their values, an engineer can explicitly shape the desired behavior of the controlled system. For instance, increasing the diagonal elements of Q will drive the corresponding states more aggressively towards zero, while increasing the diagonal elements of R will lead to more conservative control actions, prioritizing energy efficiency or actuator saturation avoidance over rapid state convergence.

The problem of finding the optimal control $u(t)$ that minimizes this cost function J for the linear system $\dot{x}(t) = Ax(t) + Bu(t)$ can be solved using the calculus of variations, or more directly, through dynamic programming and Pontryagin's Minimum Principle. The solution reveals a remarkable property: the optimal control law is a linear state feedback law. That is, at any time t, the optimal control $u^(t)$ is a linear function of the current state $x(t)$:

$u^(t) = -K(t) x(t)$

where $K(t)$ is the time-varying feedback gain matrix. This result is profound because it means we do not need to know the future state trajectory to determine the current optimal control; only the current state is required. This characteristic is fundamental to designing controllers that can operate in real-time.

The derivation of this feedback law involves constructing the Hamiltonian for the LQR problem. The system dynamics are $\dot{x} = Ax + Bu$. The running cost is $L(x, u) = x^T Q x + u^T R u$. The terminal cost is $\Phi(x(t f)) = x(tf)^T Sf x(tf)$. The Hamiltonian is:

$H(x, u, \lambda, t) = L(x, u) + \lambda(t)^T (Ax(t) + Bu(t))$

$H(x, u, \lambda, t) = x^T Q x + u^T R u + \lambda^T (Ax + Bu)$

where $\lambda(t)$ is the costate vector. According to Pontryagin's Minimum Principle, the optimal control $u^(t)$ must minimize the Hamiltonian. To find this minimizing control, we differentiate H with respect to u and set it to zero (assuming R is invertible and u is unconstrained for now):

$\frac{\partial H}{\partial u} = 2u^T R + \lambda^T B = 0$

Taking the transpose of both sides:
$2R u + B^T \lambda = 0$
$2R u = -B^T \lambda$
$u = -\frac{1}{2} R^{-1} B^T \lambda$

Since we are looking for $u^(t)$, let's denote λ as $\lambda(t)$:

$u^(t) = -\frac{1}{2} R^{-1} B^T \lambda(t)$

This equation shows that the optimal control is proportional to the costate vector $\lambda(t)$. This is a key insight from PMP. However, the costate dynamics are given by:

$\dot{\lambda}(t) = -\frac{\partial H}{\partial x} = -(2x^T Q + \lambda^T A)^T = -2Qx - A^T \lambda$

And the state dynamics are:

$\dot{x}(t) = Ax + Bu$

Substituting $u^(t)$ into the state equation:

$\dot{x}(t) = Ax + B (-\frac{1}{2} R^{-1} B^T \lambda(t))$
$\dot{x}(t) = Ax - \frac{1}{2} B R^{-1} B^T \lambda(t)$

We now have a coupled system of linear differential equations for $x(t)$ and $\lambda(t)$:

$\dot{x}(t) = Ax - \frac{1}{2} B R^{-1} B^T \lambda(t)$
$\dot{\lambda}(t) = -A^T \lambda(t) - 2Qx(t)$

These are augmented by boundary conditions. $x(0)$ is given. The boundary condition for $\lambda(t_f)$ is derived from the terminal cost:

$\lambda(t
f) = \frac{\partial \Phi}{\partial x(tf)} = 2Sf x(tf)$

This system is a two-point boundary value problem (TPBVP), where conditions are specified at both the initial time ($x(0)$) and the final time ($\lambda(t_f)$). A standard approach to solving such TPBVPs is to assume a linear relationship between the costate and the state at the final time, and then propagate this relationship backward in time.

Let's hypothesize that the relationship between $\lambda(t)$ and $x(t)$ remains linear throughout the interval, i.e., $\lambda(t) = P(t) x(t)$ for some matrix $P(t)$. Substituting this into the costate and state equations:

$\dot{\lambda}(t) = \dot{P}(t) x(t) + P(t) \dot{x}(t)$

$-A^T \lambda(t) - 2Qx(t) = \dot{P}(t) x(t) + P(t) \dot{x}(t)$
$-A^T P(t) x(t) - 2Qx(t) = \dot{P}(t) x(t) + P(t) (Ax(t) - \frac{1}{2} B R^{-1} B^T P(t) x(t))$

Rearranging terms to group by $x(t)$:

$0 = (\dot{P}(t) + P(t)A - \frac{1}{2} P(t) B R^{-1} B^T P(t) + A^T P(t) + 2Q) x(t)$

For this equation to hold for all $x(t)$ (not identically zero), the term in the parenthesis must be zero:

$\dot{P}(t) + P(t)A + A^T P(t) - P(t) B R^{-1} B^T P(t) + 2Q = 0$

This is a matrix differential equation known as the **Riccati equation**. It governs the evolution of the matrix $P(t)$. The boundary condition for $P(t)$ is derived from the terminal condition for $\lambda(t)$:

$\lambda(t
f) = P(tf) x(t_f)$
$2S*f x(tf)* = P(t*f) x(tf)*$
Thus, $P(t*f) = 2Sf*$.

The Riccati equation is typically solved backward in time from t_f to

0. Once $P(t)$ is obtained, the optimal control law $u^(t)$ can be expressed in terms of $x(t)$ and $P(t)$:

$u^(t) = -\frac{1}{2} R^{-1} B^T \lambda(t) = -\frac{1}{2} R^{-1} B^T P(t) x(t)$

This gives us the time-varying feedback gain matrix:

$K(t) = \frac{1}{2} R^{-1} B^T P(t)$

So, the optimal control is $u^(t) = -K(t) x(t)$.

The Infinite-Horizon LQR Problem and the Algebraic Riccati Equation (ARE)

A very common and practically important scenario is the infinite-horizon LQR problem, where the time horizon $t_f \to \infty$. The objective is to maintain the system's state at zero indefinitely while minimizing control effort. In this case, the performance index becomes:

$J = \int_{0}^{\infty} (x(t)^T Q x(t) + u(t)^T R u(t)) dt$

For the infinite-horizon problem, if the system is stabilizable (meaning the unstable modes of A can be controlled by B) and detectable (meaning the unobservable states can be inferred from the outputs, which for LQR typically means Q must penalize all states that B can influence), the optimal feedback gain matrix $K(t)$ becomes time-invariant, $K(t) = K$. This means $P(t)$ also converges to a constant matrix, P. The Riccati differential equation then simplifies to the **Algebraic Riccati Equation (ARE)**:

$P A + A^T P - P B R^{-1} B^T P + Q = 0$

Solving this algebraic equation for P yields a unique, symmetric, positive semi-definite matrix P (provided the system is stabilizable and detectable). Once P is found, the constant optimal feedback gain is given by:

$K = R^{-1} B^T P$

And the optimal control law is a time-invariant state feedback:

$u^(t) = -K x(t)$

The closed-loop system dynamics with this optimal controller are:

$\dot{x}(t) = Ax + B u^(t) = Ax + B (-K x(t)) = (A - BK) x(t)$

The matrix $(A - BK)$ is guaranteed to be stable (all its eigenvalues have negative real parts) if the original system is stabilizable and detectable, and Q and R are chosen appropriately. This means that the LQR controller inherently stabilizes the system.

Example 1: Stabilizing an Inverted Pendulum

Consider a simplified model of an inverted pendulum. Let the state be $x = [p, \theta, \dot{p}, \dot{\theta}]^T$, where p is the horizontal position of the cart, θ is the angle of the pendulum from the vertical (upward) equilibrium, $\dot{p}$ is the cart velocity, and $\dot{\theta}$ is the angular velocity. The control input u is the force applied to the cart. The linearized dynamics around the unstable upright equilibrium can be represented in state-space form $\dot{x} = Ax + Bu$.

Let's assume simplified dynamics for illustration (actual derivations are more complex):

$A = \begin{pmatrix}
0 & 0 & 1 & 0 \\
0 & 0 & 0 & 1 \\
0 & -g/l & 0 & 0 \\
0 & g/l & 0 & 0
\end{pmatrix}$, $B = \begin{pmatrix}
0 \\
0 \\
1/m \\
0
\end{pmatrix}$
where g is acceleration due to gravity, l is the pendulum length, and m is the mass of the pendulum bob. For simplicity, assume $g/l = 1$ and $1/m = 1$.

$A = \begin{pmatrix}
0 & 0 & 1 & 0 \\
0 & 0 & 0 & 1 \\
0 & -1 & 0 & 0 \\
0 & 1 & 0 & 0
\end{pmatrix}$, $B = \begin{pmatrix}
0 \\
0 \\
1 \\
0
\end{pmatrix}$

We want to stabilize the pendulum in the upright position ($\theta=0, \dot{\theta}=0$) and keep the cart at the origin ($p=0, \dot{p}=0$). We use an infinite-horizon LQR formulation with a cost function:

$J = \int_{0}^{\infty} (x^T Q x + u^T R u) dt$

We need to choose Q and R. A typical choice might penalize position and velocity errors, and control effort. For example:

$Q = \text{diag}(1, 100, 1, 1)$
Here, $Q{22}=100$ heavily penalizes the angle error θ, making it a primary objective to keep the pendulum upright. $Q{11}, Q{33}, Q{44}$ penalize cart position, cart velocity, and angular velocity, respectively.
$R = \text{diag}(1)$ (or simply $R=1$)
This penalizes the applied force u.

The problem reduces to solving the ARE:

$P A + A^T P - P B R^{-1} B^T P + Q = 0$
with $R=1$.
$P \begin{pmatrix}

0 & 0 & 1 & 0 \\
0 & 0 & 0 & 1 \\
0 & -1 & 0 & 0 \\
0 & 1 & 0 & 0
\end{pmatrix} + \begin{pmatrix}
0 & 0 & 0 & 0 \\
0 & 0 & -1 & 1 \\
1 & 0 & 0 & 0 \\
0 & 1 & 0 & 0
\end{pmatrix} P - P \begin{pmatrix}
0 \\
0 \\
1 \\
0
\end{pmatrix} \begin{pmatrix}
0 & 0 & 1 & 0
\end{pmatrix} P + \begin{pmatrix}
1 & 0 & 0 & 0 \\
0 & 100 & 0 & 0 \\
0 & 0 & 1 & 0 \\
0 & 0 & 0 & 1
\end{pmatrix} = 0$

This is a set of 10 coupled non-linear algebraic equations for the 10 independent entries of the symmetric matrix P. Solving this numerically (using tools like MATLAB's `lqr` or Python's `control.lqr`) yields the matrix P.

Let's assume, after numerical solution, we obtain a specific P. The optimal feedback gain K is then calculated as:
$K = R^{-1} B^T P = \begin{pmatrix}
1 & 0 & 0 & 0
\end{pmatrix} P$

Suppose the resulting K is $K = \begin{pmatrix} k
1 & k2 & k3 & k4 \end{pmatrix}$. The optimal control law would be:
$u^(t) = -k1 p(t) - k2 \theta(t) - k3 \dot{p}(t) - k4 \dot{\theta}(t)$

This control law uses all state variables to maintain the pendulum's stability. For instance, if the pendulum starts to fall (θ increases), the controller will apply a force to counteract it. If the cart moves away from the center (p increases), the controller will adjust the force to bring it back. The specific magnitudes of $k
1, k2, k3, k4$ are determined by the relative weighting of state errors and control effort in Q and R. The large penalty on θ ($Q{22}=100$) would typically result in a significant gain $k2$.

Example 2: Pitch Control of an Aircraft

Consider a simplified longitudinal dynamics model of an aircraft. The relevant states might be pitch angle θ, pitch rate $q = \dot{\theta}$, angle of attack α, and velocity V. However, for a typical autopilot design focusing on pitch hold, we might simplify the state to just θ and q. The control input is the elevator deflection δ_e.

The linearized dynamics around a steady flight condition can be approximated by:

$\dot{\theta} = q$
$\dot{q} = M{\deltae} \deltae + M{\theta} \theta + M_q q$

where $M

{\deltae}$ is the elevator effectiveness, $M{\theta}$ is the pitch restoring moment coefficient, and Mq is the pitch damping coefficient.
Let the state vector be $x = [\theta, q]^T$. The control input is $u = \delta_e$.
$A = \begin{pmatrix}
0 & 1 \\
M{\theta} & Mq
\end{pmatrix}$, $B = \begin{pmatrix}
0 \\
M{\deltae}
\end{pmatrix}$

The objective is to maintain a desired pitch angle, say $\theta {ref}$. We can achieve this by designing an LQR controller for the system in deviation from the reference: let $\tilde{\theta} = \theta - \theta{ref}$ and $\tilde{q} = q - 0 = q$. The system dynamics for $\tilde{\theta}$ and $\tilde{q}$ are:
$\dot{\tilde{\theta}} = \dot{\theta} - \dot{\theta}_{ref} = q - 0 = \tilde{q}$
$\dot{\tilde{q}} = M{\deltae} \deltae + M{\theta} (\tilde{\theta} + \theta{ref}) + Mq \tilde{q} = M{\deltae} \deltae + M{\theta} \tilde{\theta} + M{\theta} \theta{ref} + M_q \tilde{q}$
Since θ{ref} is a constant desired pitch, $M{\theta}\theta_{ref}$ is a constant term. If we want to drive $\tilde{\theta}$ and $\tilde{q}$ to zero, we can effectively ignore the constant term and use the linearized system for deviations.
$\dot{x} = Ax + Bu$, where $x = [\tilde{\theta}, \tilde{q}]^T$ and $u = \delta_e$.

We want to minimize the integrated cost:

$J = \int_{0}^{\infty} (x^T Q x + u^T R u) dt$

A suitable choice for Q might be:

$Q = \begin{pmatrix}
Q_{\theta} & 0 \\
0 & Q_{q}
\end{pmatrix}$
where $Q{\theta}$ penalizes deviations in pitch angle and $Q{q}$ penalizes pitch rate. For example, $Q{\theta} = 100$ and $Q{q} = 1$.
$R = \begin{pmatrix} R{\deltae} \end{pmatrix}$
where $R{\deltae}$ penalizes elevator deflection. For instance, $R{\deltae} = 0.1$.

The task is to solve the ARE:

$P A + A^T P - P B R^{-1} B^T P + Q = 0$
for the 2×2 matrix P.
$A = \begin{pmatrix} 0 & 1 \\ M{\theta} & Mq \end{pmatrix}$, $B = \begin{pmatrix} 0 \\ M{\deltae} \end{pmatrix}$, $R^{-1} = 1/R{\deltae}$.

After solving for $P = \begin{pmatrix} p
{11} & p{12} \\ p{12} & p{22} \end{pmatrix}$, the gain matrix K is:
$K = R^{-1} B^T P = \frac{1}{R{\deltae}} \begin{pmatrix} 0 & M{\deltae} \end{pmatrix} \begin{pmatrix} p{11} & p{12} \\ p{12} & p{22} \end{pmatrix} = \frac{M{\deltae}}{R{\deltae}} \begin{pmatrix} p{12} & p{22} \end{pmatrix}$

Let $K = \begin{pmatrix} k
{\theta} & k{q} \end{pmatrix}$. The optimal control is:
$\deltae^(t) = -K x(t) = -(k{\theta} \tilde{\theta}(t) + k_{q} \tilde{q}(t))$

This indicates that the elevator deflection is controlled by a linear

combination of the pitch angle error and the pitch rate. This is a classic pitch-attitude-hold autopilot structure. A positive pitch error $\tilde{\theta}$ would typically require a negative elevator deflection (to push the nose down) and vice versa. A positive pitch rate $\tilde{q}$ would also typically require a corrective elevator deflection to damp the rotation. The specific gains $k
*{\theta}$ and $k*{q}$ are determined by the LQR tuning parameters Q and R, balancing the desire for precise pitch hold against the limits on elevator deflection.

Properties and Advantages of LQR

The LQR framework offers several desirable properties that contribute to its widespread use:

1.
Optimality: The controller derived from LQR is optimal with respect to the specified quadratic cost function. This provides a rigorous guarantee of performance within the given model and cost metric.

2.
Stability Guarantee: For a controllable and observable (or stabilizable and detectable) linear system, the infinite-horizon LQR controller guarantees closed-loop stability. This means that regardless of the initial state, the system will converge to the desired equilibrium (usually the origin). This is a critical property for safety-critical applications.

3.
Robustness: LQR controllers exhibit a degree of robustness to modeling errors and external disturbances. The gain margin is generally at least 6 dB, and the phase margin is at least 60 degrees for single-input systems

when Q and R are positive definite. This robustness can be quantified further using concepts like Structured Singular Value (SSV) analysis, demonstrating that LQR controllers can tolerate significant variations in system parameters before instability occurs.

4.
Systematic Tuning: The matrices Q and R provide an intuitive way to tune the controller's performance. By adjusting the relative weights of state errors versus control effort, engineers can shape the system's response, achieving trade-offs between speed of response, overshoot, damping, and control energy consumption. For example, increasing the penalty on a specific state in Q will make the controller prioritize reducing that state's error.

5.
Basis for Advanced Techniques: LQR serves as a fundamental building block for many more advanced control strategies. For instance, it is the basis for Linear Quadratic Gaussian (LQG) control (which combines LQR with a Kalman filter for state estimation in the presence of noise) and Model Predictive Control (MPC), where LQR often provides a good initial guess or a local linearization solution.

6.
Solution Tractability: The solution to the LQR problem, especially the infinite-horizon case, involves solving a linear matrix equation (ARE), which can be done efficiently and reliably using numerical algorithms. The resulting controller is a simple state feedback law, which is computationally inexpensive to implement.

Limitations of LQR

Despite its strengths, LQR also has limitations:

1.
Linearity Assumption: LQR is inherently designed for linear systems. While it can be applied to nonlinear systems by linearizing them around an operating point, its optimality guarantees only hold for that specific linear model. Performance may degrade significantly for large deviations from the operating point where nonlinearities become dominant.

2.
Quadratic Cost Function: The optimality is tied to the quadratic cost function. If the true performance objectives are not well-represented by a quadratic penalty, the LQR controller might not yield the truly optimal behavior for those objectives. For instance, hard constraints on state or control variables (e.g., actuator saturation) are not directly handled by the standard LQR formulation, although the weighting matrix R can be used to implicitly penalize large control inputs, making saturation less likely.

3.
Full State Feedback Requirement: Standard LQR requires knowledge of the entire state vector $x(t)$. In many practical systems, not all states are directly measurable. This necessitates the use of state estimators, such as Kalman filters, leading to LQG controllers, which may have reduced robustness properties compared to LQR.

4.
Model Dependence: The performance of an LQR controller is entirely dependent on the accuracy of the system model (A and B matrices). Significant modeling errors can lead to suboptimal or even unstable closed-loop performance.

In conclusion, the Linear Quadratic Regulator provides a powerful, theoretically sound, and practically effective method for designing controllers for linear systems. Its ability to guarantee stability and optimality with respect to a quadratic cost, coupled with its systematic tuning and robustness properties, makes it an indispensable tool in the control engineer's arsenal. While its assumptions limit its direct applicability to nonlinear systems with hard constraints, it remains a crucial benchmark and a foundational technique that underpins many modern advanced control methodologies. The systematic way it balances performance objectives with control effort makes it an excellent starting point for understanding and implementing optimal control strategies.

Chapter 2: Introduction to Convex Optimization

In the realm of mathematical optimization, the concept of convexity plays a pivotal role. It provides a powerful framework that simplifies the search for optimal solutions and guarantees that any locally optimal solution is, in fact, globally optimal. This property is exceptionally valuable across various engineering disciplines, including control systems, where problems often translate into optimization tasks. For instance, Model Predictive Control (MPC) relies heavily on solving optimization problems at each time step to determine the best control actions, and the tractability of these problems is significantly enhanced if they are convex.

To appreciate the significance of convexity, we must first define its two fundamental components: convex sets and convex functions. These concepts are deeply intertwined, and their properties are what lend the power to convex optimization.

Convex Sets: The Foundation of Feasibility

A set is considered convex if, for any two points within the set, the line segment connecting these two points lies entirely within the set. Imagine a shape. If you can pick any two points inside that shape and draw a straight line between them without the line ever leaving the shape, then the shape represents a convex set. Mathematically, a set $C \subseteq \mathbb{R}^n$ is convex if for any two points $x_1, x_2 \in C$, and for any scalar λ such that $0 \le \lambda \le 1$, the point $\lambda x_1 + (1-\lambda) x_2$ is also in C. The term $\lambda x_1 + (1-\lambda) x_2$ represents any point on the line segment connecting x_1 and x_2.

The geometric interpretation is intuitive: convex sets are "solid" or "unbroken" in a certain sense. They do not contain any "holes" or "indentations" that would cause a line segment connecting two interior points to pass outside the set.

Let's consider some examples to illustrate this concept:

The Ball: An example of a convex set is a closed ball in $\mathbb{R}^n$, defined as $\{x \in \mathbb{R}^n \mid \|x - xc\| \le r\}$, where xc is the center and $r > 0$ is the radius. If you take any two points within this ball, the line segment connecting them will also remain within the ball. Similarly, an open ball $\{x \in \mathbb{R}^n \mid \|x - x_c\| < r\}$ is also convex.

The Hyperplane and Half-Spaces: A hyperplane, defined by $\{x \in \mathbb{R}^n \mid a^T x = b\}$ for a non-zero vector a, is a convex set. A closed half-space, defined by $\{x \in \mathbb{R}^n \mid a^T x \le b\}$ or $\{x \in \mathbb{R}^n \mid a^T x \ge b\}$, is also convex. This can be readily verified: if $a^T x1 \le b$ and $a^T x2 \le b$, then for $0 \le \lambda \le 1$, $a^T (\lambda x1 + (1-\lambda) x2) = \lambda a^T x1 + (1-\lambda) a^T x2 \le \lambda b + (1-\lambda) b = b$. Thus, the entire line segment remains within the half-space.

Polyhedra: A polyhedron is the intersection of a finite number of closed half-spaces. Since the intersection of convex sets is always a convex set, polyhedra are convex sets. This is particularly relevant in optimization, as many constrained optimization problems are defined over polyhedral feasible regions. For example, a simple box defined by $l*i \le* xi \le u_i$ for $i=1, \dots, n$ is a polyhedron and therefore a convex set.

The Ellipsoid: An ellipsoid, defined as $\{x \in \mathbb{R}^n \mid (x-x*c)^T P (x-x*c) \le 1\}$, where P is a positive definite matrix, is another important example of a convex set.

Conversely, examples of non-convex sets include:

A Ring (Annulus): If you pick two points on opposite sides of the hole in the center of a ring, the line segment connecting them will pass through the hole, which is outside the ring.

A Star-Shaped Set: A set where there is at least one point from which all other points in the set are visible without obstruction. However, it might not be the case that all pairs of points can be connected by a line segment within the set.

A Set with a Hole: Any set that contains "empty space" that is not part of the set, and which can be intersected by a line segment connecting two points within the set.

The properties of convex sets are fundamental. For instance, if $C *1$ and $C*2$ are convex sets, then their intersection $C*1 \cap C*2$ is also convex. This property is crucial in defining the feasible region of optimization problems, which is often formed by the intersection of various convex constraints.

Convex Functions: The Shape of Simplicity

A function $f: C \to \mathbb{R}$, where C is a convex set, is called a convex function if for any two points $x_1, x_2 \in C$, and for any scalar λ such that $0 \le \lambda \le 1$, the following inequality holds:

$f(\lambda x_1 + (1-\lambda) x_2) \le \lambda f(x_1) + (1-\lambda) f(x_2)$

Geometrically, this means that the line segment connecting any two points on the graph of the function lies above or on the graph itself. Another way to visualize this is by considering the "epigraph" of a function, which is the set of points lying above or on the graph of the function: $\text{epi}(f) = \{(x, y) \in C \times \mathbb{R} \mid f(x) \le y\}$. A function f is convex if and only if its epigraph is a convex set.

If the inequality $f(\lambda x_1 + (1-\lambda) x_2) < \lambda f(x_1) + (1-\lambda) f(x_2)$ holds strictly for $0 < \lambda < 1$ and $x_1 \neq x_2$, the function is called strictly convex.

A function f is concave if $-f$ is convex. This means that the line segment connecting two points on the graph lies below or on the graph: $f(\lambda x_1 + (1-\lambda) x_2) \ge \lambda f(x_1) + (1-\lambda) f(x_2)$.

First-Order Condition for Convexity

If a function f is differentiable on a convex set C, it is convex if and only if for all $x
1, x2 \in C$:

$f(x
2) \ge f(x1) + \nabla f(x1)^T (x2 - x_1)$

Here, $\nabla f(x
1)$ is the gradient of f at $x1$. This inequality states that the first-order Taylor approximation of f at $x1$ (which is a linear function) is a global underestimator of f. Geometrically, the tangent hyperplane to the graph of f at any point $x1$ lies below or on the graph of f everywhere.

Second-Order Condition for Convexity

If a function f is twice differentiable on a convex set C, it is convex if and only if its Hessian matrix $\nabla^2 f(x)$ is positive semi-definite for all $x \in C$. The Hessian matrix is the matrix of second-order partial derivatives.

$\nabla^2 f(x) = \begin{pmatrix}

\frac{\partial^2 f}{\partial x1^2} & \frac{\partial^2 f}{\partial x1 \partial x2} & \cdots & \frac{\partial^2 f}{\partial x1 \partial x_n} \\ \frac{\partial^2 f}{\partial x2 \partial x1} & \frac{\partial^2 f}{\partial x2^2} & \cdots & \frac{\partial^2 f}{\partial x2 \partial x_n} \\ \vdots & \vdots & \ddots & \vdots \\

\frac{\partial^2 f}{\partial x*n* *partial* x1} & \frac{\partial^2 f}{\partial x*n* *partial* x2} & \cdots & \frac{\partial^2 f}{\partial x_n^2} \end{pmatrix}$

For a function $f: \mathbb{R}^n \to \mathbb{R}$, $\nabla^2 f(x)$ is an $n \times n$ symmetric matrix. The condition $\nabla^2 f(x) \succeq 0$ (positive semi-definite) means that for any vector $v \in \mathbb{R}^n$, $v^T \nabla^2 f(x) v \ge 0$.

If the Hessian matrix is positive definite ($\nabla^2 f(x) \succ 0$), then the function is strictly convex.

Examples of Convex Functions:

1.
Linear Functions: A function $f(x) = a^T x + b$ is both convex and concave. Its Hessian is the zero matrix, which is positive semi-definite.

2.
Quadratic Functions: A function of the form $f(x) = x^T P x + q^T x + r$, where P is an $n \times n$ matrix, is convex if and only if the matrix P is positive semi-definite ($P \succeq 0$). If P is positive definite ($P \succ 0$), the function is strictly convex.
For instance, $f(x) = x^2$ is convex on $\mathbb{R}$. Its second derivative is $f''(x) = 2$, which is positive.
Consider a quadratic cost function relevant to control: $J(u) = u^T R u$, where R is a positive definite matrix. The Hessian of $J(u)$ with respect to u is $2R$. Since $R \succ 0$, $2R \succ 0$, so $J(u)$ is strictly convex. This is why quadratic cost functions are popular in

optimization and control – they are well-behaved and guarantee a unique minimum.
The squared Euclidean norm $\|x\|^2 = x^T x$ is also strictly convex, as its Hessian is $2I$, which is positive definite.

3.
Exponential Function: $f(x) = e^{ax}$ for $a \in \mathbb{R}$ is strictly convex. The second derivative is $a^2 e^{ax} \ge 0$. If $a \neq 0$, it is strictly convex.

4.
Norms: Any norm on $\mathbb{R}^n$ is a convex function. For example, the Euclidean norm $\|x\|*2 = \sqrt{x1^2 + \dots + xn^2}$ is convex. The $L1$* norm $\|x\|*1 = \sum*{i=1}^n |x*i|$ and the $L*\infty$ norm $\|x\|*\infty = \max*i |x_i|$ are also convex.

Operations that Preserve Convexity:

Convexity is a robust property that is preserved under several common operations:

Non-negative Weighted Sum: If $f*1, \dots, f*k$ are convex functions and $\alpha*1, \dots, \alpha*k \ge 0$, then the function $F(x) = \sum*{i=1}^k \alpha*i f_i(x)$ is also convex. This is why linear combinations of convex functions result in new convex functions.

Composition with an Affine Mapping: If $f: \mathbb{R}^n \to \mathbb{R}$ is convex, and $g: \mathbb{R}^m \to \mathbb{R}^n$ is an

affine mapping (i.e., $g(x) = Ax + b$), then the composite function $h(x) = f(g(x))$ is convex.
Example: If $f(y) = y^T P y$ with $P \succeq 0$, and $y = Ax + b$, then $h(x) = (Ax+b)^T P (Ax+b)$ is convex.

Pointwise Maximum: If $f1, \dots, fk$ are convex functions, then their pointwise maximum $F(x) = \max(f1(x), \dots, fk(x))$ is also convex. This is very useful in constructing complex convex functions. For example, the $L\infty$ norm $\|x\|\infty = \max(|x1|, \dots, |xn|)$ is the maximum of $2n$ linear functions (xi and $-xi$), and is therefore convex.

Minimization: If $f(x, y)$ is a convex function of x for each y, then the function $g(x) = \inf_y f(x, y)$ is convex. This is known as "integrating out" a variable, but when it's minimization over a discrete set or a continuous set, it results in convexity.

The Power of Convexity in Optimization

The reason convexity is so central to optimization is encapsulated by a fundamental theorem:

Theorem: If f is a convex function and C is a convex set, then any local minimum of f over C is also a global minimum.

Proof Sketch: Suppose $x^$ is a local minimum, meaning there exists an $\epsilon > 0$ such that $f(x^) \le f(x)$ for all $x \in C$ with $\|x - x^\| \le \epsilon$. Now, assume for contradiction that $x^$ is not a global minimum. Then there exists some $x{true} \in C$ such that $f(x{true}) < f(x^)$. Consider a point x on the line segment connecting $x^$ and $x{true}$, such that x is within the ϵ-ball around $x^$. Let $x = \lambda x{true} + (1-\lambda) x^$, for some $0 < \lambda < 1$ and $\|x - x^\| \le \epsilon$. By convexity of f, we have $f(x) = f(\lambda x{true} + (1-\lambda) x^) \le \lambda f(x{true}) + (1-\lambda) f(x^)$. Since $f(x{true}) < f(x^)$, we can write $\lambda f(x{true}) + (1-\lambda) f(x^) < \lambda f(x^) + (1-\lambda) f(x^) = f(x^)$. Thus, $f(x) < f(x^)$. This contradicts the assumption that $f(x^) \le f(x)$ for all x in the ϵ-ball around $x^$, because x is in that ball. Therefore, $x^$ must be a global minimum.

This theorem is profoundly important. In non-convex optimization, finding a global optimum is generally very difficult, as algorithms can get stuck in local minima. For convex problems, any algorithm that finds a local minimum is guaranteed to find the global minimum. This drastically simplifies the design of optimization algorithms. Algorithms like gradient descent, when applied to convex problems, are guaranteed to converge to the global minimum (or a set of global minima if the function is not strictly convex).

Convex Optimization Problems

A general optimization problem can be stated as:

Minimize $f_0(x)$
Subject to $f_i(x) \le 0$ for $i=1, \dots, m$

And $h_j(x) = 0$ for $j=1, \dots, p$

where $x \in \mathbb{R}^n$ is the optimization variable, $f
0$ is the objective function, fi are the inequality constraint functions, and h_j are the equality constraint functions.

A convex optimization problem is one where:

1. The objective function f_0 is convex.
2. The inequality constraint functions f_i are convex.
3. The equality constraint functions h_j are affine (linear plus a constant).

The feasible region of a convex optimization problem, defined by $\{x
\mid f
*i(x) \le 0, h*j(x) = 0\}$, must also be a convex set. This is because:
The set $\{x \mid f_i(x) \le 0\}$ is the sublevel set of a convex function, which is always a convex set.
The set $\{x \mid h*j(x) = 0\}$ is the intersection of two half-spaces (since $h*j$ is affine), which is a convex set.
The feasible region is the intersection of these convex sets, and hence, it is convex.

When all these conditions are met, the optimization problem is convex, and any local minimum found is guaranteed to be a global minimum. This makes solving convex optimization problems computationally tractable, even for very large-scale problems. Modern solvers can handle millions of variables and constraints efficiently.

Relevance to Control Systems

In control systems, many problems can be formulated as convex optimization problems. A prominent example is Model Predictive Control (MPC). At each time step, MPC solves an optimization problem to find a sequence of future control inputs that minimizes a cost function over a finite horizon, subject to system dynamics and constraints. If the system dynamics are linear, the cost function is quadratic, and the constraints are linear (or define a convex set), the resulting optimization problem is convex. This guarantees that the optimizer will find the best possible control action for the current state, enabling real-time decision-making.

For instance, consider a linear system:

$\dot{x}(t) = Ax(t) + Bu(t)$
with constraints:
$l \le u(t) \le u$ (input constraints)
$lx \le x(t) \le ux$ (state constraints)

And a quadratic cost function:

$J = \int_{0}^{T} (x(t)^T Q x(t) + u(t)^T R u(t)) dt + x(T)^T S_f x(T)$

If we discretize this system and the horizon T, the problem becomes minimizing this cost subject to the discrete-time dynamics and constraints. The objective function is convex (sum of convex quadratic terms and a terminal term which is also convex if $S_f \succeq 0$). The constraints, being linear inequalities and equalities (after discretization), define a convex feasible set. Thus, the MPC problem for linear systems with quadratic costs and linear constraints is a convex optimization problem.

The ability to efficiently solve these problems is what makes MPC a powerful and widely adopted control strategy, especially in industries like automotive, aerospace, and process control, where handling constraints and optimizing performance is critical. Without the guarantee of convexity, finding optimal control signals in real-time would be computationally prohibitive.

In summary, convexity is not merely a mathematical curiosity; it is the bedrock upon which efficient and reliable optimization algorithms are built. Its presence transforms computationally intractable problems into solvable ones, making it an indispensable concept for anyone working in fields that leverage optimization for decision-making and control. Understanding convex sets and convex functions allows us to identify these "nice" problems and leverage the powerful tools available for their solution. Convex Sets: The Geometric Landscape of Feasibility

At the heart of optimization lies the concept of a feasible region – the set of all possible solutions that satisfy the problem's constraints. For an optimization problem to be considered "convex," this feasible region must possess a specific geometric property: it must be a convex set. But what exactly defines a convex set?

Intuitively, a convex set is one that has no "dents" or "holes." If you can pick any two points within the set and draw a straight line connecting them, every point on that line segment must also lie entirely within the set. Mathematically, this is captured by the following definition:

A set $C \subseteq \mathbb{R}^n$ is
convex if for any two points $x1, x2 \in C$, and for any scalar λ satisfying $0 \le \lambda \le 1$, the point $\lambda x1 + (1-\lambda) x2$ is also in C.

The term $\lambda x
1 + (1-\lambda) x2$ is a parametric representation of the line segment connecting $x1$ and $x2$. The condition states that for any λ between 0 and 1 (inclusive), the resulting point must be a member of the set C.

Let's explore some common examples to build our intuition:

Euclidean Balls: A closed Euclidean ball centered at xc with radius $r > 0$, defined as $\{x \in \mathbb{R}^n \mid \|x - xc\|2 \le r\}$, is convex. For any two points $x1, x2$ within this ball, the line segment connecting them will remain within the ball. The same holds for open balls ($\|x - xc\|_2 < r$).

Hyperplanes and Half-Spaces: A hyperplane in $\mathbb{R}^n$, defined by $\{x \in \mathbb{R}^n \mid a^T x = b\}$, where $a \neq 0$, is a convex set. Consider any two points $x1, x2$ on the hyperplane. Then $a^T x1 = b$ and $a^T x2 = b$. For any $\lambda \in [0, 1]$, $a^T(\lambda x1 + (1-\lambda) x2) = \lambda a^T x1 + (1-\lambda) a^T x2 = \lambda b + (1-\lambda) b = b$. Thus, the entire line segment lies on the hyperplane.
Similarly, closed half-spaces, defined by $\{x \in \mathbb{R}^n \mid a^T x \le b\}$ or $\{x \in \mathbb{R}^n \mid a^T x \ge b\}$, are convex. If $a^T x1 \le b$ and $a^T x2 \le b$, then for any $\lambda \in

[0, 1]$, $a^T(\lambda x*1 + (1-\lambda)* x2) = \lambda a^T x*1 + (1-\lambda) a^T* x2 \le \lambda b + (1-\lambda) b = b$. This confirms the convexity of half-spaces.

Polyhedra: A polyhedron is a set defined as the intersection of a finite number of closed half-spaces. Since the intersection of convex sets is always a convex set, all polyhedra are convex. This is a crucial property, as many practical optimization problems, especially those involving linear programming and constrained control, involve polyhedral feasible regions. For example, a simple box defined by lower and upper bounds on each variable, $l*i \le* xi \le u_i$ for $i=1, \dots, n$, is a polyhedron and therefore a convex set.

Ellipsoids: An ellipsoid, defined as $\{x \in \mathbb{R}^n \mid (x-x*c)^T P (x-x*c) \le 1\}$, where P is a symmetric positive definite matrix, is another important class of convex sets.

Examples of sets that are
not convex include:
A Crescent Moon Shape: You can easily find two points on the opposite tips of the crescent such that the line segment connecting them passes outside the crescent.
A Star-Shaped Region: While there might be points from which all other points are visible (a property called star-shapedness), it doesn't guarantee that any two arbitrary points can be connected by a straight line segment within the set.
Any Set with a Hole: If a set contains a void, and you pick two points on opposite sides of the void, the line segment connecting them will pass through the void and thus outside the set.

The operations under which convexity of sets is preserved are also significant:

Intersection: The intersection of any collection of convex sets is convex. This property is fundamental, as the feasible region of an optimization problem is often defined by the intersection of multiple constraint sets. If each constraint defines a convex set, their intersection will also be convex.
Union: The union of convex sets is not generally convex. For instance, the union of two disjoint balls is not convex.
Affine Transformations: If C is a convex set and A is a matrix and b is a vector, then the set $\{Ax+b \mid x \in C\}$ is also convex. This means that scaling, rotating, and translating convex sets preserves their convexity.

Convex Functions: The Smooth Landscape of Optimization Objectives

While convex sets define the boundaries of our search space, convex functions describe the "shape" of the objective we want to minimize (or maximize). A function is convex if its graph curves upwards or is flat, never downwards.

Formally, a function $f: C \to \mathbb{R}$, defined on a convex set C, is
convex if for any two points $x1, x2 \in C$, and for any scalar λ satisfying $0 \le \lambda \le 1$, the following inequality holds:

$f(\lambda x *1 + (1-\lambda) x*2) \le \lambda f(x*1) + (1-\lambda) f(x*2)$

Geometrically, this inequality means that the line segment connecting any two points on the graph of the function lies above or on the graph itself. The value of the function at any point between $x *1$ and $x*2$ is less than or equal to the value on the line segment connecting $f(x*1)$ and $f(x*2)$.

If the inequality holds strictly for $0 < \lambda < 1$ and $x *1 \neq x*2$ (i.e., $f(\lambda x*1 + (1-\lambda) x*2) < \lambda f(x*1) + (1-\lambda) f(x*2)$), the function is called **strictly convex**. Strictly convex functions have a unique minimum.

A function f is **concave** if $-f$ is convex. This implies that the line segment connecting two points on the graph of a concave function lies below or on the graph.

Characterizing Convexity Using Derivatives

For differentiable functions, we have more concrete ways to check for convexity:

1. **First-Order Condition:** If a function f is differentiable on a convex set C, it is convex if and only if for all $x*1, x*2 \in C$: $f(x*2) \ge f(x*1) + \nabla f(x*1)^T (x*2 - x_1)$

Here, $\nabla f(x1)$ is the gradient of f at $x1$. This condition means that the tangent hyperplane to the graph of f at any point x_1 lies entirely below or on the graph of f.

2.
Second-Order Condition: If a function f is twice differentiable on a convex set C, it is convex if and only if its Hessian matrix, $\nabla^2 f(x)$, is positive semi-definite for all $x \in C$. The Hessian is the matrix of second partial derivatives:
$$ \nabla^2 f(x) = \begin{pmatrix}
\frac{\partial^2 f}{\partial x1^2} & \frac{\partial^2 f}{\partial x1 \partial x2} & \cdots & \frac{\partial^2 f}{\partial x1 \partial x_n} \\
\frac{\partial^2 f}{\partial x2 \partial x1} & \frac{\partial^2 f}{\partial x2^2} & \cdots & \frac{\partial^2 f}{\partial x2 \partial x_n} \\
\vdots & \vdots & \ddots & \vdots \\
\frac{\partial^2 f}{\partial xn \partial x1} & \frac{\partial^2 f}{\partial xn \partial x2} & \cdots & \frac{\partial^2 f}{\partial x_n^2}
\end{pmatrix} $$
The condition $\nabla^2 f(x) \succeq 0$ means that for any non-zero vector $v \in \mathbb{R}^n$, $v^T \nabla^2 f(x) v \ge 0$. If $\nabla^2 f(x) \succ 0$ (positive definite) for all x, the function is strictly convex.

Let's illustrate with some common examples of convex functions:

Affine Functions: A linear function $f(x) = a^T x + b$ is both convex and concave. Its Hessian is the zero matrix, which is positive semi-definite.

Quadratic Functions: A quadratic function $f(x) = x^T P x + q^T x + r$ is convex if and only if its matrix P is positive semi-definite ($P \succeq 0$). If P is positive definite ($P \succ 0$), the function is strictly convex. This is particularly relevant in control systems, where quadratic cost functions are widely used. For instance, the term $u(t)^T R u(t)$ in the LQR cost, with $R \succ 0$, ensures that the control effort is penalized quadratically, making the cost function convex with respect to the control input. Similarly, $x(t)^T Q x(t)$ with $Q \succeq 0$ makes the state cost convex.

Exponential Function: The function $f(x) = e^{ax}$ (for any real a) is strictly convex. Its second derivative is $a^2 e^{ax}$, which is always non-negative and positive if $a \neq 0$.

Norms: Any norm on $\mathbb{R}^n$ is a convex function. This includes the Euclidean norm $\|x\|*2$, the $L*1$ norm $\|x\|*1 = \sum /x*i|$, and the $L*infty$ norm $\/x\/*\infty = \max |x_i|$. These norms are often used in regularization techniques in machine learning and in defining constraints in control.

Key operations that preserve convexity of functions include:

Non-negative Weighted Sum: If $f*1, \dots, f*k$ are convex functions and $\alpha*1, \dots, \alpha*k \ge 0$, then their weighted sum $F(x) = \sum*{i=1}^k \alpha*i f_i(x)$ is also convex.
Composition with an Affine Map: If f is convex and $g(x) = Ax+b$ is an affine map, then $f(g(x))$ is convex.
Pointwise Maximum: The function $F(x) = \max(f*1(x), \dots, f*k(x))$, where each f_i is convex, is itself convex. This is a powerful tool for constructing complex convex functions from simpler ones.
Minimization: If $f(x, y)$ is convex in x for each y, then $g(x) = \inf_y f(x, y)$ is convex.

The Uniqueness Guarantee: Why Convexity Matters

The defining characteristic that makes convex optimization so powerful is the guarantee it provides regarding the nature of optimal solutions.

Theorem: For a convex optimization problem, any local minimum is also a global minimum.

This is a profound statement. In non-convex optimization, algorithms might find a solution that is better than all nearby solutions (a local minimum), but there could be another, much better solution elsewhere in the feasible region (a global minimum). Finding this global minimum can be extremely challenging. However, in convex optimization, if an algorithm finds
any minimum, it is guaranteed to be *the* minimum.

This property significantly simplifies the task of solving optimization problems. It means we don't need to worry about getting trapped in suboptimal solutions. Algorithms like gradient descent, when applied to convex problems, are guaranteed to converge to the global optimum (or a set of global optima if the function is not strictly convex). This tractability makes convex optimization a cornerstone of many advanced engineering applications.

Consider a general optimization problem:

Minimize $f_0(x)$

Subject to $f_i(x) \le 0$, $i=1, \dots, m$
$h_j(x) = 0$, $j=1, \dots, p$

This problem is a
convex optimization problem if:
1. The objective function f_0 is convex.
2. The inequality constraint functions f_i are convex.
3. The equality constraint functions h_j are affine (linear).

The feasible region, defined by the constraints, must also be a convex set. This holds true if $f
*i$ are convex and $h*j$ are affine, as the sublevel sets of convex functions are convex, and the sets defined by affine equalities are convex (specifically, they are affine subspaces, which are a special type of convex set). The intersection of convex sets is convex, so the entire feasible region is convex.

Convexity in Action: Model Predictive Control

A prime example of where convexity is critical in practice is Model Predictive Control (MPC). At each control interval, an MPC controller must solve an optimization problem to determine the best sequence of future control inputs over a prediction horizon, subject to the system's dynamics and constraints.

For a linear system:

$x*{k+1} = A*xk + Bu_k$
with constraints such as:
$l \le u_k \le u$ (input constraints)

$l_x \le x_k \le u_x$ (state constraints)

and a quadratic cost function over a finite horizon N:

$J = \sum_{k=0}^{N-1} (x_k^T Q x_k + u_k^T R u_k) + x_N^T S x_N$

The objective function J is convex if $Q \succeq 0$ and $R \succeq 0$. The system dynamics define linear equality constraints on the state and input sequence. The input and state constraints define polyhedra (convex sets). Therefore, the entire optimization problem solved by the MPC at each step is a convex optimization problem.

This convexity is what allows MPC to be implemented in real-time. Specialized optimization solvers can efficiently find the optimal control sequence, even for complex systems with many states and constraints. If the problem were non-convex, finding a guaranteed optimal solution within the short time available at each control step would be computationally infeasible for most applications. The guarantee of finding a global optimum simplifies controller design and ensures predictable performance.

In essence, convexity provides the mathematical guarantee that the "easy path" through the feasible region (the minimum of a convex function) is indeed the best path, and that we have reliable computational tools to find it. This is why understanding and identifying convexity is a fundamental step in formulating and solving many modern optimization and control problems.

The inherent structure of convex problems imbues them with a set of properties that are not merely mathematically elegant but also profoundly impactful from a computational and practical standpoint.

These properties collectively transform the often arduous task of optimization into a problem class that is, in many respects, amenable to efficient and reliable solution methods. The bedrock of this tractability lies in the special relationship between local and global optimality. For any optimization problem, we are typically interested in finding a global minimum – a solution that achieves the lowest possible objective function value across the entire feasible region. However, many optimization algorithms operate by iteratively improving a current solution. If a solution is better than all its immediate neighbors, it is called a local minimum. In the vast landscape of non-convex problems, a local minimum can be a misleading trap, offering a suboptimal solution while a far superior global minimum remains undiscovered. This distinction is what renders many non-convex optimization problems notoriously difficult, often falling into the category of NP-hard problems, where finding a guaranteed optimal solution in polynomial time is believed to be impossible.

In stark contrast, the introduction of convexity fundamentally alters this scenario. As established by a core theorem in optimization theory, for a convex objective function minimized over a convex set, *every local minimum is also a global minimum*. This is not a trivial observation; it is the lynchpin of convex optimization's computational advantage. The proof, sketched previously, demonstrates that if a point is a local minimum and the function and set are convex, then any deviation from that point, no matter how small, leads to a worse or equal objective value. If there were a better point elsewhere in the feasible region, the convexity of the function and the set would imply that points on the line segment connecting the local minimum and this better point would also yield better values, contradicting the local optimality.

This property has profound implications for algorithm design. Instead of needing sophisticated global search strategies that are often

computationally prohibitive, we can employ algorithms that are designed to find
a minimum. Techniques such as gradient descent, subgradient methods, and interior-point methods, when applied to convex problems, are guaranteed to converge to a global minimum. The convergence rate is often polynomial in the problem's input size, meaning that as the problem gets larger (more variables, more constraints), the time required to find a solution grows predictably and manageably, rather than exponentially or unpredictably as is common with non-convex problems. This polynomial-time solvability is a hallmark of convex optimization and a major reason for its widespread adoption in fields requiring high-performance computation.

Furthermore, the concept of feasibility in convex problems is also well-behaved. A convex optimization problem is defined by a convex objective function and a feasible region that is a convex set. The feasibility of a problem refers to whether there exists at least one point that satisfies all the constraints. For convex problems, the geometric nature of the feasible set simplifies analysis. If a problem is feasible, there is generally a "well-behaved" path towards optimal solutions. While a problem could theoretically be feasible but have an unbounded objective (meaning the objective can be made arbitrarily small), for many practical problems, particularly those with constraints that "bound" the problem (e.g., constraints that force variables into a compact region), a finite global minimum exists. The existence of a minimum is often guaranteed under mild conditions, such as the objective function being coercive (growing to infinity as variables go to infinity) or the feasible set being compact.

The implications for control systems are particularly striking. In applications like Model Predictive Control (MPC), where optimization is performed repeatedly in real-time, the guarantee of a global optimum and polynomial-time solvability is not a luxury but a necessity. When an

MPC controller decides on the next control action, it solves an optimization problem. If this problem is convex, the controller can be confident that it is choosing the truly optimal control input given the current state and predictions, rather than merely a locally good one. This reliability is essential for safety-critical systems. For instance, an autonomous vehicle's trajectory planning system must ensure that it finds the globally optimal path that avoids obstacles and minimizes travel time, not just one that looks good from a particular vantage point. The convexity of the underlying optimization formulation for such tasks enables this level of assurance.

The computational efficiency derived from convexity also enables larger-scale applications. Problems that might be intractable with non-convex formulations can become manageable with convex counterparts. This allows engineers to model and control more complex systems, incorporate a greater number of constraints, and achieve higher levels of performance. For example, in power systems optimization, managing the economic dispatch of electricity generation across a grid often involves solving very large convex optimization problems to minimize generation costs while meeting demand and respecting generator limits. The ability to solve these problems quickly and reliably ensures efficient energy distribution and stability of the grid.

To further appreciate the robustness of convex optimization, consider the properties of its optimal solutions. For a strictly convex function over a convex set, the global minimum is unique. This means there is only one point that achieves the minimum value. If the objective function is convex but not strictly convex, there might be a set of points that all achieve the same minimum value. This set of optimal solutions itself forms a convex set. This characteristic is also highly valuable. For example, in some control scenarios, having multiple equivalent optimal control strategies might offer flexibility in operation. The fact that this set of optima is convex means that any convex combination of these optimal solutions is also an optimal solution, providing a rich set of choices.

The tractability of convex problems is not solely due to the local-to-global minimum property but also stems from the well-defined nature of their feasibility and the properties of their optimal value function. For instance, the optimal value function, which maps problem parameters to the minimum achievable objective value, is often itself a convex function. This property is instrumental in sensitivity analysis and parameter tuning, allowing us to understand how changes in problem parameters affect the optimal solution.

In summary, the properties stemming from convexity – guaranteed global optimality from local minima, polynomial-time solvability, and well-behaved feasibility and optimal solution sets – are what make convex optimization a cornerstone of modern computational science and engineering. They provide a bridge between theoretical optimality and practical computability, enabling sophisticated decision-making and control in a wide array of applications. The subsequent sections will delve deeper into specific algorithms and problem classes within this framework, but the fundamental advantages conferred by convexity remain the guiding principle. Without these properties, many of the advanced optimization techniques used today, particularly in real-time control and large-scale data analysis, would simply not be feasible. The assumption of convexity, where applicable, is the most powerful tool in the optimization toolkit for ensuring both theoretical correctness and computational efficiency.

The elegance and computational tractability of convex optimization problems stem from their fundamental mathematical structure. While the previous discussion highlighted the overarching benefits of convexity, it is crucial to understand the specific forms these problems often take in practice. These well-defined classes of convex optimization problems are the workhorses that enable robust and efficient solutions across diverse engineering and scientific disciplines. By recognizing and formulating problems within these structures, we unlock the power of specialized algorithms that guarantee optimality and deliver rapid convergence.

Among the most fundamental and widely encountered convex optimization problems is Linear Programming (LP). An LP problem is characterized by a linear objective function that is to be minimized or maximized, subject to a set of linear equality and inequality constraints. Mathematically, a standard LP can be expressed as:

Minimize $c^T x$

Subject to $Ax \le b$
and $x \ge 0$

Here, x is the vector of decision variables, c is a vector of coefficients defining the objective function, A is a matrix representing the constraint coefficients, and b is a vector of constraint upper bounds. The constraint $x \ge 0$ is a non-negativity constraint, which is common but not strictly necessary for convexity. If we allow x to be unbounded in both positive and negative directions, we are dealing with a general linear program. The feasible region of an LP is a polyhedron, which is a convex set. Since the objective function is linear, it is also a convex function (in fact, it is both convex and concave). This combination of a linear objective and a polyhedral feasible region makes LPs convex optimization problems.

The significance of Linear Programming cannot be overstated. Its simplicity belies its power, and it forms the basis for many complex decision-making processes. Applications abound in areas such as resource allocation, production planning, scheduling, and network flow problems. For instance, a manufacturing company might use an LP to determine the optimal production quantities of different products to maximize profit, given constraints on raw material availability, machine capacity, and labor hours. In logistics, LPs are used to find the most cost-effective way to transport goods from various origins to multiple destinations, a problem known as the transportation problem. The Simplex method, developed by George Dantzig in the late 1940s, was one of the first algorithms to efficiently solve LPs, and it remains a cornerstone of computational optimization. While the Simplex method is not a polynomial-time algorithm in the worst case, it performs remarkably well in practice. Later developments, such as interior-point methods, provided the first polynomial-time algorithms for solving LPs, offering theoretical guarantees on computational complexity.

Closely related to Linear Programming is Quadratic Programming (QP). In a QP problem, the objective function is quadratic, while the constraints remain linear. A standard form for a QP is:

Minimize $\frac{1}{2} x^T P x + q^T x$

Subject to $Ax \le b$
and $x \ge 0$

Here, P is a matrix, q is a vector, A is a matrix, and b is a vector. For the problem to be a convex optimization problem, the objective function must be convex. This is achieved when the matrix P is positive semidefinite. If P is positive definite, the problem is strictly convex, guaranteeing a unique global minimum. QP problems appear in various applications, including portfolio optimization in finance, where investors aim to minimize risk (variance, a quadratic function of asset returns) for a given level of expected return, subject to budget and other constraints. In machine learning, QP formulations are central to Support Vector Machines (SVMs) for classification and regression tasks, particularly in finding the optimal hyperplane that separates data points. Solving QP problems can be done using specialized algorithms like active-set methods or interior-point methods tailored for QPs. The convexity ensures that any local minimum found by these algorithms is indeed the global minimum.

Moving to a more general class, Second-Order Cone Programming (SOCP) problems extend LPs and QPs. SOCP problems involve minimizing a linear objective function over an intersection of affine linear constraints and second-order cones. A second-order cone, also known as a Lorentz cone or ice-cream cone, is a set defined by:

$K = \{ (x, t) \in \mathbb{R}^{n+1} \mid ||x||_2 \le t \}$

where $||x||_2$ is the Euclidean norm of the vector x. An SOCP problem can be formulated as:

Minimize $c^T x$

Subject to $Ai x \le bi$, for $i = 1, \dots, m$
and $x \in K_j$, for $j = 1, \dots, p$

where K_j are second-order cones. A key insight is that a convex quadratic objective function can be reformulated into a linear objective over an expanded set of variables and second-order cone constraints. This means that any QP with a convex objective function can be cast as an SOCP. The power of SOCP lies in its ability to model problems involving norms and quadratic terms in a convex manner. Applications include robust optimization, where parameters are not known exactly but are known to lie within a certain uncertainty set (often ellipsoidal, which can be represented using SOC constraints), and control problems. For example, designing a controller that guarantees stability for a system under certain parameter uncertainties can often be formulated as an SOCP. Portfolio optimization with "robust" return estimates can also be framed as an SOCP. Interior-point methods are highly effective for solving SOCP problems efficiently.

The most general class of convex optimization problems within this discussion is Semidefinite Programming (SDP). SDP problems involve minimizing a linear objective function over the intersection of affine linear constraints and the cone of positive semidefinite matrices. The standard form of an SDP problem is:

Minimize $Tr(CX)$

Subject to $Tr(Ai X) = bi$, for $i = 1, \dots, m$
and $X \succeq 0$

Here, X is a symmetric matrix variable, C and $A

*i$ are given symmetric matrices, $b*i$ are scalars, and $Tr(\cdot)$ denotes the trace of a matrix. The constraint $X \succeq 0$ means that X must be a positive semidefinite matrix. The set of positive semidefinite matrices forms a convex cone. SDPs can be viewed as a generalization of LPs. In fact, LPs can be formulated as SDPs by considering diagonal matrices. The ability of SDPs to handle matrix inequalities makes them extremely powerful for modeling problems that were previously intractable.

Applications of SDPs are vast and include combinatorial optimization (e.g., finding approximate solutions to the Max-Cut problem), control theory (e.g., H-infinity control, linear matrix inequalities (LMIs) that describe stability and performance properties), and quantum information science. For instance, in robust control, conditions for the stability and performance of a linear system with uncertain parameters are often expressed as LMIs, which are a special case of SDPs. These problems can arise when designing controllers for systems where precise models are unavailable or subject to variations. The development of interior-point methods for SDPs has been a significant achievement, allowing for the solution of problems that were once considered computationally prohibitive. While generally more computationally intensive than LPs or QPs, the ability of SDPs to capture complex structural relationships makes them indispensable for certain advanced applications.

The relationship between these problem classes is hierarchical: LPs are a subset of QPs (with $P=0$), QPs with convex objectives are a subset of SOCPs, and SOCPs can be formulated as SDPs. This hierarchy means that algorithms developed for more general classes can also solve problems from less general classes, although specialized algorithms for LPs and QPs are often more efficient. Understanding these standard convex optimization problem types – LP, QP, SOCP, and SDP – provides a powerful framework for recognizing and solving a wide range of optimization challenges encountered in engineering and beyond. Each class offers a unique balance of modeling power and computational tractability, enabling practitioners to select the most appropriate tool for their specific needs. The continuous development of efficient algorithms for these problems fuels their increasing adoption and impact across science and industry.

The framework of convex optimization, with its guaranteed convergence to a global optimum and efficient solution methods, is further enriched by the concept of duality. Duality, in essence, provides a complementary perspective on an optimization problem, often leading to deeper theoretical insights and practical algorithmic advantages. It allows us to reformulate a problem in a way that might be easier to solve, or to derive bounds on the optimal value, which can be invaluable for verifying the quality of a solution.

At the heart of duality lies the Lagrangian, a mathematical construct that combines the objective function of an optimization problem with its constraints. For a general optimization problem, specifically a minimization problem of the form:

Minimize $f_0(x)$

Subject to $f_i(x) \le 0$, for $i = 1, \dots, m$
and $h_j(x) = 0$, for $j = 1, \dots, p$

where $x \in \mathbb{R}^n$ is the vector of decision variables, $f 0$ *is the objective function,* fi are the inequality constraint functions, and h_j are the equality constraint functions. The Lagrangian of this problem is defined as:

$L(x, \lambda, \nu) = f
0(x) + \sum{i=1}^m \lambda*i f*i(x) + \sum*{j=1}^p \nu*j h_j(x)$

Here, $\lambda = (\lambda
*1, \dots, \lambda*m)$ is a vector of Lagrange multipliers associated with the inequality constraints, and $\nu = (\nu*1, \dots, \nu*p)$ is a vector of Lagrange multipliers associated with the equality constraints. The Lagrange multipliers $\lambda*i$ are typically restricted to be non-negative ($\lambda*i \ge 0$), reflecting the nature of inequality constraints.

From the Lagrangian, we define the
Lagrangian dual function, denoted by $g(\lambda, \nu)$, as the minimum of the Lagrangian over x, for fixed values of λ and ν:

$g(\lambda, \nu) = \inf
{x \in \mathbb{R}^n} L(x, \lambda, \nu) = \inf{x \in \mathbb{R}^n} \left(f*0(x) + \sum*{i=1}^m \lambda*i f*i(x) + \sum*{j=1}^p \nu*j h_j(x) \right)$

The infimum is taken because the Lagrangian might not attain a minimum for some x. The dual function $g(\lambda, \nu)$ has a crucial property: it is always a concave function, regardless of the convexity of the original problem's objective and constraint functions. This concavity is a fundamental result and is key to how duality is exploited.

The

Lagrangian dual problem is then formed by maximizing the dual function $g(\lambda, \nu)$ subject to the implicit constraints on λ and ν:

Maximize $g(\lambda, \nu)$

Subject to $\lambda \ge 0$

This dual problem is itself a convex optimization problem (specifically, a maximization of a concave function, which is equivalent to minimizing a convex function). The variables in the dual problem are the Lagrange multipliers λ and ν.

Let $p^
*$ be the optimal value of the original (primal) minimization problem and d^* be the optimal value of the dual maximization problem. A fundamental relationship between these values is **weak duality**, which states that for any feasible primal solution x and any dual feasible solution (λ, ν) (i.e., $\lambda \ge 0$), the following inequality holds:

$g(\lambda, \nu) \le p^$

This means that the optimal value of the dual problem, $d^
*$, is always less than or equal to the optimal value of the primal problem, p^*:

$d^
*\le p^*$

This inequality is remarkably general and holds for any optimization problem, not just convex ones. It is a direct consequence of the definition of the dual function. If we consider a primal feasible \$x\$, then \$f i(x) \le 0\$ and \$hj(x) = 0\$. For \$\lambda \ge 0\$, we have \$\lambdai fi(x) \le 0\$ and \$\nuj hj(x) = 0\$. Therefore, \$L(x, \lambda, \nu) = f0(x) + \sum \lambdai fi(x) + \sum \nuj hj(x) \le f0(x)\$. Since \$g(\lambda, \nu)\$ is the infimum of \$L(x, \lambda, \nu)\$ over all \$x\$, it follows that \$g(\lambda, \nu) \le L(x, \lambda, \nu)\$. Combining these, we get \$g(\lambda, \nu) \le f0(x)\$ for any primal feasible \$x\$ and dual feasible \$(\lambda, \nu)\$. Thus, \$d^ = \sup{\lambda \ge 0} g(\lambda, \nu) \le \inf{x \text{ feasible}} f0(x) = p^\$.

The concept of weak duality is powerful because it provides a lower bound on the optimal value of the primal problem. If we can find a dual feasible solution \$(\lambda, \nu)\$ and compute \$g(\lambda, \nu)\$, this value serves as a lower bound for \$p^
\$. This is useful for assessing the quality of approximate solutions. If we find a primal feasible \$x\$ with objective value \$f0(x)\$, and a dual feasible \$(\lambda, \nu)\$ with \$g(\lambda, \nu)\$, then we have \$g(\lambda, \nu) \le p^ \le f0(x)\$. The gap \$f_0(x) - g(\lambda, \nu)\$ quantifies how far our primal solution is from the true optimum, and how far the dual solution's value is from the true optimum.

For convex optimization problems, this relationship can be significantly strengthened. If the original problem is a convex optimization problem (i.e., \$f
0, \dots, fm\$ are convex and \$h1, \dots, hp\$ are affine), and if a constraint qualification is satisfied, then **strong duality** holds. A common and useful constraint qualification is the Slater's condition: there exists a strictly feasible point \$x\$, meaning \$fi(x) < 0\$ for all \$i=1, \dots, m\$, and \$hj(x)=0\$ for all \$j=1, \dots, p\$. If Slater's condition holds for a convex problem, then:

\$d^

*= p^*$

This means that the optimal value of the dual problem is equal to the optimal value of the primal problem. This equality is a cornerstone of convex optimization, implying that by solving the dual problem, we can find the optimal value of the primal problem.

The importance of strong duality lies not only in its theoretical implications but also in its algorithmic consequences. Many optimization algorithms, particularly those designed for convex problems, implicitly or explicitly work with the dual problem or leverage the duality gap. For instance, algorithms like the cutting-plane method or the Benders decomposition method can be viewed as solving the dual problem. Furthermore, the KKT conditions (Karush-Kuhn-Tucker conditions), which are necessary optimality conditions for general nonlinear programming problems, become sufficient optimality conditions for convex problems under certain constraint qualifications, and these conditions are intimately linked to duality.

The KKT conditions for the problem stated earlier are:

1. Stationarity: $\nabla_x L(x^, \lambda^, \nu^) = 0$
2. Primal feasibility: $f*i(x^) \le 0$ for $i=1, \dots, m$, and $h*j(x^) = 0$ for $j=1, \dots, p$.
3. Dual feasibility: $\lambda_i^ \ge 0$ for $i=1, \dots, m$.
4. Complementary slackness: $\lambda*i^ f*i(x^) = 0$ for $i=1, \dots, m$.

If the problem is convex and satisfies a constraint qualification (like Slater's condition), then any primal-dual pair $(x^
, \lambda^, \nu^*)$ that satisfies the KKT conditions is an optimal solution to the primal and dual problems, respectively, and $p^* = d^ = *L(x^,

\lambda^, *nu^*)$. The complementary slackness condition, $\lambda*i^*
fi(x^) = 0$, is particularly insightful. It means that for any inequality constraint $fi*(x) \le 0$, if the constraint is not active at the optimum (i.e., $fi*(x^*) < 0$), then its corresponding Lagrange multiplier must be zero ($\lambdai^* = 0$). If a constraint is active at the optimum ($fi(x^*) = 0$), then its Lagrange multiplier $\lambda_i^$* can be positive.

The Lagrange multipliers themselves have significant interpretations. In the context of economics, they can be interpreted as shadow prices. Consider a resource that is limited and is used in an optimization problem to produce goods or services. If the constraint on this resource is binding at the optimal solution, its Lagrange multiplier can be interpreted as the marginal value of an additional unit of that resource. For example, if $\lambda
*i^$ is the multiplier for a constraint on the amount of a certain raw material, and $\lambda*i^ = \$50$, it suggests that if we had one more unit of this raw material available, the optimal objective value (e.g., profit) could increase by approximately \$50. This interpretation is valid when the changes are small and the problem is differentiable. These dual variables provide valuable sensitivity information, indicating how the optimal solution changes with small perturbations in the problem data (e.g., right-hand side of constraints).

This sensitivity analysis aspect is crucial in engineering design and decision-making. For instance, in structural engineering, if we are optimizing the design of a bridge to minimize material cost subject to strength and deflection constraints, the Lagrange multipliers associated with the stress and deflection constraints can tell us how much the cost would increase if we needed to withstand slightly higher stresses or accommodate slightly larger deflections. In finance, for portfolio optimization, the dual variables can relate to the risk-free rate or other market factors.

Let's revisit the example of a Linear Programming (LP) problem:

Minimize $c^T x$

Subject to $Ax \le b$
and $x \ge 0$

The Lagrangian is $L(x, \lambda, \nu) = c^T x + \lambda^T (Ax - b) + \nu^T (-x)$, where $\lambda \ge 0$ and $\nu \ge 0$.

The dual function is $g(\lambda, \nu) = \inf_x (c^T x + \lambda^T Ax - \lambda^T b - \nu^T x)$
$g(\lambda, \nu) = \inf_x \left((c^T + \lambda^T A - \nu^T)x - \lambda^T b \right)$

For this expression to have a finite infimum, the coefficient of x must be zero. If $(c^T + \lambda^T A - \nu^T) \ne 0$, the infimum is $-\infty$ (since x can be arbitrarily negative if the coefficient is negative). Thus, for a finite infimum, we must have $c^T + \lambda^T A - \nu^T = 0$.

So, $g(\lambda, \nu) = -\lambda^T b$ under the condition $c^T + \lambda^T A - \nu^T = 0$.

The dual problem is:

Maximize $-\lambda^T b$
Subject to $\lambda \ge 0$, $\nu \ge 0$, and $c^T + \lambda^T A - \nu^T = 0$.

The condition $c^T + \lambda^T A - \nu^T = 0$ can be rewritten. Let

$\mu = -\lambda$. Then $\mu \le 0$. The condition becomes $c^T + \mu^T A = \nu^T$. Since $\nu \ge 0$, we have $c^T + \mu^T A \ge 0$.

The dual problem becomes:
Maximize $-\lambda^T b$
Subject to $\lambda \ge 0$ and $c + A^T \lambda \ge 0$.
This is equivalent to:
Minimize $\lambda^T b$
Subject to $A^T \lambda \ge -c$ and $\lambda \ge 0$.

This is the standard dual form of the LP problem. The variables λ are the dual variables for the primal LP. Notice that the dual problem is also an LP. For LPs, weak duality always holds, and strong duality holds (i.e., $p^ = d^$) without any constraint qualification needed. The dual variables λ can be interpreted as shadow prices for the constraints $Ax \le b$.

Let's consider a convex Quadratic Programming (QP) problem:

Minimize $\frac{1}{2} x^T P x + q^T x$

Subject to $Ax \le b$
and $x \ge 0$

where P is positive semidefinite.

The Lagrangian is $L(x, \lambda, \nu) = \frac{1}{2} x^T P x + q^T x + \lambda^T (Ax - b) - \nu^T x$ (here, $\nu \ge 0$ for the $x \ge 0$ constraints).
The dual function is $g(\lambda, \nu) = \inf_x \left(\frac{1}{2} x^T P x + (q^T + \lambda^T A - \nu^T)x - \lambda^T b \right)$.

To find the infimum, we take the gradient with respect to x and set it to zero:

$\nabla_x L = Px + q + A^T \lambda - \nu = 0$.
If P is positive definite, $x = -P^{-1}(q + A^T \lambda - \nu)$.
If P is positive semidefinite but not positive definite, the infimum might be attained over a subspace. For simplicity in demonstrating duality, let's assume P is positive definite.

Substituting this x back into L:

$g(\lambda, \nu) = \frac{1}{2} (-P^{-1}(q + A^T \lambda - \nu))^T P (-P^{-1}(q + A^T \lambda - \nu)) + (q^T + \lambda^T A - \nu^T)(-P^{-1}(q + A^T \lambda - \nu)) - \lambda^T b$
$g(\lambda, \nu) = -\frac{1}{2} (q + A^T \lambda - \nu)^T P^{-1} (q + A^T \lambda - \nu) - (q + A^T \lambda - \nu)^T P^{-1}(q + A^T \lambda - \nu) - \lambda^T b$
$g(\lambda, \nu) = -\frac{1}{2} (q + A^T \lambda - \nu)^T P^{-1} (q + A^T \lambda - \nu) - \lambda^T b$

This expression is concave in λ and ν. The dual problem is to maximize $g(\lambda, \nu)$ subject to $\lambda \ge 0$ and $\nu \ge 0$.

The dual problem for a convex QP is also a convex optimization problem. For a convex QP with a constraint qualification (like Slater's condition, if A has full row rank and there is a strictly feasible point $x>0$), strong duality holds, meaning $p^ = d^$.

The dual variables λ in this QP context also carry economic interpretations. If we relax the constraints $Ax \le b$ and $x \ge 0$ and consider them with non-negative multipliers, the dual variables

λ would represent the marginal cost or benefit associated with relaxing these constraints. For example, if A represents resource usage per unit of product, and b is the total available resource, λ could represent the "cost" or "value" of these resources in achieving the optimal objective (e.g., minimizing cost or maximizing profit).

The concept of duality is not merely an academic exercise; it underpins many powerful algorithms and provides crucial insights. For instance, the famous Simplex algorithm for LPs can be interpreted as navigating between primal and dual feasible solutions. Interior-point methods, widely used for LPs, QPs, SOCPs, and SDPs, often generate primal and dual solutions that converge simultaneously. The duality gap, $p^ - d^$, is a primary measure of convergence in these algorithms. When the duality gap is sufficiently small, we are close to the optimal solution.

Furthermore, duality is essential for proving optimality conditions and for developing decomposition techniques. For problems with special structures, such as those arising in network flow or large-scale systems, the dual problem might be decomposable into smaller, more manageable subproblems.

Consider the case where the primal problem is infeasible. In such a scenario, the dual problem must be unbounded (i.e., $d^ = +\infty$ for a minimization problem). Conversely, if the dual problem is infeasible, the primal problem must be unbounded ($p^ = -\infty$ for a minimization problem). If both primal and dual problems are feasible, then weak duality guarantees $d^ \le p^$. Under convexity and a constraint qualification, strong duality ensures $d^ = p^$. If the primal is infeasible and the dual is unbounded, there is no x satisfying primal constraints and no (λ, ν) satisfying dual constraints.

The dual problem can be used to derive bounds on the optimal value, which is particularly useful when the original problem is computationally challenging. For example, in combinatorial optimization problems that can be relaxed into convex optimization problems (e.g., SDP relaxations for NP-hard problems), the dual of the relaxed problem provides a lower bound on the optimal value of the original combinatorial problem. This bound can be used to evaluate the quality of approximate solutions obtained by solving the relaxation or by other heuristic methods.

The relationship between primal and dual variables can also be used to gain insights into the problem structure. For example, in problems with many variables and few constraints, the dual problem might have fewer variables and more constraints, potentially offering a different perspective on the problem's complexity.

The development of duality theory has been a significant factor in the success and widespread adoption of convex optimization. It provides a rigorous mathematical foundation for understanding optimality, for designing efficient algorithms, and for interpreting the results of optimization in a meaningful way across various scientific and engineering disciplines. The ability to derive bounds, interpret dual variables as sensitivity measures or shadow prices, and to sometimes solve a more tractable dual problem, makes duality a cornerstone of modern optimization theory and practice.

The elegance of duality lies in its symmetry and the profound connection it establishes between primal and dual formulations. For convex problems, this connection is not just one of inequality but often of equality, transforming the quest for an optimal solution into a search for a point where primal and dual objectives meet. This meeting point, often characterized by the satisfaction of KKT conditions, represents the optimal equilibrium, a state where all constraints are optimally balanced, and marginal costs and benefits are precisely aligned. The dual problem offers a different lens through which to view this equilibrium, and often, solving one problem provides direct insights into the solution of the other, a testament to the deep structural properties of convex optimization.

The quest for optimal solutions in convex optimization problems, as we've established, relies heavily on the theoretical underpinnings of convexity and duality. However, translating these theoretical guarantees into practical results requires robust and efficient algorithms. This subsection delves into some of the most prominent algorithmic approaches employed to tackle convex optimization problems, exploring their core mechanics, convergence characteristics, and computational implications. Understanding these algorithms is paramount for any engineer or researcher seeking to leverage the power of convex optimization in real-world applications, from control system design to resource allocation and machine learning.

One of the most powerful classes of algorithms for convex optimization is
interior-point methods (IPMs). These methods are known for their remarkable efficiency and ability to solve a wide range of convex problems, including linear programming (LP), quadratic programming (QP), second-order cone programming (SOCP), and semidefinite programming (SDP), often to high precision. The fundamental idea behind IPMs is to approach the optimal solution from the "interior" of the feasible region, rather than from the boundary. This is typically achieved by introducing a barrier function that penalizes movement towards the boundary of the feasible set.

Consider a general convex optimization problem:

Minimize $f_0(x)$
Subject to $f_i(x) \le 0$, for $i = 1, \dots, m$
and $Ax = b$

where $f
0, \dots, fm$ are convex functions, and A is a matrix. In an interior-point method, we first replace the inequality constraints $fi(x) \le 0$ with a logarithmic barrier term added to the objective function. For each inequality constraint $fi(x) \le 0$, we introduce a term $-\mu \log(-fi(x))$ into the objective, where $\mu > 0$ is a barrier parameter. The term $\log(-fi(x))$ is convex because $-fi(x)$ is concave and the logarithm is concave, but $-\log$ of a concave function is convex. Thus, $-\mu \log(-fi(x))$ is convex for $\mu > 0$. The new objective function becomes:

$F
\mu(x) = f0(x) - \mu \sum{i=1}^m \log(-fi(x))$

The optimization problem is now to minimize $F
\mu(x)$ subject to the equality constraints $Ax = b$. Note that to stay in the interior of the feasible region, we must have $fi(x) < 0$ for all i, ensuring that the logarithm is well-defined.

The core of the algorithm involves iteratively solving a sequence of these barrier problems. Typically, μ is reduced gradually towards zero. At each iteration, the algorithm finds an approximate minimizer of $F
\mu(x)$ subject to $Ax=b$. This is often done by solving a Newton system derived from the first-order optimality conditions of the perturbed problem. Let $x\mu^$ be the minimizer of $F_\mu(x)$ subject to $Ax=b$. The optimality conditions are:

$\nabla f
0(x) - \mu \sum{i=1}^m \frac{1}{-fi(x)} \nabla fi(x) + A^T \nu = 0$
$Ax = b$

This system of equations is nonlinear and is typically solved using Newton's method. In each step of Newton's method, we linearize this system around the current iterate $x
k$ and solve for a search direction Δx and dual variables $\Delta \nu$. The update is then $x{k+1} = xk + \alpha \Delta x$ and $\nu{k+1} = \nuk + \alpha \Delta \nu$, where α is a step size chosen to maintain feasibility ($fi(x{k+1}) < 0$) and ensure sufficient decrease in $F\mu(x)$.

After finding an approximate solution for a given μ, the barrier parameter is reduced (e.g., $\mu
{new} = \sigma \mu{old}$, where $\sigma \in (0,1)$ is a reduction factor), and the process is repeated. As μ approaches zero, the minimizers $x_\mu^$ converge to the optimal solution of the original problem.

The computational complexity of interior-point methods is often characterized by the number of iterations required, which is typically small and grows only logarithmically with the problem size, and the cost per iteration, which is dominated by solving the Newton system. For LPs, the cost per iteration is often polynomial in the number of variables and constraints, leading to polynomial-time algorithms. For more general convex problems, the complexity can be higher, but IPMs still offer significant advantages over other methods for many classes of problems.

A crucial aspect of IPMs is their ability to exploit the structure of the problem. For instance, in LPs, the Newton system can be solved very efficiently. For QPs, the system is also manageable. For more complex problems like SDPs, the Newton system can become quite large, and specialized techniques are needed to solve it efficiently.

While interior-point methods are powerful, they can be computationally expensive, especially for very large-scale problems, due to the dense nature of the Newton system. This is where
first-order methods come into play. These algorithms rely primarily on the gradient of the objective function (and sometimes its Hessian, but not in a way that requires inverting it). They are generally simpler to implement and can be more amenable to distributed or parallel computation.

The most basic first-order method is
gradient descent. For a convex problem with a differentiable objective function $f(x)$, gradient descent iteratively updates the current estimate x_k as follows:

$x
{k+1} = xk - \alpha*k \nabla f(*xk)$

where $\nabla f(x
*k)$ is the gradient of f at $*xk$, and $\alpha*k > 0$ is the step size. The goal is to choose $\alpha*k$ such that the objective function decreases at each step. For unconstrained convex problems, a common choice for α_k is a fixed step size (if the Lipschitz constant of the gradient is known) or a line search procedure to find a suitable step size.

The convergence rate of standard gradient descent depends on the properties of the objective function, specifically its Lipschitz constant (smoothness). If the objective function f is L-smooth (i.e., $\|\nabla f(x) - \nabla f(y)\| \le L \|x-y\|$ for all x, y), then gradient descent with a constant step size $\alpha \le 1/L$ converges to the minimum at a sublinear rate of $O(1/k)$, meaning the error after k iterations is proportional to $1/k$. For many applications, this rate is too slow.

To accelerate convergence,
accelerated gradient descent methods have been developed. The most well-known is Nesterov's accelerated gradient method. Instead of just using the gradient at the current point x_k, Nesterov's method uses information from the previous iterate. The update rule involves two steps: first, a "look-ahead" step based on a momentum term, and second, a gradient step. For a smooth convex function f, the update rules are:

$y
k = x{k-1} + \beta*k (x*{k-1} - x*{k-2})$ (momentum step, $y*k$ is the look-ahead point)
$x*k = y*k - \alpha*k \nabla f(y*k)$ (gradient step)

The coefficients $\alpha
*k$ and $\beta*k$ are carefully chosen. For example, one common variant uses $\beta*k = (1 - 1/\sqrt{L/\mu}) / (1 + 1/\sqrt{L/\mu})$ and $\alpha*k = 1/L$ where L is the Lipschitz constant of the gradient and μ is related to the strong convexity parameter. With optimal choices of these parameters, Nesterov's method achieves a much faster convergence rate of $O(1/k^2)$ for smooth convex functions. This quadratic improvement in the convergence rate is significant for large-scale problems, as it means that to reduce the error by a factor of 10, one needs 10 times fewer iterations instead of 100 times fewer iterations with standard gradient descent.

Another powerful class of first-order methods is
coordinate descent. These methods update variables one at a time (or a block of variables at a time), which can be advantageous when the

objective function is separable or when computing the full gradient is expensive. For a function \$f(x*1, \dots,* xn)\$, coordinate descent updates one coordinate \$x_i\$ while keeping all other coordinates fixed. The update rule for the \$i\$-th coordinate is:

\$x
i^{k+1} = \arg\min{z} f(x*1^k, \dots, x*{i-1}^k, z, x*{i+1}^k, \dots, x*n^k)\$

This means that at each step, we perform a one-dimensional optimization along one coordinate direction. If the objective function is separable, i.e., \$f(x) = \sum
*{i=1}^n f*i(x*i)\$, then minimizing \$f\$ with respect to \$x*i\$ is simply minimizing \$f*i(x*i)\$, which can be done efficiently.

There are two main variants of coordinate descent:

1. **Cyclic coordinate descent**: The coordinates are updated in a fixed cyclic order (e.g., \$x*1, x*2, \dots, x*n, x*1, x_2, \dots\$).
2. **Randomized coordinate descent**: A coordinate is chosen uniformly at random at each step to be updated.

Randomized coordinate descent often exhibits better convergence properties and is more amenable to theoretical analysis, especially for non-separable functions. For smooth convex functions, randomized coordinate descent can achieve a convergence rate of \$O(1/k)\$, similar to standard gradient descent, but potentially with lower computational cost per iteration if the function is structured such that partial derivatives or one-dimensional minimizations are cheaper than computing the full gradient. If the function is also strongly convex, the convergence rate can be geometric (linear).

A significant advantage of coordinate descent arises in problems where the objective function is not necessarily smooth but has a structure that allows for efficient one-dimensional minimization along coordinate directions. For example, in problems involving L1 regularization (like in Lasso regression), where the objective function has a non-differentiable term at zero, coordinate descent can effectively handle the non-smoothness.

The choice of algorithm often depends on the specific characteristics of the convex optimization problem at hand. For problems with a moderate number of variables but potentially complex constraints, interior-point methods are often the preferred choice due to their robustness and guaranteed convergence rates. They are particularly well-suited for problems where high precision is required.

On the other hand, for very large-scale problems, especially those encountered in machine learning and big data analytics, first-order methods like accelerated gradient descent and randomized coordinate descent become more appealing. Their lower per-iteration cost and potential for parallelization can make them significantly faster in practice, even if they require more iterations to reach the same level of accuracy. Accelerated methods offer a significant speedup over standard gradient descent, while coordinate descent can be advantageous when the problem has inherent separability or when evaluating the full gradient is prohibitive.

Beyond these core algorithms, there are numerous variants and hybrid approaches. For instance, stochastic gradient descent (SGD) is a popular variant of gradient descent used when the objective function is a sum of a large number of terms (e.g., in empirical risk minimization). SGD approximates the gradient using only a small random subset (a mini-batch) of the terms, drastically reducing the computational cost per iteration, albeit at the expense of convergence guarantees and requiring careful tuning of the learning rate schedule.

Practical implementation of any of these algorithms requires careful consideration of several factors:

Step Size Selection: For gradient-based methods, choosing an appropriate step size (α_k) is crucial. Too large a step size can lead to overshooting the minimum or even divergence. Too small a step size results in slow convergence. Techniques like constant step size (if bounds on gradient Lipschitz constant are known), backtracking line search, or adaptive step size rules (like Adam or RMSprop in stochastic settings) are employed.
Termination Criteria: Algorithms need a way to stop. Common termination criteria include:
Gradient Norm: Stopping when the norm of the gradient is below a certain tolerance (e.g., $\|\nabla f(x_k)\| \le \epsilon$). This is effective for unconstrained problems.
Small Change in Solution: Stopping when the change in the iterate is small (e.g., $\|x{k+1} - xk\| \le \epsilon$).
Small Change in Objective Value: Stopping when the objective function value changes minimally between iterations (e.g., $|f(x{k+1}) - f(xk)| \le \epsilon$).
Duality Gap: For problems where duality is readily available, stopping when the duality gap ($p^ - d^$) is below a tolerance is a strong indicator of optimality. This is particularly relevant for interior-point methods and some other algorithms.
Initialization: The starting point (x_0) can influence the convergence speed and, for non-convex problems, the final solution. For convex

problems, most algorithms are guaranteed to converge to the global minimum, but a good initial guess can significantly shorten the time to reach it.

Numerical Precision: The choice of floating-point precision (e.g., single vs. double precision) can impact the stability and accuracy of the algorithms, especially for ill-conditioned problems.

The selection and tuning of these algorithmic parameters are often problem-dependent and may require experimentation. However, the theoretical convergence guarantees provide a solid foundation for understanding the behavior of these methods and for making informed choices. As computational power continues to grow and algorithms become more sophisticated, the ability to efficiently solve complex convex optimization problems will remain a critical capability in a wide array of engineering and scientific disciplines. The interplay between theoretical understanding and algorithmic innovation ensures that convex optimization continues to be a vibrant and essential field.

Chapter 3: Learning System Models from Data

The preceding chapters have laid a robust foundation in the theoretical underpinnings of control systems, exploring concepts such as stability, controllability, and observability, and have delved into the power of optimization techniques for designing controllers that meet specific performance criteria. However, a critical aspect of deploying these control strategies in the real world hinges on our ability to accurately represent the dynamic behavior of the systems we aim to control. In many practical scenarios, the precise mathematical equations governing a physical system are either unknown, too complex to derive analytically, or change over time. This is precisely where the discipline of **system identification** emerges as an indispensable tool.

System identification is the scientific discipline of modeling dynamical systems based on observed input-output data. It provides a systematic framework for transforming raw experimental measurements into mathematical models that capture the essential dynamic characteristics of a system. These models are not merely academic curiosities; they are the bedrock upon which effective simulation, prediction, and, most importantly, robust control system design are built. Without a reasonably accurate model, a controller designed based on theoretical assumptions might perform poorly or even destabilize the actual system. The goal is to bridge the gap between the ideal, often simplified, models used in theoretical analysis and the complex, sometimes unpredictable, reality of physical systems.

The process of system identification can be broadly segmented into several key stages, each with its own set of challenges and considerations. These stages typically include data collection, model structure selection, parameter estimation, and model validation.

The journey begins with
data collection. This is perhaps the most fundamental step, as the quality and informativeness of the data directly dictate the quality of the resulting model. The objective here is to excite the system's dynamics using appropriate input signals and to record the system's corresponding outputs. The choice of input signal is critical. It must be sufficiently rich to reveal the system's behavior across its operating range. A common mistake is to use inputs that are too simple or that do not sufficiently perturb the system, leading to models that are only accurate within a very narrow operating regime or that fail to capture important dynamic modes. For instance, applying a constant input to a system with significant inertia might not reveal its response to changes. Therefore, signals like step inputs, impulse inputs, ramps, sinusoidal sweeps, or even pseudo-random binary sequences (PRBS) are often employed, depending on the system's characteristics and the objectives of the identification. The sampling rate for data acquisition is also paramount; it must be sufficiently high to capture the fastest dynamics of interest, adhering to the Nyquist-Shannon sampling theorem. Furthermore, noise is an ever-present contaminant in real-world measurements. Understanding the nature and level of this noise is important for selecting appropriate modeling techniques and for interpreting the uncertainty in the identified model.

Once adequate data has been gathered, the next crucial step is
model structure selection. This involves deciding on the mathematical form of the model that will be used to represent the system. This is a crucial decision point that balances model complexity with the need to accurately fit the observed data. Common model structures include:

Transfer Function Models: These are widely used in classical control theory, particularly for single-input, single-output (SISO) systems. A

transfer function $G(s)$ describes the relationship between the Laplace transform of the output $Y(s)$ and the Laplace transform of the input $U(s)$, often represented as a ratio of two polynomials in s:
$$ G(s) = \frac{B(s)}{A(s)} = \frac{bm s^m + b{m-1} s^{m-1} + \dots + b0}{s^n + a{n-1} s^{n-1} + \dots + a_0} $$
Here, m and n are the orders of the numerator and denominator polynomials, respectively. The choice of orders m and n defines the complexity of the model. For example, a first-order system with a time delay might be represented by:
$$ G(s) = \frac{K e^{-\tau s}}{T s + 1} $$
where K is the gain, τ is the time delay, and T is the time constant.

State-Space Models: These models provide a more comprehensive description of the system's internal state. For a linear time-invariant (LTI) system, the state-space representation is given by:
$$ \dot{x}(t) = Ax(t) + Bu(t) $$
$$ y(t) = Cx(t) + Du(t) $$
where $x(t)$ is the state vector, $u(t)$ is the input vector, and $y(t)$ is the output vector. The matrices A, B, C, and D define the system's dynamics. State-space models are particularly useful for multi-input, multi-output (MIMO) systems and are fundamental in modern control theory.

Autoregressive (AR), Moving Average (MA), and Autoregressive Moving Average (ARMA) Models: These are commonly used in time series analysis and signal processing, and can be adapted for system identification. An ARMA model relates the current output to past outputs and past inputs:
$$ y(t) + a1 y(t-1) + \dots + an y(t-n) = b0 u(t) + b1 u(t-1) + \dots + b_m u(t-m) + e(t) $$

where $e(t)$ is a white noise process representing unmodeled dynamics or measurement noise. When the input $u(t)$ is zero, it becomes an AR model. When only the input terms are present, it becomes an MA model.

Non-linear Models: For systems exhibiting non-linear behavior, more complex model structures are required, such as Hammerstein-Wiener models (a linear dynamic system preceded by a static non-linearity and followed by another static non-linearity), neural networks, or other machine learning-based models.

The selection of the model structure is often an iterative process, guided by prior knowledge of the system, preliminary analysis of the data (e.g., impulse response plots), and performance criteria. Overly simple models will fail to capture the essential dynamics, leading to poor predictive capabilities. Conversely, overly complex models can overfit the noise in the data, resulting in models that perform poorly on new, unseen data. Model order selection criteria, such as the Akaike Information Criterion (AIC) or the Bayesian Information Criterion (BIC), can provide quantitative guidance during this phase.

Once a model structure has been chosen, the next stage is **parameter estimation**. This is the core of the identification process, where the unknown parameters within the selected model structure are determined by minimizing the difference between the model's output and the actual system's output when subjected to the same input. This difference is typically quantified by a cost function, often the sum of squared errors (SSE) between the predicted and measured outputs:

$$ J(\theta) = \sum_{t=1}^{N} (y_{measured}(t) - y_{model}(t; \theta))^2 $$

where θ represents the vector of unknown model parameters (e.g., coefficients of the polynomials in a transfer function, or the matrices in a state-space model), and N is the number of data points.

A variety of estimation algorithms can be employed, depending on the model structure and the properties of the noise. Some of the most common include:

Least Squares Estimation: This is a widely used technique when the model is linear in its parameters, such as linear transfer function models or linear state-space models. It directly seeks to minimize the SSE. For linear models, least squares provides an analytical solution, making it computationally efficient. For example, in a transfer function model where the output $y(t)$ can be expressed as a linear combination of parameters and known data terms:
$$ y(t) = \phi(t)^T \theta $$
where $\phi(t)$ is a regression vector containing past inputs and outputs, and θ is the parameter vector, the least squares estimate is given by:
$$ \hat{\theta} = (\Phi^T \Phi)^{-1} \Phi^T Y $$
where Φ is the matrix formed by stacking $\phi(t)^T$ for all time steps, and Y is the vector of measured outputs.

Maximum Likelihood Estimation (MLE): This is a more general approach that aims to find the parameters that maximize the probability of observing the given data, assuming a specific probability distribution for the noise. If the noise is assumed to be independent and identically distributed (i.i.d.) with a Gaussian distribution, MLE is equivalent to least squares. MLE can handle more complex noise models and is often used for ARX, ARMAX, and Box-Jenkins model structures.

Prediction Error Methods (PEM): This is a broad class of methods that includes least squares and MLE as special cases. The core idea is to minimize the prediction error, which is the difference between the actual output and the output predicted by the model one step ahead. Different model structures lead to different prediction error formulations. PEM is very flexible and can be applied to a wide range of linear and non-linear models.

Instrumental Variables (IV): This method is particularly useful when the noise is correlated with the input or when there is feedback, which can bias standard least squares estimates. IV methods introduce "instrumental variables" that are correlated with the input but uncorrelated with the noise, allowing for consistent parameter estimation.

Recursive Least Squares (RLS): For systems whose dynamics change over time or for online identification where data arrives sequentially, recursive algorithms are necessary. RLS is a popular choice that updates the parameter estimates iteratively as new data points become available, without needing to reprocess the entire dataset. This is crucial for adaptive control applications.

Non-linear Estimation Techniques: For non-linear model structures (e.g., neural networks), gradient-based optimization methods, such as backpropagation, are commonly used to iteratively adjust the parameters to minimize the prediction error. These methods often require careful initialization and can be susceptible to local minima.

The final stage in the system identification process is **model validation**. This is a critical step to assess whether the identified model is adequate for its intended purpose. Validation involves testing the model's performance on a separate set of data that was not used during the estimation phase. Common validation techniques include:

Simulation: The identified model is used to simulate the system's response to various inputs, and this simulated response is compared visually or quantitatively against the actual system's response (using the validation data). Metrics like the Mean Squared Error (MSE) or Normalized Mean Squared Error (NMSE) between the simulated and actual outputs are often computed.

$$ NMSE = \frac{\sum_{t=1}^{N_{val}} (y_{measured}(t) - y_{model}(t))^2}{\sum_{t=1}^{N_{val}} (y_{measured}(t) - \bar{y}_{measured})^2} $$

where N_{val} is the number of data points in the validation set, and $\bar{y}_{measured}$ is the mean of the measured validation output. A low NMSE indicates good predictive performance.

Residual Analysis: The residuals, defined as the difference between the measured output and the model's predicted output on the validation data, are analyzed. Ideally, the residuals should resemble white noise, meaning they are uncorrelated with themselves and with the input signal. Statistical tests can be performed to check for autocorrelation (indicating that the model has not captured all the dynamic information) and cross-correlation between residuals and inputs (indicating dependence that the model should have captured).

Pole-Zero Analysis: For linear models, the location of poles and zeros in the complex plane provides insights into the system's stability and dynamic characteristics (e.g., speed of response, damping). These can be compared to expectations or to estimates from other identification methods.

Frequency Domain Analysis: Comparing the frequency response (Bode plots, Nyquist plots) of the identified model with that estimated from data can reveal discrepancies, particularly at certain frequencies.

Comparison with Prior Knowledge: The identified model's parameters and behavior should be physically plausible and consistent with any existing knowledge about the system. For instance, a model of a heating system should not predict instantaneous temperature changes.

If the validation tests indicate that the model is not adequate, the process must be revisited. This might involve collecting more or different types of data, choosing a different model structure (e.g., increasing the order, including time delays, or switching to a non-linear model), or employing a different estimation algorithm.

The importance of system identification is pervasive across numerous engineering and scientific domains. In the automotive industry, accurate models of engine dynamics, vehicle suspension, or battery behavior are essential for developing advanced driver-assistance systems (ADAS), improving fuel efficiency, and designing effective powertrain control. In aerospace, identifying the aerodynamic characteristics of an aircraft or the dynamics of a satellite's attitude control system is fundamental to flight control and mission success. Industrial process control relies heavily on identified models of chemical reactors, distillation columns, or power plants to maintain product quality, optimize throughput, and ensure safety. In robotics, models of manipulator dynamics and joint friction are crucial for precise motion control and path planning. Even in fields like economics and biology, system identification techniques are applied to model the behavior of markets or the dynamics of biological systems.

Let's consider a simple example: identifying a first-order system with a time delay. Suppose we have a temperature control system where an electric heater (input) controls the temperature of a fluid in a tank (output). The heater is controlled by adjusting a voltage signal, and the temperature is measured by a sensor. We want to build a model of this system to design a controller that maintains a desired temperature.

We might choose a first-order plus dead time (FOPDT) model structure:

$$ G(s) = \frac{K e^{-\tau s}}{T s + 1} $$

Here, K is the steady-state gain (change in temperature per unit change in heater voltage), T is the dominant time constant of the fluid/tank system, and τ is the time delay (e.g., due to sensor response or signal propagation). The parameters to be estimated are K, T, and τ.

To collect data, we could apply a step change to the heater voltage from an initial level to a new level, and record the temperature over time. Let's say we apply a step increase in voltage from $V1$ to $V2$. The temperature will initially remain constant for a duration τ, and then gradually rise, eventually settling at a new steady-state temperature T_{ss} according to:

$$ T_{ss} = T_{initial} + K (V2 - V1) $$

The time constant T dictates how quickly the temperature reaches its new steady-state value after the delay period.

From the recorded input-output data, we can visually estimate these parameters. The time delay τ is the time from the voltage step until the temperature starts to change. The steady-state gain K can be calculated as the total change in temperature divided by the change in voltage: $K = (T
{ss} - *T*{initial}) / (V*2* - *V*1)$. The time constant T can be estimated by observing the time it takes for the temperature to reach approximately 63.2% of its total change after the delay has elapsed. Alternatively, more sophisticated methods like least squares can be used to fit the FOPDT model to the data, minimizing the error between the model's predicted temperature and the measured temperature.

After estimation, we would validate the model using a different step input, or perhaps a series of pulses, and compare the model's predictions to the actual system's response. If the model accurately predicts the temperature rise and settling time for this new input, it is likely a reasonable representation for control design purposes.

Extending this to more complex systems, such as a multi-variable process with multiple heaters and sensors, leads to state-space models or MIMO transfer function representations. For instance, a chemical plant might have inputs like flow rates of reactants, temperature setpoints, and pressures, and outputs like product concentration, purity, and energy consumption. Identifying such a system involves exciting different inputs and observing their effects on various outputs, potentially simultaneously. This requires careful experimental design and the use of multivariate identification techniques.

The choice between different model structures and estimation methods is often dictated by the application's requirements. If the primary goal is simple simulation or feedback control design for a relatively linear system, a transfer function or state-space model might suffice. If accurate prediction of future behavior is paramount, or if the system's dynamics are significantly influenced by noise, more complex models like ARMAX or Box-Jenkins, estimated using maximum likelihood or prediction error methods, might be necessary. For systems with known non-linearities, specific non-linear model structures or data-driven machine learning approaches are often employed.

In essence, system identification is an empirical science that complements theoretical modeling. It allows us to learn the behavior of systems directly from observations, making it a cornerstone of modern control engineering and a vital bridge between mathematical theory and practical implementation. The subsequent sections will delve deeper into specific techniques for parameter estimation and model validation, providing the tools needed to effectively build and trust data-driven models.

The journey from understanding a physical system to creating a functional mathematical model is intrinsically tied to the quality and integrity of the data we collect. As we move from theoretical constructs to empirical learning, the focus must sharpen on the practicalities of acquiring and preparing that essential data. This involves meticulous attention to detail in how we gather measurements, from the instruments we use to the very rhythm of their recordings, and subsequently, in how we clean and transform these raw observations into a format that facilitates accurate learning. The effectiveness of any system identification endeavor, and indeed, the reliability of the control systems designed upon its findings, hinges critically on the diligence applied during these initial, yet foundational, phases: data acquisition and preprocessing.

Data Acquisition: The Foundation of Empirical Modeling

The process of data acquisition is not merely about recording numbers; it is about capturing the dynamic essence of a system through its interactions with the environment and externally applied stimuli. This necessitates a thoughtful approach to selecting the right tools and strategies to ensure that the collected data is both representative and informative.

Sensor Selection and Characterization: The choice of sensors is paramount. Each sensor transduces a physical phenomenon into an electrical signal, and its accuracy, precision, bandwidth, and linearity directly influence the data's fidelity. For instance, when monitoring temperature in a chemical reactor, a thermocouple might be suitable for a wide range of temperatures but may have a slower response time compared to a resistance temperature detector (RTD). If the system exhibits rapid temperature fluctuations, an RTD might be preferred, provided its temperature range and accuracy are sufficient. Furthermore, sensors introduce their own dynamics and noise characteristics. Understanding these limitations – their inherent noise floor, their response time (which introduces a delay or filtering effect), and their calibration drift – is crucial. A sensor that is poorly calibrated will lead to systematically biased data, while a sensor with insufficient bandwidth will fail to capture fast dynamics, effectively low-pass filtering the true signal. This characterization can be done through offline calibration against known standards or by analyzing the sensor's behavior when subjected to known inputs, which itself can be a mini-system identification problem. The goal is to understand the sensor's transfer function or its error characteristics so that these can be accounted for, either in the data preprocessing or by incorporating them into the system model itself.

Sampling Rate and Resolution: The Nyquist-Shannon sampling theorem dictates that to accurately reconstruct a signal, the sampling frequency must be at least twice the highest frequency component present in the signal. In practice, however, this is often insufficient. To capture the transient behavior of a system without aliasing, and to allow for effective filtering of high-frequency noise, a sampling rate significantly higher than the Nyquist rate is typically employed. For example, identifying the dynamics of a fast-acting robotic arm might require sampling rates in the kilohertz range, while monitoring the temperature of a large industrial furnace might only necessitate sampling every few seconds or even minutes. The "rule of thumb" often suggests sampling at 5 to 10 times the bandwidth of the system dynamics of interest. The resolution of the analog-to-digital converter (ADC) also plays a role. A higher resolution (more bits) means finer quantization levels, reducing quantization error, which can be significant for signals with small dynamic ranges or those requiring high precision. For example, measuring a small but critical pressure variation in a process might require an ADC with 16-bit or higher resolution, whereas monitoring a large, slowly varying level might be adequately served by a 10-bit or 12-bit converter.

Experimental Design and Excitation Signals: The quality of the data is not solely dependent on the sensors and sampling but also on how the system is "excited." A system's dynamics can only be revealed if it is perturbed in a way that excites those dynamics. Applying a constant input, for instance, will not reveal how a system responds to changes. Therefore, the selection of appropriate excitation signals is a critical aspect of experimental design.

Step Inputs: A simple yet effective way to probe a system's response. A step input from a baseline to a new level can reveal the steady-state gain, time constant, and time delay of a system, especially for first-order or second-order systems. However, if the system is highly non-linear or has multiple operating regimes, a single step might not be sufficient.
Impulse Inputs: Theoretically, an impulse input excites all frequencies equally. In practice, true impulses are impossible. Approximations using short-duration, high-amplitude pulses can be used, but they can also excite non-linearities and are sensitive to noise.
Ramp Inputs: Similar to step inputs but provide a continuously changing stimulus, which can be useful for systems with integrating characteristics.
Sinusoidal Sweeps: By applying sinusoids of increasing or decreasing frequency, one can effectively map out the system's frequency response. This is particularly useful for identifying resonant frequencies, bandwidth, and phase lags, which are crucial for controller design. The range of frequencies to sweep and the duration of each sinusoid need to be carefully chosen to excite all relevant dynamics.
Pseudo-Random Binary Sequences (PRBS): These signals switch between two levels (e.g., 0 and 1, or low and high voltage) at regular intervals, but the timing of the switches follows a specific pseudo-random pattern. PRBS signals have excellent correlation properties, meaning they tend to "look like" white noise when correlated with themselves. This property makes them very effective for probing linear system dynamics, as they excite a wide range of frequencies and are robust to noise. The length of the PRBS sequence and the switching interval (bit duration) are important parameters. A longer sequence

provides more data and better statistical properties, while the bit duration should be chosen to match the system's time constants.
Other Perturbation Signals: Depending on the system and the objective, other signals like chirp signals (where frequency changes linearly over time) or specific, designed trajectories that are known to excite critical modes of operation can be employed.

The amplitude of the excitation signal is also important. It must be large enough to elicit a measurable response and excite the relevant dynamics, but not so large that it saturates the system or drives it into non-linear regions that are not of primary interest. For systems with multiple inputs and outputs (MIMO), the design becomes more complex, requiring coordinated excitation of multiple inputs, possibly simultaneously, to identify interactions between different parts of the system.

Data Preprocessing: Refining Raw Measurements

Once the data has been acquired, it is rarely in a state suitable for direct use in model identification. Raw data often contains artifacts, inaccuracies, and characteristics that can mislead the identification algorithms, leading to suboptimal or erroneous models. Preprocessing is the crucial step of cleaning and transforming the data to mitigate these issues and prepare it for estimation.

Noise Filtering: Measurement noise is an inherent aspect of any real-world data acquisition process. It can stem from various sources, including electromagnetic interference, sensor imperfections, or analog-to-digital conversion. Noise can obscure the underlying system dynamics and cause parameter estimates to be highly uncertain. Various filtering techniques can be employed:

Moving Average Filter: A simple filter that replaces each data point with the average of itself and its neighbors within a specified window. While easy to implement, it can significantly attenuate high-frequency components but also introduce phase lag and distort sharp transients.
Savitzky-Golay Filter: This filter fits a low-degree polynomial to a moving window of data points and then computes the smoothed point from the fitted polynomial. It can preserve the shape and height of peaks better than a simple moving average, making it suitable for noisy data where signal features are important.
Low-Pass Filters (Butterworth, Chebyshev): These are more sophisticated filters designed to attenuate frequencies above a certain cutoff. The cutoff frequency must be carefully chosen – too high and noise remains, too low and genuine system dynamics are removed. Designing digital filters often involves translating analog filter designs or using specialized algorithms.
Kalman Filter: For systems where a dynamic model of the noise or the underlying signal is available, a Kalman filter can provide optimal state estimation in the presence of Gaussian noise. It is particularly powerful when dealing with time-varying systems or when combining information from multiple sensors.
Wavelet Denoising: This technique decomposes the signal into different frequency components using wavelets and then thresholds or shrinks the coefficients corresponding to noise, effectively separating the signal from the noise. It is often effective at preserving signal features while removing noise.

The choice of filter depends on the nature of the noise and the characteristics of the system dynamics being preserved. It is crucial to remember that filtering can also alter the system's dynamics, particularly its phase response. Therefore, it's often advisable to perform filter design and analysis in the frequency domain, ensuring that the filter's characteristics align with the system's bandwidth of interest and that unwanted distortions are minimized.

Outlier Removal: Outliers are data points that deviate significantly from the general trend of the data, often due to transient faults, sensor malfunctions, or data transmission errors. They can disproportionately influence parameter estimates, especially in methods like least squares, leading to a severely biased model.

Statistical Methods: Techniques like Z-score or modified Z-score can identify points that are a certain number of standard deviations away from the mean. However, these are sensitive to the outliers themselves skewing the mean and standard deviation.
Interquartile Range (IQR): This method identifies points that fall outside a certain range defined by the first and third quartiles of the data. It is more robust to extreme values than standard deviation-based methods.
Visual Inspection: For smaller datasets or for critical segments of data, a manual review by an experienced analyst can be invaluable in spotting anomalies that automated methods might miss.
Model-Based Detection: After an initial model is estimated, its predictions can be compared to the actual data. Large discrepancies might indicate outliers that were not removed in an earlier stage.

It's important to investigate the cause of an outlier before removing it. Sometimes, an apparent outlier might represent a genuine, albeit rare, system behavior or a critical event that the model should ideally capture or at least be aware of. Simply removing such points might lead to a model that is too simplistic or fails to represent important aspects of the system.

Detrending: Many real-world systems exhibit slow drifts in their operating point over time due to factors like aging components, environmental changes, or gradual shifts in setpoints. These trends, if not removed, can be misinterpreted by the identification algorithm as part of the system's dynamic response, leading to incorrect parameter estimates.

Linear Detrending: This involves fitting a straight line to the data and subtracting it. This is suitable if the trend is approximately linear.
Polynomial Detrending: For more complex trends, a higher-order polynomial can be fitted and subtracted.
High-Pass Filtering: Applying a high-pass filter with a very low cutoff frequency can effectively remove slow drifts while preserving the faster dynamics of interest.
Differencing: For non-stationary data, taking the difference between consecutive samples ($y(t) - y(t-1)$) can often render the series stationary by removing trends. This is equivalent to setting the DC gain of the system to zero in the identified model, which might be appropriate if only the dynamic behavior is of interest.

When detrending, especially using differencing, it is crucial to remember that this operation changes the nature of the model being identified. For example, identifying a system from differenced data will result in a model that represents the
change in the system's output rather than the absolute output, which can affect the interpretation of parameters like steady-state gain.

Normalization and Scaling: Normalization can be important for several reasons. It can bring data from different sensors or different units into a comparable range, which can improve the performance of certain estimation algorithms (e.g., gradient-based methods used in neural networks) and prevent numerical instability.

Min-Max Scaling: This scales the data to a fixed range, typically [0, 1] or [-1, 1]. The formula is:

$$ X{normalized} = \frac{X - X{\min}}{X{max} - X{\min}} $$

This is useful when the absolute magnitude of the data is less important than its relative variations.

Standardization (Z-score Normalization): This scales the data to have zero mean and unit variance:

$$ X_{standardized} = \frac{X - \mu}{\sigma} $$

where μ is the mean and σ is the standard deviation. This is often preferred when the algorithm assumes data is centered around zero and has comparable variances.

Again, the choice of scaling technique depends on the estimation algorithm and the desired properties of the resulting model. If the physical units and magnitudes of the parameters are important for interpretation or for subsequent control design, then raw or appropriately scaled data should be used, and the estimation algorithm should be robust to variations in data scale. For instance, if a steady-state gain of 50 degrees Celsius per Volt is physically meaningful, scaling the output temperature to [0, 1] might obscure this direct physical interpretation of the parameter.

Data Segmentation: For time-series data, it is often beneficial to segment it into distinct periods. Identification typically requires data that is "stationarity-like" within the segment, meaning the underlying system dynamics are not changing significantly during the data collection window. If a system undergoes a significant change (e.g., a change in operating setpoint, a failure, or a maintenance intervention), data from before and after the change should ideally be treated as separate datasets for identification. This leads to the concept of using separate datasets for estimation and validation. The data used for parameter estimation should be representative of the system's behavior under typical operating conditions. A separate "validation" dataset, collected under different but relevant conditions or at a different time, is then used to assess the model's generalization capability.

Case Study Snippet: Data Preparation in Chemical Process Monitoring

Consider a chemical plant producing a specialty polymer. The process involves several reactors, distillation columns, and heat exchangers, with numerous sensors monitoring temperature, pressure, flow rates, and chemical concentrations. The goal is to develop a predictive maintenance model and an advanced control system to optimize product yield and quality.

1.
Data Acquisition Challenges:
Sensor Drift: Temperature sensors in the high-temperature reactors may drift over time, requiring recalibration. This drift can manifest as a slow, non-linear trend in the recorded temperature.
Noise: Pressure sensors in a turbulent flow regime might exhibit significant high-frequency noise. Concentration sensors, especially those

using spectroscopy, can also be susceptible to noise from varying optical paths or sample matrix effects.

Sampling Mismatch: Flow rate sensors might be sampled at 1 Hz, while crucial concentration sensors in a slow reaction might be sampled every 5 minutes. Integrating this data for identification requires careful consideration of time synchronization and interpolation.

Operational Changes: The plant might switch between producing different grades of polymer, which involves significant changes in setpoints and operating conditions. Data collected during these transitions can be highly non-stationary and may not be representative of steady-state operation.

2.

Preprocessing Steps Applied:

Detrending: Temperature data from sensors prone to drift are detrended using polynomial fitting to remove the slow drift component, allowing the identification of the dynamic response to control actions.

Noise Filtering: Pressure data is passed through a Savitzky-Golay filter to smooth out high-frequency noise while preserving sharp changes that might indicate control valve adjustments or process upsets. Concentration data might be filtered using a low-pass Butterworth filter to remove noise without excessively delaying the capture of slow chemical dynamics.

Outlier Removal: Spikes in flow rate measurements, possibly due to temporary sensor malfunctions or transient flow disturbances, are identified using the IQR method and removed. Any data points where multiple critical sensors simultaneously report physically impossible values (e.g., negative temperature) are also flagged and removed.

Normalization: For a machine learning model predicting product quality based on multiple input features (temperature, pressure, flow rates), all features are standardized (zero mean, unit variance) to ensure that features with larger inherent scales (like pressure in Pascals) do not dominate the learning process.

Data Segmentation: Data is segmented based on major operational shifts, such as a change in the primary reactant being used or a significant shutdown/startup cycle. Identification and control design are then performed on segments corresponding to the intended operating regime.
Synchronization: When combining data from sensors with different sampling rates, methods like zero-order hold (for faster to slower) or linear interpolation (for slower to faster, with caution) are used to align the time series, ensuring that corresponding input and output points are contemporaneous.

By meticulously executing these data acquisition and preprocessing steps, engineers can transform raw, noisy, and potentially misleading measurements into a clean, informative dataset. This prepared data serves as the solid empirical foundation upon which robust and accurate system models can be built, paving the way for effective control system design and reliable operational insights. The effort invested in this stage is not an overhead; it is an essential prerequisite for successful system identification and, by extension, for achieving optimal performance and safety in real-world engineering applications.

Parametric Model Structures

Having meticulously prepared our data, we now turn our attention to the core task of model building: selecting and fitting a mathematical structure that can effectively capture the system's dynamics. This chapter has thus far emphasized the empirical foundation of system identification, focusing on data acquisition and preprocessing. Now, we transition to the "model" part of "learning system models from data." Within the broad landscape of system identification, a significant and historically foundational approach involves the use of

parametric models. These models are characterized by their representation of the system's behavior using a finite, predetermined mathematical structure, where the system's dynamics are described by a specific set of adjustable parameters. The objective of the identification process, in this context, is to estimate the values of these parameters from the collected data.

The appeal of parametric models lies in their interpretability and the potential for compact representation. Unlike non-parametric models, which can be very flexible but often lack clear physical meaning, parametric models aim to embody prior knowledge about the system's underlying physics or structure. The parameters often correspond to physical quantities like mass, stiffness, damping, time constants, gains, or delays, making the resulting model intuitively understandable and facilitating insights into the system's behavior. Furthermore, once a parametric model structure is chosen, the identification problem often reduces to a well-defined mathematical optimization task, aiming to find the parameter values that best fit the observed data according to some defined criterion.

The choice of a parametric model structure is a critical decision that profoundly influences the success of the identification process. This choice is typically guided by a combination of factors:

Prior Knowledge and Physical Understanding: If there is existing theoretical knowledge about the system, such as physical laws governing its behavior (e.g., Newton's laws for mechanical systems, energy balance for thermal systems, conservation laws for chemical processes), this knowledge can strongly suggest a particular model structure. For instance, if we are modeling the motion of an object under forces, a

structure derived from Newton's second law, potentially involving mass-spring-damper elements, would be a natural starting point. Similarly, if we know a process involves diffusion and reaction, a structure reflecting these phenomena might be chosen.
Data Characteristics: Even without deep theoretical knowledge, the patterns observed in the preprocessed data can offer clues about the appropriate model structure. The presence of oscillatory behavior might suggest a second-order model, while a slow, gradual response might indicate a first-order system with a long time constant. The delay observed between input excitation and output response is another crucial characteristic that informs model structure selection.
Model Complexity and Parsimony: A fundamental principle in modeling is parsimony: the simplest model that adequately explains the data is generally preferred. Overly complex models, with too many parameters, are prone to overfitting the noise in the data, leading to poor generalization to unseen data. Conversely, a model that is too simple may fail to capture essential dynamics, resulting in a poor fit. The goal is to strike a balance, choosing a structure that is complex enough to represent the significant dynamics but not so complex as to be indistinguishable from noise.
Intended Application: The purpose for which the model will be used is also a key consideration. If the model is intended for simulation, accuracy across a wide range of operating conditions is paramount. If it's for control design, the model needs to accurately represent the dynamics relevant to the controller's bandwidth and stability margins. For fault detection, specific dynamic behaviors or deviations might need to be explicitly represented.

Two primary categories of parametric model structures are widely used in system identification:
transfer function models and **state-space models**.

Transfer Function Models

Transfer function models are a cornerstone of linear time-invariant (LTI) system analysis and identification, particularly in the context of single-input, single-output (SISO) systems. They describe the relationship between the Laplace transform of the input signal and the Laplace transform of the output signal, assuming zero initial conditions. For discrete-time systems, the equivalent is the Z-transform. A general LTI system can be represented by a rational function in the complex variable s (for continuous time) or z (for discrete time), known as the transfer function $G(s)$ or $G(z)$, respectively.

$$ G(s) = \frac{B(s)}{A(s)} = \frac{b_m s^m + b_{m-1} s^{m-1} + \dots + b_1 s + b_0}{a_n s^n + a_{n-1} s^{n-1} + \dots + a_1 s + a_0} $$

In discrete time, this becomes:

$$ G(z) = \frac{B(z)}{A(z)} = \frac{b_m z^m + b_{m-1} z^{m-1} + \dots + b_1 z + b_0}{a_n z^n + a_{n-1} z^{n-1} + \dots + a_1 z + a_0} $$

Here, $A(s)$ and $B(s)$ (or $A(z)$ and $B(z)$) are polynomials in s (or z). The order of the denominator polynomial, n, typically corresponds to the order of the system's dynamics (e.g., number of energy storage elements). The order of the numerator polynomial, m, is usually less than or equal to n. The coefficients of these polynomials (a_i and b_i) are the parameters that need to be estimated.

Several common transfer function model structures are distinguished by how they relate the current and past inputs and outputs, often incorporating a noise term. These structures are particularly prevalent in the context of time-series analysis and are often formulated in a way that is amenable to regression-based estimation techniques.

ARX (AutoRegressive with eXogenous input) Model: This is one of the simplest and most widely used parametric model structures. It relates the current output $y(t)$ to its own past values and to past and present values of the input $u(t)$, plus an additive noise term $e(t)$. In discrete time, the ARX model is formulated as:

$$ A(z) y(t) = B(z) u(t) + e(t) $$

where $A(z) = 1 + a_1 z^{-1} + \dots + a_n z^{-n}$ and $B(z) = b_1 z^{-1} + \dots + b_m z^{-m}$. The polynomials are typically defined with $A(0)=1$. The parameter n represents the order of the autoregressive part (how many past outputs influence the current output), and m represents the order of the exogenous part (how many past inputs influence the current output). The term z^{-k} represents a delay of k time steps. The noise term $e(t)$ is typically assumed to be white noise. The ARX model can be rewritten in a regression form:

$$ y(t) = -a_1 y(t-1) - \dots - a_n y(t-n) + b_1 u(t-1) + \dots + b_m u(t-m) + e(t) $$

This form clearly shows that if we know the past outputs and inputs, and the parameters (a_i, b_i), we can predict the current output. The presence of $u(t-k)$ terms implies a delay of at least one sample in the input's effect. To explicitly model a time delay d, the $B(z)$ polynomial is often written as $B(z) = z^{-d} B'(z)$, where $B'(z)$ includes terms from z^0 up to z^{m-1} or $z^{m'-1}$. In this case, the equation becomes:

$$ y(t) = -a_1 y(t-1) - \dots - a_n y(t-n) + b_1 u(t-d-1) + \dots + b_{m'} u(t-d-m') + e(t) $$

The ARX model is computationally efficient and can be estimated using straightforward linear least squares if the noise is white and uncorrelated with the input.

ARMAX (AutoRegressive Moving Average with eXogenous input) Model: This structure extends the ARX model by including past noise terms in the prediction of the current output. The model is given by:

$$ A(z) y(t) = B(z) u(t) + C(z) e(t) $$

where $C(z) = 1 + c_1 z^{-1} + \dots + c_k z^{-k}$. The regression form is:

$$ y(t) = -a_1 y(t-1) - \dots - a_n y(t-n) + b_1 u(t-1) + \dots + b_m u(t-m) + e(t) + c_1 e(t-1) + \dots + c_k e(t-k) $$

The ARMAX model can capture more complex noise dynamics, which is important when the noise is colored (i.e., not white). This makes it suitable for systems where unmodeled dynamics or disturbances have a persistent effect. However, the presence of the noise terms $e(t-i)$ makes direct linear least squares estimation impossible because $e(t)$ is unobserved. Estimation typically requires iterative methods such as maximum likelihood or prediction error methods.

Output Error (OE) Model: The OE model structure directly models the output as a filtered version of the input, with additive noise applied after the filtering. This structure is particularly well-suited when the noise is known to be solely measurement noise and not related to unmodeled system dynamics. The equation is:

$$ y(t) = \frac{B(z)}{F(z)} u(t) + e(t) $$

Here, $B(z)$ and $F(z)$ are polynomials representing the numerator and denominator of the system's transfer function, and $e(t)$ is assumed to be white noise. The regression form depends on the orders of $B(z)$ and $F(z)$. For example, if $B(z) = b_1 z^{-1} + \dots + b_m z^{-m}$ and $F(z) = 1 + f_1 z^{-1} + \dots + f_k z^{-k}$, then the output $y(t)$ can be expressed as:

$$ F(z) y(t) = B(z) u(t) + F(z) e(t) $$
$$ y(t) = -f_1 y(t-1) - \dots - f_k y(t-k) + b_1 u(t-1) + \dots + b_m u(t-m) + e(t) $$
Notice that the noise term here is $e(t)$, not $F(z)e(t)$. The key difference from ARX is that the output is considered a filtered input plus *independent* noise, whereas ARX implies a feedback loop of noise. The OE model assumes that the input $u(t)$ is independent of the noise $e(t)$. This can be a strong assumption but is often valid when the input is an actively controlled signal or a known excitation. Estimation for OE models is also typically done using iterative prediction error methods.

Box-Jenkins (BJ) Model: The BJ model is a more general structure that attempts to decouple the modeling of the system dynamics from the modeling of the noise. It is formulated as:
$$ y(t) = \frac{B(z)}{F(z)} u(t) + \frac{G(z)}{F(z)} e(t) $$
where $B(z)$, $F(z)$, and $G(z)$ are polynomials. The $B(z)/F(z)$ part represents the system's input-output relationship, and the $G(z)/F(z)$ part models the noise. The $F(z)$ polynomial appears in both the system and noise transfer functions, linking them. The regression form can be derived:
$$ F(z) y(t) = B(z) u(t) + G(z) e(t) $$
$$ y(t) = -f_1 y(t-1) - \dots - f_k y(t-k) + b_1 u(t-d) + \dots + b_m u(t-d-m+1) + e(t) + g_1 e(t-1) + \dots + g_k e(t-k) $$
where d is the time delay. The BJ model is quite flexible, allowing for independent modeling of the system dynamics and the noise spectrum. However, like ARMAX and OE, it requires iterative estimation methods because the noise terms $e(t)$ are not directly observed. The flexibility comes at the cost of higher model complexity and potentially more challenging identification.

The choice among these transfer function structures depends on the assumptions one can make about the noise and the system's inherent structure.

If the noise is believed to be white and uncorrelated with the input, and the system has a simple causal relationship with the input, ARX can be a good starting point due to its simplicity and linear estimation.
If the noise is thought to be colored (not white), ARMAX or BJ might be more appropriate, but at the cost of iterative estimation.
If the noise is primarily measurement noise and is independent of the input, the OE model offers a direct way to model the system dynamics without being confounded by noise correlations.
The BJ model provides the most general framework among these, allowing separate parameterizations for the system and noise dynamics, but demands careful consideration of polynomial orders and the delay.

When selecting orders (n, m, k, d) for these polynomials, a common approach is to start with low orders and progressively increase them, evaluating the model's fit and complexity. Techniques like cross-validation, information criteria (e.g., AIC, BIC), or residual analysis (checking if the residuals are indeed white noise) are employed to guide this selection.

State-Space Models

While transfer functions are excellent for describing the input-output relationship of LTI systems, especially in SISO cases, state-space models offer a more general and powerful framework. They are particularly well-suited for MIMO (Multiple-Input Multiple-Output) systems, time-varying systems, and systems where internal states are of interest. A state-space representation describes the system's behavior through a set of first-order differential equations (for continuous time) or difference equations (for discrete time) that define the evolution of internal "state variables."

For a discrete-time LTI system, the state-space representation is given by:

$$ x(t+1) = A x(t) + B u(t) $$

$$ y(t) = C x(t) + D u(t) $$

Here:

$x(t)$ is the state vector of dimension $N \times 1$, representing the internal state of the system at time t. The dimension N is the order of the state-space model.
$u(t)$ is the input vector of dimension $P \times 1$.
$y(t)$ is the output vector of dimension $Q \times 1$.
A is the state matrix ($N \times N$), describing how the current state influences the next state.
B is the input matrix ($N \times P$), describing how the input influences the next state.
C is the output matrix ($Q \times N$), describing how the state influences the output.
D is the feedforward matrix ($Q \times P$), describing how the input directly influences the output.

These matrices (A, B, C, D) contain the parameters of the state-space model. The identification problem then becomes estimating the elements of these matrices.

The state-space representation is more general than the transfer function representation:

1. **MIMO Systems:** It naturally handles systems with multiple inputs and outputs ($P>1$, $Q>1$).
2. **Internal States:** It explicitly models the internal states, which can be useful for observer design, state estimation, and understanding internal system dynamics.
3. **System Order:** The order of the state-space model (N) is not necessarily directly related to the number of input/output channels but rather to the number of independent energy storage elements or dynamic modes within the system.

A key challenge with state-space models is determining the appropriate order N. If N is too small, the model will not capture all essential dynamics. If N is too large, the model becomes over-parameterized and prone to overfitting. Techniques for selecting N include:

Singular Value Decomposition (SVD) of Hankel Matrices: This is a powerful non-parametric approach that can reveal the intrinsic order of a system from input-output data. By constructing a Hankel matrix from past input-output sequences, its singular values provide information about the number of linearly independent modes. The number of dominant singular values often indicates the intrinsic system order.
Information Criteria: Similar to transfer function models, criteria like AIC or BIC can be used to select the order N that balances model fit with complexity.
Iterative Refinement: Starting with a low-order model and progressively increasing the order, while monitoring validation performance, is also a common strategy.

Once the order N is chosen, the matrices A, B, C, D can be estimated. Standard methods for state-space system identification often involve:

Subspace Identification Methods: These methods aim to estimate the state trajectories and the system matrices by directly working with block-Hankel matrices of past and future input-output data. They can be very effective for identifying the state-space representation directly, often without explicitly computing the transfer function first, and are generally robust to noise. Popular algorithms include N4SID (Numerical Algorithms for Subspace State-Space System IDentification) and CVA (Canonical Variate Analysis). These methods typically avoid the iterative optimization required by prediction error methods used for transfer functions.
Prediction Error Methods: Similar to transfer function models, prediction error methods can be applied to state-space models. In this approach, a state-space model is used to predict the output, and an optimization algorithm is used to minimize the difference between the predicted and actual outputs. This usually involves iterative numerical optimization.

Choosing Between Transfer Function and State-Space Models

The decision between using a transfer function or a state-space representation often depends on the nature of the problem and the tools available.

Simplicity and Interpretability (SISO): For SISO systems, transfer functions like ARX, ARMAX, OE, and BJ are often conceptually simpler to understand and estimate, especially if linear regression techniques can be applied (as in ARX). The parameters often have more direct physical interpretations (poles and zeros).
Generality and MIMO (State-Space): State-space models offer a more unified framework for MIMO systems, multivariable dynamics, and internal state analysis. Subspace identification methods provide direct, often non-iterative, ways to estimate these models.
Noise Handling: OE and BJ models explicitly address noise dynamics in ways that can be advantageous when noise characteristics are complex. State-space models can also incorporate noise through state-space noise models (e.g., linear stochastic state-space models), allowing for Kalman filtering-like interpretations.

Illustrative Examples

Let's consider two examples to illustrate the application of these parametric model structures.

Example 1: Modeling the Response of a Heat Exchanger

Imagine a simple heat exchanger where hot fluid flows through a pipe, transferring heat to a surrounding shell containing a cooler fluid. We are interested in modeling how the outlet temperature of the cooler fluid ($y(t)$) responds to changes in the flow rate of the hot fluid ($u(t)$), which directly affects the heat transfer rate.

Prior Knowledge: We know that heat transfer processes are typically characterized by delays (as the heat propagates through the system) and time constants (related to thermal inertia and capacitance). The system is likely to be stable and exhibit a first-order or second-order response. We might expect that an increase in hot fluid flow rate will eventually lead to an increase in the cooler fluid's outlet temperature, but with some delay and smoothing.

Data Characteristics: Suppose our preprocessed data shows that when we increase the hot fluid flow rate, the cooler fluid outlet temperature rises gradually after a noticeable lag, eventually settling to a new steady-state value.

Model Selection:

A **transfer function model** seems appropriate. Given the expected delay and smoothing, a model like ARX or OE would be a good candidate. Let's consider an ARX model with a delay d and polynomial orders. We might hypothesize a structure like:

$$ y(t) = -a1 y(t-1) + b1 u(t-d) + e(t) $$

Here, $A(z) = 1 + a1 z^{-1}$ and $B(z) = b1 z^{-d}$. The parameter $a1$ would be related to the time constant of the cooler fluid, and $b1$ would relate to the gain of the system at that specific delay. The delay d would capture the transport lag. We could start with $d=1$ and then explore higher delays based on visual inspection of the data or autocorrelation analysis of residuals. We might also consider a second-order denominator ($n=2$) if the response shows a more complex lag or oscillatory tendency.

Alternatively, a **state-space model** could be used. If we assume the system has two dominant energy storage elements (e.g., the thermal mass of the pipe and the thermal mass of the cooler fluid), we might propose a second-order state-space model ($N=2$):

$$ \begin{bmatrix} x_1(t+1) \\ x_2(t+1) \end{bmatrix} = \begin{bmatrix} a_{11} & a_{12} \\ a_{21} & a_{22} \end{bmatrix} \begin{bmatrix} x_1(t) \\ x_2(t) \end{bmatrix} + \begin{bmatrix} b_1 \\ b_2 \end{bmatrix} u(t) $$
$$ y(t) = \begin{bmatrix} c_1 & c_2 \end{bmatrix} \begin{bmatrix} x_1(t) \\ x_2(t) \end{bmatrix} + d u(t) $$

Here, x_1 and x_2 would represent internal thermal states. The A, B, C, D matrices would be estimated. If we suspect a significant input delay, we might need to augment the state vector or use a transfer function structure that explicitly handles delay. Subspace identification methods would be very effective here for estimating the A, B, C, D matrices and determining if $N=2$ is indeed appropriate.

Example 2: Modeling the Vibration of a Mechanical Structure

Consider a beam subjected to an external force $u(t)$, and we measure its displacement $y(t)$ at a specific point. We want to identify a model of its vibrational behavior.

Prior Knowledge: Mechanical structures, especially beams and plates, are known to exhibit natural frequencies and damping ratios corresponding to their modes of vibration. We expect the system to be oscillatory.
Data Characteristics: When a force is applied, the displacement measurement shows damped oscillations, gradually returning to rest if the force is removed. The dominant frequency of oscillation and the rate at which the oscillations decay are key characteristics.
Model Selection:
A second-order **transfer function model** (in continuous time, represented in discrete time) is a very common and appropriate choice for a single mode of vibration:

$$ G(s) = \frac{b_0}{s^2 + a_1 s + a_0} $$

In discrete time, this could be mapped to an ARX structure $y(t) = -a_1' y(t-1) - a_2' y(t-2) + b_1' u(t-1) + b_2' u(t-2) + e(t)$, where the discrete-time parameters (a_1', a_2', b_1', b_2') are related to the continuous-time parameters (a_0, a_1, b_0) and the sampling time. The discrete-time polynomial $A(z) = 1 + a_1' z^{-1} + a_2' z^{-2}$ would have roots related to the damping ratio and natural frequency. If the structure has multiple modes of vibration that are excited by the input, we would need a higher-order transfer function or a state-space model.

A **state-space model** is ideal for capturing multiple vibration modes. If we believe the structure has two significant modes, we might opt for a fourth-order state-space model ($N=4$).

$$ x(t+1) = A x(t) + B u(t) $$

$$ y(t) = C x(t) $$

Here, the matrix A would have eigenvalues corresponding to the natural frequencies and damping ratios of the modes. The matrices B and C would describe how the input force excites these modes and how the displacement measurement captures their combined effect. Subspace identification methods are well-suited for extracting these modal characteristics directly from vibration data. If the system were subjected to multiple forces and we measured displacements at multiple points, a state-space model would be almost essential, with $P>1$ and $Q>1$.

In practice, the process of choosing a parametric model structure is iterative. One might start with a simple ARX model, analyze its residuals, and if they show structure or if the fit is poor, consider a higher-order ARX, an ARMAX, an OE, a BJ, or a state-space model. The goal is to find a model that is parsimonious, accurately represents the system's dynamics, and generalizes well to unseen data, ultimately serving the intended purpose of the identification. The rich set of parametric structures available provides engineers with a powerful toolkit to translate empirical observations into interpretable mathematical descriptions of dynamic systems.

Non-Parametric Model Structures

While parametric models provide a structured and often interpretable representation of a system, they are contingent on making strong prior assumptions about the system's underlying mathematical form. In many real-world scenarios, our knowledge about the system's internal workings might be limited, or the system dynamics could be inherently complex, making it challenging to select an appropriate parametric structure a priori. It is in these situations that **non-parametric models** emerge as invaluable tools. Unlike their parametric counterparts, non-parametric models do not impose a rigid mathematical structure determined by a fixed number of parameters. Instead, they aim to represent the system's input-output relationship in a more direct and flexible manner, often by characterizing the system's response directly in the time or frequency domain. This approach allows for a data-driven exploration of system dynamics without being constrained by preconceived notions of linearity, order, or specific equation forms.

The fundamental idea behind non-parametric modeling is to characterize the system's behavior by directly estimating its response to specific types of input signals. Two of the most common and informative non-parametric representations are the **impulse response function (IRF)** and the **frequency response function (FRF)**.

The

impulse response function, often denoted as $h(t)$ for continuous-time systems or $h[k]$ for discrete-time systems, provides a complete description of a Linear Time-Invariant (LTI) system's dynamics. It is defined as the system's output when the input is a Dirac delta function (for continuous time) or a unit impulse (for discrete time). The beauty of the impulse response lies in its ability to fully characterize the system's behavior, meaning that if we know the impulse response, we can predict the output for *any* arbitrary input signal through the process of convolution:

For a continuous-time system:

$$ y(t) = \int_{-\infty}^{\infty} h(\tau) u(t-\tau) d\tau $$

For a discrete-time system:

$$ y[k] = \sum_{i=-\infty}^{\infty} h[i] u[k-i] $$

In system identification, the goal is to estimate $h(t)$ or $h[k]$ from measured input-output data. If the system is causal (its output depends only on past and present inputs), then $h(t)=0$ for $t<0$ (or $h[k]=0$ for $k<0$). For stable LTI systems, the impulse response typically decays to zero over time. Practically, when estimating an impulse response from data, we are often interested in a finite portion of this response, representing the significant part of the system's memory or lag. The length of this estimated impulse response directly relates to the system's dynamics: a short impulse response implies a system with fast dynamics and short memory, while a long impulse response indicates slower dynamics and a longer memory.

Estimating the impulse response directly from data often involves exciting the system with an input signal and then analyzing the resulting output. If we can ensure the input signal is sufficiently "rich" and uncorrelated with noise, and if the system is LTI, then the impulse response can be recovered using correlation techniques. Specifically, if the input signal $u(t)$ is white noise (or is made to appear white relative to the system's dynamics through cross-correlation), the impulse response $h(t)$ is proportional to the cross-correlation function between the input and the output:

$$ R_{yu}(\tau) = \int_{-\infty}^{\infty} y(t) u(t-\tau) dt $$

If $u(t)$ is white noise with power spectral density $\Phi_{uu}(\omega) = N_0$ (a constant), then:

$$ R_{yu}(\tau) = N_0 h(\tau) $$

Thus, by computing the cross-correlation between the measured input and output signals, and assuming the input is white noise, we can directly obtain an estimate of the impulse response. In practice, we don't always have perfect white noise inputs. However, by using a sufficiently broadband input signal and carefully computing the cross-correlation, we can still obtain a good estimate of the impulse response. The length of the impulse response we choose to estimate dictates the complexity of the non-parametric model. A longer impulse response allows for capturing more complex dynamics but requires more data and can be more susceptible to noise.

The **frequency response function (FRF)**, denoted as $G(j\omega)$ for continuous-time systems or $G(e^{j\omega T})$ for discrete-time systems (where ω is the angular frequency and T is the sampling period), provides another powerful non-parametric representation. It describes how a system modifies sinusoidal inputs at different frequencies in terms of their amplitude and phase. If $u(t) = A \cos(\omega0 t + \phi)$, then for an LTI system, the steady-state output will be $y(t) = |G(j\omega0)| A \cos(\omega0 t + \phi + \angle G(j\omega0))$. The FRF is essentially the Fourier Transform of the impulse response.

$$ G(j\omega) = \mathcal{F}\{h(t)\} = \int_{-\infty}^{\infty} h(t) e^{-j\omega t} dt $$

The FRF is particularly useful for understanding a system's behavior across a range of frequencies, highlighting characteristics like resonance (peaks in the magnitude response), anti-resonance, bandwidth, and attenuation or amplification at different frequencies. It is a cornerstone of classical control theory and signal processing.

Non-parametric estimation of the FRF from data typically involves analyzing the system's response to sinusoidal inputs or estimating the power spectral densities of the input and output signals. When using a broadband input signal, the FRF can be estimated by computing the ratio of the cross-power spectral density between the input and output ($S {yu}(\omega)$) to the input's auto-power spectral density ($S{uu}(\omega)$):

$$ G(j\omega) \approx \frac{S {yu}(\omega)}{S{uu}(\omega)} $$

The power spectral densities are computed using the Discrete Fourier

Transform (DFT) of the input and output signals. For discrete-time systems, this relationship is:

$$ G(e^{j\omega T}) \approx \frac{\Phi_{yu}(e^{j\omega T})}{\Phi_{uu}(e^{j\omega T})} $$

where Φ_{yu} and Φ_{uu} are the cross-power and auto-power spectral densities, respectively. Estimating these spectral densities robustly often involves techniques like the Periodogram method or more advanced methods like Welch's method, which average over segments of the data to reduce variance.

The primary advantage of non-parametric models, such as the impulse response and frequency response, lies in their flexibility. They do not require prior knowledge about the system's order or the specific functional form of its dynamics. This makes them ideal for:

Exploratory Analysis: When faced with a new or poorly understood system, non-parametric models can provide initial insights into its fundamental characteristics, such as its bandwidth, dominant time scales, and general response shape.
Complex Systems: For systems with highly nonlinear dynamics, or where the underlying mechanisms are very complex and not easily expressible in simple parametric forms (e.g., certain biological systems, fluid dynamics, or complex chemical reactions), non-parametric methods offer a way to capture observed input-output behavior without oversimplification.
Model Validation: Non-parametric representations can serve as a benchmark against which the performance of parametric models is

evaluated. If a parametric model fails to accurately reproduce the non-parametric FRF or IRF, it suggests that the chosen parametric structure is inadequate.
System Characterization: Even if a parametric model is ultimately desired, the non-parametric FRF can reveal important information for its selection, such as the required bandwidth or the presence of specific modes that need to be represented.

However, non-parametric models also come with their own set of challenges and limitations. One significant drawback is their **lack of interpretability** in terms of physical parameters. An impulse response or a frequency response plot, while informative about the system's behavior, doesn't directly tell us the mass of a component, the stiffness of a spring, or the time constant of a thermal process. The estimated impulse response can consist of hundreds or thousands of values, making it unwieldy for direct use in control design or for conveying simple system properties. Furthermore, the estimation of non-parametric models, especially robustly from noisy data, can be computationally intensive and requires careful selection of parameters for the estimation algorithms themselves (e.g., length of impulse response to estimate, windowing functions for spectral estimation, segment lengths for averaging).

The choice between estimating an impulse response or a frequency response often depends on the specific application. If the goal is to understand the system's behavior in the time domain, to predict its response to arbitrary time-domain signals, or to design controllers based on time-domain specifications, the impulse response might be more directly useful. If the focus is on understanding how the system amplifies or attenuates signals at different frequencies, analyzing stability margins, or designing controllers in the frequency domain, then the frequency response is the natural choice. Importantly, these two representations are fundamentally linked through the Fourier Transform, so one can be derived from the other.

Let's consider a practical example to illustrate the concept of non-parametric modeling. Suppose we are studying a suspension system in an automobile. We apply a known force profile $u(t)$ to the wheel (e.g., a bump on the road) and measure the vertical displacement of the car body $y(t)$.

Example: Non-parametric Modeling of an Automotive Suspension

Our objective is to characterize the dynamic response of the suspension system without making strong assumptions about its exact mechanical structure (e.g., exact spring constants, damping coefficients, or whether it's perfectly linear).

1.
Data Acquisition: We apply a series of controlled force inputs $u(t)$ to the wheel and record the corresponding car body displacements $y(t)$ over a sufficient duration. The input signal should be sufficiently "rich," meaning it excites a wide range of frequencies relevant to the suspension's operation. This could involve driving over different types of road surfaces or using a specialized actuator to generate specific force profiles.

2.
Impulse Response Estimation: We can estimate the impulse response $h(t)$ of the suspension system. If we assume the applied force is a good approximation of white noise over the relevant frequency range, we can

compute the cross-correlation between $u(t)$ and $y(t)$. The resulting cross-correlation function, scaled appropriately, will provide an estimate of $h(t)$. This $h(t)$ would show how the car body displacement evolves over time following a very brief, sharp impact on the wheel. We would likely observe an initial transient response, followed by damped oscillations characteristic of the suspension's natural frequency and damping. The length of the estimated $h(t)$ would reflect how long the system "remembers" the impact – how long it takes for the oscillations to decay. For instance, we might estimate $h(t)$ for up to 2 seconds, capturing several oscillation cycles.

3.
Frequency Response Function Estimation: Alternatively, or in conjunction, we can estimate the FRF, $G(j\omega)$. Using the recorded data, we would compute the power spectral density of the input force, $S{uu}(\omega)$, *and the cross-power spectral density between the force and displacement,* $S{yu}(\omega)$. The ratio $\frac{S{yu}(j\omega)}{S{uu}(j\omega)}$ would give us an estimate of the FRF, $G(j\omega)$. Plotting the magnitude $|G(j\omega)|$ versus frequency would reveal the system's "gain" at different frequencies. We would expect to see a peak in the magnitude response at the natural frequency of the suspension. The width of this peak would be related to the damping ratio. The plot would also show how the suspension attenuates high-frequency inputs (like sharp bumps) and potentially amplifies low-frequency inputs (like gradual slopes). Analyzing the phase response $\angle G(j\omega)$ would provide further information about the phase shifts introduced by the suspension at different frequencies.

Why Non-Parametric? A suspension system is mechanically complex. It involves springs, dampers, and linkages, and its behavior can be influenced by factors like tire pressure, load, and temperature. While one could attempt to build a detailed parametric model based on first principles, it might be very complex and require many assumptions. Using non-parametric methods allows engineers to quickly characterize the system's actual observed input-output behavior. This non-parametric representation can then inform the choice of a parametric model. For example, if the FRF shows a clear resonant peak at 2 Hz, this strongly suggests that a second-order parametric model (representing a single oscillatory mode) would be a suitable candidate. If multiple peaks are observed, it indicates the presence of multiple modes, pointing towards a higher-order parametric model or a multi-input multi-output (MIMO) state-space representation.

The practical implementation of non-parametric identification involves several considerations. For impulse response estimation using cross-correlation, the choice of the input signal's duration and bandwidth is crucial. A signal that is too short or too narrow-band will not adequately excite all the system's dynamics, leading to an incomplete impulse response estimate. Conversely, using a very long signal might be computationally prohibitive or introduce time-varying effects if the system's dynamics change over time. The length of the impulse response we choose to estimate also plays a role. Estimating too few points might miss important dynamics, while estimating too many points can lead to overfitting of noise, especially at the tail end of the response.

For frequency response estimation, methods like the Fast Fourier Transform (FFT) are commonly used to compute the DFT of the input and output signals. However, the basic FFT-based spectral estimation (the Periodogram) can have high variance, meaning that small changes in the data can lead to significant variations in the estimated spectrum. To mitigate this, techniques like
Welch's method are employed. Welch's method divides the data into overlapping segments, computes the periodogram for each segment

(often after applying a window function to reduce spectral leakage), and then averages these periodograms. This averaging process reduces the variance of the spectral estimate, providing a smoother and more reliable FRF. The degree of overlap between segments and the length of the segments are tunable parameters that affect the trade-off between variance reduction and frequency resolution.

Another important aspect is the handling of **noise**. Real-world measurements are almost always contaminated with noise, which can significantly distort both impulse response and frequency response estimates. If the noise is uncorrelated with the input signal, cross-correlation and spectral ratio methods can still yield reasonable estimates. However, if the noise is correlated with the input or is generated by unmodeled dynamics within the system (colored noise), then the simple non-parametric methods described might produce biased results. In such cases, more advanced identification techniques, including parametric models that explicitly account for noise (like ARMAX or BJ models), or specialized non-parametric approaches designed for noisy environments, might be necessary.

Despite these challenges, non-parametric models remain a fundamental tool in the system identification arsenal. They provide a direct, model-structure-agnostic way to probe a system's dynamics, offering invaluable insights when prior knowledge is scarce or when dealing with highly complex phenomena. They serve as a crucial first step in understanding a system and as a benchmark for validating more structured, parametric models. By examining the impulse and frequency responses, engineers can gain a deep understanding of a system's transient behavior, its steady-state characteristics across different frequencies, and identify key dynamic features that must be captured by any subsequent parametric model. This exploration without the burden of a predefined structure is what makes non-parametric modeling a powerful complement to parametric approaches.

For example, in fields like neuroscience, understanding how a neuron responds to different electrical stimuli might involve non-parametric estimation of its impulse response to probe synaptic delays and integration times. In acoustics, the impulse response of a concert hall can be measured to characterize its reverberation properties, which are crucial for its sound quality, and this impulse response is often presented as a non-parametric function of time. Similarly, in geophysics, the impulse response of the Earth's subsurface to seismic waves is estimated to infer geological structures. These applications highlight the broad utility of non-parametric models in domains where the underlying physical models are either extremely complex or not the primary focus of the investigation. The emphasis is on characterizing the input-output relationship directly from observed data.

Having established methods for learning system models from data, the subsequent and critical phase is **model validation**. This step is paramount, especially in demanding fields like aerospace, where the reliability and accuracy of a model directly impact the safety and performance of critical systems such as flight control, guidance, and navigation. A model that fits the data used for its identification remarkably well might still fail catastrophically when deployed in a slightly different operating condition or when subjected to novel inputs. Therefore, validating a model involves rigorously testing its ability to accurately represent the system's behavior beyond the confines of the data it was trained on. This subsection will delve into several key techniques employed for robust model validation, ensuring that the learned models are not just statistical artifacts of the training set but are indeed faithful representations of the underlying system dynamics.

The primary objective of model validation is to ascertain whether the identified model is a parsimonious and accurate representation of the true system. This involves assessing its goodness-of-fit to the data used for identification, as well as its predictive capability on new, independent data. A model that overfits the training data will likely exhibit poor performance when confronted with unseen data, failing to generalize. Conversely, an underfitting model will not capture the essential dynamics of the system, regardless of the data. Model validation techniques help us distinguish between these scenarios and build confidence in the selected model structure and its estimated parameters.

One of the most fundamental and widely used approaches for model validation is
residual analysis. Residuals, often denoted by $\epsilon(k)$ for discrete-time systems or $\epsilon(t)$ for continuous-time systems, are the differences between the actual measured output of the system and the output predicted by the identified model. Mathematically, if $ym(k)$ *is the measured output and* $\hat{y}(k)$ *is the model's predicted output, then the residual is* $\epsilon(k) = ym(k) - \hat{y}(k)$. The properties of these residuals provide profound insights into how well the model has captured the system's dynamics.

For an identified model to be considered valid, the residuals should ideally behave like white noise. This means that the residuals should be:

1. **Zero Mean:** The average value of the residuals should be close to zero. This indicates that the model is not systematically over- or under-predicting the system's output.
2. **Uncorrelated:** The residuals should not exhibit any discernible pattern or correlation with themselves at different time lags. In other words, the value of a residual at one time instant should not provide any information about the value of a residual at another time instant. This implies that the model has accounted for all systematic dynamics

present in the data, and what remains is random noise or unpredictable variations.

3. **Independent:** Ideally, residuals should also be independent of the input signal. This means that the model's prediction errors should not be systematically related to the system's inputs. If there is a correlation between residuals and inputs, it suggests that the model has not adequately captured how the input influences the output.

The concept of **whiteness** of residuals is particularly crucial. A white noise signal is characterized by a constant power spectral density across all frequencies, meaning it contains no predictable information. If the residuals of a model are white, it implies that all systematic dynamic relationships between the input and output have been accounted for by the model. Any remaining variation in the output is attributable to random noise or unmodeled stochastic disturbances.

To statistically assess the whiteness of the residuals, several tests can be employed. A common practice is to examine the **autocorrelation function (ACF)** of the residuals. The ACF measures the correlation of a signal with a delayed version of itself. For a white noise process, the ACF should be zero for all non-zero lags. Therefore, if the estimated ACF of the residuals shows significant spikes at lags other than zero, it indicates that the residuals are correlated, and thus, the model is inadequate. Statistical tests, such as the **Ljung-Box test**, can be used to formally assess whether the autocorrelations up to a certain lag are significantly different from zero. The Ljung-Box test calculates a test statistic based on the sum of the squared autocorrelations, and compares it to a chi-squared distribution to determine statistical significance. A high p-value suggests that the residuals can be considered white.

Beyond checking for self-correlation, it's also important to check for

correlations between the residuals and the input signal. This is often done by computing the
cross-correlation function (CCF) between the residuals ($\epsilon(k)$) and the input signal ($u(k)$). If the model is valid and the input signal is persistently exciting (i.e., it sufficiently excites all modes of the system), then the CCF between residuals and input should ideally be zero for all leads and lags. If significant correlations are observed, it suggests that the model has failed to capture certain input-dependent dynamics. Statistical tests can also be applied to the CCF to formally assess its significance.

Consider an example in aerospace where we have identified a linear time-invariant (LTI) model for the pitch rate response of an aircraft to aileron deflection. After estimating the model's parameters using flight test data, we compute the residuals as the difference between the actual measured pitch rate and the pitch rate predicted by our LTI model for the same aileron input. We then analyze the ACF of these residuals. If the ACF shows a prominent spike at lag 3, it might indicate that the model has missed a dynamic mode that causes a correlated error with a period of approximately 3 sample times. This would suggest that our chosen LTI model structure is insufficient, and perhaps a higher-order model or a model that accounts for specific aerodynamic effects not captured by the initial structure is needed. Furthermore, we would examine the CCF between the residuals and the aileron deflection. If this CCF is non-zero, it might imply that the linearity assumption is violated, or that the gain of the pitch rate response to aileron deflection depends on the magnitude of the deflection, which our linear model cannot represent.

Another critical aspect of model validation is evaluating the model's **predictive capability**. While residual analysis focuses on the fit to the data used for identification, predictive validation assesses how well the model forecasts future system behavior. This is often achieved through

simulation-based validation using data that was *not* used during the model identification process. This is sometimes referred to as using a "validation set" or "test set."

The process typically involves splitting the available system data into two parts: an identification set and a validation set. The model is identified using the identification set. Once the model is finalized, it is then used to predict the system's output for the input sequences present in the validation set. The predicted outputs are then compared to the actual measured outputs in the validation set. The same residual analysis techniques (ACF of prediction errors, CCF with input, Ljung-Box tests) can be applied to these
prediction errors (which are essentially residuals computed on unseen data).

The success of this validation hinges on the quality of the data split. The validation data should be representative of the operating conditions under which the model is expected to perform. If the validation data comes from a significantly different operating regime than the identification data, the model's performance on this validation set might not be indicative of its true capabilities. In aerospace, this could mean using data from different flight phases, altitudes, or speeds for validation compared to identification. For instance, if a model is identified using data from straight and level flight, its validation using data from aggressive maneuvers would be crucial.

Beyond visual inspection of prediction error plots and ACF/CCF analysis, quantitative metrics are often used to assess the model's predictive performance. For example, metrics like the
Mean Squared Error (MSE) or the **Root Mean Squared Error (RMSE)** between the predicted and actual outputs on the validation set can provide a single scalar value summarizing the prediction accuracy.

However, it's important to note that MSE or RMSE alone can be misleading. A low MSE on the validation set is desirable, but it doesn't guarantee that the underlying model assumptions are met. For example, a model could still have correlated residuals even with a low MSE if the correlations are weak or the overall prediction error magnitude is small. Therefore, these quantitative metrics should always be used in conjunction with statistical tests and graphical methods.

A more advanced form of predictive validation is **one-step-ahead prediction versus simulation**. In one-step-ahead prediction, the model uses the actual measured inputs and outputs up to time $k-1$ to predict the output at time k. This is closely related to the residual analysis on the identification data, assuming no explicit validation set is used. In contrast, **simulation** involves using the model itself to generate future outputs. Starting from known initial conditions, the model uses its own predicted output at time $k-1$ (along with the input at time k) to predict the output at time k. This process is repeated for multiple future time steps. Simulation allows for evaluating the model's long-term predictive behavior and its ability to capture evolving dynamics. If a model is used for long-term forecasting or for simulating system behavior over extended periods, its performance in simulation mode is critical. The prediction errors in simulation mode tend to accumulate and can reveal instabilities or inaccuracies that might not be apparent in one-step-ahead prediction.

Let's consider a more specific aerospace application: modeling the dynamics of an unmanned aerial vehicle (UAV) for an autonomous landing system. Suppose we have collected flight data including control surface deflections (elevator, rudder, ailerons) and the resulting changes in the UAV's pitch, roll, and yaw angles, as well as its velocity components.

First, we might identify a parametric model (e.g., a state-space model) using a portion of this data. The identification process would involve selecting a model order, estimating state matrix, input matrix, output matrix, and possibly a noise covariance matrix.

After obtaining the model parameters, we would proceed with validation.

1. **Residual Analysis on Identification Data:**
We feed the input sequences from the identification dataset into our identified UAV model and compare its predicted states (e.g., pitch angle) with the actual measured pitch angles. The difference forms the residuals.
We compute the ACF of these residuals. If the ACF shows significant correlations, it suggests that the identified model has not fully captured the complex aerodynamic interactions that influence pitch angle. For instance, a strong correlation at a particular lag might point to a missing damping term or an unmodeled time delay in the aerodynamic forces.
We compute the CCF between the residuals and the input control surface deflections. A non-zero CCF could indicate that the model's assumption of linearity is incorrect, or that the control surface effectiveness is not constant but varies with other states (like airspeed or angle of attack), which the linear model fails to capture. For a UAV, this is particularly relevant, as aerodynamic forces are highly dependent on angle of attack, which is often not explicitly modeled or is assumed to be implicitly handled by linear approximations.
We apply statistical tests like the Ljung-Box test to formally reject or fail to reject the hypothesis that the residuals are white noise.

2.
Simulation-Based Validation using Unseen Data:

We take the remaining flight data (the validation set) that was not used for identification. This data should ideally cover scenarios relevant to landing, such as approach paths with varying glide slopes, wind gusts, and different throttle settings.
We initialize our identified UAV model with the states from the beginning of the validation dataset.
We then simulate the UAV's response to the control surface inputs recorded in the validation dataset, predicting the trajectory (pitch, roll, yaw, velocities) over time. This simulation would proceed by using the model's predicted state at time \$k\$ and the actual input at time \$k\$ to predict the state at time \$k+1\$.
We compare the simulated trajectory with the actual measured trajectory from the validation dataset. The differences are the prediction errors.
We analyze the ACF and CCF of these prediction errors. If the model is good, these errors should also be white and uncorrelated with inputs. However, due to the accumulation of errors in simulation, these residual characteristics might be more pronounced than in the identification phase. A growing variance in prediction errors over the simulation horizon is a strong indicator of model inadequacy for long-term prediction.
We calculate quantitative metrics like RMSE between the simulated and actual states over the validation dataset. A low RMSE for pitch, roll, and yaw angles would suggest good fidelity in capturing the rotational dynamics. Similarly, RMSE for velocity components would assess translational dynamics.

A particularly important aspect in aerospace is the handling of **uncertainty**. Even if a model passes all residual tests and shows good predictive performance on a validation set, there will always be some degree of uncertainty associated with its parameters and structure. Model validation techniques help to quantify this uncertainty and ensure that the model's limitations are understood.

One way to incorporate uncertainty is through **parameter uncertainty analysis**. If the model identification process yields confidence intervals for the estimated parameters, these can be used to assess the sensitivity of the model's output to parameter variations. Monte Carlo simulations can be performed by drawing parameter values from their estimated distributions and observing the range of model responses. This gives an idea of the "spread" in model predictions due to parameter uncertainty.

Furthermore, the choice of model structure itself introduces uncertainty. If we selected a linear model, but the system is inherently nonlinear, validation might reveal discrepancies that suggest the need for a nonlinear model. Methods exist to assess **model structure uncertainty**, such as comparing different model structures (e.g., linear vs. nonlinear, different orders of parametric models) using information criteria (like AIC or BIC) or by comparing their performance on the validation set.

In the context of aerospace control systems, an under-validated model can have severe consequences. Imagine a model of an aircraft's engine thrust that is identified using data from nominal operating conditions. If this model is used to design a thrust-vectoring control system for a fighter jet, and it fails to accurately predict thrust under extreme angles of attack or during rapid throttle changes (conditions not adequately represented in the identification data), the resulting control system could lead to instability, loss of control, or mission failure. Therefore, rigorous validation using diverse and representative datasets is not merely a procedural step but a fundamental requirement for safety and efficacy.

Another facet of validation, particularly relevant when comparing a complex parametric model against a simpler non-parametric representation (as discussed in the previous section), is the **comparison against benchmarks**. A non-parametric model, such as the Frequency Response Function (FRF) or Impulse Response Function (IRF) estimated directly from data, can serve as an excellent benchmark. After identifying a parametric model, its FRF or IRF can be computed and compared graphically to the non-parametric estimates. Significant deviations in magnitude or phase (for FRF) or in the shape and decay of the response (for IRF) would immediately flag potential issues with the parametric model. For instance, if the FRF of a parametrically identified aircraft model does not match the non-parametrically estimated FRF around the aircraft's natural frequencies (e.g., phugoid or short period modes), it suggests that the parametric model has not correctly captured these critical dynamic behaviors.

Moreover, expert judgment plays a role. Experienced control engineers and aerodynamicists can often review the validated model and its predictions, checking for consistency with known physical principles and established aircraft behavior. For example, if a validated model predicts an unexpectedly high damping ratio for a particular mode, or suggests a control surface effectiveness that contradicts aerodynamic theory, it might warrant further investigation and re-validation.

In summary, model validation is a multifaceted process that extends well beyond simply checking how well a model fits the data used for its estimation. It involves a comprehensive suite of techniques designed to ensure that the model is not only statistically sound but also practically reliable for its intended application. Key components include:

Residual analysis: Examining the statistical properties of the differences between measured and predicted outputs, focusing on whiteness and absence of correlation with inputs.

Simulation-based validation: Testing the model's predictive accuracy on new, unseen data, evaluating its performance in forecasting future system behavior.
Quantitative metrics: Using measures like MSE or RMSE to numerically assess prediction errors.
Uncertainty quantification: Understanding the confidence in parameter estimates and potential variations in model behavior.
Comparison with benchmarks: Leveraging non-parametric models or known system characteristics to verify the parametric model's fidelity.
Expert review: Incorporating domain knowledge to assess the physical plausibility and expected behavior of the model.

By systematically applying these validation techniques, engineers can build confidence in the identified system models, mitigating risks and ensuring that the models are suitable for critical applications such as the design and implementation of robust control systems in aerospace vehicles. Without thorough validation, even the most sophisticated identification algorithms can lead to models that, while appearing accurate on training data, are fundamentally flawed and unreliable in real-world deployment.

Chapter 4: Learning Residual Dynamics

When we engage in the process of modeling complex dynamical systems, particularly those encountered in fields like manufacturing automation, it's a rare occasion indeed when our identified model perfectly encapsulates every nuance of the system's behavior. The inherent nature of real-world processes—be it the intricate interplay of mechanical components, the subtle influence of environmental factors, or the presence of unmeasured disturbances—means that any model we derive from data will, to some extent, be an approximation. This approximation inherently leaves a gap, a set of behaviors or characteristics that our primary model fails to account for. These are what we refer to as **residual dynamics**.

Residual dynamics, in essence, represent the "leftovers" of the system's behavior after we have fitted our chosen model. They are the discrepancies between the true system output and the output predicted by our model. While our previous discussions on model validation focused on ensuring that the residuals of a *good* model behave like random noise, here we pivot to a different perspective: what if these residuals themselves contain significant, predictable information? This is the domain of residual dynamics. Instead of simply discarding these unexplained variations as noise, we can investigate them further. The central idea is that these residual dynamics, while perhaps secondary to the dominant behaviors captured by the primary model, still represent a structured, deterministic component of the system's response. Understanding and, crucially, modeling these residual dynamics can unlock significant improvements in control system performance and robustness, especially in scenarios where the primary model's limitations are frequently encountered.

Consider a robotic arm designed for precision assembly in a manufacturing line. We might develop a primary model that captures the arm's gross kinematic and dynamic behavior—its inertia, actuator responses, and basic trajectory following. This model would likely be based on simplified physics or identified from data under relatively clean operating conditions. However, this model might not fully account for subtle effects such as:

Flexural vibrations: The physical structure of the arm might exhibit slight bending or torsional oscillations that are not captured by the rigid-body dynamics model. These vibrations, while small, can introduce undesirable jitter into the end-effector's motion, impacting assembly precision.
Coulomb friction and stiction: The friction in the joints is often complex, non-linear, and can vary with operating conditions. A simplified friction model might not accurately represent the stick-slip behavior or the changes in friction at low speeds.
Actuator nonlinearities: Real-world actuators might have dead zones, saturation limits, or hysteresis that are not fully represented in a linear actuator model.
Unmodeled load variations: The mass or inertia of the part being handled might change dynamically, and the primary model might not be updated in real-time to reflect this.
Environmental disturbances: Air currents, vibrations from other machinery on the factory floor, or thermal expansion could all introduce small, but systematic, deviations from the primary model's predictions.

These phenomena are not entirely random. They often exhibit their own dynamics, influenced by the state of the system and the inputs applied. For instance, flexural vibrations will have their own natural frequencies and damping characteristics. Friction effects are highly dependent on velocity and position. Actuator nonlinearities are a direct consequence of the actuator's physical properties and control signals. These predictable, yet unmodeled, behaviors constitute the residual dynamics of the system.

The significance of residual dynamics becomes particularly pronounced when the primary model's assumptions are violated. In the robotic arm example, if the arm is commanded to move rapidly or to handle a much heavier part than anticipated during identification, the errors predicted by the primary model will likely be larger and more structured. These structured errors are precisely the manifestations of the residual dynamics. If we can capture these dynamics, we can implement control strategies that compensate for them.

This leads to the concept of **augmenting** our control system design. Instead of solely relying on the primary model, we can aim to design a control law that incorporates compensation for these residual dynamics. One common approach is to structure the control problem hierarchically. The primary controller, designed based on the primary model, handles the dominant system behavior. A secondary controller, designed specifically to address the residual dynamics, then acts to further refine the system's response, reducing the errors left by the primary controller.

To effectively model residual dynamics, we first need to quantify them. This is where the insights from model validation become directly applicable. If, after fitting a primary model and performing standard validation checks, the residuals still exhibit clear patterns – perhaps a noticeable autocorrelation at specific lags, or a systematic relationship with the input signal or system states – these patterns are indicative of residual dynamics. Instead of concluding that the primary model is inadequate and needs to be discarded, we can treat these structured residuals as data from which to identify a *residual model.*

For example, if the residuals of the robotic arm's position control show a persistent oscillation at a certain frequency, this suggests a missed vibratory mode. We could then attempt to identify a dynamical model specifically for this oscillatory behavior, perhaps a second-order system (mass-spring-damper analogy) whose parameters (frequency and damping) can be estimated from the residual time series. Similarly, if the residuals show a clear bias at low velocities, this might indicate a need for a friction model component that is more sophisticated than the one included in the primary model.

The process would typically involve the following steps:

1. **Identify a primary model:** This is done using standard system identification techniques on a set of training data.
2. **Validate the primary model:** Apply the techniques discussed previously. Examine residuals for whiteness and absence of correlation with inputs.
3. **Analyze persistent patterns in residuals:** If residuals are not white noise, or if their correlation with inputs or states is significant, these patterns point to residual dynamics. Visual inspection of ACF/CCF plots, alongside statistical tests, is crucial here.
4. **Identify a residual model:** Treat the structured residuals as the output of a new system (the "residual system") driven by the same inputs or states as the original system, or perhaps by past residuals. Use system identification techniques again, this time on the residual data, to find a model for these dynamics. The complexity of the residual model will depend on the observed patterns. It could range from a simple static gain (representing a bias or offset) to a complex dynamic model capturing oscillations or delays.
5. **Augment the control strategy:** Design a composite control law that combines the controller based on the primary model with a controller designed to act on the residual model's predictions. This could take the form of feedforward compensation, where the residual controller's

output is added to the primary controller's output, or a feedback loop that specifically targets the error predicted by the residual model.

Let's consider a more concrete manufacturing scenario: an automated conveyor belt system that transports components. We identify a primary model to control the belt speed based on the desired throughput and the position of components on the belt. This model might be a simple proportional-integral (PI) controller, assuming linear dynamics and constant load. However, in practice, we might observe:

Speed fluctuations: When a heavier load of components accumulates on the belt, the motor might struggle to maintain the exact speed, leading to slight, but noticeable, variations.
Belt stretching/slipping: Over time, especially with high tension or during rapid acceleration/deceleration, the belt material itself can exhibit dynamic behavior (elasticity, slight slippage) that affects the precise motion of the belt surface.
Sensor noise and delays: The sensors measuring belt speed or component position might introduce noise or have inherent delays, which are not fully handled by a simple PI controller.

If we analyze the residuals (the difference between the actual belt speed and the speed commanded by the PI controller), we might find they are correlated with the total weight of components on the belt, or with the rate of change of belt speed. This indicates the presence of residual dynamics.

To address this, we could:

Model the weight dependency: If we have a way to estimate the total weight of components on the belt (e.g., from upstream vision systems or

load cells), we could identify a static gain relating this weight to a speed correction term. This would be a simple residual model.
Model the belt elasticity: If speed fluctuations show oscillatory behavior, especially during transients, we might identify a simple second-order dynamics model to represent the belt's elastic response. This residual model could then be used to predict these oscillations and pre-emptively adjust the motor command.
Combine controllers: The primary PI controller handles the basic speed regulation. A secondary controller, designed based on the identified residual models (e.g., a proportional term for weight compensation, a resonant controller for oscillations), would then be added. This composite controller would aim to cancel out the effects of the residual dynamics, leading to a much smoother and more accurate belt speed.

The power of this approach lies in its adaptability. It allows us to build increasingly accurate system representations without necessarily having to start from scratch with a highly complex, nonlinear, or multi-physics model. By first capturing the dominant dynamics and then systematically addressing the remaining, structured discrepancies, we can achieve a level of performance that might otherwise be unattainable. This is particularly valuable in manufacturing where systems are often subject to wear and tear, changing operational conditions, or the need for adaptation to new product variants, all of which can introduce unmodeled dynamics.

The identification of residual dynamics can be approached using various system identification techniques. Depending on the observed nature of the residuals, one might opt for:

Linear Regression Models: If the residuals appear to be linearly related to external signals (e.g., weight of load, ambient temperature) or past residual values, simple linear regression can be used. For example, if the residual speed error $e(t)$ is found to be proportional to the current load $L(t)$, we can model this as $e(t) \approx K \cdot L(t)$, where K is estimated from data.

ARX/ARMAX/OE Models: If the residuals exhibit autocorrelations, suggesting internal dynamics, these standard parametric models can be applied to the residual time series. For instance, an ARX model of the form $e(t) = a*1 e(t-1) + b*1 u*{res}(t-d)$ could be used, where $e(t)$ are the residuals, $u*{res}(t)$ is an input signal (e.g., the output of the primary controller, or the actual system input), and $a*1, b*1, d$ are parameters to be estimated.

State-Space Models: For more complex residual dynamics, a state-space representation can be particularly powerful. We can define a set of "residual states" that evolve over time. For example, a residual model for belt vibration might be a 2-state system representing position and velocity of the vibration amplitude:

$\dot{x}*{res}(t) = A*{res} x*{res}(t) + B*{res} u*{residual*\input}(t)$

$y*{res}(t) = C*{res} x*{res}(t) + D*{res} u*{residual*\input}(t)$

Here, $x*{res}$ would represent the unmodeled vibratory modes, and $y*{res}$ would be the residual error in speed. The input $u*{residual*\input}$ could be the output of the primary controller or the actual command signal.

The challenge often lies in determining the appropriate complexity for the residual model. Overly simple models might not capture the essential dynamics, while overly complex ones can lead to overfitting the residuals, which might not generalize well to new operating conditions. This is where careful validation of the *residual model itself* becomes important, using data that was not used for its identification, similar to the validation of the primary model.

Consider the implications for robust control design. In many modern control architectures, particularly those aiming for high performance and adaptability, the accuracy of the nominal model is paramount. However, real-world systems are inherently uncertain and subject to unmodeled dynamics. If a controller is designed solely based on a simplified model, it might perform poorly when faced with these unmodeled effects. By explicitly identifying and modeling residual dynamics, we gain a more accurate representation of the system's potential deviations. This richer model can then be used in advanced control design frameworks, such as:

Model Predictive Control (MPC): MPC relies on a predictive model of the system's future behavior. If this model accurately incorporates residual dynamics, MPC can anticipate and compensate for them, leading to improved tracking and disturbance rejection. For example, if the residual model predicts an upcoming speed fluctuation due to accumulated load, the MPC can proactively adjust the control input to counteract it before it significantly affects the belt speed.
H-infinity control or Robust Control: These techniques are designed to provide stability and performance guarantees in the face of model uncertainty. By explicitly representing unmodeled dynamics as structured uncertainty bounds (e.g., using weighting functions that capture the frequency content and magnitude of residual dynamics), we can design controllers that are robust to these specific types of deviations. The identified residual dynamics provide the necessary information to define these uncertainty bounds more accurately than generic assumptions.
Adaptive Control: Adaptive control systems adjust their parameters online to cope with changing system dynamics. If the adaptation mechanism is designed to track and compensate for residual dynamics

as they emerge or change, the system can maintain high performance over time, even under varying conditions. The identified residual dynamics can inform the design of the adaptation rules.

The concept of residual dynamics is thus not merely an academic exercise in system identification; it is a practical bridge between simplified modeling and the demanding requirements of real-world control applications, especially in industries like manufacturing where precision, efficiency, and adaptability are critical. It allows us to incrementally improve our understanding and control of complex systems by systematically dissecting and addressing the unmodeled components of their behavior. This layered approach to modeling and control, where a primary model is augmented by compensation for residual dynamics, offers a pathway to achieving higher levels of automation and performance.

In summary, residual dynamics represent the predictable, yet unmodeled, behaviors of a system that remain after a primary model has been identified. They arise from unmodeled nonlinearities, subtle physical effects like vibrations or friction, environmental disturbances, and sensor limitations. Instead of treating these discrepancies as mere noise, understanding and modeling residual dynamics allows for the design of augmented control systems that can compensate for these effects. This typically involves identifying a residual model from the structured patterns observed in the primary model's residuals and then integrating this residual model into the control strategy, often through hierarchical control, feedforward compensation, or advanced robust/adaptive control frameworks. This approach is particularly relevant in industrial automation, enabling higher precision, improved efficiency, and greater adaptability in complex manufacturing processes.

The journey into understanding and controlling complex dynamical systems invariably leads us to confront the inherent limitations of our models. While a primary model, derived through rigorous analysis or empirical identification, captures the dominant behaviors, a subtle yet significant portion of the system's actual response often eludes it. These discrepancies, what we term residual dynamics, are not random noise but often carry structured information that, if harnessed, can dramatically enhance control performance. To effectively leverage this information, a crucial first step is to systematically identify and understand the myriad sources that give rise to these residual dynamics. This deeper understanding informs not only the choice of residual modeling techniques but also the very design of our augmented control strategies, guiding us toward more precise and robust system operation.

One of the most pervasive sources of residual dynamics stems from **unmodeled high-frequency dynamics**. Real-world physical systems are typically composed of elements operating across a wide spectrum of frequencies. For instance, a mechanical system might involve the primary motion of large components, which are well-captured by a low-frequency model. However, the same system might also contain smaller, lighter components or flexible structures that exhibit rapid vibrations or oscillations at much higher frequencies. These high-frequency modes, even if their amplitudes are small, can significantly influence the overall system response, especially during transient maneuvers or when excited by external forces. When a primary model is deliberately simplified by filtering out or neglecting these high-frequency modes to reduce complexity or improve numerical stability, the behavior attributable to these neglected modes becomes a significant component of the residual dynamics. For example, in the context of industrial robotics, a model focusing on the gross joint movements of a robotic arm might omit the flexural vibrations of the arm links. These vibrations, occurring at frequencies orders of magnitude higher than the joint dynamics, can lead to unwanted jitter at the end-effector. A primary controller based solely on the low-frequency joint model will fail to suppress these vibrations, and their effect will manifest as structured residuals in the position or force control loops. Similarly, in aerospace applications, a model of an aircraft's rigid body dynamics will not account for the flutter modes of the wings or the acoustic vibrations induced by the engines. These high-frequency phenomena represent unmodeled dynamics that can contribute to residual behavior, particularly under extreme flight conditions. Identifying these sources requires a careful consideration of the physical underpinnings of the system and an awareness of phenomena that might be naturally truncated during model simplification.

Another significant contributor to residual dynamics is the inherent **nonlinearity** present in virtually all physical systems, which is often approximated or entirely ignored by employing linear models for simplicity. Many real-world phenomena exhibit behaviors that deviate from linear superposition or proportionality. These nonlinearities can manifest in various forms, including saturation, dead zones, hysteresis, and complex relationships between inputs and outputs. When a linear model is used to represent a fundamentally nonlinear system, the errors arising from this linearization process become a crucial part of the residual dynamics. Consider a common example in actuators: many electric motors exhibit a "dead zone" where a small input voltage does not produce any significant torque output due to internal friction or backlash. A linear model would assume that torque is directly proportional to voltage across the entire operating range. When this linear model is used for control, the system will exhibit sluggishness or no response when the input voltage is within the dead zone. This unresponsibly leads to a structured error that depends on the input signal's magnitude, clearly indicating a residual dynamic. Similarly, friction in mechanical systems is notoriously nonlinear, often exhibiting characteristics like static friction (stiction), Coulomb friction, and viscous friction, each with different dependencies on velocity and applied force.

A simplified linear friction model will invariably fail to capture these complexities, and the resulting discrepancies will contribute to the residual dynamics. Hysteresis, where the output depends not only on the current input but also on the history of past inputs (e.g., in magnetic materials or certain types of valves), is another potent source of nonlinear residual dynamics. Even seemingly linear systems can exhibit subtle nonlinearities when operated at their limits, such as actuator saturation or structural yielding. Identifying these nonlinearities often involves examining the residuals' behavior under varying input amplitudes and system states, looking for systematic deviations that a linear model cannot explain.

External disturbances and noise also play a critical role in shaping residual dynamics, though it's important to distinguish between truly random noise and structured disturbances that can be considered part of the residual dynamics. While random noise, such as sensor quantization errors or inherent electronic noise, is often assumed to be white and uncorrelated, structured external disturbances are systematic influences from the environment that are not part of the system's internal dynamics but directly affect its output. These can include things like ambient temperature fluctuations affecting material properties, vibrations transmitted from the environment, variations in material feedstock, or unexpected external forces. For instance, in a manufacturing process involving precise temperature control of a chemical reactor, fluctuations in the ambient room temperature can introduce heat losses or gains that are not accounted for by the internal thermal model of the reactor. These external thermal influences will cause the actual reactor temperature to deviate from the model's prediction, and these deviations constitute residual dynamics. Similarly, in automated guided vehicles (AGVs) operating in a warehouse, unexpected impacts from other moving equipment or variations in floor surface friction can introduce transient forces or accelerations that are not predicted by the AGV's primary motion model. These external forces are distinct from the internal dynamics of the vehicle's propulsion and steering systems and will manifest as residual behavior in its trajectory. Even what appears as sensor noise might, upon closer inspection, reveal structured components related to the operating environment, such as electromagnetic interference at specific frequencies. Distinguishing between random noise and structured disturbances is key: random noise is typically additive and difficult to model deterministically, while structured disturbances often have a predictable relationship with observable environmental factors or system states, making them amenable to being modeled as part of the residual dynamics.

Over time, systems can experience **parameter variations or drift**, leading to a divergence between the initially identified model and the system's current behavior. Physical components degrade, materials change their properties, and environmental conditions evolve. These slow, gradual changes in the system's underlying parameters introduce a form of residual dynamics that is time-varying. For example, in a manufacturing assembly line, the wear and tear on robotic end-effectors or tooling can lead to changes in their effective mass, inertia, or friction characteristics. A model identified at the beginning of the production run might no longer accurately represent the system after weeks or months of operation. The resulting deviations in the robot's motion or force control performance will be a manifestation of this parameter drift, forming residual dynamics. Similarly, in process control, the fouling of heat exchangers or the degradation of catalysts in a chemical reactor can lead to changes in heat transfer coefficients or reaction rates. These changes will alter the system's dynamic response, causing the original model's predictions to become increasingly inaccurate over time. The accumulation of debris in fluidic systems, the stretching or loosening of conveyor belts, or the gradual aging of electronic components can all contribute to parameter drift. If these drifts are slow relative to the control system's bandwidth, they can often be treated as a form of residual dynamic that needs to be identified and compensated for, perhaps through online parameter estimation or adaptive control techniques. The challenge here is to differentiate between slow parameter drift and sudden, unpredictable events. While both lead to model mismatch, their modeling and compensation strategies may differ significantly.

Finally, the **actuator and sensor nonlinearities** themselves, beyond their general contribution as a source of system nonlinearity, deserve specific attention as distinct entities contributing to residual dynamics. Actuators are the components that exert influence on the system, while sensors are responsible for providing feedback. Both are physical devices with inherent limitations and nonlinear behaviors that are often simplified in ideal models. Actuator nonlinearities, as previously hinted at, can include saturation (limiting the maximum output, e.g., maximum motor torque or valve opening), dead zones (requiring a minimum input to produce any output), quantization (discrete output levels), and hysteresis (output depends on input history). For instance, a hydraulic actuator might have a nonlinear relationship between the command signal and the flow rate, or it might exhibit stiction at low velocities. A primary model might treat the actuator as a simple proportional gain, overlooking these critical nonlinearities. The resulting errors, particularly in situations where the actuator is operating near its limits or at very low speeds, will form a significant part of the residual dynamics.

Sensor nonlinearities are equally important. A sensor might have a nonlinear response curve, meaning that a unit change in the measured physical quantity does not always correspond to the same unit change in the sensor's output. For example, a pressure transducer might be more sensitive in a certain pressure range than others. It might also exhibit biases, offsets, or delays that are not perfectly linear. In some cases, sensor noise itself can have structured components. For instance, a tachometer used to measure rotational speed might produce erroneous readings when the speed fluctuates rapidly, or it might be susceptible to electromagnetic interference at certain frequencies. If a primary model assumes a perfectly linear and instantaneous sensor with no noise, the deviations caused by these real-world sensor characteristics will contribute to the residual dynamics. The consequences of these nonlinearities can be particularly severe in control loops that rely heavily on accurate feedback. For example, in high-precision motion control, unmodeled sensor bias or nonlinear gain can lead to significant tracking errors.

In summary, the genesis of residual dynamics is multifaceted, arising from the irreducible complexities of physical systems that are often distilled away in simplified models. High-frequency dynamics, pervasive nonlinearities, structured external disturbances, gradual parameter drift, and the inherent limitations of actuators and sensors all contribute to the gap between model prediction and reality. Recognizing these distinct sources is not merely an academic exercise; it is a pragmatic necessity. It allows us to move beyond simply acknowledging model inadequacy and to systematically investigate the nature of the "leftover" dynamics. This analytical approach informs our choices regarding the complexity and form of the residual model we will attempt to identify, and ultimately, guides us in designing control strategies that can effectively compensate for these predictable deviations, pushing the boundaries of system performance and robustness in demanding engineering applications.

Having dissected the myriad origins of residual dynamics – from the subtle vibrations of unmodeled high-frequency modes to the pervasive influence of nonlinearities, external disturbances, parameter drift, and actuator/sensor limitations – we now pivot from identification to characterization. The challenge at hand is to translate these identified discrepancies into actionable mathematical models. The overarching philosophy guiding this endeavor is one of parsimony: we seek the simplest possible mathematical representation that effectively captures the essence of these residual dynamics, thereby enhancing the overall model's predictive power without introducing undue complexity. This often means moving beyond the realm of perfect fidelity and embracing pragmatic approximations that yield significant improvements in control performance.

One of the most elementary yet surprisingly effective approaches to modeling residuals is through the addition of simple **stochastic noise models**. This strategy is particularly relevant when the residual dynamics, after accounting for known deterministic sources, appear largely random or when the dominant component of the discrepancy is sensor noise or unmodeled high-frequency noise that is difficult to capture with a deterministic structure. The assumption here is that the residual, denoted by $r(t)$, can be approximated as a random process, often modeled as additive noise. The simplest form of this is Gaussian white noise, $\epsilon(t) \sim \mathcal{N}(0, \sigma^2)$, where σ^2 is the variance. This implies that the residual is uncorrelated over time and has a constant mean of zero. While this might seem overly simplistic, it can be a powerful baseline. For instance, in a robotic manipulator, even after modeling the rigid body dynamics and known joint nonlinearities, there might be persistent, small-amplitude deviations in the end-effector's position. If these deviations do not exhibit clear temporal correlation or dependence on specific system states (beyond what is already captured), modeling them as additive Gaussian noise can be a reasonable first step. The primary model $y_{model}(t)$ *is augmented by this noise term:* $y_{actual}(t) \approx y_{model}(t) + \epsilon(t)$. The parameters of this noise model, primarily its variance, can be estimated from the observed residuals. This approach acknowledges uncertainty and adds a probabilistic dimension to the model, which can be crucial for designing robust controllers that account for this irreducible uncertainty.

However, true system residuals are rarely just uncorrelated noise. Often, they possess some underlying temporal structure, indicating that the "noise" is, in fact, correlated and perhaps even deterministic in nature. In such cases, modeling the residual as a **low-order linear dynamical system** driven by persistent excitation can be highly effective. The idea is to represent the residual dynamics as a separate, often simpler, dynamical system whose inputs are not directly the system's primary control inputs, but rather some form of persistent excitation. This excitation can be an artifact of the system's operation, external stimuli, or even previously unmodeled aspects of the primary inputs. Let the primary model's output be $y{model}(t)$ and the actual system output be $y{actual}(t)$. The residual is $r(t) = y{actual}(t) - y{model}(t)$. We can then model this residual as a linear system:

$$ \dot{z}(t) = Ar z(t) + Br u_{ext}(t) $$

$$ r(t) = Cr z(t) + Dr u_{ext}(t) $$

Here, $z(t)$ is the state of the residual dynamics, and $u{ext}(t)$ represents the "external excitation" driving these dynamics. The crucial aspect is identifying what constitutes $u{ext}(t)$. In many practical scenarios, $u{ext}(t)$ might be related to the primary input $u(t)$, but not in a straightforward linear way, or it might be derived from other system states or measured quantities that were not fully utilized by the primary model. A common strategy is to hypothesize that $u{ext}(t)$ is a signal that "excites" the unmodeled dynamics. If the system operates with inputs that ensure a rich spectrum of frequencies is present over time (i.e., persistent excitation), then the residual dynamics can be identified using standard linear system identification techniques.

Consider the example of unmodeled aerodynamic forces on an aircraft. While the primary model might capture the rigid body dynamics of the aircraft, subtle aerodynamic effects like vortex shedding or buffetting at certain flight conditions can lead to residuals. If these phenomena are excited by a range of control surface movements or atmospheric

disturbances, then the residual dynamics can be identified as a linear system. The "persistent excitation" might be the combined effect of pilot inputs, gusts, and autopilot commands over a period of time. By observing the residual $r(t)$ (e.g., deviations in roll rate or angle of attack from the primary model's prediction) and correlating it with the historical excitation signals, a low-order linear model for $r(t)$ can be obtained. The matrices $A
*r, B*r, C*r, D*r$ can be estimated using methods like subspace identification or prediction error methods, assuming a sufficient amount of data with rich excitation. The order of this residual model (i.e., the dimension of $z(t)$) is typically kept low, perhaps one or two states, to maintain simplicity. For instance, a simple first-order lag could represent a residual damping effect, while a second-order system might capture a residual oscillatory mode.

Another powerful yet relatively simple approach to modeling residuals is by incorporating
polynomial terms to capture basic nonlinearities that might have been overlooked or oversimplified in the primary model. While advanced nonlinear modeling techniques exist, using polynomial expansions offers a balance between capturing essential nonlinear behavior and maintaining model tractability. If the residual $r(t)$ is observed to systematically depend on certain system states $x(t)$ or inputs $u(t)$ in a nonlinear fashion, we can approximate this relationship using polynomials. For example, if the residual velocity error in a robot arm is observed to increase quadratically with the arm's velocity, we can model it as:
$$ r(t) = c1 v(t) + c2 v(t)^2 + c_3 v(t)^3 + \dots $$
where $v(t)$ is the system's velocity and c_i are coefficients to be identified. This can be seen as a Taylor series expansion of the residual dynamics around some operating point. More generally, the residual can be modeled as a function of system states and inputs:
$$ r(t) \approx f_{poly}(x(t), u(t)) $$

where $f{poly}$ is a polynomial function. For instance, if we have a system with states $x1, x_2$ and input u, a polynomial residual model might look like:
$$ r(t) = \theta0 + \theta1 x1(t) + \theta2 x2(t) + \theta3 u(t) + \theta4 x1(t)^2 + \theta5 x1(t) x_2(t) + \dots $$
The coefficients θ_i are then identified using regression techniques, treating the polynomial terms as regressors and the observed residuals as the dependent variable. This is akin to constructing a linear regression model where the features are powers and products of the system states and inputs.

This polynomial approach is particularly useful for capturing phenomena like:

Cubic or higher-order velocity-dependent effects: Beyond simple viscous damping (linear velocity dependence), real systems can exhibit drag forces that scale with velocity in more complex ways, especially at higher speeds. Polynomial terms can capture these effects.
State-dependent friction: While Coulomb friction is often modeled as a piecewise constant term, more nuanced friction models can involve velocity-dependent components that are nonlinear. Polynomial terms can approximate these.
Geometric nonlinearities: In mechanical systems, the relationship between joint angles and end-effector positions can be nonlinear. If the primary model uses a simplified kinematic model, the residual might capture these geometric nonlinearities.
Control signal nonlinearities not captured by simple dead zones or saturation: For example, if an actuator's response is slightly nonlinear even within its operating range, polynomial terms can approximate this.

An illustrative example involves modeling residual forces in an active suspension system for a vehicle. The primary model might account for spring and damper forces as linear functions of displacement and velocity. However, higher-order effects due to tire deformation, complex fluid dynamics within the dampers at high velocities, or even minor structural flexibilities can contribute to residual forces. If these residual forces are observed to be correlated with vehicle velocity and acceleration, a polynomial model can be employed. For instance, a residual force $f_{res}(t)$ could be modeled as:

$$ f{res}(t) = cv v(t)^3 + ca a(t) + c{va} v(t) a(t) + \dots $$
where $v(t)$ is the suspension velocity and $a(t)$ is the acceleration. The coefficients c_i are identified from experimental data. This polynomial representation allows the controller to anticipate and counteract these nonlinear residual forces, leading to a smoother and more stable ride.

It's important to note the relationship between these simple models and the more complex sources of residuals discussed previously. Additive noise models are suitable when residuals are largely stochastic and uncorrelated. Low-order linear systems are effective when residuals exhibit temporal correlation and can be driven by external excitation, often representing simplified dynamics of neglected modes or complex interactions. Polynomial models are best suited for capturing systematic nonlinear deviations that are directly dependent on system states or inputs, providing a piecewise linear approximation of potentially complex nonlinear functions.

The choice of which simple model to employ depends heavily on the characteristics of the observed residuals. Visual inspection of time-series plots of residuals can reveal patterns. If they appear random, an additive noise model might suffice. If there's a visible correlation with past values or inputs, a linear dynamical model might be appropriate. If residuals consistently increase or decrease in a predictable way with system states (e.g., velocity, position), polynomial terms become a strong candidate.

Furthermore, these simple models can often be combined. For instance, a residual might be modeled as a low-order linear system with additive noise, or a polynomial model might be augmented with stochastic terms.

$$ r(t) \approx f_{poly}(x(t), u(t)) + \epsilon(t) $$

or

$$ \dot{z}(t) = A_r z(t) + B_r u_{ext}(t) $$

$$ r(t) = C_r z(t) + D_r u_{ext}(t) + \epsilon(t) $$

The goal remains to achieve a satisfactory balance between model accuracy and complexity.

A practical consideration when using these simple models is the need for adequate excitation. For identifying stochastic noise, continuous operation and measurement are key. For linear dynamical models, the system must be subjected to inputs that sufficiently "excite" the dynamics of interest. This means that the input signals should contain a broad range of frequencies relevant to the residual dynamics. If the system is always operated with very slow, smooth inputs, any fast residual dynamics might remain unobserved and unmodeled. Similarly, for polynomial models, the range of operating states and inputs encountered during identification must cover the range where the polynomial approximation is intended to be valid. Extrapolating a polynomial model far beyond the range of its training data can lead to significant inaccuracies.

Let's consider a more detailed example involving a simple two-wheel mobile robot. The primary model might accurately describe the robot's kinematic relationship between wheel velocities and its linear and angular velocity. However, real robots often exhibit residual unmodeled dynamics. These could include:

1.
Wheel slippage: Especially on slippery surfaces or during rapid acceleration/deceleration, wheels might slip, leading to a deviation between the commanded wheel speeds and the actual robot motion. This slippage might be more pronounced at higher speeds or under larger lateral forces.
2. **Motor nonlinearities:** Beyond simple saturation, the relationship between motor voltage and torque can be nonlinear, especially at low voltages (dead zone) or due to electromagnetic effects.
3. **Friction:** Anisotropic friction effects, where friction depends on the direction of motion or the steering angle, can be significant.
4. **Battery voltage droop:** As the battery discharges, its voltage drops, affecting motor performance. This can manifest as a gradual reduction in speed capability, a form of parameter drift, but can also cause instantaneous nonlinearities in torque output.

Suppose we have identified a primary kinematic model for the robot. We then observe the actual trajectory and compare it to the trajectory predicted by the primary model. The differences form the residual dynamics.

Scenario 1: Residuals dominated by random fluctuations.
If the observed residuals in position and orientation are small and appear erratic, with no clear correlation with velocity or other states, we might initially model them as additive Gaussian noise. We collect data over a period of operation and compute the mean and variance of the residual. If the mean is close to zero, we can assume zero bias. The

variance σ^2 of the position residuals and the angular residuals would be estimated. This σ^2 would then inform the controller about the expected level of unpredictable error.

Scenario 2: Residuals exhibit dependence on velocity.

Suppose we plot the residual linear velocity error against the commanded linear velocity. We observe that the error is not zero-mean but increases or decreases approximately linearly with velocity. This suggests a residual viscous damping or driving effect. We could model this residual velocity as:

$$ v{residual}(t) = kv v_{commanded}(t) $$

where kv *is a coefficient identified from data. If the residual error shows a quadratic dependence on velocity, e.g.,* $v{residual}(t) = kv v{commanded}(t)^2$, then a polynomial term is warranted. If the residual error is more complex, involving both velocity and acceleration, or the robot's orientation relative to its direction of motion, a more elaborate polynomial model might be needed:

$$ v{residual}(t) = \theta1 v(t) + \theta2 v(t)^2 + \theta3 \omega(t) + \theta_4 \cos(\phi(t)) v(t) $$

where $v(t)$ is velocity, $\omega(t)$ is angular velocity, and $\phi(t)$ is orientation. The coefficients θ_i would be found using linear least squares regression on the observed residuals.

Scenario 3: Residuals show temporal correlation.

If the residual position error doesn't immediately settle to zero after a change in command, but instead exhibits a decaying oscillation or a slow drift, it suggests unmodeled dynamics. This could be due to the inertia of unmodeled parts of the drivetrain, the compliance of the wheels, or resonance effects. We could hypothesize that the residual error $e(t)$ behaves like a first-order or second-order system:

$$ \taur \dot{e}(t) + e(t) = u{residual}(t) $$

or
$$ \ddot{e}(t) + 2\zetar \omega{nr} \dot{e}(t) + \omega{nr}^2 e(t) = u{residual}(t) $$
Here, $u{residual}(t)$ is an unmodeled driving force or disturbance. If this disturbance is assumed to be zero or a simple function of the primary command, we can then identify the parameters $\taur$ (time constant), ω{nr} (natural frequency), and $\zetar$ (damping ratio) from the observed residual behavior. The driving term $u_{residual}(t)$ could itself be modeled, perhaps as a filtered version of the primary input or as a low-order linear system driven by the primary input.

The key advantage of these simple models – additive noise, low-order linear dynamics, and polynomial approximations – is their interpretability and ease of integration into existing control frameworks. An additive noise model can be used to define probabilistic bounds on performance, guiding the design of robust controllers. A linear dynamical model for residuals can be augmented to the primary system's state-space representation, potentially allowing for more sophisticated control design techniques that account for these dynamics. Polynomial terms can be incorporated into the control law directly, effectively "pre-distorting" the control signal to counteract the anticipated nonlinear behavior.

For example, if a residual velocity error $v {residual}(t) = kv v{commanded}(t)$ is identified for the mobile robot, the control law can be modified. Instead of commanding a velocity $v{cmd}$, the controller might command $v{cmd} - kv v{cmd}$, or more accurately, adjust the desired velocity to achieve the intended outcome. If the primary controller aims for a velocity $v{ref}$, and the residual causes the actual velocity to be $v{actual} = v{ref} + kv v{ref}$, then the controller might need to output a command that, when processed by the (nominal) system and the residual, yields v_{ref}. This often involves inverting the identified residual model.

The process of modeling residuals with these simple methods typically involves:

1.
Data Collection: Acquire system data under various operating conditions, including inputs, states, and outputs.
2. **Primary Model Prediction:** Use the existing primary model to predict the system's output for the collected input data.
3. **Residual Calculation:** Compute the difference between the actual observed output and the predicted output: $r(t) = y{actual}(t) - y{model}(t)$.
4. **Residual Analysis:** Analyze the computed residuals for patterns:
Statistical properties: Mean, variance, autocorrelation.
Correlation with states/inputs: Plot residuals against system states ($x(t)$) and inputs ($u(t)$). Look for trends, nonlinear relationships.
Time-domain behavior: Examine temporal correlations, oscillations, decay rates.
5. **Model Selection:** Based on the analysis, choose an appropriate simple model structure: additive noise, linear dynamical system, or polynomial model.
6. **Parameter Identification:** Estimate the parameters of the chosen model using the residual data and system states/inputs. Techniques include:
Least squares: For additive noise (estimating variance) and polynomial models (estimating coefficients).
System identification methods (e.g., prediction error method, subspace identification): For linear dynamical models.

7. **Model Validation:** Evaluate the performance of the identified residual model by comparing its predictions to new residual data or by assessing the improvement in the overall system model's prediction accuracy.

This iterative process allows for a progressive understanding and modeling of the discrepancies, moving from simple stochastic approximations to more structured, albeit still simplified, deterministic representations of the unmodeled behavior. The ultimate goal is to create an augmented model that is sufficiently accurate to significantly improve control performance without becoming intractable or overly reliant on precise, hard-to-obtain information about the residual dynamics. This pragmatic approach is a cornerstone of effective control system design in the face of imperfect models.

Having established the foundational approaches for modeling residual dynamics—ranging from simple stochastic noise to linear dynamical systems and polynomial approximations—we now transition to a more powerful and flexible paradigm: the application of machine learning. When residual dynamics exhibit complex, highly nonlinear, or intricate temporal dependencies that elude the grasping power of traditional analytical or parametric methods, machine learning algorithms offer a compelling alternative. These data-driven techniques excel at learning complex mappings directly from observed system behavior, providing an avenue to capture subtle patterns and interactions that might otherwise remain unmodeled. This section delves into how various machine learning methodologies can be employed to learn residual dynamics, thereby enhancing the accuracy and robustness of our overall system models.

One of the most versatile machine learning tools for modeling residual dynamics is the
feedforward neural network (FNN), also known as a multi-layer perceptron (MLP). An FNN can be trained to approximate any

continuous function, making it a potent candidate for learning the often-intricate relationship between system states, inputs, and the resulting residuals. The core idea is to train an FNN to map a set of input features—typically system states $x(t)$ and control inputs $u(t)$ at a given time instant—to the observed residual $r(t)$. The FNN consists of an input layer, one or more hidden layers with nonlinear activation functions (e.g., ReLU, sigmoid, tanh), and an output layer that produces the residual prediction.

The architecture of the FNN can be tailored to the complexity of the residual dynamics. For instance, a shallow network (one hidden layer) might suffice for moderately complex residuals, while deeper networks with multiple hidden layers can capture more intricate nonlinearities. The training process involves minimizing a loss function, typically the mean squared error (MSE) between the predicted residuals and the actual observed residuals, using an optimization algorithm like gradient descent or its variants (e.g., Adam, RMSprop). The training data comprises pairs of input features $(x(t), u(t))$ and corresponding residual values $r(t)$.

Consider an autonomous vehicle navigating an urban environment. The primary vehicle dynamics model might capture the basic kinematics and tire forces. However, residuals can arise from complex interactions with the road surface (e.g., varying friction due to water, oil, or debris), unpredictable aerodynamic effects at different speeds and wind conditions, and the nuanced behavior of tire deformation under combined longitudinal and lateral loading. These residual forces can significantly affect the vehicle's trajectory and are notoriously difficult to model analytically.

A feedforward neural network can be employed to learn these residual forces. The input features to the network could include:

Current vehicle states: longitudinal velocity, lateral velocity, yaw rate, steering angle, tire slip angles.
Control inputs: throttle command, brake command, steering command.
Environmental factors (if measurable): road surface type, estimated friction coefficient, wind speed and direction.

The output of the FNN would be a prediction of the residual forces acting on the vehicle, perhaps decomposed into longitudinal and lateral components. By training this network on a dataset collected from diverse driving scenarios, the FNN can learn to predict these complex residual forces, which can then be used to augment the primary vehicle model for improved simulation accuracy or to inform a more sophisticated control system that compensates for these unmodeled effects. For example, if the FNN predicts a large residual lateral force due to a slippery patch and aggressive steering, the controller could adjust its steering and throttle commands to maintain stability. The prediction horizon of an FNN is typically limited to its input features; it does not inherently have memory of past states beyond what is explicitly provided in its input vector. This makes it suitable for learning instantaneous relationships but less so for residuals with significant temporal memory.

When residual dynamics exhibit strong **temporal dependencies**, meaning the current residual is influenced by past states or residuals, **recurrent neural networks (RNNs)** become particularly advantageous. RNNs are designed to process sequential data, incorporating a "memory" mechanism that allows information from previous time steps to influence current predictions. This memory is achieved through recurrent connections that feed the output of a hidden layer (or a transformed version of it) back into itself at the next time step.

Among various RNN architectures, Long Short-Term Memory (LSTM) and Gated Recurrent Unit (GRU) networks are especially effective at capturing long-range temporal dependencies, mitigating the vanishing gradient problem that can plague simpler RNNs. These architectures employ gating mechanisms that selectively control the flow of information, allowing the network to learn which past information is relevant and should be retained and which should be forgotten.

Imagine modeling the residual vibrations in a flexible robotic arm. The primary model might capture the rigid-body dynamics and perhaps some fundamental bending modes. However, unmodeled effects such as structural damping characteristics that change with temperature, micro-vibrations from external sources, or complex interactions between different flexible modes can manifest as residuals in the arm's end-effector position or velocity. These residuals often exhibit persistent oscillatory behavior and decay patterns that depend on the arm's history of motion.

An LSTM network can be trained to predict these residual vibrations. The input sequence to the LSTM could consist of past system states and control inputs over a window of time. The LSTM's hidden state, updated at each time step, would implicitly learn to represent the "state" of the residual dynamics. The network could be trained to output:

The predicted residual position or velocity at the current time step.
A sequence of future residual states, enabling short-term prediction of vibrations.

The training data would comprise sequences of states and inputs collected while the robot arm performs various movements. The LSTM would learn to recognize patterns in these sequences that correspond to specific types of residual vibrations and to predict their evolution. For instance, if the arm has just executed a rapid, sweeping motion, the LSTM, by remembering the high velocities and accelerations from that motion, could predict a decaying oscillatory residual vibration that might not be captured by a simple linear model. This capability is crucial for precise robotic manipulation, where unmodeled vibrations can lead to settling errors and reduced accuracy.

Another powerful machine learning approach for modeling residual dynamics, particularly when uncertainty quantification is important, is the use of
Gaussian Processes (GPs). GPs offer a non-parametric Bayesian approach to regression that learns a distribution over functions. Instead of learning a single function, a GP learns a probability distribution from which functions can be sampled. This inherent probabilistic nature allows GPs to provide not only a prediction of the residual but also a measure of uncertainty associated with that prediction.

A Gaussian Process regression model for residual dynamics defines a prior over functions f, such that f is distributed according to a multivariate Gaussian distribution. When trained on data, the GP posterior distribution is updated to reflect the observed residuals. For a set of observed data points (X, y), where $X = \{x
*1, \dots, x*n\}$ are input features (e.g., system states and inputs) and $y = \{*y1, \dots, y*n\}$ are the corresponding residuals, the GP predicts the residual $y*$ at a new input $x*$ as a Gaussian distribution with a mean $\mu*$ and variance $\sigma*^2$.

The key component of a GP is its
covariance function, also known as the kernel. The kernel defines the smoothness and structure of the functions that can be learned. For modeling residual dynamics, kernels can be chosen to reflect expected properties of the residuals. For example:
Squared Exponential (RBF) kernel: Implies that functions are infinitely differentiable and smooth, suitable for residuals that are generally well-behaved.
Matern kernels: Offer varying degrees of smoothness, allowing for modeling of less smooth residual behaviors.
Periodic kernels: Can capture any cyclical or repeating patterns in the residuals.
Combinations of kernels: Multiple kernels can be combined to model residuals with mixed characteristics (e.g., smoothness and periodicity).

Consider the example of modeling residual aerodynamic forces on a high-aspect-ratio wing in a wind tunnel. The primary model might be based on linear aerodynamics or a simplified unsteady aerodynamic model. However, complex phenomena like vortex shedding, stall delay, and aeroelastic effects can lead to residuals in lift and drag that are highly dependent on angle of attack, airspeed, and even the history of the flow. These residuals can be highly nonlinear and difficult to parameterize.

A Gaussian Process can be employed to learn the residual lift and drag. The input features to the GP would include:

Angle of attack (α).
Airspeed (V).
Mach number (M).
Reynolds number (Re).

Parameters related to unsteady motion (e.g., reduced frequency, if applicable).

The GP, trained on experimental data, would provide a mean prediction of the residual forces and an associated uncertainty. This uncertainty can be extremely valuable. For instance, if the GP predicts a large residual force with high uncertainty at a new operating point (e.g., a novel combination of speed and angle of attack), it signals to the controller that the model is extrapolating beyond its reliable knowledge, potentially necessitating a more conservative control action or triggering an alert for further data collection. This uncertainty information is crucial for designing robust controllers that can adapt to varying levels of model accuracy. Furthermore, by examining the learned function's properties derived from the GP, one can gain insights into the underlying physics of the residual dynamics.

Beyond standard FNNs, RNNs, and GPs, other machine learning techniques can also be applied. For instance, **Support Vector Machines (SVMs)**, particularly in their regression formulation (SVR), can be used to model nonlinear residuals, although they typically provide point estimates without inherent uncertainty quantification like GPs. **Ensemble methods**, such as Random Forests or Gradient Boosting Machines, can combine the predictions of multiple simpler models to achieve improved accuracy and robustness. These methods can be particularly effective in capturing complex interactions between input features that might be missed by a single model.

The successful application of machine learning to residual modeling hinges on several critical factors:

1.

Data Quality and Quantity: Machine learning models are data-hungry. Sufficiently large, diverse, and accurate datasets are essential for training models that can generalize well to unseen operating conditions. The data must adequately cover the range of system states and inputs where residual dynamics are expected to be significant.

2.
Feature Engineering: The choice of input features for the machine learning model is paramount. If important state variables or external influences are omitted, the model's ability to learn the residual dynamics will be severely hampered. This might involve domain expertise to identify key predictors or employing automated feature selection techniques. For instance, in modeling residual vibrations, features related to past velocities and accelerations might be more informative than just current positions.

3.
Model Selection and Architecture: Choosing the right type of machine learning model (FNN, RNN, GP, etc.) and configuring its architecture (number of layers, neurons, kernel choice, activation functions) requires careful consideration of the nature of the residuals. Is the residual predominantly dependent on current states, does it have strong temporal memory, or is uncertainty quantification critical?

4.
Training and Validation: Rigorous training and validation procedures are necessary to prevent overfitting. This involves splitting the data into training, validation, and testing sets and using appropriate regularization techniques. Cross-validation can provide a more robust estimate of model performance.

5.

Integration with Control Systems: The ultimate goal is to use the learned residual model to improve control. This often involves augmenting the primary system model with the machine learning model's predictions. For controllers, this might mean using the predicted residual to adjust control commands in real-time (e.g., feedforward compensation) or to estimate bounds on system performance for robust control design. In simulation, the learned residual model enhances the fidelity of the simulated system behavior.

For example, consider a complex manufacturing process, such as semiconductor wafer fabrication. The precision required is extremely high, and subtle deviations from the ideal process can lead to defects. The primary process model might describe the intended chemical reactions, thermal profiles, and mechanical movements. However, residuals can arise from factors like variations in material properties, minute vibrations in machinery, temporal drift in sensor readings, and complex fluid dynamics in deposition chambers.

A
Recurrent Neural Network (LSTM) could be particularly effective here.
The inputs to the LSTM might include:
Current setpoints for temperature, pressure, gas flow rates.
Historical values of these setpoints and actual process measurements over a recent time window.
Sensor readings from vibration monitors.
Information about the specific wafer batch being processed (e.g., material composition, previous processing history).

The LSTM could be trained to predict residual deviations in key output metrics, such as film thickness uniformity, defect density, or process completion time. By learning the temporal correlations and dependencies within the process data, the LSTM can anticipate deviations before they become significant enough to cause a defect. This allows for proactive adjustments to the process parameters, either by the control system directly or by flagging the need for human intervention. For instance, if the LSTM detects a pattern in sensor readings that historically precedes a drop in film uniformity, it can signal an early warning or trigger a fine-tuning of gas flow rates. The ability of LSTMs to "remember" past process conditions is crucial, as many defects are a consequence of cumulative effects or specific sequences of events rather than isolated occurrences.

Alternatively,
Gaussian Processes might be employed if quantifying the uncertainty in process outcomes is critical. Suppose the primary model predicts a certain yield rate for a batch. A GP trained on historical data, including process parameters and actual yields, could provide a more refined prediction of the yield for a new batch, along with a confidence interval. This uncertainty estimate could inform decisions about production scheduling, quality control sampling, or when to halt the process for recalibration. For instance, if the GP predicts a high probability of a low yield for a particular wafer batch due to unusual sensor readings, the system might automatically divert that batch for more intensive inspection or reject it outright. The interpretability offered by GP kernels can also provide insights into which process parameters are most influential in contributing to yield variations.

The use of machine learning for residual modeling represents a significant advancement over simpler methods. While additive noise, linear dynamics, and polynomial approximations offer valuable insights and are often sufficient for many applications, they struggle to capture the full spectrum of complex, emergent behaviors that characterize many real-world systems. Machine learning, with its capacity to learn arbitrary, highly nonlinear mappings from data, opens up new possibilities for achieving a more faithful representation of system dynamics. This enhanced fidelity is not merely an academic exercise; it has direct implications for improving control performance, enhancing simulation accuracy, and enabling more robust and adaptive system operation in increasingly complex and unpredictable environments. The ongoing research in areas like deep learning, reinforcement learning, and explainable AI promises even more sophisticated and insightful methods for modeling residual dynamics in the future.

The integration of learned residual dynamics into the control design loop represents a crucial step in translating data-driven modeling insights into tangible improvements in system performance. Having established methods to capture these often-elusive unmodeled dynamics, the focus now shifts to how these learned models can actively inform and enhance control strategies. This integration can manifest in several forms, each tailored to leverage the specific characteristics of the residual model and the control objectives.

One of the most direct and effective approaches is **feedforward compensation**. In this paradigm, the learned residual model acts as a predictive element, anticipating the deviations from the nominal dynamics before they significantly impact the system's output. The controller then uses these predictions to proactively generate corrective control actions. For a system modeled as $\dot{x} = f(x, u) + r$, where r is the residual, a controller typically aims to steer the system towards a desired trajectory x_d by choosing u. Without accounting for r, the control law might be designed based on the nominal dynamics $f(x, u)$ alone, leading to tracking errors or poor disturbance rejection when r is present.

By incorporating the learned residual model, which provides an estimate $\hat{r}(x, u, \text{past data})$, the control law can be augmented. A common strategy is to introduce a feedforward component to the control input u. If the residual r can be roughly inverted or compensated for, the control law could be structured as $u = u {\text{nominal}}(x, u{\text{ref}}) + u{\text{residual-comp}}(x, u{\text{ref}}, \hat{r})$. Here, $u{\text{residual-comp}}$ is specifically designed to counteract the predicted residual. For instance, if the residual can be approximated as a force or torque $r \approx G \cdot \hat{r}{force}$, then the control system can compute an opposing force/torque command to cancel its effect. The input to the residual model for prediction might include current states $x(t)$, control inputs $u(t)$, and potentially historical information if using an RNN-based residual model. The output $\hat{r}$ then informs the additive control effort.

A compelling example of this feedforward compensation can be seen in **power grid frequency regulation**. The nominal dynamics of a power grid are complex, involving generators, loads, transmission lines, and control systems. However, unmodeled phenomena, such as sudden load changes not perfectly captured by aggregated models, generator governor dynamics that deviate from ideal behavior, or even the effects of renewable energy intermittency not fully accounted for in simplified models, can manifest as residuals. These residuals can cause frequency deviations that need to be rapidly corrected to maintain grid stability.

If a machine learning model (e.g., an RNN trained on historical grid data) has learned to predict these residual frequency-affecting influences based on current grid conditions (e.g., total load, generation mix, frequency deviation history), this prediction can be fed to the automatic generation control (AGC) system. The AGC can then preemptively adjust the output of controllable generators to counteract the predicted residual. For instance, if the learned model predicts an impending drop in frequency due to a confluence of factors that the primary model overlooks, the AGC can be instructed to increase generation slightly ahead of time. This anticipatory action can significantly reduce the peak frequency deviation and the time it takes to return to the nominal frequency, thereby improving overall grid stability and the quality of power delivered to consumers. The feedforward component derived from the residual model acts as a "look-ahead" mechanism, providing a crucial advantage over purely feedback-based control that can only react to deviations after they have occurred.

Beyond direct compensation, learned residual models can also be instrumental in **robust control design**. Many robust control techniques, such as $\mathcal{H}_\infty$ control or quantitative feedback theory (QFT), rely on explicit characterizations of uncertainties and disturbances. Traditionally, these uncertainties are often represented by bounds on model parameters or additive noise terms. However, machine learning models, particularly Gaussian Processes, can provide a more nuanced representation of residuals, including their statistics and, crucially, their uncertainty.

When a Gaussian Process is used to model residuals, it not only provides a mean prediction μ but also a variance σ^2 associated with that prediction. This variance quantifies the model's confidence in its prediction at a given operating point. Robust control design can then leverage this uncertainty information. For instance, a controller can be designed to be robust against the *worst-case* residual within a confidence bound derived from the GP. This means that even if the actual residual is at the upper end of the predicted uncertainty range, the controller will still maintain stability and acceptable performance. This is particularly valuable in scenarios where the residual dynamics are highly variable or where operating conditions may push the system into regimes where the residual model's accuracy is inherently lower.

Consider a sophisticated aerospace system, such as an unmanned aerial vehicle (UAV) operating in uncertain atmospheric conditions. The primary aerodynamic model might be well-established, but residuals can arise from unpredictable wind gusts, atmospheric turbulence, or complex aeroelastic effects that are difficult to model analytically. If a GP is trained to predict these residual aerodynamic forces based on flight conditions (e.g., airspeed, altitude, angle of attack), the resulting uncertainty estimates can inform the design of a flight controller. A robust controller designed using this GP information would aim to maintain stable flight and accurate trajectory tracking not just under nominal conditions, but also in the face of these unpredictable, learned residual disturbances. The controller would be less prone to overreacting to noise or misinterpreting low-uncertainty predictions, while still being sufficiently conservative when facing high-uncertainty residual estimates, which might indicate novel or extreme atmospheric phenomena. This principled approach to incorporating uncertainty is a significant advantage of integrating GP-based residual models into control design.

Furthermore, the uncertainty information can also guide adaptive control strategies. If the residual model indicates high uncertainty in a particular operating region, an adaptive controller could shift its control gains or even switch to a more conservative control law. Conversely, if the residual is predicted with high confidence and low uncertainty, the adaptive controller might relax its constraints or employ more aggressive control actions to optimize performance.

Another powerful integration strategy involves **adaptive control schemes**. In these systems, the controller parameters are updated online in response to observed system behavior, which implicitly includes the effects of residual dynamics. When a learned residual model is available, it can provide a more informed basis for adaptation. Instead of solely relying on the error between the desired and actual states, an adaptive controller can use the predicted residual to better estimate the true system dynamics or the extent of the unmodeled part.

One way to achieve this is through **model reference adaptive control (MRAC)**, where the controller aims to make the system's output track a reference model. If the system dynamics deviate from the reference model due to residuals, the adaptation law in MRAC adjusts controller parameters. By incorporating a learned residual model, the adaptation law can be made more efficient and less sensitive to noise. For example, if the residual model predicts a certain type of deviation, the adaptation mechanism can be steered to correct for that specific deviation more quickly and accurately.

Consider an industrial robot arm performing precise pick-and-place operations. Residuals can arise from factors like thermal expansion of the arm, wear and tear on actuators, or subtle variations in payload mass. These residuals can cause the arm's end-effector to deviate from its commanded trajectory. An adaptive controller can be employed to compensate for these changes. If a learned model (e.g., an FNN or RNN) has captured the relationship between operating conditions (e.g., arm configuration, speed, temperature) and the residual errors, this model can provide valuable information for adaptation.

An adaptive controller could, for instance, use the predicted residual to adjust the proportional, integral, and derivative (PID) gains of its joint controllers. If the learned residual model predicts that, for a certain arm configuration and movement, a particular type of residual error is likely, the controller can proactively modify its gains to better counteract it. For instance, if it predicts a tendency for overshoot due to residual flexibility, it might slightly increase damping in the controller. Moreover, if the residual model is capable of learning how these residuals evolve over time, an adaptive controller could exploit this to anticipate and compensate for drifting behavior. This contrasts with traditional adaptive controllers that might slowly adjust gains based on accumulated tracking errors, potentially allowing significant deviations to occur before correction. By using the learned residual model, the adaptation can be more targeted and rapid, leading to improved tracking accuracy and reduced settling times, which are critical for high-performance robotic applications.

The integration of learned residual dynamics can also extend to **learning-based predictive control** strategies, such as Model Predictive Control (MPC). In MPC, a model of the system is used to predict future behavior over a finite horizon, and an optimization problem is solved to determine the optimal control sequence. The accuracy of these predictions is paramount.

If a learned residual model is incorporated into the MPC framework, the predictions become significantly more faithful. The MPC can then optimize control actions not just based on the nominal system dynamics but also by anticipating the influence of learned residuals. For example, if the learned residual model predicts a specific disturbance or deviation at a future time step, the MPC can factor this into its optimization and compute a control input that mitigates its impact.

Consider the process control of a complex chemical reactor. The nominal model might describe the primary reaction kinetics, heat transfer, and fluid flow. However, residuals can arise from complex, time-varying catalyst deactivation, unpredictable mixing patterns, or sensor drift. An

MPC framework enhanced with a learned residual model could predict these deviations. If the learned model anticipates a drop in reaction rate due to catalyst deactivation at a certain point in the future, the MPC can adjust feed rates, temperature, or pressure proactively to maintain the desired product yield and quality. This predictive capability, informed by the learned residual dynamics, allows the MPC to achieve superior performance compared to an MPC relying solely on the nominal model, especially in the presence of unmodeled nonlinearities and disturbances. The optimization problem within MPC can also be designed to explicitly penalize deviations that are predicted by the residual model, further ensuring that the control actions are tailored to counteract these learned unmodeled effects.

The practical implications of effectively integrating learned residual dynamics are substantial and span various engineering domains. In **autonomous systems**, such as self-driving vehicles or drones, accurate modeling of residual forces (e.g., wind, aerodynamic effects, tire-road interactions) is crucial for safe and efficient navigation. By incorporating learned residuals into their control systems, these vehicles can achieve better tracking of desired trajectories, exhibit smoother responses to external disturbances, and operate more reliably in a wider range of environmental conditions. For example, a vehicle's control system might use a learned model to predict residual aerodynamic drag variations due to changing wind conditions or road surface friction, and adjust throttle and steering commands to maintain speed and lane position with increased precision.

In

robotics, learned residual dynamics can dramatically improve the precision and dexterity of manipulators. Residual vibrations, friction nonlinearities, or joint flexibility are common challenges. By learning these effects, controllers can achieve faster settling times, reduce endpoint errors, and enable more delicate tasks. For instance, in semiconductor manufacturing, where nanometer-level precision is required, learned residual models of robotic arms can compensate for micro-vibrations and thermal drifts, ensuring that components are placed with exquisite accuracy.

For
energy systems, as highlighted with power grid frequency regulation, learned residuals can lead to more stable and efficient operation. This extends to other areas like renewable energy integration, where forecasting residual power output from wind or solar farms due to complex atmospheric interactions can improve grid balancing and reduce reliance on fossil fuel backup. Similarly, optimizing the operation of industrial processes, such as those in chemical plants or manufacturing lines, can benefit immensely. Learned residuals in flow rates, temperature profiles, or reaction kinetics can be used to proactively adjust parameters, leading to higher yields, reduced waste, and improved product quality.

Finally, the advancement of learned residual models and their integration into control design also has implications for
system identification and understanding. By analyzing the predictions and uncertainties of these learned models, engineers and scientists can gain deeper insights into the underlying physics and emergent behaviors of complex systems. This knowledge can, in turn, inform the development of more accurate first-principles models or guide the design of improved sensors and actuators, creating a virtuous cycle of model improvement and control enhancement. The journey from recognizing unmodeled dynamics to actively using data-driven models to control them is a testament to the evolving synergy between machine learning and control theory.

Chapter 5: Reinforcement Learning for Control Loops

In the realm of control systems, particularly when dealing with complex, dynamic environments, the pursuit of optimal control strategies has long been a central theme. While traditional methods like PID control, optimal control, and robust control have achieved remarkable success, they often rely on accurate analytical models of the system dynamics. However, as we've explored, real-world systems are rarely perfectly described by such models. Unmodeled dynamics, disturbances, and uncertainties can significantly degrade performance. This is where the principles of Reinforcement Learning (RL) offer a powerful and complementary approach. RL provides a framework for an agent to learn how to behave in an environment so as to maximize some notion of cumulative reward. It is an area of machine learning concerned with how intelligent agents ought to take actions in an environment to maximize the notion of cumulative reward. This paradigm shifts the focus from explicitly designing a controller based on a known model to learning a control policy through experience.

At its core, Reinforcement Learning is about learning through interaction and feedback. Imagine a simple scenario: a child learning to ride a bicycle. The child (the agent) tries to pedal and steer (actions) in the world (the environment). Initially, their movements are clumsy, leading to wobbles and perhaps a fall (negative reward or penalty). Through these experiences, the child gradually learns which actions lead to maintaining balance and forward motion (positive reward) and which lead to instability. Over time, they develop a sophisticated strategy, a policy, for riding the bicycle effectively. This trial-and-error process, guided by feedback in the form of success or failure, is the essence of RL.

Let's formalize these concepts. In RL, we have an **agent**, which is the learner or decision-maker. This agent interacts with an **environment**, which is everything external to the agent. At each discrete time step, the agent perceives the current **state** of the environment. The state (st) *is a representation of the environment at a particular moment in time. Based on this state, the agent chooses an* **action** (at) to perform. This action influences the environment, causing it to transition to a new state ($s{t+1}$). *Crucially, after taking an action, the agent also receives a* **reward** ($r{t+1}$), which is a scalar feedback signal indicating how good or bad the action was in that state. The agent's objective is to learn a **policy** (π), which is a mapping from states to actions, that maximizes the expected cumulative reward over time. This cumulative reward is often referred to as the return, and it's typically discounted, meaning that immediate rewards are valued more highly than future rewards. The discount factor, denoted by γ (where $0 \le \gamma < 1$), determines how much future rewards are down-weighted. The goal is to find a policy $\pi^$ that maximizes the expected discounted return: $E\left[\sum{t=0}^{\infty} \gamma^t R{t+1} | S_0 = s, \pi\right]$.

Consider a simple control problem: a robotic arm tasked with picking up a specific object from a table. The state might include the joint angles of the arm, the position and orientation of its end-effector, and perhaps the visual input from a camera identifying the object. The available actions could be controlling the torque or velocity of each joint. When the arm attempts to grasp the object, it receives a reward. If it successfully picks up the object, the reward might be positive and significant. If it misses, knocks the object over, or collides with something, the reward would be negative. Through repeated attempts, the robotic arm's control system, acting as the RL agent, learns a policy that dictates how to move its joints in response to the current state to maximize the chances of a successful pick-up.

In the context of control loops, the environment is the physical system we are trying to control. The state might be the measured outputs of the system, such as temperature, pressure, position, or velocity. The actions are the control signals that we can apply to the system, like adjusting a valve, applying a voltage, or commanding a motor. The reward signal would be designed to reflect the desired performance objectives. For instance, if the goal is to maintain a setpoint temperature, a positive reward could be given when the temperature is close to the setpoint, and a negative reward when it deviates. The RL agent would then learn a policy that maps the measured system states to control actions that keep the temperature near the desired value.

The power of RL lies in its ability to learn optimal or near-optimal control policies even when the underlying system dynamics are unknown or too complex to model accurately. This is in stark contrast to traditional control methods that require a precise mathematical model. In RL, the "model" is implicitly learned through experience. The agent explores the state-action space, observes the consequences of its actions (state transitions and rewards), and gradually refines its policy to favor actions that lead to higher cumulative rewards. This makes RL particularly well-suited for problems where analytical modeling is difficult or impossible, such as in robotics, autonomous driving, game playing, and complex industrial processes.

Let's delve deeper into the core components of the RL framework.

The Agent: The agent is the entity that learns and makes decisions. It can be a software program, a robot, or any system that interacts with an environment. The agent's goal is to learn a policy that maximizes its long-term cumulative reward.

The Environment: The environment is everything outside the agent. It's the system or world with which the agent interacts. The environment receives actions from the agent and, in return, provides the agent with the next state and a reward. The environment can be static or dynamic, deterministic or stochastic. In control systems, the physical plant (e.g., a motor, a chemical reactor, a drone) is typically considered the environment.

The State (s): The state is a description of the current situation of the environment. It's the information available to the agent at a given time step to make decisions. A good state representation should capture all relevant information needed to predict future outcomes. For example, in controlling a self-driving car, the state might include the car's position, velocity, the positions and velocities of other vehicles, traffic light status, and road curvature. In a simpler example, like controlling a thermostat to maintain room temperature, the state could simply be the current room temperature. However, for more complex systems, the state can be high-dimensional and may involve time-series data.

The Action (a): An action is a decision made by the agent. It's what the agent does to influence the environment. The set of possible actions can be discrete (e.g., "turn left," "turn right," "apply brake") or continuous (e.g., a specific throttle percentage, a joint torque value). The choice of actions directly impacts the system's behavior and the subsequent rewards. In our robotic arm example, actions might be the specific voltages applied to the motors of each joint.

The Reward (r): The reward is a scalar feedback signal that the environment provides to the agent after it takes an action. It indicates the immediate desirability of the action taken in the given state. Rewards can be positive (encouraging certain behaviors) or negative (discouraging others). Designing an appropriate reward function is a critical aspect of applying RL, as it directly shapes the learned policy. For instance, in training a robot to walk, a reward might be given for forward progress and maintaining balance, while a penalty is incurred for falling.

The Policy (π): The policy is the agent's strategy or behavior. It defines how the agent chooses actions based on the current state. A policy can be deterministic, mapping each state to a single action, or stochastic, mapping each state to a probability distribution over actions. The goal of RL is to find an optimal policy, $\pi^$, which maximizes the expected cumulative reward. Mathematically, a policy is often represented as $\pi(a|s)$, the probability of taking action a in state s.

The Value Function: While the policy tells us what action to take, value functions help us evaluate how good a state or a state-action pair is.
State-Value Function ($V^\pi(s)$): This function estimates the expected cumulative reward starting from state s and following policy π. It answers the question: "How good is it to be in state s if I follow policy π from now on?"
Action-Value Function ($Q^\pi(s, a)$): This function estimates the expected cumulative reward starting from state s, taking action a, and then following policy π thereafter. It answers the question: "How good is it to take action a in state s and then follow policy π?" The Q-function is particularly useful because if we know the optimal Q-function, $Q^(s, a)$, we can easily derive the optimal policy by

simply choosing the action a that maximizes $Q^(s, a)$ for any given state s.

The fundamental learning process in RL involves an agent interacting with its environment over a sequence of time steps. At each step t:

1. The agent observes the current state S_t.
2. Based on its current policy π, the agent selects an action A_t.
3. The agent performs action A_t.
4. The environment transitions to a new state $S{t+1}$ *and provides a reward* $R{t+1}$ to the agent.
5. The agent uses this information ($St, At, R{t+1}, S{t+1}$) to update its policy or value functions, aiming to improve its future decision-making.

This cycle continues, allowing the agent to gather experience and refine its strategy. The exploration-exploitation trade-off is a crucial challenge in RL. The agent needs to
explore the environment to discover potentially better actions and states, but it also needs to **exploit** its current knowledge to take actions that are known to yield high rewards. Strategies like ϵ-greedy exploration (where the agent chooses a random action with probability ϵ and the best-known action otherwise) are commonly used to balance this trade-off.

To illustrate further, consider a simple grid world problem. Imagine a 3x3 grid. The agent starts at a certain cell, and its goal is to reach a target cell. Some cells might be obstacles, and others might be terminal states with rewards.

States: The individual cells in the grid. For a 3x3 grid, there are 9 states.
Actions: Move up, down, left, right.
Environment: The grid itself, including the rules for movement (e.g., cannot move into walls, terminal states).

Reward: A positive reward for reaching the target cell, a negative reward for hitting an obstacle or falling into a pit, and perhaps a small negative reward for each step taken to encourage efficiency.
Policy: A mapping from each cell (state) to a direction (action).

An RL agent would start with a random policy. It would move around the grid, receive rewards, and update its policy. For instance, if it repeatedly moves into a wall and receives a penalty, it will learn to avoid actions that lead to walls from certain states. If it finds a path to the target cell that yields a positive reward, it will reinforce the actions along that path. Over many episodes (trials), the agent would converge to a policy that reliably leads to the target cell while avoiding negative consequences.

In the context of control systems, the states are usually continuous and high-dimensional. For example, controlling a quadcopter involves states like its position, velocity, orientation, and angular rates. The actions are the control inputs to the motors. The reward function would need to be carefully designed to encourage stable flight, accurate trajectory tracking, and efficient energy consumption. Designing such a reward function is often an iterative process.

The framework of Markov Decision Processes (MDPs) is fundamental to formalizing RL problems. An MDP is defined by a tuple (S, A, P, R, γ), where:

S is the set of all possible states.
A is the set of all possible actions.
$P(s'|s, a)$ is the transition probability function, representing the probability of transitioning to state s' from state s after taking action a. This embodies the dynamics of the environment.

$R(s, a, s')$ is the reward function, specifying the reward received when transitioning from s to s' via action a. Often, this is simplified to $R(s, a)$ or $R(s)$.
γ is the discount factor, $0 \le \gamma < 1$.

Many real-world environments are not fully observable, meaning the agent doesn't have complete information about the state. These are modeled as Partially Observable Markov Decision Processes (POMDPs). In such cases, the agent might maintain a belief state, which is a probability distribution over possible states, based on the history of observations and actions. However, for many control applications, it's often possible to design a state representation that is sufficiently informative, allowing the problem to be treated as an MDP.

The ultimate goal in RL is to find the optimal policy $\pi^
*$, which maximizes the expected discounted cumulative reward from any starting state. This involves learning either the optimal value function ($V^*(s)$ or $Q^*(s, a)$) or directly learning the optimal policy ($\pi^*(a|s)$). Algorithms like Q-learning, SARSA, and Policy Gradients are standard techniques used to achieve this.

For instance, Q-learning is a model-free, off-policy algorithm that learns the optimal action-value function $Q^(s, a)$. It updates its estimate of $Q(s, a)$ based on observed transitions:

$Q(S*t, A*t) \leftarrow Q(S*t, A*t) + \alpha \left[R*{t+1} + \gamma \max*{a'} Q(S*{t+1}, a') - Q(S*t, A_t) \right]$
Here, α is the learning rate, controlling the step size of the update. The term $R*{t+1} + \gamma \max*{a'} Q(S*{t+1}, a')$ is the "target" value, representing the estimated optimal value achievable from the next state $S*{t+1}$. The difference between this target and the

current estimate $Q(St, At)$ is the temporal difference (TD) error, which drives the learning.

Policy gradient methods, on the other hand, directly learn the policy parameters. They adjust the policy parameters in the direction that increases the expected reward. These methods are often more suitable for continuous action spaces, which are common in control problems.

The application of RL to control loops, especially when combined with learned residual dynamics, opens up exciting possibilities for creating more intelligent, adaptive, and high-performing systems. By framing the control problem as a learning task, we can leverage the agent's ability to discover effective strategies through experience, without requiring a perfect prior model of the system. This is particularly valuable when dealing with the complexities and uncertainties that are inherent in many real-world control applications. The subsequent sections will explore how these RL principles can be concretely applied and integrated with residual learning techniques to enhance control performance.

The foundation upon which most reinforcement learning algorithms are built is the mathematical framework known as a Markov Decision Process (MDP). Understanding MDPs is not merely an academic exercise; it is essential for precisely defining the problem we aim to solve within a control loop context. It provides the language and structure to formalize the sequential decision-making problem that our learning agent faces within the dynamic environment of the control system. Without this formalization, designing effective learning strategies and evaluating their performance would be akin to navigating without a map or compass.

At its core, an MDP is characterized by a set of key components. First, we have the

state space, denoted by S. This is the set of all possible configurations or observations of the environment at any given time. For a control system, the state might encompass a wide range of variables. Consider a manufacturing plant where we are controlling a robotic arm for assembly. The state could include the position and orientation of the arm's end-effector, the current status of the workpiece it is handling, the joint angles of the robot, and perhaps even sensor readings like force or vision data that provide information about the object being manipulated. In a chemical process control scenario, states might include temperature, pressure, flow rates, and reactant concentrations within a reactor. The crucial characteristic here is that the state should ideally capture all relevant information that the agent needs to make an informed decision. The fidelity and completeness of the state representation directly impact the agent's ability to learn an effective policy. If a critical piece of information is omitted from the state, the agent might make suboptimal or even dangerous decisions because it lacks the full picture.

Second, we have the
action space, denoted by A. This is the set of all possible decisions or control signals that the agent can exert on the environment. For the robotic arm, actions might be the continuous torque commands applied to each of its joints. For a thermostat controlling room temperature, actions could be discrete choices like "increase heat by 1 degree," "decrease heat by 1 degree," or "do nothing." In a chemical plant, actions might correspond to adjusting the setpoints of flow controllers, opening or closing valves, or changing the speed of pumps. The nature of the action space—whether it is discrete or continuous—significantly influences the choice of RL algorithms. Algorithms designed for discrete action spaces might not directly apply to continuous control problems without modifications, and vice versa.

The third critical component is the

transition probability function, denoted by $P(s'|s, a)$. This function quantifies the probabilistic nature of the environment's dynamics. It specifies the probability of transitioning to a new state s' from the current state s after the agent takes action a. This is where the concept of a "model" of the environment, even if implicitly learned, comes into play. In many real-world control systems, especially those involving complex physical interactions, the transitions are not deterministic. For example, if a robot arm applies a certain force to move an object, the exact final position might be influenced by factors like friction, vibrations, or slight inaccuracies in the force sensor. Thus, the transition probability function captures this inherent uncertainty. If $P(s'|s, a)$ is known, the MDP is considered "model-based." If it is unknown and must be learned through interaction, the problem becomes "model-free," which is where most of reinforcement learning's power lies in practice. When the environment is deterministic, $P(s'|s, a)$ would be 1 for a single s' and 0 for all others, given (s, a).

The fourth component is the
reward function, denoted by $R(s, a, s')$. This function assigns a scalar value, the reward, to each transition. It is the primary mechanism by which we communicate our control objectives to the RL agent. The reward function encodes what we want the agent to achieve. A positive reward signifies a desirable outcome, encouraging the agent to repeat the actions that led to it. Conversely, a negative reward (often called a penalty) signifies an undesirable outcome, discouraging such actions. In our manufacturing example, a positive reward might be given when the robotic arm successfully places a component in the correct position, while a negative reward would be associated with dropping the component, colliding with other machinery, or taking too long to complete the task. Designing an effective reward function is often one of the most challenging and crucial aspects of applying RL. A poorly designed reward function can lead to unintended behaviors, where the agent finds ways to maximize reward by exploiting loopholes in the

objective rather than achieving the desired overall goal. For example, if the goal is to reach a target quickly, a reward function that solely rewards speed might lead the agent to take reckless actions that damage the system. Therefore, the reward function must be carefully crafted to align with the true, often multi-faceted, control objectives. It's also common to simplify the reward function notation to $R(s, a)$, implying the reward depends only on the state and the action taken, or even $R(s)$, where the reward is associated with entering a particular state.

Finally, an MDP includes a
discount factor, γ, where $0 \le \gamma < 1$. This factor plays a pivotal role in how the agent values future rewards compared to immediate ones. A discount factor close to 1 means the agent is far-sighted, valuing future rewards almost as much as current ones. A discount factor closer to 0 means the agent is short-sighted, prioritizing immediate rewards above all else. In control systems, a discount factor is almost always employed. This is because real-world systems can be infinite or very long-lived, and summing an infinite series of rewards without discounting could lead to infinite total reward, making it impossible to find an optimal policy. Discounting ensures that the total expected reward remains finite and also implicitly favors actions that lead to quicker achievement of goals. For example, in controlling a robot to navigate a maze, if the robot can reach the exit in 10 steps with a reward of 100, or in 100 steps with a reward of 100, a high discount factor would likely make the shorter path more attractive.

The defining characteristic that makes a process a Markov Decision Process is the
Markov property. This property states that the future state and reward depend only on the current state and the action taken, and not on the entire history of states and actions that preceded it. Mathematically, this means:

$P(s{t+1}, r{t+1} | st, at, s{t-1}, a{t-1}, \dots, s0, a0) = P(s{t+1}, r{t+1} | st, at)$
This is a fundamental simplification that makes the problem tractable. It implies that if we know the current state and the action we are about to take, all the information needed to predict the future outcome is contained within that state-action pair. The past is "forgotten" in the sense that it does not provide any additional predictive power beyond what the current state already encapsulates. For instance, if we are controlling a robot arm and its current position and velocity are known, it doesn't matter *how* it arrived at that position and velocity; the subsequent movement will depend only on these current kinematic and dynamic parameters and the new control commands.

In practical control applications, the Markov property is often an assumption that needs to be carefully considered. If the system's dynamics are truly influenced by past events that are not reflected in the current state representation, then the system is not an MDP. For example, if a chemical reactor's catalytic activity degrades over time due to prolonged exposure to certain chemicals, and this degradation is not explicitly included in the state variables (e.g., as a "catalyst age" variable), then the future behavior (reaction rates) would depend on the history of chemical exposures, violating the Markov property. In such cases, one might need to augment the state with historical information or consider more advanced frameworks like Partially Observable Markov Decision Processes (POMDPs), where the agent operates with incomplete state information. However, for many control problems, a carefully designed state representation can often make the MDP assumption a reasonable approximation.

The ultimate goal when working with an MDP is to find an **optimal policy**, denoted by $\pi^$. *A policy, $\pi(a|s)$, is a mapping that tells the agent what action a to take when it is in state s. This mapping*

can be deterministic (e.g., "if in state s_1, always take action a_1") or stochastic (e.g., "if in state s_1, take action a_1 with probability 0.7 and action a_2 with probability 0.3"). The optimal policy π^* is the one that maximizes the expected cumulative discounted reward from any starting state. This expected cumulative reward is often referred to as the **return**, G_t, starting from time step t:
$G_t = R_{t+1} + \gamma R_{t+2} + \gamma^2 R_{t+3} + \dots = \sum_{k=0}^{\infty} \gamma^k R_{t+k+1}$

The expected return for a given policy π starting from state s is denoted by $V^\pi(s)$, the
state-value function:
$V^\pi(s) = E_\pi[G_t \mid S_t = s] = E_\pi\left[\sum_{k=0}^{\infty} \gamma^k R_{t+k+1} \mid S_t = s\right]$
Similarly, the **action-value function**, denoted by $Q^\pi(s, a)$, represents the expected return starting from state s, taking action a, and then following policy π thereafter:
$Q^\pi(s, a) = E_\pi[G_t \mid S_t = s, A_t = a] = E_\pi\left[\sum_{k=0}^{\infty} \gamma^k R_{t+k+1} \mid S_t = s, A_t = a\right]$

The relationship between the state-value function and the action-value function is:

$V^\pi(s) = \sum_{a \in A} \pi(a|s) Q^\pi(s, a)$
And the action-value function can be expressed recursively in terms of the expected next state and reward:
$Q^\pi(s, a) = E[R_{t+1} + \gamma V^\pi(S_{t+1}) \mid S_t = s, A_t = a]$
$Q^\pi(s, a) = \sum_{s' \in S} P(s'|s, a) [R(s, a, s') + \gamma V^\pi(s')]$

The Bellman equations provide a powerful recursive relationship for these value functions. The Bellman equation for V^π is:

$V^\pi(s) = \sum_{a \in A} \pi(a|s) \sum_{s' \in S} P(s'|s, a) [R(s, a, s') + \gamma V^\pi(s')]$
And for Q^π:
$Q^\pi(s, a) = \sum_{s' \in S} P(s'|s, a) [R(s, a, s') + \gamma \sum_{a' \in A} \pi(a'|s') Q^\pi(s', a')]$

These equations are fundamental because they allow us to express the value of being in a state (or taking an action in a state) in terms of the values of future states. This recursive structure is what allows RL algorithms to propagate reward information backward through time and learn optimal strategies.

The optimal state-value function, $V^*(s)$, and the optimal action-value function, $Q^*(s, a)$, satisfy similar Bellman equations, but with maximization over actions:
$V^*(s) = \max_{a \in A} Q^*(s, a)$
$Q^*(s, a) = \sum_{s' \in S} P(s'|s, a) [R(s, a, s') + \gamma V^*(s')]$

The optimal policy π^* can be derived directly from the optimal action-value function $Q^*(s, a)$:
$\pi^*(a|s) = \begin{cases} 1 & \text{if } a = \arg\max_{a'} Q^*(s, a') \\ 0 & \text{otherwise} \end{cases}$
(for deterministic policies)

Thus, a significant portion of reinforcement learning research focuses on how to estimate these value functions, particularly $Q^*(s, a)$, or how to learn the policy $\pi^*(a|s)$ directly, without necessarily computing the full value functions explicitly. This is where algorithms like Q-learning, SARSA, and various policy gradient methods come into play. They are all designed to solve the MDP by finding the optimal policy, effectively navigating the complexities of sequential decision-

making in uncertain environments, a problem deeply relevant to enhancing the performance and adaptability of control loops in fields such as advanced manufacturing, robotics, and autonomous systems. The formalization provided by MDPs ensures that our learning agent has a well-defined objective and a clear understanding of its operational context.
Value-based reinforcement learning algorithms represent a cornerstone in the field, focusing on the estimation of optimal value functions. The core idea is to determine the "goodness" of being in a particular state, or the "goodness" of taking a specific action in a particular state. This goodness is quantified by the expected cumulative future reward, discounted over time. By learning these value functions, the agent can then derive an optimal policy, which dictates the best action to take in any given state to maximize its long-term reward. This approach is particularly intuitive for control problems where understanding the long-term consequences of actions is paramount.

Two seminal algorithms that exemplify the value-based approach are Q-learning and SARSA (State-Action-Reward-State-Action). Both algorithms are designed to learn the optimal action-value function, denoted as $Q^(s, a)$, which represents the maximum expected future discounted reward an agent can receive starting from state s, taking action a, and then following the optimal policy thereafter. The distinction between them lies primarily in how they update their estimates and the nature of the policy they implicitly follow during learning.

Let's delve into Q-learning. Q-learning is an
off-policy temporal difference (TD) learning algorithm. This means it learns the value of the optimal policy independently of the policy that the agent is currently following to explore the environment. The agent might be acting randomly or following a suboptimal policy to gather data, but

Q-learning aims to converge to the true optimal $Q^$ function. The update rule for Q-learning is as follows:

$Q(s, a) \leftarrow Q(s, a) + \alpha \left[r + \gamma \max_{a'} Q(s', a') - Q(s, a) \right]$

Here:

$Q(s, a)$ is the current estimate of the action-value function for state s and action a.
α is the learning rate, a value between 0 and 1, determining how much new information overrides old information. A smaller α means slower learning but potentially more stable convergence.
r is the immediate reward received after taking action a in state s and transitioning to state s'.
γ is the discount factor, as previously discussed, which weighs the importance of future rewards.
s' is the next state observed after taking action a in state s.
$\max_{a'} Q(s', a')$ represents the maximum expected future reward from the next state s', considering all possible actions a' that can be taken from s'. This is the crucial part that makes Q-learning off-policy. It assumes that from state s', the agent will take the action that yields the highest Q-value, which is indicative of the optimal policy.

The term $\left[r + \gamma \max
*{a'} Q(s', a') - Q(s, a) \right]$ is the TD error. It represents the difference between the "target" value ($r + \gamma \max*{a'} Q(s', a')$) and the current estimate $Q(s, a)$. The target value is an estimate of the true value of $Q(s, a)$, derived from the immediate reward and the estimated value of the *best* possible action in the next state. The learning rate α controls how much this TD error is used to update the current estimate.

Consider an example of optimizing traffic light control. Let's assume a simplified intersection with a few approach lanes and discrete actions for the traffic lights (e.g., "go green for North-South," "go green for East-West"). The state could be defined by the number of cars waiting in each lane and the current light phase. The reward could be negative of the total waiting time of all cars, or proportional to the number of cars that pass through the intersection.

Suppose the current state s represents a situation where there are many cars waiting on the North-South road and few on the East-West road, and the current action a is "keep North-South green." The agent receives a reward r (e.g., negative of cars waiting). It then observes the next state s'. In Q-learning, to update $Q(s, a)$, the agent looks at all possible actions a' in state s'. Let's say the possible actions in s' are "switch to East-West green" ($a'
*1$) and "keep North-South green" ($a'*2$). The agent would then estimate the value of being in state s' by taking the maximum of $Q(s', a'*1)$ and $Q(s', a'*2)$. This maximum value is then used as part of the target to update $Q(s, a)$. Even if the agent is currently following a policy that might switch to East-West green in state s', the Q-learning update will use the *best possible* action's value from s' for its update. This allows Q-learning to learn the optimal policy directly, irrespective of the exploration policy.

Now let's turn to SARSA. SARSA is an
on-policy TD control algorithm. Unlike Q-learning, SARSA learns the value of the policy that the agent is *currently following.* This means that the updates are based on the action actually taken in the next state, rather than the best possible action. The name SARSA comes from the tuple of information used in its update rule: State, Action, Reward, State', Action'.

The update rule for SARSA is:

$Q(s, a) \leftarrow Q(s, a) + \alpha \left[r + \gamma Q(s', a') - Q(s, a) \right]$

The key difference from Q-learning lies in the term $Q(s', a')$, where a' is the
actual action taken by the agent in state s' according to its current policy π. The policy π used for exploration is typically an ϵ-greedy policy, where with probability ϵ the agent chooses a random action (exploration) and with probability $1-\epsilon$ it chooses the action with the highest Q-value (exploitation).

Continuing the traffic light example with SARSA: If the agent is in state s, takes action a (e.g., "keep North-South green"), receives reward r, and transitions to state s', SARSA will then choose an action a' from state s' based on its current policy π. For instance, if the policy is ϵ-greedy, the agent might choose to
continue with "North-South green" in state s' (if it's the greedy action or chosen by chance) or it might switch to "East-West green" (either greedily or by chance). Whatever action a' is chosen in s' according to the *current policy*, that specific $Q(s', a')$ value is used in the SARSA update for $Q(s, a)$.

The implication of this difference is significant. Q-learning, by using $\max_{a'} Q(s', a')$, is inherently optimistic and learns the optimal policy regardless of the exploration strategy. SARSA, on the other hand, learns the value of the policy being followed, including its exploration steps. If the exploration policy is suboptimal (e.g., frequently takes actions that lead to poor outcomes), SARSA will converge to the value function of that suboptimal policy. However, if the exploration probability ϵ is gradually decreased to zero over time (a process called annealing), SARSA can also converge to the optimal policy. SARSA is generally considered safer for real-world applications, especially when exploration can lead to dangerous states, because it accounts for the actual consequences of the exploration policy. For example, in a robotic control scenario, if exploring a new action might lead to a collision, SARSA would learn to avoid such sequences of actions and states, whereas Q-learning might still learn the optimal path assuming the collision never happens or is immediately corrected by some external force.

Both Q-learning and SARSA operate by iteratively updating their Q-value estimates. Initially, the Q-values are often initialized arbitrarily (e.g., to zero) or with small random values. Through repeated interactions with the environment, the agent experiences transitions (s, a, r, s', a') (for SARSA) or (s, a, r, s') (for Q-learning) and uses these experiences to refine its Q-value estimates. Over many episodes or steps, these estimates are expected to converge to the true Q-values, $Q^(s, a)$.

The convergence properties of Q-learning and SARSA depend on several factors, including the learning rate α, the discount factor γ, the exploration strategy, and the nature of the state and action spaces. For discrete and finite MDPs, under certain conditions (e.g., α is annealed appropriately, and all state-action pairs are visited infinitely often), both algorithms are guaranteed to converge to their respective optimal value functions.

A key aspect of these value-based methods is their reliance on discrete state and action spaces for tabular implementations. When the state space is continuous or very large, representing $Q(s, a)$ directly in a table becomes infeasible due to memory limitations and the curse of dimensionality. In such cases, function approximation techniques, such as neural networks, are employed to estimate the Q-values, leading to algorithms like Deep Q-Networks (DQN). However, for problems with naturally discrete and manageable state-action spaces, tabular Q-learning and SARSA are powerful and interpretable tools.

Let's re-examine the traffic light control example to illustrate the practical considerations and advantages of value-based methods. Consider an intersection with two approaches (North-South and East-West) and two possible phases: Phase 1 (North-South green) and Phase 2 (East-West green).

The state s can be represented by a tuple (n, e), where n is the number of cars waiting on the North-South approach and e is the number of cars waiting on the East-West approach.
The actions a are the phases: $a*1$ (Phase 1) and $a*2$ (Phase 2).
The reward r can be defined as the negative of the total number of cars waiting in the intersection after the lights have been green for a certain duration, or the negative of the sum of waiting times.
Suppose a standard traffic light cycle is 60 seconds for each phase. A simple MDP formulation might discretize time into 5-second intervals. At each interval, the agent observes the state (n, e), chooses an action (which phase to be green), and receives a reward. The transition to the next state depends on the current state, the chosen action, and the arrival of new cars.

Q-learning in Traffic Lights:
Let's say the agent has been running Q-learning for a while, and its Q-table has some entries.

Current state $s = (10, 2)$. Current action $a = a_1$ (North-South green). After 5 seconds, 3 more cars arrive on North-South. Reward $r = -(10+3+2) = -15$ (assuming reward is total waiting cars).
The new state is $s' = (13, 2)$.
Now, for the Q-learning update for $Q(s, a)$, we need $\max*{a'} Q(s', a')$. Suppose the possible actions in s' are $a'*1$ (N-S green) and a'_2 (E-W green).
Let's assume the agent has learned:
$Q(s'=(13,2), a'_1=\text{N-S green}) = 50$
$Q(s'=(13,2), a'_2=\text{E-W green}) = 70$
Then $\max_{a'} Q(s', a') = 70$.
The Q-learning update would be:
$Q(10, 2; a*1) \leftarrow Q(10, 2; a*1) + \alpha [-15 + \gamma \times 70 - Q(10, 2; a_1)]$

SARSA in Traffic Lights:
Using the same scenario: current state $s = (10, 2)$, action $a = a_1$ (N-S green), reward $r = -15$, next state $s' = (13, 2)$.
Now, SARSA needs to determine the next action a' from s' based on its current policy. Let's assume SARSA uses an ϵ-greedy policy with $\epsilon = 0.1$.
Suppose for state $s'=(13, 2)$, the Q-values are $Q(s', a'*1) = 50$ and $Q(s', a'*2) = 70$.
With probability $1-\epsilon = 0.9$, SARSA chooses the greedy action a'_2 (E-W green), since $70 > 50$.
With probability $\epsilon = 0.1$, SARSA chooses a random action, say a'_1 (N-S green).
Let's assume in this instance, SARSA chooses a'_2 (E-W green).
Then the SARSA update for $Q(s, a)$ uses $Q(s', a'_2)$:
$Q(10, 2; a*1) \leftarrow Q(10, 2; a*1) + \alpha [-15 + \gamma \times Q(s'=(13,2), a'*2=\text{E-W green}) - Q(10, 2; a*1)]$

$Q(10, 2; a_1) \leftarrow Q(10, 2; a_1) + \alpha [-15 + \gamma \times 70 - Q(10, 2; a_1)]$

Notice that in this particular step, both Q-learning and SARSA used the value 70 in their update. However, the difference becomes apparent if SARSA had chosen a'_1 (N-S green) from s'. In that case, the update would have used $Q(s', a'_1)=50$:
$Q(10, 2; a_1) \leftarrow Q(10, 2; a_1) + \alpha [-15 + \gamma \times 50 - Q(10, 2; a_1)]$
This would lead to a more conservative update, reflecting the actual (potentially suboptimal) action taken.

The choice between Q-learning and SARSA often depends on the specific requirements of the control system. If the primary goal is to find the absolute best control strategy, even if it requires aggressive exploration, Q-learning might be preferred. However, if safety and stability during learning are critical, and the system cannot tolerate potentially high penalties during exploration, SARSA offers a more robust approach by learning the value of the policy that is actually being executed.

The effectiveness of these algorithms hinges on the quality of the state representation and the reward function. A well-designed state space should capture all relevant information about the environment's dynamics. A poorly chosen state space might lead to the Markov property being violated, or the learning problem becoming intractable. Similarly, the reward function must accurately reflect the control objectives. Misaligned reward functions can lead to agents learning undesirable behaviors, a phenomenon known as "reward hacking." For instance, if a traffic light controller is rewarded solely for minimizing the number of cars currently waiting at any instant, it might oscillate between phases rapidly, keeping waiting times low for short periods but causing overall system inefficiency and driver frustration. A better reward function would consider average waiting times, throughput, or a combination of factors over a longer horizon.

Moreover, the initialization of the Q-table plays a role, especially in smaller problems or during the initial stages of learning. Initializing all Q-values to zero is a common practice. However, if the goal is to encourage exploration, or if there are known initial "good" policies, these can be incorporated into the initialization. For instance, one could initialize Q-values based on a simple heuristic or a pre-existing control system's performance.

The learning rate α is another hyperparameter that significantly impacts convergence. A constant α that is too high can cause oscillations and prevent convergence. Conversely, a constant α that is too low will lead to very slow learning. A common strategy is to use a decaying learning rate, where α starts at a relatively high value and gradually decreases over time, allowing for rapid initial learning followed by fine-tuning. For example, $\alpha
t = \frac{1}{t}$ or $\alphat = \alpha_0 e^{-\beta t}$.

The discount factor γ determines the agent's horizon. A γ close to 0 makes the agent myopic, focusing on immediate rewards, while a γ close to 1 makes it far-sighted, considering long-term consequences. In many control problems, a high γ is desirable to encourage sustained performance and long-term stability. However, a γ too close to 1 can sometimes make learning unstable, especially in conjunction with large state spaces or function approximation.

The exploration strategy is paramount for ensuring that the agent discovers good policies. While ϵ-greedy is simple and effective, other strategies exist, such as Boltzmann exploration (soft-max selection based on Q-values) or Upper Confidence Bound (UCB) exploration, which balance exploration and exploitation more sophisticatedly. For traffic control, an ϵ-greedy strategy might translate to: with 90% probability, choose the action (phase) that the Q-table currently suggests is best for the given traffic conditions; with 10% probability, randomly pick either phase. This ensures that even if the N-S phase appears optimal most of the time, the system will still occasionally try the E-W phase to see if it yields better long-term results, especially when traffic patterns change.

Value-based methods like Q-learning and SARSA provide a robust framework for learning optimal control policies in discrete domains. Their core strength lies in systematically improving estimates of state-action values, which are then used to guide decision-making. By understanding the Bellman equation and the iterative update process, engineers can design agents that adapt to complex, dynamic environments, leading to more efficient, responsive, and autonomous control systems across a wide range of applications, from traffic management to resource allocation and robotics. The ability to learn from experience, without explicit programming of control logic for every possible scenario, is what makes these value-based RL algorithms so transformative for modern control challenges.

Further considerations for these algorithms in practice include handling non-stationarity in the environment. If the traffic patterns change seasonally, or if new road construction alters flow, the underlying MDP might shift. Both Q-learning and SARSA can adapt to these changes, provided the learning rate is maintained appropriately and the agent continues to explore. However, rapid changes might require faster adaptation mechanisms, potentially involving adjustments to the learning rate or a more aggressive exploration strategy.

In summary, value-based RL algorithms, exemplified by Q-learning and SARSA, offer a powerful paradigm for control loop optimization. They focus on learning the expected future reward associated with state-action pairs, enabling agents to make decisions that maximize long-term performance. Q-learning, being off-policy, learns the optimal policy directly, while SARSA, an on-policy method, learns the value of the policy it is currently executing. The choice between them involves trade-offs between learning speed, optimality, and safety during exploration. With careful design of state representations, reward functions, and hyperparameter tuning, these algorithms can address complex control challenges in discrete state-action spaces effectively.

Policy-based reinforcement learning algorithms represent a distinct and powerful approach to tackling control problems, fundamentally differing from value-based methods by directly optimizing the control policy itself. Instead of learning the "value" of taking an action in a given state and then deriving a policy from these values, policy-based methods aim to learn the policy parameters that directly map states to actions. This direct optimization allows for a more natural handling of continuous action spaces, which are prevalent in many real-world control systems, such as those found in robotics, autonomous vehicles, and industrial process control.

At its core, a policy-based approach seeks to find a policy, often denoted as $\pi(a|s; \theta)$, which is a probability distribution over actions a given a state s, parameterized by a set of weights θ. The objective is to adjust these parameters θ such that the expected cumulative reward is maximized. This expected reward, often denoted as $J(\theta)$, is a function of the policy parameters. The key idea behind policy-based algorithms is to employ gradient ascent to update θ in the direction that increases $J(\theta)$. This is achieved through policy gradient methods.

The foundational concept is the policy gradient theorem, which provides a way to compute the gradient of the expected reward with respect to the policy parameters. The theorem states that:

$\nabla
\theta J(\theta) = \mathbb{E}{\pi\theta} \left[\sum{t=0}^T
\nabla\theta \log \pi\theta(at/st) A^{\pi\theta}(st, a_t) \right]$

where:

$\mathbb{E}{\pi\theta}$ denotes the expectation over trajectories generated by the policy π_θ.
$\nabla\theta \log \pi\theta(at/st)$ is the gradient of the log probability of taking action at in state st under policy π_θ. This term is often referred to as the "score function."
$A^{\pi\theta}(st, at)$ is the advantage function, which estimates how much better it is to take action at in state st compared to the average action under the policy $\pi\theta$. A common and practical approximation for the advantage function is the return from time t onwards, $Gt = \sum{k=t}^\infty \gamma^{k-t} r_k$, or a baseline-subtracted return to reduce variance.

The policy gradient theorem essentially tells us that to increase the expected reward, we should increase the probability of taking actions that lead to higher-than-average returns and decrease the probability of taking actions that lead to lower-than-average returns. The $\nabla *theta \log \pi*\theta(*at*/*st*)$ term acts as a direction vector for updating the policy parameters. If an action taken in a particular state leads to a good outcome, the gradient term will push the parameters towards increasing the likelihood of that action in that state. Conversely, if an action leads to a poor outcome, the gradient term will push the parameters towards decreasing the likelihood of that action.

One of the earliest and most fundamental policy gradient algorithms is REINFORCE, also known as the Monte Carlo Policy Gradient. REINFORCE uses the full Monte Carlo return G_t (the cumulative discounted reward from time step t to the end of the episode) as an estimate for the advantage function. The update rule for REINFORCE is:

$\theta
*{t+1} \leftarrow \theta*t + \alpha \nabla*\theta \log \pi*\theta(a*t*/*s*t) G_t$

Here, α is the learning rate. The algorithm proceeds by sampling an entire episode using the current policy $\pi
*\theta$. For each time step t in the episode, the gradient of the log probability of the action taken, $\nabla*\theta \log \pi*\theta(a*t|*st)$, is multiplied by the total discounted reward $G*t$ obtained from that time step onwards. This product is then used to update the policy parameters.

Let's consider an example to illustrate REINFORCE. Suppose we are training a robotic arm to reach a target location. The state s could be the joint angles and velocities of the robot. The action a could be the torque applied to each joint. The reward might be negative of the distance to the target at the end of an episode, with small penalties for energy consumption during the movement.

In this scenario, the policy $\pi_\theta(a|s)$ would be a probability distribution over joint torques given the robot's current configuration. For instance, it could be a Gaussian distribution where the mean and variance are functions of the state s and are parameterized by θ. When REINFORCE runs an episode:

1. The robot starts in an initial configuration (s_0).
2. At each time step t, the policy $\pi*theta(at|st)$ is sampled to select a joint torque command $a*t$.
3. The robot executes $a*t$, transitions to a new state $s*{t+1}$, and receives a reward r_t.
4. This continues until the episode ends (e.g., the arm reaches the target or a time limit is exceeded).
5. The total discounted reward G_t is calculated for each time step.
6. For each step t, the gradient $\nabla*theta \log \pi*\theta(a*t*/*s*t)$ is computed. This gradient indicates how to change the parameters θ to make the specific torque command $a*t$ more or less likely in state $s*t$.
7. The update $\theta \leftarrow \theta + \alpha \nabla*theta \log \pi*\theta(a*t*/*s*t) G*t$ is performed. If $G*t$ is positive (meaning the trajectory up to that point is on a path to a good outcome), the parameters are adjusted to make action $a*t$ more likely in state $s*t$. If $G*t$ is negative, the parameters are adjusted to make $a*t$ less likely.

A key challenge with REINFORCE, and indeed with many policy gradient methods, is the high variance of the gradient estimates. The G_t term, being a full episodic return, can vary significantly between episodes, even if the policy is only slightly perturbed. This high variance can slow down learning or even prevent convergence.

To mitigate this high variance, several enhancements to the basic

REINFORCE algorithm have been developed. One of the most effective is the introduction of a baseline. A baseline $b(s
t)$ is a function that estimates the value of being in state st (e.g., a state-value function $V(s_t)$). The policy gradient can be rewritten as:

$\nabla
\theta J(\theta) = \mathbb{E}{\pi\theta} \left[\sum{t=0}^T
\nabla\theta \log \pi\theta(at|st) (Gt - b(st)) \right]$

The crucial insight here is that subtracting a baseline $b(s
t)$ from the return Gt does not change the expected value of the gradient, because the expectation of the baseline term itself, $\mathbb{E}{\pi\theta}[\nabla\theta \log \pi\theta(at|st) b(st)]$, is zero if $b(st)$ is not dependent on the action at. However, if $b(st)$ is chosen appropriately, it can significantly reduce the variance of the term $(Gt - b(st))$. A common choice for $b(st)$ is an estimate of the state-value function $V(st)$, which represents the expected return from state st onwards. This leads to the concept of the advantage function $A(st, at) = Q(st, at) - V(st)$, where Q is the action-value function. Using $A(st, at)$ instead of G_t generally leads to more stable learning.

When using an estimated state-value function $\hat{V}(s_t; w)$ (parameterized by w), the update rule becomes:

$\theta
{t+1} \leftarrow \thetat + \alpha \nabla\theta \log \pi\theta(at|st) (Gt - \hat{V}(st; w))$

This approach necessitates learning both the policy parameters θ and the value function parameters w. This leads to actor-critic methods. In actor-critic architectures, the "actor" is the policy network (parameterized by θ) that decides which action to take, and the

"critic" is the value function network (parameterized by w) that evaluates the actor's actions. The critic learns to estimate the state-value function, and its estimates are used to guide the actor's policy updates. The critic can also be trained using temporal difference (TD) learning. For example, the TD error $\delta
t = rt + \gamma \hat{V}(s{t+1}; w) - \hat{V}(st; w)$ can be used as an estimate of the advantage, leading to the update:

$\theta
{t+1} \leftarrow \thetat + \alpha \nabla\theta \log \pi\theta(at|st)
\delta_t$

This TD-based advantage estimate is more efficient than using the full Monte Carlo return G_t because it allows for online updates after each step, rather than waiting until the end of an episode.

The effectiveness of policy-based methods is particularly pronounced in continuous action spaces. In such scenarios, value-based methods like Q-learning struggle. For example, if the action space is the real-valued torque to apply to a robot's motor, discretizing this space into a finite number of bins can lead to a combinatorial explosion of states if combined with a continuous state space, or it can result in poor performance if the bins are too coarse. Policy gradient methods, on the other hand, can naturally output continuous actions. For instance, the policy network can be designed to output the parameters of a probability distribution (e.g., mean and standard deviation of a Gaussian distribution) from which the action is sampled. This makes them directly applicable to continuous control problems.

Consider an example of controlling the throttle of a vehicle for optimal fuel efficiency and speed. The state could include current speed, engine

RPM, throttle position, and road incline. The action would be the continuous value of the throttle opening (e.g., a value between 0 and 1). A value-based method would need to discretize the throttle opening, leading to suboptimal control. A policy gradient method, however, can directly learn a policy $\pi_\theta(a|s)$ that outputs, for instance, the parameters of a Gaussian distribution for the throttle action. The actor-critic framework would then learn to adjust these parameters to maximize fuel efficiency while maintaining desired speed. The critic would estimate the expected fuel consumption from a given state, and the actor would use this information to adjust the throttle policy.

Another advantage of policy-based methods is that they can learn stochastic policies. A stochastic policy, which outputs a probability distribution over actions, can be beneficial in situations where the optimal policy is inherently uncertain or when exploration is needed. For example, in a game like poker, the optimal strategy often involves bluffing, which is a form of stochasticity. While deterministic policies can be used in continuous action spaces by having the policy network output a single value, learning a stochastic policy can facilitate exploration and can sometimes lead to better convergence in complex environments.

However, policy-based methods are not without their challenges. The issue of high variance in gradient estimates, as mentioned with REINFORCE, remains a concern, even with actor-critic methods. While baselines and TD learning help, variance can still be substantial, requiring careful hyperparameter tuning and potentially long training times. Furthermore, policy-based methods can suffer from convergence to local optima. Since they perform gradient ascent, they might converge to a suboptimal policy if the initial policy is far from optimal and the policy landscape has multiple local maxima.

To address the issues of variance and exploration in policy gradient methods, several advanced algorithms have been developed. Among the most influential are Trust Region Policy Optimization (TRPO) and Proximal Policy Optimization (PPO). These algorithms aim to improve the stability of policy updates by constraining the change in the policy at each step.

TRPO, for example, imposes a constraint on the Kullback-Leibler (KL) divergence between the old and new policy. This KL divergence measures the difference between two probability distributions. By limiting the KL divergence, TRPO ensures that the policy update is not too large, preventing drastic changes that could lead to performance collapse. The update is performed using a constrained optimization problem, which is solved using a conjugate gradient method.

PPO, developed by OpenAI, offers a simpler and more computationally efficient alternative to TRPO while achieving similar performance. PPO introduces a "clipped surrogate objective function" that discourages large policy updates. The objective function in PPO is defined as:

$L^{CLIP}(\theta) = \hat{\mathbb{E}}
t \left[\min(rt(\theta) \hat{A}t, \text{clip}(rt(\theta), 1-\epsilon, 1+\epsilon) \hat{A}_t) \right]$

where:

$rt(\theta)$ *is the ratio of the new policy probability to the old policy probability:* $rt(\theta) = \frac{\pi\theta(at|st)}{\pi{\theta{old}}(at|s_t)}$.

$\hat{A}_t$ is the estimated advantage function.
ϵ is a hyperparameter (e.g., 0.1 or 0.2) that defines the clipping range.

The clipping mechanism ensures that if the ratio $r_t(\theta)$ goes beyond the range $[1-\epsilon, 1+\epsilon]$, the objective function is clipped, effectively limiting how much the policy can change in a single update step. This objective function is typically optimized using standard gradient ascent methods, making PPO easier to implement and more scalable than TRPO. PPO has become a popular choice for many continuous control tasks due to its balance of performance, stability, and ease of use.

Let's revisit the robotic arm example with PPO. Suppose the robot arm is tasked with picking up and placing objects. The state includes camera input (pixel data), joint angles, and end-effector pose. The action is the continuous torque applied to each joint.

1. The policy network (actor) outputs the parameters of a Gaussian distribution for each joint torque.
2. The value network (critic) estimates the expected future reward (e.g., reward for successfully grasping and placing the object).
3. The robot executes actions sampled from the policy for a number of time steps, collecting trajectories of states, actions, rewards, and value estimates.
4. The advantage is estimated using the TD error derived from the critic's predictions.
5. The PPO clipped objective function is computed, incorporating the advantage estimates and the policy ratio.
6. The policy parameters θ and value parameters w are updated using gradient ascent on the PPO objective and a standard TD loss for the critic, respectively.

The clipping in PPO prevents the policy from changing too drastically in response to a single high-advantage or low-advantage experience. For instance, if the robot arm momentarily applies a torque that by chance leads to a very high reward, PPO will limit how much the policy adjusts to favor that specific torque, ensuring that the learned policy remains generally robust and does not overfit to rare lucky events. This is crucial for continuous control where small changes in action can have significant effects.

The application of policy-based RL in control loops is vast and continues to expand. For instance, in autonomous driving, controlling steering, acceleration, and braking involves continuous action spaces and complex dynamics. Policy gradient methods can learn sophisticated driving behaviors, adapting to different road conditions, traffic densities, and pedestrian interactions. The policy can be trained to balance multiple objectives, such as reaching the destination quickly, ensuring passenger comfort, minimizing fuel consumption, and adhering to traffic laws.

In industrial automation, policy-based RL can optimize the control of complex manufacturing processes. For example, controlling the temperature, pressure, and flow rates in a chemical reactor to maximize yield and minimize energy usage. The state would include sensor readings from the reactor, and the actions would be continuous adjustments to control valves and heaters. A policy gradient algorithm could learn to maintain optimal operating conditions even in the presence of disturbances or variations in raw material properties.

The direct learning of policies also offers advantages in terms of interpretability, to some extent. While neural network policies can be complex, understanding the learned mapping from states to actions can sometimes be more intuitive than inferring a policy from learned value functions, especially when dealing with high-dimensional state spaces or continuous actions where value-based representations become intractable. For example, visualizing the learned policy for a robot arm might reveal specific movement patterns or strategies that are understandable to a human engineer.

In summary, policy-based reinforcement learning algorithms, epitomized by policy gradient methods like REINFORCE, actor-critic architectures, and advanced algorithms such as PPO, provide a direct and powerful framework for optimizing control policies. Their ability to directly parameterize and optimize policies makes them particularly well-suited for continuous action spaces, a common characteristic of physical control systems. By iteratively adjusting policy parameters to increase expected rewards, these methods enable agents to learn complex control strategies from experience. While challenges like variance and convergence to local optima exist, ongoing research and algorithmic advancements, particularly in trust-region methods and clipped objectives, are continuously improving their stability and effectiveness, making policy-based RL a vital tool in the modern control engineer's arsenal.

The inherent challenges of both pure value-based and pure policy-based reinforcement learning methods in control applications have spurred the development of hybrid approaches that aim to leverage the advantages of each. Actor-critic methods represent a significant advancement in this direction, seamlessly integrating policy optimization with value function estimation. At their core, actor-critic architectures consist of two main components: an "actor" and a "critic."

The

actor is responsible for learning and executing the policy. It directly maps states to actions, much like the policy networks discussed previously. The actor's objective is to learn a parameterized policy, $\pi_\theta(a|s)$, that maximizes the expected cumulative reward. This component directly controls the system's behavior.

The
critic, on the other hand, learns a value function. This value function can be either a state-value function $V(s)$ or an action-value function $Q(s, a)$. The critic's role is to evaluate the actions taken by the actor. It provides feedback to the actor, guiding its policy updates. Crucially, the critic's learning is typically done using temporal difference (TD) methods, which are more sample-efficient than Monte Carlo methods, as they can learn from incomplete episodes.

The interplay between the actor and critic is what gives these methods their power. The critic observes the actor's actions and the resulting state transitions and rewards, and uses this information to refine its value estimates. These refined value estimates are then used by the actor to update its policy parameters. Specifically, the critic's evaluation informs the actor about how to adjust its policy to achieve higher future rewards. For instance, if the critic estimates that a particular action taken in a certain state led to a lower-than-expected outcome, it signals to the actor that this action might be suboptimal in that state, prompting a policy update to decrease the probability of taking such an action in the future. Conversely, actions leading to better-than-expected outcomes will have their probabilities increased.

A common way the critic informs the actor is through the **temporal difference (TD) error**. For a state-value function critic, the TD error at time step t is defined as:

$$\delta_t = r_t + \gamma V(s_{t+1}) - V(s_t)$$

where r_t is the immediate reward, γ is the discount factor, $V(s_{t+1})$ is the critic's estimated value of the next state, and $V(s_t)$ is the critic's estimated value of the current state. This TD error can be interpreted as an estimate of the advantage function: how much better is the immediate reward plus the discounted future value, compared to the current estimated value of the state. A positive TD error suggests that the action taken led to a better-than-expected outcome, while a negative TD error indicates a worse-than-expected outcome.

The actor then uses this TD error, δ_t, to update its policy parameters θ. The policy gradient update rule, when using the TD error as an advantage estimate, becomes:

$$\theta_{t+1} = \theta_t + \alpha \nabla_\theta \log \pi_\theta(a_t|s_t) \delta_t$$

Here, α is the actor's learning rate. This update rule means that if δ_t is positive, the parameters are adjusted to increase the probability of taking action a_t in state s_t. If δ_t is negative, the parameters are adjusted to decrease this probability. The use of the TD error as a proxy for the advantage function is a key innovation, as it allows for online learning—updates can be made after each step or a small batch of steps, rather than waiting for the end of an entire episode, as is required by pure Monte Carlo policy gradient methods like REINFORCE. This makes actor-critic methods significantly more sample-efficient and suitable for continuous control tasks where episodes can be very long or even infinite.

Consider a practical application in robotics: controlling a robotic manipulator for assembly tasks. The state s might include the robot's joint angles, velocities, and the position and orientation of the object to be manipulated, often derived from sensor data like cameras and encoders. The action a would be the continuous torques or forces to be applied to each joint.

In an actor-critic setup for this task:

1. **The Actor (Policy Network):** This network takes the robot's current state as input and outputs the parameters of a probability distribution for each joint torque. For instance, it might output the mean and standard deviation of Gaussian distributions, from which the torques are sampled. This stochastic policy is important for exploration.
2. **The Critic (Value Network):** This network takes the robot's current state as input and outputs an estimate of the expected future reward, $V(s)$. This represents how "good" it is to be in the current state, assuming optimal play from both the actor and critic thereafter.

The learning process would unfold as follows:

The robot starts in an initial configuration.
At each time step t, the actor samples an action a_t *from its policy distribution* $\pi_\theta(a_t|s_t)$.
The robot executes a_t, *leading to a transition to state* s_{t+1} and receiving a reward r_t. This reward could be, for example, positive if the robot successfully moves the object closer to its target position and negative if it collides with something or drops the object.

The critic uses st, at, rt, and $s{t+1}$ to compute the TD error: $\deltat = rt + \gamma V(s{t+1}; w) - V(st; w)$, where w are the critic's network parameters. The critic also updates its parameters w to minimize the TD error, effectively learning a more accurate value function.
The actor uses the calculated δ_t as an estimate of the advantage to update its policy parameters θ, pushing the policy towards actions that are likely to yield positive TD errors (i.e., better-than-expected outcomes).

This cycle repeats. The actor and critic learn concurrently, with the critic providing increasingly accurate guidance to the actor, leading to a more effective policy over time. The choice of value function (state-value vs. action-value) influences the specific implementation, but the fundamental principle of a critic evaluating an actor's actions remains.

One of the earliest and most influential actor-critic algorithms is the **Advantage Actor-Critic (A2C)** algorithm. A2C is a synchronous, deterministic update algorithm. In A2C, the critic learns the state-value function $V(s)$, and the advantage function is estimated using the TD error: $A(st, at) \approx \deltat = rt + \gamma V(s{t+1}) - V(st)$. The policy update then uses this advantage estimate:

$\theta \leftarrow \theta + \alpha \nabla
\theta \log \pi\theta(at|st) (rt + \gamma V(s{t+1}) - V(s_t))$

The critic's parameters w are updated to minimize the squared TD error:

$w \leftarrow w - \beta \nabla
w (rt + \gamma V(s{t+1}) - V(st))^2$

where β is the critic's learning rate. A2C typically performs updates after collecting a batch of experiences. The "advantage" in its name comes from the fact that it uses an estimate of the advantage function (the TD error) for policy updates.

Building upon A2C, the
Asynchronous Advantage Actor-Critic (A3C) algorithm introduced parallelism to actor-critic methods, significantly enhancing their scalability and training speed. A3C utilizes multiple worker threads, each running an instance of the environment and its own actor-critic agent. These workers interact with their respective environments asynchronously. Each worker updates a global network of parameters at its own pace.

The asynchronous nature of A3C is key. While one worker might be in the middle of an episode, another might have just finished one. When a worker computes a gradient update based on its experiences, it asynchronously applies this update to the global network. This means that other workers are constantly learning from a network that is being updated by diverse experiences from different environments. This staggered update process effectively decorates the learning process, reducing the correlation between consecutive updates and mitigating the high variance issues often associated with policy gradients.

The A3C architecture typically uses multiple actors, each interacting with its own copy of the environment. These actors are collecting data and performing gradient updates on a shared global set of parameters. The critic in A3C also learns from the collected experiences, predicting the value function. The TD error derived from these predictions is used to update the policy (actor) and to train the value function (critic). The use of multiple, asynchronous updates from various environmental conditions and states helps to decorrelate the data and stabilize training, making A3C a powerful algorithm for complex, high-dimensional control problems.

A notable aspect of A3C is its use of multiple "actors," each operating independently and asynchronously. Each actor interacts with its own instance of the environment, generates experience, and computes policy gradients and value function updates. Periodically, these local updates are applied to a shared global set of parameters. This asynchronous approach allows for efficient exploration of the state-action space and can lead to faster convergence than synchronous methods, especially in environments where collecting data is time-consuming.

Consider the problem of controlling an unmanned aerial vehicle (UAV) for surveillance. The state might include the UAV's position, velocity, altitude, battery level, and sensor readings (e.g., camera feed). The actions would be continuous commands for pitch, roll, yaw, and throttle.

In an A3C implementation for this UAV control:

Multiple worker processes are launched, each simulating a UAV in a slightly different scenario (e.g., different wind conditions, different starting points, different target areas).
Each worker's actor network learns a policy $\pi_\theta(a|s)$ to output control commands.
Each worker's critic network learns to estimate the value function $V(s)$, predicting future mission success or time until battery depletion.
As each worker collects experience (state, action, reward, next state), it calculates the TD error $\delta_t = r_t + \gamma V(s_{t+1}; w) - V(s_t; w)$.

The reward r_t could be based on proximity to the target, energy consumption, or successful detection of surveillance targets.
The worker uses δ_t to compute gradients for the actor and critic parameters.
These gradients are then asynchronously applied to a central, shared global network. The actor and critic parameters of each worker are periodically synchronized with the global network.

This asynchronous update mechanism allows A3C to effectively leverage parallel computing resources. By having multiple agents exploring the environment simultaneously and contributing to the global learning process, A3C can learn robust policies much faster than if a single agent were to collect all the data sequentially. The diversity of experiences from different workers also helps to decorrelate the data, which is crucial for stabilizing policy gradient learning. For instance, if one worker encounters a rare but critical situation (e.g., a sudden gust of wind), its experience contributes to the global policy update, making the learned policy more resilient to such events for all workers.

The advantage function estimation is central to both A2C and A3C. While the TD error δ_t is a common and effective estimate, more sophisticated advantage estimation techniques can be employed. For example, using a k-step TD return can provide a better estimate of the true advantage:

$$A_t^k = \sum_{i=0}^{k-1} \gamma^i r_{t+i} + \gamma^k V(s_{t+k}) - V(s_t)$$

This k-step return is a form of bootstrapping that balances the bias of single-step TD with the variance of full Monte Carlo returns. By adjusting k, one can interpolate between these extremes. Using such enhanced advantage estimates can further improve the stability and performance of actor-critic methods.

Another variation and important development in the actor-critic family is
Asynchronous Advantage Actor-Critic (A3C) and its synchronous counterpart, **Advantage Actor-Critic (A2C)**. A3C, as described, uses asynchronous updates from multiple worker threads, each running a copy of the environment. This parallelism is a major advantage for speeding up training on multi-core processors. A2C, on the other hand, is a synchronous version where all workers collect data in parallel, then all gradients are aggregated and applied in a single update step. While A2C might be simpler to implement and debug, A3C often achieves better performance due to its effective handling of correlated updates.

The benefits of actor-critic methods, and specifically A2C/A3C, are particularly evident in complex control scenarios where an accurate value function estimate is difficult to obtain, or where the policy space is vast and continuous. For example, in aerospace applications like controlling the attitude of a satellite or the trajectory of a hypersonic vehicle, the dynamics are highly non-linear and subject to external disturbances. A pure policy gradient method might struggle with high variance, while a pure value-based method would face challenges in discretizing the continuous control actions. Actor-critic methods offer a robust middle ground. The actor learns the control policy, while the critic learns to predict the expected mission outcome or time to failure, guiding the actor's exploration and exploitation. The asynchronous nature of A3C allows for efficient exploration of the complex flight dynamics and failure modes, leading to safer and more efficient control strategies.

The "advantage" in these algorithms refers to the use of an estimate of the advantage function, $A(s, a) = Q(s, a) - V(s)$, for policy updates. The TD error, $\delta
t = rt + \gamma V(s{t+1}) - V(st)$, serves as a biased but low-variance estimate of the advantage. By using this estimate, the actor is encouraged to take actions that lead to outcomes better than predicted by the value function. This is crucial: instead of just maximizing absolute returns, the actor learns to improve upon the current baseline value. This focus on improvement relative to expectations is what helps to reduce variance in the policy gradient.

For instance, if the critic accurately estimates $V(s)$ for most states, then a positive TD error means that the action taken resulted in a state and reward that, when combined, were unexpectedly good. Conversely, a negative TD error means the outcome was unexpectedly poor. The policy gradient update then directs the actor to increase the probability of actions that lead to positive surprises and decrease the probability of actions that lead to negative surprises. This relative improvement framing is a powerful mechanism for stable policy learning in control systems.

Furthermore, actor-critic methods can be extended to use generalized advantage estimation (GAE), which provides a more flexible way to balance bias and variance in advantage estimation. GAE uses a parameter λ to interpolate between single-step TD error and Monte Carlo returns. The GAE advantage estimate is given by:

$\hat{A}
t^{GAE(\gamma, \lambda)} = \sum{l=0}^{\infty} (\gamma \lambda)^l
\delta_{t+l}$

where $\delta
{t+l} = r{t+l} + \gamma V(s{t+l+1}) - V(s{t+l})$ is the TD error at time $t+l$. When $\lambda=0$, GAE reduces to the standard TD error (one-step advantage). When $\lambda=1$, GAE approximates the Monte Carlo advantage. By tuning λ, one can achieve a trade-off between bias and variance, often leading to more stable and effective learning. Algorithms like Proximal Policy Optimization (PPO) and Trust Region Policy Optimization (TRPO), which were discussed in the context of policy gradients, often incorporate GAE within their actor-critic frameworks.

The integration of actor-critic architectures into control loops provides a powerful framework for learning complex behaviors directly from interaction. The actor's ability to handle continuous action spaces is paramount for many physical control problems, while the critic's efficient learning of value functions, often via TD methods, provides stable and informative guidance. The advent of asynchronous algorithms like A3C further democratized the use of these powerful methods by enabling efficient training on commodity hardware. These methods are now a cornerstone in fields ranging from robotics manipulation and locomotion to autonomous navigation and advanced process control, offering a robust path to optimizing control policies in dynamic and uncertain environments. The continuous development of these algorithms, including enhancements in advantage estimation and trust-region optimization, ensures their continued relevance and growing impact in the field of intelligent control.

Chapter 6: Deep Reinforcement Learning for Control

The inherent complexity of modern control systems, characterized by high-dimensional state spaces and continuous, often intricate action spaces, presents a formidable challenge for traditional Reinforcement Learning (RL) algorithms. Imagine attempting to control a fleet of autonomous vehicles navigating a dense urban environment. The 'state' encompasses not just the position and velocity of each vehicle, but also the positions, velocities, and intentions of all other vehicles, pedestrians, cyclists, traffic light statuses, road conditions, and even weather. This vast and dynamic information landscape is far beyond what can be reasonably represented in a tabular format, where each state-action pair is explicitly stored. Similarly, the 'actions' - steering angle, acceleration, braking intensity - are continuous, leading to an infinite number of possibilities. Traditional RL methods, such as Q-learning or SARSA with tabular representations, simply cannot scale to such problems. They would require an astronomically large table, rendering them computationally intractable and impractical. Even simpler function approximators, like linear models, would struggle to capture the complex, non-linear relationships between states, actions, and rewards in these scenarios.

The limitations of traditional RL methods stem from their fundamental assumptions about the structure of the problem. Tabular methods assume a discrete and manageable number of states and actions. When these assumptions are violated, the curse of dimensionality takes hold, leading to an exponential increase in the required memory and computation. This is precisely where Deep Reinforcement Learning (DRL) emerges as a powerful paradigm shift. DRL integrates the representational power of deep neural networks with the learning capabilities of RL. Instead of relying on explicit tables or simple linear functions, DRL employs deep neural networks as function approximators for either the value function (e.g., Q-values or state-values) or the policy itself.

The genius of deep neural networks lies in their ability to automatically learn hierarchical representations and extract salient features from raw, high-dimensional input data. Consider the visual input from a camera mounted on a robot arm attempting to grasp an object. A traditional RL agent would require extensive manual feature engineering – identifying edges, shapes, textures, and relative positions of the object and the arm. This process is tedious, error-prone, and may miss crucial subtle cues. A deep neural network, however, can be fed the raw pixel data from the camera image. Through its layers of convolutional filters and non-linear activations, it can learn to progressively identify increasingly complex visual features: first, basic edges and corners, then object parts, and eventually, a representation of the object's pose and the robot arm's configuration relative to it. This automatic feature extraction capability is a game-changer for control problems involving rich sensory inputs like images, LiDAR scans, or complex time-series sensor data. The network learns to distill the essential information from the raw data, effectively compressing the high-dimensional input into a low-dimensional, meaningful representation that can then be used by the RL algorithm to make decisions.

This ability to handle raw, high-dimensional sensory input without manual feature engineering dramatically broadens the scope of problems amenable to RL. It allows agents to learn directly from pixels, sound, or other complex, unstructured data streams, mimicking how humans and animals learn through direct sensory experience. For instance, in controlling a robotic manipulator, the state can be directly represented by camera images, joint sensor readings, and force feedback. The deep neural network at the core of the DRL agent can process this multi-modal input to infer the necessary information about the environment and the agent's own state, without requiring explicit programming of object recognition or inverse kinematics modules.

The success of DRL has been spectacularly demonstrated in domains that were previously thought to be intractable for AI. The most prominent examples include playing complex board games and video games. In the game of Go, a game with an astronomical number of possible board positions (far exceeding that of chess), DeepMind's AlphaGo and AlphaZero systems, employing deep convolutional neural networks combined with Monte Carlo Tree Search, achieved superhuman performance. These systems learned to evaluate board positions and select moves not by being programmed with human strategies, but by learning from self-play. The neural networks in AlphaGo learned to represent the complex game state and predict move probabilities and game outcomes.

Similarly, DRL agents have achieved remarkable success in mastering a wide array of Atari 2600 video games. In these games, the agent receives raw pixel data from the screen as its state and outputs joystick and button presses as its actions. Algorithms like Deep Q-Networks (DQN) were pivotal in this breakthrough. DQN combined a deep convolutional neural network with a Q-learning framework. The neural network served as the function approximator for the Q-function, mapping raw screen pixels to the expected future rewards for each possible action. Techniques like experience replay (storing past transitions and sampling them randomly for training) and target networks (using a separate, delayed network for Q-value targets) were crucial for stabilizing the learning process. The fact that a single DRL architecture could learn to play so many diverse games, often surpassing human scores, underscored the generality and power of deep learning for approximating value functions in complex state spaces.

These successes in games, while not directly control problems in the physical sense, provide crucial insights and motivation for DRL in control. Games often share key characteristics with real-world control tasks:

1. **High-Dimensional State Spaces:** Game screens, like sensor data from robots or vehicles, are high-dimensional.
2. **Complex Dynamics:** The rules and outcomes of games, like physical system dynamics, can be intricate and non-linear.
3. **Delayed Rewards:** Actions taken early in a game or control task may only yield rewards much later, requiring sophisticated temporal credit assignment.
4. **Need for Strategic Planning:** Effective play or control often requires long-term planning, not just reactive responses.

The deep neural networks used in these game-playing agents learn to capture the underlying patterns and strategies by processing large amounts of experience. In control applications, this translates to learning control policies directly from raw sensor data without explicit modeling of the system dynamics or environment. This is a fundamental departure from traditional control theory, which often relies on building precise mathematical models of the system. While model-based control can be highly effective when a good model is available, it becomes exceedingly difficult or impossible in scenarios with complex, uncertain, or unknown dynamics. DRL offers an alternative: learning directly from interaction, effectively building an implicit model or, more precisely, learning a policy that is robust to the complexities of the underlying dynamics.

The transition from success in games to physical control problems involves several key considerations. Physical systems often have continuous action spaces, which require extensions to algorithms like DQN. Algorithms like Deep Deterministic Policy Gradient (DDPG), Twin Delayed Deep Deterministic Policy Gradient (TD3), and Soft Actor-Critic (SAC) were developed to handle continuous action spaces by employing actor-critic architectures where the actor outputs continuous actions and the critic evaluates them. Furthermore, safety, sample efficiency, and real-world deployment challenges become paramount. Unlike a game where an occasional mistake might lead to a loss, a mistake in a physical control system, such as an autonomous car or a surgical robot, could have catastrophic consequences. This has spurred research into safe DRL, robust DRL, and methods for improving sample efficiency, such as model-based DRL approaches that learn a model of the environment to generate more training data.

The ability of deep neural networks to handle high-dimensional, unstructured data is not merely an advantage; it is a necessity for tackling many modern control challenges. Consider an autonomous drone tasked with inspecting a wind turbine. The drone's sensors might include high-resolution cameras, thermal cameras, and LiDAR. The state space would be formed by the combination of these diverse data streams, along with the drone's own inertial measurement unit (IMU) readings for position, orientation, and velocity. A traditional RL agent would struggle immensely to process this information. It would require a sophisticated perception system to identify the turbine components, detect damage (e.g., cracks, corrosion, thermal anomalies), and determine the drone's relative position and orientation to these components.

Deep neural networks, integrated into a DRL framework, can learn this perception-action loop end-to-end. A convolutional neural network (CNN) could process the visual and thermal camera feeds to identify the turbine structure and highlight areas of interest or potential defects. A recurrent neural network (RNN) or transformer could then process sequences of these perceived features along with the IMU data to estimate the drone's state within the complex 3D geometry of the turbine and predict future states. The RL component, guided by the learned representations, would then output the appropriate control commands (e.g., adjustments to rotor speeds and control surfaces) to maintain a stable flight path, navigate around the turbine, and position the sensors optimally for inspection. The rewards could be designed to incentivize thorough inspection, efficient coverage of the turbine surface, and safe operation.

The challenges in such applications are manifold. The dynamics of the drone are complex, influenced by aerodynamic forces, wind gusts, and the drone's own movements. The visual appearance of damage can vary greatly depending on lighting conditions, angle of observation, and the type of defect. The state space is massive and continuous, and the action space is also continuous. Deep RL provides a framework to learn effective control policies directly from this complex interplay of sensory input and physical dynamics. The deep learning component acts as a powerful feature extractor and state estimator, reducing the high-dimensional sensory data into a manageable representation, while the RL component learns to map these learned states to optimal control actions through trial and error, guided by a carefully defined reward signal. This end-to-end learning capability, enabled by DRL, is what makes it a transformative technology for advanced control systems, moving beyond the limitations of handcrafted features and explicit system modeling.

The journey from foundational Reinforcement Learning (RL) principles to the sophisticated capabilities of Deep Reinforcement Learning (DRL) is marked by significant algorithmic innovations. While earlier chapters have laid the groundwork for understanding RL's core concepts and the limitations of traditional approaches when faced with the complexities of real-world control problems, this section delves into one of the most pivotal advancements: Deep Q-Networks (DQN). DQN stands as a testament to the power of combining deep neural networks with Q-learning, enabling agents to learn optimal policies in environments characterized by high-dimensional state spaces, a scenario where tabular Q-learning falters dramatically.

At its heart, Q-learning aims to learn an action-value function, denoted as $Q(s, a)$, which represents the expected cumulative future reward of taking action a in state s and following an optimal policy thereafter. In traditional Q-learning, this function is typically stored in a table where each entry corresponds to a unique state-action pair. The update rule for $Q(s, a)$ is given by the Bellman equation:

$$Q(s, a) \leftarrow Q(s, a) + \alpha [r + \gamma \max_{a'} Q(s', a') - Q(s, a)]$$

where α is the learning rate, r is the immediate reward, γ is the discount factor, and s' is the next state. However, as previously discussed, the sheer number of states and actions in many practical control systems renders a tabular representation infeasible due to the curse of dimensionality. This is where DQN introduces its groundbreaking solution: using a deep neural network to approximate the Q-function, $Q(s, a; \theta)$, where θ represents the weights and biases of the neural network. The network takes the state s as input and outputs Q-values for all possible actions.

The architecture of a DQN typically involves a deep neural network, often a Convolutional Neural Network (CNN) for image-based inputs (like in video games or from camera sensors) or a Multilayer Perceptron (MLP) for vector-based state representations. For instance, in the context of Atari games, the input to the CNN would be the raw pixel data of the game screen, and the output would be a vector of Q-values, one for each joystick action. The network is trained to minimize a loss function that quantifies the difference between the predicted Q-values and a target Q-value. The target Q-value is derived from the Bellman equation, but with a crucial modification to stabilize learning:

$$y_i = r_i + \gamma \max_{a'} Q(s'_{i}, a'; \theta^{-})$$

The loss function is then typically the Mean Squared Error (MSE) between the current Q-value prediction and this target:

$$L(\theta) = \frac{1}{N} \sum_{i=1}^{N} (y_i - Q(s_i, a_i; \theta))^2$$

where (s_i, a_i, r_i, s'_i) are transitions sampled from the agent's experience, and N is the batch size.

However, directly applying this Q-learning update rule to a neural network presents significant challenges. Two primary issues arise:

1.
Correlated Data: In standard supervised learning, training data is typically assumed to be independent and identically distributed (i.i.d.). However, in RL, consecutive samples generated by the agent's policy are

highly correlated. If the agent is following a particular policy, the states it visits will often be similar to the previous state, and the actions taken will be correlated. Training a neural network on such correlated data can lead to oscillations and instability, as the network may become overly sensitive to recent experiences and fail to generalize effectively.

2.
Non-Stationary Targets: The target Q-values, y_i, depend on the network's own parameters θ. As the network learns and its parameters θ change, the target values also change, making the learning process non-stationary. This is akin to training a supervised learning model where the labels are constantly shifting. If the network is trying to learn to predict values that are themselves being updated by the very same network, it can lead to divergence and unstable learning.

To combat these issues, DQN introduces two key innovations: Experience Replay and Target Networks.

Experience Replay

Experience replay addresses the problem of correlated data by decoupling the learning process from the agent's current policy. Instead of training on the most recent transition, DQN stores past experiences (transitions of (s, a, r, s')) in a large memory buffer, often referred to as the "experience replay buffer." During training, mini-batches of transitions are randomly sampled from this buffer. This random sampling breaks the temporal correlations inherent in sequential experiences, presenting the neural network with a more diverse and less correlated set of data points for each training step. This has a similar effect to using an i.i.d. dataset, which is more amenable to standard gradient descent optimization.

The experience replay buffer acts as a form of memory for the agent, allowing it to learn from past interactions without being constrained by its immediate sensory input or action history. This is particularly beneficial in environments where exploration is sparse or where certain states are rarely encountered. By replaying these experiences multiple times, the agent can consolidate its learning and gain a more robust understanding of the environment's dynamics and reward structure.

The size of the experience replay buffer is a hyperparameter that needs careful tuning. A larger buffer can provide more diverse data and better decorrelation but requires more memory. Conversely, a smaller buffer might not be sufficient to break correlations effectively. The sampling strategy from the buffer can also be varied, though uniform random sampling is the most common approach. Prioritized experience replay is an extension that samples transitions more frequently if they are deemed more "important" (e.g., if they lead to larger temporal difference errors), further accelerating learning.

Target Networks

The non-stationarity of target Q-values is addressed by introducing a separate "target network." This target network has the same architecture as the main Q-network but its parameters, denoted by θ^{-}, are updated much less frequently. Specifically, the parameters of the target network are periodically copied from the main

Q-network (e.g., every few thousand steps). This means that for a period of time, the target network's Q-values remain fixed, providing stable targets for the main network's training.

During the update step, the target Q-value is calculated using the target network:

$$y_i = r_i + \gamma \max_{a'} Q(s'_{i}, a'; \theta^{-})$$

The loss function then becomes:

$$L(\theta) = \frac{1}{N} \sum_{i=1}^{N} (r_i + \gamma \max_{a'} Q(s'_{i}, a'; \theta^{-}) - Q(s_i, a_i; \theta))^2$$

By using a separate, slowly updating target network, the target values become more stable during the training of the main network. This effectively transforms the problem into a supervised learning task where the labels (the target Q-values) are updated less frequently, making the learning process more convergent and less prone to divergence. The frequency of target network updates is another crucial hyperparameter. If updated too frequently, the stability advantage is lost. If updated too infrequently, the target values can become outdated and hinder learning.

The combination of experience replay and target networks forms the core of the DQN algorithm, enabling it to learn effectively from high-dimensional sensory inputs. This was a breakthrough demonstrated powerfully in mastering Atari 2600 games, where agents trained with

DQN could achieve super-human performance by learning directly from raw pixel data.

DQN in Practice: Examples and Extensions

The impact of DQN has been profound, extending beyond video games to various control problems. Let's consider two illustrative examples: autonomous navigation and industrial robotics.

Autonomous Navigation in Simulated Environments

Imagine an autonomous robot tasked with navigating a complex, simulated indoor environment. The robot is equipped with a depth camera and LiDAR sensors, providing rich, high-dimensional state information. The objective is to reach a target destination while avoiding obstacles.

In this scenario, the state s could be a combination of processed sensor data: a top-down occupancy grid map generated from LiDAR scans and a depth image from the camera, potentially concatenated or processed through separate CNNs. The actions a would be discrete commands like "move forward," "turn left," "turn right," "stop." The reward function could be designed to provide a positive reward for reaching the goal, a small negative reward for each time step to encourage efficiency, and a large negative reward for collisions.

A DQN agent can be trained to learn a policy for navigation. The experience replay buffer would store tuples of (state, action, reward, next state), where the state is represented by the sensor data. The target network would provide stable Q-value targets for training. Over many training episodes, the DQN agent would learn to associate specific sensor readings with optimal actions, such as turning away from detected obstacles or moving towards the general direction of the goal.

The challenge here is the high dimensionality of the sensor data. A raw depth image can have thousands of pixels, and LiDAR can provide hundreds of points. A CNN is well-suited to process these inputs, learning to extract relevant features like the presence and proximity of walls, doorways, and obstacles. The network would learn to recognize patterns that indicate danger (e.g., a close obstacle directly ahead) and opportunities (e.g., a clear path towards the goal).

The discrete action space (e.g., 4-5 movement commands) is also suitable for a standard DQN. However, if a more continuous control were desired (e.g., controlling linear and angular velocity directly), extensions to DQN would be necessary, which we will discuss later. The success of DQN in such simulations demonstrates its ability to learn complex spatial reasoning and decision-making from raw sensor inputs without explicit path planning algorithms or handcrafted navigation rules.

Controlling Industrial Robots for Assembly Tasks

Consider an industrial robot arm tasked with a delicate assembly operation, such as picking up a small component from a feeder and placing it precisely into a fixture. The robot's state could be represented by joint angles, velocities, and visual feedback from a camera mounted on the end-effector. The actions would be the torques or target joint velocities for each actuator.

While this scenario often involves continuous action spaces, a simplified version can illustrate DQN's applicability. Suppose the actions are discretized: "move joint X by small increment," "move joint X by large increment," "hold." The reward could be positive upon successful placement, negative for dropped components or collisions, and small negative for time.

The visual input from the camera is crucial for detecting the component and the fixture, and for fine-tuning the placement. A CNN can process these images to identify the component's pose and the target location. The DQN would learn to map the combined joint states and visual features to the appropriate discrete joint commands.

The experience replay mechanism would allow the robot to learn from successful and unsuccessful attempts, improving its ability to grasp and place the component reliably. The target network would ensure stable learning, especially important when dealing with the precise and potentially unforgiving dynamics of a robotic arm.

DQN, with its ability to learn from high-dimensional, noisy sensory data and its stabilizing techniques, can enable robots to perform tasks that were previously difficult or impossible to program explicitly. It can adapt to variations in component presentation or minor shifts in fixture alignment, something traditional, model-based control might struggle with without extensive recalibration.

Limitations and Further Developments

Despite its successes, standard DQN has limitations. The most significant is its reliance on discrete action spaces. Many real-world control problems, such as controlling the throttle of a vehicle or the angle of a robotic gripper, require continuous actions. Adapting DQN to continuous action spaces is a subject of ongoing research and has led to the development of various extensions and alternative algorithms.

One direct approach is to discretize the continuous action space. For example, instead of allowing any steering angle, one might discretize it into a few options like "sharp left," "slight left," "straight," "slight right," "sharp right." However, this discretization can lead to a loss of precision and can increase the number of actions, potentially making learning more difficult. Moreover, the "curse of dimensionality" can re-emerge if the action space is large.

To address this, more advanced DRL algorithms have been developed that can handle continuous action spaces directly. Algorithms like Deep Deterministic Policy Gradient (DDPG), Twin Delayed Deep Deterministic Policy Gradient (TD3), and Soft Actor-Critic (SAC) employ actor-critic architectures. In these methods, an "actor" network learns the policy (i.e., directly outputs continuous actions), while a "critic" network learns the value function (e.g., Q-values or state-values) to guide the actor's learning. These algorithms are crucial for applying DRL to a wider range of physical control tasks.

Another area of active research is improving sample efficiency. DQN, like many off-policy RL algorithms, can be quite sample-inefficient, meaning it requires a large amount of interaction data to learn an effective policy. This is particularly problematic in real-world applications where data collection can be expensive, time-consuming, or even dangerous. Model-based DRL approaches aim to alleviate this by learning a model of the environment's dynamics, which can then be used to generate synthetic experiences for training, thereby reducing the need for real-world interactions.

Furthermore, ensuring safety during the learning process and deployment is a paramount concern in physical control systems. DQN, by its nature, learns through trial and error, which can involve potentially unsafe actions. Research into safe RL aims to incorporate constraints and safety guarantees into the learning process, ensuring that the agent operates within acceptable bounds even during exploration.

In summary, Deep Q-Networks represent a foundational breakthrough in Deep Reinforcement Learning, demonstrating that deep neural networks can effectively approximate value functions in high-dimensional state spaces. The ingenious use of experience replay and target networks provided the necessary stabilization mechanisms to overcome the inherent challenges of applying gradient-based learning to the non-i.i.d. and non-stationary data generated by RL agents. While DQN primarily operates with discrete action spaces, its success paved the way for numerous extensions and inspired the development of entirely new DRL architectures that have since been applied to a vast array of complex control problems, from autonomous systems to sophisticated robotics. It stands as a pivotal stepping stone in the evolution of intelligent agents capable of learning and acting in complex environments.

Policy gradient methods represent a fundamentally different approach to reinforcement learning compared to value-based methods like Deep Q-Networks (DQN). While DQN learns an approximation of the optimal action-value function (the Q-function), policy gradient methods directly learn a policy, denoted by $\pi(a|s; \theta)$, which maps states s to a probability distribution over actions a. The parameter vector θ here represents the weights and biases of a neural network that parameterizes the policy. The objective is to find the policy parameters θ that maximize the expected cumulative reward. This direct optimization of the policy offers several advantages, particularly in scenarios involving continuous action spaces, which are ubiquitous in real-world control applications.

The core idea behind policy gradient methods is to adjust the policy parameters θ in the direction that increases the expected return. This is achieved by computing the gradient of the expected return with respect to θ. The gradient tells us how a small change in each parameter will affect the overall performance of the policy. By iteratively updating θ in the direction of this gradient, the policy gradually improves. The mathematical formulation for the expected return $J(\theta)$ for a given policy π_θ can be expressed as:

$J(\theta) = \mathbb{E}
{\tau \sim \pi\theta} \left[\sum{t=0}^T rt \right]$

where τ represents a trajectory (a sequence of states, actions, and rewards) generated by the policy π_θ. The objective is to maximize $J(\theta)$. Using the log-derivative trick, the gradient of $J(\theta)$ can be written as:

$\nabla
\theta J(\theta) = \mathbb{E}{\tau \sim \pi\theta} \left[\sum{t=0}^T
\nabla\theta \log \pi\theta(at/st) (rt + \gamma r{t+1} + \dots) \right]$

This gradient can be approximated by sampling trajectories from the environment using the current policy. The term $(r
t + \gamma r{t+1} + \dots)$ is the cumulative future reward from time step t onwards, often referred to as the "return to go" or G_t. A common approximation of the gradient uses a single sampled trajectory:

$\nabla
\theta J(\theta) \approx \frac{1}{N} \sum{i=1}^N \sum{t=0}^{Ti}
\nabla\theta \log \pi\theta(a{i,t}/s{i,t}) G_{i,t}$

where N is the number of sampled trajectories, $T
i$ is the length of the i-th trajectory, and $G{i,t}$ is the return to go for the t-th step of the i-th trajectory.

Actor-Critic Methods and Deep Deterministic Policy Gradient (DDPG)

While the basic policy gradient update is conceptually simple, it suffers from high variance. The return G_t can vary significantly across different trajectories, leading to noisy gradient estimates and slow or unstable learning. Actor-critic methods were introduced to mitigate this variance. In an actor-critic setup, there are two components: an "actor" that learns the policy and an "critic" that learns a value function (either the state-value function $V(s)$ or the action-value function $Q(s,a)$) to estimate the expected return. The critic's estimates are then used to guide the actor's updates, providing a lower-variance signal.

One prominent actor-critic algorithm designed for continuous action spaces is the Deep Deterministic Policy Gradient (DDPG). DDPG is an off-policy algorithm that combines ideas from DQN and deterministic policy gradients. Instead of learning a stochastic policy that outputs probabilities for each action, DDPG learns a deterministic policy, $\mu(s;\theta^\mu)$, which directly outputs a specific action $a = \mu(s;\theta^\mu)$. This is particularly useful in control tasks where a precise action command is often desired.

DDPG employs an actor-critic architecture with deep neural networks for both the actor and the critic. The actor network, parameterized by θ^μ, takes the state s as input and outputs a continuous action a. The critic network, parameterized by θ^Q, takes both the state s and an action a as input and outputs the Q-value, $Q(s,a;\theta^Q)$.

To stabilize learning, DDPG also utilizes the techniques introduced in DQN: experience replay and target networks.

1.
Experience Replay: Transitions (s, a, r, s') are stored in a replay buffer. During training, mini-batches of transitions are sampled randomly from this buffer. This breaks temporal correlations and improves sample efficiency, allowing the algorithm to learn from past experiences even if the current policy has moved on.

2.
Target Networks: Similar to DQN, DDPG uses target networks for both the actor and the critic to provide stable targets. Let $\theta^{\mu'}$ and $\theta^{Q'}$ be the parameters of the target actor and target critic networks, respectively. These target networks are soft updates of the main networks. Instead of copying weights directly, their parameters are slowly updated by Polyak averaging:

$\theta^{\mu'} \leftarrow \tau \theta^\mu + (1-\tau) \theta^{\mu'}$

$\theta^{Q'} \leftarrow \tau \theta^Q + (1-\tau) \theta^{Q'}$

where τ is a small constant (e.g., 10^{-3}). This soft update mechanism ensures that the target values change gradually, promoting stability.

The DDPG algorithm updates the critic and actor networks iteratively. The critic is trained to minimize the mean squared Bellman error, similar to DQN, but using the target Q-value computed by the target critic and the action chosen by the target actor:

The target Q-value for a transition (s, a, r, s') is:

$y = r + \gamma Q'(s', \mu'(s'; \theta^{\mu'}); \theta^{Q'})$

The critic loss is:

$L(\theta^Q) = \frac{1}{N} \sum_i \left(y_i - Q(s_i, a_i; \theta^Q) \right)^2$

The actor is trained to maximize the expected Q-value of the actions it proposes. This is done by taking the gradient of the Q-function with respect to the actor's parameters, using the chain rule:

$\nabla {\theta^\mu} J(\theta^\mu) = \frac{1}{N} \sum i \nabla a Q(s, a; \theta^Q)|{s=si, a=\mu(si;\theta^\mu)} \nabla{\theta^\mu} \mu(si; \theta^\mu)$

This update encourages the actor to output actions that the critic estimates as having higher Q-values.

Example: Autonomous Vehicle Steering Control

Consider controlling the steering of an autonomous vehicle. The state s could include sensor readings like current speed, steering angle, road curvature estimates from cameras, and distance to lane boundaries. The action a is the desired steering angle, which is a continuous value within a certain range (e.g., $[-30^\circ, 30^\circ]$).

A DDPG agent can be trained to learn a steering policy. The actor network would take the vehicle's state as input and output a specific steering angle. The critic network would evaluate the "goodness" of a given steering angle in a given state, estimating the future reward (e.g., staying in lane, smooth driving, reaching destination).

During training, the vehicle would interact with the environment (either a simulator or the real world, carefully). For example, if the vehicle is drifting too much to the right, the critic would learn that a larger negative steering angle (turning left) is preferable in that state. The actor, guided by the critic's feedback, would adjust its output to steer more to the left when such a state is encountered. The experience replay buffer would store many such interactions, allowing the DDPG agent to learn from diverse driving scenarios. The use of target networks ensures that the learning process remains stable, preventing drastic changes in the critic's evaluation or the actor's commands that could lead to erratic driving behavior. The continuous nature of the steering command is naturally handled by the DDPG's deterministic policy output.

Example: Controlling a Robotic Arm for Grasping

In robotic manipulation, DDPG can be used to control the continuous joint velocities or end-effector trajectories of a robotic arm. The state s might include joint angles, joint velocities, and potentially visual information from cameras. The action a would be a vector of desired joint velocities or torques for each motor.

Suppose the task is to grasp an object. The DDPG agent would learn a policy that controls the arm's movements to approach, grasp, and lift the object. The actor would output continuous velocity commands for each joint. The critic would estimate the expected future reward, which might be defined as a large positive reward for successfully grasping and lifting the object, and negative rewards for dropping the object, colliding with obstacles, or taking too long.

The DDPG agent would explore various grasping strategies by trying different sequences of joint velocity commands. The experience replay buffer would store successful and unsuccessful grasp attempts. The critic would learn to identify which joint movements are more likely to lead to a successful grasp. For instance, if the critic observes that a gentle, steady approach to the object leads to a higher Q-value, the actor will be trained to produce such movements. The stability provided by target networks is crucial for robotic control, as it prevents abrupt and potentially damaging changes in motor commands.

Proximal Policy Optimization (PPO)

While DDPG is effective for continuous action spaces, policy gradient methods, in general, can be sensitive to the step size of the policy update. If the policy is updated too much, it can lead to performance collapse. If updated too little, learning can be very slow. Proximal Policy Optimization (PPO) is a policy gradient method that aims to improve stability and reliability by limiting the magnitude of policy updates. It is designed to be easier to implement and tune than some other advanced policy gradient methods while achieving competitive performance.

PPO comes in two main variants: PPO-Clip and PPO-Penalty. The PPO-Clip variant, which is more commonly used, uses a clipped surrogate objective function to prevent excessively large policy updates. The core idea is to ensure that the new policy does not deviate too far from the old policy within a single update step.

Let $\pi
*\theta$ be the current policy and $\pi*{\theta*{old}}$ be the policy from which data was collected. The advantage function $A*t$ estimates how

much better an action at is compared to the average action in state st:

$A
t = Q(st, at) - V(st)$

where $V(s_t)$ is an estimate of the state-value function, often learned by a separate critic network. The surrogate objective function in PPO-Clip is defined as:

$L^{CLIP}(\theta) = \mathbb{E}
t \left[\min(rt(\theta) At, \text{clip}(rt(\theta), 1-\epsilon, 1+\epsilon) A_t) \right]$

where:

$rt(\theta) = \frac{\pi\theta(at/st)}{\pi{\theta{old}}(at/st)}$ is the probability ratio between the new policy and the old policy.
A_t is the estimated advantage function.
ϵ is a hyperparameter (e.g., 0.1 or 0.2) that defines the clipping range.

The term $\text{clip}(r
t(\theta), 1-\epsilon, 1+\epsilon)$ restricts the ratio $rt(\theta)$ to be within the range $[1-\epsilon, 1+\epsilon]$. The objective is to maximize this clipped objective. If the advantage At is positive, it means the action was good, and we want to increase the probability of taking that action. However, we limit how much we can increase it by clipping the ratio $rt(\theta)$ to $1+\epsilon$. If the advantage A_t is negative, it means the action was bad, and we want to decrease its probability. Again, we limit how much we can decrease it by clipping the ratio to $1-

\epsilon$. This clipping mechanism effectively discourages large policy updates that could destabilize learning.

PPO can also be used with a value function loss and an entropy bonus to encourage exploration. The full objective function typically includes:

$J(\theta) = L^{CLIP}(\theta) - c
*1 L^{VF}(\theta) + c*2 S\pi$

where:

$L^{VF}(\theta)$ is the mean squared error loss for the value function critic, typically $(V(*st) - V*{target})^2$.
$S\pi$ is the entropy of the policy, which is added to encourage exploration.
$c*1$ and $c*2$ are coefficients to balance these terms.

PPO is an on-policy algorithm, meaning it collects a batch of data with the current policy and then performs several gradient updates on that data before collecting new data. This differs from off-policy algorithms like DDPG or DQN that can reuse data extensively. However, PPO's ability to perform multiple gradient updates per batch of data makes it relatively sample-efficient for an on-policy method.

Example: Multi-Robot Coordination

Consider a scenario involving a team of robots tasked with a coordinated operation, such as search and rescue or formation control. Each robot needs to decide on its actions (e.g., movement direction, speed, communication strategy) based on its local observations and potentially the states of its neighbors. The actions are often continuous, like desired velocity vectors.

PPO is well-suited for such multi-agent reinforcement learning problems. Each robot can be equipped with a PPO agent. The state for a robot might include its own position and velocity, sensor readings about its surroundings, and information about the states of nearby robots. The action would be its control commands. The reward could be shared among the robots for achieving a common goal, or individual rewards could be given based on contributions.

The PPO-Clip objective ensures that each robot's policy doesn't change too drastically in response to a single observation or a small set of experiences. This is crucial for stable coordination. If one robot suddenly changes its behavior drastically, it could destabilize the entire team. The clipped surrogate objective limits how much any single robot can deviate from its previous coordinated behavior, promoting emergent stable team behavior. The inclusion of an entropy bonus can encourage robots to explore different communication strategies or movement patterns, potentially leading to more robust and efficient coordination.

Example: Chemical Reactor Control

In chemical engineering, controlling complex processes like a chemical reactor requires precise management of multiple continuous variables, such as temperature, pressure, and flow rates. The goal is to optimize yield, minimize energy consumption, and ensure safety.

A PPO agent can be employed to learn a control policy for such a reactor. The state s would comprise sensor readings from the reactor, including temperatures at various points, flow rates of reactants, pressure, and chemical concentrations. The actions a would be the setpoints for control valves, heaters, or pumps, which are continuous values.

The PPO algorithm can learn to maintain optimal operating conditions. For example, if the temperature starts to deviate from the target, the PPO agent will adjust the heating or cooling input. The critic network will estimate the value of being in a particular state (e.g., temperature, flow rates) and the expected future rewards. The PPO-Clip objective ensures that these adjustments are smooth and do not cause drastic changes in the reactor's dynamics, which could lead to instability or hazardous conditions. The ability to handle continuous actions makes PPO directly applicable to controlling these physical processes. The reward function could be designed to incentivize high product yield and low energy usage, guiding the PPO agent towards an economically optimal control strategy.

Comparison with Value-Based Methods (DQN)

Policy gradient methods, particularly those leveraging deep networks like DDPG and PPO, offer distinct advantages over value-based methods like DQN, especially in control tasks.

One of the most significant differences lies in how they handle action spaces. DQN is inherently designed for discrete action spaces. While continuous actions can be approximated by discretization, this approach can lead to a loss of precision and suffer from the curse of dimensionality if the action space is large. Policy gradient methods, on the other hand, can directly output continuous actions, making them naturally suited for a wide range of physical control problems where actions are continuous (e.g., motor torques, throttle position, steering angles). DDPG, by learning a deterministic policy, is particularly adept at this. PPO, by learning a stochastic policy, can also output continuous actions (typically sampled from a Gaussian distribution parameterized by the policy network) and is known for its ability to learn complex control tasks with high reliability.

Sample efficiency is another point of comparison. DQN, being an off-policy algorithm with experience replay, can be quite sample-efficient. It can reuse past experiences many times for learning. DDPG, also off-policy with experience replay and target networks, inherits this sample efficiency. PPO, being an on-policy algorithm, typically requires new samples for each policy update. However, PPO's ability to perform multiple gradient updates on a single batch of data, combined with its stable updates, often makes it more sample-efficient than basic policy gradient methods and competitive with off-policy methods in many practical scenarios. The stability of PPO's updates means that it can learn effectively from a batch of data without catastrophic forgetting or policy collapse, which can plague simpler on-policy methods.

Variance reduction is a key challenge in policy gradient methods. Basic policy gradients can have very high variance, leading to slow and unstable learning. Actor-critic methods, like DDPG, address this by using a critic to provide a lower-variance estimate of the return. PPO further enhances stability by clipping the policy updates, preventing large, destabilizing changes that would otherwise be driven by high-variance advantage estimates. DQN, by learning Q-values, implicitly deals with variance by averaging over future states and actions. However, the process of learning a Q-function can itself be prone to instability when using deep networks, as seen in the development of experience replay and target networks.

Finally, policy gradient methods are generally considered to be better at learning stochastic policies, which can be advantageous in environments with inherent randomness or where exploration is crucial. While PPO learns a stochastic policy, DDPG learns a deterministic policy. Stochastic policies can also be learned by DQN variants (e.g., by sampling actions from a distribution derived from Q-values), but policy gradient methods are often more directly optimized for this. For control tasks that require exploration and adaptation to unexpected events, learning a stochastic policy can be more robust.

In summary, policy gradient methods, particularly when implemented with deep neural networks as in DDPG and PPO, offer a powerful and flexible framework for tackling complex control problems. Their ability to handle continuous action spaces, coupled with techniques for stabilizing learning and improving sample efficiency, makes them indispensable tools in the modern reinforcement learning landscape. They represent a significant advancement from value-based methods, enabling agents to learn directly how to act in environments that were previously intractable for algorithms like DQN.

Model-Based Deep Reinforcement Learning

Up to this point, our exploration of Deep Reinforcement Learning (DRL) has primarily focused on model-free approaches. These methods, such as Deep Q-Networks (DQN), policy gradient algorithms like Proximal Policy Optimization (PPO), and actor-critic methods like Deep Deterministic Policy Gradient (DDPG), learn directly from interactions with the environment without explicitly building a representation of its underlying dynamics. They treat the environment as a black box, generating actions and learning from the received rewards and state transitions. While incredibly successful and widely applicable, model-free methods often require a significant number of interactions with the environment to achieve proficient performance. This can be a substantial limitation in real-world scenarios where data collection is expensive, time-consuming, or even hazardous, such as in robotics, autonomous driving, or complex industrial control.

This inherent data inefficiency has motivated the development of model-based DRL techniques. The central idea behind model-based DRL is to leverage a learned model of the environment's dynamics. This model, often a deep neural network, attempts to capture how the environment transitions from one state to another given a particular action, and potentially what rewards are associated with those transitions. By learning this model, the agent gains an understanding of the environment's "rules." This understanding can then be utilized in several ways to enhance the learning process and improve decision-making. The integration of learned models with deep learning architectures has opened up new avenues for tackling challenging control problems with improved sample efficiency.

One of the most straightforward ways to utilize a learned model is for **synthetic data generation**. Once an agent has learned a model of the environment's dynamics, it can use this model to simulate interactions. Instead of relying solely on real-world experiences, the agent can generate numerous "imagined" trajectories by querying its learned model. These synthetic experiences can then be used to train a model-free agent (e.g., a DQN or PPO agent) more effectively. The learned model acts as a simulator, allowing the agent to explore a wider range of scenarios and learn from many more data points than would be possible through real-world interaction alone. This approach is particularly beneficial in situations where real-world data is scarce. For example, a robot learning to grasp an object might initially collect a limited set of real grasps. With a learned dynamics model, it can then simulate thousands of additional grasps, exploring different approaches and refining its policy based on this augmented dataset. The key here is that the model needs to be sufficiently accurate for the synthetic data to be useful; a poor model can lead to compounding errors and hinder learning.

Model learning process: The process of learning an environment model typically involves training a neural network to predict the next state and/or reward given the current state and action. Let the state space be $\mathcal{S}$ and the action space be $\mathcal{A}$. The model, parameterized by ϕ, aims to approximate the transition function $P(s'|s, a)$ and the reward function $R(s, a)$. A common approach is to train a neural network, denoted f_ϕ, to predict the next state distribution or a deterministic next state:

$$s'_{pred} = f_\phi(s, a)$$

and a separate network, g_ϕ, to predict the reward:

$$r_{pred} = g_\phi(s, a)$$

These networks are typically trained using supervised learning on a dataset of collected state-action-next state-reward tuples: \$(s
i, ai, s'i, ri)\$. The loss function for training the model parameters \$\phi\$ would then be a combination of state prediction error (e.g., mean squared error for deterministic predictions, or cross-entropy for discrete states) and reward prediction error:

\$L(\phi) = \sum
i \left\| s'i - f\phi(si, ai) \right\|^2 + \sumi \left(ri - g\phi(si, ai) \right)^2\$

Once trained, this model \$f
\phi\$ *can be used to generate transitions. For example, starting from a state \$s\$, an action \$a\$ is chosen, and the model predicts the next state \$s'*{pred} = f*phi(s, a)\$ and reward \$r*{pred} = g_\phi(s, a)\$. This predicted transition can then be fed into a model-free learning algorithm.

Example: Robotic Manipulation with Learned Dynamics

Consider a robotic arm tasked with assembling components. The state might include joint angles, velocities, and the positions of the components. The action would be the torques or velocities applied to the robot's joints. Collecting sufficient data to learn a robust policy for all possible assembly configurations and interaction dynamics can be prohibitive.

A model-based DRL approach would first train a dynamics model. The robot collects a set of interaction data \$(s *t, a*t, *s{t+1}, r*t)$. This data is used to train a neural network that predicts $s{t+1}$ *and* rt given st *and* at. Once this dynamics model is learned, it can be used to generate a large amount of synthetic data. For instance, if the current policy suggests a particular set of joint torques, the learned model can predict the resulting joint angles and sensor readings for a short horizon into the future. This simulated data can then be used to train a model-free policy learning algorithm (like PPO or DDPG) that operates on the simulated environment. This allows the policy to explore various strategies and learn from a much larger dataset without requiring physical robot interactions for every learning step. The critical aspect is that the model needs to accurately capture the physics of the robot and its interaction with the environment, including contact forces and friction, to ensure that the learned policy generalizes well to the real world. Techniques like learning probabilistic transition models or incorporating uncertainty estimates in the model can further improve the robustness of this approach.

Another significant paradigm in model-based DRL involves **planning with a learned model**. Instead of just using the model for data augmentation, the agent uses it to "look ahead" and plan its actions. This is inspired by traditional planning algorithms in AI, but here the planning is performed using a model that was itself learned from data.

A prime example of this is the **Model Predictive Control (MPC)** framework. In MPC, at each time step, the agent uses its learned model to simulate a sequence of future actions and their predicted outcomes over a finite horizon. It then selects the action that optimizes a cost function (which can be directly related to the RL reward) over this horizon. Only the first action in the planned sequence is executed in the real environment. Then, the agent observes the new state, and the entire process is repeated. This receding horizon approach allows the agent to adapt to changing conditions and correct its planned trajectory based on new information.

The integration of deep learning with MPC in model-based DRL allows for the learning of complex, non-linear dynamics models that can then be used for planning. The planning process itself can be computationally intensive, especially for long horizons. Techniques like Monte Carlo Tree Search (MCTS), popularized in game playing (e.g., AlphaGo), can be adapted to work with learned models. In this context, MCTS can explore the state-action space, guided by the learned model, to find optimal or near-optimal action sequences. The learned model provides the transitions and rewards needed to expand the search tree, enabling more informed decisions than random exploration.

A more advanced and integrated approach is exemplified by algorithms like
MuZero. MuZero represents a significant step forward by learning a model that is specifically optimized for planning within the reinforcement learning context. Unlike traditional model-based methods that aim to accurately predict future states and rewards, MuZero learns a model that is sufficient for planning. This model comprises three main components:

1.
Representation Function (h): This function takes raw observations (e.g., images) and converts them into a learned state representation that captures relevant information for decision-making. $h(o_t) = s_t$.

2.
Dynamics Function (g): This function predicts the next state representation and reward, given the current state representation and an action. Importantly, this dynamics model is "learned" in a latent space, not necessarily in the observation space. $g(s_t, a_t) = (s_{t+1}, r_t)$,

where $s*{t+1}$ is the next state representation and $r*t$ is the predicted reward.

3.
Prediction Function (f): This function predicts the policy (action probabilities) and the value (expected future reward) from a given state representation. $f(s*t) = (p*t, v*t)$, where $p*t$ is the policy distribution and v_t is the value estimate.

MuZero uses these learned components to perform planning using Monte Carlo Tree Search (MCTS). During MCTS, the agent uses the learned dynamics function g to simulate future transitions and rewards in the learned latent space. The prediction function f is used to guide the MCTS search by providing initial policy and value estimates for new states encountered during the search. The key innovation of MuZero is that the learned model is trained end-to-end with the policy and value networks, optimizing the model parameters such that they are useful for MCTS, rather than just for accurate state prediction. This means MuZero can learn to play games like Go, Chess, Shogi, and Atari without being given the rules of the game. The learned model implicitly encodes the rules through its predictive capabilities during planning.

The planning process in MuZero typically unfolds as follows:

When deciding on an action in a real state $s*t$ (represented by $s*t = h(o_t)$):
1. The MCTS algorithm is initiated from the current state representation s_t.
2. For each node in the MCTS tree, the agent uses the dynamics function g to simulate transitions and rewards to explore potential future states and actions. The prediction function f provides the initial policy and value estimates for the nodes.

3. The MCTS search expands the tree by balancing exploration (trying new actions) and exploitation (following promising paths).
4. After a sufficient number of simulations, the MCTS outputs a refined policy distribution over actions from the root node.
5. The agent selects an action based on this MCTS-derived policy.
6. The selected action is executed in the real environment, and a new observation o_{t+1} is received.
7. The entire process is repeated for the next time step.

Crucially, MuZero's training involves generating trajectories using its learned model for planning. The policy is updated to match the improved policy derived from MCTS, and the value function is updated to match the outcomes of the MCTS simulations. The dynamics model is trained to accurately predict the results of these simulated trajectories. This end-to-end training allows the model to learn representations and dynamics that are directly beneficial for planning and decision-making.

Example: Mastering Atari Games with MuZero

Consider the task of playing Atari games, where states are raw pixel observations, and actions are discrete joystick movements. Traditional DQN learns a Q-function directly from pixels, requiring a vast number of game frames to learn effective policies. MuZero, on the other hand, learns a compact latent representation of the game state and uses a learned dynamics model for planning.

When MuZero is presented with a game screen (observation $o t$), *its representation function h converts it into a latent state $s*t$. Then, for planning, MuZero uses its dynamics function g to "imagine" sequences of actions and their consequences. For instance, if playing

Breakout, and the current state involves the ball nearing the paddle, MuZero might use MCTS to simulate moves like "move left," "move right," or "do nothing." The dynamics model g predicts how the ball and paddle positions would change, and the reward function predicts any score changes. The prediction function f estimates the value of these imagined future states. After many simulations, MCTS suggests the optimal action, perhaps "move right," to intercept the ball. This planned action is then executed in the real game.

During training, MuZero collects these experiences, including the observations, actions taken, and the MCTS-derived policies. The representation, dynamics, and prediction networks are trained jointly. The dynamics model, for example, learns to predict the next latent state and reward when given a current latent state and an action. This allows MuZero to learn powerful policies with significantly fewer game frames compared to purely model-free approaches like DQN. The learned latent states are not necessarily interpretable in terms of pixel configurations but are effective for predictive modeling and planning.

The power of model-based DRL, especially in the vein of MuZero, lies in its ability to combine the strengths of model-free learning with explicit reasoning and planning capabilities. By learning a model of the environment and using it for planning, agents can achieve higher sample efficiency, exhibit better generalization, and make more robust decisions, particularly in complex domains with long horizons or sparse rewards. The learned model acts as an internal simulator, allowing the agent to explore and learn without the constraints of real-world interaction costs. This is a crucial step towards developing more intelligent and data-efficient AI systems for a wide range of applications.

Challenges and Future Directions: Despite the promise, model-based DRL faces challenges. The accuracy of the learned model is paramount. If the model is inaccurate, planning based on it can lead to suboptimal or even catastrophic decisions. This is known as the "model bias" problem. Techniques to mitigate this include:

Ensemble of Models: Training multiple models and using their predictions to reduce uncertainty or average out errors.
Model Uncertainty Estimation: Quantifying the confidence in the model's predictions and using this information during planning. Actions leading to states where the model is uncertain might be avoided or explored more cautiously.
Directly Optimizing the Model for Planning: As in MuZero, training the model parameters such that they are most useful for the planning algorithm (like MCTS), even if they don't provide the most accurate pixel-level predictions.

Furthermore, learning accurate models for high-dimensional, continuous state and action spaces remains a significant research area. The computational cost of planning, especially for long horizons or in complex environments, can also be a bottleneck.

Future research in model-based DRL is likely to focus on developing more robust and efficient model learning techniques, improving the integration of learned models with advanced planning algorithms, and addressing the challenges of model bias and uncertainty. The trend towards hybrid approaches that leverage the complementary strengths of model-free and model-based methods is also expected to continue. For instance, one might use a learned model to generate synthetic data for a model-free agent, while simultaneously using the model for short-horizon planning. This synergistic combination holds immense potential for pushing the boundaries of what DRL can achieve, especially in safety-critical and data-scarce real-world applications. The ability to "reason" about the consequences of actions through a learned internal model is a critical step towards more general artificial intelligence.

The transformative capabilities of Deep Reinforcement Learning (DRL) are perhaps most vividly illustrated in the realm of robotics and autonomous systems. These domains present a confluence of challenges that DRL is uniquely positioned to address: high-dimensional sensory inputs, complex, often non-linear dynamics, and the necessity for robust decision-making in real-time. Traditional control methods, while foundational, often struggle with the sheer complexity and variability encountered in real-world robotic applications. They typically rely on precise mathematical models of the system and its environment, which are difficult to derive and maintain for systems exhibiting intricate behaviors or operating in unpredictable settings. DRL, by contrast, learns policies directly from interaction, bypassing the need for explicit, hand-engineered models and demonstrating remarkable adaptability.

One of the most significant areas where DRL has made profound inroads is in robotic manipulation. The ability to grasp and manipulate a diverse array of objects, often with different shapes, textures, and weights, is a hallmark of advanced robotic intelligence. Consider the task of grasping an object. A robot needs to perceive the object's geometry, determine the optimal grasp points and forces, and execute a precise movement sequence. This involves processing complex visual data from cameras, potentially tactile information from sensors, and coordinating multiple degrees of freedom in the robot's arm and gripper. DRL agents, trained using a combination of vision and robotic state information, have demonstrated remarkable success in learning robust grasping policies. For instance, research has shown DRL agents learning to grasp objects from a large, diverse set of items, often outperforming classical grasp planning methods that require detailed object models. The learning process typically involves training an agent to map raw sensor inputs (like camera images) to motor commands (like joint torques or gripper forces). By receiving rewards for successful grasps and penalties for failures, the agent iteratively refines its policy. The sample efficiency can be significantly improved by leveraging simulation environments that mimic real-world physics and sensor noise, allowing for rapid data generation before deployment on a physical robot. This approach not only reduces the time and cost of training but also enhances safety by allowing exploration of potentially unstable grasp configurations in a virtual setting. The use of end-to-end learning, where the DRL agent directly maps pixels to actions, has been particularly impactful, simplifying the traditional pipeline of perception, planning, and control into a single, learned function.

Beyond static manipulation, DRL has also revolutionized robotic locomotion. Teaching robots to walk, run, and navigate challenging terrains is a critical objective for applications ranging from exploration and disaster relief to agriculture and logistics. Quadrupedal robots, inspired by animals, are particularly adept at traversing uneven landscapes, but developing stable and agile gaits is a formidable control problem. DRL offers a powerful framework for learning these complex motor skills. Agents can be trained to control the torques or positions of a quadruped's joints based on sensory feedback such as joint encoders, accelerometers, and gyroscopes. The reward function typically incentivizes forward progress, stability, and energy efficiency, while penalizing falls or undesirable body postures. Early successes in this area involved learning basic walking gaits in simulation. However, recent advancements have enabled robots to learn highly dynamic behaviors like jumping, turning, and recovering from disturbances. One notable aspect is the ability of DRL to learn policies that are robust to variations in terrain and external perturbations. By training in environments with diverse simulated obstacles, slopes, and even simulated "kicks" to the robot, the learned policies can generalize to unseen conditions. For example, a quadruped robot trained with DRL can learn to adapt its gait on the fly to navigate rocks, uneven ground, or slippery surfaces, exhibiting a level of adaptability that would be extremely difficult to achieve with traditional control design. The continuous learning aspect of DRL is also crucial here; a robot can continue to refine its locomotion skills even after deployment, adapting to wear and tear or new environmental challenges.

Autonomous driving represents another frontier where DRL is making significant contributions. The task of navigating complex urban environments, interacting with other vehicles, pedestrians, and traffic signals, requires a sophisticated decision-making system capable of handling a vast state space and making rapid, safe choices. While classical approaches often rely on modular pipelines (perception, prediction, planning, control), DRL offers the potential for end-to-end learning, directly mapping sensor inputs (LiDAR, cameras, radar) to driving commands (steering, acceleration, braking). DRL agents can learn to handle nuanced driving scenarios that are difficult to pre-program. For instance, learning to merge into dense traffic, navigate unprotected turns, or react appropriately to sudden events like a pedestrian stepping into the road can be trained using DRL. Rewards are designed to encourage safe, efficient, and comfortable driving, penalizing collisions, traffic violations, and jerky maneuvers. The high dimensionality of sensory data, particularly from cameras and LiDAR, makes DRL a natural fit. Deep neural networks within the DRL framework can extract relevant features from these rich inputs, enabling the agent to perceive its surroundings and make informed decisions. Furthermore, DRL's ability to learn from experience is invaluable for capturing the subtle behaviors and predictions of other road users, which are often difficult to model explicitly. While fully autonomous driving using DRL is still an active area of research and development,

DRL components are increasingly being integrated into advanced driver-assistance systems (ADAS) and sophisticated simulation platforms for testing and validation. These systems can learn to handle edge cases and optimize driving strategies in ways that surpass traditional rule-based systems.

The application of DRL in robotics and autonomous systems extends to numerous other domains. In aerial robotics, DRL has been used to train autonomous drones for complex navigation tasks, such as performing aggressive maneuvers in cluttered environments or autonomously inspecting infrastructure. For example, drones can learn to fly through narrow gaps, avoid obstacles at high speeds, and even land precisely on designated targets. The visual perception capabilities of DRL are particularly useful for drones operating in GPS-denied environments or requiring visual servoing for precise movements. In underwater robotics, DRL can enable autonomous vehicles to navigate complex underwater terrains, avoid collisions with obstacles, and perform tasks like sample collection in dynamic ocean currents. The control of robotic manipulators in unstructured environments, such as disaster sites or construction zones, is another area where DRL is proving its worth. Robots can learn to pick up and move debris, operate tools, and interact with their surroundings in a more intelligent and adaptive manner.

A key factor contributing to the success of DRL in these applications is its inherent ability to handle high-dimensional, continuous state and action spaces. Traditional control methods often require significant simplification or discretization of the state and action spaces, which can lead to a loss of fidelity and performance. DRL, by leveraging deep neural networks, can directly process raw sensor data (like images or point clouds) and output continuous control signals (like joint torques or velocities). This end-to-end learning paradigm simplifies the overall system design and allows for the discovery of complex control strategies that might be unintuitive to human engineers.

Furthermore, the adaptability of DRL agents is crucial for real-world deployment. Robots operating in dynamic environments are subject to changes in lighting conditions, object appearances, and physical interactions. DRL policies, through continuous learning or fine-tuning, can adapt to these changes, maintaining performance over time. This is in contrast to traditional controllers that may need recalibration or redesign when operating conditions deviate significantly from their design parameters.

The use of simulation environments, powered by sophisticated physics engines, plays a critical role in enabling DRL for robotics. These simulators allow for rapid and safe exploration of the state-action space, generating vast amounts of training data without the risk of damaging expensive hardware or causing safety incidents. Techniques like domain randomization, where simulation parameters (e.g., friction, lighting, textures) are varied during training, help to bridge the "sim-to-real" gap, ensuring that policies learned in simulation generalize effectively to the real world. However, this gap remains a significant challenge, and ongoing research focuses on improving sim-to-real transfer through more accurate simulation models, adaptive learning techniques, and robust policy optimization.

The integration of DRL into robotics and autonomous systems is not without its challenges. Ensuring safety and reliability remains a paramount concern, especially for safety-critical applications like autonomous driving. The "black box" nature of deep neural networks can make it difficult to provide formal guarantees about system behavior. Research into explainable AI (XAI) and formal verification methods for DRL is crucial to build trust and enable widespread adoption. Moreover, the computational resources required for training complex DRL models can be substantial, necessitating specialized hardware and efficient algorithms. Finally, the practical aspects of deploying and maintaining DRL-based systems in the field, including data collection, model updates, and failure detection, are active areas of engineering and research.

Despite these challenges, the impact of DRL on robotics and autonomous systems is undeniable. It has unlocked new levels of performance and autonomy, enabling robots to perform tasks that were previously considered impossible. As DRL algorithms continue to advance in terms of sample efficiency, robustness, and safety, we can expect to see even more sophisticated and capable robots and autonomous systems emerge, reshaping industries and our daily lives. The ability to learn complex behaviors from raw sensory data and adapt to dynamic, unpredictable environments positions DRL as a cornerstone technology for the future of intelligent machines.

Chapter 7: Safety-Aware Learning and Constraint Handling

The pervasive integration of learning-based systems into modern engineering applications, particularly those that interact with the physical world, brings forth a critical imperative: the unwavering focus on safety. Traditional control systems, while often less adaptable to novel scenarios, benefit from a rich history of formal verification and rigorous mathematical guarantees. Their behavior, within defined operating envelopes, can be meticulously analyzed and proven safe under specific conditions. This predictability has been the bedrock upon which safety-critical systems, from aircraft autopilots to industrial robotic arms, have been built. However, the very power of learning systems—their ability to adapt, generalize, and discover emergent behaviors—also introduces inherent uncertainties that challenge these established paradigms.

When a learning system, especially one powered by deep neural networks, encounters a situation outside its training distribution, its response can be unpredictable. This unpredictability is not merely an academic concern; it carries significant implications for real-world deployment. Consider the domain of autonomous vehicles. A failure in perception or decision-making could lead to a collision, endangering occupants, other road users, and pedestrians. In industrial settings, a malfunctioning robotic arm might deviate from its intended path, causing damage to expensive machinery or severe injury to human operators. In aerospace, an unexpected control command from a learning-based autopilot could have catastrophic consequences. The potential for failure in these scenarios transcends mere inconvenience; it directly impacts human safety, economic stability, and public trust.

The complexity arises from the nature of learning itself. Many modern learning algorithms, particularly deep reinforcement learning (DRL) agents, operate as "black boxes." While their performance can be impressive during training and in simulated environments, understanding the precise reasoning behind a particular decision or action, especially when it deviates from expected behavior, can be exceptionally difficult. This lack of interpretability makes it challenging to apply the same formal safety verification techniques that are standard in classical control. We cannot simply prove that a neural network policy will always remain within safe bounds because its internal workings are not transparent to mathematical analysis in the same way as a PID controller or a state-machine.

The criticality of safety is amplified in safety-critical domains where the cost of failure is unacceptably high. These are environments where even a small probability of a severe outcome necessitates extraordinary measures. Automotive safety standards, for instance, are exceptionally stringent, requiring extensive validation and redundancy. Similarly, in aviation and medical devices, the burden of proof for safety is immense. Introducing learning systems into these domains therefore requires a fundamental shift in our approach to safety assurance. It moves beyond simply optimizing for performance metrics like speed or efficiency and places safety as a non-negotiable, primary objective that must be integrated throughout the entire development lifecycle.

This necessitates a proactive strategy for safety. It means anticipating potential failure modes, not just for known scenarios, but also for those that might arise from novelty. This involves a deep understanding of the learning algorithm's limitations, the characteristics of the data it was trained on, and the properties of the environment in which it will operate. It calls for developing new methodologies that can provide assurances about the system's behavior, even when faced with uncertainty or unforeseen circumstances. The challenge is to harness the power of learning systems while simultaneously building robust safeguards that prevent catastrophic outcomes. This subsection serves as the foundational statement for the subsequent exploration of these vital safety-aware learning techniques and constraint handling mechanisms. It frames the problem, highlighting why safety is not an afterthought but a core design principle when deploying intelligent systems in the real world, setting the stage for the deeper dives into specific solutions that lie ahead.

The fundamental divergence between traditional control and learning-based systems in terms of safety assurance can be starkly illustrated by considering their respective design philosophies. Classical control engineering often relies on a predictive, model-based approach. System dynamics are mathematically modeled, and controllers are designed to ensure stability and adherence to desired trajectories. Safety is then often a direct consequence of this rigorous mathematical design. For instance, in a linear control system, stability can be proven using Lyapunov functions, guaranteeing that the system will not diverge uncontrollably. Even in more complex non-linear systems, established tools exist for analyzing stability margins and ensuring that control inputs remain within physical limits. The system's behavior is, in essence, an open book, amenable to formal analysis and verification before deployment.

Learning systems, in contrast, often learn their behavior through interaction and experience, particularly in the case of reinforcement learning. While this allows them to discover highly effective strategies in complex environments, it also means that their internal decision-making logic might not be directly interpretable or easily verifiable through traditional mathematical proofs. An agent might learn a policy that relies on subtle correlations in the training data that are not fully understood by the human designers. When confronted with a novel input, the network might extrapolate in an unintended and unsafe manner. For example, a DRL agent trained to control a robotic arm might learn to exploit a particular contact dynamic that is only present under specific, rare circumstances. If this agent is deployed in an environment where that dynamic is absent or modified, its learned policy could lead to unexpected and potentially hazardous movements.

The implications of this unpredictability are profound, especially in safety-critical applications. Consider the development of an autonomous driving system. While the goal is to achieve human-level or superhuman driving performance, the introduction of learning components means that ensuring safety requires more than just verifying that the learned policy performs well on average. It demands assurance that the system will not engage in dangerous behavior, even in rare, out-of-distribution scenarios. This could include situations like encountering unusual road debris, experiencing sensor malfunctions under specific weather conditions, or interacting with erratic human drivers whose behavior falls outside the typical patterns observed during training.

The challenge is compounded by the sheer scale and complexity of many real-world engineering problems. Modern robotic systems, for instance, operate with numerous degrees of freedom, interact with dynamic environments, and process high-dimensional sensor data. Traditional control methods might struggle to provide robust and adaptive control for such systems without significant simplification or manual tuning, which can be time-consuming and may not achieve optimal performance. Learning systems offer a path to overcoming these limitations, but their deployment must be accompanied by a robust framework for safety.

This safety framework needs to go beyond mere performance

evaluation. It involves understanding the limits of the learned policy, identifying potential failure modes, and developing mechanisms to either prevent the system from entering unsafe states or to mitigate the consequences of an unsafe action. This could involve incorporating safety constraints directly into the learning process, developing independent safety monitors that can override the learned policy when necessary, or utilizing formal methods to certify that certain safety properties are maintained.

The economic and societal impact of failures in learning systems is also a significant driver for prioritizing safety. A single high-profile accident involving an autonomous vehicle or a malfunctioning industrial robot can erode public trust, lead to significant financial penalties, and result in stringent regulatory hurdles that can stifle innovation. Therefore, building a strong safety case for learning systems is not just a technical requirement but a business and ethical imperative. It ensures that the transformative potential of these technologies can be realized responsibly.

This emphasis on safety sets the stage for exploring the various techniques that are being developed to address these challenges. It highlights the need for a paradigm shift in how we design, validate, and deploy intelligent systems, moving from a primary focus on performance to an equally, if not more, critical focus on guaranteed safe operation, especially in the face of uncertainty and novelty. The subsequent sections will delve into the specific methods and strategies employed to achieve this crucial balance between learning and safety.

The "black box" nature of many deep learning models, particularly neural networks, presents a fundamental hurdle for traditional safety verification methods. In fields like aerospace and automotive engineering, safety certification often relies on formal proofs and rigorous mathematical analysis. These methods typically require that the system's behavior can be precisely modeled and that its outputs can be provably bounded or constrained. For instance, control engineers might use tools like formal methods, reachability analysis, or state-space modeling to demonstrate that a system will remain within safe operating parameters under all foreseeable conditions.

However, when a learning system, such as a deep neural network controlling a robotic arm or an autonomous vehicle, is involved, applying these tools directly becomes extremely challenging. The complex, non-linear mappings learned by these networks are often difficult to characterize analytically. We may not fully understand why a specific input leads to a particular output, making it hard to provide formal guarantees about its behavior, especially when faced with inputs that differ significantly from the training data. This lack of interpretability means that even if a system performs exceptionally well during extensive testing, there remains an inherent uncertainty about its behavior in novel or unexpected situations—the very situations where safety is most critical.

Consider the example of an autonomous vehicle navigating a busy intersection. A traditional system might rely on explicit rules and models for predicting the behavior of other vehicles and pedestrians. If a pedestrian suddenly deviates from a predictable path, a rule-based system might still have a defined response. In contrast, a learning-based system might encounter an unprecedented scenario for which its learned policy offers no clear, safe guidance. The network might extrapolate based on superficial similarities to training data, leading to an incorrect or dangerous decision. The potential consequences—a collision, injury, or worse—underscore the paramount importance of addressing this unpredictability.

The risks associated with deploying learning systems in safety-critical applications are not hypothetical. They represent a tangible threat that demands a proactive and robust approach to safety engineering. This is particularly true in domains where failure can result in severe harm to humans or extensive damage to property. Think of industrial automation, where robots collaborate with humans on assembly lines. A misstep by a robotic arm due to an unpredictable learning algorithm could lead to serious injuries. In healthcare, learning systems are being explored for diagnostic assistance and even surgical robotics. Here, the stakes are extraordinarily high, and any compromise in safety is unacceptable.

The criticality of safety in these contexts cannot be overstated. It shifts the focus from merely achieving high performance to guaranteeing a minimum level of safe operation under all conditions, including those that are unforeseen. This necessitates a fundamental re-evaluation of the development and validation processes for learning-based systems. It implies that research and development efforts must not only focus on improving the learning algorithms' accuracy and efficiency but also on developing mechanisms to ensure their predictability, robustness, and accountability.

This involves moving beyond empirical testing, which can only cover a finite subset of possible scenarios, towards more principled approaches that can provide stronger assurances. It may involve integrating domain knowledge and safety constraints into the learning process itself, developing techniques for monitoring the system's behavior at runtime and intervening when necessary, or exploring methods that can provide a degree of explainability for the decisions made by the learning system. The challenge is to build trust in these powerful, yet inherently complex, artificial intelligence systems by demonstrating that their deployment is safe, reliable, and responsible. This foundational understanding of the criticality of safety is what motivates the subsequent exploration of specific techniques designed to achieve these objectives.

In the pursuit of deploying learning-based systems into safety-critical applications, the abstract notion of "safety" must be translated into concrete, actionable requirements. This transformation is achieved through the rigorous formulation of safety constraints. These constraints serve as the mathematical bedrock upon which safe operation is built, defining the boundaries within which the system is permitted to operate and the undesirable outcomes it must actively avoid. Without a precise, formalized definition of what constitutes safe behavior, any attempt to guarantee it would remain elusive.

The landscape of engineering systems is replete with various categories of constraints, each reflecting different aspects of operational and design limitations. A primary and often paramount concern is **state constraints**. These define the permissible ranges for the system's internal variables, essentially dictating the operational envelope. For instance, in the context of an autonomous vehicle, state constraints might dictate that the vehicle's velocity must remain below a certain threshold on residential streets, or that its pitch and roll angles should not exceed values that would compromise stability. For an industrial robot, joint angles must stay within their physical limits to prevent mechanical damage or exceeding the workspace boundaries. Similarly, in a chemical process, the temperature and pressure of reactors must be maintained within a specific band to ensure stable operation and prevent runaway reactions or material failure. Mathematically, these constraints are typically expressed as inequalities. A state variable, $x

\in \mathbb{R}^n$, might be constrained to lie within a set $\mathcal{X}$, such that $x \in \mathcal{X}$. This set $\mathcal{X}$ can be defined by a series of linear or non-linear inequalities:
$$ li \leq xi \leq u_i \quad \text{for } i=1, \dots, n $$
or more generally, by a function $g(x) \leq 0$. For example, ensuring a robotic arm's end-effector stays within a designated safe work cell $\mathcal{W}$ can be formulated as:
$$ p_{\text{end-effector}}(q) \in \mathcal{W} $$
where $p_{\text{end-effector}}(q)$ is the end-effector position in Cartesian space as a function of the joint angles q.

Beyond the internal states, the actions taken by the system, dictated by its control policy, are also subject to significant limitations. These are known as
control constraints or **actuator constraints**. Actuators, whether they are motors, valves, or thrusters, have finite physical capabilities. They cannot instantaneously change their output, nor can they produce infinite forces or torques. For an electric motor, this might mean a limit on the maximum voltage or current it can accept, or a maximum rate at which its speed can change (slew rate). In a hydraulic system, a valve might have a maximum flow rate or be unable to open or close instantaneously. These constraints are crucial for preventing damage to the hardware and for ensuring that the system's response is physically realizable. Control constraints are typically formulated as bounds on the control input vector $u \in \mathbb{R}^m$. This can be represented as:
$$ u{\min, i} \leq ui \leq u_{\max, i} \quad \text{for } i=1, \dots, m $$
or more generally, $u \in \mathcal{U}$, where $\mathcal{U}$ is a convex or non-convex set representing the feasible control actions. For example, if a learning algorithm were to control the throttle of a vehicle, the throttle position would be constrained between 0% and 100%. Similarly, the steering angle of a vehicle is physically limited. For a drone, the maximum thrust that can be generated by its rotors is a hard

limit. Failure to respect these constraints can lead to actuator saturation, which can destabilize the system or lead to undesirable performance.

The third significant category encompasses
performance constraints. While state and control constraints focus on preventing physical damage or system instability, performance constraints relate to the quality and desirability of the system's behavior. These are often more nuanced and can sometimes be expressed as trade-offs. Examples include ensuring that oscillations are kept within acceptable bounds, that settling times for tracking trajectories are within a certain limit, or that energy consumption is minimized. While often framed as optimization objectives, they can also be critical for safety. For instance, excessive oscillations in an aircraft's control surfaces could lead to structural fatigue or passenger discomfort, bordering on unsafe. In a robotic manipulator, rapid, jerky movements (high jerk) can not only be unsafe for human interaction but can also put undue stress on the mechanical components. These constraints can be more complex to formulate mathematically, sometimes involving norms of signals over time, frequency-domain specifications, or conditional statements. For example, a constraint on overshoot for a step response might be formulated as:
$$ \frac{y_{\max} - y_{\text{final}}}{y_{\text{final}}} \leq \epsilon $$
where $y_{\max}$ is the maximum value achieved by the output y and y_{final} is the final steady-state value. Another example could be a constraint on the rate of change of a state variable, reflecting a smoothness requirement:
$$ |\dot{x}_i(t)| \leq M_i \quad \forall t $$
for some predefined bounds M_i.

In the context of machine learning, particularly reinforcement learning, these constraints can be incorporated in several ways. One common approach is to modify the

reward function. For state constraints, any deviation into an unsafe region can be penalized with a large negative reward. For control constraints, exceeding the limits can also incur significant penalties. For performance constraints, deviations from desired performance (e.g., excessive oscillation) can lead to reduced rewards. For example, if a robot arm's joint velocity ω must satisfy $|\omega| \leq \omega_{\max}$, the reward function $R(s, a)$ could include a term like:
$$ R{\text{penalty}}(s, a) = -\lambda \sum{i} \max(0, |\omegai(s, a)| - \omega{\max, i})^2 $$
where λ is a weighting factor. This additive penalty encourages the agent to learn policies that keep the joint velocities within safe limits.

However, relying solely on reward shaping can be problematic. If the penalty for violating a constraint is not sufficiently large or if the agent rarely encounters violations during training, it might still learn unsafe behaviors. Moreover, this approach does not offer formal guarantees. Therefore, more direct methods of constraint handling are often preferred, especially for hard constraints.

One such method is
constraint projection or **clipping**. When a control command u is generated by the learning policy, it can be clipped to the feasible set $\mathcal{U}$:
$$ u{\text{clipped}} = \text{clip}(u, u{\min}, u_{\max}) $$
Similarly, if a state variable x violates its bounds, it can be projected back onto the feasible set. While simple, clipping can lead to undesirable effects, such as saturating actuators and causing the system to behave differently than intended by the policy, potentially leading to oscillatory behavior or reduced performance.

Another powerful approach is to integrate constraints directly into the optimization problem during policy learning. This is often seen in Model

Predictive Control (MPC) frameworks, where the future trajectory is optimized subject to system dynamics and constraints. For learning-based MPC, the learning agent might learn a model of the system and/or a policy that directly optimizes an objective function that includes constraint satisfaction. For example, if a learning algorithm is trained to find optimal control parameters for an MPC controller, the objective function would explicitly incorporate the cost of constraint violations.

Furthermore, constraints can be represented not just as simple inequalities but also as logical conditions. For instance, a constraint might be: "If the vehicle is in a school zone AND the time is between 8 AM and 4 PM, THEN the speed must be below 25 mph." Such logical constraints can be incorporated into formal verification methods or adapted into penalty functions, though their integration into standard gradient-based learning can be more complex.

Consider the concrete example of a drone operating in an urban environment.

State Constraints: The drone's altitude might be constrained to be above a minimum safe altitude (e.g., 10 meters) to avoid ground obstacles and below a maximum ceiling (e.g., 150 meters) due to regulations or battery limitations. Its horizontal position must remain within a predefined geofenced area. Its velocity in all axes should not exceed certain limits to ensure stable flight and prevent excessive forces on the airframe.
Control Constraints: The motors have a maximum thrust and a minimum thrust (to maintain stability). The rate of change of motor commands (e.g., PWM signals) is also limited due to the physical inertia of the motors and electronic speed controllers (ESCs). The maximum tilt

angle of the drone is also a control constraint, dictating how aggressively it can maneuver.
Performance Constraints: While not strictly safety, rapid acceleration or deceleration can be considered undesirable performance that might also impact safety indirectly by making the drone's motion less predictable to external observers or by stressing components. Smooth transitions between waypoints are often desired.

Formulating these constraints mathematically allows us to guide the learning process. For example, if a learning algorithm is used to tune the parameters of a PID controller for the drone's attitude stabilization, the reward function could penalize any instance where the tilt angle exceeds, say, 45 degrees or where the motor command rate of change exceeds a physical limit. If a state variable x is constrained to be in $\mathcal{X}$, the objective function J could be augmented:

$$ J' = J + \alpha \sum{k} \max(0, c(xk, u_k)) $$
where $c(xk, uk)$ represents a measure of constraint violation at time step k, and α is a penalty coefficient. For a state constraint $x \in \mathcal{X}$, c could be the distance from x to $\mathcal{X}$. For a control constraint $u \in \mathcal{U}$, c could be the distance from u to $\mathcal{U}$.

The precise formulation of these constraints is paramount. A poorly defined constraint, or one that is too easily violated by the learning process, will not adequately ensure safety. For instance, if the penalty for exceeding a joint velocity limit is too low, the reinforcement learning agent might learn to exploit that limit to achieve faster task completion, even if it means occasional, brief over-velocities. Conversely, an overly aggressive penalty could make the learning problem intractable or lead to excessively conservative behavior that severely hinders performance. Therefore, careful consideration of the system's physics, actuator capabilities, and desired operational boundaries is necessary for effective constraint formulation. This mathematical translation of safety requirements is the critical first step in developing learning systems that can be trusted in real-world, safety-sensitive applications.

When we move from simply acknowledging constraints to actively managing them within a learning or control framework, we enter the realm of **constrained optimization techniques**. The previous discussion established the necessity and various forms of constraints – state, control, and performance. Now, we must explore the mathematical machinery that allows us to respect these boundaries while still pursuing optimal system behavior. These techniques are the workhorses that translate abstract safety requirements into actionable control policies, ensuring that the learned system operates within the designated safe envelope.

At the heart of constrained optimization lies the challenge of finding the best solution to an objective function while simultaneously satisfying a set of conditions. For many engineering problems, this translates to minimizing or maximizing a cost or performance metric subject to a variety of equality and inequality constraints. A fundamental mathematical tool for dealing with such problems is the method of **Lagrange multipliers**.

Consider a general optimization problem:

$$ \min_{x} f(x) $$
subject to:
$$ g_i(x) \leq 0, \quad i = 1, \dots, m $$
$$ h_j(x) = 0, \quad j = 1, \dots, p $$
Here, $f(x)$ is the objective function we wish to optimize, $g_i(x)$ *are inequality constraints, and* $h_j(x)$ are equality constraints. The domain of x is typically a subset of $\mathbb{R}^n$.

The method of Lagrange multipliers introduces a set of new variables, known as Lagrange multipliers (often denoted by Greek letters like λ for inequality constraints and ν for equality constraints), to convert a constrained optimization problem into an unconstrained one, or at least a problem where the constraints are handled implicitly within the structure of the optimization. For equality constraints, we form the Lagrangian function:

$$ \mathcal{L}(x, \nu) = f(x) + \sum{j=1}^{p} \nuj h_j(x) $$
The key insight is that at an optimal solution $x^$, *if the gradients of the constraints are linearly independent, then the gradient of the objective function must be a linear combination of the gradients of the active constraints (those that are binding at x^*). This condition can be expressed by setting the gradient of the Lagrangian with respect to x to zero:
$$ \nablax \mathcal{L}(x, \nu) = \nablax f(x) + \sum{j=1}^{p} \nuj \nablax hj(x) = 0 $$
Combined with the original equality constraints $h_j(x) = 0$, this system of equations can be solved for x and ν.

For inequality constraints, the situation is slightly more complex, leading to the Karush-Kuhn-Tucker (KKT) conditions. The Lagrangian is extended to include multipliers for inequality constraints as well:

$$ \mathcal{L}(x, \lambda, \nu) = f(x) + \sum{i=1}^{m} \lambdai gi(x) + \sum{j=1}^{p} \nuj hj(x) $$
The KKT conditions provide necessary conditions for optimality for constrained optimization problems. They are:
1. **Stationarity:** The gradient of the Lagrangian with respect to x must be zero:
$$ \nablax \mathcal{L}(x, \lambda, \nu) = \nablax f(x) + \sum{i=1}^{m} \lambdai \nablax gi(x) + \sum{j=1}^{p} \nuj \nablax hj(x) = 0 $$

2. **Primal Feasibility:** The original constraints must be satisfied:
$$ g_i(x) \leq 0, \quad i = 1, \dots, m $$
$$ h_j(x) = 0, \quad j = 1, \dots, p $$
3. **Dual Feasibility:** The multipliers for inequality constraints must be non-positive:
$$ \lambda_i \leq 0, \quad i = 1, \dots, m $$
(Note: Some formulations use $\lambda_i \ge 0$ and define the Lagrangian as $f(x) - \sum \lambda_i g_i(x)$. The convention used here is consistent with minimizing $f(x)$ and ensuring $g_i(x) \le 0$. The important aspect is that the multipliers have a sign associated with the inequality direction.)
4. **Complementary Slackness:** For each inequality constraint, either the constraint is inactive (i.e., $g_i(x) < 0$) *and its multiplier is zero* ($\lambda_i = 0$), or the constraint is active (i.e., $g_i(x) = 0$) *and its multiplier can be non-zero* ($\lambda_i \leq 0$). This is expressed as:
$$ \lambda_i g_i(x) = 0, \quad i = 1, \dots, m $$

The KKT conditions are powerful because they encompass the conditions under which an optimal solution can exist. For convex optimization problems (where the objective function f is convex, and the feasible region defined by the constraints is a convex set), the KKT conditions are also sufficient for optimality. This means that any point x satisfying the KKT conditions is a global minimum.

In the context of machine learning and control, these conditions provide a theoretical foundation for developing algorithms that can find optimal policies while respecting constraints. For instance, if we are training a neural network to output control signals, and the network's output must satisfy certain bounds (control constraints) or lead to system states within acceptable limits (state constraints), the optimization process can be guided by principles derived from KKT conditions. Many optimization solvers used in machine learning, such as Sequential Quadratic

Programming (SQP) or Interior-Point Methods, are designed to find solutions that satisfy these conditions.

However, directly applying Lagrange multipliers and KKT conditions can be computationally intensive, especially for problems with a large number of variables or complex, non-linear constraints. Furthermore, for dynamic systems, the constraints often evolve over time, and a static optimization approach might not be sufficient. This is where techniques specifically designed for dynamic systems, such as Model Predictive Control (MPC), become indispensable.

Model Predictive Control (MPC) represents a paradigm shift in how constraints are handled in dynamic systems. Instead of solving a single, large optimization problem for the entire future horizon, MPC solves a finite-horizon optimization problem at each time step, using a model of the system's dynamics. The first control move from the optimal sequence is applied to the system, and then the entire process is repeated at the next time step, taking into account the new system state. This "receding horizon" approach makes MPC inherently suitable for real-time control of systems with evolving states and constraints.

At each time step k, MPC aims to find a sequence of control inputs $u_k, u_{k+1}, \dots, u_{k+N-1}$ over a prediction horizon N, to optimize a cost function J, subject to the system's dynamics and various constraints. The system dynamics are typically represented by a discrete-time model:

$$ x_{k+i+1} = f(x_{k+i}, u_{k+i}) $$

where x_{k+i} is the state at time step $k+i$, and u_{k+i} is the control input.

The optimization problem at time step k can be formulated as:

$$ \min*{uk, \dots, u*{k+N-1}} *\sum*{i=0}^{N-1} L(x*{k+i}, u*{k+i}) + M(x_{k+N}) $$
subject to:
$$ x*{k+i+1} = f(x*{k+i}, u_{k+i}), \quad i = 0, \dots, N-1 $$
$$ x_{k+i} \in \mathcal{X}, \quad i = 0, \dots, N $$
$$ u_{k+i} \in \mathcal{U}, \quad i = 0, \dots, N-1 $$
and potentially other path constraints, terminal constraints, or stage costs L that penalize deviations from a desired trajectory or enforce performance. M is a terminal cost function.

The crucial aspect of MPC for safety is its explicit handling of constraints. The state constraints ($x
{k+i} \in \mathcal{X}$) and control constraints ($u{k+i} \in \mathcal{U}$) are directly incorporated into the optimization problem. This means that the optimizer is actively seeking a control sequence that *guarantees* that, according to the model, the system will remain within the feasible sets for the entire prediction horizon.

Let's elaborate on how MPC handles different types of constraints:

State Constraints: If the system is required to stay within a safe operating region $\mathcal{X}$, this is modeled as $x*{k+i} \in \mathcal{X}$ for all i in the prediction horizon. If $\mathcal{X}$ is defined by inequalities, e.g., $l*j \leq x*j \leq u*j$, these are directly added as constraints to the MPC optimization problem. For example, if a drone's altitude must stay between 10m and 150m, then $10 \leq x_{\text{altitude}}(k+i) \leq 150$ for all i in the horizon. MPC will find control actions that ensure this during its prediction.

Control Constraints: Actuator limits, such as maximum motor torque or voltage, are naturally handled by ensuring $u{k+i} \in \mathcal{U}$ for all i. If u is a vector with limits $u{\min,j} \leq uj \leq u{\max,j}$, these are simply included as bounds in the optimization. This prevents the controller from commanding physically impossible actions and avoids actuator saturation, which can lead to unpredictable behavior.

Performance Constraints: These can be integrated in various ways. For example, a constraint on the rate of change of a state variable, $|\dot{x}j(t)| \leq Mj$, can be approximated in discrete time as $|xj(k+i+1) - xj(k+i)| \leq Mj \Delta t$. Alternatively, performance objectives can be embedded in the stage cost $L(x{k+i}, u_{k+i})$, penalizing undesirable behavior like large oscillations or slow response times.

The power of MPC lies in its predictive nature and its explicit constraint handling. By optimizing over a horizon and re-planning at each step, it can react to disturbances and changes in the system state while continuously ensuring that future predicted behavior remains feasible and safe according to the model. This makes it a robust framework for safety-critical applications.

However, MPC also has its challenges. The computational burden of solving an optimization problem at each sampling instant can be significant, especially for fast-dynamics systems or long prediction horizons. The performance of MPC is also highly dependent on the accuracy of the system model. If the model is inaccurate, the predictions may not reflect the true system behavior, and constraints might be violated in reality even if they are satisfied by the MPC optimization.

The integration of machine learning with MPC has emerged as a powerful avenue to address these challenges. Learned models can potentially capture complex, non-linear dynamics more accurately than traditional analytical models. Furthermore, machine learning can be used to learn the MPC control law itself, or parts of it, to speed up computation.

For instance, a
learned dynamics model can replace the analytical $f(x_{k+i}, u_{k+i})$ in the MPC formulation. This learned model, often a neural network, can be trained offline or online using system data. The MPC optimization then proceeds using this learned model, with the explicit constraints still being enforced. This approach benefits from the predictive power of machine learning while retaining the rigorous constraint satisfaction guarantees of MPC.

Another approach involves using
deep reinforcement learning (DRL) to learn an approximation of the MPC control policy. Instead of explicitly solving the optimization problem at each step, a DRL agent learns to directly map system states to control actions that would be generated by an MPC controller. This can significantly reduce online computation. However, ensuring that a learned DRL policy strictly adheres to hard constraints can be challenging. Techniques like constrained DRL, which incorporate constraint satisfaction into the learning objective or reward function, are crucial here.

For instance, if we want to learn a policy $\pi(x)$ that mimics an MPC controller, we can train π to minimize the difference between its output $u = \pi(x)$ and the MPC-generated optimal control

$u_{\text{MPC}}(x)$, while also penalizing any constraint violations. The objective might look something like:

$$ \min{\pi} \mathbb{E}{x \sim \mathcal{D}} \left[\| \pi(x) - u_{\text{MPC}}(x) \|^2 + \alpha \cdot \text{ConstraintViolation}(x, \pi(x)) \right] $$
where $\mathcal{D}$ is a distribution of system states, and $\text{ConstraintViolation}$ is a function that quantifies how much the state or control constraints are violated. The term α acts as a penalty multiplier.

More advanced methods directly embed the KKT conditions or other optimization problem structures into the neural network architecture or loss function, creating so-called **"differentiable optimization layers"**. These layers allow gradients to flow through the optimization process, enabling end-to-end training of policies that implicitly solve constrained optimization problems.

For example, a neural network can be trained to output the parameters of a control trajectory that satisfies dynamic equations and constraints, effectively learning to solve a constrained optimal control problem. The output of the network would be the sequence of control inputs, and the loss function would penalize deviations from the dynamics, constraint violations, and any performance cost.

The choice of constrained optimization technique depends heavily on the specific application, the system dynamics, the nature of the constraints (hard vs. soft, linear vs. non-linear), and the available computational resources. For systems with relatively slow dynamics and well-defined models, traditional MPC offers strong guarantees. For faster systems or those with highly complex, potentially unknown dynamics, learned approaches integrated with robust constraint handling mechanisms are becoming increasingly vital.

The underlying principle remains consistent: effective safety in learning-based systems is not an emergent property but a direct consequence of explicitly formulating and rigorously satisfying constraints. Whether through the analytical rigor of Lagrange multipliers and KKT conditions, the receding horizon optimization of MPC, or sophisticated learning algorithms that internalize optimization principles, the ability to handle constraints is paramount for deploying these systems into the real world. This mathematical and algorithmic backbone provides the confidence that the system will not only perform its intended task but will do so without compromising safety.

Safe Reinforcement Learning Algorithms

While traditional reinforcement learning (RL) excels at finding policies that maximize cumulative reward, it often overlooks the critical aspect of safety. An RL agent, by its very nature, explores the state-action space to discover optimal behaviors. This exploration, if unchecked, can lead to catastrophic failures, leading the system into unsafe states or executing dangerous actions. Recognizing this fundamental limitation, a significant body of research has emerged focused on developing **safe reinforcement learning (Safe RL)** algorithms. These algorithms aim to integrate safety guarantees directly into the learning process, ensuring that the agent operates within predefined safe boundaries, not just during deployment but also during the learning and exploration phases.

One of the primary strategies in Safe RL is to directly incorporate safety constraints into the RL optimization framework. This can be conceptualized as a constrained Markov Decision Process (CMDP) rather than a standard MDP. In a CMDP, alongside the objective of maximizing expected cumulative reward, there are one or more additional objectives that must be kept below certain thresholds. These additional objectives typically represent the costs associated with constraint violations. For instance, in a robotic manipulation task, the primary reward might be to successfully grasp an object, while a secondary cost could be the energy consumed or the proximity of the robot's end-effector to sensitive areas.

A prominent class of algorithms in this domain is **Constrained Policy Optimization (CPO)** and its variants. CPO, inspired by Trust Region Policy Optimization (TRPO), aims to find a policy that maximizes expected reward while ensuring that the expected cost of a set of safety constraints remains below a specified limit. The core idea is to perform policy updates in a way that guarantees monotonic improvement of the reward and bounded violation of the costs. This is achieved by formulating the optimization problem such that each policy update also enforces a constraint on the Kullback-Leibler (KL) divergence between the old and new policies, similar to TRPO. This KL constraint prevents excessively large policy changes that could lead to drastic performance degradation or safety violations.

More formally, a CMDP can be defined by a tuple $(\mathcal{S}, \mathcal{A}, P, r, c, \gamma, \rho)$, where $\mathcal{S}$ is the state space, $\mathcal{A}$ is the action space, $P(s'|s,a)$ is the transition probability, $r(s,a)$ is the reward function, $c
j(s,a)$ are the cost functions for J constraints, γ is the discount factor, and ρ is the initial state distribution. The goal is to find a policy $\pi(a|s)$ that maximizes the expected cumulative discounted reward $R(\pi) = \mathbb{E}{\pi}[\sum{t=0}^{\infty} \gamma^t r(st, at)]$ subject to $Cj(\pi) = \mathbb{E}{\pi}[\sum{t=0}^{\infty}

\gamma^t *cj(s*t, a*t)] \leq d*j$ for all $j=1, \dots, J$, where d_j are the safety thresholds.

Algorithms like CPO and
Proximal Policy Optimization (PPO), when adapted for CMDPs, can tackle this problem. For instance, a generalized version of PPO for CMDPs involves optimizing a surrogate objective that includes both rewards and costs. The objective at each step typically involves solving a constrained optimization subproblem. This subproblem aims to find a policy update that improves the reward while staying within a "trust region" (often defined by a KL divergence bound) and satisfying the cost constraints. The dual problem arising from the Lagrangian relaxation of the CMDP can also be used to derive optimization objectives. For example, one might alternate between optimizing the policy for a fixed set of Lagrange multipliers (which penalize constraint violations) and updating the Lagrange multipliers based on the realized constraint violations.

Consider an example in autonomous driving. The primary reward could be associated with reaching the destination quickly and smoothly. Safety constraints would include not colliding with other vehicles, not exceeding speed limits, and maintaining a safe distance from the car ahead. A CMDP formulation would assign negative rewards (costs) for collisions, speeding tickets, or tailgating. A Safe RL algorithm, like CPO, would then learn a driving policy that maximizes the travel speed and smoothness while ensuring that the probability and severity of these safety-critical events remain below predefined acceptable levels. The exploration phase would be particularly critical here; the algorithm must learn about dangerous situations without actually causing an accident.

Another powerful approach to achieving safety in RL involves the use of

safety layers or safety shields. This paradigm decouples the learning agent from the direct control of the system. The RL agent proposes an action based on its learned policy. This proposed action is then intercepted by a safety layer, which acts as a guardian. The safety layer evaluates the proposed action based on a predefined safety model or set of rules. If the action is deemed safe, it is passed on to the system. If, however, the action is predicted to lead to an unsafe state or violate a constraint, the safety layer overrides it with a safe fallback action.

The design of these safety layers can vary significantly. A simple safety layer might enforce hard constraints on the action space, such as preventing the agent from commanding a motor to exceed its torque limit or a robot arm from moving into a forbidden region. More sophisticated safety layers can leverage a learned predictive model of the system's dynamics and safety properties. For instance, a predictive safety layer could use a learned model to forecast the next state resulting from the proposed action. If this predicted state is unsafe, the safety layer intervenes.

Let's take the example of a drone navigation task. An RL agent might learn a policy to fly through a complex environment. A safety layer could monitor the proposed control commands. If the RL agent suggests a command that would cause the drone to descend too rapidly, potentially leading to a crash, the safety layer would intercept it and command a gentler descent or a hover maneuver. This safety layer can be designed using various techniques, including formal verification methods, model-based predictive control, or even another learned model trained specifically for safety verification. The advantage of this modular approach is that it can often be implemented without retraining the core RL agent, and it provides a more interpretable mechanism for ensuring safety.

The challenge with safety layers lies in their ability to comprehensively cover all potential unsafe scenarios, especially in complex, high-dimensional environments. If the safety layer's model of safety is incomplete or inaccurate, it might fail to prevent hazardous situations or, conversely, might be overly conservative and prevent the agent from achieving its goals. Therefore, the design and validation of the safety layer itself are critical.

A more rigorous, mathematically grounded approach to safety in learning controllers involves
Lyapunov-based safety guarantees. This framework originates from classical control theory and provides formal stability guarantees for dynamical systems. A Lyapunov function $V(x)$ for a system is a scalar function of the state x that is positive definite (i.e., $V(x) > 0$ for $x \neq 0$ and $V(0) = 0$) and whose time derivative along the system's trajectories is negative semi-definite ($\dot{V}(x) \leq 0$). If such a function can be found, it implies that the system is stable and will not diverge from its equilibrium point.

In the context of Safe RL, Lyapunov theory can be adapted to ensure that the system remains within a predefined safe region. A set D is considered safe if, for any state x within D, the system's evolution under the learned policy will also keep the state within D. This can be formalized by selecting a Lyapunov function such that $V(x)$ is positive within the safe set D and becomes zero or negative at the boundary of D. The goal of the Safe RL algorithm then becomes learning a policy π such that the time derivative of $V(x)$ along the trajectories generated by π is non-positive within D.

The process typically involves learning a control policy π and, concurrently, learning a Lyapunov function candidate V. The learning objective can be formulated to minimize a combination of the standard RL reward and a penalty term that encourages $\dot{V}(x) \leq 0$. This penalty can be implemented by sampling states and actions, computing the predicted next state using a learned dynamics model or by direct interaction, and then penalizing any observed positive $\dot{V}$.

For instance, consider a robot arm that needs to avoid collisions with its environment. The safe set D would be the region of free space. A Lyapunov function could be designed such that it increases as the robot arm approaches obstacles. The Safe RL agent would then aim to learn a policy that minimizes the expected distance to obstacles while ensuring that the time derivative of this "obstacle-distance" Lyapunov function remains non-positive, meaning the robot arm never gets closer to obstacles than it already is.

The challenge in Lyapunov-based methods is often in finding suitable Lyapunov functions for complex, high-dimensional systems, and in ensuring that the learned policy strictly satisfies the $\dot{V}(x) \leq 0$ condition across the entire state space, not just at sampled points. Techniques like
Sum-of-Squares (SOS) programming can be used to analytically verify Lyapunov stability for polynomial systems, and these principles can inspire robust learning algorithms. Some research explores learning parameterized Lyapunov functions, where the parameters are optimized alongside the policy parameters to satisfy the Lyapunov conditions.

Furthermore,
Robust Safe RL aims to provide guarantees even in the presence of model uncertainty or external disturbances. This can be achieved by designing policies that are inherently robust to perturbations or by

explicitly modeling the uncertainty and incorporating it into the safety constraints. For example, one might seek a policy that guarantees safety not just for a single system model, but for a whole family of possible models. This often leads to more conservative policies but provides stronger assurances in uncertain environments.

Another line of research focuses on
offline Safe RL, where the learning agent learns from a fixed dataset of previously collected experiences without further interaction with the environment. This is particularly relevant in domains where online exploration is prohibitively expensive or dangerous, such as healthcare or critical infrastructure. In offline settings, the primary challenge is to avoid extrapolating to unseen state-action pairs that might lead to unsafe outcomes, a phenomenon known as "distribution shift." Algorithms in this category often employ techniques to penalize or down-weight actions that are dissimilar to those present in the dataset, or to estimate the uncertainty in the learned policy and restrict exploration to regions where confidence is high.

For example, an offline Safe RL algorithm for learning a medical treatment policy might be trained on historical patient data. The RL agent's goal is to maximize patient recovery (reward), while safety constraints would include avoiding treatments known to cause severe side effects or contraindications. The offline nature means the algorithm cannot directly experiment with new treatment combinations. Therefore, it must rely on the existing data to infer safe and effective policies. This often involves estimating the reliability of the learned value functions or Q-functions and ensuring that the chosen policy is supported by sufficient data, thus mitigating risks associated with extrapolation.

The overarching theme across these diverse Safe RL algorithms –

constrained policy optimization, safety layers, Lyapunov-based methods, robust, and offline approaches – is the explicit and rigorous incorporation of safety considerations. Safety is not an afterthought; it is a fundamental design principle. While the theoretical underpinnings and practical implementations vary, the goal remains the same: to enable intelligent agents to learn and operate effectively in the real world without compromising human safety or system integrity. The continued advancement in these areas is crucial for unlocking the full potential of RL in safety-critical applications.

Ensuring the safety of learned controllers, particularly those developed using reinforcement learning or other machine learning paradigms, is paramount, especially when these systems are deployed in safety-critical applications. Even the most sophisticated safety-aware learning algorithms are not inherently infallible. The process of learning itself can be susceptible to unforeseen circumstances, data biases, or limitations in the fidelity of the learned models. Therefore, a robust and comprehensive framework for **verification and validation (V&V)** is an indispensable component of the safe AI development lifecycle. This V&V process moves beyond simply observing the system's behavior during training or a limited set of deployment tests; it involves a rigorous examination of the system's properties and performance under a wide spectrum of conditions, aiming to provide a high degree of confidence in its safety guarantees.

The verification aspect of V&V focuses on mathematically proving that the learned controller adheres to specified safety properties. This often draws upon techniques from the field of **formal methods**, which provide mathematical tools to reason about the correctness of systems. For learned controllers, this can be a significant challenge because their behavior is often defined by complex, high-dimensional neural networks rather than explicit, analyzable mathematical equations. Nevertheless, several approaches are being explored to bridge this gap.

One promising avenue is the application of **model checking**. Model checking is an automated technique for verifying finite-state systems. While learned controllers are typically not finite-state, researchers are developing techniques to create abstractions or simplified models of the learned controller that can be amenable to model checking. This might involve converting neural network policies into equivalent finite-state automata under certain discretization of states and actions, or using abstract interpretation to bound the possible outputs of the network for given inputs. The goal is to prove properties such as: "For any state within the safe operating region, the controller will never take an action that leads to a violation of constraint X."

Another formal verification technique is **symbolic verification**. This approach attempts to find analytical proofs of safety properties. For example, if the system dynamics and the learned controller can be represented using polynomial functions, techniques like **Sum-of-Squares (SOS) programming** can be employed to prove properties such as the existence of a Lyapunov function that guarantees stability within a safe set. While this often requires significant simplifying assumptions about the system and the controller (e.g., linearity or polynomial approximations), it can provide strong, mathematically rigorous safety guarantees for those specific scenarios. Research is ongoing to extend these techniques to more complex, non-linear systems and deep neural network controllers, perhaps by using network dissection or symbolic regression to approximate the behavior of neural networks with more analyzable functions.

Beyond formal verification, which aims for mathematical certainty, **validation** plays a crucial role in building confidence. Validation encompasses a range of testing methodologies designed to assess the learned controller's performance and safety in practical scenarios. **Simulation-based testing** is the cornerstone of this validation process. However, simply running simulations under typical operating conditions is insufficient. A comprehensive validation strategy requires going beyond nominal scenarios to probe for weaknesses and potential failures.

Extensive simulation-based testing involves creating a vast number of diverse simulation environments and scenarios. This includes testing across a wide range of initial conditions, environmental parameters, and system dynamics variations. If the learned controller is for an autonomous vehicle, simulations would cover diverse weather conditions, road surfaces, traffic densities, and pedestrian behaviors. For a robotic arm, this would mean testing in cluttered environments, with varying object properties, and under different external forces. The key is to ensure that the training data and scenarios are representative of the operational domain, but also to deliberately explore the boundaries of this domain.

A particularly important subset of simulation-based testing is **adversarial testing**. In adversarial testing, the goal is to intentionally create scenarios that are designed to challenge and potentially break the learned controller. This can involve introducing:

Perturbations: Small, seemingly innocuous changes to sensor inputs or system parameters that might be overlooked by a standard test suite but could cause a learned system to misbehave. For instance, subtle changes in lighting conditions for an autonomous driving perception system, or minor actuator noise for a robotic control system.
Out-of-distribution (OOD) scenarios: Situations that are significantly different from what the agent encountered during training. This is a

critical area because machine learning models often perform unpredictably when faced with data that deviates substantially from their training distribution. Adversarial testing aims to discover these OOD vulnerabilities by crafting scenarios that push the boundaries of the learned model's understanding. This could involve simulating rare but critical events, such as unexpected sensor failures, sudden environmental changes, or the appearance of novel objects or agents.
"Red teaming" the system: Employing human experts or even other AI agents to actively search for failure modes. This collaborative approach leverages human creativity and intuition, as well as computational power, to identify scenarios that might not be immediately obvious.

The effectiveness of adversarial testing often depends on the ability to generate these challenging scenarios systematically. Techniques from generative modeling, reinforcement learning itself (where another agent tries to find failures), or optimization methods can be used to automatically discover adversarial examples. The insights gained from these adversarial tests are invaluable for identifying weaknesses that need to be addressed, either by retraining the model with more diverse data, refining the safety constraints, or improving the verification mechanisms.

Furthermore,
formal robustness analysis plays a vital role in understanding how sensitive the learned controller is to uncertainties and disturbances. Unlike adversarial testing, which often seeks to find *a* failure, robustness analysis aims to quantify the extent of uncertainty that the system can tolerate while remaining safe. This can involve methods that bound the worst-case performance degradation or safety violation under a specified range of perturbations. For example, one might want to prove that the system's error remains within a certain bound, or that a critical

safety metric (like distance to an obstacle) never falls below a threshold, even if sensor readings are corrupted by noise up to a certain level.

This type of analysis can often be formulated as an optimization problem: maximize the disturbance while ensuring safety constraints are met, or conversely, find the minimum required safety margin given the expected level of disturbance. Techniques like **scenario optimization** or **robust convex optimization** (when applicable to approximations of the learned controller) can be used here. The results of formal robustness analysis provide a more quantitative understanding of the system's reliability and can help in setting appropriate operational envelopes and safety margins for deployment.

A crucial aspect of validation is ensuring the safety of the system under **edge cases and disturbances not encountered during training**. The training process is, by its nature, limited by the data available and the scenarios explored. Real-world deployments, however, are unpredictable. Therefore, validation must actively seek out these novel situations. This often involves:

Scenario Generation: Developing sophisticated methods to automatically generate a vast array of potential scenarios, including rare events, combinations of common events that might interact unexpectedly, and situations that push the system to its operational limits. This can involve techniques like Monte Carlo sampling of parameters, evolutionary algorithms for scenario discovery, or using generative models trained on real-world data to synthesize new, plausible scenarios.
Anomaly Detection during Testing: Implementing anomaly detection mechanisms within the simulation environment itself. If the learned controller's behavior or the resulting system state deviates significantly from expected patterns or norms established during training, this can

flag a potential issue that requires further investigation, even if it doesn't immediately trigger a predefined safety violation.

"What-if" Analysis: Developing frameworks that allow engineers to pose hypothetical "what-if" questions about system behavior. For example, "What would happen if sensor X failed at this specific moment?" or "What if agent Y suddenly performed this unexpected maneuver?" The ability to explore these "what-if" scenarios quickly and efficiently in simulation is a powerful validation tool.

The entire verification and validation process should be iterative. Insights gained from failed verification attempts or validation tests should feed back into the learning process. This might involve:

Retraining with augmented data: Incorporating new data from challenging simulation scenarios or identified edge cases into the training dataset.

Refining safety constraints: Adjusting the parameters of safety layers, cost functions, or CMDP constraints based on observed failures.

Improving the system model: If the validation highlights discrepancies between the simulation model and the real-world system (or the assumed dynamics), efforts should be made to improve the fidelity of the simulation environment.

Enhancing the verification methods: If formal verification fails due to overly complex learned controllers, research might focus on developing more interpretable or approximate models of the controller for verification purposes.

Ultimately, the goal of this rigorous V&V process is to **gain trust in AI-augmented control systems**. For these systems to be adopted in safety-critical domains like autonomous driving, aviation, medical robotics, or industrial automation, stakeholders – including regulators, operators, and the public – need to have a high degree of confidence that they will operate safely and reliably under all foreseeable circumstances. Verification provides mathematical assurances, while validation offers empirical evidence of safe behavior across a broad spectrum of operational conditions. By combining these methodologies, we can move towards deploying intelligent control systems that are not only effective but also demonstrably safe, fostering wider acceptance and enabling the realization of their transformative potential. This multifaceted approach, encompassing formal proof, extensive simulation, adversarial exploration, and robustness analysis, forms the bedrock of responsible AI development in critical applications.

Chapter 8: AI-Augmented Model Predictive Control (MPC)

Model Predictive Control (MPC) stands as a cornerstone in advanced control system design, particularly favored for its sophisticated approach to managing complex, dynamic systems operating under constraints. At its heart, MPC is an optimization-based control strategy that leverages a predictive model of the system to make optimal control decisions over a finite future horizon. The fundamental principle of MPC is the **receding horizon optimization**. Instead of calculating a single, open-loop optimal control sequence for all future time, MPC computes an optimal sequence of control inputs over a defined prediction horizon. However, only the first control input from this computed sequence is applied to the actual system. At the next time step, the entire process is repeated: the system's current state is measured, a new prediction is made, and a new optimal control sequence is calculated over the shifted horizon. This iterative, receding-horizon approach allows MPC to continuously adapt to disturbances and unmodeled dynamics, ensuring that the control actions remain optimal with respect to the most up-to-date information about the system's state.

The efficacy of MPC hinges on the quality of its **prediction model**. This model, which can be derived from first principles (e.g., physics-based equations) or learned from data, encapsulates the system's dynamics—how its states evolve over time in response to control inputs and external disturbances. A more accurate prediction model leads to more reliable future state predictions, thereby enabling more effective optimization and constraint satisfaction. For instance, in managing the energy storage of a hybrid electric vehicle (HEV), the prediction model would capture how the battery's state of charge changes based on the power demanded by the vehicle and the power generated by the internal combustion engine or regenerative braking, considering factors like battery degradation and temperature.

Central to the MPC framework is the

cost function, often referred to as the objective function or performance index. This function mathematically quantifies the desired system behavior over the prediction horizon. It typically includes terms that penalize deviations from a desired setpoint or trajectory, excessive control effort, and undesirable states. By minimizing this cost function, MPC seeks to achieve the best possible performance according to the defined objectives. In the HEV example, the cost function might penalize high fuel consumption, battery degradation, and excessive emissions, while simultaneously aiming to maintain the battery's state of charge within a desired range for optimal operation and longevity.

A critical and distinguishing feature of MPC is its inherent ability to explicitly handle
constraints. Real-world systems are almost always subject to operational limitations, such as actuator saturation (e.g., a motor cannot exceed its maximum torque), state variable limits (e.g., temperature must stay within a certain range), or safety boundaries. MPC directly incorporates these constraints into the optimization problem. This is typically achieved by defining feasible regions for the system states and control inputs. The optimization algorithm then searches for a control sequence that not only minimizes the cost function but also ensures that all predicted states and control actions remain within these predefined limits throughout the prediction horizon. This constraint-handling capability is what makes MPC particularly well-suited for safety-critical applications and systems with demanding operational requirements.

The combination of these elements—receding horizon optimization, an accurate prediction model, a well-defined cost function, and explicit constraint handling—allows MPC to exhibit several advantageous properties. Firstly, it is
proactive, meaning it anticipates future system behavior and takes preemptive control actions to achieve desired outcomes or avoid undesirable situations. This forward-looking nature is in contrast to

reactive controllers that primarily respond to current errors. Secondly, MPC is inherently **optimal** with respect to the defined cost function and constraints over the prediction horizon. Thirdly, its ability to manage constraints ensures that the system operates within safe and feasible boundaries, thereby enhancing **robustness and safety**.

Consider the energy management of an HEV as a running example to illustrate these principles. The objective is to optimize the power split between the electric motor and the internal combustion engine to minimize fuel consumption and emissions while maintaining the battery's state of charge (SoC) within an acceptable range, say 40% to 70%. The MPC controller would:

1.
Predict future driving conditions: Using a combination of historical data and real-time traffic information, the controller might predict the required acceleration, deceleration, and speed profile for the next, say, 30 seconds.
2. **Model system dynamics:** A model would describe how the battery SoC changes based on the power drawn by the motor and the power generated by the engine or regenerative braking. It would also model the fuel consumption of the engine as a function of its operating point.
3. **Define cost function:** The cost function would penalize fuel usage and emissions, and significantly penalize any predicted SoC falling outside the [40%, 70%] range. It might also penalize rapid switching between engine and motor operation.
4. **Incorporate constraints:** Constraints would include the maximum power output of the motor and engine, the maximum charge/discharge rate of the battery, and the SoC limits themselves.
5. **Optimize and Recede:** The MPC would then solve an optimization problem to find the engine torque and motor torque commands over the 30-second horizon that minimize the cost function while respecting all

constraints. Only the first set of commands (e.g., torque for the next 1 second) would be applied. At the next time step, the vehicle's actual state (current speed, SoC) would be measured, the prediction horizon would slide forward, and a new optimization would be performed.

This receding horizon approach ensures that if, for instance, the vehicle encounters unexpected uphill terrain (requiring more power than predicted), the controller can adapt its strategy to maintain the SoC within its bounds, potentially by increasing engine power or reducing regenerative braking, while still striving for overall fuel efficiency.

The inherent strengths of MPC—its predictive capabilities, optimization-driven control, and robust constraint management—make it a powerful tool for a wide array of applications, from industrial process control and robotics to automotive systems and aerospace. However, the performance of traditional MPC is critically dependent on the accuracy of its underlying prediction model and its ability to solve the optimization problem in real-time. When models are highly complex, nonlinear, or subject to significant uncertainty, or when rapid computational solutions are required for high-speed systems, the effectiveness of standard MPC can be challenged. It is in these scenarios, where traditional methods encounter limitations, that the integration of Artificial Intelligence (AI) offers a transformative pathway to enhance and extend the capabilities of MPC. AI, particularly machine learning, can address these challenges by improving model accuracy, accelerating optimization, and enabling more sophisticated decision-making within the MPC framework. This forms the core motivation for exploring AI-augmented MPC, which we will delve into in the subsequent sections.

The performance of any Model Predictive Control (MPC) system is intrinsically linked to the fidelity of its predictive model. This model acts as the "eyes" of the controller, forecasting how the system will behave under various control actions over the future horizon. In traditional MPC, this model is often derived from first principles – that is, from fundamental physical laws, chemical reactions, or engineering principles governing the system's operation. While this approach can yield highly accurate models for well-understood systems, it presents significant challenges in several critical areas.

Firstly, deriving accurate first-principles models for complex, nonlinear systems can be an arduous, time-consuming, and expertise-intensive undertaking. Consider, for instance, a sophisticated chemical reactor where numerous concurrent and sequential reactions occur, influenced by factors such as temperature, pressure, reactant concentrations, catalyst activity, and even subtle mixing effects. Capturing all these intricate interactions and their dependencies through differential equations requires deep domain knowledge and can result in a model that is not only difficult to formulate but also computationally expensive to simulate. Even minor deviations from ideal operating conditions or unforeseen environmental changes can render such a model suboptimal.

Secondly, real-world systems are rarely perfectly represented by simplified analytical models. There are always "unmodeled dynamics" – factors and behaviors that are either unknown, too complex to model analytically, or exhibit stochastic characteristics that are hard to capture with deterministic equations. These unmodeled dynamics can include sensor noise, actuator nonlinearities (like dead zones or hysteresis), external disturbances that are difficult to measure or predict, and subtle material property variations. When the MPC controller's prediction model fails to account for these effects, its predictions will diverge from the actual system behavior. This divergence leads to suboptimal control actions, potential constraint violations, and a degradation of overall system performance and stability. For example, in the chemical reactor scenario, subtle changes in raw material purity or ambient temperature might affect reaction rates in ways not explicitly accounted for in a physics-based model, leading to deviations in product quality or throughput.

This is precisely where Artificial Intelligence (AI), and particularly machine learning (ML) techniques, offer a powerful paradigm shift for developing and enhancing the prediction models used in MPC. Instead of relying solely on first principles, AI-driven approaches leverage system data to learn the underlying dynamics. This data-driven system identification allows us to build models that can inherently capture complex nonlinearities and effectively incorporate the influence of unmodeled dynamics, leading to a significant improvement in predictive accuracy.

The fundamental idea is to use historical or actively collected data from the system – consisting of input sequences, corresponding output sequences, and potentially state measurements – to train a model that mimics the system's behavior. This trained model then serves as the prediction model within the MPC framework. The advantage is that the model learns directly from observed reality, making it more adept at representing the system's true operational characteristics, even those that are difficult to articulate mathematically from first principles.

Several machine learning techniques are particularly well-suited for learning complex system dynamics for MPC applications. Among the most prominent are Neural Networks (NNs) and Gaussian Processes (GPs).

Neural Networks, inspired by the structure of the human brain, are powerful function approximators capable of learning highly nonlinear relationships between inputs and outputs. For system identification, a neural network can be trained to predict the next state or output of a system given its current state and control inputs. Various architectures are employed, depending on the nature of the system dynamics. For instance, Recurrent Neural Networks (RNNs), including Long Short-Term Memory (LSTM) and Gated Recurrent Unit (GRU) networks, are particularly adept at modeling sequential data and temporal dependencies, making them ideal for learning the dynamics of dynamic systems where past behavior influences future outcomes. A typical application might involve feeding a sequence of past states and control actions into an RNN to predict the system's state at the next time step. The network's parameters (weights and biases) are adjusted during training to minimize the difference between its predicted outputs and the actual observed outputs from the system data.

For example, imagine training an LSTM network to predict the temperature evolution in a complex industrial oven. The inputs to the LSTM would be a history of control signals applied to the heating elements and cooling fans, along with any measured internal temperatures from previous time steps. The output would be the predicted temperature at the next time step. By training this LSTM on extensive operational data collected from the oven, the network can learn to implicitly account for factors such as thermal inertia, heat losses through insulation, interactions between heating zones, and even the impact of opening/closing the oven door, without these physical phenomena being explicitly programmed into its architecture. This learned LSTM model then becomes the prediction engine for an AI-augmented MPC controller, enabling more accurate temperature forecasts and thus more precise control.

Another powerful class of models for learning system dynamics is Gaussian Processes (GPs). GPs provide a non-parametric, probabilistic approach to modeling. Unlike neural networks, which learn a point estimate of the function, GPs model a distribution over functions. This inherent probabilistic nature offers several advantages for MPC. Firstly, it provides not just a prediction but also an estimate of the uncertainty associated with that prediction. This uncertainty information can be invaluable for MPC, allowing the controller to make more informed decisions, especially when operating near constraints or in situations where prediction confidence is low. The controller can potentially adopt a more conservative strategy when uncertainty is high, or it can actively explore regions where uncertainty is large to gather more information.

A GP model defines a prior distribution over functions, and this prior is updated based on observed data to form a posterior distribution. This means that as more data is observed, the GP model becomes more confident in its predictions. For system identification, a GP can be trained to map current system states and control inputs to future system states. The training process involves finding the GP hyperparameters that best fit the observed input-output data. The resulting GP can then be used to predict the system's state at a future time, along with a measure of the prediction variance.

Consider again the chemical reactor example. A GP could be trained to predict the concentration of a key intermediate product over the next hour, given the current concentrations of reactants, catalyst loading, and the flow rates of feed streams. The GP would learn the complex reaction kinetics and mass transfer dynamics from historical batch data. Crucially, the GP would also output an uncertainty associated with its concentration prediction. If the MPC controller is tasked with maintaining the intermediate concentration within a narrow target range, and the GP predicts a high probability of exceeding this range with low uncertainty, the controller will take aggressive action to counteract it. Conversely, if the prediction is within the range but has high uncertainty, the MPC might proceed with a less aggressive control action, or trigger additional data acquisition to reduce uncertainty.

The integration of these data-driven models into the MPC framework involves replacing or augmenting the traditional first-principles model with the learned model. During the MPC optimization step at each control interval, the AI-learned model is queried to predict the system's trajectory over the receding horizon. This prediction is then used within the optimization problem, alongside the cost function and constraints, to determine the optimal control sequence.

The benefits of using AI-learned prediction models for MPC are manifold:

1.
Enhanced Predictive Accuracy: By learning from data, these models can capture intricate nonlinearities and subtle dynamics that are often missed or oversimplified in physics-based models. This leads to more accurate predictions of future system behavior.
2. **Adaptability to Unmodeled Dynamics:** The data-driven nature allows these models to implicitly learn the effects of disturbances, parameter variations, and other unmodeled phenomena, making the MPC more robust to real-world uncertainties.
3. **Modeling of Complex Systems:** For systems where first-principles modeling is infeasible or prohibitively difficult (e.g., biological systems, complex fluid dynamics, or intricate chemical processes), AI-based

system identification provides a practical path to obtaining a functional prediction model.

4. **Reduced Modeling Effort:** While data collection and model training require effort, it can often be significantly less demanding than deriving and validating a comprehensive, high-fidelity first-principles model.

5. **Incorporation of Probabilistic Information (with GPs):** Gaussian Processes can provide valuable uncertainty estimates, enabling more sophisticated and robust control strategies that account for prediction confidence.

Illustrating this with a more detailed hypothetical scenario involving a complex chemical reactor:

System: A continuous stirred-tank reactor (CSTR) performing an exothermic, irreversible reaction: A + B -> C. The reaction rate is sensitive to temperature, reactant concentrations, and catalyst activity. The reactor has a jacket for cooling.

Traditional MPC Approach: A first-principles model would be derived based on mass and energy balance equations.

Mass Balances: Differential equations describing the change in concentrations of A, B, and C based on inflow rates, reaction rates, and outflow.

Energy Balance: A differential equation describing the change in reactor temperature based on inflow/outflow enthalpies, heat of reaction, and heat transfer to the cooling jacket.

Reaction Rate Kinetics: An Arrhenius-type equation for the rate constant, dependent on temperature, and potentially including terms for reactant concentrations.

Cooling Jacket Model: An equation relating the jacket coolant flow rate and temperature to the heat removal rate.

Challenges with First-Principles Model:
The exact activation energy and pre-exponential factor of the reaction might not be precisely known or may vary due to catalyst degradation.
Mixing efficiency within the CSTR might not be uniform and could be difficult to model accurately.
Heat transfer coefficients might vary with fouling on the heat exchanger surfaces.
External disturbances like fluctuations in feed concentration or temperature are hard to model deterministically.

These inaccuracies in the first-principles model would lead to suboptimal control of reactor temperature and product concentration. The MPC might over- or under-cool the reactor, leading to reduced yield, increased by-product formation, or even safety concerns if temperature runaway occurs.

AI-Augmented MPC Approach:
1. **Data Collection:** Collect historical operational data from the CSTR. This includes:
Inputs: Feed flow rates of A and B, coolant flow rate, setpoints for temperature.
States: Reactor temperature, concentrations of A, B, and C (measured by online sensors).
Outputs: Reactor temperature, concentrations at the outlet.
2. **Model Selection and Training:** Choose a suitable AI model, for instance, a Long Short-Term Memory (LSTM) network or a Gaussian Process model.

LSTM Training: Train the LSTM to predict the next state (temperature, concentrations) given the current state and control inputs (coolant flow rate, feed rates) over a short time horizon. The LSTM learns the temporal dependencies and complex, potentially nonlinear, relationships directly from the data. It implicitly captures how changes in coolant flow affect temperature, how temperature affects reaction rate, and how concentrations evolve, without needing explicit kinetic equations.
GP Training: Train a GP to map current states and control inputs to future states. This would provide predictive mean values for temperature and concentrations, along with associated uncertainty bounds.
3. **Integration into MPC:** Replace the first-principles prediction model within the MPC with the trained AI model.
At each control step, the current measured state of the reactor is fed into the AI model.
The AI model forecasts the reactor's temperature and concentrations over the prediction horizon, considering the control actions being optimized.
The MPC optimization problem then uses these AI-generated predictions to minimize the cost function (e.g., maximizing product yield, minimizing energy consumption for cooling) while respecting constraints (e.g., maximum allowable temperature, minimum reactant concentration).
4. **Performance Enhancement:** With an AI-learned model that more accurately reflects the reactor's actual behavior, including its thermal inertia, reaction kinetics influenced by subtle factors, and heat transfer characteristics, the MPC controller can:
More precisely maintain the reactor temperature at its optimal setpoint, leading to higher yield and potentially reduced by-product formation.
Respond more effectively to disturbances, such as fluctuations in feed composition or ambient temperature, because the learned model implicitly accounts for the system's dynamic response to such changes.
Operate closer to constraints if desired, with higher confidence due to the more accurate predictions. If GPs are used, the uncertainty estimates

can inform conservative control actions when necessary, preventing constraint violations.

This AI-augmented approach transforms MPC from a controller relying on potentially simplified or incomplete physical understanding to one that learns and adapts from direct observation of the system's performance. This makes it particularly valuable for legacy systems where upgrading sensors or instrumentation to better support first-principles modeling might be impractical, or for novel processes where fundamental understanding is still evolving. The ability of AI models to ingest large datasets and identify subtle patterns is a powerful enabler for achieving high-performance control in challenging, real-world applications. The process of selecting the appropriate AI architecture, preparing the data, training the model, and validating its performance is crucial for success, but the potential rewards in terms of improved system efficiency, safety, and robustness are substantial.

The efficacy of any Model Predictive Control (MPC) system is not solely dictated by the accuracy of its predictive model; the judicious formulation of the cost function and the definition of constraints are equally paramount. These elements act as the controller's guiding principles, shaping its objectives and delineating the boundaries of acceptable operation. While traditional MPC relies on analytically defined cost functions and explicit constraints derived from engineering specifications or safety requirements, the advent of AI offers a powerful avenue to imbue these components with greater intelligence, adaptability, and alignment with nuanced operational goals. This subsection delves into the ways in which AI, particularly machine learning techniques, can augment the design and online adaptation of both the cost function and the constraints within an MPC framework.

One of the most compelling applications of AI in this domain lies in the learning of cost functions that better reflect desired system behavior, especially when such behavior is difficult to articulate purely through mathematical objectives. In many control scenarios, especially those involving human interaction or subjective performance metrics, the "optimal" outcome is not merely about minimizing error or energy consumption. It might also encompass aspects like comfort, smoothness of operation, aesthetic appeal, or adherence to implicit human preferences. Traditional methods often struggle to capture these qualitative aspects. For instance, in the control of an autonomous vehicle, minimizing deviations from a planned trajectory might be the primary objective. However, a human driver would also naturally aim for a smooth, comfortable ride, avoiding abrupt accelerations or braking, and maintaining a predictable lane position. Defining a cost function that precisely quantifies "smoothness" or "comfort" analytically can be a complex endeavor, often requiring subjective tuning of weighting factors.

AI, through techniques such as learning from expert demonstrations or inferring preferences from user feedback, offers a data-driven approach to bridge this gap. One prominent method is Imitation Learning, where an AI model is trained to mimic the behavior of an expert operator. In the context of autonomous driving, this would involve collecting data of a skilled human driver performing various maneuvers - driving on highways, navigating city streets, parking, and responding to traffic. The AI system, often employing deep reinforcement learning or supervised learning architectures, learns to map the current state of the vehicle and its environment to control actions that are consistent with the human driver's actions. The underlying "cost function" implicitly learned by the AI in such scenarios is not an explicit mathematical formula but rather a representation of the driving policy that successfully emulates the human expert. By analyzing the sequences of control inputs and system states from the expert demonstrations, the AI can learn to prioritize factors like smooth acceleration, gentle braking, and appropriate steering inputs, effectively internalizing a cost function that embodies these desirable, albeit implicitly defined, objectives.

Consider a more detailed example of trajectory planning for an autonomous vehicle. A purely analytical MPC might aim to minimize the integral of the squared error between the vehicle's position and a pre-defined path, along with a term for control effort. However, this can lead to jerky motions if the path itself is not perfectly smooth or if rapid corrections are needed. Using imitation learning, data from human drivers executing the same path would be recorded. The AI would observe how a human driver modulates acceleration, braking, and steering to achieve a smooth and efficient traversal. Through training, the AI learns a policy. When this policy is integrated into an MPC framework, it can effectively guide the trajectory generation. The "cost" associated with a particular control action might be implicitly higher if it leads to a state that the learned policy would consider undesirable – for instance, a state that would typically precede a harsh acceleration in the human demonstration data. This allows the MPC to generate trajectories that are not only accurate but also perceptibly smoother and more comfortable for passengers, aligning better with human expectations of good driving.

Beyond imitation, Reinforcement Learning (RL) from Human Feedback (RLHF) or direct preference learning can be employed. In RLHF, after an initial policy is learned (perhaps through imitation learning or initial RL), human evaluators provide feedback on the generated behaviors. This feedback can range from simple binary preferences (e.g., "Behavior A is better than Behavior B") to more granular ratings. This preference data is then used to train a "reward model" or "preference model" that quantitatively scores different system behaviors. This learned reward model essentially acts as a learned cost function, providing a more nuanced and human-aligned objective for the MPC optimization. The MPC can then use this learned reward model within its optimization loop to find control actions that maximize the expected reward, thereby achieving performance that is more in line with human judgment.

For example, in a robotic arm application tasked with a delicate assembly operation, a human operator might provide feedback on various attempts by the robot. The human might prefer an assembly sequence that involves slower movements but avoids any slight tremor that could risk damaging the components, even if a slightly faster, albeit riskier, sequence could technically complete the task. RLHF would allow the AI to learn this preference for steadiness over speed, and the learned reward model would then guide the MPC to generate control signals that prioritize smooth, tremor-free movements, even if it means a longer task completion time. The cost function effectively becomes a proxy for human judgment of "good performance" in that specific task.

Furthermore, AI can play a significant role in the online adaptation and refinement of constraints. Constraints in MPC are critical for ensuring safety, maintaining operational limits, and achieving desired performance. They can be hard constraints (e.g., maximum joint torque, minimum fluid level) or soft constraints (penalized in the cost function if violated). In dynamic and uncertain environments, or for systems with complex and evolving operational envelopes, defining and maintaining these constraints can be challenging. AI techniques can help in learning these constraints from data or in adapting them dynamically.

One area where AI can be particularly valuable is in learning "implicit constraints" that arise from complex system interactions or safety considerations that are not easily expressed as simple mathematical inequalities. Consider a multi-agent system, such as a fleet of drones coordinating for surveillance or delivery. While individual drone flight envelopes (e.g., maximum speed, climb rate) are known, the collective behavior introduces complex inter-agent constraints: collision avoidance, maintaining formation, or ensuring adequate separation. Learning these emergent constraints from data can be more effective than trying to model all possible inter-agent interactions analytically. By observing successful and unsuccessful coordination scenarios, AI models can learn to predict the likelihood of collisions or suboptimal formations based on the current states and intended actions of multiple agents. This learned predictive capability can then be used to formulate or adapt constraints within the MPC framework for each individual drone, ensuring that their planned trajectories respect not only their own operational limits but also the emergent safety requirements of the collective.

Another important application is in learning constraints related to comfort and driver experience in autonomous vehicles. Beyond the cost function influencing smoothness, actual operational constraints might need to be adapted. For instance, the acceptable range of lateral acceleration might be dynamically adjusted based on the road conditions (e.g., tighter constraint on wet surfaces) or even passenger preferences (e.g., more lenient constraint if "sport mode" is selected). AI can learn these mappings from historical data or explicit driver input. A predictive model, trained on data correlating road surface information, vehicle dynamics, and driver feedback (e.g., subjective comfort ratings), could predict the maximum safe and comfortable lateral acceleration for a given situation. This prediction can then be used to dynamically adjust the lateral acceleration constraint within the MPC's optimization problem in real-time.

Moreover, AI can be instrumental in identifying and adapting to unknown or evolving operational limits. In many industrial processes, the exact limits of safe operation might not be perfectly known due to factors like material degradation, unforeseen operating conditions, or subtle interactions between different system components. AI-based anomaly detection or predictive maintenance techniques can monitor system behavior for subtle signs of impending issues or performance degradation. If an AI system detects patterns indicative of increased wear on a particular actuator or a potential for a cascading failure, it can infer that the current operating constraints might need to be tightened. This information can then be used to dynamically modify the constraints within the MPC. For example, if an AI model predicts an increased risk of actuator overheating due to an anomaly in its operational signature, it could signal the MPC to reduce the maximum allowable command signal for that actuator, thereby preventing failure. This proactive constraint adaptation, driven by AI insights, can significantly enhance the robustness and safety of the control system.

Consider the scenario of a manufacturing process involving robotic manipulators. The reach and payload capacity of these robots are well-defined. However, factors like tool wear, minor misalignments in fixtures, or variations in the material being handled can subtly alter the effective operational envelope. An AI system monitoring the robot's end-effector forces, motor currents, and vibration patterns might detect deviations from nominal behavior that correlate with an increased risk of component stress or reduced precision. This intelligence can be fed back to the MPC, which then adjusts its constraints on, for instance, the maximum speed of movement or the acceptable force applied during an operation. This adaptive constraint management ensures that the robot operates within safe and effective boundaries, even under conditions not fully anticipated by the initial analytical model.

The process of learning cost functions and constraints using AI typically involves several key stages. Firstly, appropriate data needs to be collected. This data can originate from various sources: historical operational logs, expert demonstrations, human feedback sessions, simulations, or dedicated data collection experiments. The quality and relevance of this data are critical for the success of the learning process. Secondly, a suitable AI model architecture is chosen. For learning cost functions that emulate expert behavior, imitation learning models or RL-based approaches with reward shaping are common. For learning constraints, classification models (to predict feasibility) or regression models (to predict boundary values) might be employed, often coupled with anomaly detection techniques. Thirdly, the model is trained using the collected data. This involves optimizing the model's parameters to either mimic expert actions, accurately predict human preferences, or correctly classify safe versus unsafe states. Finally, the learned cost function or constraints are integrated into the MPC framework. This might involve using the learned reward model directly as the objective function for the optimizer, or it could involve translating learned feasibility predictions into dynamic hard or soft constraints that the MPC must satisfy.

The integration of AI-learned cost functions and constraints into MPC offers several significant advantages. It allows for the control system to be more closely aligned with human-centric objectives, such as comfort and natural interaction, which are often difficult to formalize analytically. It enables the controller to adapt to dynamic and uncertain environments by learning and refining operational boundaries in real-time, thereby enhancing safety and robustness. Furthermore, it provides a powerful mechanism for incorporating knowledge that is implicitly held by expert operators or that emerges from complex system interactions, going beyond what can be readily captured by first-principles modeling alone. This synergy between AI and MPC opens up new possibilities for designing intelligent control systems that are not only efficient and precise but also intuitive and safe in their operation across a wide spectrum of applications. The iterative refinement of these learned components, driven by continuous data collection and retraining, allows the MPC system to evolve and improve its performance over time, adapting to changing conditions and user expectations.

The computational burden associated with solving the complex optimization problem at the heart of Model Predictive Control (MPC) can, in certain scenarios, present a significant bottleneck. This is particularly true for systems that operate at high frequencies, demanding rapid decision-making, or for models that are inherently complex, involving numerous states, inputs, and a multitude of constraints. In such cases, the time required to compute the optimal control sequence for the prediction horizon might exceed the available sampling period, rendering traditional MPC implementation infeasible. This critical limitation underscores the imperative to explore innovative approaches that can accelerate the optimization process, thereby extending the applicability of MPC to a broader spectrum of demanding control tasks. It is within this context that Artificial Intelligence (AI), with its capacity for learning, approximation, and pattern recognition, emerges as a transformative force, offering potent solutions to alleviate the computational load of MPC optimization solvers.

The core idea behind leveraging AI for MPC optimization solvers is to replace or augment the computationally intensive, first-principles optimization algorithms with faster, AI-driven surrogates. Instead of re-solving the entire optimization problem from scratch at every control interval, AI models can be trained to approximate the optimal control actions or even the entire optimal control sequence. This approach fundamentally shifts the computational paradigm from explicit, time-consuming optimization to rapid inference. The training phase, which can be computationally demanding and time-consuming, is performed offline, utilizing historical data, simulation results, or data generated by a traditional MPC controller operating under various conditions. Once trained, the AI model can then predict the desired control inputs in near real-time, offering a significant speed advantage.

One of the most direct ways AI can accelerate MPC is through the development of surrogate models. These are essentially machine learning models that are trained to mimic the behavior of the MPC's optimization solver. The input to the surrogate model typically consists of the current system state and any relevant disturbances or setpoint information, while its output is the predicted optimal control action(s). Various machine learning techniques can be employed for this purpose, including neural networks (deep learning architectures like multi-layer perceptrons, recurrent neural networks, or convolutional neural networks, depending on the nature of the state and control inputs), support vector machines, or even ensemble methods.

Consider, for instance, an advanced robotics application, such as the precise manipulation of delicate components on an assembly line. These robots often require extremely fast response times and complex trajectory planning to achieve high throughput and accuracy. A traditional MPC controller for such a system might involve a quadratic programming (QP) problem or a more general nonlinear programming (NLP) problem to determine the optimal joint torques or velocities at each time step. The complexity of the robot's dynamics, along with kinematic constraints, gravity compensation, and collision avoidance, can make the online solution of these optimization problems computationally prohibitive for high sampling rates (e.g., in the kilohertz range).

To address this, an AI surrogate model can be trained. The training data would consist of pairs of system states (robot joint positions, velocities, end-effector pose, etc.) and the corresponding optimal control actions computed by a meticulously tuned, offline MPC solver for a wide range of operating scenarios. The AI model, perhaps a deep neural network, learns the complex mapping from these states to optimal actions. Once trained, this neural network can predict the required joint torques or velocities in a matter of microseconds through a forward pass, a task that would take orders of magnitude longer for a traditional optimizer. This drastically reduces the computational overhead, enabling the robot to operate at much higher frequencies with MPC-based control, leading to improved performance, increased speed, and enhanced precision. The effectiveness of this approach hinges on the comprehensiveness of the training data; it must adequately cover the expected range of system states and operating conditions to ensure the surrogate model generalizes well and makes accurate predictions in real-world scenarios.

Another significant AI-driven approach involves using machine learning predictors to approximate the optimal control actions directly, or to provide a strong initial guess for the traditional optimization solver, thereby accelerating its convergence. This is often referred to as "warm-starting" the optimizer. Instead of starting the optimization from an arbitrary point (or zero), the AI predictor provides a highly informed initial guess, significantly reducing the number of iterations required for the solver to converge to a satisfactory solution. This hybrid approach retains the guarantee of optimality (or near-optimality) provided by the traditional solver while benefiting from the speed of AI inference for initialization.

Let's elaborate on the warm-starting concept. In many iterative optimization algorithms, such as interior-point methods or gradient descent variants commonly used in MPC, the initial guess for the solution plays a crucial role in both the speed of convergence and the ability to avoid local minima. If the optimizer starts from an initial control trajectory that is already close to the optimal one, it can reach the solution much faster. An AI model can be trained to predict this initial optimal trajectory. The input to this predictor would again be the current system state and desired setpoints. The output would be a predicted sequence of control inputs over the prediction horizon. This predicted trajectory is then used as the starting point for the MPC's online optimization solver.

For instance, consider the control of a complex chemical process, such as distillation columns, where precise temperature and pressure profiles must be maintained over multiple stages. The dynamic model of a distillation column can be highly nonlinear and involve significant time delays. An MPC controller is often employed to manage these dynamics, but the computational cost of solving the nonlinear optimization problem for a long prediction horizon can be substantial. By employing an AI predictor to generate an initial guess for the control inputs across the entire horizon, the subsequent optimization problem can be solved much more rapidly. The AI predictor, trained on past operational data or simulation results, provides a reasonable starting point, guiding the optimizer towards the true minimum in fewer iterations. This acceleration can allow for a longer prediction horizon or faster sampling rates, leading to improved disturbance rejection and tighter control of product quality.

Furthermore, AI can be employed to learn the constraints themselves, or to provide feasibility information to the solver, thereby simplifying the optimization problem. In some advanced AI-MPC integration schemes, the AI might learn a mapping from system states to the set of feasible control actions or to the parameters of the cost function and constraints that would lead to a feasible and desirable outcome. This can significantly reduce the search space for the optimizer or even allow for a shift from a constrained optimization problem to an unconstrained one if the AI can effectively guarantee feasibility.

A compelling example of AI augmenting the optimization solver can be seen in predictive control strategies for electric vehicle powertrains. Managing the battery state of charge, motor efficiency, and regenerative braking requires optimizing control actions over a horizon that accounts for driving conditions, traffic, and driver behavior. The optimization problem involves maximizing energy efficiency while adhering to battery thermal limits, motor torque limits, and desired acceleration profiles. When operating in dynamic urban environments, the rapid changes in speed and traffic patterns necessitate frequent re-optimization.

An AI model, such as a Recurrent Neural Network (RNN) or a Long Short-Term Memory (LSTM) network, can be trained to predict the optimal control sequence for the electric motor and braking system given the current vehicle state (speed, battery charge, temperature) and upcoming traffic information (derived from sensors or navigation data). This trained network acts as a rapid controller. For situations where higher precision is required or when the AI's prediction is uncertain, the predicted control sequence can be fed as a warm start to a traditional MPC optimizer. The optimizer then refines this initial guess to ensure strict adherence to all constraints and to potentially achieve a slightly better objective function value than the AI alone might achieve. This synergistic approach combines the speed of AI inference for common scenarios with the robustness and optimality guarantees of traditional MPC for critical adjustments, effectively creating a faster and more capable control system.

The choice of AI architecture and training methodology is critical for the success of these acceleration techniques. For learning surrogate models or direct control action predictors, supervised learning is often employed, where the AI is trained on input-output pairs derived from a high-fidelity simulation or a well-tuned offline MPC. Techniques like data augmentation and curriculum learning can be used to ensure the AI is robust to variations in operating conditions. For warm-starting, the AI predictor needs to generate a trajectory that is not only close to the optimal but also feasible, or at least a good starting point for the optimizer to recover feasibility quickly. This might involve training the AI predictor with an objective that penalizes infeasibility or guides it towards a "good enough" feasible solution.

Another facet of AI-driven optimization acceleration involves decomposing the complex MPC problem into smaller, more manageable subproblems that can be solved in parallel or sequentially with AI assistance. For instance, in a distributed MPC setting for a large-scale system (like a smart grid or a multi-robot system), each agent might have its own local MPC, but they need to coordinate to achieve a global objective. AI can be used to predict the communication requirements, estimate the impact of other agents' actions, or even solve parts of the local optimization problem that are independent of the others.

Consider a fleet of autonomous delivery drones. Each drone operates with its own MPC to navigate its assigned delivery route, avoid obstacles, and manage its battery. However, they must also coordinate to avoid aerial collisions and optimize overall fleet efficiency. A central AI system could analyze the planned routes and current states of all drones and predict potential conflict zones. This information can be used to adjust the local MPC constraints for each drone, such as tightening proximity constraints or slowing down certain drones proactively. Alternatively, an AI can learn to predict the "market price" of certain resources (like airspace or charging stations) that the local MPCs then factor into their cost functions, effectively decentralizing the coordination logic in a computationally efficient manner.

The development of AI-driven optimization solvers for MPC is an active area of research and development. While AI offers tremendous potential for acceleration, it's important to acknowledge the challenges. These include:

1.
Generalization and Robustness: Ensuring that the AI model performs reliably across the entire operating envelope, including unseen or rare conditions, is paramount. Poor generalization can lead to suboptimal or even unsafe control actions. Extensive validation and testing are crucial.
2. **Data Requirements:** Training effective AI models often requires large amounts of high-quality data. Generating this data, especially from real-world systems, can be expensive and time-consuming. Simulation plays a vital role here, but sim-to-real gaps must be addressed.
3. **Interpretability and Verification:** Understanding why an AI model makes a particular prediction can be difficult, especially for deep neural networks. This lack of interpretability can be a barrier in safety-critical applications where formal verification of the control system's behavior is required. Research into explainable AI (XAI) is addressing this.

4. **Stability Guarantees:** Traditional MPC often provides formal stability and performance guarantees. Retaining these guarantees when replacing or augmenting the solver with AI-based methods is a significant theoretical challenge. Techniques are emerging that combine AI with Lyapunov methods or other formal verification tools to provide such guarantees.
5. **Computational Resources for Training:** While inference is fast, the initial training of complex AI models can require substantial computational resources.

Despite these challenges, the benefits of using AI to accelerate MPC optimization solvers are undeniable. The ability to deploy MPC on faster systems, implement more complex models, or achieve higher performance through tighter control loops makes AI a critical enabler for the next generation of intelligent control systems. By intelligently integrating AI, the computational bottleneck of MPC can be significantly alleviated, paving the way for its widespread application in fields ranging from autonomous driving and robotics to industrial automation and smart infrastructure management, where real-time responsiveness and computational efficiency are paramount. The ongoing research in hybrid AI-MPC architectures, which strategically combine the strengths of AI inference and traditional optimization, promises to deliver control solutions that are both highly performant and computationally tractable.

Case Study: AI-Augmented MPC for Turbines

The pursuit of enhanced efficiency and reliability in energy generation systems has consistently driven innovation in control methodologies. Wind turbines, as prime examples of complex electromechanical systems operating in highly variable and unpredictable environments, present a compelling testbed for advanced control strategies. The inherent nonlinearities of aerodynamics, the stochastic nature of wind turbulence, and the stringent demands of minimizing structural loads while maximizing power output necessitate sophisticated control approaches. Traditional Model Predictive Control (MPC) has been a cornerstone in addressing these challenges, offering a powerful framework for anticipating future system behavior and optimizing control actions over a defined horizon. However, the computational intensity of solving the underlying optimization problems, especially when dealing with highly detailed, nonlinear models that accurately capture the turbine's dynamics and environmental interactions, can become a limiting factor for achieving the fastest possible response times and the most intricate control strategies. This is precisely where the integration of Artificial Intelligence (AI) into MPC, as discussed in preceding sections, offers transformative potential, and the application to wind turbines provides a vivid illustration of these benefits.

In the context of wind turbines, the core control objective is multifaceted: to efficiently extract kinetic energy from the wind and convert it into electrical power, while simultaneously safeguarding the turbine's structural integrity by mitigating excessive loads on the blades, tower, and drivetrain. These objectives are often in tension. For instance, aggressive control actions designed to maximize power capture during gusty wind conditions can inadvertently amplify fatigue-inducing stresses. Conversely, overly conservative control strategies aimed at load reduction might lead to significant underutilization of available wind energy, particularly during periods of high wind speeds where the turbine is designed to operate in a power-limiting regime. Furthermore, the wind itself is a capricious input. Its speed and direction fluctuate rapidly and unpredictably, influenced by atmospheric turbulence, terrain, and weather patterns. Accurate prediction of these wind characteristics over the MPC's prediction horizon is crucial, yet inherently challenging. Traditional MPC controllers often rely on simplified aerodynamic models and simplified turbulence models, which, while computationally tractable, may not fully capture the complex, nonlinear interactions between the wind flow and the rotating blades. This can lead to suboptimal control decisions, either by failing to extract the maximum available power or by imposing unnecessary structural stress.

The AI-augmented MPC approach seeks to address these limitations by leveraging machine learning to enhance the predictive and optimization capabilities of the controller. One primary avenue involves the development of more accurate and computationally efficient system models. Instead of relying solely on first-principles physics-based models, which can be computationally expensive to simulate and integrate into the MPC optimization loop, AI can be employed to learn these dynamics directly from data. For wind turbines, this data can come from a variety of sources: SCADA (Supervisory Control and Data Acquisition) data from operational turbines, high-fidelity computational fluid dynamics (CFD) simulations, or data generated by a well-tuned traditional MPC controller operating in a simulated environment. Machine learning algorithms, particularly deep neural networks such as Recurrent Neural Networks (RNNs) or Long Short-Term Memory (LSTM) networks, are adept at capturing complex temporal dependencies and nonlinear relationships. By training these networks on vast datasets, they can learn to accurately predict the turbine's response to different control inputs (e.g., blade pitch angle, generator torque) under varying wind conditions, including the intricate effects of turbulence and unsteady aerodynamics.

These learned AI models can serve several purposes within the AI-augmented MPC framework for wind turbines. Firstly, they can act as highly accurate surrogate models for the turbine's aerodynamics and structural dynamics. When integrated into the MPC's prediction horizon, these AI surrogates can provide faster and more accurate predictions of future states compared to traditional physics-based models. This acceleration is critical. By reducing the time required to predict the system's trajectory, the MPC optimization solver has more computational budget available for finding a better control trajectory, or it can operate with a longer prediction horizon. A longer horizon, in turn, allows the controller to "see" further into the future, anticipating changes in wind speed and direction more effectively, and consequently making more proactive and optimal control decisions. For instance, an AI-trained aerodynamic model might learn to better predict the lift and drag forces on the blades as a function of wind speed, blade pitch, and rotational speed, accounting for stall effects and dynamic inflow phenomena that are often simplified in conventional models. This improved predictive accuracy directly translates into better power output optimization.

Secondly, AI can be used to improve the prediction of external disturbances, most notably the wind itself. While purely physics-based wind forecasting models exist, integrating AI can further enhance their accuracy. Machine learning models can be trained to learn complex spatio-temporal patterns in wind data from meteorological sources, radar, lidar, and existing turbine SCADA data. These models can potentially capture local micro-climate effects and rapid turbulence fluctuations that are difficult to model using traditional methods. By providing more accurate and granular wind forecasts as inputs to the MPC, the controller can make more informed decisions regarding pitch angle adjustments and torque commands. For example, if an AI predictor forecasts a rapid gust of wind followed by a lull, the MPC can pre-emptively adjust the pitch angle to manage the incoming surge of power and then relax it during the lull, thereby smoothing power output and reducing transient structural loads. This proactive management is far more effective than reacting to measurements after the wind has already impacted the turbine.

Thirdly, AI can directly assist in solving the optimization problem itself, as discussed in the previous chapter. In wind turbine control, the optimization problem typically involves minimizing a cost function that penalizes deviations from the power maximization setpoint and structural load exceedances, subject to operational constraints (e.g., maximum rotational speed, maximum pitch angle, structural stress limits). This can be a computationally intensive nonlinear optimization problem. An AI model, trained on data generated by a traditional MPC, can learn to predict the optimal control actions (e.g., sequences of pitch angles and generator torques) directly for a given system state and wind forecast. This trained AI model then acts as a rapid inference engine, providing near-instantaneous control commands. To maintain the rigor and robustness of MPC, this AI-generated command can be used as a warm start for a traditional MPC optimizer. The optimizer then refines this initial guess, ensuring that all constraints are strictly met and potentially achieving a slightly more optimal solution than the AI alone might provide. This hybrid approach offers the best of both worlds: the speed and adaptability of AI for quick decision-making in dynamic conditions, and the guaranteed performance and constraint satisfaction of MPC for ensuring safety and reliability.

A specific challenge in wind turbine control is handling the stochastic nature of wind turbulence. While average wind speed can be predicted with some accuracy, the rapid, chaotic fluctuations within that average are harder to model. These fluctuations are critical because they are the primary drivers of fatigue loads on the turbine components. Traditional MPC, with its discrete time steps and limited prediction horizon, often struggles to fully account for the impact of high-frequency turbulence. AI, however, can be trained to recognize patterns indicative of turbulent bursts and their likely effects on the turbine. For instance, an AI model might learn from high-frequency sensor data that a certain pattern of rapid fluctuations in wind speed and direction is highly correlated with increased blade root bending moments. Armed with this knowledge, the AI-augmented MPC can then proactively adjust the pitch and torque to counteract these predicted loads, even if the exact magnitude and timing of the turbulent event are uncertain. This is a form of predictive load mitigation that goes beyond the capabilities of controllers relying on simpler turbulence models.

Consider a scenario where a wind turbine is operating in a site known for its significant atmospheric turbulence. A traditional MPC might experience limitations in its ability to react quickly enough to turbulent gusts, potentially leading to high peak loads. An AI-augmented MPC, equipped with an AI-trained aerodynamic model and an AI-enhanced wind turbulence predictor, can significantly improve performance. The AI turbulence predictor might identify a high probability of a turbulent shear event within the next few seconds. Based on this prediction and its learned understanding of how such events impact the turbine, the AI component of the controller might suggest an immediate, small adjustment to the blade pitch angle, perhaps increasing it slightly. This proactive pitch adjustment, executed before the full impact of the gust is felt, can effectively dampen the resulting power surge and, more importantly, reduce the peak bending moments on the blades. Once the gust passes, the AI can then guide the controller to return to optimal power extraction mode. The AI-generated pitch command can also be used as a warm start for the MPC optimizer, which would then verify and refine this command, ensuring it adheres to all operational constraints and potentially finding a slightly better fine-tuning of the pitch and generator torque to optimize power output during the transition. This iterative process, driven by AI's predictive power and MPC's optimization rigor, leads to smoother power output, reduced fatigue loads, and extended turbine lifespan.

The practical implementation of AI-augmented MPC for wind turbines involves careful consideration of several factors. Firstly, the data used for training the AI models must be representative of the turbine's operational environment. This includes data from various wind conditions, operational modes (e.g., power production, idling, shutdown), and fault scenarios. High-fidelity simulations are invaluable for generating diverse training data, especially for extreme or rare events that may not be well-represented in historical operational data. However, it is crucial to address the "sim-to-real" gap, ensuring that the AI models generalize well to the real-world system's nuances. Model validation and continuous online learning are therefore essential.

Secondly, the integration strategy of AI and MPC needs to be carefully designed. A common approach is to use AI for:

1. **Improved System Dynamics Prediction:** Replacing or augmenting physics-based models within the MPC prediction step with AI-learned models.
2. **Enhanced Disturbance Forecasting:** Using AI to predict wind speed, direction, and turbulence more accurately.
3. **Fast Control Action Generation:** Employing AI as a direct controller or as a warm-start provider for the MPC optimizer.

Each of these integration strategies has its own trade-offs in terms of computational requirements, performance gains, and the complexity of achieving formal guarantees. For instance, replacing the entire MPC optimization with a direct AI inference model offers the highest speed but may sacrifice the rigorous constraint satisfaction and optimality guarantees that are characteristic of MPC. Conversely, using AI solely as a warm-start for a traditional MPC solver retains the guarantees but might not provide as significant a speedup as a fully AI-driven approach. A balanced hybrid approach often strikes the right chord, utilizing AI for its predictive power and speed where appropriate, and relying on MPC for its robustness and optimality verification.

Thirdly, the issue of interpretability and safety is paramount in the wind energy sector. While deep learning models can achieve remarkable predictive accuracy, their "black box" nature can be a concern. Operators and regulators need to understand why a controller is making certain decisions, especially when those decisions could impact safety or grid stability. Research into Explainable AI (XAI) techniques is crucial for providing insights into the AI's decision-making process. Furthermore, methods for formally verifying the stability and safety of AI-augmented MPC systems are an active area of research. This might involve combining AI with Lyapunov stability analysis or using formal methods to bound the error introduced by AI approximations. For critical systems like wind turbines, ensuring that AI integration does not compromise safety is non-negotiable.

The performance improvements resulting from AI-augmented MPC for wind turbines can be substantial and span multiple dimensions. Increased power output is a direct benefit, achieved by more precisely tracking the optimal power curve across a wider range of wind conditions and by better exploiting available wind energy during periods of high wind speed. Reduced structural loads, particularly fatigue loads, lead to extended turbine lifespan and lower maintenance costs. Smoother power output contributes to improved grid stability and reduced wear and tear on drivetrain components. The ability to operate the turbine more effectively in turbulent environments, where traditional controllers might struggle, unlocks the potential for greater energy capture in sites previously considered less viable.

For example, consider a large offshore wind farm. The collective control of multiple turbines in close proximity can lead to complex aerodynamic interactions, such as wake effects, where the turbulence generated by one turbine significantly impacts the performance and loads of downstream turbines. An AI-augmented MPC, designed to consider these inter-turbine interactions and their impact on the local wind field, can optimize the operation of the entire farm, not just individual turbines. This might involve slightly "de-tuning" upstream turbines to reduce their wake impact on downstream ones, a trade-off that AI can precisely quantify and optimize based on real-time wind conditions and power demands. Such coordinated control, enabled by AI's ability to process complex, multi-variable interactions, can lead to substantial aggregate increases in energy production for the entire farm. The AI can learn the complex wake dynamics from simulation and operational data, providing a more accurate prediction of how pitch and torque adjustments at one turbine will affect others, thus facilitating coordinated optimization.

In summary, the case study of AI-augmented MPC for wind turbines highlights the tangible benefits of integrating machine learning into advanced control systems for complex, dynamic environments. By leveraging AI to enhance model accuracy, improve disturbance forecasting, and accelerate optimization, it becomes possible to achieve unprecedented levels of performance in terms of power generation, structural load mitigation, and operational safety. The ongoing development in this area, focusing on data-driven modeling, robust integration strategies, and formal verification of AI-MPC systems, promises to further unlock the potential of renewable energy sources and pave the way for more intelligent and efficient industrial control solutions. The ability to dynamically adapt to the inherent variability of the wind, making precise, predictive control decisions in near real-time, is a testament to the transformative power of AI in modern control engineering.

Chapter 9: Learning for Adaptive Control

In the realm of control systems, a fundamental challenge arises when the system being controlled is not static. Many real-world systems, from the complex aerodynamics of an aircraft to the intricate dynamics of a chemical reactor, are subject to variations. These variations can stem from a multitude of sources: changes in operating conditions, environmental factors, wear and tear on components, or inherent nonlinearities that manifest differently at different operating points. A controller designed to perform optimally under one set of conditions might exhibit degraded performance, or even instability, when those conditions change. This is where the concept of **adaptive control** emerges as a crucial paradigm.

Adaptive control addresses this challenge by endowing the controller with the ability to
learn and *adjust* its own behavior online, in real-time, as the system evolves or as new information becomes available. Unlike conventional controllers, which are typically designed with fixed parameters based on a nominal model of the system, an adaptive controller actively monitors the system's performance and modifies its control law to ensure that desired objectives are met, even in the face of uncertainty or variation. The core motivation is to maintain satisfactory levels of performance—be it stability, speed of response, or accuracy—despite the inherent uncertainties that plague many practical control applications. This adaptability is not merely a desirable feature; for many complex systems, it is an absolute necessity for reliable and efficient operation.

Consider, for instance, the challenge of controlling an aircraft's autopilot. As an aircraft ascends, its speed changes, its fuel is consumed (altering its weight and center of gravity), and aerodynamic conditions like air density and temperature vary significantly. These changes alter the aircraft's dynamic characteristics. A fixed-gain autopilot, tuned for cruise conditions, would likely perform poorly and could even become unstable during ascent or descent. An adaptive autopilot, however, continuously estimates the aircraft's current aerodynamic parameters and adjusts its control gains accordingly, ensuring stable and precise flight throughout the entire mission profile. Similarly, a power management system in a flexible manufacturing plant might need to adapt to the changing power demands of various machines coming online or offline, or to fluctuations in the availability and price of electricity from the grid.

The fundamental principle behind adaptive control is the continuous interaction between the controller and the system it manages. The controller observes the system's behavior, typically through measurements of its states or outputs, and compares this behavior to the desired behavior. Based on this comparison, an adaptation mechanism within the controller updates the controller's parameters. This update is guided by an adaptation law, which dictates how the parameters should be modified to improve performance or reduce the error between the actual and desired system responses. This process creates a feedback loop not just for control, but also for adaptation, allowing the controller to dynamically reshape itself to better suit the prevailing system dynamics.

At its heart, adaptive control aims to overcome the limitations imposed by uncertainties in system models. These uncertainties can be broadly categorized. Firstly, there are **parameter uncertainties**, where the structure of the system model is known, but some of its coefficients (parameters) are not precisely known or are subject to drift. For example, the friction in a robotic arm might change over time due to wear, or the mass of a payload being manipulated might vary. Secondly, there are **unmodeled dynamics**, where the controller design relies on a simplified model that omits certain high-frequency dynamics, delays, or nonlinearities that are present in the actual system. Thirdly, **external disturbances** can significantly affect system behavior, and an adaptive controller can implicitly or explicitly account for their impact by adjusting its response.

The contrast with fixed-gain controllers is stark. A conventional controller, designed using techniques like PID (Proportional-Integral-Derivative) control or linear-quadratic regulation, relies on a set of constant gains. These gains are typically determined during the design phase based on a mathematical model of the system that represents its behavior under nominal or average conditions. While such controllers can perform admirably when the system adheres closely to its model, their performance degrades substantially when significant deviations occur. They lack the inherent ability to compensate for unexpected changes, requiring manual retuning or a complete redesign for different operating regimes. This makes them less suitable for systems that are inherently variable or operate in unpredictable environments.

The field of adaptive control encompasses a rich variety of approaches, each with its strengths and weaknesses. Some of the most prominent categories include model reference adaptive control (MRAC), self-tuning regulators (STR), and extremum seeking control. In MRAC, the goal is to make the controlled system behave like a reference model, which dictates the desired performance. The adaptation mechanism adjusts the controller parameters to minimize the difference between the actual system output and the output of the reference model. Self-tuning regulators, on the other hand, explicitly estimate the system parameters online and then use these estimates to design a controller, often using traditional control design techniques. Extremum seeking control is used to find the optimal operating point of a system by iteratively adjusting a control parameter to maximize or minimize an output performance measure, even when the underlying system dynamics are unknown or changing.

The development of adaptive control strategies has been significantly influenced by advancements in related fields, particularly system identification and machine learning. System identification provides the tools and techniques necessary for estimating system parameters and dynamics from measured data, which is a prerequisite for many adaptive control algorithms. Machine learning, with its powerful methods for learning complex patterns and relationships from data, has opened up new avenues for designing more sophisticated and robust adaptation mechanisms. This intersection is particularly evident in modern approaches to adaptive control, where data-driven learning plays an increasingly central role in shaping the controller's intelligence.

The need for adaptive control is pervasive across numerous engineering disciplines. In aerospace, beyond autopilots, adaptive control is employed in flight control systems for highly agile aircraft (like fighter jets) whose aerodynamic characteristics change dramatically with speed and altitude, and for unmanned aerial vehicles (UAVs) operating in unpredictable environments. In robotics, adaptive control is essential for manipulators handling payloads of varying mass, for legged robots that must adapt to uneven terrain, and for robots operating in close proximity to humans where safety and adaptability are paramount. In process control, for example, controlling chemical reactors often involves dealing with variations in catalyst activity, reactant concentrations, and temperature profiles. Adaptive controllers can ensure consistent product quality and safe operation in such dynamic environments. Even in areas like automotive engineering, adaptive cruise control systems that maintain a set distance from the vehicle ahead, or active suspension systems that adjust to road conditions, embody adaptive control principles.

The core idea is to achieve robustness not by designing a controller that is inherently very conservative and performs adequately across all possible conditions (which often leads to suboptimal performance in nominal conditions), but by designing a controller that can actively track and compensate for the changing system characteristics. This allows for higher performance in nominal conditions while still maintaining stability and acceptable performance when deviations occur. The "intelligence" of an adaptive controller lies in its ability to learn from experience and adjust its strategy accordingly, making it a powerful tool for tackling the inherent complexity and variability of the real world. The quest for more efficient, reliable, and autonomous systems continues to drive innovation in adaptive control, making it an increasingly vital area of study and application.

The pursuit of robust and high-performance control in the face of uncertainty has led to the development of sophisticated adaptive control techniques. Among these, Model Reference Adaptive Control (MRAC) stands out as a foundational and widely explored methodology. The core philosophy of MRAC is to imbue a control system with a desired dynamic behavior, dictated by a "reference model," and then to continuously adjust the controller's parameters so that the actual plant output converges to, and tracks, the output of this idealized reference model. This approach elegantly sidesteps the need for an explicit, accurate model of the plant being controlled during the initial design phase. Instead, the focus shifts to defining the desired performance characteristics, which are encapsulated within the reference model.

At its heart, MRAC operates on a simple yet powerful principle: error minimization. We define a reference model, which is a mathematical representation of the desired closed-loop system response. This model takes the same reference input as the actual plant and generates a "desired" output trajectory. The adaptive controller then manipulates the plant's input signals, attempting to force the actual plant output to match this desired trajectory. The discrepancy between the actual plant output and the reference model output, known as the tracking error, serves as the crucial feedback signal for the adaptation mechanism. This mechanism's sole purpose is to adjust the controller's parameters in such a way that the tracking error is progressively reduced, ideally to zero.

Let's consider a typical MRAC setup. We have a plant, described by its dynamics, which we aim to control. Let's denote the plant's state-space representation as:

$$ \dot{x}_p(t) = A_p x_p(t) + B_p u(t) $$
$$ y_p(t) = C_p x_p(t) $$

where $x_p(t)$ is the plant state, $u(t)$ is the control input, and $y_p(t)$ is the plant output. The matrices A_p, B_p, and C_p represent the plant dynamics. In a classic MRAC scenario, these matrices are not precisely known or are subject to change.

The reference model, on the other hand, is chosen to exhibit the desired performance. It is typically a stable linear system, often represented as:

$$ \dot{x}_m(t) = A_m x_m(t) + B_m r(t) $$
$$ y_m(t) = C_m x_m(t) $$

Here, $x_m(t)$ is the reference model's state, $y_m(t)$ is the desired output, $r(t)$ is the reference input, and A_m, B_m, C_m are matrices defining the desired dynamics. Crucially, the reference model is not adapted; its parameters are fixed and define the target performance. The goal is to design a controller $u(t) = K(t) x_p(t)$ (or a more general structure $u(t) = f(x_p(t), \theta(t))$, where $\theta(t)$ are adjustable controller parameters) such that $y_p(t) \to y_m(t)$ as $t \to \infty$.

The control law is often structured to incorporate adjustable parameters. For a linear time-invariant (LTI) plant and a linear controller, the control input might be a linear combination of the plant states, with time-varying gains:

$$ \dot{u}(t) = \theta^T(t) \xi(t) $$

where $\theta(t)$ is a vector of adjustable controller parameters and $\xi(t)$ is a vector of signals derived from the plant's state or input. For example, $\xi(t)$ could be the plant's state vector $x_p(t)$ *or a filtered version of it. The objective is to find an adaptation law for* $\dot{\theta}(t)$ *such that the tracking error* $e(t) = y_p(t) - y_m(t)$ asymptotically vanishes.

The adaptation law is the "brain" of the MRAC system. It dictates how the controller parameters $\theta(t)$ are updated based on the observed tracking error. The design of this adaptation law is intimately linked to ensuring the stability of the overall adaptive system. Early and influential adaptation laws were derived using Lyapunov stability theory and the so-called MIT rule. The MIT rule, named after the Massachusetts Institute of Technology, provides a direct way to derive an adaptation law by minimizing the integral of the squared tracking error. If we consider the error $e(t)$ and its time derivative $\dot{e}(t)$, and assume a controller structure $u = \theta^T \xi$, then the rate of change of the error can be expressed in terms of $\dot{\theta}$. The MIT rule proposes updating θ in the direction that reduces the performance index $J = \frac{1}{2} e^2$. This leads to an update rule of the form:

$$ \dot{\theta}_i(t) = -\gamma \frac{\partial e(t)}{\partial \theta_i} e(t) $$

where γ is a positive adaptation gain. This is essentially a gradient descent approach applied to the error. However, calculating

$\frac{\partial e(t)}{\partial \theta_i}$ can be challenging as it often requires knowledge of the plant dynamics, which is precisely what MRAC aims to avoid needing explicitly.

To circumvent this, researchers developed techniques to express the error dynamics in a form that allows for parameter adaptation without complete plant knowledge. A common strategy involves rewriting the plant dynamics in a form where the control input is augmented with unknown parameters, which are then compensated by the adaptive controller. For instance, if the plant is linear and can be expressed as:

$$ yp^{(n)}(t) + a{n-1} yp^{(n-1)}(t) + \dots + a0 yp(t) = b0 u(t) $$

where the coefficients ai and $b0$ are unknown, the reference model would be:

$$ ym^{(n)}(t) + a'{n-1} ym^{(n-1)}(t) + \dots + a'0 ym(t) = b'0 r(t) $$

with known coefficients $a'i$ and $b'0$. The control law is structured as $u(t) = \theta^T(t) \xi(t)$, where $\theta(t)$ contains estimates of the unknown parameters. The adaptation law is then derived to drive the error $e(t) = yp(t) - ym(t)$ to zero.

A more formal and rigorous approach to proving stability in MRAC relies heavily on Lyapunov's direct method. The core idea is to construct a Lyapunov function $V(t)$ for the augmented system (plant, controller, and reference model) that is positive definite and whose time derivative $\dot{V}(t)$ is negative semi-definite. If $\dot{V}(t)$ is negative definite, then the system state (including the tracking error and parameter errors) will asymptotically converge to zero. The construction of such a Lyapunov function often involves analyzing the error dynamics, which can be manipulated into a form suitable for Lyapunov analysis.

Consider a simplified case where the plant is a first-order system with an unknown gain and time constant:

$$ \frac{y_p(s)}{u(s)} = \frac{b}{s+a} $$
where a and b are unknown. The reference model could be:
$$ \frac{ym(s)}{r(s)} = \frac{bm}{s+a_m} $$
with known am and bm. The goal is to have $yp(t) \to ym(t)$. A common controller structure is $u(t) = \theta1(t) r(t) + \theta2(t) yp(t)$. The challenge is to design adaptation laws for $\dot{\theta}1(t)$ and $\dot{\theta}_2(t)$ that ensure stability and convergence.

Let's delve deeper into the structure of adaptation laws derived from stability considerations. A key result in MRAC theory, particularly for linear systems, involves defining the error dynamics. Let $e(t) = y p(t) - ym(t)$. If the plant can be expressed in a specific form, the error dynamics can often be written as:
$$ \dot{e}(t) = Am e(t) + Bm \Delta(t) $$
where $\Delta(t)$ is a term that depends on the difference between the actual controller and an ideal controller whose parameters are not known. The adaptive control law aims to force $\Delta(t)$ to zero. For instance, if the ideal control law were $u{ideal} = \theta{ideal}^T \xi$, and the adaptive law uses $u = \theta^T \xi$, then $\Delta(t)$ might be related to $(\theta_{ideal} - \theta)^T \xi$.

A common approach for updating θ uses a formulation that ensures $\dot{V}(t) \le 0$. For example, a gradient-based adaptation law might look like:

$$ \dot{\theta}(t) = - \Gamma \xi(t) e(t) $$
where Γ is a positive definite matrix. However, this simple form requires the tracking error $e(t)$ to be directly proportional to the parameter error $(\theta - \theta_{ideal})$. For more complex systems, a Kalman filter-like structure or other observers might be incorporated to estimate states or parameters that are not directly measurable, leading to more sophisticated adaptive laws.

One of the most influential adaptation laws is the Lyapunov redesign method. This involves defining a controller of the form $u(t) = \theta^T(t) \xi(t)$ and choosing a Lyapunov function that incorporates the tracking error and the parameter error. By carefully analyzing the time derivative of the Lyapunov function, one can derive an update law for $\theta(t)$ that guarantees the Lyapunov function decreases, thus ensuring stability. A typical structure derived from this method for a system of the form $\dot{x} = Ax + bu$ with $u=\theta^T\xi$ and reference model $\dot{x}
m=*A*xm+br$ might yield an adaptation law:
$$ \dot{\theta}(t) = - \Gamma \xi(t) (C(x*p* - *x*m))^T $$
where C is a matrix to extract the output, and Γ is a positive definite matrix. The key is that the error term is related to the output error and its transformation, allowing for the Lyapunov function to be constructed.

The MRAC framework has been extended to handle various plant structures and uncertainties. For example, in systems with unknown high-frequency gain, the control law and adaptation mechanism need to be carefully designed to ensure stability. Similarly, systems with relative degree greater than one (meaning the output is related to higher-order derivatives of the input) require more complex reference models and control structures.

A significant challenge in MRAC is the potential for parameter drift or "wind-up" in the adaptation mechanism when the system is not persistently exciting. If the input signals to the adaptation law ($\xi(t)$ and $e(t)$) do not provide sufficient information about the unknown plant parameters, the estimated parameters may not converge to their true values or may diverge. Techniques like "leaky adaptation" (adding a small decay term to the adaptation law) or using a "zeta-on-off" strategy (disabling adaptation when the error is small) have been proposed to mitigate these issues, although they can sometimes lead to slower adaptation or suboptimal performance.

Let's illustrate the application of MRAC with a more concrete example, such as controlling a chemical process. Consider a simple exothermic continuous stirred-tank reactor (CSTR) where the reaction rate depends on temperature and reactant concentration. The temperature dynamics might be represented by a nonlinear differential equation. For the purpose of MRAC, we can often linearize the system around an operating point or use a simplified linear model that captures the dominant dynamics. However, the kinetic parameters or heat transfer coefficients might be uncertain or drift over time due to catalyst deactivation or fouling.

Suppose the linearized temperature dynamics can be approximated by a second-order system:

$$ \ddot{T}(t) + a_1 \dot{T}(t) + a_0 T(t) = b_0 u(t) $$

where $T(t)$ is the reactor temperature, $u(t)$ is the manipulated variable (e.g., coolant flow rate), and a_1, a_0, b_0 are parameters that are not precisely known or may vary. The desired reference model for temperature control could be:

$$ \ddot{T}_m(t) + a'_{1} \dot{T}_m(t) + a'_{0} T_m(t) = b'_{0} T_{ref}(t) $$

Here, $T_{ref}(t)$ is the desired setpoint temperature profile, and a'_1, a'_0, b'_0 are chosen to yield a stable and responsive temperature response (e.g., critically damped).

The adaptive controller would then be designed to adjust its parameters to make $T(t)$ track $T_m(t)$. A common controller structure for this second-order system might involve a proportional-derivative (PD) controller with adaptive gains:

$$ u(t) = \theta1(t) (T{ref}(t) - T(t)) + \theta2(t) (\dot{T}{ref}(t) - \dot{T}(t)) $$
Here, $\theta1(t)$ and $\theta2(t)$ are the adaptive gains. For this specific structure, and assuming a specific form for the plant's unknown parameters and output equation, an adaptation law can be derived.

A more general approach for a plant $\frac{Y(s)}{U(s)} = \frac{b(s)}{a(s)}$ and reference model $\frac{Y m(s)}{R(s)} = \frac{bm(s)}{am(s)}$, *where* $a(s)$ *and* $b(s)$ *are polynomials of degree* n *and* m *respectively, and* $am(s)$ and $bm(s)$ *are the desired polynomials, requires a controller of the form* $u(t) = \phi^T(t) \omega(t)$, *where* $\phi(t)$ *are the adaptive parameters and* $\omega(t)$ *are regressor signals derived from the reference input and the plant's output and its derivatives. The adaptation law is designed to minimize the error* $e(t) = yp(t) - y_m(t)$.

The stability proofs for MRAC systems are often complex and depend heavily on the assumed plant structure, the controller structure, and the adaptation law. For linear systems with known relative degree and bounded unknown parameters, rigorous proofs of asymptotic tracking can be established using Lyapunov methods. However, for nonlinear systems, time-varying parameters beyond a certain class, or under external disturbances, achieving guaranteed stability and tracking can be significantly more challenging, often requiring extensions of the basic MRAC framework.

One significant extension is the development of MRAC with a priori bounds on parameters. If we know that the unknown parameters lie within a certain range, this information can be used to design more robust adaptation laws. For example, if a parameter is known to be positive, the adaptation law can be constrained to keep the estimated parameter positive, preventing it from crossing zero and causing instability.

The practical implementation of MRAC involves several considerations. Firstly, the choice of the reference model is critical. A poorly chosen reference model (e.g., one that demands faster response than the plant can physically achieve) will lead to persistent errors or even instability. Secondly, the choice of adaptation gain (Γ or γ) influences the speed of adaptation and the robustness to noise. A higher gain leads to faster adaptation but can also amplify noise, potentially destabilizing the system. Conversely, a lower gain makes the system more robust to noise but slows down adaptation.

Thirdly, the regressor signals $\xi(t)$ (or $\omega(t)$ in more general formulations) must be sufficiently "rich" or "persistently exciting" for the parameters to converge to their correct values. If the system is only subjected to inputs that do not excite all the unknown dynamics, the adaptation mechanism might fail to identify the parameters accurately. This is a common issue in practical applications where system behavior might be constrained by operational modes or external conditions.

Furthermore, the presence of noise in the measured outputs is a major concern for MRAC. Standard adaptation laws can be very sensitive to noise, leading to parameter estimates that oscillate around their true values or even diverge. Various filtering techniques are often employed to preprocess the signals before they are fed into the adaptation law, or the adaptation law itself might be modified to incorporate noise rejection properties. For instance, the adaptation law might be averaged over time or implemented with a smoother update mechanism.

Despite these challenges, MRAC remains a powerful paradigm for adaptive control. Its ability to define desired performance through a reference model, rather than requiring an explicit plant model for the controller itself, makes it attractive for systems with significant uncertainties. The theoretical foundations, particularly regarding stability proofs for linear systems, are well-established, providing a solid basis for understanding and designing MRAC controllers. The ongoing research in robust adaptation, handling nonlinearities, and integrating MRAC with other learning techniques continues to expand its applicability to increasingly complex real-world problems. The fundamental idea of learning from error to match a desired behavior is a core concept that continues to drive innovation in adaptive control.

The adaptive control landscape is rich with methodologies designed to tackle the inherent uncertainties and time-varying nature of real-world dynamical systems. While Model Reference Adaptive Control (MRAC) focuses on directly shaping the system's response to match that of a predefined reference model, another powerful paradigm, Self-Tuning Regulators (STR), adopts a slightly different, yet complementary, strategy. STRs offer a distinct approach to achieving adaptive control by explicitly identifying a model of the plant and then using this estimated model to design or re-tune a controller. This methodology is particularly appealing in scenarios where the underlying plant dynamics might be complex or difficult to characterize analytically for direct MRAC synthesis, yet amenable to model identification.

At its core, a Self-Tuning Regulator operates on a fundamental principle of separation: it divides the adaptation process into two distinct, yet tightly coupled, stages. The first stage involves an online parameter estimation algorithm that continuously observes the system's behavior and updates a mathematical model representing the plant. This model, typically a simplified representation of the actual system, captures its essential dynamics and is updated in real-time as new data becomes available. The second stage then utilizes this updated model in a controller design algorithm. This algorithm recalculates the controller parameters, ensuring that the control system's performance remains optimal or satisfactory despite changes in the plant or its environment. This dual-rate operation—one rate for parameter estimation and another for controller re-tuning—is a hallmark of STRs and allows for a flexible and robust approach to adaptive control.

The structure of a typical STR can be visualized as a feedback loop where the plant output is fed back not only to the controller but also to a parameter estimation block. This estimation block processes the system's inputs and outputs to refine its internal model of the plant. Subsequently, this updated plant model is passed to a controller synthesis module, which then computes the new control law. The overall process can be considered a form of "implicit" adaptation, in contrast to MRAC's "explicit" matching of a reference model. In STRs, the desired performance is not directly specified by a reference model but rather by the controller synthesis algorithm, which aims to achieve certain performance objectives (e.g., stability, desired bandwidth, disturbance rejection) based on the estimated plant model.

A critical component of any STR is the parameter estimation algorithm. The success of the entire adaptive system hinges on the accuracy and speed with which this algorithm can identify the plant's parameters. Among the most widely used and well-understood techniques for online parameter estimation is the Recursive Least Squares (RLS) algorithm. RLS is an iterative method that updates parameter estimates based on incoming data, minimizing the sum of squared errors between the actual system output and the output predicted by the current model. Unlike batch least squares, which requires all data points to be processed simultaneously, RLS updates the parameter estimates with each new data sample, making it ideal for real-time applications.

The RLS algorithm, when applied to linear system identification, typically aims to estimate parameters in a model of the form:

$$ y(k) = \phi^T(k) \theta $$

where $y(k)$ is the current output (or a filtered version of it), $\phi(k)$ is a vector of past inputs, outputs, and possibly external reference signals (known as the regressor vector), and θ is the vector of unknown plant parameters to be estimated. The RLS algorithm provides a computationally efficient recursive update for θ:

$$ \hat{\theta}(k) = \hat{\theta}(k-1) + K(k) [y(k) - \phi^T(k) \hat{\theta}(k-1)] $$

$$ K(k) = P(k-1) \phi(k) [1 + \phi^T(k) P(k-1) \phi(k)]^{-1} $$

$$ P(k) = [I - K(k) \phi^T(k)] P(k-1) $$

Here, $\hat{\theta}(k)$ is the estimate of the parameter vector at time step k, $K(k)$ is the Kalman gain, and $P(k)$ is the covariance matrix of the parameter estimates. The term $y(k) - \phi^T(k) \hat{\theta}(k-1)$ represents the prediction error—the difference between the actual output and the output predicted by the model with the previous parameter estimates. The Kalman gain $K(k)$ determines how much of this prediction error is used to update the parameter estimates. The covariance matrix $P(k)$ reflects the uncertainty in the parameter estimates; it decreases as more data becomes available and the estimates become more confident.

For a system with time-varying parameters, the standard RLS algorithm can be modified to incorporate a "forgetting factor" (λ). This factor allows the algorithm to give more weight to recent data and less weight to older data, enabling it to track parameter variations. The update equations for RLS with a forgetting factor are:

$$ \hat{\theta}(k) = \hat{\theta}(k-1) + K(k) [y(k) - \phi^T(k) \hat{\theta}(k-1)] $$
$$ K(k) = P(k-1) \phi(k) [\lambda + \phi^T(k) P(k-1) \phi(k)]^{-1} $$
$$ P(k) = \frac{1}{\lambda} [I - K(k) \phi^T(k)] P(k-1) $$
A value of $\lambda = 1$ corresponds to standard RLS with no forgetting. Values of λ slightly less than 1 (e.g., 0.95 to 0.99) allow the algorithm to adapt to gradual parameter changes, but at the cost of increased sensitivity to noise and potentially less precise estimates if the parameters are actually constant.

Another important aspect of parameter estimation in STRs is the choice of the model structure. The model must be complex enough to capture the essential dynamics of the plant but simple enough for accurate and efficient online identification. Common choices include ARX (AutoRegressive with eXternal input), ARMAX (AutoRegressive Moving Average with eXternal input), and state-space models. For instance, an ARX model for a single-input, single-output (SISO) system can be expressed as:

$$ A(q^{-1}) y(k) = B(q^{-1}) u(k) + e(k) $$
where $y(k)$ is the output, $u(k)$ is the input, $e(k)$ is a white noise disturbance, and $A(q^{-1})$ and $B(q^{-1})$ are polynomials in the backward shift operator q^{-1}. Rearranging this equation leads to a linear regression form suitable for RLS:
$$ y(k) = -\sum_{i=1}^{na} a_i y(k-i) + \sum_{j=0}^{nb} b_j u(k-j) + e(k) $$
The parameter vector θ would then contain the coefficients $[a_1, \dots, a_{na}, b_0, \dots, b_{nb}]$, and the regressor vector $\phi(k)$ would contain the past outputs $[y(k-1), \dots, y(k-na)]$ and past inputs $[u(k), \dots, u(k-nb)]$. The order of the polynomials (na, nb) needs to be

determined based on prior knowledge of the system or through system identification experiments.

Once the parameters of the plant model are estimated, the second crucial stage of the STR comes into play: the controller synthesis. The goal here is to design a controller whose parameters are derived from the current estimates of the plant model, such that the closed-loop system meets predefined performance specifications. This stage is often referred to as the "tuner" or "self-tuner." The specific method used for controller synthesis depends heavily on the chosen controller structure and the desired performance objectives.

A widely adopted approach is the pole-placement method. In this strategy, the parameters of the controller are calculated such that the poles of the overall closed-loop system are placed at desired locations in the complex plane. These desired pole locations are typically chosen to achieve a specific transient response, such as a certain rise time, settling time, and damping ratio. For an n-th order plant and a controller that, when combined with the plant, results in an $(n+m)$-th order closed-loop system, the goal is to place these $(n+m)$ poles at specified locations.

Consider a plant described by the ARX model $A(q^{-1}) y(k) = B(q^{-1}) u(k)$. A common controller structure is the Proportional-Integral-Derivative (PID) controller, but in the STR context, it's often more practical to use a more general controller structure that can be directly synthesized from the identified model. A popular choice is a controller of the form:

$$ R(q^{-1}) u(k) = T(q^{-1}) r(k) - S(q^{-1}) y(k) $$

where $r(k)$ is the reference signal, and $R(q^{-1})$, $S(q^{-1})$, and $T(q^{-1})$ are polynomials in q^{-1}. For a stable controller, $R(q^{-1})$ is typically chosen to be monic (the coefficient of q^{-1} is 1) and stable. The polynomial $S(q^{-1})$ is chosen to influence the closed-loop poles, while $T(q^{-1})$ can be used to shape the response to the reference signal.

The closed-loop system equation is obtained by substituting the controller into the plant equation:

$$ A(q^{-1}) y(k) = B(q^{-1}) [T(q^{-1}) r(k) - S(q^{-1}) y(k)] / R(q^{-1}) $$
$$ R(q^{-1}) A(q^{-1}) y(k) = B(q^{-1}) T(q^{-1}) r(k) - B(q^{-1}) S(q^{-1}) y(k) $$
$$ [R(q^{-1}) A(q^{-1}) + B(q^{-1}) S(q^{-1})] y(k) = B(q^{-1}) T(q^{-1}) r(k) $$
The characteristic polynomial of the closed-loop system is given by:
$$ \Psi(q^{-1}) = R(q^{-1}) A(q^{-1}) + B(q^{-1}) S(q^{-1}) $$
The controller design then involves choosing $\Psi(q^{-1})$ as a desired polynomial with roots at the desired locations, and then solving the Diophantine equation:
$$ \Psi(q^{-1}) = R(q^{-1}) \hat{A}(q^{-1}) + \hat{B}(q^{-1}) S(q^{-1}) $$
for the controller polynomials $S(q^{-1})$ and potentially $R(q^{-1})$ and $T(q^{-1})$ (if R and T are not fixed a priori), using the estimated plant polynomials $\hat{A}(q^{-1})$ and $\hat{B}(q^{-1})$. The degree of $S(q^{-1})$ is typically chosen such that the degree of $\Psi(q^{-1})$ is fixed. For example, if $\hat{A}(q^{-1})$ has degree na, $\hat{B}(q^{-1})$ has degree nb, $R(q^{-1})$ has degree nr, and we want the closed-loop system to have degree n_{cl}, then the degree of $S(q^{-1})$ is $n_{cl} - na - n_r$.

Another important control design strategy within STRs is Generalized

Minimum Variance (GMV) control. GMV control aims to minimize a cost function that includes a weighted sum of the future output and control effort. The standard GMV cost function is:

$$ J = E \{[y(k+d) - w(k+d)]^2 + \rho u^2(k)\} $$

where d is the system delay, $w(k+d)$ is a setpoint or desired trajectory, and ρ is a weighting factor that balances output performance against control effort. By minimizing this cost function using the estimated plant model, an optimal control law can be derived. The resulting controller parameters are then updated in real-time.

The practical implementation of STRs brings forth several considerations. One of the primary challenges is the "dual-rate" nature of the system. The parameter estimation and controller synthesis algorithms operate at different rates. Parameter estimation often needs to be performed at a high rate (e.g., the sampling rate of the system) to capture fast-changing dynamics. In contrast, controller re-tuning might be done less frequently to avoid excessive computation and to ensure that the estimated model is sufficiently reliable. A common strategy is to estimate parameters at each sampling instant but re-tune the controller only after a certain number of samples or when a significant change in the estimated parameters is detected.

The stability of STRs is a complex issue and often harder to guarantee rigorously compared to MRAC, especially for general plant models and controller design methods. The overall stability of the closed-loop system depends on the convergence properties of the parameter estimates and the performance of the controller synthesized from these estimates. Theoretical results on the stability of STRs often rely on assumptions such as:

1. The identified plant model converges to the true plant model asymptotically.
2. The desired controller specifications are achievable with the identified model.
3. The signals in the system are sufficiently "rich" to allow for accurate parameter estimation.

If the parameter estimates are poor, or if the controller design algorithm is sensitive to small errors in the model, the adaptive system may become unstable or exhibit poor performance. Techniques like using a forgetting factor in RLS, implementing checks for parameter estimate validity (e.g., ensuring estimated denominator polynomial is stable), or using a "freeze" mode where controller parameters are held constant when parameter estimation is unreliable, are employed to enhance robustness and stability.

A significant advantage of STRs lies in their practical applicability and interpretability. By explicitly identifying a plant model, STRs provide insights into the system's behavior, which can be valuable for diagnostics and process understanding. This contrasts with MRAC, where the plant model is implicitly adapted, and direct interpretability of intermediate parameters can be less straightforward. The controller synthesis stage also allows for direct specification of control objectives, such as pole locations or variance minimization, which can be more intuitive for control engineers accustomed to traditional control design methods.

Consider the application of STRs in controlling robotic manipulators. Robotic arms are inherently nonlinear systems with dynamics that can vary significantly due to changing payloads, friction in joints, and external forces. A common approach for adaptive robot control involves identifying a dynamic model of the manipulator. This model typically relates joint torques (control inputs) to joint positions, velocities, and accelerations (outputs and their derivatives). The model usually takes the form:

$$ M(\mathbf{q}) \ddot{\mathbf{q}} + C(\mathbf{q}, \dot{\mathbf{q}}) \dot{\mathbf{q}} + G(\mathbf{q}) = \tau $$
where $\mathbf{q}$ is the vector of joint positions, $\dot{\mathbf{q}}$ and $\ddot{\mathbf{q}}$ are velocities and accelerations, $M(\mathbf{q})$ is the inertia matrix, $C(\mathbf{q}, \dot{\mathbf{q}})$ represents Coriolis and centrifugal forces, $G(\mathbf{q})$ is the gravity vector, and τ is the vector of applied joint torques.

Many of the terms in this dynamic model, such as the inertia matrix elements and friction coefficients, are unknown or can change. STRs can be employed by linearizing this dynamic model around a working point or by parametrizing the unknown terms. For example, the equation can be rewritten in a linear-in-the-parameters form:

$$ \tau = Y(\mathbf{q}, \dot{\mathbf{q}}, \ddot{\mathbf{q}}) \mathbf{\theta} $$
Here, $\mathbf{\theta}$ is a vector of unknown dynamic parameters (e.g., mass, inertia, friction coefficients), and $Y(\mathbf{q}, \dot{\mathbf{q}}, \ddot{\mathbf{q}})$ is a matrix of known terms derived from the robot's state. The STR would then use an online estimation algorithm (like RLS) to estimate $\mathbf{\theta}$ based on observed joint trajectories and applied torques. Once $\mathbf{\theta}$ is estimated, a controller (e.g., a computed-torque controller or a PID controller with adaptive gains) can be synthesized using the estimated parameters to achieve desired joint position tracking.

For instance, a computed-torque controller aims to achieve a desired dynamic behavior by calculating the required torques based on the robot's dynamics. If the dynamics are unknown, an adaptive computed-torque controller would use estimated parameters:

$$ \tau{adaptive} = \hat{M}(\mathbf{q}) \ddot{\mathbf{q}}d + \hat{C}(\mathbf{q}, \dot{\mathbf{q}}) \dot{\mathbf{q}}_d + \hat{G}(\mathbf{q}) $$
where $\hat{M}$, $\hat{C}$, and $\hat{G}$ are computed using the estimated parameter vector $\hat{\mathbf{\theta}}$. This adaptive controller would then attempt to make the actual robot dynamics match the desired dynamics specified by $\ddot{\mathbf{q}}_d$. The RLS algorithm would continuously update $\hat{\mathbf{\theta}}$ as the robot operates.

Another common scenario where STRs shine is in process control, such as in chemical plants or power systems. These systems often exhibit slow dynamics, significant time delays, and parameters that drift over time due to aging equipment, catalyst deactivation, or changing operating conditions. For example, controlling the temperature in a distillation column involves complex interactions and nonlinearities. A simplified linear model of the column dynamics can be identified using STR. The model might describe the relationship between the steam flow rate to the reboiler (control input) and the temperature at a particular tray (output).

Suppose the identified model is a first-order plus dead-time (FOPDT) model:

$$ G(s) = \frac{K e^{-\theta s}}{\tau s + 1} $$
where K is the process gain, τ is the time constant, and θ is the time delay. In a discrete-time setting, this can be approximated by an ARX model. An STR would continuously update estimates for K, τ, and θ. Based on these estimates, a controller, such as a

PID controller, would be re-tuned. A common adaptive PID tuning rule derived from an FOPDT model is the Internal Model Control (IMC) tuning rule, which can be adapted to STRs. If $\hat{K}, \hat{\tau}, \hat{\theta}$ are the current estimates, the PID parameters (proportional gain K_p, integral time T_i, derivative time T_d) can be calculated using formulas that ensure the closed-loop system has a desired response speed, often dictated by a filter time constant λ. For instance, a common set of tuning rules is:

$$ K_p = \frac{\hat{\tau} + 0.5 \hat{\theta}}{\lambda + 0.5 \hat{\theta}} \frac{1}{\hat{K}} $$

$$ T_i = \hat{\tau} + 0.5 \hat{\theta} $$

$$ T_d = \frac{0.5 \hat{\theta} \hat{\tau}}{\hat{\tau} + 0.5 \hat{\theta}} $$

The adaptation rate is governed by how frequently these parameters are recomputed. A slower re-tuning rate (larger λ or re-tuning only when parameter estimates change significantly) provides more robustness to noise, while a faster rate allows quicker adaptation to process changes.

The choice between STR and MRAC often comes down to the specific application and the engineer's preferences. STRs provide a more explicit model-based design process, which can be easier to understand and debug, and they are particularly well-suited for systems where a reasonable parametric model can be identified. MRAC, on the other hand, excels in situations where defining a target performance via a reference model is more straightforward than obtaining an accurate plant model, or when direct stability guarantees are paramount, often leveraging more sophisticated theoretical tools for adaptation law design.

In summary, Self-Tuning Regulators represent a powerful and practical class of adaptive control strategies. By employing a recursive parameter estimation algorithm to build and continuously update an internal model of the plant, and then using this model within a controller synthesis framework, STRs can effectively track changing system dynamics and maintain desired performance levels. Techniques like Recursive Least Squares provide robust methods for online parameter identification, while pole-placement and minimum variance control offer established strategies for controller re-design. Despite the challenges in guaranteeing stability in all scenarios, the interpretability, flexibility, and proven effectiveness of STRs in diverse applications, from robotics to process control, solidify their importance in the field of adaptive control.

The evolution of adaptive control has been significantly propelled by the integration of machine learning paradigms. While traditional adaptive controllers, such as Self-Tuning Regulators (STRs) and Model Reference Adaptive Controllers (MRACs), rely on pre-defined mathematical structures and parameter updates, machine learning offers a more flexible and powerful toolkit for learning complex adaptation behaviors. This section delves into the realm of learning-based adaptation strategies, exploring how techniques rooted in artificial intelligence can empower control systems to adapt to their environments in more sophisticated and efficient ways.

One of the primary avenues through which machine learning enhances adaptive control is by enabling the representation and learning of highly nonlinear adaptation laws. Traditional methods often assume a linear relationship between system parameters and control actions, or they rely on analytical derivations that may not capture intricate system behaviors. Machine learning models, particularly neural networks, excel at approximating arbitrary nonlinear functions. This capability allows them to learn complex mappings from system states, past control actions, and performance errors to the required control adjustments, even in the presence of highly coupled and nonlinear dynamics. Instead of relying on explicit identification of a plant model and then synthesizing a controller, a neural network can directly learn the control law or an adaptation mechanism that modifies an existing control law.

Consider a scenario where a robotic manipulator operates in an environment with unpredictable and rapidly changing payloads, friction, and external forces. A traditional adaptive controller might struggle to keep up if these changes are significant and deviate from the model assumptions. A learning-based approach, however, could employ a neural network trained to predict the necessary adjustments to the control torques based on sensory feedback. This network could be trained online, continuously updating its weights as new data becomes available. For instance, if a payload is unexpectedly added to the robot's end-effector, the sudden increase in required torque would result in a performance error. The neural network would observe this error, along with the current state of the robot (joint positions, velocities), and adjust its internal parameters to generate the correct torque in subsequent control cycles. This learned adaptation can be far more rapid and nuanced than what might be achievable with a purely parametric adjustment scheme.

This direct learning of control policies or adaptation mechanisms can be achieved through various machine learning frameworks.
Online learning is particularly relevant here. In contrast to batch learning, where models are trained on a fixed dataset, online learning algorithms update model parameters incrementally as new data points arrive. This is crucial for adaptive control, as the system's dynamics and environment can change continuously. Algorithms like stochastic gradient descent (SGD) or its variants (e.g., Adam, RMSprop) are commonly used for online training of neural networks. When applied to adaptive control, the neural network might take the current state and error signals as input and output corrections to the controller gains or

directly compute control commands. The "loss function" for the gradient descent update would be designed to penalize deviations from the desired performance (e.g., tracking error, overshoot, settling time).

For example, in an adaptive cruise control (ACC) system for vehicles, the goal is to maintain a safe following distance from the vehicle ahead while also considering fuel efficiency and passenger comfort. The dynamics of vehicle platoons are complex, influenced by factors such as road gradient, wind resistance, tire wear, and the driving styles of other vehicles. A traditional ACC might use a fixed-gain PID controller or a simple gain-scheduling approach. A learning-based ACC, however, could utilize a neural network to learn optimal acceleration and braking commands. This network could be trained online using data from sensors (radar, cameras) and vehicle dynamics (speed, acceleration). If the system encounters a sudden deceleration from the lead vehicle or a change in road conditions, the neural network, through its online learning mechanism, can adapt its output more effectively than a pre-programmed gain schedule. The learning objective might be to minimize a weighted sum of tracking error, jerk (rate of change of acceleration for comfort), and fuel consumption.

Reinforcement Learning (RL) offers another powerful framework for learning-based adaptation. In RL, an agent learns to make a sequence of decisions by interacting with an environment to maximize a cumulative reward signal. This is a natural fit for control problems, where the control system (the agent) needs to learn optimal actions (control inputs) based on observed states and received rewards (performance feedback). For adaptive control, RL can be used to learn adaptation rules or even the entire control policy directly.

In the context of adaptation, RL can be used to learn how to adjust the parameters of a base controller (e.g., a PID controller) or to directly output control signals. If we consider a reinforcement learning agent that observes the system's state, it can learn a policy $\pi(a|s)$ that maps states to actions. This policy can be directly the control input, or it can be an adaptation adjustment. For instance, a deep reinforcement learning algorithm could learn a policy that, given the current tracking error, its derivative, and perhaps some estimate of the system's uncertainty, outputs a multiplicative factor to adjust the gains of a fixed-structure controller. The reward function would be designed to encourage good performance (low error) and penalize aggressive control actions or instability.

Consider the challenge of controlling a fleet of autonomous drones for tasks like aerial surveillance or delivery in a dynamic urban environment. The atmospheric conditions (wind speed and direction), battery levels, and communication quality can change rapidly, affecting the drones' flight dynamics and control effectiveness. Reinforcement learning can be employed to develop adaptive control policies for each drone. The "state" for the RL agent might include the drone's current position and velocity, its estimated battery level, and environmental parameters like wind. The "action" could be the control signals to the drone's motors, or it could be an adjustment to the gains of a low-level flight controller. The "reward" would be shaped to reward successful mission completion (e.g., reaching the target location, maintaining formation, timely delivery) while penalizing deviations from the desired trajectory, excessive energy consumption, or unsafe maneuvers. Through continuous interaction and learning, the RL agent can develop sophisticated adaptation strategies to cope with the unpredictable changes in the operational environment.

A particularly advanced concept in learning-based adaptation is

meta-learning, often referred to as "learning to learn." Instead of learning a specific control task or adaptation rule from scratch for a given system, meta-learning aims to train a model that can quickly adapt to new tasks or systems with minimal additional data. In the context of adaptive control, this means training a meta-learner that can, given a new system or a new operating condition, rapidly learn an effective adaptation strategy or control policy.

Imagine a scenario where a manufacturing plant needs to control a multitude of similar but not identical machines, each with slightly different wear characteristics or operating parameters. Training a separate adaptive controller for each machine from scratch would be time-consuming and data-intensive. A meta-learning approach could be used to train a "meta-controller" that learns the underlying commonalities across these machines. When a new machine is introduced, the meta-controller would leverage its prior "learning to learn" experience to quickly fine-tune an adaptation mechanism or a control policy for that specific machine, requiring only a small amount of data from the new machine's operation. The meta-learner could be trained on a diverse set of simulated or real-world machine behaviors, learning to infer efficient adaptation strategies. This allows for rapid deployment of adaptive control on a large scale.

The process typically involves two phases: a "meta-training" phase and a "meta-testing" (or adaptation) phase. During meta-training, the meta-learner is exposed to a variety of control tasks (e.g., controlling different simulated machines with varying parameters). It learns to generate a good initial set of parameters for an adaptation module or to learn an initialization that allows for rapid fine-tuning. During meta-testing, when faced with a new task (a new machine), the meta-learned initialization is used, and then a few gradient updates (or other optimization steps) are performed using data from the new machine to adapt the control strategy quickly. This "few-shot" adaptation capability is a hallmark of meta-learning.

Furthermore, these learning-based strategies can be integrated with traditional adaptive control techniques, creating hybrid approaches. For instance, a neural network could be used to learn the adaptation law for the parameters of an existing STR, rather than relying on fixed rules like RLS with a forgetting factor. The neural network could analyze the prediction error and the estimated parameter uncertainty from the RLS algorithm and then propose optimal adjustments to the forgetting factor or even directly modify the parameter estimates to achieve faster convergence or better robustness. This allows the system to benefit from the interpretability and structure of traditional methods while gaining the flexibility and learning power of neural networks.

An example of such a hybrid approach could be an adaptive PID controller where the gains (K_p, K_i, K_d) *are adjusted by a neural network. The neural network would take the current tracking error, its integral, its derivative, and possibly other system states as input. Its output would be the changes to be applied to* K_p, K_i, K_d. The training of this neural network could be done offline using system simulations or online using reinforcement learning. The goal would be to achieve a desired performance (e.g., minimizing a cost function involving error, control effort, and perhaps a measure of smoothness) more effectively than simple gain-scheduling or pre-defined adaptive rules.

The use of machine learning in adaptive control is not without its challenges. One significant concern is the **guarantee of stability**. While traditional adaptive controllers often come with theoretical stability proofs under certain conditions, guaranteeing the stability of a closed-loop system with a learned adaptation law can be much more difficult. Neural networks can exhibit complex behaviors, and their training process can be sensitive to hyperparameter choices, initialization, and the data distribution. Ensuring that the learned adaptation law does not lead to oscillations or divergence requires careful design of the learning objective, regularization techniques, and potentially formal verification methods adapted for neural network controllers. Researchers are actively developing techniques to provide stability guarantees, such as using Lyapunov-based approaches for neural network training or designing neural network architectures that inherently promote stability.

Another consideration is
sample efficiency. While online learning and RL can adapt to new conditions, they often require a significant amount of data to learn effectively. In real-world systems where data acquisition can be slow, costly, or even dangerous, this can be a bottleneck. Meta-learning and techniques that leverage prior knowledge or system structure can help mitigate this issue by enabling faster adaptation with less data.

Finally, the
interpretability of learned adaptation strategies can be a concern. While traditional adaptive controllers offer a degree of transparency into how parameters are updated, neural networks can often operate as "black boxes," making it difficult to understand why a particular adaptation decision is made. This can hinder debugging, validation, and trust in safety-critical applications. Research into explainable AI (XAI) is crucial in this context, aiming to develop methods that can shed light on the decision-making process of learned controllers.

Despite these challenges, the potential benefits of learning-based adaptation strategies are immense. They open up possibilities for controlling highly complex, nonlinear, and rapidly changing systems that were previously intractable with traditional methods. From optimizing energy consumption in smart grids to enabling more agile and responsive autonomous vehicles, learning-based adaptive control promises to be a cornerstone of future intelligent systems. As research continues to advance in areas like robust learning, sample-efficient RL, and verifiable AI, the integration of machine learning into adaptive control is poised to unlock new levels of performance, efficiency, and autonomy across a vast spectrum of applications.

The integration of machine learning into adaptive control, while offering unprecedented flexibility and performance potential, also introduces a distinct set of challenges that require careful consideration and innovative solutions. Unlike the well-established theoretical frameworks that underpin many classical adaptive control techniques, systems that learn to adapt often operate in a less predictable manner, necessitating new approaches to ensure reliable and safe operation. Among the most critical concerns is the **guarantee of stability** in the presence of learning-based adaptation mechanisms. Traditional adaptive controllers, particularly those with explicit model reference or self-tuning structures, often come with rigorous mathematical proofs of stability under specific assumptions about the plant dynamics and the adaptation law. However, when the adaptation law itself is learned, for instance, through a neural network, these guarantees become significantly harder to establish. Neural networks, by their nature, can exhibit highly complex and nonlinear behaviors. The learning process itself, often driven by optimization algorithms like stochastic gradient descent, can be sensitive to initial conditions, learning rates, and the specific data encountered. This sensitivity means that the learned adaptation strategy could, under certain circumstances, push the system into unstable operating regimes, leading to oscillations or even divergence. This is particularly concerning in safety-critical applications such as aerospace, autonomous driving, or industrial process control, where instability can have catastrophic consequences. Researchers are actively exploring methods to bridge this gap, drawing inspiration from areas like Lyapunov stability theory. The aim is to develop learning algorithms or network architectures that intrinsically promote stability, or to design verifiable neural network controllers where formal proofs of stability can be provided. This might involve constraining the output of the neural network, using specific activation functions, or employing regularization techniques during training that penalize behaviors leading to instability.

A related and pervasive issue is the impact of **persistent disturbances and unmodeled dynamics**. While adaptive control inherently aims to compensate for uncertainties, learning-based approaches can be particularly vulnerable to disturbances that are not transient but rather continuously present or slowly varying. Consider a scenario where a sensor in an industrial process is persistently biased, or an external force is continuously applied to a robotic arm. If a learning algorithm is tasked with adapting the controller parameters to minimize the error caused by this disturbance, it may incorrectly attribute the persistent error to a change in the system's fundamental dynamics. This can lead to the adaptation mechanism continually adjusting parameters in a way that not only fails to reject the disturbance but also potentially destabilizes the system or degrades performance for other aspects of the control task. In essence, the learner can be "fooled" into identifying a non-existent system change, leading to inappropriate adaptations. This challenge is exacerbated in systems with significant nonlinearities or complex interactions, where the effect of a disturbance might be highly state-dependent. Traditional adaptive controllers sometimes employ techniques like forgetting factors in recursive least squares estimation to mitigate the impact of past, potentially irrelevant data, allowing them to focus on more recent information. However, in learning-based systems, selecting the appropriate "forgetting" mechanism or its learned equivalent is not trivial. A forgetting factor that is too aggressive might make the system overly sensitive to noise, while one that is too conservative might lead to slow adaptation to genuine system changes.

Another significant challenge, particularly for neural network-based learners, is the phenomenon of **catastrophic forgetting.** This occurs when a model trained on a sequence of tasks or data distributions sequentially overwrites the knowledge acquired from earlier tasks with new information from later tasks. In the context of adaptive control, this is highly problematic. Imagine a system that needs to adapt to changing operating conditions over time. If the system first adapts to a light load and then to a heavy load, without proper safeguards, the adaptation mechanisms learned for the light load might be completely erased when adapting to the heavy load. Consequently, if the system subsequently reverts to operating under a light load, it may perform poorly because it has "forgotten" how to handle that condition. This "all-or-nothing" forgetting prevents the accumulation of a robust, generalized adaptive capability. Ideally, an adaptive system should be able to retain its proficiency across a wide range of past operating conditions, even if it is currently operating under different circumstances. Addressing catastrophic forgetting is an active area of research in machine learning. Techniques such as experience replay (storing and replaying past data), elastic weight consolidation (regularizing updates to prevent drastic changes to important parameters), and synaptic intelligence (tracking the importance of parameters for previous tasks) are being explored and adapted for control applications. The goal is to enable systems to learn new adaptations without sacrificing previously acquired knowledge, leading to a more stable and versatile adaptive capability.

The inherent trade-off between **adaptation speed and robustness** presents a fundamental design dilemma in adaptive control, and learning-based approaches are not exempt from this. Rapid adaptation is desirable when system dynamics change quickly or unpredictably. However, very fast adaptation can make the system overly sensitive to noise and disturbances, leading to erratic control actions and potential instability, as discussed earlier. Conversely, a more robust adaptation mechanism, one that is less susceptible to noise and more conservative in its parameter updates, will naturally be slower to respond to genuine changes in the system's dynamics. This creates a delicate balancing act. In many practical applications, the rate at which the system dynamics are expected to change is not known a priori or can vary significantly. For instance, an autonomous vehicle operating in varying weather conditions might experience rapid changes in tire grip during a sudden rain shower, requiring fast adaptation, but in dry conditions, the changes might be much slower and more gradual. Learning-based controllers need mechanisms to dynamically adjust their adaptation rate. This could involve learning a "meta-parameter" that controls the learning rate or the forgetting factor based on the perceived level of system uncertainty or the rate of change in performance error. Techniques that analyze the statistics of the error signal or explicitly estimate the uncertainty in the system model can inform such dynamic adjustments. For example, if the estimation error is consistently high and fluctuating, it might indicate rapid system change, prompting a faster adaptation rate. If the error is low and stable, a slower, more robust adaptation rate might be preferred.

Furthermore, the practical implementation of learning-based adaptive control in industrial settings brings its own set of considerations. **Sample efficiency**, as alluded to previously, is paramount. Real-world industrial processes often generate data slowly. Running a complex simulation to gather millions of data points for training might be feasible offline, but for online adaptation in a live plant, the amount of data that can be collected and processed within a control cycle is limited. This necessitates the use of highly sample-efficient learning algorithms. Techniques that leverage prior knowledge, such as pre-training on simulations that accurately capture the plant's physics or using model-based reinforcement learning where a learned model of the system dynamics guides exploration, become crucial. **Data quality and availability** are also critical. Sensors can be noisy, subject to drift, or even fail entirely. If the learning algorithm relies on faulty data, its adaptations will be misguided. Robust data preprocessing, outlier detection, and fault detection mechanisms are essential complements to learning-based adaptive controllers.

The
initialization of learned controllers is another practical hurdle. Many learning algorithms, especially neural networks, are sensitive to their initial weights. A poor initialization can lead to slow convergence, getting stuck in local optima, or even initial instability. Strategies like using pre-trained models from similar systems, employing transfer learning, or using more sophisticated initialization techniques that consider the expected dynamics of the problem can significantly improve the initial performance and the speed of subsequent adaptation. For example, a controller for a robotic arm designed to handle varying payloads could be initialized with weights learned from controlling a similar arm with known payload characteristics.

The interpretability of learned adaptation strategies, or the lack thereof, poses a significant challenge for
validation and certification, particularly in safety-critical domains. While a human engineer might understand why a traditional PID controller's gains are being adjusted according to a specific rule, the complex interplay of weights and activations within a neural network can obscure the reasoning behind a particular adaptation. This makes it difficult to perform thorough validation, debug unexpected behaviors, and gain the necessary confidence for certification. This is where the field of **Explainable AI (XAI)** becomes indispensable. Developing methods that can provide insights into the decision-making process of learned adaptive controllers – perhaps by highlighting which input features are most influential in a given adaptation decision, or by

visualizing the learned internal representations – is crucial for building trust and enabling widespread adoption of these advanced control techniques in regulated industries. Techniques such as LIME (Local Interpretable Model-agnostic Explanations) or SHAP (SHapley Additive exPlanations) can be adapted to provide post-hoc explanations for the actions of learned controllers.

Furthermore, the
computational complexity associated with running sophisticated learning algorithms online can be a limiting factor, especially for embedded control systems with limited processing power. While modern hardware is increasingly capable, the real-time requirements of many control applications demand highly efficient algorithms and optimized implementations. Model compression, quantization, and specialized hardware accelerators are all areas that contribute to making complex learned controllers feasible for deployment in resource-constrained environments.

Finally, the presence of
non-stationarity in the learning process itself needs to be managed. While adaptive control aims to handle non-stationarity in the plant dynamics, the learning algorithm's parameters are also changing over time. If the learning rate is too high, the adaptation can become unstable. If it's too low, it might not keep up with system changes. The effective management of this internal non-stationarity, through careful tuning of learning rates, momentum terms, and regularization, is key to achieving reliable performance. Techniques such as curriculum learning, where the learner is exposed to progressively more challenging tasks or data distributions, can also help in building robust learned adaptation capabilities by guiding the learning process in a structured manner. The interplay between the learning algorithm and the evolving system dynamics requires a holistic approach to design and analysis.

In summary, while machine learning has opened exciting new frontiers for adaptive control, the path to widespread, reliable deployment is paved with significant challenges. Ensuring stability in the face of learned adaptation, mitigating the impact of persistent disturbances, preventing catastrophic forgetting, balancing adaptation speed with robustness, achieving sample efficiency, managing data quality, initializing learned models effectively, providing interpretability for validation, and addressing computational constraints are all critical areas that require ongoing research and development. Overcoming these hurdles will be essential to unlock the full potential of learning-based adaptive control for creating more intelligent, resilient, and autonomous systems across a vast array of applications. The focus on robust estimation, formal verification of learned policies, and developing more sample-efficient and interpretable learning algorithms will be crucial in navigating these complexities and realizing the promise of adaptive control in the era of artificial intelligence.

Chapter 10: Learning for Robust Control

The quest for intelligent control systems that can operate reliably and safely in the face of the inherent unpredictability of the real world has led to the development of various sophisticated techniques. While adaptive control, particularly when augmented with machine learning, offers remarkable flexibility and the potential for highly responsive behavior, it often operates under the assumption that the underlying system dynamics, while potentially unknown, are at least consistent. However, many practical systems are characterized by a significant degree of uncertainty, which can stem from a multitude of sources. These uncertainties are not merely fleeting disturbances; they can be persistent, evolving, or simply inherent to the system's design and operating environment. It is in this context that the field of **robust control** emerges as a cornerstone for ensuring reliable system performance. Robust control theory provides a rigorous framework for designing controllers that are not only effective under ideal conditions but also maintain stability and acceptable performance levels when faced with a predefined set of uncertainties.

At its heart, robust control seeks to answer a fundamental question: how can we design a controller that guarantees a certain level of performance, not just for a single, perfectly known model of the system, but for an entire *set* of possible models representing the plausible variations and uncertainties? This is a critical distinction from traditional control design, which often focuses on achieving optimal performance for a single nominal model. In robust control, the objective shifts from optimizing performance for a precise representation to ensuring acceptable performance across a spectrum of possibilities. This concept is often articulated as the trade-off between **nominal performance** and **robust performance**. Nominal performance refers to how well a controller performs when applied to the exact, idealized model of the system used in its design. Robust performance, on the other hand, quantifies how well the controller maintains its desired behavior when the actual system deviates from this nominal model within specified bounds. A controller that offers excellent nominal performance might be highly sensitive to even minor deviations, leading to poor robust performance. Conversely, a controller designed for robustness might exhibit slightly degraded nominal performance but will remain stable and functional across a wider range of conditions. The goal in robust control is to achieve a satisfactory balance, ensuring that the system is both well-behaved under normal circumstances and resilient to expected deviations.

The uncertainties that robust control aims to address can manifest in various forms. One of the most common is **parameter uncertainty**. In many physical systems, certain physical parameters, such as mass, friction coefficients, resistance, or capacitance, are not known with perfect precision. These parameters might be subject to manufacturing tolerances, environmental variations (like temperature changes affecting material properties), or aging effects. For instance, in an automotive suspension system, the stiffness and damping coefficients of the shock absorbers can vary due to wear and tear, temperature, and manufacturing variations. A robust controller for such a system would be designed to maintain acceptable ride comfort and handling regardless of these parameter variations within a defined range. This type of uncertainty can often be represented by bounding the possible range of values for each uncertain parameter.

Beyond simple parameter variations, robust control also grapples with **unmodeled dynamics**. Real-world systems are often infinitely complex, and any mathematical model used for control design is necessarily a simplification. There are always higher-order modes, nonlinearities, delays, or interactions that are neglected in the nominal model to make the design problem tractable. These neglected dynamics, collectively termed unmodeled dynamics, can significantly impact system behavior, especially at higher frequencies. For example, the flexible modes of a robotic arm or the complex fluid dynamics in a chemical reactor might be simplified or entirely ignored in an initial model. If these unmodeled dynamics are not properly accounted for in the control design, they can lead to unexpected oscillations or even instability. Robust control techniques provide ways to represent and bound the uncertainty introduced by these unmodeled dynamics, often in the frequency domain, ensuring that the controller remains stable and performs adequately even when these neglected aspects of the system become significant. This is particularly relevant in the design of controllers for high-performance aerospace vehicles, where aerodynamic effects that are difficult to model precisely can become dominant.

The theoretical underpinnings of robust control often rely on concepts from linear systems theory, particularly
H-infinity (H∞) control and **Linear Matrix Inequalities (LMIs)**. H∞ control, for instance, provides a systematic framework for designing controllers that minimize the worst-case effect of disturbances and uncertainties on the system's output. It frames the control problem as an optimization problem in which the controller seeks to minimize the H∞ norm of a specific transfer function that encapsulates the interconnection of the plant, the controller, and the uncertainties. This norm represents the maximum amplification from exogenous inputs (like disturbances and noise) to the controlled outputs. By minimizing this norm, the H∞ controller effectively limits the worst-case gain from uncertainties to performance outputs, thereby guaranteeing a level of robust performance.

LMIs offer a powerful computational tool for solving robust control design problems. Many robust control specifications, including H∞ performance, robustness to structured uncertainties, and even some aspects of robust stability, can be formulated as LMI problems. LMIs are a class of convex optimization problems that can be solved efficiently using numerical algorithms. This mathematical tractability is a significant advantage, allowing for the automated design of robust controllers for complex systems where manual design would be exceedingly difficult or even impossible. The ability to translate robust control objectives into a solvable LMI problem has been a key factor in the widespread adoption of robust control techniques in various engineering disciplines.

A classic example illustrating the need for robust control can be found in the operation of spacecraft. Satellites in orbit are subject to a dynamic and often unpredictable environment. The gravitational forces from celestial bodies, solar radiation pressure, atmospheric drag (even in very thin upper atmospheres), and internal disturbances from moving parts all contribute to variations in the satellite's trajectory and attitude. Furthermore, the physical properties of the satellite itself can change over time due to thermal expansion and contraction, fuel consumption, or the deployment of components. A controller designed solely for the initial, perfectly modeled state of the satellite might quickly become inadequate as these external and internal factors come into play. A robust controller, however, would be designed to maintain stable attitude control and precise orbital positioning despite these environmental variations and potential changes in the satellite's dynamics. For instance, it must ensure that the attitude control system remains stable and responsive whether the satellite is passing through the Earth's shadow (affecting thermal properties) or is subjected to increased solar radiation pressure. This requires the controller to be insensitive to a defined range of parameter uncertainties and external disturbances.

Another compelling scenario is the control of unmanned aerial vehicles (UAVs) operating in challenging environments. UAVs, especially those designed for reconnaissance, delivery, or agricultural monitoring, often fly in the presence of wind gusts, varying air density due to altitude changes, and potential damage to aerodynamic surfaces. The exact aerodynamic coefficients of the UAV can change significantly with airspeed and angle of attack, and these are often hard to model precisely over the entire flight envelope. A robust control system for a UAV would aim to maintain stable flight and execute planned trajectories accurately, even when subjected to strong, intermittent wind disturbances or experiencing slight variations in wing shape due to minor impacts or material fatigue. The controller must be robust to uncertainties in aerodynamic parameters and the effects of external forces, ensuring safe operation and mission success. This often involves designing controllers that can actively reject disturbances while maintaining stability, even when the underlying aerodynamic model is not perfectly known.

The principles of robust control are not confined to traditional linear systems. Extensions to nonlinear systems, referred to as **robust nonlinear control**, have also been developed. These techniques aim to provide similar guarantees of stability and performance in the presence of uncertainties for systems exhibiting nonlinear behavior. However, the design and analysis of robust nonlinear controllers are generally more complex and can be computationally intensive. Techniques such as feedback linearization, sliding mode control, and control Lyapunov functions are often employed and extended to achieve robust performance for nonlinear systems. For example, in robotics, where systems are inherently nonlinear due to terms like Coriolis forces and gravity, robust control is essential for manipulators operating in uncertain environments. A robot arm tasked with grasping objects of varying mass and friction properties would benefit from a robust controller that can adapt its gripping force and trajectory planning to ensure a secure grasp without damaging the object, even if the object's exact properties are not known beforehand.

While robust control offers powerful guarantees, it is important to acknowledge its limitations and the inherent trade-offs involved. Designing for robustness often means sacrificing some degree of optimal performance in the nominal case. A controller that is designed to be very insensitive to uncertainty might be less agile or responsive than one tuned for a specific, known system. The degree of uncertainty that can be tolerated is also finite; if the actual system deviates too far from the bounds defined in the robust control design, performance will degrade, and stability may be lost. Therefore, an accurate characterization of the system's uncertainties is crucial for effective robust control design. Overestimating uncertainties can lead to overly conservative controllers, while underestimating them can lead to control failures.

In many modern applications, particularly those involving autonomous systems, the strengths of robust control are increasingly being integrated with the adaptive capabilities offered by machine learning. While robust control provides a solid foundation of guaranteed stability and performance bounds in the presence of uncertainties, machine learning can be used to fine-tune these controllers, adapt to uncertainties that are not well-characterized, or learn optimal parameters within the robust framework. For instance, a robust controller might provide baseline stability, while a learned component could adjust certain parameters to improve performance under specific operating conditions that were not fully anticipated during the initial robust design phase. This synergistic approach, combining the guarantees of robust control with the flexibility of learning, is a promising direction for developing highly reliable and intelligent control systems capable of operating effectively across a vast spectrum of real-world complexities. The development of controllers that are both robust to well-defined uncertainties and capable of learning to adapt to unforeseen circumstances represents a significant frontier in control engineering, paving the way for more autonomous and resilient systems in critical applications.

The design of controllers that can guarantee performance in the face of system variations is fundamentally reliant on the ability to accurately and systematically represent these uncertainties. Without a clear definition of what constitutes "uncertainty," the concept of robustness remains ill-defined, and the resulting controller's guarantees become tenuous. This subsection delves into the prevalent methodologies for modeling these uncertainties, which form the bedrock upon which robust control designs are built. These frameworks provide a structured language to describe the plausible deviations of a real system from its idealized mathematical model, thereby enabling the design of controllers that can effectively cope with such variations.

One of the most intuitive ways to represent uncertainty is through **interval uncertainty**. This approach is particularly well-suited for situations where the exact value of a system parameter is unknown, but its range of possible values is bounded. For instance, a resistor in an electronic circuit might have a nominal resistance of 100 ohms but be specified as having a tolerance of ±5%. In an interval uncertainty model, this parameter would be represented as belonging to the interval [95, 105] ohms. This can be generalized to multiple parameters. If a system's behavior is described by a set of parameters $\theta = [\theta1, \theta2, ..., \thetan]$, and each parameter $\thetai$ is known to lie within an interval $[\underline{\thetai}, \overline{\thetai}]$, then the set of all possible parameter values forms a hyper-rectangle in the parameter space. This representation is straightforward and often directly reflects manufacturing tolerances or known environmental operating ranges. For example, in the design of an autopilot for an aircraft, the lift and drag coefficients of the wings might not be precisely known due to variations in atmospheric conditions (temperature, humidity) and slight imperfections in the wing's surface. If these coefficients are known to vary within certain bounds, interval uncertainty provides a direct way to model this. The controller would then need to ensure stable flight and accurate trajectory tracking for all possible combinations of these coefficients within their respective intervals. While conceptually simple, handling interval uncertainty in complex systems can lead to a very large set of possible models, which can be computationally challenging to analyze directly.

A more mathematically sophisticated and widely adopted framework for modeling uncertainty, especially in the context of linear time-invariant (LTI) systems, is
norm-bounded uncertainty. This approach is central to the H-infinity control framework and is particularly powerful for representing uncertainties that may not be confined to simple parameter variations but can also encompass unmodeled dynamics. Norm-bounded uncertainty assumes that the deviation of the actual system from its nominal model can be represented by an additive or multiplicative perturbation, denoted by Δ. The key aspect is that the "size" or "magnitude" of this perturbation is bounded in some mathematical norm. For example, in additive uncertainty, the true system's transfer function $G(s)$ might be related to the nominal model $\hat{G}(s)$ by $G(s) = \hat{G}(s) + \Delta(s)$. The uncertainty is then characterized by bounding the norm of $\Delta(s)$, such as the H-infinity norm $\| \Delta \|{\infty}$. *The H-infinity norm of a stable transfer function is its peak gain over all frequencies. Therefore,* $\| \Delta \|{\infty} \leq \gamma$ means that the magnitude of the uncertain part of the system, when viewed as a transfer function itself, is bounded by γ across all frequencies. This is incredibly useful because it can represent a wide range of uncertainties. For instance, unmodeled high-frequency dynamics, which are often neglected in model reduction, can be effectively bounded using this approach. If we suspect that neglected dynamics contribute at most a certain amount of gain at all frequencies, we can use norm-bounded uncertainty to encapsulate this.

The H-infinity framework, in particular, leverages this norm-bounded uncertainty to formulate robust control problems. The goal is often to find a controller $K(s)$ such that the closed-loop system, incorporating the nominal plant $\hat{G}(s)$ and an uncertainty $\Delta(s)$ satisfying $\| \Delta \|
*{\infty} \leq \gamma$, remains stable and achieves a certain performance level. This performance is typically measured by another H-infinity norm, representing the worst-case gain from exogenous inputs (like disturbances) to the system outputs. The robust control problem then becomes finding a controller $K(s)$ that minimizes this worst-case gain, subject to the condition that the closed-loop system is stable for all Δ with $\| \Delta* \|{\infty} \leq \gamma$. This allows designers to specify a maximum acceptable level of uncertainty and then design a controller that guarantees performance as long as the actual uncertainty stays within those bounds. For an aircraft autopilot, norm-bounded uncertainty can represent variations in aerodynamic coefficients across different flight regimes or atmospheric conditions. Instead of bounding each coefficient individually, one can bound the overall effect of these variations on the aircraft's dynamics using a suitable norm, which is often more practical when dealing with complex interdependencies. The transfer function from pilot input to aircraft response, for instance, can be modeled with an uncertainty block that has a bounded H-infinity norm, ensuring acceptable handling qualities regardless of the precise aerodynamic conditions within the defined bounds.

Beyond deterministic bounds,
stochastic uncertainty offers another perspective, particularly relevant when dealing with random processes or uncertainties that are best described by probability distributions. In this framework, system parameters or disturbances are modeled as random variables or stochastic processes with known statistical properties, such as mean, variance, or autocorrelation functions. For example, wind gusts acting on

an aircraft can be modeled as a stochastic process. While the exact magnitude and timing of each gust are unpredictable, their statistical characteristics might be known from historical data or meteorological models. Similarly, sensor noise is almost always modeled as a stochastic process. Robust control techniques can be extended to handle stochastic uncertainty, often by aiming for performance guarantees in an average sense (e.g., minimizing the expected value of a performance metric) or by ensuring that performance degrades gracefully with a low probability.

Quantifying stochastic uncertainty often involves statistical estimation techniques. If data is available from system operation or from a similar system, methods like maximum likelihood estimation or Bayesian inference can be used to estimate the parameters of the probability distributions governing the uncertainties. For instance, if an autonomous vehicle is operating in an environment with varying road friction, data collected over numerous driving scenarios could be used to build a probabilistic model of the friction coefficient. The control system would then be designed to maintain stability and track trajectories while accounting for this probabilistic variation. Techniques like Kalman filtering and its extensions (e.g., Extended Kalman Filter, Unscented Kalman Filter) are inherently designed to handle stochastic noise in measurements and can be used as part of a control system that explicitly models and accounts for stochastic uncertainties in the system's state and dynamics.

The practical challenge in all these modeling approaches lies in **quantifying the uncertainty**. This quantification can stem from various sources:

1. Prior Knowledge and Specifications: As mentioned, manufacturing tolerances, material properties, and operating environment constraints often provide direct bounds or statistical information about uncertainties. Regulatory standards or safety requirements in critical applications like aviation or automotive control often mandate conservative estimates for uncertainties. For an autopilot, the Federal Aviation Administration (FAA) might specify maximum allowable variations in aerodynamic parameters for certification, guiding the uncertainty modeling process.

2. Experimental Data and System Identification: When prior knowledge is insufficient, experimental data becomes crucial. Techniques from system identification are employed to estimate the system's dynamics and characterize the uncertainties. This can involve applying specific input signals to the system and observing the output, then using algorithms to infer the model parameters and their variability. For example, to model uncertainty in the dynamics of a robotic manipulator, one might perform a series of controlled movements with varying payloads and record the joint torques and positions. Statistical analysis of this data can reveal not only the nominal dynamics but also the variance or range of parameters like inertia or friction.

3. Model Reduction and Neglected Dynamics: When complex models are simplified for control design, the neglected terms represent unmodeled dynamics. Robust control techniques often require bounding the impact of these neglected dynamics. Frequency-domain system identification techniques, coupled with knowledge of the ignored dynamics (e.g., higher-order modes, nonlinearities), can be used to establish bounds on the uncertainty introduced by model reduction. For instance, if a model is simplified by neglecting modes above a certain frequency, robust control techniques might assume that the unmodeled dynamics in that high-frequency range do not introduce more than a certain amount of gain, as indicated by the frequency response of the neglected part.

The choice of uncertainty model significantly influences the design process and the resulting controller's characteristics. Interval uncertainty is conceptually simple but can lead to overly conservative designs if the intervals are large. Norm-bounded uncertainty, particularly within the H-infinity framework, offers a powerful way to handle a broad class of uncertainties and provides a direct link to performance optimization, but it requires careful selection of the norm and the bounding factor. Stochastic uncertainty is essential for systems with inherent randomness but often leads to performance guarantees in a probabilistic sense rather than absolute worst-case guarantees.

The process of creating a robust controller is iterative: a model of the uncertainty is created, a controller is designed based on this model, and then the controller's performance is evaluated against the set of admissible uncertainties. If the performance is not satisfactory, either the uncertainty model needs to be refined (perhaps by incorporating more data or prior knowledge to tighten the bounds) or the controller design must be revisited, potentially accepting a larger trade-off between nominal performance and robustness. For the robust design of aircraft autopilots, this iterative process is paramount. An initial uncertainty model might be based on known variations in air density with altitude and temperature. A controller is designed for this. However, during flight testing, unexpected wind shear conditions might reveal performance degradation. This prompts a revision of the uncertainty model to include a more aggressive representation of wind disturbances, leading to a redesign of the autopilot to ensure its robustness against these more extreme, albeit less frequent, events. The careful and systematic modeling of uncertainties is thus not just a preliminary step but an integral, ongoing part of achieving truly reliable and resilient control systems.

The pursuit of control systems that reliably perform under a spectrum of unpredictable conditions has led to the development of sophisticated methodologies. Among these, H-infinity (H∞) control stands out as a powerful and mathematically rigorous framework designed to explicitly address uncertainty and guarantee performance in a worst-case sense. Unlike classical control techniques that often focus on nominal system behavior, H∞ control prioritizes robustness by actively minimizing the influence of disturbances and model uncertainties on the system's outputs. This approach is particularly vital when dealing with complex systems where precise modeling is challenging, and unmodeled dynamics are a significant concern. The core idea is to design a controller that limits the maximum gain from all possible exogenous inputs (including disturbances and noise) to the system's performance outputs.

At the heart of H∞ control lies the concept of minimizing the
$\mathcal{H}
*{\infty}$ norm of a carefully constructed closed-loop transfer function. This norm, in essence, quantifies the peak amplification from an input signal to an output signal across all frequencies. By focusing on this worst-case gain, H∞ control provides a guarantee on performance that holds true regardless of the specific realization of uncertainty, as long as it adheres to predefined bounds. The general problem in H∞ control is to find a controller K such that for a given system, the $\mathcal{H}*{\infty}$ norm of the closed-loop transfer function from an exogenous input vector w to a regulated output vector z is less than or equal to a specified level γ. Mathematically, this can be expressed as:

$$ \|T
{zw}(s; P, K)\|{\infty} < \gamma $$

where $T_{zw}(s; P, K)$ represents the closed-loop transfer function from w to z, P is the system describing the plant and its uncertainties, and K is the controller. The objective is typically to find a stabilizing controller K that minimizes this γ, thereby achieving the best possible worst-case performance.

To effectively apply H∞ control, the system's dynamics, uncertainties, and performance objectives must be cast into a standardized framework. This is commonly achieved through a generalized plant representation. This generalized plant encapsulates the nominal system dynamics, the exogenous inputs (disturbances, noise, reference signals), the measured outputs used for feedback, and the regulated outputs whose performance is to be guaranteed. The design process often involves shaping the frequency response characteristics of critical closed-loop transfer functions using weighted functions. These weights are instrumental in translating high-level performance specifications into concrete constraints on the system's frequency response.

Two particularly important transfer functions shaped by H∞ control are the sensitivity function S and the complementary sensitivity function T. For a standard feedback configuration with a plant G and a controller K, the sensitivity function is defined as $S = (I + GK)^{-1}$, and the complementary sensitivity function is $T = GK(I + GK)^{-1} = I - S$. The sensitivity function S governs the rejection of disturbances and noise at the output, and the tracking of reference signals. A small S at low frequencies is desirable for good disturbance rejection and tracking. The complementary sensitivity function T, on the other hand, characterizes the closed-loop system's response to inputs and is also related to robustness to multiplicative uncertainties, particularly at high frequencies. A small T at high frequencies is often desired to attenuate the effects of unmodeled dynamics, which tend to dominate at these frequencies.

In the context of H∞ control, performance specifications are often translated into constraints on the norms of these weighted functions. For instance, a specification requiring good disturbance rejection might translate into a constraint on the weighted sensitivity function, such as $\|W_1 S\|_{\infty} < 1$, where W_1 is a weighting function designed to penalize sensitivity at frequencies where disturbance rejection is critical. Similarly, a requirement for robustness against multiplicative uncertainty might be formulated as $\|W_2 T\|_{\infty} < 1$, where W_2 is a weighting function that penalizes the complementary sensitivity function at frequencies where uncertainty is significant. The overall H∞ control problem then becomes finding a stabilizing controller K that satisfies these weighted norm constraints simultaneously, along with any other imposed constraints, such as limiting the control effort.

The mathematical formulation of the H∞ control problem typically involves setting up a linear fractional transformation (LFT) representation of the closed-loop system. The generalized plant P is defined such that when it interacts with a controller K, the resulting closed-loop system T_{zw} has the desired structure. This structure allows for the systematic analysis of stability and performance. The problem then reduces to finding a controller K that stabilizes the system and makes $\|T_{zw}\|_{\infty} < \gamma$.

Solving the H∞ control problem to find such a controller K can be achieved through several methods. A classical approach relies on solving two coupled algebraic Riccati equations (AREs). These AREs arise from the standard loop-shifting techniques and the duality between the $\mathcal{H}_{2}$ and $\mathcal{H}_{\infty}$ optimal control problems. The solutions to these AREs provide information about the structure and achievable performance level γ. If the solutions are well-behaved (e.g., positive semi-definite matrices, if the system is represented in state-space), then a controller exists. The controller itself can then be constructed from the solutions of the Riccati equations.

More modern and computationally efficient approaches leverage the power of Linear Matrix Inequalities (LMIs). LMIs offer a convex optimization framework, meaning that finding a solution is guaranteed, and efficient numerical solvers exist. The $H\infty$ control problem can be reformulated as a set of LMIs. For instance, a condition for the existence of a stabilizing controller K of a certain order that achieves $\|T_{zw}\|_{\infty} < \gamma$ can be expressed as the feasibility of a single LMI involving the system matrices and the parameter γ. If this LMI is feasible for a given γ, then such a controller exists. The LMI formulation is particularly appealing because it naturally handles multiple performance objectives and constraints in a unified framework. It can also be extended to mixed-sensitivity problems, where constraints are imposed on linear combinations of S and T, and to controller order reduction.

The LMI approach typically involves defining a Lyapunov function candidate and using its properties along with the system dynamics and the $\mathcal{H}_{\infty}$ *norm bound to derive the LMIs. For a discrete-time linear system, for example, the condition for stability and* $\mathcal{H}_{\infty}$ performance often involves finding a symmetric positive definite matrix X and a matrix Y such that certain matrix inequalities hold. These inequalities encode the system's stability and the bound on the $\mathcal{H}_{\infty}$ norm. The search for the minimum achievable

γ can be performed using a bisection search algorithm on γ, where for each tested value of γ, the feasibility of the corresponding LMI is checked.

The solution obtained from these Riccati equations or LMIs typically yields a controller structure that can be quite complex, often of a higher order than the original plant. This is a characteristic trade-off: achieving guaranteed worst-case performance often necessitates a more sophisticated controller. However, techniques exist for controller reduction, allowing designers to approximate the full-order H∞ controller with a lower-order one while attempting to preserve a significant portion of the robustness and performance guarantees. This is crucial for practical implementation, especially in systems with limited computational resources.

The application of H∞ control is widespread, ranging from aerospace and automotive systems to process control and robotics. For instance, in aircraft control, H∞ techniques are employed to design autopilots that maintain stable flight and precise trajectory tracking despite variations in atmospheric conditions, aerodynamic parameters, and the presence of unmodeled structural dynamics. Consider an aircraft experiencing turbulence. The turbulence acts as an external disturbance, and the variations in lift and drag coefficients due to changing air density and speed represent model uncertainty. An H∞ controller can be designed to minimize the impact of this turbulence on critical outputs like attitude and altitude, ensuring passenger comfort and flight safety. The weighting functions would be chosen to penalize deviations from desired attitude and altitude at low frequencies (where turbulence is most impactful) and to ensure stability at high frequencies where unmodeled dynamics are more likely to cause problems.

In the automotive industry, H∞ control can be used for developing robust electronic stability control (ESC) systems. These systems need to maintain vehicle stability under aggressive maneuvers or on slippery surfaces. The dynamics of a vehicle can change significantly with speed, tire wear, and road surface conditions. An H∞ controller can provide stability guarantees across a range of these operating conditions by minimizing the worst-case lateral acceleration or yaw rate deviations in response to driver inputs and external disturbances like wind gusts. The design would incorporate weighting functions to ensure rapid response to steering inputs while maintaining stability and limiting excessive lateral forces.

For robotic systems, H∞ control can be applied to achieve precise and robust manipulation. A robot arm operating in an industrial setting may encounter variations in payload mass, friction in joints, or external forces due to contact with its environment. An H∞ controller can ensure that the robot's end-effector follows its intended trajectory accurately and with minimal vibration, even when these uncertainties are present. The performance objectives might include tracking accuracy of the end-effector position and limiting the torque applied by the motors to prevent damage. The robustness guarantee ensures that the robot can operate reliably in its intended workspace, potentially with varying loads.

A key advantage of H∞ control is its ability to systematically handle unmodeled dynamics. In many real-world systems, the mathematical models derived from first principles or system identification are simplifications of reality. These models often neglect high-frequency modes, nonlinearities, or parasitic effects that can become significant under certain operating conditions. H∞ control allows designers to explicitly account for the potential impact of these unmodeled dynamics by bounding their contribution using norms, typically the $\mathcal{H}{\infty}$ norm. By assigning a suitable weighting function $W2$, the designer can specify the maximum allowable gain of the complementary sensitivity function T at high frequencies. If the uncertainty is known to be dominated by high-frequency effects, W_2 would be chosen to be large at high frequencies, forcing T to be small and thus mitigating the influence of these unmodeled dynamics.

The design process with H∞ control involves a careful selection of weighting functions $W
1$ and $W2$. These functions are crucial for translating performance requirements into a solvable control problem. A common strategy is to use rational functions that emphasize specific frequency ranges. For example, to achieve good low-frequency disturbance rejection, $W1$ *might have a high-pass filter characteristic, allowing the sensitivity function S to be small at low frequencies. Conversely, to reject high-frequency noise and avoid exciting high-frequency unmodeled dynamics,* $W2$ might have a low-pass filter characteristic, ensuring that T is small at high frequencies. The trade-off between performance and robustness is often managed by adjusting the magnitudes and frequency characteristics of these weighting functions. A more aggressive performance requirement (e.g., demanding very small S at low frequencies) might necessitate a controller that is less robust or has higher control effort, and vice versa.

The iterative nature of robust control design is also prominent in H∞ control. After an initial controller is designed based on the chosen weighting functions and the generalized plant, its performance is analyzed. This analysis involves checking if the $\mathcal{H}_{\infty}$ norm constraint is met and evaluating the closed-loop system's response to various disturbances and uncertainties. If the performance is not satisfactory, or if the controller exhibits excessive control effort, the weighting functions may need to be adjusted, or the generalized plant representation itself might need refinement to more accurately capture the system's behavior and uncertainties. This iterative refinement process, guided by both analytical tools and simulation, is essential for arriving at a controller that effectively balances performance, robustness, and implementability.

Despite its power, H∞ control is not without its challenges. The synthesis of optimal H∞ controllers can be computationally intensive, especially for high-order systems. Furthermore, the resulting controllers can be of high order, requiring further reduction for practical implementation. The selection of appropriate weighting functions can also be somewhat ad hoc and requires significant engineering judgment and experience. However, the guarantees provided by H∞ control – namely, stability and performance in the face of specified uncertainties – make it an indispensable tool in the robust control engineer's arsenal, especially for critical applications where reliability is paramount. The framework offers a principled approach to quantifying and managing uncertainty, leading to controllers that are demonstrably more resilient to the imperfections of the real world.

The preceding discussion has firmly established the foundational principles and methodologies of H-infinity control, a powerful framework for designing controllers that guarantee performance in the presence of bounded uncertainties. We've explored its reliance on worst-case analysis, the generalized plant representation, the critical role of weighting functions in shaping sensitivity and complementary sensitivity functions, and the mathematical tools, including algebraic Riccati equations and linear matrix inequalities, used for controller synthesis. The inherent robustness guarantees offered by H∞ control make it indispensable for critical applications where reliable operation under uncertainty is paramount. However, even with its rigorous mathematical underpinnings, the practical application of H∞ control often involves a degree of art alongside science, particularly in the selection of weighting functions and the handling of complex, potentially nonlinear, or time-varying uncertainties that may not fit neatly into the standard linear, time-invariant (LTI) framework. This is precisely where the integration of machine learning presents a compelling new frontier for advancing robust control design.

The advent of machine learning, with its unparalleled ability to discern intricate patterns and relationships from data, offers novel avenues to augment and even surpass traditional robust control techniques. Rather than solely relying on
a priori analytical models of uncertainty, machine learning can be employed to learn these uncertainties from operational data, or to directly search for controller parameters that exhibit robustness across a wide spectrum of potential operating conditions and disturbances. This paradigm shift moves beyond designing controllers for *predefined* uncertainty sets to creating controllers that can *adapt* or *learn* to be robust in more dynamic and complex environments. The core idea is to leverage the data-driven capabilities of AI to enhance the robustness, performance, and adaptability of control systems, particularly in scenarios where analytical modeling is intractable or insufficient.

One significant contribution of machine learning to robust control lies in its capacity to develop more accurate and comprehensive models of uncertainty. Traditional H∞ design often assumes that uncertainties belong to a known, bounded set, such as a structured or unstructured norm-bounded uncertainty. While effective, this assumption can be restrictive. Machine learning, particularly techniques like Gaussian Processes (GPs) or deep neural networks (NNs), can learn complex, nonlinear, and even time-varying uncertainty models directly from observed system behavior. For instance, if we consider the uncertainties affecting a robotic manipulator, such as variations in friction that change with temperature and lubrication, or unpredictable external forces acting on the end-effector, these might be difficult to capture with simple parametric bounds. A Gaussian Process, trained on experimental data of the manipulator's response under varying conditions, could learn a probabilistic model of these uncertainties. This learned uncertainty model, which inherently quanties the confidence in its predictions, can then be integrated into a robust controller design framework. Instead of a fixed bound $\Delta(s)$, the controller might be designed to be robust against an uncertainty representation $f(x)$ learned by a GP, where $f(x)$ provides both a predicted deviation and its variance. This allows for a more refined and less conservative robust control design, as the controller can exploit knowledge about the structure and confidence of the uncertainty, rather than treating it as an opaque worst-case scenario.

Furthermore, neural networks are proving invaluable for representing and approximating complex functions that arise in robust control. Consider the scenario where the optimal robust controller's structure or parameters are implicitly defined by a complex optimization problem that is computationally prohibitive to solve online. A neural network can be trained offline to approximate this solution. For example, in a model predictive control (MPC) framework that aims for robust performance, the receding horizon optimization problem might be challenging to solve within the required sampling time. A neural network can be trained to directly predict the control actions or the state feedback gains that would result from solving this optimization problem for a given system state and disturbance estimate. This "learning to optimize" approach can significantly reduce the online computational burden while retaining much of the robustness properties of the original MPC formulation. The neural network essentially learns a policy that is inherently robust because it has been trained to produce control actions that are optimal over a set of simulated scenarios encompassing various disturbances and uncertainties.

Reinforcement learning (RL) represents another powerful branch of machine learning that is revolutionizing the way we think about robust control. RL algorithms learn optimal control policies through trial-and-error interactions with an environment, aiming to maximize a cumulative reward signal. This intrinsic exploration and exploitation mechanism makes RL naturally suited for discovering control strategies that are resilient to disturbances and variations. In the context of robust control, the "environment" can be a high-fidelity simulator that incorporates a wide range of uncertainties and disturbances, or even a real-world system with safety constraints. The reward function can be designed to penalize deviations from desired performance metrics, excessive control effort, and system instability under adverse conditions.

For instance, consider the challenge of designing a robust trajectory planner for an autonomous vehicle operating in complex urban environments. The vehicle's dynamics are subject to variations in road friction (due to rain, ice, or tire wear), sensor noise (affecting localization and obstacle detection), and external disturbances (like wind gusts or unexpected pedestrian movements). A traditional approach might involve extensive offline testing and tuning of parameters to ensure safety across a predefined set of conditions. With reinforcement learning, however, an agent can learn a policy for generating safe and efficient trajectories by interacting with a sophisticated simulator. This simulator can systematically introduce diverse scenarios, such as sudden braking of a lead vehicle, abrupt changes in road surface, or temporary sensor dropouts. The RL agent, tasked with reaching a destination while minimizing travel time and maximizing passenger comfort, will learn to adapt its planned path and control actions to mitigate the effects of these uncertainties. The learned policy, encapsulated within a neural network, will implicitly encode robust behaviors: it will learn to maintain safe distances, adjust speed based on perceived risks, and recover from minor deviations caused by disturbances. The key is that the robustness is not explicitly programmed but emerges from the learning process that optimizes performance across a multitude of simulated adverse conditions.

The application of deep reinforcement learning (DRL) to robust control is particularly promising. Deep neural networks can serve as powerful function approximators for both the policy (mapping states to actions) and the value function (estimating future rewards). This allows RL algorithms to handle high-dimensional state and action spaces characteristic of complex physical systems. For example, in the control of unmanned aerial vehicles (UAVs) that operate in unpredictable weather conditions, DRL can learn policies that maintain stable flight and execute complex maneuvers despite significant wind disturbances and sensor noise. The UAV's state might include its position, velocity, attitude, and sensor readings, while the actions could be control surface deflections or motor thrust commands. By training in a simulated environment that faithfully models aerodynamic uncertainties and atmospheric turbulence, the DRL agent can learn to proactively counteract gusts and maintain desired flight paths, achieving a level of robustness that might be difficult to achieve with classical robust control design alone, especially when nonlinearities and unmodeled dynamics are significant.

Another avenue where machine learning enhances robust control is through learning residual dynamics or nonlinearities. In many practical systems, the linearized LTI model used for H∞ design captures the dominant dynamics well, but there are residual nonlinearities or unmodeled dynamics that can degrade performance or even compromise stability under certain conditions. Machine learning models, such as neural networks, can be trained to learn these residual dynamics.

This learned residual model can then be incorporated into the control design. For instance, the learned residual model could be used to augment the reference signal for a robust linear controller, effectively "pre-compensating" for the predictable nonlinear effects. Alternatively, the residual model could be used to inform an adaptive control law, allowing the controller gains to be adjusted in real-time to compensate for deviations from the nominal model. This hybrid approach, combining the guaranteed robustness of a linear controller with the adaptive capabilities of machine learning to handle unknown or unmodeled nonlinearities, offers a potent strategy for achieving superior performance.

Consider a system with significant friction, such as a robotic joint or a linear motor. The friction can be highly nonlinear, depending on velocity, direction of motion, and even temperature. A standard H∞ controller might be designed based on a linearized model around an operating point, providing some robustness to friction variations. However, its performance might suffer when the system operates at different velocities or experiences significant changes in friction. A machine learning model, such as a neural network, can be trained offline or online to accurately predict the friction force based on the current state (e.g., velocity, position). This learned friction model can then be used in several ways:

1. **Feedforward Compensation:** The predicted friction force can be directly subtracted from the control command, effectively cancelling out a significant portion of the friction. A robust linear controller then only needs to handle the remaining, smaller residual dynamics and uncertainties.
2. **Adaptive Control:** The parameters of the friction model can be updated online based on observed system behavior, and these updated parameters can be used to adjust the control law.

3. **Model Augmentation for Robust Design:** The learned friction model can be incorporated into a more comprehensive nonlinear model used for robust control design, potentially leading to a more accurate generalized plant and a more effective robust controller.

The integration of machine learning into robust control also opens up possibilities for optimizing the uncertainty models themselves. Instead of treating uncertainty sets as fixed, one could imagine a system that learns to characterize the *relevant* uncertainties for a given task or environment. For example, a system might learn that for a particular type of maneuver, only certain types of sensor noise are significant, while others are negligible. This learned knowledge about the structure and magnitude of pertinent uncertainties could then be used to design a more tailored and less conservative robust controller. This could involve using machine learning to define a "risk-aware" uncertainty set, where probabilities or confidence levels are assigned to different types of disturbances, allowing the controller to make decisions that balance performance with the likelihood of encountering specific adverse conditions.

Let's delve deeper into the concept of learning uncertainty models. Suppose we are designing a robust controller for an industrial process, such as a chemical reactor. The process is subject to variations in feed composition, catalyst activity, and ambient temperature. Traditional robust control might bound these variations within specific ranges. However, historical data might reveal correlations between these uncertainties. For example, a drop in catalyst activity might often be accompanied by a slight increase in ambient temperature due to reduced cooling efficiency. A machine learning model, such as a Bayesian network or a recurrent neural network, could learn these probabilistic dependencies. This learned model provides a richer description of the uncertainty than simple independent bounds. A robust controller designed using this richer uncertainty model could potentially achieve better performance because it can anticipate and account for these correlated variations, rather than just reacting to the worst-case independent realization of each uncertainty.

Furthermore, the realm of robust trajectory planning for robotic systems offers fertile ground for machine learning. Consider a robot arm tasked with assembling a complex product. The arm needs to navigate through a cluttered workspace, pick up components, and perform precise insertions. The uncertainties here are manifold: variations in component dimensions, unpredictable forces during grasping, potential collisions with other objects, and inaccuracies in robot kinematics and sensor readings. A reinforcement learning agent can be trained to learn a robust grasping and manipulation policy. The agent could be rewarded for successful grasps, accurate insertions, and for avoiding collisions, while being penalized for dropped components or collisions. By training in a simulated environment that incorporates variations in component properties, lighting conditions affecting vision sensors, and random perturbations of object positions, the RL agent can develop a policy that is resilient to these factors. This learned policy, perhaps a deep neural network, would output a sequence of robot actions (joint velocities, gripper commands) that are inherently robust. For instance, it might learn to apply just the right amount of force during grasping, to adjust its trajectory slightly to avoid a perceived obstruction, or to re-attempt a grasp if initial sensor feedback suggests a slip.

The concept of "learning to be robust" also extends to situations where the system's dynamics are inherently difficult to model, such as soft robotic systems or systems operating in highly fluid or granular environments. These systems often exhibit complex, nonlinear behaviors that defy simple analytical description. Machine learning, particularly techniques like deep learning and Gaussian processes, can learn surrogate models of these systems from experimental data. Once a sufficiently accurate surrogate model is learned, it can be used within a robust control design framework. For example, a deep neural network could be trained to predict the output of a soft robotic gripper given the actuator commands. This neural network model, along with estimated bounds on its prediction error (e.g., using ensemble methods or techniques like MC-Dropout), can then form the basis of a generalized plant for H∞ control or be used to train a robust reinforcement learning agent. The robustness then comes from the ability of the control system to account for the uncertainty in the learned model itself.

Moreover, machine learning can be utilized to enhance the robustness of existing controllers. For instance, a classical PID controller might be adequate for nominal conditions but struggles with significant disturbances or parameter variations. By employing machine learning, one could train a neural network to act as an "intelligent supervisor" or a "residual compensator" that augments the output of the PID controller. This neural network could learn to predict the deviations from the desired behavior caused by disturbances or model changes and generate corrective actions to improve the overall system's robustness. This is a form of composite control, where a robust linear controller is combined with a data-driven component that addresses the limitations of the linear model.

In the context of aerospace applications, consider the challenge of robustly controlling a flexible aircraft wing. The wing's dynamics are complex, involving aeroelastic effects that are difficult to model precisely and can change with flight conditions. Machine learning can be used to learn these complex aeroelastic interactions from flight data or high-fidelity simulations. A Gaussian Process, for example, could learn a probabilistic model of the wing's response to control surface deflections under various aerodynamic loads. This learned model, which quantifies the uncertainty in the aeroelastic response, can then be used to design a robust flight control system. The controller could be designed using an H∞ framework where the generalized plant incorporates the learned aeroelastic uncertainty model, or a reinforcement learning agent could be trained to achieve stable and responsive flight across a range of simulated aeroelastic conditions. The resulting control system would be more resilient to the unpredictable behavior of flexible structures.

Another significant area is the application of machine learning to robust control of power systems. Grid stability is paramount, and controllers must be robust to a wide array of disturbances, including sudden load changes, generator trips, and faults. The dynamics of interconnected power grids are complex and highly nonlinear. Machine learning techniques can be employed to learn predictive models of grid behavior or to develop adaptive control strategies that respond to changing conditions. For instance, reinforcement learning could be used to train a controller for dynamic voltage stability, learning policies that optimally adjust generator outputs and transformer tap positions to maintain voltage within acceptable limits under various stress scenarios. The learning process would expose the agent to a multitude of simulated disturbances, forcing it to develop strategies that are inherently robust to unpredictable grid events.

The challenges associated with integrating machine learning into robust control are also worth noting. A primary concern is the "black-box" nature of many machine learning models, particularly deep neural networks. While they can achieve impressive performance, understanding *why* they make certain decisions or *how* they guarantee robustness can be difficult. This lack of interpretability can be a barrier in safety-critical applications where formal verification and clear explanations of behavior are required. Research in explainable AI (XAI) is actively addressing this, aiming to provide insights into the decision-making processes of ML models. Another challenge is the need for large amounts of data for training, and ensuring that this data adequately represents the range of operating conditions and uncertainties the system will encounter in practice. Furthermore, guaranteeing the stability and performance of hybrid systems combining ML components with classical control methods requires new theoretical frameworks and rigorous analysis techniques.

Despite these challenges, the synergy between machine learning and robust control holds immense potential. By leveraging the data-driven pattern recognition capabilities of AI, we can develop controllers that are not only robust to known, bounded uncertainties but also adaptable to novel situations, capable of learning complex nonlinear dynamics, and optimized for performance across a broader spectrum of real-world conditions. This fusion promises to unlock new levels of performance, reliability, and autonomy for control systems across a vast array of applications, from autonomous vehicles and advanced robotics to resilient power grids and complex industrial processes. The future of robust control is increasingly looking towards intelligent, learning-based solutions that can navigate the inherent complexities and uncertainties of the physical world with unprecedented efficacy.

The preceding sections have thoroughly explored the integration of machine learning for *designing* robust controllers, leveraging its capabilities to model uncertainties, optimize policies, and adapt to dynamic environments. Now, we pivot our attention to a crucial, yet distinct, aspect: the *analysis* of robustness in control systems that have already been designed or trained using learning-based methodologies. While the previous discussions focused on how learning can *introduce* robustness, this subsection is dedicated to *evaluating* the robustness that has been achieved, or to identify its limitations. This shift in perspective is paramount for ensuring the safety, reliability, and trustworthiness of intelligent control systems, especially when deployed in safety-critical domains such as autonomous navigation, advanced robotics, medical devices, and critical infrastructure management.

When a control system relies on machine learning, particularly deep neural networks or reinforcement learning agents, its internal workings can often be opaque. This "black-box" nature poses a significant challenge for traditional robustness analysis techniques, which are typically predicated on well-defined analytical models of the controller and the plant. For a learning-based controller, simply knowing its input-output relationship from empirical testing might not be sufficient to guarantee its behavior under unseen or adversarial conditions. Therefore, specialized methods are required to probe, test, and formally or semi-formally verify its robustness. These methods aim to quantify how susceptible a learned policy is to perturbations, whether they arise from sensor noise, environmental changes, variations in the plant dynamics, or deliberate adversarial manipulation.

One primary avenue for analyzing the robustness of learning-based controllers involves adapting and extending formal verification techniques. Traditionally, formal methods have been used to prove properties of systems with known, deterministic behaviors. However, applying these to systems involving neural networks, which can exhibit complex, nonlinear mappings, is a significant research challenge. For neural network controllers, robustness analysis often translates to verifying that for any small perturbation within a defined bound applied to the network's input (e.g., noisy sensor readings, slightly altered system state), the network's output (the control command) remains within acceptable bounds, or that the closed-loop system state does not enter an unsafe region. Techniques such as Abstract Interpretation,

Reachability Analysis, and Satisfiability Modulo Theories (SMT) solvers are being adapted to handle the piecewise linear or polynomial nature of neural network computations. For instance, reachability analysis can compute a provable bound on the set of all possible output values for a given range of input perturbations. If this set of outputs is within the safe control limits, then the controller is robust with respect to those specific input perturbations. Similarly, SMT solvers can be used to search for counterexamples: specific input perturbations that lead to undesirable system behavior. The development of efficient and scalable formal verification methods for neural networks remains an active area of research, with significant efforts directed towards handling larger networks and more complex system dynamics. The goal is to move beyond empirical testing, which can only demonstrate the presence of robustness, not its absolute guarantee.

Beyond formal verification, a powerful class of techniques for robustness analysis centers on adversarial attacks. This paradigm views robustness as the ability of a learned policy to maintain performance even when subjected to deliberate, worst-case perturbations designed to cause failure. This is analogous to adversarial attacks in machine learning classification, where tiny, imperceptible changes to an image can fool the classifier. In the context of control, an "adversary" might try to manipulate sensor readings, introduce unmodeled dynamics, or inject false information to destabilize the system or force it to violate performance constraints. Evaluating robustness through adversarial attacks involves formulating an optimization problem where the adversary seeks to find the worst possible perturbation within a given budget (e.g., a bound on the magnitude of the perturbation) that maximally degrades the controller's performance or leads to instability. The control system's robustness is then assessed by its ability to withstand these optimized adversarial inputs.

For example, consider an autonomous vehicle controlled by a deep neural network policy. An adversary might subtly alter the perceived distance to an obstacle or the estimated velocity of another vehicle by introducing carefully crafted noise to the sensor inputs. The goal would be to cause the autonomous vehicle to brake too late, swerve unexpectedly, or otherwise enter an unsafe state. Robustness analysis then involves simulating this scenario: can we find an adversarial perturbation to the sensor inputs (within a realistic noise bound) that leads to a collision or a violation of safety rules? If such a perturbation exists, the controller is not robust to this specific attack. Conversely, if no such perturbation can be found within the defined bounds, the controller exhibits a degree of robustness against that attack. This adversarial perspective is particularly valuable for identifying potential vulnerabilities that might not surface during standard testing with random noise or nominal operating conditions. It pushes the boundaries of testing by actively seeking out failure modes.

Simulation-based approaches offer a more empirical, yet highly practical, method for analyzing the robustness of learning-based controllers. This involves systematically introducing various forms of uncertainty and disturbances into a high-fidelity simulation environment and observing the closed-loop system's performance. Unlike simple Monte Carlo simulations that might sample from a nominal distribution of uncertainties, robustness analysis through simulation often employs more targeted strategies. This can include:

Worst-Case Scenario Simulation: Designing specific scenarios that are known or suspected to be challenging for the control system. This might involve combining multiple unfavorable conditions simultaneously, such as low sensor accuracy, aggressive maneuvers, and unexpected environmental changes.

Sensitivity Analysis: Varying individual parameters or input signals within their expected ranges and quantifying the impact on performance metrics. This helps identify which sources of uncertainty have the most significant effect on robustness.

Stochastic Simulation with Extreme Value Theory: Instead of just sampling from distributions, employing statistical techniques like Extreme Value Theory (EVT) to generate and analyze extreme, rare events that are likely to stress the controller. This can provide insights into the tail behavior of performance degradation.

System Identification under Perturbation: Using data collected during perturbed operation to identify the system's current dynamics and then evaluating how the learned controller performs with this updated model.

For instance, in the development of a robust controller for a robotic surgical instrument, extensive simulations would be conducted. These would include variations in tissue properties (stiffness, elasticity), unexpected instrument vibrations, slight inaccuracies in camera tracking, and variations in the surgeon's control inputs. The simulation would be designed to replicate a wide spectrum of potential failure modes, and the performance of the learned controller would be quantified based on metrics like accuracy of tissue manipulation, time to complete a task, and the occurrence of any unintended movements. By running thousands or even millions of these simulations, researchers can build a statistical profile of the controller's robustness and identify operating regimes where its performance might degrade unacceptably.

Moreover, the analysis of robustness for learning-based controllers can involve developing metrics that quantify performance degradation under uncertainty. Instead of a binary pass/fail, these metrics aim to provide a continuous measure of robustness. For example, one could define a "robustness score" that averages performance across a spectrum of simulated disturbances. A controller that maintains high performance across a wide range of disturbances would have a higher score. Alternatively, one could analyze the "margin" of safety. For a task that requires a certain minimum distance to an obstacle, the margin of safety could be defined as the minimum distance the system maintains throughout a set of challenging scenarios. A larger margin indicates greater robustness. This quantitative approach allows for comparison between different learned controllers and helps in setting design targets for desired levels of robustness.

The interpretability of learned models also plays a role in robustness analysis. While deep neural networks are often considered black boxes, techniques from Explainable AI (XAI) can provide insights into *why* a controller behaves in a certain way, which can aid in understanding its robustness. For example, techniques like SHAP (SHapley Additive exPlanations) or LIME (Local Interpretable Model-agnostic Explanations) can help identify which input features or internal states are most influential in the controller's decision-making process. If robustness analysis reveals a vulnerability, XAI can help pinpoint the specific conditions or internal states that lead to this vulnerability, guiding further development or refinement of the learning process. Understanding the salient features that drive a controller's actions can also help in designing more effective adversarial attacks or in developing targeted simulation scenarios.

In the context of medical devices, such as insulin pumps or automated drug delivery systems, robustness analysis is not merely a performance metric but a critical safety requirement. For an AI-powered insulin pump, robustness means maintaining precise blood glucose control even with variations in patient diet, exercise, stress levels, sensor noise, and potential pump malfunctions. Analysis would involve simulating scenarios like a missed meal, an unexpected strenuous workout, or a temporary sensor dropout. The learned control policy would need to be rigorously tested to ensure it does not lead to dangerous hypoglycemia or hyperglycemia. Formal methods might be used to prove that the blood glucose level will always remain within a safe physiological range under a specified set of environmental and physiological uncertainties. Adversarial analysis could explore how small, potentially sensor-induced, errors might mislead the pump into administering an incorrect dose. The ultimate goal is to provide a high degree of assurance, backed by rigorous analysis, that the device will operate safely and effectively under a wide variety of real-world conditions.

Furthermore, robustness analysis is intrinsically linked to the concept of uncertainty quantification within the learning process itself. If the learning algorithm provides not just a point estimate of the control action but also a measure of uncertainty associated with that estimate (e.g., variance in a Gaussian Process, or confidence intervals from ensemble methods), this information can be leveraged for robustness analysis. A controller that consistently signals high uncertainty in its predictions for certain operating regimes might indicate an area where its robustness is questionable, prompting further investigation or the implementation of fallback safety mechanisms. This internal awareness of uncertainty can be a powerful tool for self-assessment of robustness.

The practical implementation of robustness analysis for learning-based controllers often involves a multi-faceted approach, combining elements of formal verification, adversarial testing, and extensive simulation. There is no single silver bullet. The choice of methods depends heavily on the application domain, the criticality of safety, the available computational resources, and the specific characteristics of the learned controller. For instance, a reinforcement learning policy trained for a video game might be analyzed primarily through simulation and adversarial attacks, while a neural network controller for an autonomous vehicle would likely require a much more stringent combination of formal verification (for critical safety properties) and exhaustive simulation.

The development of standardized benchmarks and methodologies for robustness evaluation of learned controllers is an ongoing endeavor in the research community. This includes creating diverse datasets of challenging scenarios, defining clear metrics for performance degradation, and developing tools that automate parts of the analysis process. As machine learning continues to permeate safety-critical control applications, the ability to rigorously and confidently analyze the robustness of these learned systems will be paramount for their widespread adoption and public trust. The focus shifts from simply demonstrating that a learning system can perform well under nominal conditions, to providing evidence that it will continue to perform acceptably, or fail gracefully, even when faced with the unpredictable and often adversarial nature of the real world. This analytical rigor complements the learning-based design approaches, ensuring that intelligent control systems are not only capable but also dependable.

Chapter 11: Hybrid Systems and Learning

In our exploration of advanced control systems, we've delved into the power of machine learning to design controllers that can adapt, optimize, and learn from data. We've discussed how these learned controllers can enhance robustness by modeling uncertainties and responding dynamically to changing environments. Now, our focus shifts to a more fundamental question: how do we analyze and understand the behavior of control systems that are inherently complex, often exhibiting a blend of continuous and discrete characteristics? This leads us to the fascinating realm of hybrid dynamical systems.

Hybrid dynamical systems represent a broad and powerful framework for modeling systems that exhibit both continuous and discrete behaviors. Many real-world phenomena and engineered systems cannot be adequately described by either purely continuous or purely discrete models. Instead, they possess dynamics that evolve smoothly over time, governed by differential equations, interspersed with abrupt changes or switches that occur at discrete points in time. These switches can be triggered by events, logic conditions, or the inherent nature of the system's operation, leading to a composite behavior that is characteristic of hybrid systems.

The essence of a hybrid system lies in its ability to operate in different "modes" or "regimes." Within each mode, the system's behavior is typically described by a set of continuous dynamics, often expressed as ordinary differential equations (ODEs) or differential algebraic equations (DAEs). These ODEs capture how the system's state variables evolve smoothly over time, such as position, velocity, temperature, or voltage. However, these continuous dynamics do not persist indefinitely. At certain points, the system can transition from one mode to another. These transitions are governed by discrete dynamics, which can be triggered by various conditions. For instance, a transition might occur when a continuous state variable crosses a predefined threshold, when an external event signal is received, or when a logical condition becomes true. Upon transition, the system's continuous dynamics can change, potentially leading to a completely different set of ODEs or a modification of the existing ones. The state variables themselves may also be reset or altered during a mode switch.

The prevalence of hybrid systems in engineering and science is remarkable. Consider a robotic manipulator tasked with assembling a product. During its operation, the robot might have different modes: a "pick-and-place" mode where it grasps an object, a "moving" mode where it transports the object, and a "placing" mode where it positions the object. Each of these modes involves continuous motion governed by its joint velocities and accelerations. The transitions between these modes are discrete events: the gripper closing, the gripper opening, or reaching a target position. Another common example is a thermostat controlling a heating system. The system has a continuous model of room temperature and heating dynamics. However, the controller operates in discrete modes: "heating on" and "heating off." The transition occurs when the temperature crosses the setpoint plus some hysteresis band.

Power electronics converters are another rich source of hybrid dynamical systems. A DC-DC converter, for instance, uses semiconductor switches to regulate voltage. The circuit's behavior depends on the state of these switches. When a switch is on, the circuit follows a specific set of ODEs describing current and voltage dynamics through inductors and capacitors. When the switch turns off, the circuit's dynamics change, governed by a different set of ODEs. The switching instants are precisely controlled, creating a hybrid system where continuous electrical dynamics are interleaved with discrete switching events. This allows for efficient power conversion but necessitates a hybrid modeling approach for analysis and control design.

Manufacturing processes often exhibit hybrid characteristics. An automated assembly line might have distinct phases of operation, such as "loading," "machining," and "unloading." Each phase involves continuous physical movements and interactions governed by physical laws. However, the progression from one phase to the next is a discrete event, often triggered by the completion of a task or a sensor signal. The control system needs to manage both the continuous motion within each phase and the discrete transitions between them to ensure efficient and accurate production.

In the context of aerospace engineering, aircraft have distinct flight phases such as takeoff, climb, cruise, descent, and landing. Each phase has different aerodynamic properties and requires different control strategies. The transition between these phases are discrete events. Even within a single phase, there might be sub-modes. For example, during landing, an aircraft might transition between an approach mode, a flare mode, and a touchdown mode.

The modeling of hybrid systems is a specialized area of control theory. Several formalisms exist to represent these systems, each offering different levels of abstraction and analytical power. One common approach is the "state-space" representation, where the system's state is augmented to include both continuous variables (often denoted by $x \in \mathbb{R}^n$) and a discrete variable representing the current mode (often denoted by $q \in Q$, where Q is a finite set of modes). For each mode $q *i \in Q$, there is a set of continuous dynamics $fi*(x, u)$ and a set of possible discrete transitions. A transition from mode $qi*$ to mode $qj*$ might be triggered by a condition $g*{ij}(x, u)$, which depends on the continuous state and control inputs. Upon satisfying the condition $g*{ij}$, the system transitions to mode $qj*$, and the continuous state might undergo a reset $x^+ = r*{ij}(x)$.

A fundamental challenge in dealing with hybrid systems is their inherent complexity. The interplay between continuous and discrete dynamics can lead to emergent behaviors that are difficult to predict from analyzing the continuous or discrete parts in isolation. For example, a system might appear stable in each continuous mode, but the switching logic could inadvertently create oscillations or instability when transitions occur frequently or under specific conditions. This necessitates a unified analytical framework that can capture the coupled nature of these dynamics.

The analysis of hybrid systems often involves understanding properties such as stability, reachability, and performance. Stability in hybrid systems is a nuanced concept. A system might be stable in each of its continuous modes, but the overall hybrid system could be unstable if transitions are not managed properly. For instance, a system might be stable when operating in a specific mode, but if the trigger for switching out of that mode is delayed, the continuous dynamics could push the system state into an undesirable or unsafe region before the transition occurs. Conversely, if transitions are too rapid, the system might not have enough time to settle into its intended behavior in the new mode, leading to oscillations or erratic behavior.

Reachability analysis, which aims to determine the set of all possible states that a system can reach from a given initial set of states, is particularly important for hybrid systems. Due to the discrete transitions, the set of reachable states can evolve in a highly complex, non-convex manner, growing and splitting as the system moves between modes. Understanding reachability is crucial for safety verification, as it allows us to determine if the system can ever enter an unsafe state.

The development of control strategies for hybrid systems is also an active area of research. Traditional control techniques, such as PID control or linear quadratic control, are often designed for systems with fixed dynamics. For hybrid systems, controllers must be able to adapt their behavior based on the current mode and trigger appropriate transitions. This has led to the development of specialized control techniques, including:

Mode-dependent control: Where the control law is explicitly designed to be different for each mode.
Switched control: Where the controller itself is a switching system, selecting control laws based on the system's state and logic.
Event-triggered control: Where control actions or state updates are performed only when specific events occur, rather than at fixed time intervals. This can lead to more efficient computation and communication.
Model Predictive Control (MPC) for hybrid systems: MPC can be extended to handle hybrid dynamics by incorporating discrete modes and transitions into the optimization problem. This allows for optimizing control actions over a future horizon while respecting the hybrid nature of the system.

The integration of machine learning with hybrid dynamical systems is a particularly promising frontier. As discussed in previous sections, machine learning excels at modeling complex, nonlinear relationships from data. This capability is directly applicable to hybrid systems in several ways:

First, machine learning can be used to learn the continuous dynamics within each mode. If the underlying physics of a particular mode is not well understood or is too complex to model analytically, a neural network or another data-driven model can be trained to approximate the ODEs. This learned model can then be used for analysis or control design.

Second, machine learning can be employed to learn the switching logic or the conditions that trigger transitions between modes. Instead of manually defining threshold conditions, a classifier or a reinforcement learning agent could be trained to predict the optimal time to switch modes based on observed system behavior and desired performance objectives. For example, in a robotic system, a learned policy might decide when to switch from a precise manipulation mode to a faster movement mode based on the task progress and estimated time to completion.

Third, reinforcement learning is exceptionally well-suited for developing controllers for hybrid systems. A reinforcement learning agent can learn a policy that maps the system's state (including both continuous variables and the current mode) to control actions. The agent's reward function can be designed to encourage efficient transitions between modes and maintain desirable performance within each mode. This allows the RL agent to discover complex switching strategies and control laws that might be difficult to design manually. For instance, an RL agent could learn to control a multi-stage chemical process, deciding not only the continuous control inputs (e.g., flow rates, temperatures) but also when to activate or deactivate specific stages (discrete transitions).

Consider the example of an adaptive cruise control (ACC) system in a vehicle. This system inherently exhibits hybrid behavior. There are continuous dynamics related to the vehicle's speed, acceleration, and distance to the vehicle ahead. However, the ACC system operates in distinct modes: "following," "accelerating to set speed," and "braking." The transitions between these modes are triggered by discrete events, such as the detection of a slower vehicle, the road becoming clear, or the driver setting a new desired speed. A traditional ACC system relies on carefully tuned rules and thresholds to manage these modes. However, a more sophisticated, hybrid-aware ACC could leverage machine learning. A learned model could predict the trajectory of surrounding vehicles more accurately, informing more precise predictions of when mode switches are necessary. A reinforcement learning agent could be trained to optimize not just for maintaining a set distance, but also for passenger comfort (smoothness of acceleration/deceleration) and fuel efficiency, learning a nuanced policy that manages the transitions between following, accelerating, and braking modes in a way that is superior to rule-based systems. The state for the RL agent would include current speed, distance to lead vehicle, relative speed, throttle/brake pedal position, and the current ACC mode.

Another compelling application of hybrid systems and machine learning is in the field of autonomous robotics. A legged robot, for instance, moves by coordinating discrete events: lifting a foot, swinging it forward, placing it down, and shifting weight. Each of these actions is associated with continuous dynamics of joint torques, velocities, and body posture. The robot's gait is a sequence of these discrete events. Machine learning, particularly reinforcement learning, has shown great promise in enabling robots to learn complex gaits that are robust to uneven terrain and external disturbances. An RL agent could learn a policy that takes the robot's current joint angles, velocities, foot contact status (discrete), and desired locomotion direction as input, and outputs desired joint torques and foot placement strategies. The reward function could penalize falling, reward forward progress, and reward energy efficiency. The learned policy implicitly encodes the hybrid dynamics of locomotion, effectively learning the timing and coordination of discrete footfalls while simultaneously controlling the continuous dynamics of body movement.

The complexity of hybrid systems also presents challenges for formal verification and robustness analysis. As we discussed earlier, analyzing the robustness of learned controllers is critical. When these controllers are applied to hybrid systems, the analysis must account for both continuous and discrete dynamics. This means that not only must the learned controller be robust to perturbations in its continuous inputs or internal states, but it must also be robust to unexpected or erroneous discrete transitions. For example, a slight sensor error might incorrectly trigger a mode switch, or a mode switch might not occur when expected due to a logic flaw. Robustness analysis in this context would need to consider:

1. **Robustness within modes:** Ensuring the learned controller performs reliably under continuous perturbations while the system is in a given mode.
2. **Robustness of transitions:** Verifying that mode transitions occur correctly, reliably, and at the appropriate times, even in the presence of noise or uncertainty.

3. **Robustness to mode mismatch:** Analyzing system behavior if the controller *believes* the system is in one mode, but it is actually in another.

This multilevel robustness analysis is a significant research challenge. Formal methods like reachability analysis can be extended to hybrid systems to provide guarantees, but scaling these methods to complex learned controllers and high-dimensional state spaces remains an active area of investigation. Adversarial analysis can also be adapted: an adversary might try to induce false mode switches or prevent necessary ones, or introduce perturbations that cause the system to behave erratically during transitions.

In summary, hybrid dynamical systems provide an essential framework for accurately modeling a vast array of real-world engineering systems that exhibit both continuous evolution and discrete changes. Their complexity arises from the intricate interplay between these two types of dynamics. Understanding and controlling these systems requires specialized analytical tools and control strategies. The integration of machine learning, particularly reinforcement learning, offers powerful new avenues for modeling the dynamics of hybrid systems, learning optimal switching logic, and developing sophisticated, adaptive controllers. As we move towards increasingly autonomous and intelligent systems, the ability to model, analyze, and control hybrid dynamical systems will become ever more critical, enabling the design of robust, safe, and efficient solutions for complex real-world problems. The next sections will further explore specific methods for analyzing and controlling such hybrid systems, building upon this foundational understanding.

The foundation for effectively analyzing and controlling any dynamical system, particularly those exhibiting hybrid characteristics, rests upon the bedrock of accurate modeling. Hybrid systems, by their very definition, blend continuous-time dynamics with discrete events and logic, creating a rich tapestry of behavior that necessitates specialized formalisms. Our endeavor to understand and manipulate these systems begins with capturing their dual nature in a mathematically rigorous and computationally tractable manner. This involves representing both the smooth, evolving aspects governed by differential equations and the abrupt, event-driven changes that characterize their discrete transitions.

One of the most intuitive and widely adopted formalisms for modeling hybrid systems is the coupling of state machines with continuous-time differential equations. In this approach, the system is conceptualized as possessing a finite set of operational "modes" or "states." Each mode corresponds to a specific configuration or regime of operation, within which the system's behavior is governed by a set of continuous dynamics. These dynamics are typically expressed as ordinary differential equations (ODEs) or differential algebraic equations (DAEs), describing how the system's state variables, such as positions, velocities, voltages, or temperatures, evolve over time. For instance, a robotic arm might have modes like "joint
*control*p," "joint*control*v," or "end*effector*grasp." In the "joint*control*p" mode, the ODEs might describe how the joint angle changes based on a proportional controller's output relative to a desired position.

However, the system does not remain indefinitely in a single mode. Discrete transitions are crucial for capturing the system's ability to switch between these operational regimes. These transitions are governed by specific conditions, often referred to as "guards" or "trigger conditions." A guard is a logical expression that depends on the continuous state variables and potentially control inputs. When this condition is met, the system is allowed to transition from its current mode to another. For example, in the robotic arm scenario, a transition from "joint *control*p" to "joint*control*v" might be guarded by the condition that the joint angle has reached its target position within a certain tolerance. The transition itself may also involve a discrete event, such as a change in the control law or a reset of certain state variables. This might be formulated as $x^+ = f(x)$, where x^+ represents the state immediately after the transition, and f is a function that maps the pre-transition state to the post-transition state. This function can be as simple as identity (no reset) or involve a specific re-initialization of certain state variables.

This state-machine-plus-ODE approach is highly versatile and finds application in numerous mechatronic systems. Consider an electromechanical actuator controlled by a pulse-width modulation (PWM) signal. The actuator has continuous dynamics related to its mechanical position and velocity, often described by second-order ODEs involving mass, damping, and spring forces, plus an input term proportional to the effective voltage. The PWM signal, however, switches discretely between an "on" state (applying a high voltage) and an "off" state (applying zero or a low voltage). The system effectively operates in two continuous modes: one when the PWM is high and another when it is low. The switching between these modes is dictated by the PWM duty cycle, which itself might be generated by a continuous-time controller or a discrete-time digital controller. The guards for transitioning between these PWM modes are simply the moments in time when the PWM signal changes its state. The continuous dynamics in each mode will differ based on the applied voltage. For instance, if $v
*{in}$ is the input voltage, the ODEs in one mode might be $\ddot{p} = \frac{1}{m}(F*{spring} + F*{damping} + k \cdot v*{in})$, while in another mode (e.g., PWM off, $v*{in}=0$), it would be $\ddot{p} = \frac{1}{m}(F*{spring} + F_{damping})$.

A more formal and powerful framework for modeling hybrid systems is the concept of

hybrid automata. This formalism extends the idea of state machines by explicitly defining states (called "locations" in automata theory) and transitions between them. Each location in a hybrid automaton is associated with:

1. **Continuous dynamics:** A set of differential equations that describe how the system's continuous state variables evolve while the system resides in that location. These are often denoted as $\dot{x} \in f_i(x, u)$ for location i, where x is the continuous state vector and u is the control input.
2. **Invariant set:** A condition that must hold for the continuous state variables as long as the system remains in that location. The system is not allowed to leave the location as long as its state x satisfies the invariant $Inv_i(x)$. If the continuous dynamics cause the state to violate the invariant, a transition must occur.
3. **Transitions:** Discrete events that cause the system to move from one location to another. Each transition is associated with:

Guard condition: A condition on the continuous state (and possibly control inputs) that must be met for the transition to be taken. For a transition from location i to location j, this is a guard $G_{ij}(x, u)$.
Reset map: A function that defines how the continuous state variables are updated immediately after the transition. This is often denoted as $x^+ \in R_{ij}(x)$.

Hybrid automata provide a rigorous mathematical structure that allows for formal analysis techniques, such as reachability analysis and model checking, to be applied. This makes them particularly valuable for safety-critical applications where formal guarantees about system behavior are paramount. For example, in modeling a charging system for an electric vehicle, different locations could represent "charging," "waiting for grid connection," and "fault state." The "charging" location would have ODEs describing the battery's voltage and current dynamics, with an invariant stating that voltage and current should remain within safe operational limits. Transitions out of "charging" could be triggered by guards like "battery full" (transitioning to "charging complete") or "over-voltage detected" (transitioning to "fault state"). The reset map for "battery full" might set a flag indicating completion, while for "over-voltage," it might shut down the charging circuit.

Another common modeling paradigm, closely related to hybrid automata and state-machine-ODE couplings, is
piecewise-defined systems. In this view, the system's dynamics are defined by a collection of continuous functions, each active over a specific region of the state space. These regions are often separated by boundaries. When the system's state trajectory crosses one of these boundaries, a discrete event occurs, potentially leading to a change in the active continuous dynamics. The "regions" and "boundaries" effectively correspond to the modes and guards of hybrid automata.

Consider a thermal management system for electronics. The system might have modes like "cooling
*on," "cooling*off," and "fan*speed*high." The continuous dynamics in each mode would describe how the temperature of the electronic component changes based on heat generation and the effectiveness of the cooling mechanism. For instance, in "cooling*off," temperature might rise according to $\dot{T} = P*{gen} - K*{ambient} \cdot (T - T*{ambient})$, where $P*{gen}$ is power generation, $K*{ambient}$ is heat dissipation to the ambient, and $T*{ambient}$ is ambient temperature. In "cooling*on," the dynamics would include an additional term representing heat removal by the cooling system, say $-K*{cooling} \cdot (T - T*{sink})$, where $T*{sink}$ is the sink temperature of the cooler. Transitions would be triggered by temperature thresholds: if T exceeds $T*{max}$, a transition to "cooling*on" might occur; if T drops below $T*{low}$, a transition back to "cooling*off" might be triggered. The "fan*speed*high" mode could represent a more aggressive cooling strategy with a larger $-*K{cooling}$ term, activated if T exceeds a higher threshold. The

piecewise definition captures this piecewise behavior: the function governing $\dot{T}$ changes depending on which region of temperature the system is currently operating in.

The core challenge in modeling hybrid systems lies in accurately representing the **interaction between continuous and discrete dynamics**. It's not enough to simply specify the ODEs within each mode and the conditions for switching. The way these components influence each other is paramount. The **jump conditions** associated with discrete transitions are a critical aspect. These conditions specify what happens to the continuous state variables precisely at the instant of a mode switch. As mentioned, this can involve resetting variables, which can drastically alter the system's trajectory and behavior. A well-defined reset map is crucial to prevent, for instance, a control system from immediately re-triggering a transition it just exited, or to properly initialize a new mode of operation.

For example, in a robotic pick-and-place operation, a robot arm might transition from a "moving" mode to a "grasping" mode. The "moving" mode involves continuous trajectory following governed by joint velocity ODEs. The transition to "grasping" is triggered when the end-effector reaches the target object's position. Upon entering the "grasping" mode, the continuous dynamics might change to reflect the closed-loop control of the gripper. Crucially, the reset map might need to update a state variable indicating whether the object has been successfully grasped. If the initial grasp attempt fails, the state might be reset to allow for a re-approach and another grasping attempt. The jump condition effectively bridges the continuous evolution leading up to the event with the new continuous evolution that begins after the event.

Another subtle but important aspect of modeling hybrid systems, especially those derived from physical systems, is ensuring **consistency across different components**. This means that the continuous dynamics in adjacent modes should be compatible in some sense, and the transition logic should be logical and physically realizable. For instance, if a system transitions from a high-speed mode to a low-speed mode, the control signals and system states should be managed such that the transition is smooth and does not cause undue stress or instability. In a power converter, if the switching logic dictates a transition from a mode where a certain inductor is charging to a mode where it is discharging, the voltages and currents must be consistent with Kirchhoff's laws at the transition instant. Inconsistencies can arise if the modeled dynamics or reset conditions do not respect the underlying physical principles.

The complexity inherent in hybrid systems modeling can be a significant hurdle. The state space can grow exponentially with the number of modes and their interconnections. Furthermore, continuous dynamics themselves can be nonlinear and high-dimensional. When combined, analyzing the global behavior of such systems can become computationally intractable. For instance, a system with 10 modes, each governed by a set of 5 ODEs, and with potential transitions between any pair of modes, can quickly become unmanageable. Each transition requires its own guard condition and reset map, leading to a combinatorial explosion of possibilities.

In mechatronic systems, this complexity is frequently encountered. Consider an automated guided vehicle (AGV) operating in a warehouse. The AGV might have modes for: "moving *straight," "turning," "picking*upload*," "dropping*offload*," and "charging." Each mode has associated continuous dynamics for linear and angular* *velocity, battery level, and position. Transitions between these modes are triggered by sensor readings (e.g., reaching a waypoint, detecting an obstacle, battery level low) and internal logic. The guards for "moving*straight" to "turning" would involve reaching a specific point and initiating a turn command. The reset map might update the vehicle's orientation. The guards for "picking*up*load" would involve reaching the designated pickup location, and the reset might engage a gripper mechanism. The overall behavior of the AGV depends critically on the correct specification of these modes, their continuous dynamics, and the precise conditions and consequences of their transitions. Ensuring that an AGV can navigate complex environments safely and efficiently requires a detailed and accurate hybrid model that captures these interactions.

To mitigate modeling complexity, researchers often employ abstraction techniques. This involves simplifying the hybrid model while preserving certain essential properties. For example, one might abstract away fine details of continuous dynamics to focus on qualitative behaviors, or aggregate multiple modes into a single, more general mode. However, abstraction can lead to a loss of precision, and the trade-off between simplicity and accuracy must be carefully considered, especially when the goal is to derive precise control laws or guarantees.

Another approach to managing complexity is the use of specialized modeling tools and languages. Formalisms like Stateflow in MATLAB/Simulink, or languages like HyVisual, provide graphical or textual interfaces for defining hybrid automata and simulating their behavior. These tools often incorporate built-in mechanisms for checking consistency and detecting common modeling errors, aiding in the creation of robust and accurate hybrid models.

The choice of modeling formalism also depends on the intended application. For purely descriptive purposes or for simple controller design, a state-machine-ODE coupling might suffice. For rigorous safety analysis and formal verification, hybrid automata offer a more powerful and mathematically grounded framework. Piecewise-defined systems provide a natural way to represent systems whose dynamics are inherently separated by state-space partitions. Regardless of the formalism chosen, the emphasis remains on capturing the interconnectedness of continuous evolution and discrete events, which is the defining characteristic of hybrid dynamical systems. The accuracy and fidelity of this model are paramount, as any subsequent analysis or control design will operate based on its representation of the system's behavior.

The inherent complexity arising from the interplay between continuous dynamics and discrete events in hybrid systems necessitates a distinct set of control strategies, diverging from those suitable for purely continuous or purely discrete systems. Effectively managing these systems requires a nuanced approach that can both regulate the smooth evolution of continuous states within operational modes and orchestrate the often abrupt transitions between these modes. This control challenge is multi-faceted, demanding careful consideration of local behavior within modes and global coordination across the entire system's operational landscape.

One fundamental approach to controlling hybrid systems is to design controllers that are mode-specific. In this paradigm, a separate continuous-time controller is developed for each distinct mode of the hybrid system. For instance, in an automated manufacturing line with modes like "assembly," "inspection," and "packaging," a dedicated controller might be responsible for regulating robot arm movements during assembly, another for ensuring quality during inspection, and a third for managing conveyor belt speeds during packaging. These mode-specific controllers are typically designed using established techniques from classical control theory, such as PID control, linear quadratic regulation (LQR), or model predictive control (MPC), tailored to the local dynamics described by the differential equations within that particular mode. The critical challenge then shifts to managing the transitions between these modes. A supervisory logic, often implemented as a discrete-state controller or embedded within the hybrid automaton's transition guards, is responsible for monitoring the system's state and issuing commands to switch from one mode to another. This logic must ensure that transitions occur under safe and appropriate conditions, determined by the guard conditions defined in the system's model. Furthermore, upon transitioning to a new mode, the corresponding continuous-time controller must be activated, and its initial state might need to be set appropriately, possibly via a reset map, to ensure a smooth and stable continuation of operation. This "controller-per-mode" strategy is intuitive and modular, allowing for specialized expertise to be applied to each operational regime. However, it can lead to complex supervisory logic as the number of modes and transitions grows, and it may not always guarantee optimal performance or stability across the entire system's operational envelope, particularly if transitions are frequent or the modes are highly interdependent.

Consider an autonomous vehicle as a prime example of a system that could benefit from mode-specific control. The vehicle might operate in distinct modes such as "highway
*driving," "city*driving," and "parking." In "highway*driving" mode, the continuous dynamics are primarily concerned with maintaining speed and lane position, perhaps using an LQR controller designed for high-speed, stable trajectories. The "city*driving" mode involves more frequent braking, acceleration, and steering maneuvers in response to traffic and pedestrians. Here, a more responsive controller, possibly a gain-

scheduled MPC that adapts to varying road conditions and traffic densities, might be employed. Finally, the "parking" mode requires precise low-speed maneuvering, possibly using a vision-based system and a path-following controller optimized for tight spaces. The transitions between these modes are triggered by discrete events: detecting a highway entrance/exit ramp, entering a city zone based on GPS, or initiating a parking maneuver. The supervisory logic would monitor GPS, speed, and sensor inputs to decide when to switch modes. Upon switching to "city_driving," the steering and throttle controllers would be reconfigured from their highway settings to their city settings, and the initial throttle command might be set to zero to ensure a smooth handover.

Beyond mode-specific controllers, a more holistic approach involves employing global optimization techniques. These methods aim to find a single control policy that is optimal over the entire hybrid system's state space and operational modes, explicitly considering the interactions between continuous and discrete behaviors. Model Predictive Control (MPC) can be extended to handle hybrid systems, often referred to as Hybrid MPC. In this framework, the optimization problem at each time step involves predicting the system's future behavior over a finite horizon, taking into account both continuous dynamics and possible discrete transitions. The controller then computes a sequence of control inputs and discrete mode switches that minimizes a cost function (e.g., minimizing energy consumption, maximizing tracking accuracy, or ensuring safety) over the prediction horizon, while satisfying system constraints. The continuous dynamics within each mode are described by differential equations, and the transitions are modeled using logic-based constraints or by incorporating discrete optimization variables. For instance, at each decision point, the Hybrid MPC might consider whether to continue in the current mode, transition to another based on predicted future states, or even change its control strategy within the current mode if it's a mode with internal parameter variations. The complexity of solving such a mixed-integer, hybrid optimization problem at each time step can be significant, often requiring specialized solvers and approximations, but it offers the potential for globally optimal and robust control.

Consider a building's HVAC (Heating, Ventilation, and Air Conditioning) system as an example where Hybrid MPC can be highly effective. The system has continuous dynamics describing the temperature evolution in different zones, influenced by ambient conditions, internal heat loads, and the HVAC equipment's operation. Discrete modes could include "heating," "cooling," "ventilation," and "idle." The control objective might be to maintain comfortable temperatures while minimizing energy consumption. A Hybrid MPC would predict temperature trajectories for various control sequences and mode selections over the next few hours. It would account for the energy cost associated with activating heating or cooling systems, the dynamics of air flow, and the constraints on temperature (e.g., never exceeding a certain threshold to avoid discomfort or equipment damage). The optimization would decide not only the fan speeds and setpoints for continuous variables but also when to switch between heating, cooling, and ventilation modes, potentially exploiting periods of lower energy prices or favorable ambient conditions.

Hierarchical control structures offer another powerful paradigm for managing the complexity of hybrid systems. In this architecture, a high-level discrete controller makes strategic decisions about which mode the system should operate in, while a lower-level continuous controller is responsible for executing the desired behavior within the selected mode. The discrete controller typically operates on a longer time scale and makes decisions based on the overall system goals, environmental conditions, and the current operational state. Its decisions are akin to setting the operating point or control law for the continuous subsystem. The continuous controller, in turn, receives commands from the discrete layer and uses its knowledge of the local continuous dynamics to achieve the specified objective. This separation of concerns simplifies the design process. The discrete controller can be designed using tools from discrete event systems or finite automata theory, focusing on logic and sequencing. The continuous controller can be designed using traditional control methods, ensuring stability and performance within its operational context.

An excellent illustration of hierarchical control is in the operation of a fleet of delivery robots in a warehouse. The high-level discrete controller might be a fleet manager responsible for assigning tasks, optimizing routes, and coordinating robot movements to avoid collisions. Based on these strategic decisions, it commands individual robots to enter specific modes, such as "navigating *to*pickup," "executing*pickup," "navigating*to*dropoff," or "charging." Once a robot is commanded into "navigating*to*pickup" mode, a lower-level continuous controller takes over. This controller is responsible for generating smooth velocity commands to follow the assigned path, using sensors like lidar and odometry to track its position and avoid dynamic obstacles not accounted for by the high-level planner. If the robot encounters an unexpected obstacle, it might signal back to the high-level manager (a discrete event) to re-plan its route or enter an "emergency*stop" mode, illustrating the feedback loop between the hierarchical layers. The discrete manager might then decide to switch the robot to a "re-routing" mode, activating a different continuous path-planning algorithm.

For systems where the discrete decisions are heavily dependent on precise state estimations and continuous dynamics, event-based control offers an intriguing alternative. Instead of operating on a fixed time schedule, event-based control systems trigger control actions only when certain events occur. These events can be related to the continuous state variables crossing specific thresholds, the detection of significant changes, or the completion of specific sub-tasks. This can lead to more efficient use of computational resources and faster responses to critical changes. For a hybrid system, this might translate to a continuous controller operating, for instance, until a certain error tolerance is reached, at which point a discrete event is generated to trigger a mode switch or a re-evaluation of the control strategy.

Consider a self-balancing robot. It operates in a continuous-time manner to maintain its balance. However, certain discrete events might dictate changes in its control strategy. For example, if the robot's tilt angle exceeds a predefined safety margin, an "emergency_stop" event is triggered, causing the continuous balancing controller to be disabled, and the robot to be commanded to fall safely or activate a braking mechanism. Conversely, if the robot successfully navigates a specific obstacle course segment (detected by its sensors, generating discrete events), the controller might switch to a more aggressive speed profile for the next segment.

The development of effective control strategies for hybrid systems is also closely intertwined with the system's model. The fidelity and accuracy of the hybrid automaton or equivalent model directly impact the controller's performance. If the model inaccurately captures the continuous dynamics within a mode, or if the guards and reset maps are not precisely defined, the resulting controller may exhibit unexpected behavior, instability, or fail to achieve the desired objectives. Techniques like system identification can be employed to refine the parameters of the continuous dynamics, while formal verification methods can help ensure that the discrete logic and transition conditions are robust.

Furthermore, the control of hybrid systems often involves uncertainties. These uncertainties can arise in the continuous dynamics (e.g., unmodeled friction, sensor noise) or in the discrete transitions (e.g., unreliable event detection). Robust control techniques must be employed to ensure satisfactory performance despite these uncertainties. This might involve designing controllers that are less sensitive to parameter variations or developing strategies that can adapt to changing conditions. For instance, in an electric vehicle charging system, uncertainties in the grid voltage or current measurements could affect the guards that trigger transitions between charging modes (e.g., fast charging, trickle charging). Robust controllers would need to account for potential measurement errors to avoid prematurely switching modes or, conversely, failing to switch when necessary.

The integration of learning capabilities into hybrid system control is a rapidly evolving area. Machine learning, particularly reinforcement learning, can be used to learn optimal control policies for hybrid systems, especially in complex environments where analytical modeling is difficult or incomplete. A reinforcement learning agent can learn to make both discrete mode-switching decisions and continuous control adjustments by interacting with the system (or a simulator) and receiving rewards based on its performance. For instance, in a robotic manipulation task involving grasping objects of varying shapes and sizes, a reinforcement learning agent could learn an optimal policy that decides when to switch from a "approach" mode to a "grasp" mode and, within the "grasp" mode, how to modulate finger forces based on sensory feedback. The agent would learn through trial and error, gradually improving its ability to balance the discrete decision of initiating a grasp with the continuous control of applying the appropriate force.

Another avenue is to use learning to adapt or fine-tune controllers designed using traditional methods. For example, a gain-scheduled controller might have its schedule optimized by a machine learning algorithm, or a model predictive controller's cost function weights could be learned to better align with user preferences or system objectives. This hybrid approach leverages the strengths of both analytical design and data-driven learning.

Consider a scenario in advanced robotics where a robot arm needs to perform delicate assembly tasks. The system has modes like "approach *part," "orient*part," "insert*part," and "release*part." While initial controllers can be designed based on the robot's kinematics and dynamics, the precise forces and timings required for successful insertion might vary subtly due to manufacturing tolerances of the parts. A reinforcement learning agent could be trained to observe tactile sensor feedback and visual cues, learning to fine-tune the continuous control within the "insert*part" mode or to decide whether to re-attempt the insertion by transitioning back to the "orient*part" mode if the initial attempt fails. This learning can happen online, adapting the robot's behavior to the specific parts it encounters during operation.

The control of hybrid systems is a rich and challenging field that draws upon diverse areas of control theory, logic, and optimization. The continuous evolution of system states within modes, coupled with the discrete jumps between these modes, presents a complex control landscape. Strategies ranging from mode-specific controllers and global optimization techniques like Hybrid MPC to hierarchical architectures and event-based control offer various ways to tackle this complexity. The effectiveness of any control strategy hinges critically on the quality of the hybrid system model. As we look to the future, the integration of machine learning and robust control principles will undoubtedly lead to even more sophisticated and adaptive control solutions for the ever-growing class of hybrid systems encountered in real-world applications.

The integration of learning into the control of hybrid systems opens up a powerful avenue for enhancing performance, adaptability, and robustness in systems exhibiting both continuous and discrete dynamics. While traditional control design relies heavily on analytical modeling and established control theory, learning-based approaches leverage data to infer system behavior, optimize control actions, and adapt to unforeseen circumstances. In the context of hybrid systems, this learning can manifest in several crucial ways: learning the transitions between discrete modes, learning optimal control policies within specific continuous modes, or a combination of both. The overarching goal is to imbue these complex systems with a degree of intelligence that allows them to operate more effectively and autonomously, particularly in dynamic and unpredictable environments.

One significant area where learning can be applied is in the learning of mode transitions. In many hybrid systems, the conditions governing switches between discrete modes are defined by predefined logical rules and guard conditions derived from a system model. However, these conditions might be simplifications of reality, or the underlying dynamics that influence these transitions might evolve over time. Learning techniques, especially those rooted in supervised or unsupervised learning from observational data, can be employed to infer these switching logic or refine existing ones. For instance, if a hybrid system operates in modes like "active" and "idle," and the transition from "active" to "idle" is governed by a threshold on a continuous state variable (e.g., power consumption), learning can be used to identify the optimal threshold from historical data that best captures when the system is truly inactive or requires a reset. Techniques like decision trees or support vector machines could learn the classification boundary that distinguishes between situations warranting a mode switch and those that do not, based on a rich set of observed continuous state variables. This is particularly relevant in systems where the "event" that triggers a discrete transition is not a sharp, easily measurable threshold but rather a more subtle, data-driven pattern. For example, in an automated manufacturing process, the decision to transition from an "inspection" mode to a "rework" mode might depend on a complex combination of sensor readings (e.g., visual, acoustic, force) that are not easily encapsulated by simple analytical guard conditions. A machine learning classifier, trained on data from successful and unsuccessful inspection outcomes, could learn to predict the likelihood of a defect with sufficient confidence to trigger the transition to "rework." This approach allows for more nuanced and data-informed mode switching, potentially leading to improved efficiency and reduced false positives or negatives.

Reinforcement learning (RL) offers a particularly potent framework for learning optimal control policies in hybrid systems, enabling the system to learn both discrete switching strategies and continuous control actions through interaction with its environment. In RL, an agent learns to make decisions by taking actions in an environment to maximize a cumulative reward signal. For hybrid systems, this translates to an RL agent learning a policy that dictates not only which control inputs to apply for the continuous dynamics within a mode but also when and to which mode to transition. The state space for such an RL agent would encompass both the continuous state variables and the current discrete mode of the hybrid system. The action space could be a combination of continuous control signals and discrete mode choices.

Consider a complex robotic system, such as a quadrupedal robot navigating challenging terrain. The robot's behavior can be decomposed into distinct modes, for instance, "standing," "walking," "trotting," and "jumping." Each of these modes involves intricate continuous dynamics governing the joint torques and leg trajectories. Furthermore, the transitions between these gaits (e.g., from "walking" to "trotting") are discrete events that must be triggered appropriately to maintain stability and efficiency. A reinforcement learning agent can be trained to learn a policy that optimally selects gaits and generates precise motor commands for each. The agent's state could include its current posture, velocity, orientation, and information about the terrain (e.g., incline, surface type). The actions would involve choosing a gait mode and applying specific torque commands to the robot's joints. Through trial and error, the agent could learn to transition seamlessly between gaits, for example, by initiating a "trot" when encountering a flatter, faster-moving section of terrain, or by switching to "standing" and then "jumping" to clear an obstacle. The reward function would be designed to encourage forward progress, maintain stability, and minimize energy consumption. This data-driven approach can discover control strategies that might be difficult to derive analytically, especially when dealing with highly non-linear dynamics and complex environmental interactions.

Another crucial application of learning in hybrid systems lies in adapting and optimizing controllers within specific continuous modes. Even when a nominal controller is designed for a particular mode, uncertainties in system parameters, external disturbances, or changes in operating conditions can degrade performance. Machine learning, particularly techniques like adaptive control and model learning, can be used to fine-tune these controllers or even learn entirely new ones. For example, if a hybrid system includes a mode for "cruise control" on a vehicle, the underlying continuous dynamics of engine response and aerodynamic drag might vary with factors like payload or wind speed. A learning algorithm could observe the vehicle's speed deviations and adjust the parameters of the cruise control's PID controller in real-time to maintain a more precise speed. This could involve learning an optimal gain schedule for the PID controller that adapts to different operating regimes within the "cruise control" mode.

Furthermore, learning can be employed to create models of the continuous dynamics within each mode, which can then be used by model-based control techniques such as Model Predictive Control (MPC). If the exact differential equations governing a mode are unknown or difficult to derive, machine learning models (e.g., neural networks, Gaussian processes) can be trained to approximate these dynamics based on collected data. These learned models can then be embedded within an MPC framework to predict future states and compute optimal control actions. For instance, in a chemical process with a "reaction" mode, where the reaction kinetics are complex and sensitive to temperature and pressure, a learned dynamics model could capture these non-linearities. This learned model would then be used by the MPC to predict how the concentrations of reactants and products evolve over time, allowing it to calculate optimal temperature and pressure setpoints to maximize yield while respecting safety constraints. The MPC, operating with the learned dynamics, can then decide on the continuous control signals required within the "reaction" mode, and its overall planning horizon can also incorporate potential switches to other modes like "separation" or "purification."

The challenge in applying learning to hybrid systems lies in ensuring that the learned behaviors are not only effective but also safe and coordinated across all operational modes and transitions. Unlike purely continuous systems where stability guarantees can be established through well-defined Lyapunov functions, the discrete jumps and mode switches in hybrid systems introduce additional complexities. A learned policy that optimizes performance within one mode might lead to instability or unsafe conditions when transitioning to another. Therefore, integrating learning with the hybrid system structure requires careful consideration.

One approach is to use learning to refine the discrete switching logic while keeping the continuous controllers analytically designed or separately learned. In this scenario, a learning algorithm might observe system trajectories and learn to predict the optimal time or condition for switching modes. For example, in a smart grid energy management system that switches between "grid-connected" and "islanded" modes based on grid stability, a learning agent could analyze sensor data to predict impending grid instability more accurately than fixed thresholds, thereby initiating the transition to "islanded" mode proactively and safely. The continuous controllers for managing energy flow within each mode would remain robustly designed.

Conversely, learning can focus on optimizing continuous controllers within modes, while the discrete mode selection adheres to established logic or a separate, more conservative learning mechanism. This is particularly useful when discrete transitions are critical for safety. For instance, in an autonomous vehicle, the mode switches for "autonomous driving" versus "manual override" are safety-critical. While the continuous control within "autonomous driving" (e.g., lane keeping, adaptive cruise control) could be refined by learning, the transition to "manual override" would likely be triggered by explicit driver input or predefined critical failure conditions, rather than purely learned heuristics. However, even in such cases, learning can play a role in making the autonomous system's behavior more predictable and comfortable, thereby reducing the likelihood of needing manual intervention.

A more integrated approach involves using reinforcement learning where the agent learns both the mode-switching policy and the continuous control policy simultaneously. This requires a carefully designed state representation and reward function that penalizes unsafe transitions or suboptimal performance across the entire hybrid system's operational envelope. For instance, if a robotic arm is tasked with assembling a complex product, a single RL agent could learn when to switch from a "picking" mode to a "placing" mode, and simultaneously learn the precise trajectory and force control within each mode. The reward function would be crafted to reward successful assembly while penalizing collisions, dropped parts, or excessive energy consumption. The state might include the position and orientation of the robot arm, the status of the part being manipulated, and visual feedback from cameras. The actions would be the selection of the next mode and the continuous control commands (e.g., joint velocities or torques). This end-to-end learning approach can potentially uncover highly optimized and synchronized behaviors that are difficult to achieve with separate learning or analytical designs.

The successful integration of learning into hybrid systems often necessitates techniques that can provide some level of safety guarantees or formal verification. While traditional machine learning can be a "black box," methods are emerging that allow for learning with safety constraints. For example, constrained reinforcement learning can incorporate explicit safety specifications into the learning process, ensuring that the learned policy never leads to unsafe states. This might involve defining a set of "forbidden" states or transitions and penalizing the agent heavily if it approaches them. Alternatively, formal methods can be used to verify the safety properties of a learned policy or to synthesize controllers that incorporate learned components while maintaining formal guarantees. This is crucial for safety-critical applications such as autonomous vehicles, medical robotics, or industrial automation.

Furthermore, the problem of learning in hybrid systems can be framed as learning a hybrid automaton itself. Instead of pre-defining the discrete modes and transition logic, learning algorithms can infer these structures from data. Techniques like learning finite automata or Markov decision processes can be adapted to learn the discrete components, while other methods can learn the continuous dynamics within identified modes. This discovery-driven approach is valuable when the underlying hybrid nature of a system is not fully understood or when the modes are emergent rather than pre-defined. For instance, analyzing the operational data of a complex manufacturing plant might reveal distinct operational regimes (modes) and the conditions under which the system transitions between them, which were not initially apparent from the system design.

In essence, learning transforms hybrid systems from passively following predefined rules to actively adapting and optimizing their behavior. It allows for the development of systems that are more resilient to uncertainties, more efficient in their operation, and capable of tackling increasingly complex tasks. Whether it's refining mode transitions, enhancing control within modes, or learning the entire hybrid control policy, the synergy between learning and hybrid systems is poised to drive significant advancements in artificial intelligence and autonomous systems across a multitude of domains, from robotics and autonomous vehicles to smart manufacturing and energy management. The ability to learn and adapt is no longer a luxury but a necessity for systems operating in the dynamic and multifaceted environments of the real world.

In the realm of modern automotive engineering, the paradigm of hybrid systems finds one of its most compelling and ubiquitous applications. Vehicles that combine internal combustion engines with electric powertrains, or even purely electric vehicles (EVs) with sophisticated energy management, are inherently hybrid in their operational structure. These systems are characterized by distinct operating modes—such as pure electric driving, hybrid driving (engine and motor working together), engine-only driving, battery charging, and various levels of regenerative braking—and by the complex, often non-linear, continuous dynamics that govern vehicle motion, powertrain operation, and energy storage. The seamless and efficient management of transitions between these modes, along with the optimization of continuous control within each mode, presents a rich landscape for the application of hybrid control theory and, crucially, for the integration of learning-based techniques.

Consider, for instance, a conventional hybrid electric vehicle (HEV). At its core, an HEV can be conceptualized as a hybrid automaton. The discrete states, or modes, might include: "engine running," "electric motor running," "engine and motor running in parallel," "engine charging the battery," "regenerative braking (battery charging)," and "auxiliary systems only (engine off, motor off)." The transitions between these modes are governed by a set of logical rules and guard conditions that depend on a variety of continuous state variables. These variables typically include the vehicle's speed, acceleration, battery state of charge (SoC), driver's torque demand (throttle position), engine speed, electric motor speed, and battery temperature. For example, a transition from "engine running" to "engine and motor running" might be triggered when the driver demands more acceleration than the engine alone can provide, while the battery SoC is sufficiently high. Conversely, a transition to "engine charging the battery" might occur when the SoC drops below a certain threshold during low-demand driving conditions.

The continuous dynamics within each mode are equally complex. In "electric motor running" mode, the dynamics involve the electrical characteristics of the motor, the power electronics, the battery output capability, and the mechanical powertrain connecting the motor to the wheels, all interacting with vehicle inertia and external forces like aerodynamic drag and rolling resistance. In "engine running" mode, the dynamics are governed by the internal combustion engine's fuel injection, ignition timing, and torque production characteristics, also coupled to the powertrain and vehicle dynamics. When both are active, the interaction between the two propulsion sources, and their respective controllers, adds another layer of complexity.

The challenge for automotive engineers is to design a control system that manages these modes and dynamics to achieve multiple, often conflicting, objectives: maximizing fuel economy (or energy efficiency for EVs), minimizing emissions, providing desired driving performance (acceleration, responsiveness), ensuring passenger comfort, and maintaining the longevity of the battery and other components. Traditional control strategies often rely on rule-based systems, lookup tables, and predefined logic developed through extensive simulation and empirical testing. While effective to a degree, these methods can struggle with the inherent uncertainties in real-world driving conditions—variations in road gradient, traffic flow, ambient temperature, tire wear, and aging of components—and may not always achieve optimal performance across the full spectrum of operational scenarios.

This is where the integration of learning, particularly artificial intelligence and machine learning, offers a transformative approach. By leveraging data collected from vehicle operation, learning algorithms can infer more accurate models of system behavior, discover optimal control policies, and adapt to changing conditions in ways that are difficult to pre-program.

One key area for AI application is in optimizing the mode transitions. The predefined guard conditions and switching logic in traditional HEVs are often designed for robustness and safety, but they might not always represent the most efficient or comfortable way to switch. For instance, a sudden engagement of the internal combustion engine can be jarring and inefficient if not managed smoothly. Machine learning algorithms, such as those based on reinforcement learning or supervised learning from large datasets of driving scenarios, can learn to predict the optimal timing and manner of mode transitions.

For example, a reinforcement learning agent could be trained to control the transitions in a parallel hybrid powertrain. The state space for this agent would include current vehicle speed, acceleration, driver's torque demand, battery SoC, engine status (on/off, speed, load), and motor status (speed, torque). The actions would involve decisions like: engage engine, disengage engine, increase/decrease engine load, adjust motor torque, or initiate regenerative braking. The reward function would be designed to penalize fuel consumption and emissions, reward smooth transitions (e.g., by penalizing abrupt changes in acceleration or engine noise), and ensure that the battery SoC remains within a desired operating range. Through millions of simulated or real-world driving cycles, the agent could learn a policy that minimizes fuel use while providing a seamless driving experience, potentially discovering transition strategies that human engineers might not have explicitly considered. For instance, it might learn to preemptively engage the engine slightly before a steep incline is encountered, based on subtle cues in the driver's throttle input, to ensure sufficient power delivery without a sudden surge.

Another significant application is in optimizing the continuous control within specific modes, especially concerning energy management. In a battery electric vehicle (BEV), the effective range and performance are heavily dependent on how intelligently the regenerative braking system is managed. Regenerative braking captures kinetic energy during deceleration and converts it back into electrical energy to recharge the battery. However, the optimal level of regeneration is not constant. It depends on the current battery SoC, temperature, the driver's deceleration demand, and even upcoming road conditions (e.g., anticipating a long downhill stretch).

AI can be employed to learn a dynamic and adaptive regenerative braking strategy. A model-based predictive control (MPC) framework, augmented with learned dynamics models, is a powerful approach here. Machine learning models, such as Gaussian Processes or neural networks, can learn the complex, non-linear relationship between battery current, voltage, temperature, SoC, and the efficiency of energy recuperation. This learned model can then be fed into an MPC controller. The MPC would predict the vehicle's trajectory and energy demand over a short future horizon, considering factors like upcoming speed limit changes, traffic light predictions (if connectivity is available), and the driver's braking input. Based on these predictions and the learned battery dynamics, the MPC could then compute an optimal braking torque profile that maximizes energy recuperation while ensuring the vehicle decelerates as intended and avoids overcharging the battery.

Furthermore, AI can learn driver behavior patterns. If the system learns that a particular driver frequently brakes at a certain point before a common intersection, it can proactively adjust the regenerative braking profile to capture more energy without surprising the driver. This learning can be achieved by analyzing historical driving data, correlating braking events with subsequent actions and vehicle states. Techniques like Recurrent Neural Networks (RNNs) or Long Short-Term Memory (LSTM) networks are well-suited for this temporal pattern recognition.

The concept of "one-pedal driving," where a strong regenerative braking effect is applied when the driver lifts their foot off the accelerator, is a feature that can be significantly enhanced with learning. Instead of a fixed regeneration strength, an AI system could learn to modulate this strength based on the immediate context. For example, if the system detects a rapid change in the accelerator pedal position indicative of a deliberate stop, it might apply stronger regeneration. Conversely, if it detects a slight lift-off during steady cruising, it might apply minimal regeneration to avoid unintended deceleration.

Beyond pure electric and conventional hybrids, consider plug-in hybrid electric vehicles (PHEVs) and advanced battery management systems. PHEVs can operate in multiple modes, including extended electric-only driving, hybrid mode, and engine-only mode, with the ability to charge the battery from the grid. The optimal strategy for PHEVs involves deciding when to use electric power, when to engage the engine, and critically, when to charge the battery. This decision-making is influenced by factors such as the current electricity price, the predicted cost of gasoline, the duration and route of the upcoming trip, and the driver's charging habits.

An AI-powered energy management system for a PHEV could learn these external factors and the driver's preferences to make optimal decisions. For instance, if the system knows that electricity prices are low overnight and high during the day, and the driver typically charges at home, it would prioritize charging the battery overnight. If the system also learns the typical commute duration and predicts that the driver will need the full electric range for the morning commute, it might choose to delay charging until later or even use the engine on the return trip if electricity prices are predicted to be high. This is a complex optimization problem that can be tackled with techniques like dynamic programming or reinforcement learning, where the state includes not only the vehicle's internal states (SoC, fuel level) but also external information (electricity prices, traffic conditions, weather).

In advanced battery management, learning plays a crucial role in estimating critical parameters like State of Health (SoH) and State of Power (SoP). These parameters are essential for predicting battery degradation, ensuring safety, and optimizing performance. Traditional methods often rely on empirical models or simplified electrochemical models. Machine learning, however, can build highly accurate models of battery behavior by learning from large datasets of voltage, current, temperature, and cycling history. Neural networks, for example, can be trained to predict SoH and SoP with remarkable accuracy, allowing the vehicle's control system to adjust charging and discharging rates to prolong battery life and prevent performance fade.

Moreover, AI can enhance the thermal management of vehicle components, including the battery, motor, and power electronics. Maintaining these components within their optimal temperature ranges is critical for efficiency, performance, and longevity. An AI controller can learn the thermal dynamics of the entire system, considering factors like ambient temperature, solar radiation, driving intensity, and the state of operation of different components. Based on this learned understanding, it can proactively manage cooling systems (e.g., fans, pumps, refrigerant circuits) to pre-condition the battery for optimal charging or performance, or to dissipate heat effectively during demanding driving conditions, thereby avoiding thermal throttling and ensuring consistent performance.

The integration of learning into automotive hybrid systems also extends to enhancing the user experience and safety. For example, learning systems can adapt the vehicle's driving characteristics to the driver's preferences. If a driver consistently prefers a more aggressive acceleration response or a softer braking feel, the AI can learn these preferences and adjust the powertrain and braking control parameters accordingly. This personalization can make the driving experience more intuitive and enjoyable.

From a safety perspective, AI can analyze sensor data to predict potential hazards and proactively assist the driver or take mitigating actions. This is particularly relevant for advanced driver-assistance systems (ADAS) and autonomous driving features, which are themselves sophisticated hybrid systems combining sensing, perception, planning, and control. For instance, in a semi-autonomous driving mode, the system might learn to anticipate sudden braking by vehicles ahead based on their acceleration patterns and distance. This predictive capability allows the hybrid control system to initiate its own braking or deceleration earlier and more smoothly than a reactive system, improving safety and passenger comfort.

The development and deployment of these AI-enhanced hybrid control systems in automotive applications face several challenges. One is the need for vast amounts of high-quality data for training. Vehicles generate a wealth of data, but collecting and labeling it appropriately for specific learning tasks can be a significant undertaking. Another challenge is ensuring the robustness and safety of learned policies. Unlike traditional, analytically derived controllers, learned policies can sometimes exhibit unexpected behaviors in novel situations. Therefore, rigorous testing, validation, and the development of safety guarantees for AI-controlled systems are paramount. Techniques like formal verification of neural networks, constrained reinforcement learning, and extensive real-world testing are crucial.

Furthermore, computational resources onboard vehicles are limited. Complex AI models require efficient implementation and often hardware acceleration. Model compression, quantization, and optimized inference engines are necessary to deploy these models in real-time within the vehicle's electronic control units (ECUs).

Despite these challenges, the trajectory of automotive technology clearly points towards an increasing reliance on hybrid systems and AI. From managing the intricate interplay of electric motors and internal combustion engines to optimizing the flow of energy within sophisticated battery systems, the principles of hybrid control, empowered by machine learning, are at the forefront of innovation. These technologies are not merely about improving efficiency; they are about creating vehicles that are more intelligent, more adaptable, safer, and ultimately, more in tune with the needs of drivers and the environment. The automotive industry is, in essence, becoming a living laboratory for the practical, large-scale application of advanced hybrid control and learning systems.

Chapter 12: Integrating Learning and Control: Frameworks and Architectures

The integration of learning, particularly through machine learning and artificial intelligence (AI), with classical control theory represents a profound evolution in engineering design. For decades, control systems have relied on analytical models derived from first principles and extensive empirical data to predict system behavior and devise strategies for stabilization and optimization. While immensely successful, these traditional approaches often encounter limitations when faced with highly complex, non-linear, or ill-defined systems, or when operating conditions exhibit significant variability and uncertainty. This is precisely where the synergy with learning becomes not just beneficial, but essential.

Learning algorithms excel at discerning intricate patterns and relationships within vast datasets, often surpassing human intuition and analytical capabilities. This innate ability allows AI to construct remarkably accurate models of system dynamics, even for phenomena that are analytically intractable or difficult to model explicitly. For instance, in a complex industrial process with numerous interacting variables and subtle, time-varying behaviors, a traditional control engineer might struggle to develop a comprehensive mathematical model. A machine learning approach, such as training a deep neural network on historical operational data, can implicitly learn these underlying dynamics. This learned model can then be used to represent the system's behavior, providing a more faithful basis for control design than a simplified analytical model might offer. This enhanced model accuracy is the bedrock upon which improved control performance is built. By understanding the system's nuances with greater fidelity, controllers can be designed to achieve tighter regulation, faster response times, and reduced deviations from desired setpoints.

Beyond mere model approximation, learning imbues control systems with the crucial capability of adaptation. Real-world systems are rarely static. Components age, environmental conditions fluctuate, and unexpected disturbances arise. Classical controllers, unless specifically designed with adaptive mechanisms (which themselves can be complex to tune and guarantee stability for), often struggle to cope with these shifts. Machine learning, particularly through techniques like online learning or reinforcement learning, can enable controllers to continuously update their understanding of the system and adjust their strategies accordingly. Imagine a robotic manipulator tasked with precise assembly in a dynamic manufacturing environment. If unforeseen variations occur in the positioning of parts, or if the friction characteristics of the joints change over time due to wear, a purely pre-programmed controller might fail. An adaptive learning-based controller, however, could detect these discrepancies, update its internal model of the robot's kinematics and dynamics, and modify its control commands in real-time to maintain performance. This resilience in the face of uncertainty is a hallmark of learning-enhanced control.

Furthermore, learning-based approaches can unlock levels of performance optimization that are often beyond the reach of traditional methods. Classical control design typically focuses on achieving robustness and meeting specified performance criteria, often under worst-case scenarios or defined operating ranges. However, achieving optimal performance across all possible operating conditions, especially in systems with multiple, potentially conflicting objectives (e.g., maximizing energy efficiency while minimizing response time), can be exceedingly difficult using purely analytical techniques. Reinforcement learning, for instance, excels at exploring a wide range of control strategies through trial and error (often in simulation first) and discovering policies that maximize a cumulative reward function. This reward function can be carefully crafted to balance various performance metrics. For example, in the control of a complex chemical reactor, a reinforcement learning agent could learn a policy that optimizes product yield and minimizes energy consumption by intelligently adjusting temperature, pressure, and reactant flow rates. The learned policy might involve subtle, non-intuitive control actions that are highly effective in specific operational regimes, leading to significant gains in efficiency or throughput.

The ability of machine learning to handle high-dimensional data is another significant advantage. Modern engineering systems are increasingly instrumented, generating vast streams of data from numerous sensors. Traditional control techniques can become computationally prohibitive or analytically intractable when dealing with such high-dimensional state and input spaces. Machine learning algorithms, especially deep learning architectures, are inherently designed to process and extract meaningful information from large, complex datasets. This allows for the development of controllers that can leverage a much richer set of information to make more informed decisions. Consider a fleet of autonomous vehicles. Each vehicle generates data related to its own state, its environment, and its interactions with other agents. An AI-driven control system could learn from this collective data to develop sophisticated coordination strategies, optimize traffic flow across the entire fleet, and enhance overall safety and efficiency, a task that would be practically impossible with traditional, low-dimensional control models.

However, the integration is not a one-way street; control theory offers indispensable foundations that are often nascent or absent in pure machine learning applications. One of the most critical contributions of control theory is the provision of formal tools for stability analysis.

When designing a control system, ensuring that the system remains stable—that it does not diverge uncontrollably—is paramount. Classical control theory provides well-established methodologies, such as Lyapunov stability analysis, Nyquist stability criterion, and root locus analysis, to rigorously prove the stability of a proposed controller. While reinforcement learning agents can learn effective policies, proving their stability in the presence of disturbances or under conditions outside their training data can be extremely challenging. Control theory provides the framework to rigorously assess and guarantee these essential properties.

Control theory also provides systematic design methodologies for achieving specific performance objectives. Techniques like PID control, H-infinity control, and model predictive control (MPC) offer structured ways to design controllers that meet predefined performance specifications, such as rise time, overshoot, and steady-state error. While AI can discover optimal parameters or even entire policies, it often does so in a black-box manner. Control theory can help translate desired performance metrics into tangible design specifications, which can then guide the learning process or provide a baseline against which learned policies can be evaluated and refined. For instance, an MPC controller, which inherently incorporates prediction and optimization over a future horizon, can benefit from learned models of system dynamics. The MPC framework itself, rooted in control theory, provides guarantees on performance and stability under certain conditions, which are then enhanced by the accuracy of the learned model.

Moreover, control theory is instrumental in ensuring robustness against uncertainties and disturbances. Explicit robustness analysis techniques allow engineers to quantify how much uncertainty a control system can tolerate before performance degrades unacceptably or instability arises.

This is vital for safety-critical systems where predictable behavior is non-negotiable. While machine learning can implicitly learn to cope with some uncertainty, control theory provides the tools to explicitly design for and analyze this robustness. For example, a control system designed using robust control techniques might guarantee performance within a defined range of parameter variations. If a machine learning component is introduced to fine-tune the controller, control theory can help ensure that the learned adjustments do not violate these fundamental robustness guarantees.

The combination of learning and control allows for a powerful paradigm shift: hybrid systems that leverage the strengths of both disciplines. In such systems, machine learning might be used to construct a highly accurate, adaptive model of a complex, non-linear plant. This learned model can then be embedded within a formal control framework, such as an MPC controller. The MPC would utilize the learned model to predict future system behavior and optimize control actions over a receding horizon, while the inherent structure of the MPC provides stability and performance guarantees. This creates a control system that is both highly performant and adaptable, thanks to the learned model, and rigorously designed and provably stable, thanks to the MPC framework.

Another manifestation of this synergy is in the realm of reinforcement learning with safety constraints. Standard reinforcement learning might lead an agent to discover highly efficient but potentially unsafe strategies. By incorporating concepts from robust control and formal methods, it is possible to constrain the learning process. For example, techniques like constrained reinforcement learning can be used, where the reward function is augmented with penalties for violating safety constraints, or where the state-space exploration is guided by stability principles derived from control theory. This ensures that the learned policy is not only optimal but also adheres to critical safety specifications.

Consider the example of autonomous driving. A perception system, powered by deep learning, identifies objects and predicts their trajectories. This high-dimensional, data-driven output is then fed into a motion planning and control system. While the perception is inherently learned, the planning and control layers can be designed using classical control principles, perhaps augmented with learned elements. For instance, a model predictive controller could use the perceived information to predict future states and optimize control commands (steering, acceleration, braking) while ensuring passenger comfort and adhering to traffic laws. If the learned perception model is slightly inaccurate, the robust nature of the MPC can help mitigate the consequences. Conversely, if the traditional planner struggles to adapt to dynamic traffic scenarios, a learning component could be introduced to adapt the planner's parameters or even learn entire sub-policies for specific maneuvers.

In essence, the synergy between learning and control creates a virtuous cycle. Learning provides the ability to model complex realities and discover novel, high-performing strategies. Control theory provides the framework to ensure that these strategies are safe, stable, robust, and meet predefined engineering specifications. By weaving these two domains together, engineers can design next-generation intelligent systems capable of tackling challenges that were previously insurmountable. This integration moves beyond simply applying AI to existing control problems; it represents a fundamental re-imagining of how intelligent control systems are conceived, designed, and validated, promising significant advancements across a vast spectrum of engineering disciplines. The future of advanced control lies in this intelligent fusion, where the data-driven insights of learning are grounded by the rigorous foundations of control theory.

The landscape of intelligent control systems is increasingly being shaped by architectures that harness the power of data, moving beyond purely analytical or first-principles modeling. These data-driven control architectures offer a spectrum of approaches, from those that entirely replace traditional control logic with learned models to those that judiciously augment existing frameworks with AI capabilities. Understanding these architectural paradigms is crucial for effectively integrating learning into control systems, ensuring both performance gains and the preservation of essential engineering properties like stability and robustness.

One of the most direct approaches involves purely data-driven controllers. In this paradigm, a machine learning model, typically a neural network or a Gaussian Process, is trained to directly map system states and desired setpoints to control actions. The controller essentially learns a function $u = f(x, r)$, where u is the control input, x is the system state, and r is the reference input or desired setpoint. This approach is particularly attractive for systems where obtaining an accurate analytical model is exceedingly difficult or impossible, such as in highly complex biological systems, intricate material processing, or systems with significant unmodeled dynamics. For instance, consider a complex manufacturing process involving a delicate chemical reaction where precise thermodynamic and kinetic models are hard to formulate due to numerous interacting variables and complex reaction pathways. A direct neural network controller could be trained on historical operational data, observing how different control inputs (e.g., temperature, pressure, reactant feed rates) correlated with desired outcomes (e.g., product purity, reaction yield). The trained network then acts as the controller, directly outputting the necessary adjustments to achieve the desired product quality.

However, purely data-driven controllers face significant challenges. A primary concern is the guarantee of stability and robustness. Without an explicit underlying model, it can be very difficult to mathematically prove that the learned controller will maintain stability under all possible operating conditions, especially in the presence of disturbances or sensor noise. Generalization is another hurdle; a controller trained on a specific dataset might perform poorly when faced with novel situations not represented in its training data. Furthermore, interpretability can be an issue. Understanding
why a neural network produces a particular control command can be challenging, making debugging and validation more complex compared to model-based controllers where the decision-making process is more transparent. Despite these challenges, purely data-driven controllers are a vibrant area of research, often coupled with techniques that attempt to embed some level of safety or stability guarantees, perhaps through constrained optimization during training or by using architectures designed for better generalization.

Moving along the spectrum, hybrid architectures offer a more pragmatic and often more robust integration of learning. These approaches leverage the strengths of both traditional control theory and machine learning, creating systems that are both intelligent and reliable. One prominent hybrid architecture involves learning residual dynamics. In this setup, a classical controller, perhaps a PID or a linear quadratic regulator (LQR), is designed based on a simplified or approximate linear model of the system. The actual system, however, is non-linear and complex. The discrepancy between the simplified model and the true system dynamics is then learned by a machine learning model, often a neural network, which estimates the "residual" or unmodeled dynamics. This residual can then be used to augment the output of the classical controller. If $u *{classical}$ is the control signal from the traditional controller and $u*{residual}$ is the output of the learned model estimating the unmodeled dynamics, the total control input becomes $u = u*{classical} + u*{residual}$.

This residual learning approach is powerful because it allows engineers to build upon well-understood classical control design principles while still capturing complex non-linearities and uncertainties. The classical controller provides a baseline level of performance and stability, often designed with robustness in mind. The learned residual then fine-tunes the control action, compensating for the inaccuracies of the simplified model. For example, in controlling a robotic arm, an LQR controller might be designed for nominal operating conditions. However, friction, gravity effects, and joint flexibility can significantly deviate the arm's behavior from the linear model. A neural network trained to predict the error between the LQR's commanded motion and the actual motion can then generate a correction term, $u_{residual}$, which is added to the LQR's output. This hybrid approach can lead to significantly improved tracking performance and disturbance rejection without sacrificing fundamental stability guarantees derived from the LQR design. The training of the residual model can be done offline using recorded data or, in some cases, online.

Another significant hybrid architecture involves adaptive controllers with learned adaptation rules. Classical adaptive control systems adjust controller parameters online to cope with changing system dynamics. However, the rules for updating these parameters are often derived analytically and can be conservative or limited in their ability to track rapid changes. In a data-driven adaptive architecture, machine learning models are employed to learn these adaptation rules. This could involve learning an explicit mapping from observed system behavior to the required parameter updates, or using reinforcement learning to discover optimal adaptation policies. For instance, consider a system where wear and tear gradually alter its characteristics, such as a hydraulic actuator where seal wear increases leakage. A traditional adaptive controller might slowly adjust its gains to compensate. An AI-enhanced adaptive controller could analyze sensor data (e.g., flow rates, pressure drops) and learn a more sophisticated, faster adaptation rule. A neural network could be trained to predict how much each controller parameter needs to change based on the current state and the observed deviation from the desired behavior. This learned adaptation mechanism can be more agile and effective in tracking time-varying dynamics, leading to consistently better performance over the system's lifetime.

The realm of Model Predictive Control (MPC) has also seen substantial benefits from data-driven integration, leading to AI-enhanced MPC architectures. MPC relies on an explicit model of the system to predict its future behavior over a finite horizon and then computes an optimal sequence of control inputs by solving an optimization problem. The performance of MPC is critically dependent on the accuracy of this predictive model. When the true system dynamics are complex, non-linear, or uncertain, the predictive model used in standard MPC might be inadequate. Data-driven MPC addresses this by incorporating learned models into the MPC framework.

One way this is achieved is by using a machine learning model as the predictive model within the MPC optimization. Instead of a traditional analytical state-space model, a neural network or a Gaussian Process is trained to predict the system's next state given the current state and control input: $x_{k+1} = f_{learned}(x_k, u_k)$. This learned model is then embedded within the MPC's prediction horizon. The optimization problem at each time step then becomes:

$$ \min{uk, \dots, u{k+N-1}} \sum{i=0}^{N-1} \left(x{k+i} - r{k+i} \right)^T Q \left(x{k+i} - r{k+i} \right) + u{k+i}^T R u{k+i} $$
subject to:
$x{k+i+1} = f{learned}(x{k+i}, u{k+i})$ for $i=0, \dots, N-1$
and any other system constraints.

This approach allows MPC to leverage the accuracy of data-driven models while retaining the systematic optimization and constraint handling capabilities inherent to MPC. For example, in controlling a power grid with renewable energy sources, the unpredictable nature of wind and solar power makes accurate prediction challenging. An AI-enhanced MPC could use a learned model for wind speed and solar irradiance forecasting, which then feeds into a learned model of the power plant's output and grid dynamics. The MPC would then optimize dispatch decisions to maintain grid stability and meet demand, all based on these more accurate, data-driven predictions.

Another AI-enhancement to MPC involves learning components of the cost function or constraints. The tuning of the weighting matrices (Q and R) in the MPC cost function can significantly impact performance. Machine learning can be used to learn optimal tuning parameters that adapt to different operating regimes or user preferences, effectively making the cost function itself data-driven. Similarly, learned models can be used to define complex state or input constraints that are hard to express analytically, such as dynamic safety envelopes derived from real-world accident data.

Beyond these specific architectural paradigms, broader trends are emerging. The concept of "learning to control" rather than "learning a model to control" is gaining traction. This often manifests through reinforcement learning (RL), where an agent learns a control policy directly through interaction with the environment, aiming to maximize a cumulative reward signal. While pure RL controllers can fall under the purely data-driven category, they can also be integrated into hybrid architectures. For instance, an RL agent could be used to learn the optimal parameters for a classical controller, or to learn a supervisory policy that switches between different classical controllers based on the operating condition.

Furthermore, there is a growing interest in architectures that explicitly manage uncertainty. Techniques like robust learning, Bayesian neural networks, or Gaussian Processes for control can provide not only predictions of system behavior but also measures of uncertainty associated with those predictions. This uncertainty information can then be explicitly used by the control architecture. For example, in an AI-enhanced MPC, if the learned predictive model has high uncertainty for a particular future state, the MPC might choose a more conservative control action or fall back to a robust backup controller. This allows for a more principled approach to safety and reliability in data-driven control systems.

The choice of architecture is paramount and depends heavily on the specific application, the availability of data, the criticality of safety and stability, and the desired level of performance. Purely data-driven controllers offer the highest potential for uncovering novel control strategies in highly complex systems but often come with significant challenges in validation and certification. Hybrid architectures, such as residual learning or AI-enhanced MPC, strike a balance, leveraging the power of data to improve upon established control paradigms while retaining much of their analytical rigor and guarantees. As our ability to collect and process data continues to advance, and as machine learning techniques become more sophisticated and interpretable, we can expect to see increasingly innovative and effective data-driven control architectures emerge, pushing the boundaries of what is possible in autonomous systems, robotics, industrial automation, and beyond. The future of control engineering will undoubtedly be characterized by the intelligent fusion of data-driven insights with the foundational principles of control theory.

The complexity inherent in managing and controlling large-scale, multi-agent, or multi-objective systems often necessitates a departure from monolithic control designs. Hierarchical control structures provide an elegant solution by decomposing a complex control problem into a series of nested levels, each responsible for a distinct scope of decision-making and control execution. At the highest levels, decisions are strategic and long-term, dealing with overarching goals and resource allocation. As one descends the hierarchy, the scope becomes more tactical and operational, focusing on shorter time horizons, more specific objectives, and finer-grained control actions. Integrating machine learning into such hierarchical frameworks opens up new avenues for enhanced performance, adaptability, and autonomy, allowing for the automation of strategic planning and adaptive execution that was previously the domain of human operators.

In a typical hierarchical control architecture, the top level might be concerned with overall mission planning or high-level task allocation. For instance, in an autonomous fleet of delivery drones, the highest layer could be responsible for deciding which drone should serve which customer based on factors like proximity, battery life, current workload, and predicted traffic patterns. This decision-making process can be significantly enhanced by machine learning. A learned policy, perhaps developed through reinforcement learning or trained on historical fleet performance data, could optimize these high-level assignments to maximize overall delivery efficiency and minimize response times across the entire fleet. This top-level learning module doesn't need to know the intricate details of how each drone flies; its focus is on strategic deployment and resource management. Its output would be a set of high-level commands or objectives for the level below.

The intermediate levels of the hierarchy would then translate these broad objectives into more concrete plans. If the top level has assigned a drone to a specific delivery route, an intermediate level might be responsible for generating a detailed flight path, considering airspace regulations, predicted weather conditions along the route, and potential obstacles. Machine learning can play a crucial role here as well, for example, by learning to predict optimal cruising speeds or altitudes that minimize energy consumption while adhering to time constraints. More sophisticated learning approaches could even dynamically re-plan routes mid-flight if unforeseen circumstances arise, such as sudden weather changes or the emergence of new airspace restrictions, based on real-time sensor data and learned predictive models. This level operates with a more detailed understanding of the environment but still within a defined set of objectives passed down from above.

Finally, the lowest level of the hierarchy is responsible for the actual physical execution of control commands. This typically involves low-level controllers, such as PID controllers, state-space controllers, or other classical control algorithms, tasked with ensuring the stable operation of actuators, precise trajectory tracking, and immediate response to sensor feedback. For the delivery drone example, this level would be responsible for actuating the motors to follow the planned trajectory, maintaining attitude stability, and executing take-off and landing maneuvers. While these low-level controllers are often designed using traditional engineering principles for guaranteed stability and robustness, machine learning can also be integrated here to fine-tune their performance. For example, a learned model could predict and compensate for actuator nonlinearities, sensor noise, or environmental disturbances (like wind gusts) that affect the precise execution of control commands. This learned compensation acts as a fine-tuning layer, augmenting the robust but potentially suboptimal performance of the classical controller.

One of the key advantages of integrating learning into hierarchical control is the ability to achieve a separation of concerns that simplifies design and improves modularity. The strategic decisions at the top are handled by a learning system that can adapt to changing global objectives or environmental conditions, while the low-level control remains grounded in well-established principles of stability and robustness, often augmented by learned elements for enhanced performance. This separation allows engineers to focus on designing and validating each level independently, drawing on different sets of tools and expertise. For instance, the mission planner (high-level) might be developed by AI specialists, while the flight controller (low-level) is designed by control engineers. The interface between these levels then becomes critical, defining how objectives and feedback are communicated.

Consider the application in advanced robotics, specifically in collaborative manipulation tasks. A hierarchical system might assign roles and sub-tasks to multiple robotic arms. The top-level planner, potentially a learned system, could decide which arm should pick up a certain object, which should hold a fixture, and which should perform the assembly operation, based on factors like reachability, dexterity, and the current state of the workpiece. This planner might use a form of imitation learning, trained on demonstrations of expert human assembly, or reinforcement learning, exploring different task allocations to optimize assembly time or success rate.

The intermediate levels would then decompose these high-level task assignments into specific motions. If one robot arm is tasked with picking up a bolt, the next level might generate a precise trajectory for its gripper to approach, grasp, and lift the bolt. This motion planning could involve learned path generation techniques that consider the robot's kinematic constraints and the spatial configuration of its environment, possibly informed by learned models of object dynamics or interaction forces. Machine learning can help in generating smoother, more efficient, and collision-free paths, especially in cluttered environments.

At the lowest level, classical controllers ensure that each joint of the robotic arm follows the generated trajectory accurately and stably. However, to achieve highly precise and dexterous manipulation, the classical controller might be augmented by learned compensation for unmodeled dynamics, such as joint friction, backlash, or the compliance of the object being manipulated. A neural network could learn to predict the forces exerted by the object on the gripper, allowing the controller to adjust its actions to maintain stable contact and perform delicate tasks like inserting a screw or aligning two components. The overall system benefits from the strategic intelligence of the learned planner, the sophisticated path generation of the learned motion planner, and the precise, robust execution of the learned-augmented low-level controllers.

Another compelling example is in the domain of smart grids, where optimizing energy generation, distribution, and consumption is a highly complex, multi-objective problem. A hierarchical control architecture can be employed, with different layers managing distinct aspects of the grid. At the highest level, a learning agent could act as a market operator or a grid scheduler, making decisions about which power sources (e.g., renewable, fossil fuel, storage) to dispatch to meet demand, considering economic factors, environmental impact, and grid stability constraints. This scheduler might learn optimal bidding strategies in energy markets or develop predictive models for renewable energy generation to minimize reliance on less desirable sources.

Intermediate layers could focus on regional grid management or specific types of assets. For instance, a subsystem might manage a portfolio of solar farms, learning to optimize their collective output based on weather forecasts and grid demand signals. Another layer might manage a network of electric vehicle charging stations, learning to schedule charging times to minimize peak load on the grid while satisfying user charging needs. These layers would translate the global objectives from the top into more localized control strategies.

The lowest level of this smart grid hierarchy would involve direct control of individual components, such as voltage regulators, capacitor banks, or smart inverters of distributed energy resources. Here, classical control algorithms would ensure local stability and power quality. However, machine learning can be used to enhance their adaptiveness and efficiency. For example, a learned controller could adapt the settings of a voltage regulator based on learned patterns of load fluctuations in a specific neighborhood, or optimize the charging profile of a battery storage system to maximize its lifespan and economic return based on learned usage patterns and electricity price forecasts. The integration of learning across these hierarchical levels enables the smart grid to operate more autonomously, efficiently, and resiliently in the face of fluctuating demand and supply.

The concept of hierarchical reinforcement learning (HRL) is particularly relevant here. HRL breaks down a complex task into a hierarchy of policies, where higher-level policies learn to set goals or sub-tasks for lower-level policies, which then learn how to achieve those goals. This offers a structured way to tackle problems with long time horizons and sparse rewards, which are common in many complex autonomous systems. In an HRL framework for a robot navigating a large building, a high-level policy might learn to set navigation sub-goals (e.g., "reach the elevator," "go to room 301"), while lower-level policies learn the primitive motor commands required to achieve these sub-goals, such as steering, speed control, and obstacle avoidance. This is a direct application of hierarchical control principles where learning is embedded at multiple levels of abstraction.

The communication and coordination between different levels in a hierarchical control system are critical design considerations. In learning-augmented hierarchies, this communication often involves transmitting abstract commands, goals, or desired states from higher levels to lower levels, and relaying feedback, status, or performance metrics from lower levels to higher levels. Machine learning can also be used to optimize this inter-level communication, for example, by learning the optimal level of detail or granularity for information transfer to maximize overall system performance without overwhelming either the decision-making or execution capabilities of any particular level.

For instance, a top-level strategic planner might only need to know the aggregate performance of a fleet of robots (e.g., average task completion rate, total energy consumed), rather than the precise state and control actions of each individual robot. This abstraction reduces the computational burden on the high-level planner and allows it to focus on broader strategic objectives. Conversely, a low-level controller needs detailed, real-time information about the system's state and immediate environment to ensure safe and effective execution. The learning components can help in defining these effective communication protocols.

Another significant aspect is the potential for emergent behavior and robust adaptation. When learning is integrated at multiple levels of a hierarchy, the system can exhibit a remarkable ability to adapt to unforeseen circumstances and achieve complex objectives. A high-level learned policy can re-strategize based on global performance metrics or environmental changes, while lower-level learned components can fine-tune their execution to compensate for local disturbances or variations. This layered approach to adaptation allows for both strategic and tactical flexibility. If a high-level objective (e.g., "maximize production output") becomes unattainable due to a major external factor (e.g., a supply chain disruption), the top-level planner can learn to adjust the objective itself (e.g., switch to a "minimize waste" objective), and the lower levels will then adapt their execution accordingly.

The process of training such hierarchical learning systems can also be structured. Techniques like curriculum learning, where the system is trained on progressively more difficult tasks or scenarios, can be applied. Within a hierarchy, training might start by focusing on stabilizing the low-level controllers, then training the intermediate motion planners, and finally training the high-level strategic decision-makers, or vice-versa, depending on the problem structure. Alternatively, multi-agent reinforcement learning approaches can be used where each level of the hierarchy acts as an agent interacting with other agents (other levels or parts of the environment).

In summary, hierarchical control structures provide a powerful paradigm for managing complexity, and the integration of machine learning at various levels of these hierarchies unlocks significant potential for enhanced autonomy, adaptability, and performance. By assigning distinct responsibilities to different layers - from strategic planning and task allocation at the top, to motion planning and optimization in the middle, down to precise execution and stabilization at the bottom - and embedding learning capabilities within these layers, complex systems can be designed to operate more intelligently and robustly. This decomposition allows for the application of specialized learning techniques at each level, leveraging the strengths of data-driven approaches for tasks where traditional analytical methods might be insufficient, while retaining the stability and reliability guarantees often provided by classical control for critical low-level operations. The synergy between hierarchical design and machine learning promises to be a cornerstone in the development of advanced autonomous systems across a wide array of applications.

The increasing prevalence of complex, interconnected systems, ranging from swarms of autonomous robots and sensor networks to decentralized manufacturing processes and smart power grids, brings to the forefront the critical need for effective distributed and networked control strategies. Unlike centralized systems where a single controller manages all aspects of operation, distributed systems feature multiple interacting agents, each with its own localized sensing, computation, and actuation capabilities. These agents must coordinate their actions to achieve collective goals, often in the presence of uncertainties, communication constraints, and evolving system dynamics. Integrating machine learning into this distributed paradigm offers a powerful pathway to enhance robustness, scalability, and adaptability, enabling these systems to learn from their collective experiences and adapt their behavior without explicit reprogramming of each individual agent.

One of the foundational challenges in distributed control is understanding the overall system dynamics when only local information is available to each agent. Traditional system identification methods often rely on centralized data collection and analysis, which can be infeasible in large-scale distributed networks. Learning-based approaches offer a compelling alternative through **distributed system identification**. Instead of a single entity estimating the global system model, each agent can independently learn a local model of its own dynamics and potentially estimate the influence of its neighbors. Techniques such as distributed Kalman filtering or consensus-based parameter estimation can be employed. In these methods, agents iteratively exchange their estimated parameters or model components with their neighbors. Through a consensus protocol, they gradually converge towards a shared estimate of the global system parameters, or at least a sufficient local representation that enables effective coordinated control. For instance, a fleet of autonomous ground vehicles navigating an unknown environment could collectively learn a probabilistic map of the terrain and the dynamics of inter-vehicle interactions, such as collision probabilities at certain relative velocities, without a central mapping station. Each vehicle would update its local map based on its own sensor readings and then share this information with nearby vehicles. Through repeated exchanges and averaging, a more accurate global understanding of the environment and agent interactions emerges, allowing for more sophisticated coordinated navigation and obstacle avoidance strategies to be developed and executed.

Beyond understanding the system, learning how to effectively control it in a distributed manner is paramount.

Decentralized reinforcement learning (DRL) has emerged as a pivotal area of research for this purpose. In DRL, multiple agents learn policies simultaneously, often through trial and error, to optimize a shared or individual reward signal. The fundamental challenge here is that each agent's decision-making is based on its own limited observations and the actions of other agents are not perfectly known or predictable. This creates a non-stationary environment from the perspective of any single agent, as the policies of its neighbors are constantly evolving. Nevertheless, DRL algorithms are being developed to address these complexities.

A common framework in DRL is the **multi-agent reinforcement learning (MARL)** setup, which can be broadly categorized. In a fully decentralized setting, each agent learns its policy independently, treating other agents as part of the environment. This is computationally efficient but often suffers from poor convergence due to the non-stationarity problem. More advanced MARL approaches involve some level of coordination or shared learning. For example, **Centralized Training with Decentralized Execution (CTDE)** is a popular paradigm. During the training phase, a central controller or simulator has access to global information and can use this to train individual agent policies. However, once trained, each agent acts independently based solely on its local observations. This allows for learning complex coordination strategies while maintaining the scalability and real-time operational advantages of decentralized execution.

Consider a scenario involving a team of drones tasked with monitoring a large area for anomalies. Each drone has its own sensors and can communicate with its immediate neighbors. Using CTDE, a central simulator could train each drone's policy. The simulator would observe the positions, sensor readings, and actions of all drones to train a shared value function or to guide the learning process of each individual policy.

The reward might be based on the coverage achieved and the rate of anomaly detection. Once trained, the drones would deploy and operate using their learned policies, relying only on their local sensors and communication with nearby drones to coordinate their search patterns and avoid redundant coverage. The CTDE approach enables the learning of sophisticated coordinated behaviors, such as maintaining formation, dynamically reallocating search areas based on detected anomalies, and retreating to recharge, all without requiring continuous real-time communication with a central command.

Furthermore, the integration of learning within consensus algorithms offers a potent combination for distributed systems. **Consensus algorithms** are fundamental for achieving agreement among agents on a particular value or state, even in the presence of communication noise and delays. Traditional consensus algorithms typically rely on fixed averaging or voting schemes. However, by incorporating learning, these algorithms can become more adaptive and efficient. For instance, agents can learn to adjust the weights they assign to information received from different neighbors, prioritizing more reliable or relevant sources. They can also learn optimal communication schedules or adapt their convergence criteria based on the perceived state of the network and the criticality of the task.

Imagine a distributed sensor network designed to estimate the average temperature across a vast geographical region. Each sensor node has a local temperature reading and communicates with its adjacent nodes. A learning-enhanced consensus algorithm could allow each node to learn which of its neighbors provides the most accurate and up-to-date temperature information, perhaps by observing the consistency of past readings or by implicitly learning about sensor drift or failures. The node could then dynamically adjust the weight it gives to incoming data from each neighbor during the averaging process. This learned weighting scheme would enable faster and more accurate convergence to the true average temperature, especially in a network where some sensors are prone to errors or become temporarily unavailable. This learning can be achieved through various methods, such as online gradient descent on a cost function that penalizes deviations from neighboring estimates, or through meta-learning approaches that learn to adapt the consensus protocol itself.

The practical implementation of distributed learning control systems faces significant hurdles, primarily stemming from the inherent characteristics of networked environments.
Communication delays and limited bandwidth are pervasive issues. Agents often receive information from their neighbors with a time lag, and the amount of data that can be exchanged is constrained. These limitations can significantly degrade the performance of learning algorithms, leading to oscillations, divergence, or suboptimal control. For example, if an agent learns a policy based on outdated information about its neighbors' states, its actions might become detrimental rather than beneficial to the collective goal. Researchers are developing robust DRL algorithms that are explicitly designed to handle such communication constraints. This includes techniques like learning predictive models of neighbor states, employing event-triggered communication to reduce network load, or designing policies that are inherently less sensitive to communication latency.

Another critical challenge is
maintaining stability in large-scale networks. As the number of agents increases, the complexity of their interactions grows exponentially. A local control action by one agent can propagate through the network, potentially leading to unforeseen global instabilities. Traditional stability analysis methods, which are often designed for centralized systems, become intractable for large distributed systems

with learned controllers. Therefore, new theoretical frameworks are needed to guarantee stability properties in these learning-enabled distributed control settings. This might involve developing Lyapunov-based stability proofs that account for learning uncertainties and communication delays, or employing formal verification techniques to check the safety properties of learned policies within bounded network conditions.

The concept of
emergent behavior from local learning is one of the most fascinating and powerful aspects of distributed learning control. In many cases, sophisticated and desirable global behaviors can arise spontaneously from simple, locally defined learning rules executed by individual agents. This contrasts with traditional control where global behavior is explicitly designed. For example, a swarm of robots, each programmed with a simple rule to move towards a light source while maintaining a minimum distance from its neighbors, might exhibit emergent flocking or coordinated exploration behaviors that were not explicitly programmed into any single robot. Machine learning amplifies this emergent capability. By allowing agents to adapt their local rules based on their experiences, the system can discover novel and effective coordination strategies to achieve complex objectives.

Consider a fleet of autonomous vehicles coordinating at an intersection. Instead of a central traffic light or a complex centralized coordination system, each vehicle could be equipped with a DRL agent. Each agent observes its local surroundings – the positions and velocities of nearby vehicles, and the state of the intersection. Through local learning and communication with adjacent vehicles, the agents can learn a decentralized policy that dynamically manages the flow of traffic. This could lead to emergent behaviors such as self-organizing platoons, efficient merging strategies, or adaptive clearing of the intersection based on real-time traffic density. The global behavior of orderly traffic flow emerges from the decentralized learning and interaction of individual vehicles, making the system more resilient to failures and adaptable to varying traffic conditions.

Applications of learning in distributed and networked control are diverse and impactful. In the realm of
autonomous vehicle coordination, DRL is being used to develop cooperative driving policies for fleets of vehicles, enabling them to achieve higher traffic throughput, improve safety through cooperative perception and intention sharing, and optimize energy consumption through coordinated acceleration and deceleration. In **smart grids**, distributed learning agents can manage the operation of distributed energy resources (DERs), such as solar panels, battery storage, and electric vehicles, to optimize grid stability, minimize costs, and integrate renewable energy sources more effectively. Each DER controller could learn to adapt its charging or discharging profile based on local measurements of grid voltage, frequency, and energy prices, as well as communicated information from neighboring DERs.

Another promising area is
robotic swarms, where learning enables swarms to collectively perform complex tasks such as exploration, foraging, construction, or environmental monitoring. Each robot in the swarm can learn to contribute to the collective goal based on its local interactions and a shared reward signal, leading to emergent behaviors that are robust to individual robot failures. For instance, a swarm of drones tasked with mapping an unknown area could use DRL to learn efficient coverage patterns, adapt to obstacles, and collectively decide where to focus their sensing efforts, all without central command.

The challenges associated with distributed learning control – communication limitations, stability guarantees, and the complexity of multi-agent learning – are significant. However, the potential benefits in terms of scalability, robustness, and adaptability make it a crucial area of research and development. As machine learning algorithms become more sophisticated and computational power becomes more distributed, we can expect to see increasingly intelligent and autonomous networked systems that can learn and adapt collectively to solve complex problems. This shift represents a fundamental paradigm change, moving from meticulously designed, centralized control architectures to emergent, self-organizing systems that learn and evolve in real-time. The ongoing advancements in this field promise to unlock unprecedented capabilities in a wide range of applications, from coordinating massive fleets of robots to managing the intricate dynamics of global energy infrastructures.

The integration of artificial intelligence, particularly machine learning, into the realm of control systems is no longer a purely academic pursuit. It has transitioned into a tangible engineering reality, driven by the increasing complexity of modern systems and the limitations of traditional control methodologies. To bridge the gap between sophisticated theoretical concepts and practical implementation, a growing ecosystem of frameworks, libraries, and software tools has emerged. These resources are crucial for engineers seeking to leverage the power of AI for enhanced control, enabling them to design, simulate, test, and deploy intelligent control solutions with greater efficiency and effectiveness.

At the forefront of this technological landscape are the foundational machine learning toolkits. Libraries such as **TensorFlow** and **PyTorch** have become indispensable, offering robust and flexible platforms for building, training, and deploying machine learning models. These frameworks provide high-level APIs that abstract away much of the underlying computational complexity, allowing engineers to focus on the core aspects of model design and optimization.

For instance, when developing a deep reinforcement learning agent for a complex robotic manipulator, one might use TensorFlow to define the neural network architecture that maps sensor inputs to control actions, and then employ PyTorch's autograd engine to efficiently compute gradients for policy updates. The ability to leverage pre-built neural network layers, optimization algorithms, and data handling utilities significantly accelerates the development cycle. Furthermore, these libraries are designed for scalability, supporting both CPU and GPU acceleration, which is essential for training large, data-intensive models commonly encountered in advanced control applications. Their extensive community support and continuous development ensure access to state-of-the-art algorithms and best practices.

Complementing these AI-centric libraries are specialized control system design environments and libraries.
MATLAB/Simulink has long been a cornerstone of control engineering education and industry. Its graphical modeling environment allows for the intuitive design of complex control systems, including simulation of plant dynamics, controller design, and analysis of system performance. The integration of AI capabilities within Simulink has been a significant advancement. Toolboxes like the **Deep Learning Toolbox** and the **Reinforcement Learning Toolbox** within MATLAB/Simulink enable engineers to design, train, and deploy deep learning and reinforcement learning agents directly within the familiar Simulink environment. This allows for seamless co-simulation of AI-based controllers with traditional control algorithms and physical system models. For example, an engineer could design a Simulink model of an autonomous vehicle's dynamics and then use the Reinforcement Learning Toolbox to train a decentralized braking controller that learns to optimize safety and passenger comfort based on simulated driving scenarios. The ability to generate C/C++ code directly from Simulink models further facilitates the deployment of these AI-enhanced controllers onto embedded hardware.

Beyond the integrated environments, several Python-based libraries cater specifically to control systems engineering, offering excellent complements to the major AI frameworks. The
Python Control Systems Library (python-control) is a prime example, providing a comprehensive set of tools for the analysis and design of feedback control systems. It offers functions for state-space and transfer-function representations, frequency-domain analysis, and controller synthesis. When combined with libraries like **NumPy** and **SciPy** for numerical computation and data manipulation, and the aforementioned TensorFlow or PyTorch for machine learning, Python offers a powerful and flexible open-source ecosystem for AI-enhanced control. For instance, an engineer might use `python-control` to define a linear time-invariant (LTI) model of a drone's aerial dynamics. This model could then be used to generate simulation data or to define a simplified plant model for training a reinforcement learning agent using TensorFlow. The control system library can also be used to analyze the stability and performance of the learned policy in conjunction with the drone's dynamics.

The concept of
hybrid systems, which involve both continuous and discrete dynamics, is prevalent in many AI-enhanced control applications. Frameworks that support modeling and simulation of such systems are therefore invaluable. While Simulink inherently handles hybrid systems, other specialized tools and libraries are emerging in the open-source community. These tools often focus on specific aspects, such as formal verification of hybrid automata or efficient simulation of event-driven systems. For an engineer working on a complex manufacturing system with both continuous physical processes (e.g., fluid flow, temperature control) and discrete events (e.g., machine state transitions, product arrival), a framework that can accurately model and simulate these interactions is critical for developing robust AI controllers.

Simulation platforms play a pivotal role in the development and validation of AI-enhanced control systems. Due to the safety-critical nature of many control applications, real-world testing of nascent AI controllers can be prohibitively expensive or dangerous. High-fidelity simulators allow engineers to create virtual environments that mimic the behavior of physical systems with a high degree of accuracy. This enables extensive testing of control algorithms under a wide range of operating conditions, including rare or extreme scenarios that are difficult to reproduce in the physical world. Examples of such simulators range from industrial-grade platforms like **Gazebo** and **Isaac Sim** for robotics and autonomous systems, to specialized environments for specific domains like power systems or telecommunications. These simulators often provide APIs that allow for integration with AI training frameworks. For instance, a swarm robotics simulation in Gazebo could be connected to a PyTorch-based multi-agent reinforcement learning system, allowing the simulated robots to learn coordinated behaviors in a safe and cost-effective manner. The fidelity of these simulators is crucial; a disconnect between the simulation environment and the real world (often referred to as the "sim-to-real gap") can lead to controllers that perform well in simulation but fail when deployed on physical hardware. Bridging this gap is an active area of research, involving techniques such as domain randomization, adaptive simulation parameters, and robust policy learning.

For applications involving autonomous systems, particularly in robotics and vehicles,

robot operating systems (ROS) has become a de facto standard. ROS provides a flexible framework for writing robot software. It is a collection of tools, libraries, and conventions that aim to simplify the task of creating complex and robust robot behavior across a wide variety of robotic platforms. ROS enables the development of modular control systems, where different components (e.g., perception, planning, control, actuation) can be developed and tested independently and then integrated seamlessly. The integration of AI within ROS is a natural progression. Libraries and packages exist to connect ROS nodes with TensorFlow, PyTorch, and other machine learning frameworks, allowing AI models to be used for tasks such as object recognition, path planning, or direct motor control. For example, a perception node in ROS might use a TensorFlow-trained convolutional neural network to detect and track objects, and then publish this information to a control node that uses a reinforcement learning policy to navigate a robot safely around these detected obstacles. The distributed nature of ROS also aligns well with the principles of decentralized control, facilitating the implementation of multi-agent AI strategies.

The deployment of AI-enhanced control systems onto embedded hardware introduces a unique set of challenges, often referred to as **edge AI** or **embedded AI**. Traditional machine learning models, particularly deep neural networks, can be computationally intensive and require significant memory resources, which are often scarce in embedded systems. Consequently, specialized frameworks and techniques are employed to optimize AI models for deployment on resource-constrained hardware. **TensorFlow Lite** and **PyTorch Mobile** are popular examples of libraries that enable the deployment of TensorFlow and PyTorch models, respectively, on mobile and embedded devices. These frameworks provide tools for model quantization (reducing the precision of model weights and activations), pruning (removing redundant connections), and efficient inference engines optimized for various hardware architectures, including microcontrollers and specialized AI accelerators. For a controller designed for a small, battery-powered sensor node or a compact actuator, such optimization techniques are essential to achieve real-time performance within power and computational budgets. Furthermore, the development of **TinyML** (Machine Learning on extremely resource-constrained devices) is an emerging field that pushes the boundaries of what is possible with embedded AI control.

The process of
testing and validation for AI-enhanced control systems requires a shift in perspective compared to traditional control. While traditional methods rely heavily on analytical proofs of stability and performance guarantees, AI controllers, especially those based on deep learning or reinforcement learning, often exhibit emergent behaviors that are difficult to predict through purely analytical means. Therefore, a comprehensive validation strategy typically involves a combination of approaches:

1. **Simulation-based testing**: As mentioned earlier, this is the first line of defense, allowing for extensive exploration of the state space and identification of potential failure modes. It's crucial to test not only nominal performance but also behavior under disturbances, sensor noise, and actuator uncertainty.
2. **Formal verification**: For safety-critical applications, formal methods are increasingly being employed to provide mathematical guarantees about the behavior of AI controllers. Techniques like abstract interpretation, model checking, and theorem proving can be adapted to verify properties of neural networks and reinforcement learning policies within defined operational envelopes. For example, one might formally verify that a learned adaptive cruise control system will always maintain a safe following distance under specified conditions.
3. **Hardware-in-the-loop (HIL) testing**: This involves connecting the AI controller (either in software or on target hardware) to a real-time simulator that mimics the plant dynamics. This provides a more realistic testing environment than pure simulation by including the latencies and characteristics of the actual hardware and its interfaces.
4. **Incremental deployment and online monitoring**: For systems that cannot be fully tested in simulation or HIL, a phased deployment strategy is often adopted. The AI controller might initially operate in a

supervisory or advisory role, or its performance might be closely monitored in a limited operational environment. Online monitoring tools can detect anomalies, deviations from expected behavior, or performance degradation, triggering alerts or fallback to a safe mode.

The development and deployment of AI-enhanced control systems are further supported by
model-based reinforcement learning approaches. These frameworks combine the strengths of traditional model-based control with the learning capabilities of reinforcement learning. Instead of learning a direct mapping from states to actions, or learning a value function, the agent first learns a model of the system dynamics. This learned model can then be used for planning, simulating future trajectories, and deriving control policies. Frameworks that facilitate this include libraries for system identification (which can be AI-driven itself) and planning algorithms that can leverage learned models. For example, a robot arm could learn an accurate dynamics model of its own kinematics and the interaction forces with objects it manipulates. This learned model could then be used by a planning module to compute optimal trajectories for complex manipulation tasks, potentially achieving better performance and generalization than purely model-free reinforcement learning methods, especially in scenarios with sparse rewards.

Furthermore, the increasing sophistication of AI control systems necessitates robust
experimentation platforms and orchestration tools. For developing and comparing multiple AI control strategies, managing distributed training across multiple machines, or orchestrating complex simulation environments, tools like **Kubernetes** for container orchestration, **MLflow** or **Weights & Biases** for experiment tracking and hyperparameter tuning, and specialized simulation orchestration frameworks become essential. These tools help manage the complexity

of the development lifecycle, from initial prototyping to large-scale distributed training and deployment.

In summary, the practical realization of AI-enhanced control systems relies heavily on a robust and integrated set of software tools and frameworks. From the foundational machine learning libraries like TensorFlow and PyTorch, to specialized control system design environments like MATLAB/Simulink, and open-source Python libraries, engineers have a rich toolkit at their disposal. Simulation platforms provide a safe and efficient environment for development and testing, while ROS offers a standardized framework for robotics applications. The challenges of deploying AI on embedded systems are addressed by optimization frameworks like TensorFlow Lite. Finally, rigorous testing, validation, and experimentation management are crucial for ensuring the reliability and safety of these advanced control solutions. By effectively leveraging these resources, engineers can accelerate the transition of AI-enhanced control from theoretical concepts to impactful real-world applications.

Chapter 13: Industrial Case Study: AI in Vehicle Control

The modern automobile is far more than a mere mechanical conveyance; it is a sophisticated, interconnected network of electronic control systems, each meticulously designed to enhance performance, safety, efficiency, and driver comfort. The advent of Artificial Intelligence (AI) in vehicle control is not an isolated phenomenon but rather an evolution built upon a deep foundation of established control paradigms that have been refined over decades. Understanding this foundation is crucial to appreciating the potential and the challenges of integrating AI into automotive applications. This section delves into the core vehicle control systems, tracing their evolution and highlighting their inherent complexities, thereby establishing the landscape upon which AI-driven enhancements are being implemented.

At the heart of most internal combustion engine vehicles lies the **Engine Control Unit (ECU)**, often referred to as the engine control module (ECM). This is arguably one of the earliest and most pervasive examples of a digital control system in a vehicle. The ECU's primary role is to manage and optimize the combustion process. It achieves this by continuously monitoring a multitude of sensors that measure parameters such as engine speed (RPM), throttle position, manifold absolute pressure, oxygen levels in the exhaust gases, coolant temperature, and crankshaft position. Based on this real-time data, the ECU precisely controls various actuators, including fuel injectors, ignition timing systems, and throttle valves. The objective is to achieve a delicate balance between maximizing power output, minimizing fuel consumption, and adhering to increasingly stringent emissions regulations. Traditional ECUs employ a combination of look-up tables (often referred to as "maps") and closed-loop feedback control algorithms. For instance, a PID (Proportional-Integral-Derivative) controller might be used to regulate the air-fuel ratio based on oxygen sensor feedback, ensuring efficient combustion and low emissions. The complexity of these systems has grown exponentially, with modern ECUs managing hundreds of parameters and employing sophisticated diagnostic routines to identify and report potential faults. The transition from simpler analog control to digital microprocessors allowed for much finer control and adaptability, paving the way for subsequent generations of vehicle control systems.

Building upon the fundamental engine management, safety systems have become paramount in vehicle design. Among the most critical are the **braking systems**, which have undergone significant transformation. Early vehicles relied on purely mechanical or hydraulic systems. However, the introduction of the **Anti-lock Braking System (ABS)** marked a pivotal step towards electronically controlled braking. ABS prevents the wheels from locking up during hard braking, which would lead to a loss of steering control and increased stopping distances, particularly on slippery surfaces. It achieves this by rapidly modulating brake pressure to individual wheels. Sensors at each wheel detect incipient wheel lock-up, and the ABS controller, a dedicated electronic control unit (ECU, though distinct from the engine ECU), rapidly pulses the brake pressure for that wheel, allowing it to regain traction before re-applying braking force. This process happens many times per second, significantly enhancing vehicle stability and controllability under emergency braking.

Closely related to ABS is the
Electronic Brakeforce Distribution (EBD) system. EBD works in conjunction with ABS to optimize the distribution of braking force between the front and rear wheels. The optimal distribution depends on factors such as vehicle load and deceleration rate. EBD electronically adjusts the brake pressure to the rear wheels to prevent them from locking up prematurely, as they are typically subjected to less load than the front wheels. This results in shorter stopping distances and improved overall braking stability. The integration of ABS and EBD demonstrates the increasing reliance on electronic control for

fundamental safety functions, moving beyond simple mechanical actuation to intelligent, adaptive response.

The evolution of braking systems naturally led to the development of comprehensive
Electronic Stability Control (ESC), also known as Electronic Stability Program (ESP) or Dynamic Stability Control (DSC) depending on the manufacturer. ESC is a crucial safety feature designed to prevent loss of control, particularly during cornering or evasive maneuvers. It integrates inputs from ABS wheel speed sensors, steering angle sensors, yaw rate sensors, and lateral acceleration sensors. If the system detects that the vehicle is deviating from the driver's intended path – for example, if it begins to understeer (front wheels lose grip) or oversteer (rear wheels lose grip) – ESC intervenes. It can selectively apply brake pressure to individual wheels and, in some cases, reduce engine power to help the driver regain control. For instance, if the vehicle is oversteering, ESC might apply the brake to the outer front wheel to help pivot the vehicle back into line. ESC systems are highly sophisticated, requiring precise real-time estimation of vehicle dynamics and rapid, controlled application of braking and powertrain interventions. The interconnectedness of ABS, EBD, and ESC exemplifies how multiple control systems must work in concert to achieve a higher-level safety objective.

Beyond safety, the desire for improved fuel efficiency and performance has driven the development of advanced
powertrain management systems. These systems encompass a wide range of functionalities, including transmission control, torque management, and emissions control. Modern automatic transmissions, for instance, are no longer simple hydraulic units but are controlled by sophisticated electronic modules that optimize shift points based on vehicle speed, engine load, throttle position, and driver input. The goal is to keep the engine operating within its most efficient speed range while

providing smooth and responsive acceleration. In sophisticated performance vehicles, electronic throttle control (ETC) has replaced mechanical linkages between the accelerator pedal and the throttle body. This allows the ECU greater flexibility in managing engine response, enabling features like cruise control, traction control, and smooth integration with other stability systems. Furthermore, advanced emissions control systems, involving catalytic converters, exhaust gas recirculation (EGR) systems, and particulate filters, are all precisely managed by dedicated ECUs that monitor exhaust gas composition and adjust engine parameters accordingly.

The progression from managing individual subsystems to orchestrating their collective behavior has led to the development of **Advanced Driver-Assistance Systems (ADAS)**. ADAS represents a significant leap towards automating certain driving tasks and enhancing the driver's situational awareness. One of the most common ADAS features is **Adaptive Cruise Control (ACC)**. Unlike traditional cruise control, which maintains a set speed, ACC uses radar or camera sensors to detect vehicles ahead and automatically adjusts the vehicle's speed to maintain a pre-set following distance. If the vehicle ahead slows down, ACC will reduce speed; if it speeds up or changes lanes, ACC will accelerate back to the set speed. This significantly reduces driver fatigue in highway driving.

Another critical ADAS component is **Lane Keeping Assist (LKA)**. LKA systems utilize cameras to monitor lane markings on the road. If the vehicle begins to drift out of its lane without the turn signal being activated, LKA can provide a gentle steering correction to guide the vehicle back into the center of the lane. More advanced versions might provide haptic feedback through the steering wheel to alert the driver. These systems, while still requiring driver supervision, represent an early foray into semi-autonomous control, where the vehicle takes over certain longitudinal or lateral control tasks.

The development of ADAS has been a stepping stone towards **autonomous driving functionalities**. While fully autonomous vehicles are still under development and subject to regulatory hurdles, many vehicles today offer capabilities that are precursors to full autonomy. This includes features like automatic emergency braking (AEB), where the vehicle can detect an imminent collision and automatically apply the brakes if the driver does not respond. Parking assist systems, which can automatically steer the vehicle into a parking space, are also becoming increasingly common. These systems rely on a complex interplay of sensors (cameras, radar, lidar, ultrasonic sensors), sophisticated perception algorithms (often AI-driven, which will be discussed in later chapters), and advanced control logic to interpret the environment and execute precise maneuvers.

The complexity and interconnectedness of these diverse control systems within a modern vehicle cannot be overstated. Hundreds of electronic control units (ECUs) communicate with each other over a high-speed network, typically using a vehicle-specific network protocol like **CAN (Controller Area Network)**. This distributed architecture allows for modular design and efficient communication, but it also introduces significant challenges in terms of integration, synchronization, and fault diagnosis. For example, the ESC system needs real-time information from the ABS wheel speed sensors, the steering angle sensor, and potentially even the engine ECU to modulate engine torque. The ACC system needs to communicate with the throttle control, braking system, and transmission control to adjust speed.

Each of these systems operates with specific control objectives, performance metrics, and safety constraints. Traditional control methodologies, such as PID control, state-space control, and model predictive control (MPC), have been instrumental in achieving the performance and reliability seen in today's vehicles. However, the increasing demands for more sophisticated automation, adaptive behavior in unpredictable environments, and the desire to optimize multiple conflicting objectives (e.g., safety, comfort, efficiency, performance) are pushing the boundaries of what these traditional methods can achieve alone. This is precisely where the integration of AI, particularly machine learning techniques, offers a transformative potential. AI can augment these existing control systems by providing more intelligent perception, more adaptive decision-making, and more optimized control policies, ultimately paving the way for safer, more efficient, and more autonomous vehicles. The systems described above—ECU, ABS, EBD, ESC, powertrain management, ACC, LKA, and the foundational elements of autonomous driving—form the intricate technological ecosystem within which AI is being deployed to revolutionize automotive control. Understanding this rich landscape is the essential first step in exploring how AI is reshaping the future of mobility.

The intricate dance of a vehicle traversing the road is governed by a complex interplay of forces, many of which are inherently nonlinear and highly dynamic. At the core of designing effective control systems, whether traditional or AI-driven, lies the critical need for an accurate representation of these vehicle dynamics. For decades, engineers have relied on analytical models derived from first principles of physics, incorporating detailed knowledge of tire mechanics, suspension behavior, mass distribution, and aerodynamic effects. However, these physics-based models, while powerful, often struggle to capture the full spectrum of real-world operating conditions. Factors such as varying road surface friction (from dry asphalt to wet or icy conditions), tire wear, payload variations, and even subtle atmospheric changes can significantly alter how a vehicle responds to control inputs. Developing a single, universally accurate analytical model that encompasses all these variables is a monumental, if not impossible, task. This is where the power of machine learning (ML) comes into play, offering a data-driven approach to learning vehicle dynamics directly from the vast amounts of information collected by onboard sensors.

Machine learning excels at identifying complex patterns and relationships within data that might be difficult or impossible to derive analytically. In the context of vehicle dynamics, this means leveraging sensor streams—such as wheel speed, steering angle, yaw rate, lateral acceleration, throttle position, brake pressure, and GPS data—to build predictive models of how the vehicle will behave. These learned models can then be used for a variety of purposes, including enhanced control system design, improved state estimation, and advanced prediction capabilities for safety and autonomous driving functions. The process typically involves collecting a diverse dataset that covers a wide range of driving scenarios, maneuvers, and environmental conditions. This data is then preprocessed to clean it, handle missing values, and extract relevant features. Subsequently, various ML algorithms are employed to learn the underlying dynamics.

One of the most challenging and crucial aspects of vehicle dynamics is accurately modeling tire behavior. The tire is the sole point of contact between the vehicle and the road, and its friction characteristics dictate almost every aspect of vehicle motion and control. Traditional tire models, such as the Pacejka 'Magic Formula', are highly sophisticated and empirically derived, but they require careful parameterization for different tires and conditions. ML offers a complementary approach by learning these friction models directly from sensor data. For instance, by analyzing the relationship between slip angle (the difference between the direction a tire is traveling and the direction it is pointed) and the resulting lateral forces, ML algorithms can learn to predict tire forces under varying conditions. Techniques like Recurrent Neural Networks

(RNNs) or Long Short-Term Memory (LSTM) networks are particularly well-suited for this task, as they can capture the temporal dependencies in tire behavior, considering factors like the history of slip and the rate of change of steering. By feeding these models with real-time sensor data, the vehicle's control systems can gain a more accurate, adaptive understanding of the available tire grip, allowing for more precise interventions in systems like Electronic Stability Control (ESC) or more nuanced torque distribution in advanced all-wheel-drive systems. The learned models can predict the peak friction coefficient or the curvature of the friction circle, enabling controllers to operate closer to the limit of traction without exceeding it.

Beyond tire friction, predicting the overall vehicle response to driver inputs is another critical area where ML shines. When a driver applies a certain amount of steering input and throttle, the vehicle will respond with a specific trajectory, acceleration, and yaw rate. Analytical models try to capture this, but often simplify complex phenomena. ML models, particularly deep neural networks, can learn these input-output relationships directly from data. For example, a neural network could be trained to predict the future trajectory (e.g., position and orientation) of the vehicle over a short horizon, given the current vehicle state and control inputs (steering, throttle, brake). This predictive capability is invaluable for ADAS and autonomous driving. A predictive model can anticipate where the vehicle will be in the next few seconds, allowing systems like ACC to make smoother adjustments to speed and distance, or enabling LKA to provide more proactive and less abrupt steering corrections. The network can learn to implicitly account for factors like vehicle mass, tire wear, and even the subtle effects of suspension geometry and damping, which are often simplified in analytical models.

The estimation of vehicle parameters, such as mass, center of gravity, and suspension characteristics, is also an area ripe for ML-based learning. Traditionally, these parameters are either measured during vehicle development or assumed to be within a certain range. However, the actual mass of a vehicle can vary significantly depending on passengers and cargo, impacting its braking distance and handling. ML algorithms can be trained to estimate these parameters in real-time using onboard sensor data. For instance, by analyzing the relationship between braking force, deceleration, and throttle input under different conditions, an ML model can infer the current effective mass of the vehicle. Similarly, by observing the vehicle's response to cornering and road imperfections, it might be possible to estimate changes in suspension stiffness or damping. These learned parameters can then be fed back into the control system, allowing it to adapt its behavior dynamically. For example, a braking controller could adjust its strategy based on an estimated vehicle mass, leading to more consistent stopping performance.

Modeling the complex effects of aerodynamics adds another layer of challenge to vehicle dynamics. Aerodynamic forces, particularly drag and downforce, are highly dependent on vehicle speed, shape, and orientation. While analytical models can approximate these forces, ML can refine them by learning from high-speed driving data. Neural networks trained on data from various speeds and wind conditions can provide more accurate predictions of aerodynamic drag, which is crucial for optimizing energy consumption in electric vehicles or for precisely managing powertrain output during high-speed maneuvers.

The practical implementation of learning vehicle dynamics models using ML involves several key considerations. Data acquisition is paramount. This requires robust data logging systems capable of capturing synchronized high-frequency data from a multitude of sensors. The diversity of this data is critical; it must include normal driving, emergency maneuvers, different road surfaces, varying speeds, and different loading conditions to ensure the learned model generalizes well. Data preprocessing, including noise filtering, sensor calibration checks, and feature engineering, is crucial for the success of any ML model. Feature engineering might involve creating new features from raw sensor data, such as calculating the slip ratio for each wheel, estimating the road bank angle from lateral acceleration, or deriving a measure of tire load.

Model selection is another important step. Different ML architectures are suited for different aspects of vehicle dynamics. For instance, feedforward neural networks might be sufficient for learning static relationships, while RNNs and LSTMs are better for capturing temporal dynamics. Gaussian Processes can offer not only predictions but also uncertainty estimates, which are valuable for safety-critical applications. Reinforcement learning (RL) is also emerging as a powerful tool, where an agent (the control system) learns optimal control policies by interacting with a learned or simulated environment representing the vehicle dynamics. In an RL framework, the agent learns to take actions (steering, throttle, brake) to maximize a reward signal (e.g., maintaining lane, smooth acceleration, minimizing energy consumption), and in the process, it implicitly learns the dynamics of the environment it is interacting with.

Validation and verification of these learned models are critical. Unlike physics-based models, whose behavior can often be analyzed mathematically, ML models can act as "black boxes," making it challenging to guarantee their safety and reliability. Therefore, rigorous testing is essential. This involves testing the learned models against unseen data, deploying them in simulation environments, and finally, conducting extensive real-world testing under controlled conditions. Techniques for explainable AI (XAI) are also gaining traction, aiming to provide insights into why an ML model makes certain predictions or decisions, thereby increasing trust and facilitating debugging.

Furthermore, the concept of online learning or adaptive learning is highly relevant for vehicle dynamics models. As the vehicle accumulates more driving experience or as conditions change (e.g., tire wear over time, changing weather), the learned dynamics model can be continuously updated. This allows the vehicle's control systems to remain optimized and robust over its entire lifespan. This adaptive capability is a significant advantage over static, pre-defined analytical models. For example, a model that learns a slight understeer characteristic due to worn front tires can adapt its control strategy to compensate, maintaining predictable handling.

In summary, learning vehicle dynamics models using machine learning represents a paradigm shift from purely analytical approaches. By harnessing the power of onboard sensor data, ML algorithms can capture the intricate nonlinearities and variabilities inherent in vehicle behavior that are often difficult to model with first principles alone. From refining tire friction models and predicting vehicle response to steering and throttle inputs, to estimating vehicle parameters and understanding aerodynamic effects, ML-driven dynamics models are paving the way for more intelligent, adaptive, and safer vehicle control systems. This data-driven approach promises to unlock new levels of performance, efficiency, and autonomy, enabling vehicles to better understand and interact with their complex environment.

The evolution of vehicular systems from basic mechanical assemblies to sophisticated, computationally driven machines has been nothing short of revolutionary. As we've previously explored, the ability to accurately model and predict vehicle dynamics forms the bedrock upon which advanced control systems are built. This foundation is now being augmented and, in some cases, supplanted by artificial intelligence (AI) to tackle the most intricate challenges in automotive engineering, particularly in the realm of autonomous driving. The transition from human drivers, with their innate perception, intuition, and adaptability, to automated systems necessitates AI that can replicate, and ideally surpass, human-level decision-making capabilities in dynamic and often unpredictable environments. This subsection delves into the specific applications of AI in enabling autonomous vehicles to make critical driving decisions, moving beyond mere control of steering, throttle, and brake to encompass the complex reasoning required for navigating the real world.

At the heart of any autonomous driving system lies its ability to understand the surrounding environment. This process, often referred to as perception, involves processing vast amounts of data from a suite of sensors, including cameras, LiDAR, radar, and ultrasonic sensors. AI, particularly through techniques like deep learning, has become indispensable for interpreting this raw sensor data. Convolutional Neural Networks (CNNs), for instance, are adept at analyzing images from cameras to detect and classify objects such as other vehicles, pedestrians, cyclists, traffic signs, and lane markings. Similarly, point cloud data from LiDAR is processed by specialized neural networks to create a 3D map of the environment, identifying obstacles and their precise locations. Sensor fusion, the intelligent combination of data from multiple sensor types, is another area where AI plays a pivotal role. By integrating the strengths of different sensors – for example, the precise depth information from LiDAR with the rich texture and color information from cameras, or the long-range detection capabilities of radar – AI algorithms can build a more robust and comprehensive understanding of the vehicle's surroundings, even in challenging conditions like fog or heavy rain. This perception layer is the crucial first step, providing the necessary input for the subsequent decision-making processes.

Once the environment is perceived, the next critical capability for an autonomous vehicle is to predict the future behavior of dynamic agents within that environment. This is a formidable task, as human drivers, pedestrians, and cyclists can exhibit unpredictable actions. AI models, often leveraging Recurrent Neural Networks (RNNs) or Transformer architectures, are employed to learn patterns of motion and behavior. By analyzing historical trajectories and interactions, these models can forecast the likely paths and intentions of other road users. For example, a pedestrian approaching a crosswalk might be predicted to stop or wait for a gap in traffic, or a vehicle signaling a lane change might be expected to execute that maneuver within a certain timeframe. This predictive capability is not just about anticipating immediate actions; it's also about understanding longer-term intentions. For instance, an AI might predict that a car in an adjacent lane is likely to merge into the ego vehicle's lane based on its speed, position, and the surrounding traffic flow. The accuracy of these predictions directly impacts the safety and efficiency of the autonomous vehicle's decisions, allowing it to proactively adjust its own behavior rather than reactively swerving or braking at the last moment.

The culmination of perception and prediction is the strategic decision-making process, where the autonomous vehicle determines its own course of action. This involves complex tasks such as path planning, maneuvering, merging into traffic, and avoiding obstacles. Here, AI techniques like Reinforcement Learning (RL) and advanced search algorithms have proven highly effective. In RL, an agent (the autonomous driving system) learns to make optimal decisions by trial and error, guided by a reward function that encourages safe and efficient driving behaviors. The agent interacts with a simulated environment that mimics real-world driving scenarios, receiving rewards for desirable outcomes (e.g., successfully completing a lane change, maintaining a safe distance) and penalties for undesirable ones (e.g., collisions, traffic violations). Through this iterative process, the RL agent learns a policy – a mapping from states (current environmental conditions and vehicle status) to actions (steering, acceleration, braking).

Consider the challenge of merging onto a busy highway. An AI system must not only perceive the speed and gaps in the traffic flow but also predict the behavior of approaching vehicles. Based on this, it needs to determine the optimal acceleration profile and steering angle to seamlessly integrate into the stream of traffic without causing disruption or compromising safety. This involves balancing multiple objectives: matching the speed of the highway traffic, finding a sufficiently large gap, and ensuring that the merge itself is executed smoothly and predictably for other drivers. RL agents can be trained to master such complex maneuvers by exploring a vast state-action space. They learn to evaluate potential future trajectories and select the one that maximizes expected cumulative reward, effectively learning a sophisticated driving strategy.

Another critical decision-making task is obstacle avoidance. When an unexpected obstacle, such as a fallen object or a sudden braking vehicle, appears in the path of the autonomous vehicle, the AI must react instantly and appropriately. This might involve a rapid deceleration, a swerve to an adjacent lane (if safe), or a combination of both. The decision-making process here is highly time-critical and requires rapid processing of sensor data, accurate estimation of the obstacle's trajectory and the vehicle's own capabilities, and a swift execution of control commands. AI-driven planning algorithms can explore numerous avoidance maneuvers within milliseconds, evaluating their feasibility and safety in real-time. For instance, a planning module might consider braking to a complete stop, steering to the left shoulder, or steering to the right shoulder. Each option is assessed based on factors like available space, predicted time to collision, and the potential for secondary collisions. The algorithm then selects the safest and most efficient maneuver.

Simulated driving environments play an indispensable role in the development and validation of AI decision-making systems. Training AI agents in real-world traffic is prohibitively dangerous and slow. Therefore, sophisticated simulators are used to create a wide range of driving scenarios, from routine urban navigation to complex emergency situations. These simulators can accurately model vehicle dynamics, sensor behavior, traffic patterns, and environmental conditions, allowing AI algorithms to be trained and tested on millions of miles of virtual driving. Examples of such simulations include Waymo's internal simulators, CARLA, and NVIDIA's DRIVE Sim. These platforms enable developers to rigorously evaluate the performance of their AI systems under diverse and challenging conditions, identify edge cases, and iterate on their designs without risking real-world accidents. For instance, a scenario involving a sudden tire blowout or a pedestrian darting into the road can be replayed and analyzed countless times in simulation to refine the AI's response.

Despite the remarkable progress, ensuring the safety, interpretability, and robustness of AI decision-making systems for autonomous driving remains a significant challenge. The "black box" nature of many deep learning models can make it difficult to understand why a particular decision was made, which is crucial for debugging, verification, and public trust. Efforts in Explainable AI (XAI) are underway to provide insights into the reasoning behind AI decisions, for instance, by highlighting the specific sensor inputs or learned features that influenced a decision. Furthermore, the AI must be robust to a vast array of unpredictable events and variations in the real world that may not have been encountered during training or simulation. This includes adversarial attacks, sensor failures, and novel driving situations. Techniques such as formal verification, robust control methods, and extensive real-world testing are employed to build confidence in the safety and reliability of these AI systems. The continuous learning and adaptation of these systems, as they gather more data from real-world driving, are also vital for maintaining performance and safety over time.

The integration of AI into autonomous driving decision-making represents a profound shift in how vehicles operate. It moves beyond pre-programmed rules to systems that can learn, adapt, and reason about their environment. From the nuanced interpretation of sensor data through deep learning for perception, to the predictive modeling of other road users' behaviors, and culminating in the strategic planning of maneuvers via reinforcement learning, AI is orchestrating a complex symphony of actions. The reliance on high-fidelity simulations for training and validation is paramount, allowing for the exploration of an immense number of driving scenarios in a safe and efficient manner. While challenges related to safety assurance, interpretability, and robustness persist, ongoing research and development are steadily addressing these, paving the way for a future where autonomous vehicles navigate our roads with enhanced safety, efficiency, and intelligence. The ability of AI to process information, predict outcomes, and make informed decisions in real-time is the very essence of autonomous driving, transforming our understanding of mobility and the potential of artificial intelligence in safety-critical applications.

The perception of the environment, as enabled by AI, is a multi-layered process. Beyond object detection and classification, it involves understanding the context of these objects. For example, detecting a pedestrian is one thing, but understanding their likely intention – whether they are waiting to cross, walking casually, or running – is another. Deep learning models, trained on massive datasets annotated with behavioral cues, can infer these intentions. Similarly, understanding traffic signals involves not just recognizing the color of the light but also its state (e.g., solid red, flashing yellow) and its context within the intersection. AI algorithms can also interpret complex road markings, such as directional arrows, bus lanes, or temporary construction zones, adapting the vehicle's behavior accordingly. The ability to distinguish between a parked car and a car about to pull out into traffic, or to recognize the subtle cues that indicate a cyclist is about to make a turn, are all critical aspects of an AI-powered perception system. The fusion of data from multiple sensors is crucial here. Cameras might identify a traffic light and its color, while radar can detect the presence and speed of approaching vehicles, and LiDAR can provide precise distance measurements. AI algorithms then integrate these disparate pieces of information to build a coherent and actionable understanding of the scene. For instance, if a camera detects a pedestrian looking towards the road and a LiDAR detects them at the curb, and radar shows no vehicles approaching rapidly, the AI can infer a higher probability of the pedestrian attempting to cross.

The predictive modeling of other road users is an area where AI is continually advancing. Traditional prediction methods might rely on simple kinematic models, assuming constant velocity or acceleration. However, AI, particularly with deep learning architectures like LSTMs or Transformer networks, can capture more complex, non-linear behaviors. These models can learn to anticipate abrupt changes in velocity, sudden lane changes, or unexpected turns based on learned patterns from vast amounts of real-world driving data. For example, an AI might learn that drivers approaching a specific intersection tend to brake harder if there's a slight incline, or that certain types of vehicles are more likely to perform aggressive overtakes. Furthermore, understanding the interactions between multiple agents is vital. If two vehicles are approaching each other in adjacent lanes, their future trajectories are not independent; they influence each other. AI models that can reason about these multi-agent interactions are essential for safe navigation in dense traffic. This is often framed as a game theory problem, where each agent (vehicle) is trying to optimize its own outcome, and AI can be used to predict the equilibrium strategies.

The decision-making framework itself is a rich area for AI application. Path planning, for instance, involves generating a safe, comfortable, and efficient trajectory from the current position to the destination. This is not a static process but a continuous replanning based on the evolving environment. AI algorithms can explore a multitude of potential paths, evaluating each one against various criteria: adherence to traffic laws, avoidance of static and dynamic obstacles, passenger comfort (minimizing sudden accelerations or jerky movements), and energy efficiency. For complex scenarios like navigating a crowded roundabout, the AI must consider multiple entry and exit points, the speed and intentions of vehicles already in the roundabout, and the flow of traffic approaching from different directions. Reinforcement learning is particularly well-suited for this, as it allows the agent to learn a policy that balances these competing objectives over time. The reward function can be meticulously designed to encourage safe gap acceptance, smooth merging, and efficient progression through the roundabout.

In scenarios requiring immediate reactions, such as emergency braking or evasive maneuvers, AI decision-making systems must operate with extreme speed and precision. This often involves a rapid re-evaluation of the vehicle's capabilities, the dynamics of the obstacle, and the available space. For example, if an obstacle appears directly in front of the vehicle, the AI must quickly determine if it can stop in time or if it needs to steer to avoid it. This calculation involves estimating the braking distance, considering factors like road surface conditions (friction coefficient) and tire grip, which we discussed in the context of vehicle dynamics. If a swerve is deemed necessary, the AI must also consider the safety of the adjacent lanes and the possibility of oversteering or losing control. Advanced AI planners can explore a vast decision tree of potential actions and consequences within fractions of a second, selecting the optimal path to minimize risk.

The role of simulation in AI development for autonomous driving cannot be overstated. High-fidelity simulators provide a safe and scalable environment for training and testing AI algorithms across an unprecedented range of scenarios. They allow for the generation of rare but critical events, such as sudden mechanical failures, extreme weather conditions, or unpredictable human behavior, which would be difficult or impossible to encounter consistently in real-world testing. For example, a simulator can be configured to present a scenario where a sensor momentarily fails, forcing the AI to rely on its redundancy and fallback mechanisms. Similarly, scenarios involving multiple aggressive drivers or pedestrians exhibiting erratic behavior can be simulated repeatedly to ensure the AI's robustness. The ability to inject specific types of noise or errors into sensor data within a simulation also allows for testing the AI's resilience to sensor degradation or malfunction. Furthermore, simulators enable rapid iteration on AI algorithms. Developers can make changes to the algorithms, test them in simulation, and gather feedback on their performance within minutes or hours, a process that would take months or years if relying solely on real-world testing. This accelerates the development cycle significantly, allowing for more thorough validation before deploying systems onto public roads.

The challenges of safety, interpretability, and robustness are ongoing areas of research and development. One approach to improving interpretability is through attention mechanisms in neural networks, which can highlight which parts of the input data the network is focusing on when making a decision. Another is to decompose complex AI systems into modules with well-defined functions, where the behavior of each module can be analyzed more easily. For robustness, techniques such as domain randomization in simulations (varying simulation parameters widely) and adversarial training (exposing the AI to deliberately challenging inputs) are employed. Formal verification methods, borrowed from traditional software engineering, are also being adapted to provide mathematical guarantees about the behavior of AI systems within certain operating envelopes. Ensuring that an AI system will always behave safely under all possible conditions is a grand challenge, and a combination of rigorous simulation, targeted real-world testing, and ongoing refinement is essential. The goal is not just to create AI that performs well in common situations, but AI that can reliably handle the infinite variety and unpredictability of the real world, especially in safety-critical contexts like driving.

The continuous learning and adaptation of AI systems in autonomous vehicles are crucial for their long-term effectiveness and safety. As vehicles accumulate more driving miles, they encounter new situations and gather more data. This data can be used to retrain and update the AI models, improving their performance and extending their capabilities. This process can occur both offline, in controlled development environments, and potentially online, with some limited adaptation occurring in the vehicle itself. For instance, if a vehicle encounters a new type of road hazard or a unique traffic pattern, that experience can be flagged and used to enhance the AI models in future software updates. This adaptive capability allows autonomous driving systems to evolve and improve over time, much like human drivers gain experience. However, online learning also presents its own set of challenges, particularly concerning ensuring that the learning process itself remains stable and safe, and that the system does not inadvertently learn undesirable or unsafe behaviors. Therefore, careful design and validation are necessary to manage these adaptive learning processes.

In conclusion, the journey of autonomous driving is inextricably linked to the advancements in artificial intelligence, particularly in enabling sophisticated decision-making. AI's ability to perceive, predict, and plan in complex, dynamic environments forms the core of this revolution. From the deep learning models that decode sensor data to the reinforcement learning agents that master intricate driving maneuvers, AI is providing the intelligence required for vehicles to navigate our world autonomously. The critical role of high-fidelity simulations in training and validating these systems cannot be overstated, allowing for exhaustive testing and refinement. While the pursuit of absolute safety, complete interpretability, and unwavering robustness continues, the trajectory of AI in autonomous driving is one of continuous progress, promising a future of safer, more efficient, and more accessible transportation. This ongoing synergy between AI and vehicle control is redefining not just how we drive, but how we conceive of mobility itself.

The integration of artificial intelligence into existing vehicle control systems presents a compelling paradigm shift, moving beyond the wholesale replacement of established, reliable engineering with entirely novel AI-driven architectures. Instead, this approach focuses on leveraging AI's unique capabilities to augment and refine the performance of proven control algorithms, thereby unlocking new levels of efficiency, comfort, and safety. This symbiotic relationship allows us to harness the predictive and adaptive power of AI while retaining the robustness and transparency of traditional control methodologies. The core idea is to imbue conventional systems with an intelligent layer that learns from data, anticipates future states, and subtly adjusts parameters to achieve superior outcomes.

One significant area where AI can enhance existing control systems is in the optimization of Adaptive Cruise Control (ACC). Traditional ACC systems typically rely on radar or camera sensors to detect vehicles ahead and maintain a set speed or distance. However, their performance can degrade in scenarios involving complex traffic flows, such as those found on congested highways or during sudden traffic slowdowns. AI, particularly through techniques like deep learning and predictive modeling, can significantly improve ACC's foresight. By analyzing historical traffic data, real-time sensor inputs from the vehicle's extended sensor suite (including potentially V2X communication), and even external data sources like traffic forecasts, AI models can predict future traffic conditions with remarkable accuracy. For instance, an AI system could anticipate a traffic jam forming several kilometers ahead by observing subtle changes in the speed and density of vehicles further down the road, or by analyzing patterns associated with specific times of day or events. Armed with this predictive insight, the ACC system can then proactively adjust the vehicle's speed, initiating gentle deceleration much earlier than a conventional system would. This proactive approach not only enhances safety by providing a larger buffer and avoiding abrupt braking but also dramatically improves passenger comfort by smoothing out the typical stop-and-go nature of congested highway driving. Instead of reacting to a sudden deceleration, the vehicle might gradually reduce its speed, maintaining a more consistent and comfortable driving experience. The AI's prediction of traffic flow can also inform the ACC's gap-acceptance strategy. It can learn to be more conservative when predicting a rapid increase in traffic density and more assertive when anticipating a clear stretch of road, thereby optimizing both safety and traffic throughput. This predictive capability transforms ACC from a reactive system into a more intelligent, anticipatory one.

Furthermore, AI can personalize the driving experience by learning individual driver preferences. Drivers have distinct styles when it comes to acceleration and braking – some prefer a more spirited, responsive feel, while others favor a smoother, more gradual approach. Traditional cruise control systems offer limited adjustability, often restricting users to a few predefined settings. AI, however, can learn these nuanced preferences over time. By observing the driver's manual inputs (steering, throttle, and brake commands) in various situations and correlating them with the resulting vehicle behavior and passenger comfort, AI algorithms can build a dynamic driver profile. This profile can then be used to fine-tune the parameters of the ACC system, as well as other powertrain and braking controllers. For example, if the AI observes that a particular driver consistently brakes earlier and more gently when approaching a red light, it can learn to replicate this smoother braking profile within the ACC. Similarly, if the driver tends to apply a slightly firmer throttle when merging onto a highway, the AI can adjust the ACC's acceleration profile to better match this preference when it needs to re-accelerate after a slowdown. This learning process can be achieved through supervised learning, where driver actions are labeled as "smooth" or "aggressive," or through reinforcement learning, where the AI is rewarded for actions that align with the inferred driver preferences. The result is a vehicle that feels more intuitive and responsive to its owner, enhancing the overall sense of control and satisfaction without requiring the driver to manually adjust complex settings. This personalization extends beyond ACC, potentially influencing throttle mapping for a sportier or more eco-friendly drive, or even adjusting the sensitivity of the regenerative braking in electric vehicles to mimic the feel of traditional engine braking or optimize energy recuperation based on driving style.

Another crucial area for AI enhancement lies within the Electronic Stability Control (ESC) system. ESC is a vital safety feature designed to detect and mitigate loss of traction by automatically applying brakes to individual wheels and, in some cases, reducing engine power. While ESC systems are highly sophisticated, their default tuning is often a compromise designed to work adequately across a wide range of conditions. AI can elevate ESC performance by enabling it to dynamically adapt its parameters based on a learned understanding of the road surface conditions. Traditional ESC systems rely on sensors to infer tire slip, but they may struggle to distinguish between a genuinely low-friction surface (like ice or wet leaves) and a surface where aggressive driving maneuvers are simply causing temporary wheel spin. AI, by processing a richer set of data, can provide a more nuanced estimation of the road surface. This could involve correlating tire slip data with other sensor inputs such as wheel speed sensor fluctuations, accelerometer readings, yaw rate, and even data from cameras or radar that might detect visual cues of moisture, gravel, or unevenness. By training AI models on datasets that pair these sensor readings with ground truth labels of road surface conditions (e.g., dry asphalt, wet concrete, icy patch, gravel road), the AI can learn to accurately classify the friction coefficient. Once the AI has a reliable estimate of the road surface, it can provide this information to the ESC controller. The ESC system can then adjust its intervention thresholds and control gains accordingly. For instance, on a surface detected by AI as icy, the ESC can become significantly more sensitive, intervening at much lower levels of detected slip to prevent a complete loss of control. Conversely, on a high-grip surface, the ESC might allow for slightly more wheel slip before intervening, enabling more dynamic driving maneuvers for experienced drivers while still ensuring safety. This adaptive approach means that the ESC system is no longer a one-size-fits-all solution but rather a continuously optimizing safety net that is tailored to the immediate driving environment, thereby offering a superior balance of safety and dynamic performance across an unprecedented range of conditions. The AI acts as an intelligent interpreter of the driving environment, translating complex, multi-sensor data into actionable insights that empower traditional safety systems to perform at their peak.

Beyond these specific examples, the principle of augmenting established control systems with AI can be applied broadly across vehicular engineering. Consider the integration of AI into powertrain management for improved fuel efficiency or extended electric vehicle range. While sophisticated engine control units (ECUs) and battery management systems (BMS) already employ complex algorithms, AI can enhance their predictive capabilities. An AI system could learn to predict upcoming driving demands – whether it's a steep incline, a sustained period of high-speed driving, or a series of stop-and-go traffic lights – by analyzing route data, traffic predictions, and historical driving patterns. Based on these predictions, the AI can proactively adjust engine mapping, transmission shift points, or the deployment of electric propulsion and regenerative braking to optimize energy consumption. For example, knowing that a significant climb is imminent, the AI could slightly increase battery charge levels or adjust engine parameters to ensure sufficient power is available, preventing the need for a sudden, inefficient power surge. Similarly, on a downhill section, it could more aggressively engage regenerative braking if the AI predicts that the battery has sufficient capacity. This predictive optimization leads to smoother power delivery, reduced energy waste, and ultimately, improved overall efficiency without compromising the underlying functionality of the existing control hardware and software. The AI acts as a high-level optimizer, guiding the decisions of the lower-level, established controllers to achieve superior global objectives.

The key advantage of this AI augmentation strategy is its inherent modularity and reduced risk. By building upon existing, well-tested control architectures, engineers can introduce AI capabilities incrementally. This means that if the AI component were to fail or produce unexpected results, the underlying, traditional control system would still be operational, ensuring a baseline level of safety and functionality. This is a critical consideration for safety-critical systems like those found in vehicles. Furthermore, the performance of AI models can be rigorously validated in simulation and through extensive real-world testing before being fully integrated. The learned models can be analyzed, and their decision-making processes can be subjected to scrutiny, providing a degree of interpretability that is often challenging to achieve with end-to-end AI systems. This approach allows for the best of both worlds: the reliability and predictability of established engineering principles, enhanced by the adaptive intelligence and predictive power of artificial intelligence. This synergistic approach is not about replacing proven technology but about making it smarter, more responsive, and more aligned with the complexities of modern driving environments and individual user needs.

The successful deployment of artificial intelligence in automotive control systems hinges critically on a comprehensive and multi-faceted approach to safety and validation. While AI offers unprecedented capabilities for enhancing performance, efficiency, and driver experience, the inherent complexity and data-driven nature of these systems necessitate rigorous testing and verification procedures to ensure they operate reliably and safely under all conceivable conditions. This is not merely a matter of technical diligence but a fundamental prerequisite for public trust and regulatory acceptance in the automotive sector, where the stakes for system failure are exceptionally high.

One of the foundational pillars of AI validation in automotive applications is

simulation-based testing. This methodology allows engineers to create virtual environments that replicate real-world driving scenarios with a high degree of fidelity. These simulations can range from simple, controlled environments designed to test specific algorithmic responses to complex, dynamic simulations that mimic intricate traffic flows and diverse weather conditions. The advantage of simulation lies in its ability to generate an almost infinite number of test cases, including rare and hazardous "edge cases" that are impractical, unsafe, or prohibitively expensive to reproduce in the real world. For instance, an AI-powered adaptive cruise control system's reaction to a sudden, unexpected pedestrian darting into the road can be simulated millions of times, with variations in pedestrian speed, trajectory, and environmental lighting, to ensure the AI consistently identifies the hazard and initiates an appropriate evasive maneuver or emergency braking. Similarly, the system's behavior when encountering unexpected road surface changes, such as a sudden patch of black ice or a large pothole, can be meticulously studied and refined within a simulated environment. Advanced simulation tools can also incorporate sensor noise and actuator limitations, providing a more realistic assessment of the AI's performance under imperfect conditions. Furthermore, the scalability of simulation allows for rapid iteration during the development cycle. Engineers can quickly modify AI models, re-run simulations, and analyze the results, accelerating the process of identifying and rectifying potential issues. This continuous feedback loop is essential for robust development, enabling the AI to be exposed to a vast array of scenarios, from mundane everyday driving to highly unusual and potentially dangerous situations, all within the safety of a digital realm. The ability to systematically explore the parameter space of these scenarios, varying factors such as speed, distance, sensor inputs, and environmental conditions, allows for the creation of comprehensive test matrices that thoroughly probe the AI's operational boundaries.

Building upon the insights gained from pure simulation, **Hardware-in-the-Loop (HIL) testing** bridges the gap between the virtual and the physical. In a HIL setup, the actual electronic control unit (ECU) or a representative subsystem that will be embedded in the vehicle is connected to a real-time simulator. This simulator presents the ECU with sensor data that mimics the inputs it would receive from the vehicle's physical sensors in a real-world driving scenario. The ECU then processes this data and generates control signals, which are fed back into the simulator. The simulator, in turn, calculates the resulting vehicle dynamics and returns updated sensor data to the ECU. This closed-loop testing environment allows engineers to validate the AI algorithms not only in terms of their software logic but also their interaction with the actual hardware components, including microcontrollers, communication buses, and sensor interfaces. HIL testing is particularly valuable for assessing the real-time performance of the AI and its embedded software. It can reveal timing issues, communication bottlenecks, or unexpected interactions between different hardware modules that might not surface in pure software simulation. For example, if an AI system responsible for managing regenerative braking in an electric vehicle is being tested, HIL allows engineers to simulate various battery states of charge, motor speeds, and driver inputs, and then observe how the actual control unit responds and how its commands affect the simulated vehicle behavior. This allows for the validation of critical timing and control loop performance, ensuring that the AI's commands are executed precisely and in the correct sequence, even under high computational loads. The ability to inject faults or anomalies into the simulated sensor inputs during HIL testing also provides a powerful means to verify the AI's fault-detection and fallback mechanisms, ensuring that it can gracefully handle sensor failures or erroneous data without compromising vehicle safety.

While simulation and HIL testing are indispensable for initial development and validation, they cannot entirely replace **real-world driving trials**. Ultimately, the AI system must demonstrate its safety and efficacy in the complex, unpredictable, and dynamic environment of actual roadways. These trials are conducted in a highly structured and controlled manner, often starting with closed tracks and progressing to public roads under strict safety protocols. During these trials, the AI system is typically operated in parallel with a human driver who is ready to take immediate control. Extensive data logging is a critical component of real-world testing. Every sensor reading, every AI decision, and every control command is meticulously recorded, providing a rich dataset for post-drive analysis. This data allows engineers to identify scenarios where the AI performed as expected, as well as instances where its behavior deviated from desired outcomes. For public road testing, stringent safety drivers and chase vehicles are often employed, and test routes are carefully selected to encompass a wide variety of driving conditions, including urban, rural, and highway environments, as well as different times of day and weather. The data gathered from these real-world trials serves multiple purposes: it validates the AI's performance in scenarios not fully captured by simulations, it helps to identify and address emergent behaviors, and it provides crucial evidence for regulatory approval. Moreover, real-world data is invaluable for retraining and refining AI models, enabling them to adapt to unforeseen situations and improve their performance over time. The iterative process of testing, data collection, analysis, and model refinement is central to achieving a high level of confidence in the AI system's safety and reliability. This continuous improvement cycle ensures that the AI evolves and adapts, becoming more robust and capable with each iteration of testing and deployment.

Beyond these testing methodologies, specific

techniques for verifying the safety of AI algorithms are paramount. One such technique is **formal verification**, which uses mathematical methods to prove that an AI system will always adhere to a set of safety properties, regardless of the input it receives. While challenging to apply to complex, deep learning models, formal methods can be effectively used to verify critical components or decision logic within the AI architecture. For instance, if an AI system makes a decision based on a set of rules derived from a neural network, formal methods could be used to prove that the rule-based system always adheres to predefined safety boundaries, such as maintaining a minimum following distance or avoiding excessive acceleration. Another crucial aspect is **adversarial testing**, where deliberate attempts are made to "trick" the AI system into making incorrect or unsafe decisions. This involves crafting specific inputs that are designed to exploit potential weaknesses in the AI model. For example, an adversarial attack might involve subtly altering an image captured by a camera to make an AI misclassify a stop sign as a speed limit sign. By understanding how these adversarial examples can cause failures, engineers can develop more robust AI models that are less susceptible to such manipulations. This is particularly important in automotive contexts where malicious actors or even unintended environmental factors could present deceptive inputs. Furthermore, **explainability and interpretability** are increasingly important for AI safety. While many advanced AI models, particularly deep neural networks, can operate as "black boxes," understanding *why* an AI makes a particular decision is crucial for debugging, validation, and building trust. Techniques such as LIME (Local Interpretable Model-agnostic Explanations) or SHAP (SHapley Additive exPlanations) can help to shed light on the factors that influence an AI's output, allowing engineers to scrutinize its reasoning process. If an AI-powered lane-keeping system steers erratically, explainability techniques might reveal that it was mistakenly focusing on a shadow on the road rather than the lane markings, enabling engineers to identify and correct the issue.

Addressing
edge cases is arguably one of the most challenging aspects of AI validation. Edge cases are rare, unforeseen, or unusual situations that a system might encounter, and they are often the scenarios where AI systems are most likely to fail. These could include bizarre combinations of sensor failures, unusual weather phenomena, unpredictable human behavior, or complex interactions within the traffic environment. For instance, an AI might perform flawlessly in everyday driving but struggle when faced with a combination of heavy fog, a flooded road, and a flock of birds crossing the highway simultaneously. Rigorous validation requires an intentional effort to identify, categorize, and test these edge cases. This involves not only leveraging simulation to generate diverse scenarios but also drawing upon real-world incident data, expert knowledge, and even crowdsourced observations. A systematic approach to edge case management involves defining criteria for what constitutes an edge case, developing specific test cases for each identified edge case, and meticulously analyzing the AI's performance in these situations. The goal is to ensure that the AI either handles these rare events gracefully, perhaps by reverting to a safe default mode or alerting the driver, or that its failure mode in such extreme circumstances does not lead to catastrophic outcomes. This proactive approach to identifying and mitigating risks associated with edge cases is fundamental to achieving a high level of safety assurance for AI-driven vehicle control.

Compliance with stringent
automotive safety standards, such as **ISO 26262**, is a non-negotiable requirement for any AI system intended for automotive deployment. ISO 26262, the international standard for functional safety of electrical and/or electronic systems in road vehicles, provides a comprehensive framework for managing safety risks throughout the entire lifecycle of an automotive system, from conception and design to production and operation. For AI-powered systems, applying ISO 26262 presents unique

challenges due to the probabilistic nature and the "learning" aspect of AI. The standard requires a thorough hazard analysis and risk assessment (HARA) to identify potential hazards and determine the Automotive Safety Integrity Level (ASIL) for each. This ASIL rating dictates the rigor of the safety measures and verification processes required. For AI components, this often translates into the need for extensive testing, validation, and potentially the use of AI-specific safety mechanisms. For example, if an AI system is responsible for emergency braking, and a HARA determines it requires a high ASIL (e.g., ASIL D), then the development and validation processes must be extremely thorough, with multiple layers of redundancy, stringent testing requirements, and rigorous documentation. The standard also emphasizes the importance of a safety culture within the organization and the need for clear roles and responsibilities for safety management. The integration of AI into safety-critical functions necessitates a careful consideration of how traditional safety engineering principles can be adapted and extended to accommodate the characteristics of machine learning. This might involve defining safe operating envelopes for AI models, developing robust monitoring mechanisms to detect anomalies, and establishing clear procedures for human intervention when the AI's behavior becomes uncertain or unsafe. The application of ISO 26262 to AI is an evolving field, with ongoing efforts to develop more specific guidance and best practices for AI safety.

The robust
management of data is the bedrock upon which AI safety and validation are built. The performance and reliability of AI models are directly proportional to the quality, quantity, and representativeness of the data used for their training, validation, and testing. This involves meticulous data collection strategies, ensuring that data is gathered from diverse sources and under a wide range of conditions that accurately reflect the operational environment of the vehicle. Data cleaning and preprocessing are critical steps to remove noise, correct errors, and ensure consistency.

Furthermore, establishing clear data provenance and version control is essential for traceability and reproducibility, allowing engineers to understand exactly which data was used to train a particular model and to track changes over time. For safety-critical AI, the concept of "data curation" takes on heightened importance. This involves not only ensuring the data is accurate but also that it is representative of all plausible driving scenarios, including rare events and edge cases. Techniques like data augmentation can be employed to synthetically expand the dataset, but care must be taken to ensure these augmentations do not introduce biases or unrealistic scenarios. Moreover, ethical considerations regarding data privacy and security must be rigorously addressed throughout the data management lifecycle. The integrity of the training data directly impacts the safety of the deployed AI system; any biases or deficiencies in the data can lead to biased or unsafe AI behavior. Therefore, a comprehensive data governance framework that covers collection, storage, access, usage, and archival is indispensable for ensuring the trustworthiness of the AI.

Ultimately, the journey of bringing AI into automotive control systems safely is an iterative and collaborative process. It demands a deep understanding of both traditional control engineering principles and the nuances of AI development, coupled with an unwavering commitment to safety. By employing a layered approach that combines rigorous simulation, hardware-in-the-loop testing, extensive real-world validation, advanced verification techniques, meticulous data management, and adherence to established safety standards, the automotive industry is paving the way for AI-powered vehicles that are not only smarter and more efficient but, above all, demonstrably safe. This multi-pronged strategy builds confidence in the technology, ensuring that the integration of AI into vehicle control systems enhances, rather than compromises, the fundamental safety expectations of drivers and passengers alike.

Chapter 14: Laboratory Exercises and Implementation

Establishing a functional and accessible laboratory environment is paramount for hands-on exploration of AI-augmented control systems. This section provides a practical guide to setting up such a space, focusing on readily available hardware and versatile software tools. The objective is to equip you with the necessary infrastructure to not only replicate the exercises presented in this book but also to foster your own innovative experiments. We will delve into the essential components, from microcontrollers and sensors to simulation platforms, and outline the software ecosystem that empowers development and deployment. The emphasis will be on creating an environment that is both cost-effective and sufficiently powerful to handle the complexities of modern control systems augmented with artificial intelligence.

At the heart of any embedded control system lies the microcontroller unit (MCU). For introductory and intermediate experiments, platforms like the

Arduino and **Raspberry Pi** offer excellent starting points. Arduinos, such as the Uno or Mega, are well-suited for direct hardware interfacing due to their robust analog-to-digital converters (ADCs) and straightforward digital I/O capabilities. They are ideal for tasks involving reading sensor data (e.g., potentiometers, temperature sensors, simple encoders) and controlling basic actuators (e.g., DC motors via H-bridges, servos). The Arduino IDE provides a simplified C/C++ programming environment that makes getting started with embedded programming remarkably accessible. This simplicity allows for a quick transition from conceptual understanding to tangible interaction with physical hardware, enabling immediate feedback on control algorithms implemented directly on the MCU. For instance, a basic PID controller for motor speed can be implemented and tested on an Arduino within a few hours of setup, allowing for direct observation of its response to various load conditions.

The Raspberry Pi, on the other hand, offers a more powerful, Linux-based computing platform. With its quad-core processor, ample RAM, and extensive connectivity options (USB, Ethernet, Wi-Fi, Bluetooth), it can serve as a more sophisticated controller or as a host system for more complex AI models. It excels in scenarios where higher computational demands are present, such as running real-time operating systems, processing data from multiple high-resolution sensors simultaneously, or even hosting small-scale machine learning inference directly. The Raspberry Pi's versatility allows it to act as a bridge between low-level hardware and high-level software. For example, you could use a Raspberry Pi to collect data from an Arduino-based sensor array, perform feature extraction, and then run a pre-trained neural network for object detection or state estimation. The availability of GPIO pins also allows for direct interaction with sensors and actuators, though often in conjunction with specialized driver boards or level shifters for voltage compatibility. This dual capability makes the Raspberry Pi a powerful tool for developing and testing AI algorithms that interact with the physical world.

Beyond these microcontrollers, consider dedicated simulation platforms. For rapid prototyping and algorithm development without the need for physical hardware, software-based simulation environments are invaluable.
MATLAB/Simulink remains an industry standard for control system design and simulation. Its block-diagram interface in Simulink, combined with MATLAB's powerful scripting and analysis capabilities, provides a comprehensive environment for developing, testing, and deploying control algorithms. The ability to model complex systems, simulate their dynamic behavior, and then automatically generate code for embedded targets (including many ARM-based MCUs like those found in Raspberry Pi and various development boards) makes it an exceptionally efficient

tool. For instance, you can model a robotic arm, design an AI-based trajectory planner in Simulink, and then simulate its performance before deploying it to hardware. The Control System Toolbox and Deep Learning Toolbox in MATLAB further enhance its utility for AI-augmented control.

Alternatively, open-source simulation tools can offer powerful alternatives, especially when budget is a concern.
Python, with its extensive ecosystem of libraries, has become a dominant force in both AI and scientific computing. Libraries such as **NumPy** for numerical operations, **SciPy** for scientific and technical computing (including optimization and signal processing), and **Matplotlib** for visualization are foundational. For AI development, **TensorFlow** and **PyTorch** are the leading deep learning frameworks. These libraries allow for the definition, training, and deployment of complex neural networks. When combined with the **Control Systems Library** in Python, which provides functionalities for analyzing, designing, and simulating linear control systems, you can build a robust simulation environment for AI-augmented control. Tools like **PyBullet** or **Gazebo** offer physics-based simulation environments that can be integrated with Python scripts, enabling the testing of control algorithms in a realistic virtual world. For example, one could develop a reinforcement learning agent in PyTorch, train it within a PyBullet simulation of a mobile robot, and then deploy the trained policy onto a Raspberry Pi controlling a physical robot.

When setting up your hardware, consider the necessary peripherals. A stable power supply is crucial for reliable operation of MCUs and actuators. For motor control experiments, motor driver ICs (like the L298N for DC motors) or dedicated motor controller boards are essential. Sensors are the eyes and ears of your system; for basic experiments, consider potentiometers (for position feedback), rotary encoders (for speed and position), Hall effect sensors (for proximity or magnetic field detection), infrared proximity sensors, and ultrasonic distance sensors. As you progress, you might incorporate more advanced sensors like Inertial Measurement Units (IMUs – accelerometers and gyroscopes) for motion sensing, cameras for computer vision tasks, or LiDAR for more precise environmental mapping.

The software setup is equally important. For Python-based development, installing a distribution like
Anaconda or **Miniconda** simplifies package management and environment isolation. You'll typically want to create dedicated virtual environments for each project to avoid dependency conflicts. This involves using commands like `conda create -n my*ai*control*env python=3.9` and `conda activate my*aicontrol*env`. Within this environment, you can then install the necessary libraries using `pip install numpy scipy matplotlib scikit-learn tensorflow` (or `torch` for PyTorch) and `pip install control`. For hardware interfacing with Python on a Raspberry Pi, libraries like `RPi.GPIO` or `gpiozero` are commonly used for direct GPIO control, while libraries like `pyserial` are used for communication with external devices like Arduinos via the serial port.

For Arduino development, the Arduino IDE should be installed, and you'll need to familiarize yourself with its basic structure: `setup()` for initialization and `loop()` for continuous execution. Libraries for specific sensors or actuators can be easily installed through the IDE's Library Manager. If you plan to communicate between an Arduino and a Python host (e.g., Raspberry Pi), understanding serial communication protocols is key. You'll implement `Serial.begin(baudrate)` and `Serial.print()` or `Serial.write()` on the Arduino, and `pyserial` in Python to establish and manage the connection.

Consider the physical layout of your lab space. A stable workbench, adequate lighting, and organized storage for components are essential. For experiments involving moving parts or potential hazards (e.g., high-speed motors, robotic arms), ensure a clear safety perimeter and consider incorporating emergency stop mechanisms. Cable management is not just about tidiness; it prevents accidental disconnections and reduces electrical noise. Using breadboards for prototyping allows for quick circuit modifications, but for more permanent or robust setups, consider perfboards or custom PCBs.

When interfacing hardware, pay close attention to voltage levels and current ratings. Many microcontrollers operate at 3.3V or 5V, while some sensors or actuators might require different voltages. Level shifters are often necessary to bridge these differences and prevent damage to components. Similarly, ensure your power supply can provide sufficient current for all connected devices, especially motors, which can draw significant current spikes during startup or under load. Understanding datasheets for all components is a fundamental practice in any hardware-centric lab.

The choice between an Arduino and a Raspberry Pi often depends on the task. If your primary goal is to learn direct hardware control and implement low-level algorithms, an Arduino is a fantastic starting point due to its simplicity and real-time deterministic behavior. If your project requires significant data processing, running AI models, or networking capabilities, a Raspberry Pi will be more suitable. It's also common and highly beneficial to use them in tandem: an Arduino handles the real-time sensor acquisition and low-level control loops, while a Raspberry Pi acts as the "brain," running more complex AI algorithms, processing sensor fusion data, and making higher-level decisions, communicating with the Arduino via serial.

For simulation-based work, ensure your computer meets the requirements for the chosen software. MATLAB/Simulink can be resource-intensive, particularly for large models and long simulation times. Python-based environments are generally more flexible and can run on a wider range of hardware, including laptops. However, for computationally intensive deep learning training, a dedicated GPU can significantly accelerate the process. Cloud computing platforms (e.g., Google Colab, AWS, Azure) also offer access to powerful computing resources, including GPUs, which can be leveraged for training large AI models without requiring local hardware investment.

Documentation is a critical, though often overlooked, aspect of lab setup. Keep a log of your hardware inventory, software versions, and configuration settings. Documenting your experiments, including circuit diagrams, code snippets, observed behaviors, and analysis results, is crucial for reproducibility and for tracking your progress. This practice will save you considerable time and effort in the long run, especially when revisiting projects or sharing your work.

In summary, setting up a laboratory environment for AI-augmented control systems involves a careful selection of hardware and software tools. By starting with accessible platforms like Arduino and Raspberry Pi, leveraging powerful simulation environments such as Python with its extensive AI and scientific libraries, and paying attention to practical aspects like power, interfacing, and organization, you can create a productive space for learning and experimentation. The ability to seamlessly transition between physical hardware, software simulation, and potentially hardware-in-the-loop setups will provide a comprehensive understanding of the challenges and opportunities in this exciting field.

This exercise provides a practical, hands-on investigation into a pivotal advancement in Model Predictive Control (MPC): the replacement of analytically derived models with data-driven, learned models. The motivation behind this approach stems from the inherent challenges in precisely modeling complex, nonlinear, or time-varying systems. In many real-world applications, obtaining an accurate analytical model can be difficult, time-consuming, or even impossible due to unknown dynamics, unmodeled disturbances, or changing operating conditions. Data-driven modeling, powered by machine learning techniques, offers a compelling alternative by learning the system's behavior directly from observed input-output data. This exercise will guide you through the process of collecting data, identifying a system model from this data, integrating this learned model into an MPC controller, and then evaluating its performance. By the end of this exercise, you will have a tangible understanding of how AI, specifically machine learning for system identification, can significantly enhance the capabilities and applicability of MPC.

To begin, we need a system to control and from which to collect data. For the purpose of this exercise, a simple, yet illustrative, system is recommended. Two excellent candidates are a mass-spring-damper system, which is a fundamental concept in mechanical vibrations and control, and a thermal process, such as a small heated enclosure, which exhibits distinct dynamic characteristics.

Let's consider the mass-spring-damper system. This system can be represented by a second-order ordinary differential equation:

$m\ddot{x} + c\dot{x} + kx = u(t)$
where m is the mass, c is the damping coefficient, k is the spring stiffness, x is the displacement, and $u(t)$ is the applied force (our

control input). While we can derive analytical equations of motion for this system, imagine a scenario where some of these parameters are not precisely known, or perhaps the damping is nonlinear.

Alternatively, a thermal process can be modeled as a system with thermal mass, resistance, and potentially convective losses. A simplified model might look like:

$C\frac{dT}{dt} = P*{in}* - *P*{out}$
where C is the thermal capacitance, T is the temperature, $P*{in}$ is the power input (our control), and $P*{out}$ represents heat loss to the environment, which might be a function of the temperature difference and ambient conditions. Again, modeling these heat transfer dynamics accurately can be challenging in practice.

For this exercise, you have the flexibility to implement either a physical version of these systems or to utilize a simulation environment. A physical mass-spring-damper can be constructed using readily available components: a cart on rails, a spring, a damper (e.g., a viscous damper or even a simple electromagnetic damper), and a motor to apply a controlled force (e.g., a DC motor with a lead screw or a geared mechanism). For a thermal process, a small insulated box with a heating element (e.g., a resistor or Peltier module) and a temperature sensor (e.g., a thermistor or RTD) would suffice. Controlling the power supplied to the heater via a suitable driver (e.g., a PWM output from a microcontroller) would be your control input.

If a physical setup is not feasible, or for quicker iteration, a simulation environment is highly recommended. Using MATLAB/Simulink or Python with libraries like SciPy, you can accurately simulate the dynamics of either system. For the mass-spring-damper, you would discretize the differential equation and implement a state-space representation. For the thermal system, a discrete-time model representing the temperature change over time based on power input and heat loss can be created. The advantage of simulation is the ability to precisely control the system's parameters, introduce realistic noise, and generate large amounts of data quickly. It also allows for a direct comparison: you can run an MPC with a known analytical model (derived from the simulation parameters) against an MPC using a learned model.

The first critical step is data collection. The goal is to excite the system across a range of operating conditions and record its response. This data will serve as the basis for learning the system model. A common strategy for data collection is to apply a series of test signals to the system's input and record the corresponding output and input over time.

For excitation, a Pseudorandom Binary Sequence (PRBS) is often an excellent choice. A PRBS signal is a digital signal that takes on two values (e.g., minimum and maximum control effort) and switches between them at discrete time intervals. While it might seem random, it has desirable properties: it is persistently exciting, meaning it will drive the system through a wide range of its states, and it has a flat power spectrum over a certain frequency range, which helps in identifying system dynamics across various frequencies. Alternatively, you could use a series of step changes, a chirp signal, or even a carefully designed random signal. The key is to ensure the system is adequately "exercised."

When collecting data, it is crucial to record both the input signals applied and the system's output response at a sufficiently high sampling rate. The sampling rate should be chosen to capture the relevant dynamics of the system without being excessively high, which can lead to large data files and computational burdens. A general rule of thumb is to sample at least 5 to 10 times faster than the system's dominant pole or bandwidth.

Let's outline the data collection process:

1. **Initialize the System:** Start the physical system or simulation. Ensure it is at a stable equilibrium point.
2. **Apply an Input Signal:** Introduce a chosen excitation signal (e.g., PRBS) to the system's input. This signal should span the expected range of control inputs.
3. **Record Data:** Simultaneously record the applied input signal $u(t)$ and the system's output response $y(t)$ (and potentially other measured states, if available). Record these at a fixed sampling interval Δt. Store this data as a sequence of input-output pairs: $\{(u*k, yk)\}{k=1}^N$, where $u*k$ is the input at time step $k\Delta t$ and y_k is the output.
4. **Vary Operating Conditions (Optional but Recommended):** If the system's dynamics are known to change significantly with operating point (e.g., due to nonlinearity), it is beneficial to collect data at multiple nominal operating points. This can involve setting different setpoints for the output and exciting the system around those setpoints.
5. **Add Noise:** If working with a physical system, it's natural to have sensor noise and actuator imperfections. If simulating, you might want to add realistic noise to the output and possibly the input to make the learned model more robust.

After collecting a sufficient amount of data, the next step is system identification. The objective here is to build a model that accurately maps system inputs to outputs based on the collected data. For this exercise, we will focus on using machine learning, specifically neural networks, as they are well-suited for learning complex nonlinear relationships.

A common approach is to train a feedforward neural network (also known as a Multilayer Perceptron or MLP). The network will take past input and output values as inputs and predict future output values. A standard structure for this type of prediction in discrete time involves using a "tapped delay line" approach, where the network's inputs are a concatenation of a certain number of past inputs and outputs.

Let's define the input to the neural network. If we want to predict the output at time step $k+1$, $y
{k+1}$, using inputs and outputs up to time step k, we can structure the input vector Xk as:
$Xk = [uk, u{k-1}, \dots, u{k-nu+1}, yk, y{k-1}, \dots, y{k-n_y+1}]$
where nu is the number of past input samples to consider, and ny is the number of past output samples to consider. The target output for the network would be $Yk = y{k+1}$.

The neural network can then be defined as:

$y{k+1} = f(Xk; \theta)$
where $f(\cdot; \theta)$ represents the neural network function with parameters θ. This function is typically composed of one or more layers of neurons with nonlinear activation functions (e.g., ReLU, sigmoid, tanh).

To train the neural network, we use the collected data and a suitable loss function, such as the Mean Squared Error (MSE):

$L(\theta) = \frac{1}{N} \sum{k=1}^N (y{k+1} - f(X_k; \theta))^2$

The parameters θ are then optimized using an algorithm like Stochastic Gradient Descent (SGD) or its variants (Adam, RMSprop) to minimize this loss function.

Practical Implementation of System Identification:

You can implement this using Python with libraries like TensorFlow or PyTorch.

1.
Data Preparation:
Load your collected data (input sequences and corresponding output sequences).
Create the input vectors Xk and target vectors Yk by constructing the tapped delay lines. For example, if you decide to use $nu=3$ past inputs and $ny=3$ past outputs to predict the next output, for a data sequence $u = [u1, u2, \dots, uN]$ and $y = [y1, y2, \dots, yN]$:
The first input vector $X1$ might be $[u1, u0, u{-1}, y1, y0, y{-1}]$ (assuming appropriate initial conditions $u0, u{-1}, y0, y{-1}$). A more practical approach is to start generating these sequences once you have enough initial data, e.g., $X1 = [u1, u2, u3, y1, y2, y3]$ and $Y1 = y4$.
The target vector $Y1$ would be $y4$.
You will need to decide on appropriate values for nu and ny. These are hyperparameters that can affect the model's performance. Start with values like 5 or 10 and experiment.
Split your data into training, validation, and testing sets. The training set is used to update the network's weights, the validation set is used to monitor for overfitting and tune hyperparameters (like network architecture, learning rate, nu, ny), and the testing set is used for a final, unbiased evaluation of the trained model.

Normalize your input and output data. This is crucial for neural network training, as it helps stabilize the learning process and improve convergence. Common normalization techniques include z-score normalization (subtracting the mean and dividing by the standard deviation) or min-max scaling (scaling values to a range, e.g., [0, 1] or [-1, 1]).

2.
Neural Network Architecture:
Choose the number of hidden layers and the number of neurons in each layer. For many system identification tasks, one or two hidden layers with 32 to 128 neurons each are often sufficient.
Select an activation function for the hidden layers (e.g., ReLU: `tf.nn.relu` or `torch.relu`).
The output layer should have a linear activation function if you are predicting continuous values (which is typical for system outputs).

3.
Training the Network:
Compile the model, specifying the optimizer (e.g., Adam), the loss function (e.g., MSE), and any metrics you want to track (e.g., MSE, MAE).
Train the model using the `fit` method (in Keras/TensorFlow) or a custom training loop (in PyTorch), providing the training data and validation data. Train for a sufficient number of epochs, monitoring the validation loss. Use early stopping to prevent overfitting: stop training if the validation loss starts to increase.

4.
Evaluation:
After training, evaluate the model on the held-out test set to obtain performance metrics.
Crucially, visualize the model's predictions against the actual system response on the test data. This visual inspection is often more insightful

than raw metrics. You should see the learned model closely tracking the actual system's behavior.

Integrating the Learned Model into MPC:

Now that you have a data-driven model, the next step is to integrate it into an MPC framework. Recall that MPC relies on a system model to predict future system behavior over a finite horizon and optimize control actions to minimize a cost function while satisfying constraints.

The standard MPC structure involves an inner loop where at each time step k:

1. **Measure the current state:** Obtain the current system state x_k. For our example, this might be the displacement and velocity for the mass-spring-damper, or temperature for the thermal system. If only a subset of states are measured (e.g., only position or temperature), you might need a state estimator (like a Kalman filter), but for simplicity in this exercise, we will assume the states required by the learned model are directly observable or can be inferred.
2. **Solve the optimization problem:** Use the learned model to predict the system's future states $x{k+1}, x{k+2}, \dots, x{k+Np}$ and outputs $y{k+1}, y{k+2}, \dots, y{k+Np}$ over a prediction horizon Np, *given a sequence of future control inputs* $uk, u{k+1}, \dots, u{k+Nc-1}$ *over a control horizon* Nc. The optimization problem aims to find the sequence of control inputs that minimizes a cost function:
$J = \sum{i=k+1}^{k+Np} Q(xi, ui) + \sum{i=k+1}^{k+Nc} R(u_i)$
subject to constraints on states and inputs:
$x{i+1} = f{learned}(X_i; \theta)$ (using your learned model)
$u{min} \le ui \le u_{max}$

$y{min} \le yi \le y{max}$ (if yi is directly predicted by the learned model, or derived from it)
...and other relevant constraints.

3.
Apply the first control input: Apply only the first optimal control input $u_k^$ found from the optimization to the actual system.
4. **Shift the horizon:** For the next time step, repeat the process from step 1 with the new current state.

Key Differences with Analytical MPC:

The crucial difference here lies in the prediction model used in step 2: $f {learned}(Xi; \theta)$ instead of an analytical model like $x{i+1} = A xi + B u_i$ (for linear systems) or a more complex nonlinear analytical function.

Implementation Considerations for Learned Model MPC:

State Representation: The learned model $f{learned}$ *likely operates on a specific state representation* Xk (e.g., past inputs and outputs). Ensure that the current state of the physical system can be accurately translated into this Xk *format at each time step. If your learned model predicts* $y{k+1}$ from $[uk, \dots, u{k-nu+1}, yk, \dots, y{k-ny+1}]$, and your physical system provides y_k, you'll need to store a history of past inputs and outputs to form the input vector to the learned model.
Computational Cost: Neural networks, especially larger ones, can be computationally intensive. For real-time MPC, the prediction step using the neural network must be fast enough to meet the control loop's sampling rate. This might require choosing a simpler network

architecture, using optimized neural network inference engines (e.g., ONNX Runtime, TensorRT), or deploying on hardware with sufficient processing power (like a Raspberry Pi with a GPU or a dedicated AI accelerator).

Constraint Handling: Directly incorporating complex constraints (especially state constraints) into an optimization problem solved with a neural network predictor can be challenging. Often, constraints are handled by the optimizer. If the optimizer relies on gradients of the prediction function, and the neural network is a black box, gradient estimation techniques might be needed, or the optimizer might need to be designed to handle non-differentiable functions. However, for basic input constraints, this is usually straightforward.

Horizon Lengths (N_p, N_c): The choice of prediction and control horizons remains critical. These parameters are tuned to balance performance, constraint satisfaction, and computational feasibility.

Experimental Setup and Comparison:

To effectively evaluate the performance of the MPC with a learned model, you will need to compare it against a baseline controller.

1.
Baseline Controller:

MPC with Analytical Model: If you simulated the system, you should have the true analytical model. Use this model within the MPC framework to create a baseline. If you used a physical system, you might have a nominal analytical model (even if imperfect). This provides a valuable comparison point.

Other Controllers (Optional): For further comparison, you could implement a simpler controller like a PID controller tuned for the system.

2.

Performance Metrics:

Tracking Accuracy: Quantify how well the controller maintains the system's output at a desired setpoint or follows a trajectory. Metrics include:

Integral of Squared Error (ISE): $\int e(t)^2 dt$

Integral of Absolute Error (IAE): $\int |e(t)| dt$

Root Mean Squared Error (RMSE): $\sqrt{\frac{1}{N}\sum_{k=1}^N e_k^2}$

Overshoot, Rise Time, Settling Time (for step responses).

Constraint Satisfaction: Measure the extent to which the controller violates predefined input or state constraints. This can be quantified as the number of constraint violations or the magnitude of violations.

Control Effort: Evaluate the "smoothness" or "aggressiveness" of the control signals. High-frequency switching of control inputs can be undesirable and can lead to actuator wear.

3.

Experimental Procedure:

Data Collection Phase: Collect data from your system (physical or simulated) using appropriate excitation signals.

Model Training Phase: Use the collected data to train your neural network system identification model. Validate its performance using metrics and visualizations.

MPC Implementation:

Implement the MPC controller using the **learned** model. Tune its parameters (cost function weights Q, R, horizons N_p, N_c, optimizer settings).

Implement the MPC controller using the **analytical** model (if available) for comparison. Tune its parameters similarly.

Testing Phase:

Apply a series of setpoint changes or trajectories to both MPC controllers in separate experiments.
For each experiment, record the system's output, applied control inputs, and any relevant states.
Carefully measure and record the performance metrics defined above for each controller.
Repeat tests multiple times to ensure reproducibility and account for any randomness in the system or controller.

Expected Outcomes and Analysis:

You should expect to observe differences in performance between the MPC using the learned model and the MPC using the analytical model.

Improved Tracking: If the analytical model was not perfectly accurate (due to nonlinearities, unmodeled dynamics, or parameter uncertainty), the MPC with the learned model should exhibit superior tracking accuracy. The learned model, by capturing the actual system behavior from data, can make more informed predictions, leading to more precise control.
Better Constraint Handling: With more accurate predictions, the MPC using the learned model can often push the system closer to its constraints without violating them, leading to more aggressive and efficient control. This is because the learned model "knows" what will happen when the system operates near its limits, whereas an inaccurate analytical model might make overly conservative predictions or miss critical nonlinear effects.
Robustness: A well-trained data-driven model can implicitly learn to handle unmodeled disturbances or parameter variations that were present in the training data, leading to a more robust controller.

Potential Challenges:
Generalization: The learned model's performance is highly dependent on the quality and representativeness of the training data. If the system operates in an regime not encountered during training, the learned model may not generalize well, leading to poor performance.
Computational Load: As mentioned, neural network inference can be computationally demanding, potentially limiting the achievable closed-loop bandwidth.
Extrapolation: Neural networks are generally poor at extrapolating beyond the range of their training data. If the controller tries to drive the system into states or input ranges far outside those seen during training, the predictions can become highly unreliable.

Extending the Exercise:

To deepen your understanding, consider the following extensions:

1.
State Estimation with Learned Models: Instead of directly using measured outputs, train a model that predicts future *states* from past inputs and *states*. This requires access to state measurements during training. If only a subset of states are measurable, you could combine this with a learned state estimator, where a separate neural network tries to reconstruct the full state vector from available measurements.
2. **Nonlinear System Identification:** Explore different neural network architectures (e.g., Recurrent Neural Networks like LSTMs or GRUs) that are inherently designed to handle sequential data and might capture temporal dependencies more effectively than simple MLPs.
3. **Online Learning/Adaptation:** Investigate how the learned model can be updated online as new data becomes available during operation. This allows the MPC controller to adapt to slowly changing system dynamics

or environmental conditions. Be mindful of the computational cost and stability implications of online model updates.

4. **Impact of Data Quality and Quantity:** Systematically study how the amount and quality of training data affect the performance of the learned MPC. Vary the sampling rate, the duration of data collection, the type of excitation signal, and the level of injected noise.
5. **Hybrid Models:** Explore combining analytical models with learned components. For instance, an analytical linear model could capture the dominant system dynamics, while a neural network learns to correct for the nonlinearities or unmodeled aspects. This can lead to models that are both accurate and more interpretable or extrapolative than pure neural networks. For example, a system model could be represented as $x_{k+1} = A_{learned}(x_k, u_k) x_k + B_{learned}(x_k, u_k) u_k + f_{NN}(x_k, u_k)$, where $A_{learned}$ and $B_{learned}$ might be learned parameters or matrices, and f_{NN} is a neural network representing the residual dynamics.
6. **Multiple Operating Points:** If you collected data at different operating points, train separate learned models for each region or train a single model that takes the operating point as an additional input. Evaluate how well each approach handles transitions between operating regions.

This exercise offers a profound insight into the synergy between machine learning and classical control theory. By moving from pre-defined, often simplified analytical models to data-driven, learned representations, Model Predictive Control can be extended to a far wider range of complex and challenging real-world systems. The ability to learn system dynamics directly from observations is a cornerstone of modern AI-augmented control, enabling controllers that are more accurate, more robust, and more efficient than ever before.

This exercise shifts our focus from data-driven model identification for Model Predictive Control to a fundamentally different, yet equally powerful, paradigm within artificial intelligence: Reinforcement

Learning (RL). While MPC with learned models excels when we have a clear objective and can frame control as an optimization problem over a predictive horizon, RL offers a compelling alternative when the system dynamics are complex, perhaps even unknown, and the control objective can be defined through a reward signal. Instead of explicitly modeling the system and optimizing future actions, RL agents learn to make optimal decisions through trial and error, guided by the rewards they receive. This approach is particularly well-suited for control tasks in robotics, where systems are often inherently nonlinear, exhibit complex dynamics, and where defining a precise analytical model can be exceedingly difficult.

Our goal in this exercise is to implement a reinforcement learning algorithm to enable a simulated robot to perform a specific task. We will abstract away the complexities of real-world robotics hardware, focusing instead on the core principles of RL for control. This hands-on experience will demystify the process of setting up an RL agent, defining its learning environment, and interpreting its acquired behavior. By the end of this exercise, you will have a practical understanding of how RL agents can learn to control dynamic systems without explicit programming of control laws, relying instead on a reward-driven learning process.

To begin, we need a simulated robotic system and a well-defined task. For this exercise, a simple wheeled robot is an excellent choice. Imagine a differential drive robot, common in mobile robotics research and applications. This robot is controlled by two independent motors, one for each wheel. The velocity of these wheels directly dictates the robot's linear and angular motion. The state of the robot can be described by its position (x, y coordinates) and orientation (theta angle) in a 2D plane, along with potentially the velocities of its wheels. For a more complex scenario, we could consider a robotic arm, where the state would involve the angles of its joints, and the actions would be the torques or velocities applied to those joints. However, for clarity and to focus on RL fundamentals, we will stick with the simpler wheeled robot.

The task we will assign to our simulated robot is navigation: reaching a specific target location in its environment. This is a fundamental problem in robotics and provides a clear objective for the RL agent. The agent's goal will be to learn a policy – a mapping from the robot's current state to the control actions it should take – that consistently guides the robot towards the target.

The core components of any Reinforcement Learning setup are:

1.
The Environment: This is the world in which the RL agent operates. In our case, it's the simulation of the wheeled robot and its surrounding space. The environment provides the current state to the agent and responds to the actions taken by the agent by transitioning to a new state and providing a reward.

2.
The Agent: This is the learning entity. It receives observations (states) from the environment, takes actions based on its policy, and learns from the feedback (rewards) it receives.

3.
The State Space: This defines all possible configurations or observations the agent can receive from the environment. For our wheeled robot, a basic state space might include its (x, y) position, its orientation (theta), and possibly its linear and angular velocities. It is

crucial to define a state space that provides sufficient information for the agent to make informed decisions. For navigation, knowing the robot's position relative to the target is paramount. We might also include the target's coordinates or the relative distance and angle to the target to simplify the learning problem.

4.
The Action Space: This defines all possible actions the agent can take. For our differential drive robot, actions could be continuous values representing the velocity command for the left and right wheels, or they could be discretized into a few options like "move forward," "turn left," "turn right," and "stop." The choice between continuous and discrete action spaces significantly influences the RL algorithm selection.

5.
The Reward Function: This is arguably the most critical component in guiding the learning process. It's a scalar signal that the environment provides to the agent after each action. A positive reward encourages behavior that leads to the desired outcome, while a negative reward (or penalty) discourages undesirable behavior. Designing an effective reward function is often an iterative process, requiring careful tuning to ensure it truly reflects the task objective without introducing unintended consequences.

6.
The Policy: This is what the agent learns. It's a function that maps states to actions. The ultimate goal of RL is to find an optimal policy that maximizes the cumulative reward over time.

Let's delve deeper into each of these components for our wheeled robot navigation task.

Setting Up the Simulated Environment

We will use a Python-based simulation environment. Libraries like PyBullet, MuJoCo (often accessed via OpenAI Gym), or even custom-built simulations using libraries like `pygame` or `matplotlib` can be employed. For this exercise, let's assume a simplified simulation where the robot's state (position, orientation) is updated based on simple kinematic or dynamic models.

The environment needs to:

Initialize the Robot: Place the robot at a starting position and orientation. This could be fixed or randomized for each training episode to improve generalization. Similarly, the target location can be fixed or randomized.
Simulate Physics/Kinematics: Update the robot's state (x, y, theta) based on the actions (e.g., wheel velocities) applied by the agent and the simulation's time step. For a simple kinematic model, we can use:
$x{t+1} = xt + vt \cos(\thetat) \Delta t$
$y{t+1} = yt + vt \sin(\thetat) \Delta t$
$\theta{t+1} = \thetat + \omega_t \Delta t$
where vt is the linear velocity and $\omegat$ is the angular velocity. These velocities can be derived from the individual wheel velocities. If vL and vR are the left and right wheel velocities, and r is the wheel radius, L is the distance between the wheels, then:
$vt = \frac{r}{2}(vL + v_R)$
$\omegat = \frac{r}{L}(vR - v_L)$

Detect Termination: An episode (a single attempt by the robot to reach the target) might terminate under several conditions:
Success: The robot reaches the target (within a certain tolerance).
Failure: The robot collides with an obstacle (if obstacles are present), goes out of bounds, or exceeds a maximum number of steps (to prevent infinite episodes).
Calculate Reward: At each time step, compute the reward based on the robot's current state and action.
Provide State Observation: Return the current state of the robot to the agent.

Defining the State and Action Spaces

For our navigation task, a reasonable state representation could be:

Relative Goal Position: $(x{goal} - x{robot}, y{goal} - y{robot})$. This is crucial as it tells the robot where the target is relative to its own position.
Robot's Orientation: θ_{robot}. This helps the robot understand which way it's facing.
Relative Angle to Goal: The angle between the robot's current heading and the direction pointing to the goal. This can be calculated from the robot's orientation and the relative position vector.
(Optional) Robot's Linear and Angular Velocity: Including these can help if the robot's dynamics are important and the action space is continuous.

So, a possible state vector $s
t$ could be: $[dx, dy, \theta{robot}, \alpha{goal}]$, where $dx = x{goal} - x{robot}$, $dy = y{goal} - y{robot}$, and α{goal} is the angle to

the goal. Normalizing these values to a standard range (e.g., [-1, 1]) is often beneficial for neural network-based RL agents.

The action space can be defined as:

Discrete Actions: A finite set of actions, such as:
1. Move forward a fixed distance.
2. Turn left by a fixed angle.
3. Turn right by a fixed angle.
4. Move backward.
5. Stop.

This is often easier to start with, especially when using algorithms like Q-learning.

Continuous Actions: Two continuous values representing the desired linear velocity (v) and angular velocity (ω) of the robot. This offers finer control but requires algorithms capable of handling continuous action spaces, such as Deep Deterministic Policy Gradient (DDPG), Proximal Policy Optimization (PPO), or Soft Actor-Critic (SAC).

Let's opt for the
discrete action space for our initial implementation, as it simplifies the understanding of basic RL algorithms.

Designing the Reward Function

A well-designed reward function is key to successful RL training. For navigation, we want to incentivize moving towards the goal and penalize actions that move the robot away from it or prolong the episode unnecessarily.

Here's a possible reward structure:

Reaching the Goal: A large positive reward (e.g., +100). This is the primary objective.
Getting Closer to the Goal: A small positive reward based on the reduction in distance to the goal. For example, if the distance decreased from $D{old}$ to $D{new}$, the reward could be $(D{old} - D{new}) \times \text{scaling\_factor}$. This encourages progress.
Moving Away from the Goal: A small negative reward (penalty) if the distance to the goal increases. This discourages errant movements.
Collision/Out of Bounds: A large negative reward (e.g., -50). This strongly discourages undesirable outcomes.
Time Penalty: A small negative reward at each time step (e.g., -0.1). This encourages the robot to reach the goal efficiently, rather than meandering indefinitely.

The exact values for these rewards will need tuning. A common pitfall is having a reward function that is too sparse (e.g., only rewarding reaching the goal), which makes learning very slow, or one that is too sensitive to small changes, leading to unstable learning.

Choosing an RL Algorithm

Given our choice of a discrete action space and a potentially complex state space (especially if we include velocities or use neural networks for function approximation), Q-learning is a fundamental algorithm to consider.

Q-Learning:

Q-learning is a model-free, off-policy temporal difference (TD) learning algorithm. It learns an action-value function, denoted as $Q(s, a)$, which represents the expected future cumulative reward of taking action a in state s and then following the optimal policy thereafter.

The core update rule for Q-learning is:

$Q(s
t, at) \leftarrow Q(st, at) + \alpha \left[r{t+1} + \gamma \max{a{t+1}}
Q(s{t+1}, a{t+1}) - Q(st, a_t) \right]$

Where:

s_t: The current state.
at: The action taken at state st.
$r{t+1}$: The reward received after taking action at.
$s{t+1}$: The next state after taking action at.
α: The learning rate (how much we update the Q-value based on new information), typically between 0 and 1.
γ: The discount factor (how much we value future rewards compared to immediate rewards), typically between 0 and 1.

$\max{a{t+1}} Q(s{t+1}, a{t+1})$: The maximum expected future reward from the next state $s{t+1}$, *achievable by choosing the best possible action* $a{t+1}$.

Challenges with Tabular Q-Learning:

If the state space is small and discrete (e.g., a grid world with a few cells), we can store the Q-values in a table. However, for robotics applications, the state space is often continuous or very large and discrete. In such cases, a Q-table becomes infeasible. This is where
Deep Q-Networks (DQN) comes in.

Deep Q-Networks (DQN):

DQN extends Q-learning by using a neural network to approximate the Q-function, $Q(s, a; \theta)$, where θ represents the weights of the neural network. The neural network takes the state s as input and outputs the Q-values for all possible discrete actions.

The training process for DQN involves:

1.
Experience Replay: Store transitions $(st, at, r{t+1}, s{t+1})$ in a memory buffer. During training, sample mini-batches of these transitions from the buffer. This breaks the correlation between consecutive samples and improves learning stability.
2. **Target Network:** Use a separate "target network" with weights θ^- to compute the target Q-values: $y = r{t+1} + \gamma \max{a{t+1}} Q(s{t+1}, a{t+1}; \theta^-)$. *The main network's weights*

θ *are then updated to minimize the loss:* $L(\theta) = \frac{1}{N} \sum{i=1}^N (yi - Q(s{i}, a_{i}; \theta))^2$. The target network's weights are periodically updated by copying the weights from the main network ($\theta^- \leftarrow \theta$). This also enhances stability.

DQN is a good candidate for our discrete action space navigation task.

Implementing DQN for Robot Navigation

Let's outline the practical steps for implementing DQN:

1.
Environment Setup:
Choose a simulation library (e.g., PyBullet, or a custom `gym`-like environment).
Implement the robot's state (position, orientation, relative goal info), actions (discrete commands), and the reward function as described above.
Define the termination conditions for an episode.

2.
DQN Agent Architecture:
Neural Network: Design a feedforward neural network. The input layer will have a size corresponding to the dimension of your state vector. The output layer will have a size equal to the number of discrete actions. Each output neuron will represent the Q-value for a specific action in the given state. Activation functions like ReLU for hidden layers and a linear activation for the output layer are common.

Target Network: Create an identical network structure for the target network.
Experience Replay Buffer: Implement a data structure (e.g., a `collections.deque`) to store experiences.
Optimizer: Choose an optimizer, such as Adam or RMSprop, to update the neural network weights.

3.
Training Loop:
Initialize the main network and the target network with random weights.
Initialize the experience replay buffer.
Set hyperparameters: learning rate (α), discount factor (γ), replay buffer size, batch size, target network update frequency, exploration parameters (epsilon for epsilon-greedy policy).
For each episode:
Reset the environment to get the initial state s_0.
Initialize episode reward accumulator.
For each time step t:
Choose action at: Use an epsilon-greedy policy. With probability ϵ, choose a random action (exploration). Otherwise, choose the action $at = \arg\max{a} Q(st, a; \theta)$ (exploitation). Gradually decay ϵ over episodes to shift from exploration to exploitation.
Take action a_t: Send the action to the environment.
Observe reward $r{t+1}$ and next state $s{t+1}$: The environment returns these values.
Store experience: Add the transition $(st, at, r{t+1}, s{t+1})$ to the replay buffer.
Update state: $st \leftarrow s{t+1}$.
Learn (if buffer is sufficiently full):
Sample a mini-batch of experiences from the replay buffer.
For each sampled experience $(sj, aj, r{j+1}, s{j+1})$:
Calculate the target Q-value:

If $s{j+1}$ is a terminal state, $yj = r_{j+1}$.
Otherwise, $yj = r{j+1} + \gamma \max{a'} Q(s{j+1}, a'; \theta^-)$.
Compute the loss: $Lj = (yj - Q(sj, aj; \theta))^2$.
Perform a gradient descent step on the mini-batch loss to update the main network's weights θ.
Update Target Network: Periodically copy weights from the main network to the target network.
Accumulate episode reward.
Check for episode termination.
Log episode reward and other relevant metrics.

4.
Evaluation:
After training for a sufficient number of episodes, evaluate the learned policy by disabling exploration (setting $\epsilon = 0$) and observing the robot's behavior.
Visualize the robot's path and compare its performance against the desired task.
Monitor metrics like success rate, average episode length, and cumulative reward.

Considerations and Further Enhancements

State Representation: The choice of state representation is crucial. If the robot's orientation is not included, it might not be able to learn to turn correctly. Including sensor readings (like distance to goal) can significantly speed up learning. For more complex environments with obstacles, incorporating obstacle sensor data (e.g., from simulated LiDAR or proximity sensors) into the state would be necessary.

Reward Shaping: As mentioned, reward shaping is an art. If the robot struggles to find the goal, you might need to "shape" the reward function to provide more intermediate guidance. However, be cautious, as poorly shaped rewards can lead to suboptimal policies. For instance, rewarding for being within a certain radius of the goal, or penalizing for turning away from the goal direction, can be forms of shaping.

Exploration Strategies: Epsilon-greedy is a simple exploration strategy. More advanced strategies like Boltzmann exploration or adding noise to actions (especially in continuous action spaces) can sometimes be more effective. For complex exploration problems, intrinsic motivation techniques can also be employed, where the agent is rewarded for exploring novel states or for achieving goals it sets for itself.

Hyperparameter Tuning: RL algorithms are notoriously sensitive to hyperparameters. Learning rate, discount factor, replay buffer size, batch size, exploration decay rate, and neural network architecture all play a significant role. It's common to run multiple training experiments with different hyperparameter settings to find optimal configurations.

Continuous Action Spaces and Advanced Algorithms:

If we had chosen a continuous action space (e.g., desired linear and angular velocities), we would need different algorithms.

Deep Deterministic Policy Gradient (DDPG): An actor-critic algorithm suitable for continuous action spaces. The "actor" network learns the policy (mapping states to actions), and the "critic" network learns the Q-function (evaluating the actor's actions). It uses techniques like experience replay and target networks, similar to DQN, but adapted for continuous actions.
Proximal Policy Optimization (PPO): A policy gradient method that aims to make optimization steps as large as possible without going too far, leading to more stable learning. It's known for its good performance across a wide range of tasks.
Soft Actor-Critic (SAC): An actor-critic method that incorporates an entropy maximization objective into the reward. This encourages exploration and can lead to more robust policies.

Implementing these algorithms involves managing two neural networks (actor and critic) and their respective target networks, along with specialized loss functions for policy and value updates.

Interpreting the Learned Policy:

Once the agent has been trained, it's essential to analyze its behavior.

Visualization: The most intuitive way to evaluate the learned policy is to run the robot in the simulation with exploration turned off and visualize its path. Does it move towards the goal? Does it exhibit smooth or jerky movements? Does it avoid obstacles (if applicable)?
Success Rate: Quantify how often the robot successfully reaches the target within a given number of steps.

Episode Length: How long does it take the robot to reach the goal? A shorter episode length generally indicates a more efficient policy.
Q-Value Analysis: While harder to interpret directly, examining the learned Q-values for specific states can sometimes provide insights into what the agent has learned. For example, are the Q-values for "move forward" higher when the robot is facing the goal?

Challenges and Pitfalls:

Local Optima: RL algorithms can sometimes get stuck in local optima, learning a policy that is good but not the best possible.
Instability: Training can be unstable, with performance fluctuating significantly between episodes or training runs.
Sample Inefficiency: RL algorithms, especially model-free ones, can require a very large amount of data (interactions with the environment) to learn effectively. This is why simulation is often preferred for initial training.
Reward Hacking: The agent might find unexpected ways to maximize reward that don't align with the intended task. For example, if the reward for getting closer is too high, it might just oscillate back and forth near the goal without actually reaching it.

This exercise, by guiding you through the implementation of RL for a basic robotic control task, provides a foundational understanding of how intelligent agents can learn to navigate complex environments. It highlights the importance of problem formulation – defining the state, action, and reward – and showcases the power of iterative learning through trial and error. The transition from a meticulously designed controller, as in MPC, to a learned controller, as in RL, represents a significant shift in how we approach robotics and control challenges, opening doors to solutions for problems that were previously intractable with traditional methods.

In our journey through advanced control strategies, we have explored model predictive control, leveraging system dynamics to optimize future actions, and delved into the trial-and-error learning of reinforcement learning (RL) agents for autonomous navigation. While RL offers remarkable flexibility and the ability to handle complex, even unknown, dynamics, its data-driven, emergent nature brings a critical challenge to the forefront: ensuring safety. An RL agent, by its very design, learns through exploration and exploitation, and in the initial stages of training, or even when faced with novel situations, its actions can be unpredictable and potentially hazardous. This is particularly true in physical systems, such as robotics and autonomous vehicles, where an unsafe action can lead to damage, injury, or mission failure.

This exercise directly addresses this crucial aspect of deploying learning-based controllers in real-world or safety-critical applications. We will shift our focus from merely enabling a controller to learn an optimal policy to embedding a robust safety layer that guarantees the system operates within predefined safe boundaries, regardless of the controller's proposed actions. This concept is often referred to as a "safety shield" or "safety supervisor." The core idea is to create an intelligent system that not only learns to perform a task efficiently but also possesses an inherent mechanism to prevent catastrophic failures.

Imagine a scenario where our previously trained RL agent is tasked with controlling a simulated drone. The agent has learned to perform maneuvers like hovering, ascending, descending, and perhaps even a simple form of aerial navigation. However, during training or deployment, the agent might propose an action that causes the drone to exceed its maximum velocity limits, pitch too aggressively beyond its stable angle, or descend too rapidly, leading to a crash. Without a safety layer, these actions would be executed, with potentially dire consequences. Our objective in this exercise is to implement a system that intercepts such hazardous commands and enforces safe behavior.

We will conceptualize and implement a safety layer that acts as an intermediary between the learned controller and the actual actuators of the simulated drone. This safety layer will be equipped with knowledge of the drone's safe operating envelope – the set of states and actions that are considered acceptable. When the learned controller proposes an action, the safety layer will first evaluate its safety based on the current state and the predefined safety constraints. If the proposed action is deemed safe, it will be passed on to the drone's actuators. If, however, the action is deemed unsafe, the safety layer will intervene. This intervention could take several forms: it might modify the unsafe action to the nearest safe alternative, replace it with a default safe action (like maintaining current velocity or initiating a controlled hover), or even take direct control to ensure immediate safety.

For this exercise, we will use a simplified simulated drone model. This model will have a state vector that includes parameters such as its position (x, y, z coordinates), orientation (roll, pitch, yaw angles), and velocities (linear and angular). The learned controller, for example, our RL agent, will output desired control signals, which in a real drone would typically correspond to thrust, pitch, roll, and yaw rates. The safety layer will receive these desired commands, along with the current drone state, and decide on the final commands to be sent to the simulation.

The key components of our safety layer will be:

1.

Safe Operating Envelope Definition: This is the heart of the safety mechanism. It involves mathematically defining the boundaries within which the drone must operate. This can be expressed as a set of inequalities or constraints on the state variables and/or the control inputs. For instance, we might define:

State Constraints: Maximum altitude, minimum altitude, maximum pitch/roll angles, limits on linear/angular velocities.

Control Input Constraints: Maximum motor thrust, maximum rate of change of control inputs.

These constraints are derived from the physical limitations of the drone, its components, and the mission requirements.

2.

Safety Verification Module: This module takes the current state of the drone and the control action proposed by the learning controller and checks if the resulting next state and the action itself violate any of the defined safe operating boundaries. This check might involve:

Direct Constraint Checking: Evaluating if the proposed control action exceeds limits on thrust, velocity, or angle rates.

Predictive Checking (Optional but highly desirable): Using a simplified model of the drone's dynamics, the safety layer could predict the next state resulting from the proposed action and check if this predicted state violates any state constraints. This is a more proactive approach to safety.

3.

Action Intervention Mechanism: If the safety verification module flags a proposed action as unsafe, this mechanism takes over. Its role is to provide a safe alternative action. Common strategies include:

Clipping/Saturation: If an action component exceeds a limit, it is "clipped" to the maximum or minimum allowed value. For example, if the

RL agent requests 120% thrust, the safety layer might enforce 100% thrust.

Projection: Projecting the unsafe action onto the set of safe actions. This is a more sophisticated method that ensures the resulting action is not just within bounds but also as close as possible to the original unsafe action, preserving some of the controller's intent.

Fallback Policies: In severe cases, the safety layer might switch to a predefined, robust "fallback" policy that guarantees stability, such as commanding the drone to hover or initiate a gentle descent.

4.

State Estimation and Prediction (if using predictive checking): For predictive safety checks, an accurate and reasonably fast state estimation is required. If the system dynamics are complex, a simplified linear or nonlinear model can be used for prediction. The accuracy of this prediction model directly impacts the effectiveness of the predictive safety layer.

Exercise Setup: Simulated Drone with a Safety Layer

We will build upon a simulated drone environment. This environment will allow us to:

Define the drone's state (position, orientation, velocities).
Simulate the drone's dynamics based on control inputs.
Implement predefined safe operating limits.
Incorporate mechanisms to test the safety layer, such as introducing faults or pushing the learning controller to propose extreme actions.

Defining the Safe Operating Envelope for the Drone

Let's consider a simplified drone model where the control inputs are four thrust values for individual rotors, or aggregated into commands for collective thrust, pitch, roll, and yaw. For this exercise, let's assume the learning controller outputs desired
angular velocities ($\omega{pitch}, \omega{roll}, \omega{yaw}$) *and a desired* **collective thrust** command ($T{des}$).

The state of the drone (s) can be represented by its current orientation (ϕ, θ, ψ for roll, pitch, yaw), linear velocities ($v x, vy, vz$), *and angular velocities* ($\omegax, \omegay, \omegaz$).

The safe operating envelope can be defined by constraints such as:

Pitch and Roll Angle Limits: To prevent the drone from flipping over.
$-\theta{max} \leq \theta \leq \theta{max}$
$-\phi{max} \leq \phi \leq \phi{max}$
where θ{max} *and* ϕ{max} are typically around 30-45 degrees for stable flight.

Angular Velocity Limits: To ensure smooth control and prevent instability.
$-\omega{max} \leq \omegax, \omegay, \omegaz \leq \omega_{max}$

Linear Velocity Limits: To maintain control authority and avoid high-speed instability.
$-v{max} \leq vx, vy, vz \leq v_{max}$

Collective Thrust Limits: To avoid exceeding motor capabilities or causing structural stress.
$T{min} \leq T{des} \leq T{max}$ (where $T{min}$ might be a small positive value to keep rotors spinning slowly even when commanded zero thrust, or even zero if motors can be fully stopped).

Implementing the Safety Verification and Intervention

The safety layer will continuously monitor the situation. At each control cycle:

1.
Receive State and Proposed Action: The safety layer gets the current drone state (st) and the action ($a{learned}$) proposed by the learning controller. $a{learned} = [T{des, learned}, \omega{pitch, learned}, \omega{roll, learned}, \omega_{yaw, learned}]$.

2.
Safety Check:
Check Control Input Limits:
Is $T{min} \leq T{des, learned} \leq T_{max}$?
Is $-\omega{max} \leq \omega{pitch, learned} \leq \omega_{max}$?
Is $-\omega{max} \leq \omega{roll, learned} \leq \omega_{max}$?
Is $-\omega{max} \leq \omega{yaw, learned} \leq \omega_{max}$?

Predictive State Check (using a simplified drone dynamics model): This is a more advanced check. Let's assume we have a simplified kinematic model that relates control inputs to changes in state over a small time step Δt. For instance, angular accelerations might be approximated based on control inputs, and then integrated to find

predicted angular velocities and orientations. If $a*{learned}$ is applied, what will the state $s*{t+\Delta t}$ approximately be?
Approximate the next angular velocities: $\omega*{x, t+\Delta t} \approx \omega*{x, t} + \alpha*{pitch} \Delta t$, where $\alpha*{pitch}$ is related to $\omega_{pitch, learned}$ and drone parameters.
Approximate the next orientation: For small angles, $\theta*{t+\Delta t} \approx \theta*t + \omega_{pitch, t+\Delta t} \Delta t$. More generally, quaternion or rotation matrix updates would be used.
Check if these predicted values violate constraints:
Is $-\theta*{max} \leq \theta*{t+\Delta t} \leq \theta_{max}$?
Is $-\phi*{max} \leq \phi*{t+\Delta t} \leq \phi_{max}$?
Is $-\omega*{max} \leq \omega*{x, t+\Delta t}, \omega*{y, t+\Delta t}, \omega*{z, t+\Delta t} \leq \omega_{max}$?
(Linear velocity prediction is more complex and depends on thrust and orientation, typically requiring a full dynamics model.)

3.
Action Intervention:
If all checks pass, the action is safe: $a*{safe} = a*{learned}$.
If any check fails, an intervention is triggered. A simple intervention is **clipping** the violating control inputs to their safe limits. For example, if $\omega*{pitch, learned} > \omega*{max}$, then $\omega*{pitch, safe} = \omega*{max}$. If $T*{des, learned} < T*{min}$, then $T*{des, safe} = T*{min}$. The resulting safe action a_{safe} is then computed with clipped values.
A more advanced intervention might involve projecting the action onto the feasible set, or executing a predefined emergency landing sequence if the state is already critical.

Testing the Safety Layer

To demonstrate the effectiveness of the safety layer, we need to design test scenarios. These scenarios will deliberately challenge the learning controller and the safety mechanisms:

Pushing the Controller to its Limits: We can modify the rewards or the environment to encourage the learning controller to propose actions that are close to or exceed the safe boundaries. For example, if the RL agent is rewarded for fast maneuvers, it might learn to output high angular velocities. The safety layer should then intervene, clipping these velocities to the allowed maximum.

Introducing Disturbances and Faults: We can simulate external forces acting on the drone (e.g., wind gusts) or internal faults (e.g., one motor failing, leading to unbalanced thrust). These disturbances can push the drone into unsafe states or cause the learning controller to output extreme commands in an attempt to compensate.
Wind Gust Scenario: Simulate a sudden horizontal wind gust. This will push the drone off its intended trajectory and orientation. The learning controller might try to counteract this by commanding large roll or pitch rates and thrust. The safety layer must ensure these counter-commands do not violate physical limits.
Motor Failure Scenario: Simulate the failure of one of the drone's motors. This will cause an imbalance in thrust and torques, leading to uncontrolled rotation and translation. The learning controller will likely try to compensate by adjusting the thrust of the remaining motors. The safety layer needs to ensure that the commanded thrust for the functioning motors does not exceed maximum limits and that the resulting state remains within safe bounds (or at least the system attempts a controlled descent rather than an immediate crash).

Novel State Exploration: During initial training of the RL agent, it will encounter states it has never seen before. The safety layer must be robust to these novel states and ensure that any action proposed by the agent in these unknown territories is safe. This highlights the advantage of a fixed, verifiable safety layer over a purely learned policy.

Implementation Details and Considerations

Discretization vs. Continuous Control: The choice of whether the learning controller outputs discrete actions (e.g., "increase thrust," "pitch left") or continuous actions (e.g., precise thrust and angular velocity values) affects the implementation of the safety layer. For continuous actions, clipping or projection methods are more applicable. For discrete actions, the safety layer might map unsafe discrete actions to safe ones or a default safe action. In our example, we assumed continuous control outputs from the RL agent.

Prediction Model Accuracy: If using predictive safety checks, the accuracy of the dynamics model used for prediction is crucial. An overly simplified model might miss potential safety violations, while a very complex one might be too computationally expensive to run in real-time. A trade-off is necessary. Often, simplified linear models or models that capture the dominant dynamics are sufficient for safety verification.

Computational Load: Safety verification and intervention must be performed very quickly, typically at the same frequency as the control loop. This means the safety layer's algorithms must be computationally efficient. Clipping is very fast. Projection algorithms can be more intensive, depending on the complexity of the feasible set.

Safety Layer Design Philosophy: The safety layer should be designed to be conservative. It's better to slightly restrict the performance of the learned controller than to risk an unsafe event. The goal is not to optimize performance but to guarantee safety. The learned controller is responsible for performance within the safe envelope.

Hierarchical Control: The safety layer can be viewed as a form of hierarchical control. The learning controller acts as a high-level planner or controller, proposing actions. The safety layer acts as a low-level supervisor or guardian, ensuring these proposed actions are permissible.

Formal Verification (Advanced): For extremely safety-critical applications, formal verification techniques could be employed to mathematically prove that the safety layer, under all possible inputs and conditions, will always keep the system within its safe boundaries. This is a highly advanced topic usually applied to simpler systems or specific components.

Demonstration Walkthrough

Let's illustrate with a hypothetical scenario. Suppose the drone is currently flying at a pitch angle of 15 degrees, well within the $\pm$ 45-degree limit. The learning controller, trying to execute a rapid ascent, proposes an action that includes a desired pitch rate of 60 degrees per second. Our safety parameters define a maximum allowed pitch rate of 50 degrees per second.

The safety layer receives the current state and the proposed action.

State: Pitch = 15 degrees, Pitch Rate = 5 deg/sec, etc.
Proposed Action: Pitch Rate = 60 deg/sec.

Safety Check:
The safety layer checks the proposed pitch rate: 60 deg/sec. This exceeds the maximum allowed pitch rate of 50 deg/sec.

Intervention:
Since the proposed action is unsafe, the intervention mechanism is activated. In this case, simple clipping would be applied.
Safe Action: Pitch Rate = 50 deg/sec.

The safety layer then outputs this clipped pitch rate to the drone's simulation. The drone will pitch at the maximum allowed rate, preventing it from potentially over-pitching into an unstable or unsafe configuration. The learning controller, meanwhile, would ideally receive feedback (e.g., through a modified reward or by observing that its requested action was not fully executed) that its proposed action was limited, which might influence its future learning.

Consider another scenario where the drone is near its maximum altitude limit of 100 meters. The RL agent proposes to increase collective thrust by 80%. With a simplified predictive model, the safety layer estimates that this thrust increase would cause the drone's altitude to reach 103 meters within the next control interval.

State: Altitude = 99 meters, Altitude rate = 2 m/sec.
Proposed Action: Collective Thrust = 80% (higher than current).
Predicted Next State: Altitude = 103 meters.

Safety Check:
The predicted altitude (103 meters) exceeds the maximum altitude limit (100 meters).

Intervention:
The safety layer would then modify the thrust command. It might reduce the collective thrust to a level that is predicted to keep the altitude at or below 100 meters, or it might issue a "hover" command for thrust. For example, it might cap the collective thrust to a value that is estimated to result in a zero vertical velocity or a minimal ascent.

Role of the Safety Layer in Robustness

The safety layer plays a critical role in making learning-based controllers robust. While the learning controller aims to optimize performance under nominal conditions, the safety layer acts as a safeguard against unforeseen circumstances:

Sensor Noise and Estimation Errors: If the state estimation is noisy, the learning controller might receive incorrect state information, leading it to propose unsafe actions. A well-designed safety layer can filter or bound the effects of such errors.

Model Mismatch: The learning controller might have been trained on a model that doesn't perfectly represent the real system dynamics. The safety layer, with its explicit, often simpler, and conservative bounds, can compensate for these mismatches.
Adversarial Attacks: In security-sensitive applications, an adversary might try to feed false sensor data to the learning controller to make it behave dangerously. A safety layer, if designed to be resistant to such manipulations (e.g., by checking for consistency in sensor readings or using diverse safety checks), can provide a layer of defense.

In summary, integrating a safety layer is not merely an optional addition but a fundamental requirement for deploying learning-based control systems in any application where safety is paramount. It transforms a potentially unpredictable learned policy into a reliable component of a safe autonomous system. This exercise provides hands-on experience in building such a critical safety mechanism, reinforcing the principles of robust and responsible AI in control engineering. The ability to define, verify, and enforce safety constraints is a cornerstone of trustworthy autonomous systems.In our journey through advanced control strategies, we have explored model predictive control, leveraging system dynamics to optimize future actions, and delved into the trial-and-error learning of reinforcement learning (RL) agents for autonomous navigation. While RL offers remarkable flexibility and the ability to handle complex, even unknown, dynamics, its data-driven, emergent nature brings a critical challenge to the forefront: ensuring safety. An RL agent, by its very design, learns through exploration and exploitation, and in the initial stages of training, or even when faced with novel situations, its actions can be unpredictable and potentially hazardous. This is particularly true in physical systems, such as robotics and autonomous vehicles, where an unsafe action can lead to damage, injury, or mission failure.

This exercise directly addresses this crucial aspect of deploying learning-based controllers in real-world or safety-critical applications. We will shift our focus from merely enabling a controller to learn an optimal policy to embedding a robust safety layer that guarantees the system operates within predefined safe boundaries, regardless of the controller's proposed actions. This concept is often referred to as a "safety shield" or "safety supervisor." The core idea is to create an intelligent system that not only learns to perform a task efficiently but also possesses an inherent mechanism to prevent catastrophic failures.

Imagine a scenario where our previously trained RL agent is tasked with controlling a simulated drone. The agent has learned to perform maneuvers like hovering, ascending, descending, and perhaps even a simple form of aerial navigation. However, during training or deployment, the agent might propose an action that causes the drone to exceed its maximum velocity limits, pitch too aggressively beyond its stable angle, or descend too rapidly, leading to a crash. Without a safety layer, these actions would be executed, with potentially dire consequences. Our objective in this exercise is to implement a system that intercepts such hazardous commands and enforces safe behavior.

We will conceptualize and implement a safety layer that acts as an intermediary between the learned controller and the actual actuators of the simulated drone. This safety layer will be equipped with knowledge of the drone's safe operating envelope – the set of states and actions that are considered acceptable. When the learned controller proposes an action, the safety layer will first evaluate its safety based on the current state and the predefined safety constraints. If the proposed action is deemed safe, it will be passed on to the drone's actuators. If, however, the action is deemed unsafe, the safety layer will intervene. This intervention could take several forms: it might modify the unsafe action to the nearest safe alternative, replace it with a default safe action (like maintaining current velocity or initiating a controlled hover), or even take direct control to ensure immediate safety.

For this exercise, we will use a simplified simulated drone model. This model will have a state vector that includes parameters such as its position (x, y, z coordinates), orientation (roll, pitch, yaw angles), and velocities (linear and angular). The learned controller, for example, our RL agent, will output desired control signals, which in a real drone would typically correspond to thrust, pitch, roll, and yaw rates. The safety layer will receive these desired commands, along with the current drone state, and decide on the final commands to be sent to the simulation.

The key components of our safety layer will be:

1.
Safe Operating Envelope Definition: This is the heart of the safety mechanism. It involves mathematically defining the boundaries within which the drone must operate. This can be expressed as a set of inequalities or constraints on the state variables and/or the control inputs. For instance, we might define:
State Constraints: Maximum altitude, minimum altitude, maximum pitch/roll angles, limits on linear/angular velocities.
Control Input Constraints: Maximum motor thrust, maximum rate of change of control inputs.
These constraints are derived from the physical limitations of the drone, its components, and the mission requirements. The definition of these constraints requires a thorough understanding of the system's physical properties, flight envelope, and failure modes. For instance, the

maximum pitch and roll angles are often dictated by the point at which the drone loses aerodynamic stability or its rotors start to stall or interfere with each other. Similarly, velocity limits might be imposed not just for safety but also to ensure the effectiveness of the attitude control system, which often relies on maintaining a certain level of maneuverability.

2.

Safety Verification Module: This module takes the current state of the drone and the control action proposed by the learning controller and checks if the resulting next state and the action itself violate any of the defined safe operating boundaries. This check might involve:

Direct Constraint Checking: Evaluating if the proposed control action exceeds limits on thrust, velocity, or angle rates. This is the most straightforward check and is performed directly on the control command itself. For example, if the control command is a desired thrust value, it's checked against the minimum and maximum thrust the motors can provide.

Predictive Checking (Optional but highly desirable): Using a simplified model of the drone's dynamics, the safety layer could predict the next state resulting from the proposed action and check if this predicted state violates any state constraints. This is a more proactive approach to safety. For example, if the drone is currently at 95 meters altitude and the learned controller commands an action that, according to a simplified model, would increase its altitude by 10 meters, the safety layer would predict a new altitude of 105 meters and flag it as unsafe if the maximum altitude is 100 meters. This prediction horizon can be adjusted; a longer horizon might be safer but computationally more expensive and reliant on a more accurate dynamics model.

3.

Action Intervention Mechanism: If the safety verification module flags a proposed action as unsafe, this mechanism takes over. Its role is to provide a safe alternative action. Common strategies include:
Clipping/Saturation: If an action component exceeds a limit, it is "clipped" to the maximum or minimum allowed value. For example, if the RL agent requests 120% thrust, the safety layer might enforce 100% thrust. This is simple and computationally cheap but might not always yield a desirable safe action.
Projection: Projecting the unsafe action onto the set of safe actions. This is a more sophisticated method that ensures the resulting action is not just within bounds but also as close as possible to the original unsafe action, preserving some of the controller's intent. This often involves solving a constrained optimization problem. For example, if a combination of pitch and roll commands is unsafe, projection would find the closest safe combination.
Fallback Policies: In severe cases, the safety layer might switch to a predefined, robust "fallback" policy that guarantees stability, such as commanding the drone to hover or initiate a gentle descent. This is often a last resort when the system is in a critical state.

4.
State Estimation and Prediction (if using predictive checking): For predictive safety checks, an accurate and reasonably fast state estimation is required. If the system dynamics are complex, a simplified linear or nonlinear model can be used for prediction. The accuracy of this prediction model directly impacts the effectiveness of the predictive safety layer. The choice of state variables is also critical; for instance, including angular velocities is vital for predicting changes in orientation.

Exercise Setup: Simulated Drone with a Safety Layer

We will build upon a simulated drone environment. This environment will allow us to:

Define the drone's state (position, orientation, velocities). This state representation needs to be comprehensive enough to capture all parameters relevant to safety constraints. For example, if altitude is a safety constraint, then vertical position and vertical velocity must be part of the state.
Simulate the drone's dynamics based on control inputs. This simulation should be sufficiently realistic to test the safety layer effectively, even if it's simplified for computational reasons. The simulation typically involves integrating differential equations describing the drone's motion.
Implement predefined safe operating limits. These limits should be clearly defined and verifiable. They form the basis of the safety layer's decision-making.
Incorporate mechanisms to test the safety layer, such as introducing faults or pushing the learning controller to propose extreme actions. This is crucial for validating the robustness of the safety system.

Defining the Safe Operating Envelope for the Drone

Let's consider a simplified drone model where the control inputs are four thrust values for individual rotors, or aggregated into commands for collective thrust, pitch, roll, and yaw. For this exercise, let's assume the learning controller outputs desired
angular velocities ($\omega*{pitch}, \omega*{roll}, \omega*{yaw}$) and a desired* **collective thrust** command ($T{des}$).

The state of the drone (s) can be represented by its current orientation (ϕ, θ, ψ for roll, pitch, yaw), linear velocities ($v x, vy, vz$), and angular velocities ($\omegax, \omegay, \omegaz$). The position (x, y, z) is also essential, particularly for altitude constraints.

The safe operating envelope can be defined by constraints such as:

Pitch and Roll Angle Limits: To prevent the drone from flipping over.
$-\theta{max} \leq \theta \leq \theta{max}$
$-\phi{max} \leq \phi \leq \phi{max}$
where θ{max} and ϕ{max} are typically around 30-45 degrees for stable flight. These limits are critical because exceeding them can lead to loss of control authority, as the aerodynamic forces become unpredictable or insufficient to counteract disturbances.

Angular Velocity Limits: To ensure smooth control and prevent instability.
$-\omega{max} \leq \omegax, \omegay, \omegaz \leq \omega_{max}$
These limits prevent the drone from rotating too quickly, which could induce high accelerations, lead to structural stress, or exceed the capabilities of the attitude control system.

Linear Velocity Limits: To maintain control authority and avoid high-speed instability.
$-v{max} \leq vx, vy, vz \leq v_{max}$
High linear velocities, especially in conjunction with large pitch or roll angles, can also lead to unpredictable flight dynamics and make it difficult for the control system to maintain stability.

Collective Thrust Limits: To avoid exceeding motor capabilities or causing structural stress.
$T_{min} \leq T_{des} \leq T_{max}$ (where T_{min} might be a small positive value to keep rotors spinning slowly even when commanded zero thrust, or even zero if motors can be fully stopped). These are fundamental physical limits of the propulsion system.

Altitude Limits: To ensure the drone stays within a safe operational altitude range.
$z_{min} \leq z \leq z_{max}$
This is particularly important in scenarios where the drone operates near the ground or must avoid airborne obstacles or airspace restrictions.

Implementing the Safety Verification and Intervention

The safety layer will continuously monitor the situation. At each control cycle:

1.
Receive State and Proposed Action: The safety layer gets the current drone state (s_t) and the action ($a_{learned}$) proposed by the learning controller. $a_{learned} = [T_{des, learned}, \omega_{pitch, learned}, \omega_{roll, learned}, \omega_{yaw, learned}]$. The state s_t would typically include $(x, y, z, \phi, \theta, \psi, v_x, v_y, v_z, \omega_x, \omega_y, \omega_z)$.

2.
Safety Check:
Check Control Input Limits:

Is $T{min} \leq T{des, learned} \leq T_{max}$?
Is $-\omega{max} \leq \omega{pitch, learned} \leq \omega_{max}$?
Is $-\omega{max} \leq \omega{roll, learned} \leq \omega_{max}$?
Is $-\omega{max} \leq \omega{yaw, learned} \leq \omega_{max}$?

Predictive State Check (using a simplified drone dynamics model): This is a more advanced check. Let's assume we have a simplified kinematic model that relates control inputs to changes in state over a small time step Δt. For instance, angular accelerations might be approximated based on control inputs, and then integrated to find predicted angular velocities and orientations. If $a{learned}$ *is applied, what will the state* $s{t+\Delta t}$ approximately be?
Approximate the next angular velocities: A simple model might relate control commands to angular accelerations: $\alphax \approx k{roll} \omega{roll, learned}$, $\alphay \approx k{pitch} \omega{pitch, learned}$, etc. Then, $\omega{x, t+\Delta t} \approx \omega{x, t} + \alpha_x \Delta t$.
Approximate the next orientation: For small angles, $\theta{t+\Delta t} \approx \thetat + \omega{pitch, t+\Delta t} \Delta t$. *More generally, quaternion multiplication or rotation matrix updates would be used:* $R{t+\Delta t} = R(t) \cdot \Delta R(\omega{x,t+\Delta t}, \omega{y,t+\Delta t}, \omega_{z,t+\Delta t}, \Delta t)$.
Approximate the next linear velocities and position: This is more complex and depends on current orientation and thrust. A simplified approach might assume $v{z, t+\Delta t} \approx v{z, t} + (T_{des, learned}/m - g) \Delta t$ (where m is mass and g is gravity), and then transform this acceleration to the inertial frame using the current orientation.
Check if these predicted values violate constraints:
Is $-\theta{max} \leq \theta{t+\Delta t} \leq \theta_{max}$?
Is $-\phi{max} \leq \phi{t+\Delta t} \leq \phi_{max}$?

Is $-\omega*{max} \leq \omega*{x, t+\Delta t}, \omega*{y, t+\Delta t}, \omega*{z, t+\Delta t} \leq \omega_{max}$?
Is $z*{min} \leq z*{t+\Delta t} \leq z_{max}$?
Is $-v*{max} \leq v*{x, t+\Delta t}, v*{y, t+\Delta t}, v*{z, t+\Delta t} \leq v_{max}$?

3.
Action Intervention:
If all checks pass, the action is safe: $a*{safe} = a*{learned}$.
If any check fails, an intervention is triggered. A simple intervention is **clipping** the violating control inputs to their safe limits. For example, if $\omega*{pitch, learned} > \omega*{max}$, then $\omega*{pitch, safe} = \omega*{max}$. If $T*{des, learned} < T*{min}$, then $T*{des, safe} = T*{min}$. The resulting safe action a_{safe} is then computed with clipped values.
A more advanced intervention might involve projecting the action onto the feasible set, or executing a predefined emergency landing sequence if the state is already critical or the predicted trajectory is highly dangerous. For instance, if predictive checking indicates the drone will hit the ground within 1 second, the safety layer might override all other commands and issue a hard "land now" command, potentially with limited horizontal movement.

Testing the Safety Layer

To demonstrate the effectiveness of the safety layer, we need to design test scenarios. These scenarios will deliberately challenge the learning controller and the safety mechanisms:

Pushing the Controller to its Limits: We can modify the rewards or the environment to encourage the learning controller to propose actions that are close to or exceed the safe boundaries. For example, if the RL agent is rewarded for fast maneuvers, it might learn to output high angular velocities or rapid thrust changes. The safety layer should then intervene, clipping these velocities or thrust rates to the allowed maximum, thus preventing aggressive and potentially unstable behavior. Another approach is to present the learned controller with states it has not frequently encountered during training, which can sometimes elicit extreme or unexpected actions.

Introducing Disturbances and Faults: We can simulate external forces acting on the drone (e.g., wind gusts) or internal faults (e.g., one motor failing, leading to unbalanced thrust). These disturbances can push the drone into unsafe states or cause the learning controller to output extreme commands in an attempt to compensate.
Wind Gust Scenario: Simulate a sudden horizontal wind gust. This will push the drone off its intended trajectory and orientation. The learning controller might try to counteract this by commanding large roll or pitch rates and thrust adjustments. The safety layer must ensure these counter-commands do not violate physical limits such as maximum angular velocities or thrust. For instance, if a gust pushes the drone sideways, the controller might command a large roll to correct. The safety layer must cap this roll rate to prevent instability, even if it means the drone doesn't perfectly counteract the gust immediately.
Motor Failure Scenario: Simulate the failure of one of the drone's motors. This will cause an imbalance in thrust and torques, leading to uncontrolled rotation and translation. The learning controller will likely try to compensate by adjusting the thrust of the remaining motors. The safety layer needs to ensure that the commanded thrust for the functioning motors does not exceed maximum limits and that the resulting state remains within safe bounds (or at least the system

attempts a controlled descent rather than an immediate crash). If one motor fails, the required thrust distribution for stability might be impossible to achieve within the limits of the remaining motors, in which case the safety layer should command a safe descent.

Novel State Exploration: During initial training of the RL agent, it will encounter states it has never seen before. The safety layer must be robust to these novel states and ensure that any action proposed by the agent in these unknown territories is safe. This highlights the advantage of a fixed, verifiable safety layer over a purely learned policy, which might behave erratically in uncedented situations. The safety layer acts as a universal guard, irrespective of the learned controller's familiarity with the current state.

Implementation Details and Considerations

Discretization vs. Continuous Control: The choice of whether the learning controller outputs discrete actions (e.g., "increase thrust," "pitch left") or continuous actions (e.g., precise thrust and angular velocity values) affects the implementation of the safety layer. For continuous actions, clipping or projection methods are more applicable. For discrete actions, the safety layer might map unsafe discrete actions to safe ones or a default safe action. In our example, we assumed continuous control outputs from the RL agent, making clipping and projection the most relevant intervention strategies.

Prediction Model Accuracy: If using predictive safety checks, the accuracy of the dynamics model used for prediction is crucial. An overly simplified model might miss potential safety violations, while a very complex one might be too computationally expensive to run in real-time. A trade-off is necessary. Often, simplified linear models or models that capture the dominant dynamics are sufficient for safety verification. For instance, for attitude control, the rotational dynamics are often dominant and can be modeled with reasonable accuracy without excessive complexity.

Computational Load: Safety verification and intervention must be performed very quickly, typically at the same frequency as the control loop. This means the safety layer's algorithms must be computationally efficient. Clipping is very fast. Projection algorithms can be more intensive, depending on the complexity of the feasible set and the dimensionality of the action space. Techniques like quadratic programming can be used for projection, but their computational cost must be considered.

Safety Layer Design Philosophy: The safety layer should be designed to be conservative. It's better to slightly restrict the performance of the learned controller than to risk an unsafe event. The goal is not to optimize performance but to guarantee safety. The learned controller is responsible for performance within the safe envelope. This conservative approach means that in some edge cases, the safety layer might intervene even when the learned controller's action would have been acceptable, leading to a sub-optimal but safe outcome.

Hierarchical Control: The safety layer can be viewed as a form of hierarchical control. The learning controller acts as a high-level planner or controller, proposing actions based on its learned policy. The safety layer acts as a low-level supervisor or guardian, ensuring these proposed actions are permissible before they are sent to the actuators. This separation of concerns allows for more modular design and easier verification.

Formal Verification (Advanced): For extremely safety-critical applications, formal verification techniques could be employed to mathematically prove that the safety layer, under all possible inputs and conditions, will always keep the system within its safe boundaries. This is a highly advanced topic usually applied to simpler systems or specific components, but it represents the gold standard for safety assurance.

Demonstration Walkthrough

Let's illustrate with a hypothetical scenario. Suppose the drone is currently flying at a pitch angle of 15 degrees, well within the $\pm$ 45-degree limit. The learning controller, trying to execute a rapid ascent, proposes an action that includes a desired pitch rate of 60 degrees per second. Our safety parameters define a maximum allowed pitch rate of 50 degrees per second.

The safety layer receives the current state and the proposed action.

State: Pitch = 15 degrees, Pitch Rate = 5 deg/sec, Altitude = 80 meters, etc.
Proposed Action: Pitch Rate = 60 deg/sec, Collective Thrust = 70% (assumed safe for now).

Safety Check:

The safety layer checks the proposed pitch rate: 60 deg/sec. This exceeds the maximum allowed pitch rate of 50 deg/sec. The direct control input check fails.

Intervention:
Since the proposed action is unsafe, the intervention mechanism is activated. In this case, simple clipping would be applied.
Safe Action: Pitch Rate = 50 deg/sec. The Collective Thrust remains 70%.

The safety layer then outputs this clipped pitch rate to the drone's simulation. The drone will pitch at the maximum allowed rate, preventing it from potentially over-pitching into an unstable or unsafe configuration. The learning controller, meanwhile, would ideally receive feedback (e.g., through a modified reward or by observing that its requested action was not fully executed) that its proposed action was limited, which might influence its future learning.

Consider another scenario where the drone is near its maximum altitude limit of 100 meters. The RL agent proposes to increase collective thrust by 80%. With a simplified predictive model (e.g., assuming constant mass and negligible air resistance for a short interval), the safety layer estimates that this thrust increase would cause the drone's altitude to reach 103 meters within the next control interval of $\Delta t = 0.1$ seconds.

State: Altitude = 99 meters, Vertical Velocity = 2 m/sec.
Proposed Action: Collective Thrust = 80% (higher than current).

Prediction: Let's assume a simple model where $\Delta z = vz *Delta t + 0.5 az* (\Delta t)^2$. If the acceleration a_z due to 80% thrust is, say, 5 m/s², then $\Delta z = 2 \times 0.1 + 0.5 \times 5 \times (0.1)^2 = 0.2 + 0.025 = 0.225$ meters. The predicted altitude is $99 + 0.225 \approx 99.2$ meters. If the acceleration was significantly higher, say due to a different control strategy, we could reach 103 meters. Let's adjust our hypothetical: assume the thrust command implies an upward acceleration of 15 m/s². Then $\Delta z = 2 \times 0.1 + 0.5 \times 15 \times (0.1)^2 = 0.2 + 0.075 = 0.275$ meters. Predicted altitude is $99 + 0.275 \approx 99.3$ meters. The predictive model needs to be calibrated for realistic accelerations. Let's assume a more aggressive scenario where the predicted altitude increase would indeed cross the 100m mark. For instance, if the current vertical velocity is high and the thrust causes an acceleration that, over Δt, leads to exceeding 100m. Let's say, for simplicity, the predictive model simply states: "Applying this thrust will lead to altitude > 100m in 0.1s".

Safety Check:
The predicted altitude (e.g., 103 meters) exceeds the maximum altitude limit (100 meters). The predictive state check fails.

Intervention:
The safety layer would then modify the thrust command. It might reduce the collective thrust to a level that is predicted to keep the altitude at or below 100 meters, or it might issue a "hover" command for thrust. For example, it might cap the collective thrust to a value that is estimated to result in a zero vertical velocity or a minimal ascent. This ensures the drone adheres to its altitude ceiling.

Role of the Safety Layer in Robustness

The safety layer plays a critical role in making learning-based controllers robust. While the learning controller aims to optimize performance under nominal conditions, the safety layer acts as a safeguard against unforeseen circumstances:

Sensor Noise and Estimation Errors: If the state estimation is noisy, the learning controller might receive incorrect state information, leading it to propose unsafe actions. A well-designed safety layer can filter or bound the effects of such errors. For instance, if the altitude sensor momentarily glitches and reports a very low value, the RL agent might command full thrust to ascend. A safety layer checking against a maximum altitude limit would prevent this.

Model Mismatch: The learning controller might have been trained on a model that doesn't perfectly represent the real system dynamics. The safety layer, with its explicit, often simpler, and conservative bounds, can compensate for these mismatches. A common example is unmodeled aerodynamic effects at high speeds or extreme angles.

Adversarial Attacks: In security-sensitive applications, an adversary might try to feed false sensor data to the learning controller to make it behave dangerously. A safety layer, if designed to be resistant to such manipulations (e.g., by checking for consistency in sensor readings or using diverse safety checks), can provide a layer of defense.

In summary, integrating a safety layer is not merely an optional addition but a fundamental requirement for deploying learning-based control systems in any application where safety is paramount. It transforms a potentially unpredictable learned policy into a reliable component of a safe autonomous system. This exercise provides hands-on experience in building such a critical safety mechanism, reinforcing the principles of robust and responsible AI in control engineering. The ability to define, verify, and enforce safety constraints is a cornerstone of trustworthy autonomous systems, bridging the gap between theoretical learning capabilities and practical, safe deployment.

Interpreting Results and Troubleshooting

Successfully implementing advanced control strategies, especially those involving machine learning and real-world systems, is rarely a linear process. The journey from theoretical understanding to a functioning, reliable system is often punctuated by unexpected behaviors, performance bottlenecks, and subtle errors. This section is dedicated to equipping you with the skills to navigate these challenges. We will delve into how to interpret the outcomes of your laboratory exercises, understand the underlying reasons for observed phenomena, and employ systematic troubleshooting techniques to refine your implementations.

Analyzing Performance Metrics and Identifying Anomalies

The first crucial step in understanding your system's behavior is the meticulous analysis of performance metrics. These metrics serve as quantitative indicators of how well your control system is performing its intended task. For an AI-augmented control system, these might include measures of accuracy, speed, stability, and robustness.

For Model Predictive Control (MPC): Key metrics often revolve around tracking error, control effort, and constraint violations. A persistently high tracking error, for instance, might indicate that the predictive model does not accurately capture the system's dynamics, or that the control effort is insufficient. Conversely, excessively large control efforts, even if tracking is good, could point to an overly aggressive tuning or a model that is too sensitive to small state deviations. Analyzing constraint violations is paramount; if your MPC system is frequently exceeding predefined limits (e.g., actuator saturation, state boundaries), it suggests that the predictions are too optimistic or the optimization horizon is not long enough to account for future disturbances. Visualizing the predicted trajectories against the actual system response can be incredibly insightful. Look for discrepancies between the predicted future states and the actual subsequent states. A consistent divergence suggests a model mismatch.

For Reinforcement Learning (RL) Agents: Performance is typically gauged by cumulative reward over an episode or training run. A reward that plateaus prematurely, or worse, starts to decrease after initial improvement, signals potential issues. This could manifest as an agent getting stuck in a suboptimal policy, oscillating between states, or exhibiting unstable behavior. Examining the learning curve itself - the plot of reward versus training steps or episodes - is vital. A smooth, upward trend is ideal. A noisy curve might indicate inherent stochasticity in the environment or actions, which is common but needs to be managed. A sudden drop in reward can suggest catastrophic forgetting or an abrupt change in the environment that the agent hasn't adapted to. Beyond cumulative reward, consider analyzing specific aspects of the agent's behavior. For instance, in a navigation task, you might track path efficiency, collision rates, or time to reach a goal. If an

RL agent is tasked with stabilization, metrics like settling time and overshoot are critical. Visualizing the agent's policy – how it maps states to actions – can also reveal unexpected patterns, such as an agent consistently choosing risky actions in certain situations.

For Safety Layers and Certified Controllers: The primary metric here is the absence of unsafe events. This means zero violations of hard constraints, guaranteed stability within a defined operating region, and predictable behavior under all specified conditions. Performance metrics from the underlying controller (e.g., the RL agent it's supervising) are also relevant, as the safety layer should ideally not unduly degrade performance. Look for instances where the safety layer had to intervene. Analyze the frequency and nature of these interventions. If interventions are happening too often, it might imply that the learned controller is too aggressive or that the safety envelope is defined too restrictively. If interventions are insufficient and an unsafe event occurs, the safety logic or its implementation is critically flawed.

Common Pitfalls and Diagnostic Strategies:

During the implementation and experimentation phase, several common pitfalls can hinder progress. Recognizing these and knowing how to diagnose them is key to efficient troubleshooting.

1.
Model Mismatch: This is a pervasive issue, especially when bridging simulations and real-world systems.
Symptoms: Persistent tracking errors in MPC, an RL agent failing to generalize to slightly different dynamics, oscillations, or instability that wasn't predicted by initial analysis.

Diagnosis: Compare the actual system response to the predicted response from your model. If they diverge significantly, your model needs refinement. For systems with identifiable parameters (e.g., mass, inertia, friction), try to estimate these parameters more accurately using system identification techniques. If the system is highly nonlinear or complex, consider using more sophisticated modeling approaches, such as data-driven models or hybrid systems models. In RL, if the agent performs well in simulation but poorly in a real system, it's a strong indicator of model mismatch. Techniques like domain randomization during training (varying model parameters within reasonable bounds) can help create more robust policies.

Troubleshooting:

MPC: Refine the system model used in the MPC formulation. This might involve adding neglected dynamics, improving parameter estimates, or using an extended state observer. Adjusting the prediction horizon or the weights in the cost function can also sometimes compensate for minor model inaccuracies.

RL: Retrain the agent with a more accurate model, or use techniques like transfer learning to adapt a pre-trained policy to the new dynamics. Data augmentation or domain randomization in training can make the learned policy more resilient to variations.

2.

Parameter Tuning: Control systems and learning algorithms are often sensitive to hyperparameter choices.

Symptoms: Unstable learning (oscillations, divergence), slow convergence, poor performance, or overly conservative behavior.

Diagnosis: Systematically vary key parameters and observe their effect on performance metrics. For MPC, this includes tuning weights in the cost function (e.g., tracking gain, control effort penalty) and prediction horizon. For RL, critical parameters include learning rate, discount factor, exploration rate, network architecture, and regularization.

Troubleshooting:

Systematic Search: Employ techniques like grid search, random search, or Bayesian optimization to explore the parameter space.
Rule of Thumb: Start with commonly accepted ranges for parameters (e.g., learning rates of 10^{-3} to 10^{-5} for deep RL).
Gradual Adjustment: Make small, incremental changes to one parameter at a time to understand its impact. For instance, if the system is unstable, try increasing the control effort penalty in MPC or decreasing the learning rate in RL. If performance is poor, try increasing the tracking gain or the discount factor.
Visual Inspection: Plotting performance metrics against parameter values can reveal optimal ranges.

3.
Implementation Errors (Bugs): Simple coding mistakes can lead to complex and baffling system behavior.
Symptoms: Unexpected jumps in state, control signals behaving erratically, system crashing, or results that defy physical intuition.
Diagnosis: This is often the most time-consuming but critical part of troubleshooting.
Troubleshooting:
Modular Testing: Test each component of your system independently. For example, verify that your state estimator is providing correct outputs before integrating it with the controller. Ensure your dynamics model is correctly implemented by simulating simple, known inputs.
Logging and Visualization: Log all relevant variables: state estimates, control commands, sensor readings, model predictions, and internal states of the learning algorithm. Visualize these logs to identify inconsistencies or unexpected values. Plotting control signals alongside state trajectories is particularly revealing.
Unit Tests: Write unit tests for critical functions, such as state transformations, constraint calculations, and optimization routines.
Code Review: Have a colleague or peer review your code for potential errors.

Simplify: If a complex system is not working, simplify it. Remove parts of the control logic or learning algorithm to isolate the problem. For example, if your RL agent isn't learning, try running it with a simple, fixed policy first to ensure the environment and simulation are working correctly.

4.
Numerical Instability: Issues can arise from floating-point precision, ill-conditioned matrices, or numerical methods that struggle with specific system configurations.
Symptoms: Erratic behavior, NaNs (Not a Number) or Infs (Infinity) appearing in performance metrics or control signals, or sudden divergence of algorithms.
Diagnosis: Examine the values of intermediate calculations in your algorithms. Are they becoming extremely large or small? Are matrices that are supposed to be invertible becoming singular?
Troubleshooting:
Numerical Precision: Ensure you are using appropriate data types (e.g., `double` precision floating-point numbers).
Regularization: Add small regularization terms to matrices in optimization problems (e.g., in least-squares estimation or neural network training) to improve their conditioning.
Algorithm Choice: Consider alternative numerical solvers or algorithms that are known to be more robust. For instance, some optimization libraries offer more stable solvers than others.
Scaling: Ensure that state and input variables are appropriately scaled to avoid extremely large or small numbers.

5.
Unrealistic Environment or Simulation: The simulation or experimental setup might not accurately reflect the intended problem or the real world.

Symptoms: An RL agent trained in simulation performs poorly in the real world, or control performance does not match theoretical expectations.
Diagnosis: Carefully validate your simulation environment. Are actuator dynamics, sensor noise, communication delays, and external disturbances modeled realistically? If testing on hardware, ensure sensors are properly calibrated and actuators are functioning as expected.
Troubleshooting:
Simulation Fidelity: Increase the fidelity of your simulation by incorporating more realistic models of noise, delays, and nonlinearities. Domain randomization, as mentioned before, can help bridge the sim-to-real gap.
Sensor Calibration: Recalibrate all sensors (e.g., IMU, GPS, cameras) to ensure accurate readings.
Actuator Characterization: Understand the performance limitations and nonlinearities of your actuators.
Hardware-in-the-Loop (HIL) Testing: If possible, use HIL setups to test your control algorithms with real hardware components connected to a simulated environment.

Refining System Models and Control Strategies

Once you have a handle on performance metrics and have begun diagnosing issues, the next step is to refine your models and control strategies. This is an iterative process where insights gained from analysis inform modifications.

Model Refinement:

Data-Driven Modeling: If analytical modeling is too complex or inaccurate, consider using machine learning techniques to build data-driven models. Techniques like Recurrent Neural Networks (RNNs), Long Short-Term Memory (LSTM) networks, or Gaussian Processes can learn complex system dynamics from observed input-output data. These models can then be used within an MPC framework or to improve the realism of an RL training environment.
Hybrid Models: For systems with distinct operating modes (e.g., different flight regimes for a drone), hybrid models that combine analytical components with learned components or state-dependent parameters can offer a good balance of accuracy and interpretability.
Observer Design: If direct state measurement is difficult or noisy, designing state observers (like Kalman filters or Extended Kalman Filters) to estimate the system's state from available measurements is crucial. The performance of the observer directly impacts the performance of the controller.

Control Strategy Adjustments:
MPC Tuning: If constraint violations are frequent, you might need to increase the prediction horizon to allow the controller more time to react to disturbances. If tracking error is high, adjust the weights in the cost function to prioritize state tracking over control effort reduction. Consider adding integral action if steady-state errors are a persistent problem.
RL Algorithm Selection and Tuning: The choice of RL algorithm (e.g., PPO, SAC, TD3) can significantly impact performance and stability. Experiment with different algorithms based on the problem's characteristics (e.g., continuous vs. discrete action space, deterministic vs. stochastic environment). Fine-tuning hyperparameters like the learning rate, discount factor, and entropy regularization term is often essential.

Safety Layer Enhancements: If the safety layer is too restrictive, leading to significant performance degradation, you might explore defining a more nuanced safe operating envelope, potentially using reachability analysis or formal methods to expand it slightly while maintaining safety guarantees. Alternatively, if the safety layer is not intervening sufficiently, you may need to tighten constraints or implement more sophisticated predictive safety checks.
Hierarchical Control Architectures: For complex tasks, consider decomposing the problem into a hierarchy. For example, a high-level planner (perhaps another RL agent or a rule-based system) could set waypoints or objectives, while a lower-level controller (MPC or another RL agent) handles local trajectory tracking and stabilization, with a safety layer overseeing both.

Debugging Code and Calibrating Sensors

Beyond algorithmic and model-related issues, practical implementation details like software bugs and sensor miscalibrations are frequent sources of problems.

Code Debugging Best Practices:
Version Control: Use a version control system (like Git) religiously. This allows you to track changes, revert to previous working states, and collaborate effectively.
Clear Code Structure: Write well-organized, modular code with clear function definitions and descriptive variable names. This makes it easier to understand and debug.
Assertions: Use assertion statements (`assert`) to check for conditions that should always be true during execution. This can catch errors early.

Breakpoints and Step-Through Debugging: Utilize the debugging tools provided by your IDE to set breakpoints and step through your code line by line, inspecting variable values.
Logging Levels: Implement different logging levels (e.g., DEBUG, INFO, WARNING, ERROR) so you can control the verbosity of output during different phases of testing and deployment.

Sensor Calibration:
Importance: Inaccurate sensor readings are a primary cause of poor controller performance and instability. For example, a drifting IMU can cause a drone to lose its orientation, leading to catastrophic failure.
Common Sensors and Calibration Needs:
IMU (Inertial Measurement Unit - Accelerometer & Gyroscope): Requires calibration for bias and scale factor errors. Gyroscope bias can drift over time, and accelerometers need to be calibrated against gravity.
Magnetometer: Susceptible to magnetic interference and requires hard and soft iron calibration.
GPS: While typically factory-calibrated, its accuracy can be affected by environmental factors. Understanding its typical error bounds is important.
Cameras: Require intrinsic (focal length, distortion) and extrinsic (position and orientation relative to the vehicle) calibration for computer vision tasks.
LiDAR/Radar: May require calibration for range and angle offsets.
Calibration Procedures: Many sensor manufacturers provide calibration tools or routines. Often, calibration involves exposing the sensor to known conditions (e.g., placing an IMU flat on a table to calibrate accelerometers, rotating the vehicle through specific maneuvers to calibrate gyros and magnetometers). For computer vision, specific calibration patterns (like checkerboards) are used.
Online vs. Offline Calibration: Some calibrations are done offline before operation. Others, like IMU bias tracking or magnetometer

interference estimation, can be performed online during system operation.
Validation: After calibration, always validate the sensor readings. For instance, check if accelerometer readings are consistent with gravity when the sensor is stationary, or if GPS position is stable when the vehicle is not moving.

Advanced Troubleshooting Scenarios

Sometimes, problems are not immediately obvious and require deeper investigation.

Non-Determinism: If your system's behavior changes slightly even with identical initial conditions, it could be due to non-determinism in your software (e.g., floating-point arithmetic differences across hardware, asynchronous operations, or stochastic elements in algorithms like RL exploration). Debugging non-deterministic issues often involves running the same experiment multiple times to see if the anomaly recurs and analyzing the exact sequence of events leading up to it.

Intermittent Failures: These are the most challenging. They might occur under specific environmental conditions, after a certain period of operation, or due to rare combinations of system states. Thorough logging and the ability to reproduce the failure condition are essential. Sometimes, intermittent failures can be traced to hardware issues (e.g., loose connections, overheating components).

Safety Layer Interaction: When combining a learning controller with a safety layer, their interaction can be a source of complex behavior. The learning controller might try to "fight" the safety layer, leading to oscillations or unexpected performance degradation. Understanding how the learning controller's learning process is affected by safety interventions is crucial. Does it adapt to the clipping, or does it merely learn to push harder against the safety bounds? Techniques like reward shaping or modifying the state feedback to the learning controller based on safety layer actions can help.

By systematically approaching result interpretation and employing robust troubleshooting strategies, you can gain confidence in your implementations, gain deeper insights into the complex interplay of control, learning, and physical systems, and ultimately develop more effective and reliable autonomous systems. This iterative process of testing, analyzing, and refining is the hallmark of sound engineering practice. Interpreting Results and Troubleshooting

The culmination of any laboratory exercise, particularly in the complex domain of AI-augmented control, lies not just in achieving a desired outcome, but in understanding
why that outcome occurred and how to adapt when it deviates from expectations. This subsection delves into the critical art of interpreting experimental results and systematically troubleshooting any anomalies or performance deficiencies. It's about transforming raw data and observations into actionable insights, enabling you to refine your models, tune your algorithms, and ultimately achieve robust and reliable system behavior.

Deconstructing Performance Metrics for Deeper Understanding

Performance metrics are the quantitative language through which a control system communicates its success or failure. For advanced systems that blend classical control theory with machine learning, a diverse set of metrics is often required to paint a comprehensive picture.

For
Model Predictive Control (MPC), the focus is typically on:
Tracking Error: The deviation between the desired setpoint and the system's actual state. Low, consistent tracking error indicates a well-tuned controller and an accurate system model. Persistent or growing errors can signal fundamental issues. Analyzing the root mean square error (RMSE) or maximum absolute error over time provides a good summary.
Control Effort: The magnitude and rate of change of control inputs. Excessive control effort can lead to actuator wear, increased energy consumption, and potentially instability if actuators reach their limits. Conversely, too little effort might result in sluggish performance or an inability to reject disturbances. Visualizing control signals over time alongside state trajectories is key.
Constraint Violations: This is a critical safety and performance metric. Any instance where a state variable or control input exceeds its predefined safe or operational limits indicates a failure in the predictive or optimization stage. The frequency, magnitude, and duration of these violations are vital for assessing safety.
Prediction Accuracy: Comparing the system's actual trajectory with the predictions made by the MPC's internal model over the prediction horizon offers direct insight into model fidelity. Significant divergence suggests the model needs refinement.

For

Reinforcement Learning (RL) agents, performance is often evaluated through:

Cumulative Reward: The sum of rewards obtained over an episode or a series of episodes. A steadily increasing cumulative reward during training is the primary indicator of successful learning. However, plateaus, oscillations, or decreases can signal problems.

Convergence Behavior: Observing how the cumulative reward changes over training iterations or episodes. A smooth, asymptotic convergence to a high reward is desirable. Erratic learning curves or divergence indicate instability in the learning process.

Policy Stability: In some cases, especially with continuous actions, the learned policy might become unstable, leading to jerky or unpredictable movements. Analyzing the distribution of actions taken by the agent in different states can reveal this.

Exploration vs. Exploitation Balance: In stochastic environments, an agent might get stuck in a local optimum if exploration is insufficient, or it might fail to converge if exploration remains too high. Metrics related to exploration strategy (e.g., entropy of the policy for stochastic policies) can be useful.

Task-Specific Metrics: Beyond reward, specific metrics relevant to the task are crucial. For navigation, this could be path efficiency, collision rate, success rate in reaching the goal, or time taken. For manipulation, it might be grasp success rate or task completion time.

For

Safety Layers and Certified Controllers, the paramount metric is:

Absence of Safety Violations: This is a binary outcome – either a safety critical event occurred, or it did not. The goal is to achieve a 100% safety record under all specified operating conditions and disturbances.

Performance Degradation: While safety is primary, the impact of the safety layer on the performance of the underlying (e.g., learned) controller must also be assessed. Excessive conservatism from the safety

layer can significantly hinder task performance. Metrics from the underlying controller should be tracked to quantify this trade-off.
Intervention Frequency: The number of times the safety layer had to intervene. High intervention rates might suggest that the safe operating envelope is too restrictive, or that the learned controller is consistently proposing borderline or unsafe actions.

Systematic Troubleshooting: From Symptoms to Solutions

When performance metrics fall short, or unexpected behaviors emerge, a structured approach to troubleshooting is essential to avoid wasted effort and frustration.

1. Identify the Nature of the Problem:
Is it a:
Complete Failure: The system doesn't run, crashes, or produces nonsensical outputs.
Performance Deficiency: The system runs but doesn't achieve desired performance (e.g., high error, slow convergence, frequent constraint violations).
Instability: The system exhibits oscillations, diverges, or behaves erratically.
Safety Breach: A critical safety constraint is violated.
Non-Determinism: The behavior changes unpredictably between runs.

2. Isolate the Failing Component:
Control systems are often modular. Try to isolate the problem to a specific subsystem:

Sensing/State Estimation: Are sensor readings plausible? Is the state estimator providing stable and accurate state estimates?
System Model: Is the dynamic model used by the controller accurate?
Controller Logic (MPC/RL): Is the controller algorithm itself correctly implemented and configured?
Safety Layer Logic: Is the safety verification and intervention mechanism functioning as intended?
Actuation: Are the control commands being translated into appropriate physical actions? (This is harder to diagnose directly in simulation but crucial for real-world systems).
Simulation Environment: If working in simulation, is the simulation itself accurate and bug-free?

3. Utilize Debugging Tools and Techniques:

Logging and Visualization: This is your most powerful tool. Log everything relevant: sensor readings, estimated states, raw model predictions, proposed control actions, final control commands, performance metrics, internal states of the learning algorithm (e.g., network weights, gradients), and any flags or decisions made by the safety layer. Visualize these logs: plot state trajectories against setpoints, overlay predicted states with actual states, display control inputs, and plot reward functions or loss curves over time. This graphical representation can often reveal subtle anomalies that raw numbers might obscure.
Example: If an MPC system has a high tracking error, plotting the predicted trajectory from the MPC against the actual system response can immediately show if the model is underestimating or overestimating certain dynamics. If an RL agent is oscillating, plotting its chosen actions in different states might reveal it's repeatedly commanding extreme control signals.

Unit Testing: Write small, focused tests for individual functions or modules. For instance, test your state transformation functions, constraint checking routines, or a single step of your MPC prediction. This ensures that basic building blocks are correct before integrating them into the larger system.

Step-Through Debugging: Use a debugger to execute your code line by line, inspecting variable values at each step. This is invaluable for understanding the flow of execution and pinpointing where values deviate from expectation.

Print Statements (Strategic Use): While less sophisticated than a debugger, strategically placed print statements can quickly reveal intermediate values. However, avoid excessive printing, which can clutter output and slow down execution.

4. Common Troubleshooting Scenarios and Solutions:

Model Mismatch:
Symptoms: Persistent tracking errors (MPC), poor generalization from simulation to reality (RL), oscillations around setpoints, failure to stabilize.
Diagnosis: Compare model predictions with actual system behavior. Quantify the discrepancy. If the model consistently over or underestimates certain effects (e.g., inertia, drag, sensor delays), this points to a specific area for model improvement.
Solutions:

Refine Analytical Model: Revisit system identification. Try to estimate parameters more accurately. Consider adding neglected dynamics (e.g., friction, actuator saturation, sensor noise models, aerodynamic effects).
Data-Driven Modeling: Collect more system identification data. Use techniques like Gaussian Processes, Neural Networks (e.g., LSTMs for time-series dynamics), or System Identification tools (e.g., `ssest` in MATLAB) to build or improve your model.
State Estimation: Enhance your state estimator (e.g., Kalman Filter, Extended Kalman Filter). If the model is poor, a good observer can still provide reasonable state estimates, albeit with potential lag or noise.

Parameter Tuning Issues:
Symptoms: Learning divergence or stagnation (RL), oscillations or sluggishness (MPC/RL), over-aggressive control actions, or extreme conservatism.
Diagnosis: Many parameters affect stability and performance. For RL, this includes learning rate, discount factor (γ), entropy coefficient, network architecture, and replay buffer size. For MPC, it's cost function weights, prediction horizon (N), and control horizon (M).
Solutions:
Systematic Search: Employ grid search, random search, or Bayesian optimization to explore the hyperparameter space. Define clear performance metrics to guide the search.
Start Simple: Begin with parameters recommended in literature for similar problems.
Gradual Adjustment: Change one parameter at a time and observe its effect. If instability occurs, try reducing the learning rate (RL) or increasing control effort penalties (MPC). If convergence is slow, try increasing the learning rate or discount factor.
Learning Rate Scheduling: For RL, use techniques that decrease the learning rate over time as training progresses.

Implementation Bugs:
Symptoms: Crashing, NaNs/Infs, nonsensical outputs, system behaving in ways that defy physics or logic.
Diagnosis: This is where step-through debugging and careful logging are critical. Is a variable being initialized correctly? Is a matrix inversion failing? Is array indexing correct? Is a state transformation applied in the wrong frame of reference?
Solutions:
Modular Testing: Test each function/class in isolation.
Assertions: Use `assert` statements to check preconditions and postconditions of functions.
Code Reviews: Have another person review your code. A fresh pair of eyes can often spot errors you've overlooked.
Simplify and Rebuild: If a complex module is buggy, try to implement a simplified version first. Once that works, incrementally add complexity.

Numerical Instability:
Symptoms: Values becoming extremely large (Inf) or undefined (NaN), oscillations that grow in amplitude, solver failures.
Diagnosis: Examine intermediate calculations, especially those involving matrix inversions, divisions, or exponentiation. Check for small denominators or ill-conditioned matrices.
Solutions:
Floating-Point Precision: Ensure you are using double-precision floating-point numbers (`float64`) for critical calculations.
Regularization: Add small values (e.g., 10^{-6}) to diagonal elements of matrices that are being inverted or used in inversions (e.g., covariance matrices in Kalman filters, Hessian matrices in optimization) to improve their conditioning.

Scaling: Normalize or scale state and input variables to keep them within a reasonable numerical range.
Robust Solvers: Use numerical solvers known for their stability.

Safety Layer Issues:
Symptoms: System operating unsafely despite the safety layer, or the safety layer intervening too frequently and hindering performance.
Diagnosis: Log the proposed action, the current state, the safety check results (which constraints were violated, if any), and the final, safe action.
Solutions:
Constraint Definition: Re-evaluate the strictness of your safety constraints. Are they appropriately defined based on system capabilities?
Prediction Model Accuracy (for predictive safety): If predictive checks are failing, ensure the model used for prediction is accurate enough for the prediction horizon.
Intervention Strategy: If clipping is too harsh, explore projection methods to find the closest safe action that respects more of the original controller's intent. If safety is still breached, consider more conservative fallback actions. If performance is degraded, investigate if the learned controller can be guided (e.g., through reward shaping) to propose safer actions, reducing the need for intervention.

Refining System Models and Control Strategies

Troubleshooting often reveals weaknesses in your system model or control strategy that necessitate refinement.

Model Enhancement:

System Identification: Rigorously collect data from your system (or a high-fidelity simulation) and use techniques to estimate model parameters. This can be done offline or sometimes online. For instance, an Extended Kalman Filter not only estimates states but can also estimate unknown parameters.

Data-Driven Models: If analytical modeling remains challenging, explore learning-based models. Techniques like Gaussian Processes can provide probabilistic models that capture uncertainty, which can be valuable for robust control design. Recurrent Neural Networks (RNNs) or LSTMs can learn complex, nonlinear temporal dynamics. These learned models can then be integrated into MPC or used to improve RL training realism.

Observer Tuning: If state estimation is a bottleneck, carefully tune observer parameters (e.g., Kalman gain) to balance responsiveness to new measurements with noise rejection.

Control Strategy Adjustments:

MPC Tuning: If constraint violations are prevalent, consider increasing the prediction horizon (N) to give the controller more foresight. Alternatively, adjusting weights in the cost function can influence how aggressively the controller tries to satisfy constraints versus tracking the setpoint. For instance, increasing the penalty on constraint violations will make the controller more conservative. Adding integral action can help eliminate steady-state errors.

RL Algorithm and Hyperparameter Tuning: The choice of RL algorithm can be critical. Algorithms like Soft Actor-Critic (SAC) often offer better stability and sample efficiency for continuous control tasks compared to older methods. Experimenting with different network architectures (e.g., deeper networks, different activation functions),

optimizers, and regularization techniques can also yield significant improvements. Carefully tune the discount factor (γ) – a higher γ emphasizes future rewards, which is good for long-term planning, but can also lead to instability if not balanced.
Hierarchical Control: For complex tasks, decomposing the problem into a hierarchy can simplify design and troubleshooting. A high-level agent might set intermediate goals or trajectories, while a low-level controller executes them. The safety layer can then operate at multiple levels or provide overarching safety guarantees.

Calibrating Sensors and Hardware Considerations

Even the most sophisticated control algorithms are useless if they are fed incorrect information. Sensor calibration is non-negotiable for any real-world implementation.

Importance of Calibration: Inaccurate sensor readings can lead to a completely incorrect understanding of the system's state, causing controllers to act in unintended and potentially dangerous ways. For example, a miscalibrated IMU on a drone can cause it to believe it's level when it's actually tilted, leading to erratic flight.
Common Sensors and Calibration Needs:
IMUs (Accelerometers & Gyroscopes): Require calibration for bias (offset), scale factor (gain), and potentially cross-axis sensitivities. Bias can drift over time and with temperature.
Magnetometers: Crucial for yaw estimation in many vehicles but highly susceptible to magnetic interference from nearby electronics and structural components. Calibration involves estimating hard-iron (constant offset) and soft-iron (distortion of magnetic field) effects.

GPS: While generally factory-calibrated, understanding its typical error bounds and how environmental factors (e.g., multipath interference) affect accuracy is important.
Cameras: Need intrinsic calibration (focal length, principal point, lens distortion) and extrinsic calibration (position and orientation relative to other sensors and the vehicle frame).
Lidar/Radar: May require calibration for range offsets, angle offsets, and intensity scaling.
Calibration Procedures: Manufacturers often provide specific tools and procedures. Common steps include:
Static Calibration: Exposing sensors to known static conditions (e.g., placing an IMU on a level surface to measure gravity vector for accelerometer calibration).
Dynamic Calibration: Moving the system through specific maneuvers to expose different dynamic behaviors (e.g., rotating a drone to calibrate gyroscopes, performing a figure-eight pattern for magnetometer calibration).
Online Calibration: Some parameters, like IMU bias, can be continuously estimated and updated during operation using algorithms like Kalman filtering.
Validation: After calibration, always validate. Do accelerometer readings correspond to gravity when stationary? Does the magnetometer reading change predictably when rotating the vehicle? Does the camera output make sense for simple visual scenes?

By approaching results interpretation and troubleshooting with a structured, analytical mindset, and by paying meticulous attention to practical implementation details like sensor calibration, you can navigate the complexities of advanced control systems effectively. This iterative process of analysis, diagnosis, and refinement is fundamental to developing reliable, high-performing AI-augmented control solutions.

Chapter 15: Future Trends and Conclusion

The landscape of control systems is undergoing a profound transformation, driven by rapid advancements in artificial intelligence. As we look beyond current capabilities, several emergent trends promise to redefine how we design, implement, and interact with intelligent control systems. These are not merely incremental improvements but represent potential paradigm shifts that could unlock unprecedented levels of performance, adaptability, and trustworthiness.

One of the most critical areas of development is **Explainable AI (XAI) in Control Systems**. As AI, particularly deep learning and reinforcement learning, becomes more deeply integrated into safety-critical applications such as autonomous driving, robotics, and industrial process control, the demand for understanding *why* an AI makes a particular decision becomes paramount. Traditional control systems, often based on well-understood mathematical models, offer a degree of inherent interpretability. An AI, especially a complex neural network, can act as a "black box," making it challenging to diagnose failures, guarantee safety, or gain user trust. XAI techniques aim to shed light on this black box. This includes developing methods to:

Visualize decision-making processes: Techniques like attention mechanisms in neural networks can highlight which parts of the input data were most influential for a given control action. For example, in an autonomous vehicle, XAI might show that the braking decision was primarily driven by the detection of a pedestrian in the vehicle's path, rather than, say, a shadow on the road.

Identify influential features: Understanding which sensor inputs or state variables are most critical for the AI's decisions allows engineers to focus monitoring and maintenance efforts. If an AI controller for a chemical reactor consistently relies heavily on the temperature reading from a specific sensor, that sensor's reliability becomes a critical factor.

Generate human-understandable explanations: This could involve rule extraction from trained neural networks, generating natural

language justifications for control actions, or creating simplified surrogate models that approximate the AI's behavior in specific operating regimes. For instance, a robot arm controller might explain its path planning by stating, "I am moving the arm to position X to avoid the obstacle Y while maintaining grasp on object Z."
Provide uncertainty quantification: XAI can also extend to understanding the confidence an AI has in its decision. If the AI indicates low confidence, it might trigger a fallback to a more conservative, pre-defined control strategy or alert a human operator. This is crucial for safety-critical systems where a probabilistic understanding of risk is essential.

The integration of XAI into control engineering not only facilitates debugging and validation but also paves the way for certified AI controllers. By providing formal guarantees or interpretable evidence of safe and desirable behavior, XAI can bridge the gap between the empirical performance of AI and the rigorous demands of safety certifications. Research is actively exploring how to combine formal methods with XAI to provide mathematical proofs of safety properties for AI-driven controllers.

Another transformative trend is
Lifelong Learning and Continual Adaptation. Real-world environments are rarely static. External conditions change, system dynamics can drift over time (e.g., due to wear and tear, changing payloads, or environmental factors like temperature and humidity), and new tasks or operating modes may emerge. Traditional control systems often rely on fixed, pre-tuned parameters or models that must be re-engineered if the environment changes significantly. AI, however, offers the potential for systems that can learn and adapt *on the fly*.

Lifelong learning, also known as continual learning, aims to endow AI systems with the ability to learn new knowledge and skills over time without forgetting previously acquired information - a phenomenon known as "catastrophic forgetting." This is particularly relevant for AI controllers operating in dynamic environments. Imagine a robotic manipulator tasked with grasping a variety of objects. As it encounters new object shapes or textures, it needs to update its grasping strategy without degrading its ability to grasp familiar objects. Similarly, an autonomous vehicle needs to adapt to new road conditions, traffic patterns, or even subtle changes in its own sensor characteristics over its operational lifetime.

Key challenges and research directions in lifelong learning for control include:

Avoiding Catastrophic Forgetting: Developing algorithms that can learn new tasks or adapt to new dynamics without overwriting or degrading previously learned policies. Techniques such as experience replay (storing past experiences to periodically retrain on them), regularization methods (penalizing changes to important parameters for old tasks), and dynamic network architectures (growing or repurposing parts of the network as new knowledge is acquired) are being investigated.
Online Model Updates: For model-based control, lifelong learning implies the ability to continuously update the system model based on new data. This could involve adaptive observers or online system identification techniques integrated within a learning framework.
Task Discovery and Segmentation: In open-ended environments, a system might need to autonomously identify new tasks or distinct operating regimes and adapt its control strategy accordingly. This could involve unsupervised learning techniques to segment experiences into different "modes" and applying specialized controllers or learning agents for each mode.

Transfer Learning and Meta-Learning: Leveraging knowledge gained from one task or environment to accelerate learning in new, related ones is a cornerstone of lifelong learning. Meta-learning ("learning to learn") aims to train models that can quickly adapt to new tasks with minimal data. For control, this could mean training an AI that is predisposed to learn efficient control policies for a class of robotic arms, rather than learning from scratch for each new arm.

The ability of AI controllers to continually adapt will be crucial for long-term autonomy and efficiency in complex, evolving systems, from smart grids to fleets of delivery drones.

Emerging from the realm of multi-agent systems, **Multi-Agent Reinforcement Learning (MARL)** is poised to revolutionize the control of systems composed of multiple interacting intelligent agents. This is applicable to scenarios ranging from coordinating fleets of autonomous vehicles or drones to managing distributed resources in smart grids, or even controlling robotic swarms for exploration and manipulation.

In MARL, each agent learns its own policy to maximize its individual reward, but the behavior of each agent is influenced by the actions of other agents. This creates a non-stationary environment from the perspective of any single agent, as the optimal strategy for one agent depends on the evolving strategies of all others. This presents significant challenges compared to single-agent RL.

Key areas of research and application in MARL for control include:

Cooperative Control: Agents work together towards a common goal, such as coordinating multiple robots to move a large object or managing

traffic flow to minimize congestion. Here, agents need to learn collaborative policies.
Competitive Control: Agents have conflicting objectives, such as in a simulated combat scenario or game theory applications where AI agents might play against each other.
Mixed Cooperative-Competitive Scenarios: Many real-world situations involve elements of both cooperation and competition. For example, in a smart grid, distributed energy resources might cooperate to maintain grid stability but compete to sell excess energy at the highest price.
Communication and Coordination: MARL often involves exploring how agents can effectively communicate (explicitly or implicitly) to coordinate their actions. This could involve learning communication protocols or inferring the intentions of other agents through their actions and observations.
Decentralized Execution with Centralized Training (CTDE): A popular paradigm where agents are trained using a centralized critic that has access to global information (states and actions of all agents), but during execution, each agent acts independently based on its local observations and learned policy. This balances the complexity of multi-agent learning with the practical need for decentralized control.

The application of MARL to control problems promises to enable sophisticated emergent behaviors in complex distributed systems. Instead of relying on hand-coded rules for interaction, MARL allows these interaction strategies to be learned and optimized, potentially leading to more robust and efficient collective performance.

Looking further into the future, the intersection of AI with emerging computational paradigms, particularly
Quantum Computing, hints at potentially revolutionary advancements in control system design. While still largely in the theoretical and early

experimental stages, the prospect of quantum algorithms offers capabilities far beyond classical computation for specific types of problems relevant to control.

Quantum computers excel at certain tasks that are intractable for even the most powerful classical supercomputers, such as solving systems of linear equations exponentially faster (e.g., using Harrow-Hassidim-Lloyd (HHL) algorithm) or performing optimization through quantum annealing.

How might this impact AI-augmented control?

Accelerated Optimization: Many control problems, especially in Model Predictive Control, involve solving complex optimization problems at high frequencies. Quantum optimization algorithms, such as Quantum Approximate Optimization Algorithm (QAOA) or quantum annealing, could potentially solve these optimization problems much faster, enabling higher control frequencies, longer prediction horizons, or the consideration of more complex models and constraints. This could be transformative for real-time control of highly dynamic systems.
Enhanced Machine Learning Models: Quantum Machine Learning (QML) is a burgeoning field exploring how quantum computers can enhance ML algorithms. This could involve quantum algorithms for faster training of neural networks, improved feature extraction, or novel ways to represent data and learn complex patterns that are difficult for classical ML. For control, this might lead to more powerful predictive models or more efficient RL agents.
Quantum Simulation for Control Design: Quantum computers are inherently well-suited for simulating quantum systems. While most control applications are classical, there are niche areas, such as controlling quantum phenomena for applications in quantum computing

itself or in advanced materials science, where quantum simulation will be essential.

Novel Control Paradigms: It's conceivable that quantum mechanics could inspire entirely new approaches to control design, moving beyond classical state-space representations or optimization frameworks. For instance, concepts like superposition and entanglement could potentially be leveraged in novel ways to design controllers that exhibit unique properties.

While practical, fault-tolerant quantum computers are still some years away, research in this area is crucial for understanding the potential long-term impact. Early explorations are focused on hybrid quantum-classical approaches, where quantum computers are used to accelerate specific computationally intensive sub-routines within a larger classical AI control framework. The integration of quantum capabilities could eventually unlock solutions to control problems that are currently considered intractable.

In summary, the future of AI-augmented control is bright and multifaceted. From making AI decisions transparent and trustworthy through XAI, to enabling systems that continuously learn and adapt in dynamic environments via lifelong learning, to orchestrating complex coordinated behaviors with multi-agent reinforcement learning, and perhaps even revolutionizing computational capabilities with quantum computing, these emerging trends point towards a future where intelligent control systems are more capable, resilient, and integrated than ever before. These advancements will undoubtedly continue to push the boundaries of what is possible across a vast spectrum of technological applications.

The convergence of artificial intelligence and sophisticated simulation technologies is heralding a new era in control system engineering, with

Digital Twins emerging as a pivotal element. A Digital Twin is, at its core, a dynamic virtual representation of a physical asset, process, or system. Unlike static models, Digital Twins are continuously updated with real-world data, mirroring the state and behavior of their physical counterparts in near real-time. This fidelity transforms them from mere simulation tools into powerful platforms for understanding, predicting, and optimizing the performance of complex systems. The synergistic relationship between AI-augmented control and Digital Twins is not merely an enhancement; it is a fundamental enabler of next-generation control strategies, pushing the boundaries of efficiency, reliability, and adaptability.

One of the most profound impacts of Digital Twins on AI-augmented control lies in their capacity to serve as rich, high-fidelity training and validation environments. Developing robust AI controllers, especially those based on reinforcement learning, often requires vast amounts of data and extensive trial-and-error. Training directly on a physical system can be prohibitively expensive, time-consuming, and, in many safety-critical applications, outright dangerous. Digital Twins offer a safe, cost-effective, and accelerated sandbox for this crucial development phase. An AI agent can interact with the virtual replica of a factory floor, an autonomous vehicle, or a chemical plant, exploring countless scenarios and learning optimal control policies without any risk of damaging physical hardware or disrupting ongoing operations.

Consider the development of an AI controller for a complex manufacturing process. Traditionally, tuning the parameters of a controller might involve numerous physical runs, each potentially leading to suboptimal product quality or even equipment downtime. With a Digital Twin, an AI can be exposed to a multitude of operating conditions, including edge cases and failure modes, in a compressed timeframe. For instance, a Digital Twin of a robotic assembly line can simulate variations in part dimensions, conveyor belt speeds, and actuator response times. An AI reinforcement learning agent can then be trained to robustly handle these variations, learning to adjust its movements, gripping forces, and sequencing to maintain high precision and throughput, even when faced with unexpected deviations. The learning process can be significantly sped up, as simulations can often be run orders of magnitude faster than real-time, and parallelization across multiple computational cores allows for the exploration of an immense state-action space.

Furthermore, Digital Twins provide a structured and repeatable environment for validating the performance and safety of AI controllers before deployment. Once an AI policy has been trained in simulation, the Digital Twin can be used to rigorously test its behavior under a wide array of conditions, including those that are rare or difficult to reproduce in the physical world. This validation can go beyond simple performance metrics to encompass safety checks, robustness assessments against sensor noise or actuator failures, and analyses of the AI's decision-making under stress. For example, an AI designed to manage a power grid might be tested in its Digital Twin against scenarios like sudden generator outages, unexpected demand surges, or malicious cyberattacks, ensuring it can respond safely and effectively. The detailed data logging capabilities of Digital Twins allow for thorough post-hoc analysis of any performance anomalies, which is invaluable for debugging and continuous improvement.

The iterative nature of control system design is also greatly accelerated by the use of Digital Twins. Control engineers often work in cycles of design, implementation, testing, and refinement. Digital Twins allow for rapid prototyping and testing of new control algorithms or modifications to existing ones. Instead of waiting for physical prototypes or reconfiguring complex industrial setups, engineers can deploy a new AI controller onto the Digital Twin, observe its performance immediately, and iterate on the design based on the results. This significantly shortens the design-to-deployment lifecycle, enabling faster innovation and quicker adaptation to evolving market demands or operational requirements.

Beyond training and validation, Digital Twins are instrumental in enabling advanced control strategies that leverage predictive capabilities. By continuously ingesting data from the physical system, the Digital Twin not only mirrors its current state but also becomes a powerful tool for forecasting future behavior. This predictive fidelity can be further enhanced by AI algorithms that learn to model complex dynamics, predict component degradation, and anticipate potential failures. This fusion of Digital Twin and AI leads directly to the concept of AI-enhanced predictive maintenance and proactive control.

Imagine a complex industrial pump whose performance is monitored by a Digital Twin. The twin receives real-time data on vibration, temperature, pressure, and flow rate. An AI model, trained on historical data and running within or in conjunction with the Digital Twin, can analyze these parameters to detect subtle anomalies that indicate incipient wear in a bearing or a developing seal leak. Instead of waiting for the pump to fail catastrophically or for scheduled maintenance to reveal the issue, the Digital Twin, powered by AI, can predict the probability of failure within a specific timeframe. This prediction allows for maintenance to be scheduled proactively during planned downtime, preventing costly unplanned outages and extending the operational life of the equipment.

This predictive capability extends to operational control as well. For systems like autonomous vehicles or fleets of drones, the Digital Twin can be used to predict the impact of future environmental changes or system states on the agents' performance. For instance, a Digital Twin of a city's traffic network, updated with real-time traffic flow and weather data, can be used by an AI traffic management system to predict congestion hotspots. The AI can then proactively adjust traffic light timings or reroute vehicles to mitigate the predicted congestion before it occurs. Similarly, for a fleet of delivery drones, a Digital Twin could predict potential flight path disruptions due to changing wind patterns or air traffic, allowing the AI to pre-emptively adjust routes for optimal efficiency and safety.

The relationship between AI and Digital Twins is, however, a symbiotic one. While Digital Twins provide fertile ground for AI development and deployment, AI is also revolutionizing the creation and capabilities of Digital Twins themselves. Building accurate and high-fidelity Digital Twins of complex systems can be an enormously challenging task, often requiring intricate physical modeling, domain expertise, and extensive calibration. AI, particularly techniques like machine learning and system identification, can automate and enhance various aspects of Digital Twin creation and maintenance.

Machine learning algorithms can be employed to learn the underlying dynamics of a physical system directly from observed data, potentially building more accurate and comprehensive models than traditional physics-based approaches alone, especially for systems with highly complex or poorly understood phenomena. For example, in modeling the behavior of a sophisticated battery system, where electrochemical processes are intricate, an AI might learn a more predictive model of degradation and performance characteristics than a purely analytical model could achieve. This learned model can then be integrated into the Digital Twin, significantly improving its predictive accuracy.

Furthermore, AI can be used to continuously improve the fidelity of the Digital Twin over its lifecycle. As the physical system ages or its operating conditions change, its behavior may deviate from the initial model. AI algorithms can monitor the discrepancies between the Digital Twin's predictions and the actual system's performance, automatically updating the twin's parameters or even its structure to maintain accurate representation. This concept of an "adaptive Digital Twin" ensures that the virtual replica remains a faithful and useful companion to the physical asset throughout its operational life, a feat that would be exceptionally difficult to achieve with purely manual model updates.

AI can also enhance the simulation capabilities within a Digital Twin. For instance, AI-driven generative models could be used to create realistic synthetic data representing a wide range of operational scenarios, including rare events or extreme conditions, which can then be used to further stress-test and train AI controllers within the Digital Twin environment. This capability is particularly valuable for systems where collecting sufficient real-world data for all possible scenarios is impractical or impossible.

The integration of AI and Digital Twins also has profound implications for human-machine interaction and decision support. Digital Twins can provide operators with intuitive, visual interfaces that present the current state of a complex system and highlight AI-driven insights or recommendations. For a human supervisor overseeing a fleet of autonomous robots, a Digital Twin could visualize the operational status of each robot, predict potential bottlenecks, and suggest optimal task assignments or interventions. This "explainable" aspect, where the Digital Twin visualizes the reasoning behind AI suggestions, builds trust and facilitates more informed human oversight.

In industrial settings, the combination of AI and Digital Twins is poised to drive significant improvements in operational efficiency, product quality, and safety. For complex processes like chemical manufacturing or power generation, Digital Twins can simulate the impact of different control strategies or operational parameters on yield, energy consumption, and emissions. AI can then optimize these parameters in real-time, guided by the Digital Twin's predictions, leading to more sustainable and cost-effective operations. The ability to virtually test process changes before implementing them physically minimizes risks and ensures that new operational strategies are robust and beneficial.

Looking ahead, as AI capabilities become more sophisticated and Digital Twin technologies mature, their combined impact will likely expand to encompass entire ecosystems. For example, a Digital Twin of a smart city, integrating data from traffic, energy grids, public transportation, and environmental sensors, could be used by AI to optimize city-wide operations, manage resources efficiently, and improve the quality of life for citizens. The control systems for each of these sub-systems could be developed and validated using their respective Digital Twins, with overarching coordination managed by AI leveraging the integrated city-level Digital Twin.

In summary, the advent of Digital Twins, when coupled with advanced AI, creates a powerful feedback loop that significantly enhances the design, implementation, and operation of control systems. Digital Twins provide the essential virtual environments for training and validating AI controllers safely and efficiently, enabling faster iteration and the exploration of complex scenarios. Simultaneously, AI imbues Digital Twins with greater predictive power, enabling proactive maintenance and intelligent operational adjustments, while also aiding in the very creation and ongoing refinement of these virtual replicas. This synergistic relationship is not merely an incremental improvement but a fundamental shift, paving the way for more intelligent, adaptable, and resilient control systems across a vast array of industrial and societal applications. The future of control is increasingly being shaped in the digital realm, with AI and Digital Twins acting as the architects of that transformation.

The increasing integration of AI-augmented control systems into the fabric of our daily lives and industries brings with it a complex tapestry of ethical considerations and societal impacts that demand our rigorous attention. As these systems move from theoretical concepts and specialized applications into widespread deployment, it is imperative to proactively address the potential challenges and to cultivate a framework for responsible innovation. This subsection delves into these critical aspects, aiming to foster a balanced perspective that acknowledges both the transformative potential and the inherent risks associated with this technological evolution.

One of the most immediate and widely discussed societal impacts of advanced automation, driven by AI-augmented control, is the potential for significant job displacement. As intelligent systems become capable of performing tasks that were once the exclusive domain of human workers—from manufacturing and logistics to data analysis and even creative endeavors—concerns about widespread unemployment and economic restructuring are amplified. While historical technological shifts have often led to the creation of new job categories, the speed and breadth of AI's capabilities raise questions about whether this transition will be as smooth or as equitable as in the past. The nature of work itself is likely to change, with a greater emphasis on skills that complement AI, such as critical thinking, creativity, complex problem-solving, and emotional intelligence. However, the transition period could be marked by significant societal disruption if adequate reskilling and upskilling initiatives, coupled with robust social safety nets, are not put in place. The economic benefits derived from increased productivity and efficiency must be carefully distributed to ensure that society as a whole, and not just a select few, reaps the rewards. This necessitates a societal dialogue about the future of work, the role of education, and the potential need for new economic models that can support populations in an increasingly automated world. Governments, educational institutions, and industry leaders all have a crucial role to play in navigating this transition, fostering an environment where technological advancement leads to shared prosperity rather than increased inequality.

Beyond the economic implications, the issue of algorithmic bias represents a profound ethical challenge. AI-augmented control systems learn from data, and if that data reflects existing societal biases—whether related to race, gender, socioeconomic status, or any other characteristic—the AI will invariably perpetuate and even amplify those biases. This can have serious consequences when these systems are deployed in sensitive areas such as hiring, loan applications, criminal justice, or healthcare. For instance, an AI-driven recruitment tool trained on historical hiring data might inadvertently favor male candidates for certain roles if past hiring practices were gender-biased. Similarly, an AI used for medical diagnosis could exhibit lower accuracy rates for certain demographic groups if the training data was not representative. Addressing algorithmic bias requires a multi-pronged approach. It begins with careful data curation and auditing to identify and mitigate biases in training datasets. It extends to the development of fairness-aware machine learning algorithms that are explicitly designed to avoid discriminatory outcomes. Furthermore, transparency and explainability in AI decision-making are paramount. When the reasoning behind an AI's recommendation or action can be understood, it becomes easier to identify and correct biased behavior. This also empowers individuals to challenge decisions made by AI systems. The pursuit of fairness in AI is not merely a technical problem; it is a societal imperative that requires ongoing vigilance and commitment from developers, policymakers, and users alike.

Data privacy is another critical concern that looms large with the proliferation of AI-augmented control systems. These systems often rely on vast amounts of data, much of which can be personal and sensitive. From smart home devices that collect information about daily routines to autonomous vehicles that track travel patterns, the potential for data collection and misuse is significant. The aggregation and analysis of such data by AI can reveal intimate details about individuals' lives, raising questions about surveillance, consent, and the potential for data breaches or unauthorized access. Robust data protection regulations, such as GDPR, are essential first steps, but they must be continually adapted to keep pace with technological advancements. Beyond legal frameworks, there is a need for a culture of privacy-by-design within the development of AI systems. This means embedding privacy considerations into every stage of the design and development process, ensuring that data is collected only when necessary, anonymized or pseudonymized wherever possible, and secured with state-of-the-art encryption. Furthermore, individuals need to have greater control over their data, with clear and accessible mechanisms for understanding how their data is being used and for opting out of certain types of data collection. The ethical deployment of AI requires a fundamental respect for individual privacy, recognizing that the benefits of data-driven insights must be weighed against the potential risks to personal autonomy and security.

The increasing autonomy of AI systems also brings to the forefront the complex question of accountability and responsibility, particularly in the event of failures. When an autonomous vehicle causes an accident, or an AI-controlled medical device malfunctions with adverse consequences, who is to blame? Is it the programmer who wrote the algorithm, the manufacturer that deployed the system, the owner of the system, or the AI itself? Current legal and ethical frameworks are often ill-equipped to handle these scenarios. Establishing clear lines of accountability is crucial for building public trust and ensuring that appropriate redress is available when harm occurs. This requires a careful examination of existing liability laws and, potentially, the development of new legal principles specifically tailored to autonomous systems. The concept of "explainable AI" (XAI) plays a vital role here, as understanding the decision-making process of an AI can help in attributing responsibility. Furthermore, a focus on rigorous testing, validation, and ongoing monitoring of AI systems can help prevent failures in the first place. Insurance models may also need to evolve to cover the unique risks associated with autonomous technologies. Ultimately, ensuring accountability for AI failures will require collaboration between legal scholars, ethicists, engineers, and policymakers to develop frameworks that are both just and practical.

Despite these challenges, the potential benefits of AI-augmented control systems are substantial and can lead to significant positive societal impacts. Improved safety is a prime example. In domains like transportation, AI-driven control can reduce human error, which is a leading cause of accidents. Autonomous vehicles, when fully developed and deployed responsibly, have the potential to drastically lower road fatalities. Similarly, in industrial settings, AI can monitor hazardous environments or perform repetitive tasks that are prone to causing human injury, thereby enhancing workplace safety. AI-augmented control can also drive remarkable gains in efficiency. In energy grids, AI can optimize power distribution, reducing waste and improving reliability. In agriculture, AI can enable precision farming, optimizing resource allocation for irrigation, fertilization, and pest control, leading to higher yields and reduced environmental impact. For individuals, AI-powered control systems can enhance accessibility and quality of life. Smart home technologies can assist the elderly or individuals with disabilities in performing daily tasks, promoting independence. Personalized healthcare, driven by AI analysis of patient data, can lead to more effective and tailored treatments. The potential for AI to solve complex global challenges, from climate change modeling and resource management to disease prediction and mitigation, is immense. These benefits, however, are not automatic. They depend on a conscious and deliberate effort to steer the development and deployment of these technologies towards positive societal outcomes.

This necessitates a commitment to responsible innovation and the establishment of robust governance frameworks. Responsible innovation means not only focusing on the technical feasibility and economic viability of AI-augmented control systems but also proactively considering their ethical implications and societal consequences from the outset. It involves engaging a diverse range of stakeholders—including ethicists, social scientists, policymakers, and the public—in the design and development process. Governance frameworks are essential for providing the rules of the road for AI development and deployment. These frameworks should encompass ethical guidelines, regulatory standards, and mechanisms for oversight and enforcement. They need to be flexible enough to adapt to the rapid pace of technological change while also being sufficiently robust to protect societal interests. Key elements of such frameworks might include requirements for transparency and explainability, independent auditing of AI systems, clear procedures for addressing bias and discrimination, and strong data privacy protections. International cooperation will also be vital, as AI technologies transcend national borders and present global challenges that require coordinated solutions. Building trust in AI-augmented control systems requires a transparent and inclusive approach to their governance, ensuring that these powerful technologies are developed and used for the benefit of all humanity. The path forward demands not just technological ingenuity, but also wisdom, foresight, and a deep sense of ethical responsibility.

The journey toward realizing the full potential of AI-augmented control systems is undeniably marked by remarkable achievements, yet it is equally defined by a landscape of persistent challenges and nascent open problems. These are not merely academic curiosities; they represent critical junctures that will dictate the pace, breadth, and safety of future advancements. Acknowledging and actively addressing these frontiers is paramount for moving beyond specialized applications to truly ubiquitous, reliable, and trustworthy intelligent control.

One of the most formidable hurdles lies in establishing universally applicable and provable safety guarantees for learning-based control systems. Unlike traditional control systems, where stability and performance can often be mathematically derived from system models and controller design, AI-based controllers, particularly those employing deep learning, learn their behavior from data. This data-driven nature introduces inherent uncertainties. When a controller learns a complex, non-linear mapping from sensor inputs to actuator commands, ensuring that it will behave safely and predictably under all possible operating conditions—including unseen or adversarial inputs—is exceedingly difficult. Formal verification methods, which are standard in classical control theory, often struggle to scale to the complexity of modern neural networks. Developing techniques that can provide rigorous, mathematically sound guarantees of safety, robustness, and stability for these learning systems, even in the presence of noise, disturbances, and model uncertainties, is a grand challenge. This is particularly crucial for safety-critical applications such as autonomous driving, medical robotics, and aerospace, where failure can have catastrophic consequences. Research into methods like robust control, formal methods adapted for neural networks, and uncertainty quantification within learned models is essential. The goal is to bridge the gap between the empirical performance observed during training and testing, and the absolute assurance required for deployment in high-stakes environments.

Furthermore, the insatiable appetite of many current AI control algorithms for vast amounts of data presents a significant practical limitation. Training sophisticated deep learning controllers often requires millions, if not billions, of data points, which can be prohibitively expensive or simply impossible to collect in many real-world scenarios. This data inefficiency is a major bottleneck for broader adoption, especially in domains where data acquisition is costly, time-consuming, or poses ethical concerns. Consider industrial process control, where extensive real-world experimentation might disrupt ongoing operations, or rare event detection in safety systems, where obtaining sufficient examples of failure modes is inherently difficult. Consequently, a significant research thrust is dedicated to developing more data-efficient learning techniques. This includes exploring meta-learning (learning to learn), transfer learning (leveraging knowledge from related tasks), few-shot learning (learning from very limited examples), and simulation-to-real transfer methods that can effectively bridge the gap between simulated and physical environments. The development of model-based reinforcement learning, where an agent learns a model of the environment and uses it for planning and control, also holds promise for reducing data requirements compared to purely model-free approaches. The ultimate aim is to enable AI controllers to achieve high performance with significantly less data, making advanced control accessible to a wider range of applications.

The interpretability and robustness of deep learning controllers also remain critical areas for investigation. While deep neural networks have demonstrated remarkable capabilities in learning complex control policies, their "black box" nature often makes it difficult to understand *why* a particular decision is made. This lack of transparency hinders debugging, trustworthiness, and the ability to gain insights into system dynamics. In critical applications, engineers need to be able to scrutinize the decision-making process of the controller to ensure it aligns with domain knowledge and safety principles. Moreover, deep learning models can be surprisingly brittle, exhibiting poor performance when faced with inputs that differ even slightly from their training distribution, or when subjected to adversarial attacks designed to deceive them. Developing methods for enhancing the interpretability of these controllers—such as attention mechanisms, feature visualization, and surrogate models—is crucial. Equally important is improving their robustness. This involves techniques like adversarial training, regularization methods that promote smoother decision boundaries, and incorporating domain knowledge into the network architecture. The interplay between interpretability and robustness is also a key research question: can interpretable models inherently be more robust, or are these often competing objectives?

Beyond specific algorithmic challenges, there is a pressing need for unified theoretical frameworks that seamlessly integrate the principles of classical control theory with modern machine learning. Currently, these two fields often operate in parallel, with researchers in one domain sometimes unaware of or unable to leverage the advancements in the other. Classical control offers a rich theoretical foundation for stability analysis, optimal control, and disturbance rejection, while machine learning excels at learning complex dynamics from data and adapting to changing environments. A truly synergistic approach would involve developing theoretical constructs that can harness the strengths of both. This could manifest as frameworks for learning controllers that are guaranteed to be stable, or methods for incorporating prior knowledge from physical models into the learning process to improve data efficiency and robustness. Research into areas like system identification using machine learning, learning optimal control policies within established theoretical bounds, and hybrid control architectures that combine classical and learning-based components are all steps in this direction. The goal is to create a more holistic and mathematically rigorous understanding of how to design and deploy intelligent control systems that are both data-driven and theoretically sound, paving the way for broader, more confident adoption.

The development of adaptive and online learning control strategies that can continuously learn and adapt to changing system dynamics or environments in real-time presents another significant challenge and opportunity. Many existing AI control methods are trained offline and then deployed, with limited capacity for further learning once in operation. However, real-world systems are rarely static. Manufacturing processes drift, environmental conditions fluctuate, and the performance of components degrades over time. For AI controllers to be truly effective in these dynamic settings, they must possess the ability to adapt their behavior on the fly without compromising stability or safety. This requires sophisticated online learning algorithms that can efficiently update their parameters based on new incoming data, along with mechanisms to ensure that these updates do not lead to undesirable performance or instability. The exploration of techniques such as online reinforcement learning, adaptive control methods informed by machine learning, and the development of robust online validation procedures are all vital for realizing controllers that can maintain optimal performance in perpetually evolving environments. This continuous adaptation is not just about performance enhancement; it is often a prerequisite for sustained operation and safety in complex, unpredictable scenarios.

Finally, the standardization and benchmarking of AI-augmented control systems are essential for fostering scientific progress and facilitating wider adoption. Unlike traditional control engineering, where well-established benchmarks and performance metrics exist for evaluating controllers, the rapidly evolving field of AI control often lacks agreed-upon standards. This makes it difficult to compare different approaches rigorously, to assess progress objectively, and for practitioners to choose the most suitable methods for their applications. Establishing standardized datasets, simulation environments, and performance evaluation metrics—across various application domains—is crucial for creating a common ground for research and development. This will enable researchers to benchmark their algorithms against established baselines, identify areas for improvement more effectively, and build upon each other's work. Furthermore, developing guidelines and best practices for the development, testing, and deployment of AI control systems will be critical for building confidence among end-users and regulatory bodies. This includes aspects like reproducible research, transparent reporting of model architectures and training procedures, and clear documentation of performance characteristics and limitations. The pursuit of such standardization efforts will accelerate the maturation of the field and lay the groundwork for more reliable and widespread integration of AI into control systems.

The journey through the multifaceted landscape of intelligent control systems, as explored in this book, has illuminated a path marked by profound transformation and boundless potential. We stand at a pivotal juncture where the marriage of classical control theory with the burgeoning power of artificial intelligence and machine learning is not merely an academic pursuit but a fundamental shift in engineering paradigms. This integration promises to equip engineers with an unprecedented suite of tools and methodologies, enabling the design of systems that are not only more intelligent and efficient but also remarkably adaptable and inherently robust. The implications are far-reaching, poised to redefine the capabilities and applications of automation and control across virtually every industrial sector imaginable.

The core message resonating through our exploration is one of empowered innovation. Traditional control, with its rigorous mathematical underpinnings and established frameworks for stability and performance analysis, provides a vital bedrock of reliability. Machine learning, on the other hand, offers an extraordinary ability to discern complex patterns from data, to learn intricate dynamics that defy traditional modeling, and to adapt to the ever-changing vagaries of real-world environments. The synergy between these disciplines unlocks a new era of control system design. Engineers are no longer constrained by the limitations of purely analytical models when faced with highly non-linear, uncertain, or time-varying systems. Instead, they can leverage AI algorithms to augment or even create control strategies that learn, adapt, and optimize in real-time, pushing the boundaries of what was previously thought achievable. This fusion is not about replacing established principles but about augmenting them, creating a more potent and versatile engineering toolkit.

Consider the impact on autonomous systems. Vehicles, drones, and robots are increasingly expected to navigate complex, dynamic, and unpredictable environments, often in close proximity to humans. The sophisticated perception, decision-making, and actuation required for safe and efficient operation demand more than static, pre-programmed logic. Intelligent control systems, informed by machine learning models trained on vast datasets and refined through reinforcement learning, can endow these systems with an almost intuitive grasp of their surroundings. They can anticipate the actions of other agents, react instantaneously to unforeseen obstacles, and optimize their trajectories for efficiency and safety in ways that would be impossibly complex to hardcode. This leap in capability is directly attributable to the integration of advanced AI techniques within the control loop, enabling a level of autonomy and situational awareness that was the realm of science fiction just a few decades ago.

In the realm of manufacturing and industrial automation, the benefits are equally transformative. Smart factories are increasingly reliant on intelligent control to optimize production lines, predict equipment failures, and adapt to changing product demands. AI-driven control systems can monitor myriad variables in real-time, identifying subtle deviations that signal potential issues long before they would be detectable by human operators or traditional sensors. This proactive approach minimizes downtime, reduces waste, and enhances overall equipment effectiveness (OEE). Furthermore, intelligent controllers can dynamically reconfigure production processes, allowing for rapid customization of products and agile responses to market shifts. Imagine a robotic assembly line that can seamlessly switch between manufacturing different product variants based on real-time orders, or a chemical process plant that continuously adjusts its parameters to maintain optimal yield and energy efficiency under fluctuating raw material quality and ambient conditions. These are the realities being shaped by intelligent control.

The medical field is another arena where the profound impact of intelligent control is becoming increasingly evident. From robotic surgery platforms that enhance precision and minimize invasiveness, to intelligent prosthetics that offer a more natural and intuitive user experience, AI-augmented control is revolutionizing patient care. Surgical robots, guided by advanced control algorithms, can perform intricate maneuvers with superhuman stability and accuracy. Prosthetic limbs, equipped with sophisticated sensors and learning algorithms, can interpret user intent from subtle muscle signals, allowing for fluid and natural movement. Beyond robotics, intelligent control is also being applied to optimize drug delivery systems, personalize treatment plans based on patient data, and improve diagnostic accuracy through AI-powered analysis of medical imagery. The ability of these systems to learn, adapt, and operate with a high degree of autonomy and precision opens up new therapeutic possibilities and enhances the quality of life for countless individuals.

Looking ahead, the trajectory of intelligent control systems points towards ever-greater integration and autonomy. We are moving towards a future where control systems are not just reactive but are deeply predictive and proactive. They will not only manage individual machines or processes but will orchestrate complex networks of interconnected systems, optimizing performance at a global scale. The concept of the "Internet of Things" (IoT) coupled with intelligent control envisions a world where billions of devices communicate and collaborate, coordinated by sophisticated AI algorithms to achieve unprecedented levels of efficiency, sustainability, and convenience. This might manifest as smart grids that seamlessly balance energy supply and demand from diverse renewable sources, intelligent transportation networks that optimize traffic flow and minimize congestion, or smart cities that manage resources and services with remarkable efficiency.

The role of the engineer in this evolving landscape is one of strategic oversight and creative design. While AI algorithms will automate many of the complex control tasks, the human engineer remains indispensable. The responsibility shifts towards defining the overarching objectives, specifying the constraints, ensuring safety and ethical considerations are paramount, and architecting the intelligent systems themselves. Engineers will need to develop a deep understanding of both control theory and machine learning, mastering the tools and techniques that enable the creation of these sophisticated systems. They will be the architects of intelligence, translating human needs and societal goals into actionable control strategies for machines. This requires a continuous commitment to learning and adaptation, staying abreast of the rapid advancements in both fields.

Furthermore, the development of intelligent control systems necessitates a strong emphasis on ethical considerations and societal impact. As these systems become more autonomous and pervasive, questions surrounding accountability, bias, transparency, and job displacement become increasingly important. Engineers have a crucial role to play in ensuring that these technologies are developed and deployed responsibly, with a focus on human well-being and societal benefit. This involves designing systems that are fair, equitable, and robust against misuse, as well as engaging in open dialogue about the broader implications of artificial intelligence in our lives.

In conclusion, the integration of artificial intelligence and machine learning with traditional control theory represents not just an evolution but a revolution in engineering. It empowers us with the ability to design and implement control systems that are more intelligent, adaptable, robust, and efficient than ever before. The opportunities for innovation are vast, spanning every conceivable industry and application, from the microscopic world of nanotechnology to the global scale of smart grids and interconnected economies. By embracing these advancements, fostering interdisciplinary collaboration, and maintaining a steadfast commitment to safety and ethical development, engineers are poised to shape a future of intelligent automation that is not only technologically advanced but also beneficial for humanity. The era of intelligent control is here, and its potential to drive progress and redefine our world is only just beginning to be realized. This book has aimed to provide a foundational understanding of this exciting field, encouraging a proactive and innovative approach to tackling the challenges and harnessing the immense opportunities that lie ahead. The future of control is intelligent, adaptive, and undeniably exciting.

Adaptive Control: A type of control system that adjusts its controller parameters in real-time to compensate for unknown or changing system dynamics.

Artificial Intelligence (AI): The simulation of human intelligence processes by machines, especially computer systems.

Closed-Loop Control: A control system that uses feedback from the system's output to adjust its input and achieve a desired state.

Control Theory: A branch of engineering and mathematics that deals with the behavior of dynamical systems with inputs, and how their behavior can be modified by changing various parameters.

Deep Learning: A subset of machine learning that uses artificial neural networks with multiple layers to learn representations of data.

Feedback: The process of conveying information about the present state of a system to its controller.

Fuzzy Logic: A form of many-valued logic in which the truth values of variables may be any real number between 0 and 1 inclusive.

Intelligent Control: A broad term encompassing control systems that employ AI techniques such as machine learning, fuzzy logic, or expert systems to achieve enhanced performance, adaptability, and autonomy.

Machine Learning (ML): A type of AI that allows systems to learn from data without being explicitly programmed.

Model Predictive Control (MPC): An advanced control strategy that uses a dynamic model of the process to predict future behavior and optimize control actions over a finite horizon.

Neural Network (NN): A computational model inspired by the structure and function of biological neural networks.

Optimization: The process of finding the best solution from among all available alternatives, according to some criterion.

Reinforcement Learning (RL): A type of machine learning where an agent learns to make a sequence of decisions by trying to maximize a reward it receives for its actions.

Robotics: The field concerned with the design, construction, operation, and application of robots.
Stability: The property of a control system that ensures its output remains bounded in response to bounded inputs and disturbances.
Supervisory Control: A higher level of control that sets goals or parameters for lower-level controllers.
System Dynamics: The study of the characteristic behavior of complex systems over time.
Uncertainty: In control systems, refers to unknown or imprecise knowledge about the system's parameters or behavior.

[1] Åström, K. J., & Wittenmark, B. (2008). *Advanced Adaptive Control.* Courier Corporation.
[2] Bertsekas, D. P. (2012). *Dynamic Programming and Optimal Control, Vol. I.* Athena Scientific.
[3] Bishop, C. M. (2006). *Pattern Recognition and Machine Learning.* Springer.
[4] Boyd, S., & Vandenberghe, L. (2004). *Convex Optimization.* Cambridge University Press.
[5] Goodfellow, I., Bengio, Y., & Courville, A. (2016). *Deep Learning.* MIT Press.
[6] Khosravi, A., & Nahavandi, S. (2015). *Intelligent Control Systems: Theory and Applications.* Springer.
[7] Lewis, F. L., & Syrmos, V. L. (1995). *Adaptive Control.* John Wiley & Sons.
[8] Ljung, L. (1999). *System Identification: Theory for the User.* Prentice Hall.
[9] Miller, W., & Li, W. (2007). *Intelligent Control.* CRC Press.
[10] Sutton, R. S., & Barto, A. G. (2018). *Reinforcement Learning: An Introduction.* MIT Press.
[11] Tsinias, J. (2016). *Robust Control: An Adaptive Approach.* Springer.
[12] Van Overschee, P., & De Moor, B. (1996). *N4SID: System Identification in the Time Domain.* Springer.

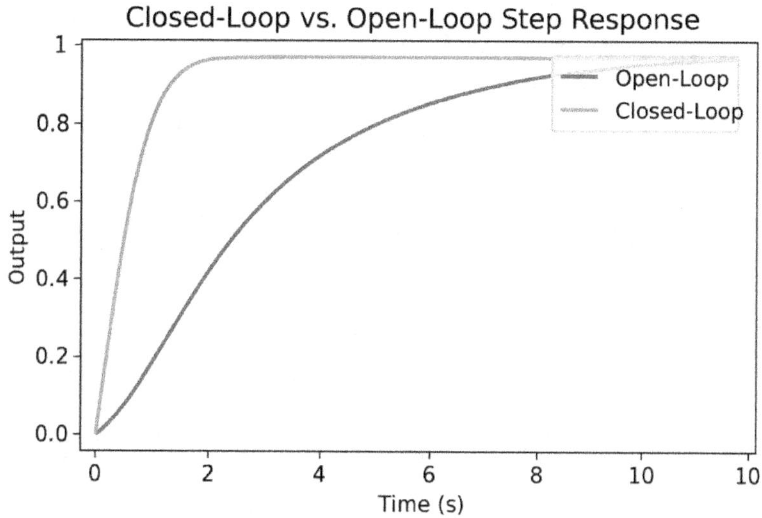

Closed-Loop vs. Open-Loop Step Response
Open-Loop
Closed-Loop
Output
Time (s)
0
0.2
0.4
0.6
0.8
1
0
2
4
6
8
10
10

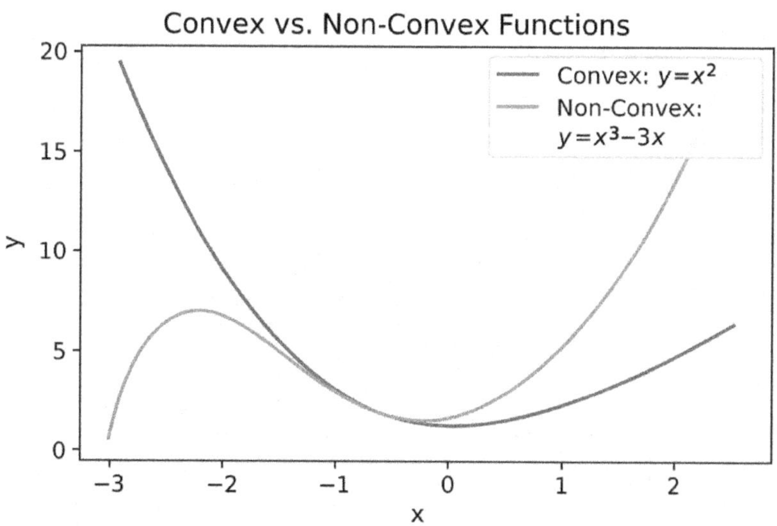

Convex vs. Non-Convex Functions
Convex: y=x²
Non-Convex:
y=x³−3x
y
x
0
5
10
15
20
−3
−2
−1
0
1
2

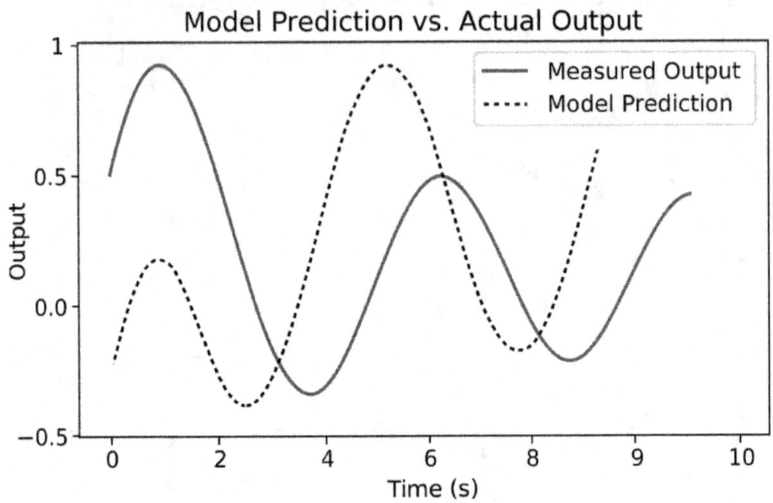
Model Prediction vs. Actual Output
Measured Output
Model Prediction
Output
Time (s)
1
0.5
0.0
−0.5
0
2
4
6
8
9
10

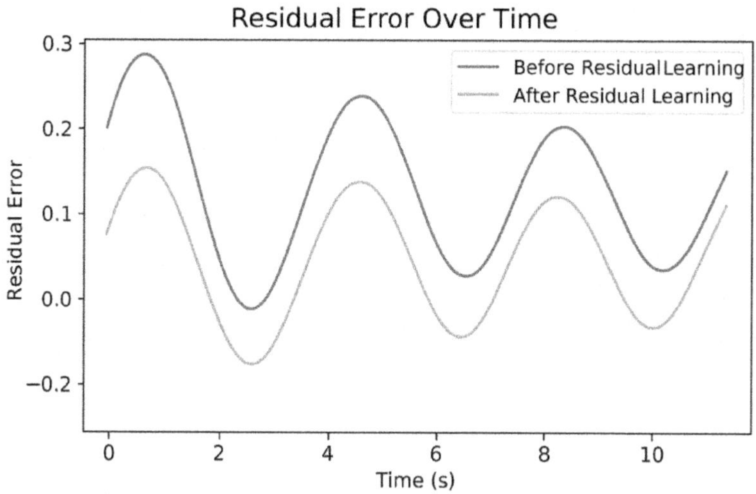
Residual Error Over Time
Before Residual Learning
After Residual Learning
Residual Error
0.3
0.2
0.1
0.0
−0.2
0
2
4
6
8
10
Time (s)

www.ingramcontent.com/pod-product-compliance
Lightning Source LLC
LaVergne TN
LVHW052013200926
848481LV00005B/1477